Palgrave Studies in Economic History

Series Editor
Kent Deng, London School of Economics, London, UK

Palgrave Studies in Economic History is designed to illuminate and enrich our understanding of economies and economic phenomena of the past. The series covers a vast range of topics including financial history, labour history, development economics, commercialisation, urbanisation, industrialisation, modernisation, globalisation, and changes in world economic orders.

Herbert S. Klein · Francisco Vidal Luna

Brazilian Crops in the Global Market

The Emergence of Brazil as a World Agribusiness Exporter Since 1950

palgrave
macmillan

Herbert S. Klein
Menlo Park, CA, USA

Francisco Vidal Luna
São Paulo, Brazil

ISSN 2662-6497 ISSN 2662-6500 (electronic)
Palgrave Studies in Economic History
ISBN 978-3-031-38588-9 ISBN 978-3-031-38589-6 (eBook)
https://doi.org/10.1007/978-3-031-38589-6

Cover credit: AFP/Stringer

This Palgrave Macmillan imprint is published by the registered company Springer Nature Switzerland AG
The registered company address is: Gewerbestrasse 11, 6330 Cham, Switzerland

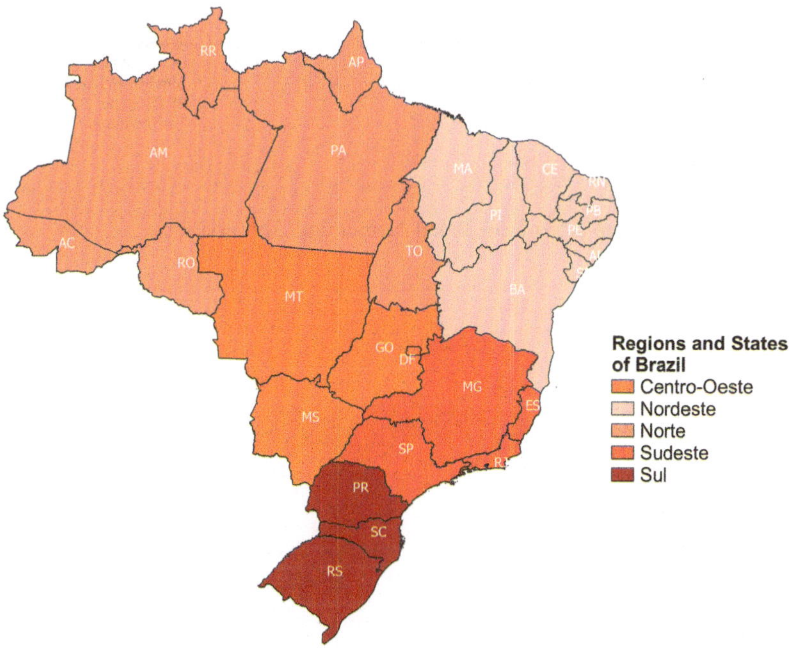

Map 1 Regions and States of Brazil

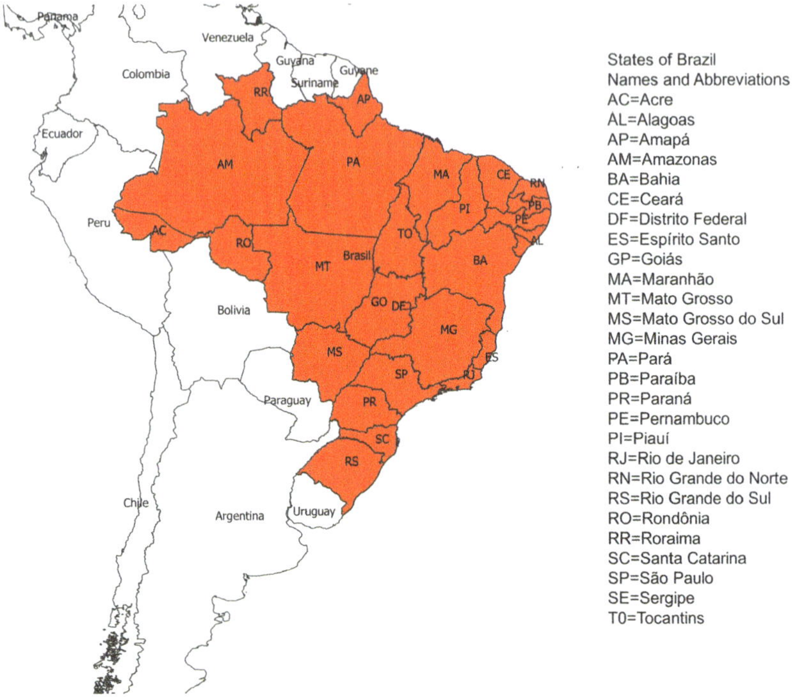

Map 2 States of Brazil Names and Abbreviations

Contents

Abbreviations

ABIEC	Associação Brasileira das Indústrias Exportadoras de Carnes
ABIOVE	Associação Brasileira das Indústrias de Óleos Vegetais [The Brazilian Vegetable Oil Industries Association]
ABPA	Associação Brasileira de Proteína Animal
ABRAFRIGO	Associação Brasileira de Frigoríficos
ABRAPA	Associação Brasileira dos produtores de algodão
ABRASEM	Associação Brasileira de Sementes e Mudas
ABTCP	Associação Brasileira Técnica de Celulose e Papel
AGENDA 21	Documento assinado na Conferência das Nações Unidas sobre o Meio Ambiente e Desenvolvimento, Rio de Janeiro, 1992
AGF	Aquisição do Governo Federal [Federal Government Acquisitions]
AGROSTAT	Estatísticas de Comércio Exterior do Agronegócio Brasileiro
ANATER	Agência Nacional de Assistência Técnica e Extensão Rural [National Agency for Technical Assistance and Rural Extension]
ANEC	Associação Nacional de Exportadores de Cereais [The National Grain Exporters Association]
ANFAVEA	Associação Nacional dos Produtores de Veículos Automotores
ANP	Agência Nacional do Petróleo, Gás Natural e Combustíveis
APTA	Agência Paulista de Tecnologias dos Agronegócios [São Paulo Agribusiness Technology Agency]
ARGENBio	Consejo Argentino para la Informacion y el Desarrollo de la Biotecnologia
ATER	Assistência Técnica e Extensão Rural
BEKP	Bleached Eucalyptus Kraft Pulp

BID	Banco Interamericano de Desenvolvimento [Inter-American Development Bank]
BIRD	Banco Internacional para Reconstrução e Desenvolvimento [International Bank of Reconstruction and Development]
BNDES	Banco Nacional de Desenvolvimento Econômico e Social
BSKP	Bleached Softwood Kraft Pulp
CAMEX	Câmara de Comércio Exterior
CEAG-SC	Centro de Assistência Gerencial de Santa Catarina
CEPAL	Comisión Económica para América Latina y el Caribe (Nações Unidas)
CEPEA	Centro de Estudos Avançados em Economia Aplicada
CIMGC	Comissão Interministerial de Mudança Global do Clima [Commission on Global Climate Change]
CNI	Confederação Nacional da Indústria
COMEXSTAT	Camex, Sistema de informações de comércio exterior
CONAB	Companhia Nacional de Abastecimento
CONAF	Corporação Florestal Nacional do Chile
CORDES	Corporación de Estudios para el Desarrollo
CORFO	Corporación de Fomento de la Producción, Chile
CPR	Certificado de Produto Rural [Rural Producer Certificate]
CTC	Centro de Tecnologia Canavieira
CTNBio	Comissão Técnica de Biosseseguranca, Tecnologia e inovações
ECO-92	Conferência das Nações Unidas sobre o Meio Ambiente e Desenvolvimento, Rio de Janeiro, 1992
EGF	Empréstimo do Governo Federal [Federal Government Loans]
EMBRAPA	Empresa Brasileira de Pesquisa Agropecuária
EPAGRI	Empresa de Pesquisa Agropecuária e Extensão Rural de Santa Catarina [Agricultural Research and Rural Extension Company of Santa Catarina]
EPAMIG	Empresa de Pesquisa Agropecuária de Minas Gerais [Agricultural Research Company of Minas Gerais]
EPE	Empresa de Pesquisa Energética
ESALQ	Escola Superior de Agricultura "Luiz de Queiróz", da Universidade de São Paulo
FAO	Food and Agriculture Organization
FAOSTAT	Food and Agriculture Organization - Statistics
FCO	Frozen Concentrated Juice
FFLCH-USP	Faculdade de Filosofia, Letras e Ciências Humanas da Universidade de São Paulo
FINEP	Financiadora de Estados e Projetos
GATT	General Agreement on Tariffs and Trade
GDP	Gross Domestic Product
GMO	Genetically Modified Organisms

IAA	Instituto do Açúcar e do Álcool
IAC	Instituto Agronômico de Campinas
IBC	Instituto Brasileiro do Café
IBGE	Instituto Brasileiro de Geografia e Estatística
ICO	International Coffee Organization
ILP	Crop-Livestock Integration
IMF	International Monetary Fund
INCRA	Instituto Nacional de Colonização e Reforma Agrária
INDEC	Instituto Nacional de Estadística y Censos de la Republica Argentina
INIA	Instituto Nacional de Investigación Agropecuaria, Uruguai
INPE	Instituto Nacional de Pesquisas Espaciais [National Institute for Space Research]
INTA	Instituto Nacional de Tecnologia Agropecuaria, Argentina [The National Agricultural Technology Institute]
IPEADATA	Instituto de Pesquisas Econômicas Aplicadas - Statistics
IPEF	Instituto de Pesquisas Florestais
LIPF	crop-livestock-forest integration systems
MAGYP	Ministerio de Agricultura, Ganaderia y Pesca, Argentina
MAPA	Ministério da Agricultura, Pecuária e Abastecimento
MATOPIBA	[region that comprises the Cerrado biome in the states of Maranhão, Tocantins, Piauí, and Bahia
MCTI	Ministério da Ciência, Tecnologia e Inovações
MERCOSUR	Mercado Comum do Sul
MGAP	Ministerio de Ganaderia, Agricultura y Pesca, Uruguai
MMA	Ministério do Meio Ambiente
MME	Ministério de Minas e Energia
MST	Movimento dos Trabalhadores Rurais sem Terra
NAFTA	North American Free Trade Agreement
NASS	National Agricultural Statistics Service
NFC	Non-Concentrated Juice
ODEPA	Oficina de Estudios y Politicas Agrarias, Chile
PGPM	Política de Garantia de Preços Mínimos [Minimum Price Guarantee Policy]
PLANO ABC	Agricultura de Baixo Carbono [Low Carbon Emission Agriculture Plan]
PNATER	Política Nacional de Assistência Técnica e Extensão Rural para a Agricultura Familiar e Reforma Agrária
PNMC	*Política Nacional sobre Mudança do Clima* [National Policy on Climate Change]
Polonoroeste	[Program for the development of the Northwest region of Brazil]
PROÁLCOOL	Programa Brasileiro de Álcool

PRONAF	Programa Nacional de Fortalecimento da Agricultura Familiar
PRONATER	Programa Nacional de Assistência Técnica e Extensão Rural para a Agricultura Familiar e Reforma Agrária
PT	Partido dos Trabalhadores
PV	Partido Verde (Green Party)
RF	Roundup Ready Flex [resistant to glufosinate and glyphosate]
RR	Roundup Ready
S.I.F	Serviço de Inspeção Federal
SEMA	Secretaria de Infraestrutura e Meio Ambiente do Estado de São Paulo
SENAR	Serviços Nacional de Aprendizado Rural
SIDRA	Sistema IBGE de Recuperação Automática
SNCR	Sistema Nacional de Crédito Rural
SOBER	Sociedade Brasileira de Economia, Administração e Sociologia Rural
TPF	Total Factor Productivity
UNDP	United Nations Development Program
UNESCO	The United Nations Educational, Scientific and Cultural Organization
UNICAMP	Universidade de Campinas
USAID	United States Agency for International Development
USDA	United States Department of Agriculture
WTO	World Trade Organization

List of Graphs

List of Maps

List of Tables

CHAPTER 1

Introduction

This is the second volume of our study of the history and modern development of Brazilian Agriculture. In our previous volume we were concerned with the causes of change and where they occurred, with only a secondary concern about the crops which were developed. In this volume we examine in detail the crops which evolved from products exclusive to a national market, to those which became international commodities on a massive scale. It was for this reason that the current volume is therefore more descriptive of change in time and place by crop or product. To understand the context of this change we have provided a summary of the major causal factors, internal and external, which influenced the changes we are analyzing. Without question the role of the government was fundamental to this entire process. It provided the credit, price support, and technology needed to modernize Brazilian agriculture. While the government support was intended to use agriculture to provide basic support to its import substitution industrialization program through cheap food and by generating foreign reserves to import machinery, it nevertheless led Brazilian agriculture to slowly and steadily modernize from the middle decades of the twentieth century. So successful was this process, in contrast to what would happen in the industry, that when the Brazilian economy was opened up to the world market in the decade of the 1990s and much of this government support structure ended,

H. S. Klein and F. V. Luna, *Brazilian Crops in the Global Market*, Palgrave Studies in Economic History,
https://doi.org/10.1007/978-3-031-38589-6_1

Brazilian agriculture was able to begin a massive export of these basic commodities. At the same time Brazilian farmers continued to supply at ever cheaper cost basic inputs for the internal market. Fortunately for Brazilian producers they would enter the world market just as a commodities boom occurred because of the extraordinary growth of the Asian economies.

Brazilian exports until quite recently were dominated by only a few special products, either mineral or agricultural. These created poles of excellence in these exporting enclaves, but in general the Brazilian economy for centuries was dominated by subsistence agriculture. Even these few agricultural exports, above all coffee and sugar, since the 1930s have been controlled by production and export quotas, just as were most of the other crops produced in Brazil. Yet it was only in the past half century that the government moved from quotas and control to a policy of modernizing this agriculture with credit, price supports, purchasing of stocks, and above all with developing a modern research program for Brazilian crops. But even as late as 1990 price controls existed on most agricultural products, import and export quotas were enforced and regulatory stocks were maintained. Since that date, however, the entire agricultural sector was opened to the world market. The result was that hundreds of agricultural products became commodities with their prices determined by the world market just as many of these Brazilian products entered the world market for the same time. Although the transition was often difficult and costly, since the 1990s Brazilian agriculture has successfully integrated into the world market on almost all its products.

Important in all these crop changes have been the settlement of the newly developed Cerrado region and the expansion of land devoted to agricultural crops in the Center-West. In the period since 1950 the number of hectares devoted to crops has gone from 19 million hectares in 1950 to 91 million hectares today.[1] At the same time the massive growth of agricultural faculties has provided both the large number of scientists working in agriculture and a large group of technically trained agronomists. To this has been added the entrepreneurial and capital coming from the traditional southern farming sectors which has provided the leadership in developing these modern farms.

It is that integration of new lands, scientific research, government support, and entrepreneurial leadership, as seen in the evolution of its major crops, which is the history we present in this current volume of our ongoing history of Brazilian agriculture. This has been a revolutionary transformation which has seen agriculture move from yields below general international standards, to yields close to the leading world producers in almost all the major crops. It is also an industry that went from employing 80% of the economically active population in 1950, to producing much higher volumes of products with only 10% of the economically active population today. Coffee, Brazil's primer agricultural export of the past two centuries is now just a small part of a mix of hundreds of products produced on Brazil's modern farms and ranches and exported to the world. Even with coffee, Brazil producers now export more coffee than any time in its history.

Here we will examine the evolution of all the major crops of the twenty-first century in which Brazil has now achieved extraordinary importance and for which it has become one of the leading challengers to the formerly world dominant agricultural producers such as the United States. Some of these crops had been produced in the country since early colonial times, while others were only introduced in the twentieth century. But the main factor has been the dramatic increase in productivity in all crops which has allowed Brazil to increase output faster than its use of land to produce these crops.

We begin this study with a brief overview of the causal factors which led to this agricultural revolution and the changing structure of agricultural production as seen in the national censuses. We then began our study of individual products with a chapter each on the major new export crops: soybeans, maize, cotton, and citrus production. We conclude the agricultural crops with sugar and the ethanol industries and the traditional coffee sector. Finally we examine two other major areas of agroindustry, that of forestry products and the evolution of the pastoral industries and the growth of a meat exporting sector.

Our administrative data comes from the relevant Brazilian Ministries as well as national and local censuses. Fundamental are the data collected by IBGE, CONAB and the various Agricultural and Trade ministries as well as reports from various Brazilian growers associations. We have also relied on international sources such as the UN, FAO, and its extraordinary data collection, as well as the USDA reports and surveys. We have found that usually there is a harmony between all these sources when dealing with crops. But in the case of animals we have found that data in the national agricultural censuses differs from those both in the retrospective tables of the national census bureau (IBGE) and in the data provided by FAO. We have therefore decided to use the census numbers only when looking at the structure of ranches, and the other non-census sources when discussion production data. Another technical issue is the problem of constant change of extra-municipal boundaries by IBGE over time. All our maps use either the traditional municipal or state boundaries, or the mesoregion boundaries which were adopted in 1989, but which have now been abandoned in the recent national censuses and replaced by new micro and macro regional groupings as of 2017.[2] Fortunately IBGE in its SIDRA database maintains these mesoregion divisions for all current and retrospective data.

The chapters are organized into essentially four sections. The first two chapters deal with the causes for the explosive growth of Brazilian agriculture in this period and with the structure of farm ownership from the first national agrarian census to the latest one of 2017. The second section has chapters dealing with all the "new" agricultural crops which have recently dominated exports: these include chapters on soybeans, maize, cotton, and citrus products. The third section deals with the traditional crops of sugar and coffee and their evolution in the recent period. The final fourth section has two chapters on forestry and pastoral industries, both of which have emerged as major new sectors in Brazilian agricultural growth.

For their support in the development of this volume we would like to thank William Summerhill, Renato Augusto Rosa Vidal, Matiko Kume Vidal and Judith H. Schiffner.

Notes

1. IBGE Censo 1950, Série Nacional, Volume 2, Brasil Censo Agrícola, vi, tab 1; and IBGE, tabela 2 "Área, Produção e Rendimento Médio—Confronto das safras de 2022 e das estimativas para 2023" at https://www.ibge.gov.br/estatisticas/economicas/agricultura-e-pecuaria/9201-levantamento-sistematico-da-producao-agricola.html?=&t=resultados.
2. IBGE, Divisão Regional do Brasil, found at https://www.ibge.gov.br/geociencias/organizacao-do-territorio/divisao-regional/15778-divisoes-regionais-do-brasil.html?edicao=16163.

CHAPTER 2

The Modernization of Brazilian Agriculture Since 1950

The emergence of Brazil as a major world agricultural producer in the late twentieth century is one of the most important developments in modern history. Until the middle of the twentieth century Brazil was a food importer and by then only exported one agricultural product of any significance into the international market. By the third decade of the twenty-first century it was the world's third largest agricultural exporter, just behind the United States and the European Union. Currently, it is among the world's top five producers of 36 agricultural products and has become the world's leading exporter of soybeans, orange juice, maize, sugar, meat (both beef and poultry), coffee, tobacco, cellulose, and ethanol, as well as being the world´s largest exporter of halal animal protein. It is now also the second largest international exporter of cotton. In the third decade of the twenty-first century, it sold nearly 300 agricultural products to more than 200 countries.[1] Although it is only the fifth largest nation in the world in terms of size and population, it has the largest quantity of arable lands of any nation in the world.[2] It is also the largest net exporter of food in the world, since it satisfies domestically almost all of its food needs and generates the highest net income of any agricultural exporting country. It is also the most important agricultural country situated in the tropics.

H. S. Klein and F. V. Luna, *Brazilian Crops in the Global Market*, Palgrave Studies in Economic History,
https://doi.org/10.1007/978-3-031-38589-6_2

Until the middle of the twentieth century a traditional agriculture was practiced in Brazil with little use of fertilizers, insecticides or machinery. Exports focused on coffee, and imports on those food imports crucial for domestic supply. The overwhelming majority of the economic active population worked in agriculture and two thirds of the population resided in rural areas. Although national production provided the basic food consumed in the country, except for wheat, efficiency was low with output per hectare well below world standards. Food prices were high and a large portion of the population was malnourished. Today Brazil exports food products and still provides a vast array of nationally consumed products at relatively low cost. Malnutrition and accompanying high post neonatal infant mortality are no longer a fundamental national problem.

As we noted in our earlier study, the 1960–1980 period can be considered the formative stage of modern Brazilian agriculture. The government began providing large public resources for financing of agriculture. It also supported farmer incomes with a minimum price guarantee policy and subsidized credit. An ambitious state research program was established and new equipment and agricultural inputs industries were subsidized. The period 1980 to 1999 represented a transition phase, marked by external and internal fiscal crises, the acceleration of inflation and a succession of failed stabilization programs. This resulted in a drastic reduction of protection for the domestic market and the end of subsidized credit for agriculture. Agricultural producers had by then achieved such productivity however, that they were able not only to survive these crises but began exporting their surplus production after satisfying the local market. Since 2000 there has been a systematic growth of Brazilian agriculture, its continued modernization and its complete integration into the world market. In this final period Brazil has established itself as a major producer and exporter of agricultural products worldwide.

Agriculture prior to 1960 was a low productivity activity. Domestic crops as well as coffee exports were produced with little utilization of machines and equipment. Modest productivity was obtained by constant renovation of the planting areas through the incorporation of virgin soils, leaving behind depleted soils. Agricultural labor was poorly qualified and badly paid, agricultural credit was limited and virgin land was the main input for agriculture. Land ownership was highly concentrated and unproductive latifundia were a striking feature of the agrarian structure. Some of these larger rural properties often had only limited agricultural production. Despite absorbing half of the economically active population of males as late as 1970,[3] work relations were considered archaic and productivity was low. Three quarters of the value of production was made up of just ten crops. Although the number of farms and land in production had been expanding since the 1920s, the amount of machinery, fertilizers and insecticides used was quite limited. Planted pastures were a small share of total available grazing areas and most animal breeds were native to the region.

Between the 1940s and the early 1960s, economists argued that the deficient structure of agriculture was the main impediment to the country's development, restricting the expansion of productive forces and allowing the survival of a backward and conservative power structure. It was argued that the high concentration of land ownership and the existence of unproductive latifundia prevented the modernization of agriculture. Agrarian reform was proposed as a solution.[4] In Brazil and in most Latin American countries, agrarian reform became the main theme in the debates about the development process in the middle of the last century. The military government which took over the country in 1964, though contrary to any change in land ownership, accepted the basic premise that Brazilian agriculture was retarding the development of the country and needed to be reformed. As a result, it developed a broad set of reforms, classified as "conservative modernization." It was conservative since it did not include changes in the structure of land ownership, nor did it challenge the power of rural elites, but it did exert pressure on unproductive landowners. It put a great deal of government resources into modernizing agriculture. At the same time, it combated the social movements that demanded agrarian reform by promoting a massive colonization of poor and landless farmers into state owned or abandoned lands.[5]

The military regime saw in agriculture an important source of inflationary pressure because of its deficiencies in the supply of agricultural products for the domestic market. They also believed that the reduction in the cost of food would be essential to contain the existing wage pressures in the evolving industrial sector. In a poor country such as Brazil, with low wages and a perverse distribution of income, food was an important component in the cost of living and therefore had a strong impact on the formation of real wages. The military government concluded that by rapid modernization, agriculture could play a crucial role in the process of industrial import substitution, through the supply of abundant and cheap food and raw materials. It could also generate exportable surpluses, thus contributing to the balance of trade. It decided to provide massive subsidized credit to rural producers to stimulate the adoption of machinery and the use of modern inputs such as new seed varieties, fertilizers, and pesticides. The process of mechanization would also have a positive effect of freeing labor from traditional agriculture so it could be used in the expanding industrial sector.

This modernization process required additional measures. Given the high costs of locally produced machinery, equipment, and inputs, which were protected by tariffs and other import restrictions, it was necessary to create a comprehensive system of subsidies to allow farmers to purchase these high priced inputs. A key program to do this was the Minimum Price Guarantee Policy (PGPM). For greater control over the behavior of supply and greater price stability, a broad system of government purchases of regulatory stocks was developed.[6] In addition, a complex public and private subsidized credit system was created, directed to the acquisition of machines and equipment in order to stimulate the use of modern inputs in agriculture.[7] The government also engaged in major road construction and opened up many frontier lands for exploitation. This system benefited commercial farmers with the interest and potential to modernize and led to important interregional migration of experienced commercial farmers from the Southern states to newly opened lands in the Center-West region. At the same time, it supported industries related to agriculture. With the expansion of industries processing agricultural and forestry products, such as meatpackers, soybean crushers, orange juice processors, and paper and cellulose mills, an important agroindustrial complex was formed, which would be of fundamental importance to the Brazilian economy and which would be the embryo of the current agribusiness complex.

Within the industrial import substitution system being created, there was significant regulation of imports which protected the domestic market from external competition. Even the products destined for the foreign market were controlled by the government, since the country also needed exportable surpluses. In addition to direct exchange rate control, and the subsidized credit, regulations were established to guide exports, in many cases through public entities such as the Sugar and Alcohol Institute (IAA) and the Brazilian Coffee Institute (IBC). There were also created special programs for regional development, in particular for the newly opened Center-West.

The government also invested heavily in modern agricultural research. In 1973, it created *Embrapa* (the Brazilian Agricultural Research Company) responsible for a massive research program aimed at providing modern technology to Brazilian agriculture. With a focus on agribusiness, and counting on hundreds of researchers trained in Brazil and overseas, *Embrapa* aimed to provide solutions for the development of tropical agriculture, from enriching soils to developing a new generation of plants and seeds adapted to local conditions. *Embrapa*'s sophisticated research work, and its effective results, explains a large part of the agricultural productivity gains obtained in the last fifty years in Brazil. The government also promoted the creation of agricultural faculties at all the major state and federal universities. The resulting research and products created by Embapa and the Agricultural Faculties were distributed throughout Brazil and involved most of the commercial crops being produced. The impact of this revolution in production and productivity can be seen from a comparison of the results of the crop year of 1976/1977 and that of 2022/2023. Even traditional products, preferentially aimed at the domestic market, such as rice, beans, and maize, showed a significant increase in productivity. Moreover all these crops increased faster in production than in land use (See Table 2.1).

Soybeans stand out among the new grains that were part of Brazil's agricultural modernization. Introduced in the late 1950s, production reached some 12 million tons in 1976/77, a level only surpassed by maize. The production of orange juice also showed rapid growth, becoming one of the main items in the list of Brazilian exports. Sugarcane expanded greatly, especially after the introduction of the Proálcool program in 1975 which promoted the production and use of ethanol. Even a traditional crop such as wheat showed exceptional growth through strong government incentives.

As can be seen in a number of comparisons, Brazil in the 1960s was far below the United States in productivity, but by the decade of the 2010s it finally surpassed the United States in output per hectare in sugar and cotton and came close to the North American level in soybean yield (see Graph 2.1). Even in maize production, while yield is still just half of that in the United States, its ability to produce two crops a year allowed Brazil in the second decade of this century to become the world's largest exporter of the product. Due to this performance, the current yields of most of the main commercial crops in Brazil are similar to those obtained in the advanced agricultural countries. Thus, in 2014, the average yield

Table 2.1 Planted area, production and productiy of the principal crops of Brazil, harvests of 1976/77 and 2022/23

Product	*Area (hectares)*		*Production (1000 tons)*		*Productivity per Hectare (kg/ha)*		*Change 1976/ 2022*	*Production*
	1976/ 77	*2022/ 23*	*1976/ 77*	*2022/23*	*1976/ 77*	*2022/ 23*	*Area*	
Cotton*	4,096	1,642	1,176	4,254	287	2,590	0.4	3.6
Peanuts**	222	212	314	802	1,413	3,782	1.0	2.6
Rice***	5,992	1,517	8,993	10,640	1,501	7,012	0.3	1.2
Oats	40	498	37	1,176	940	2,359	12.5	31.8
Barley	94	119	95	497	1,018	4,182	1.3	5.2
Beans****	4,539	2,782	2,215	2,900	488	1,043	0.6	1.3
Maize-total	11,797	22,325	19,256	126,397	1,632	5,662	1.9	6.6
Soybeans	6,949	43,242	12,145	153,538	1,748	3,551	6.2	12.6
Sorghum	178	1,054	435	2,968	2,450	2,815	5.9	6.8
Wheat	3,153	3,052	2,066	9,501	655	3,114	1.0	4.6
All Grains	37,060	76,828	46,732	313,036	1,258	4,075	2.1	6.7

Source CONAB, https://www.conab.gov.br/info-agro/safras/serie-historica-das-safras; CONAB. *Boletim da Safra de Grãos, 09/11/22*

Notes *Seed cotton

**Total for two harvests per crop year

***Total of irrigated and Dry Rice

****Total of three harvests per crop year

per hectare of soybeans in Brazil surpassed the yield of soybeans in Argentina and represents 90% of the yield obtained in the United States, while seed cotton has exceeded the North American yields since the turn of the century.[8]

This productivity has grown at an extraordinary rate in the past thirty or forty years in the production of coffee, corn, oranges, cotton, soybeans, sugar cane, and tobacco, all products in which Brazil now has a major participation in world markets. In all these products, Brazilian productivity was reaching world standards. The case of cotton, for example, was the most significant since Brazil went from 88% of the world average productivity in 1991–2000 to 171% of the average world cotton yield in 2011–2020. Even in the case of coffee, a traditional Brazilian product, productivity went from 101 to 167% of world standards in the same period. Such increases in productivity, associated with increased production, allowed for competitiveness and the generation of exportable surpluses in countless products from grains and animal proteins to orange juice (see Table 2.2).

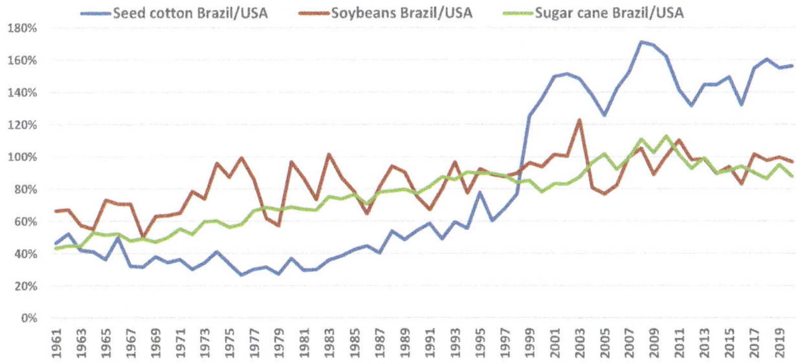

Graph 2.1 Comparison of output per hectare, Brazil/USA in selected crops, 1961–2020 (USA = 100%) (*Source* FAOSTAT)

Table 2.2 Average ten-year productivity of Principal Agricultural Crops, Brazil and World 1961–2020, in Kilograms per Hectare

Period	*Coffee, green*	*Maize*	*Oranges*	*Seed Cotton*	*Soybeans*	*Sugar cane*	*Tobacco*
Brazil							
1961–1970	447	1,325	15,035	592	1,084	44,535	881
1971–1980	546	1,488	16,229	459	1,501	50,160	1,143
1981–1990	595	1,838	19,732	751	1,730	61,086	1,425
1991–2000	647	2,498	21,815	1,420	2,175	66,459	1,645
2001–2010	1,052	3,592	22,060	3,281	2,621	75,252	1,876
2011–2020	1,536	5,166	26,450	3,895	3,071	74,540	2,063
Relation between Brazil and World Productivity							
1961–1970	101%	61%	108%	59%	84%	86%	75%
1971–1980	110%	51%	98%	40%	94%	92%	88%
1981–1990	110%	53%	122%	50%	97%	102%	96%
1991–2000	106%	61%	132%	88%	104%	106%	104%
2001–2010	142%	74%	131%	165%	112%	110%	111%
2011–2020	174%	93%	143%	172%	116%	105%	113%

Source FAOSTAT, http://www.fao.org/faostat/en/#data/QC

Some of this growth was accounted by the expansion of agriculture into new regions formerly of little agricultural value, this was especially important in the North and Center-West regions. Land planted in seasonal crops increased by 4.9% and 5.0% per annum respectively in these two regions between 1974 and 2021 (see Graph 2.2). This was due to

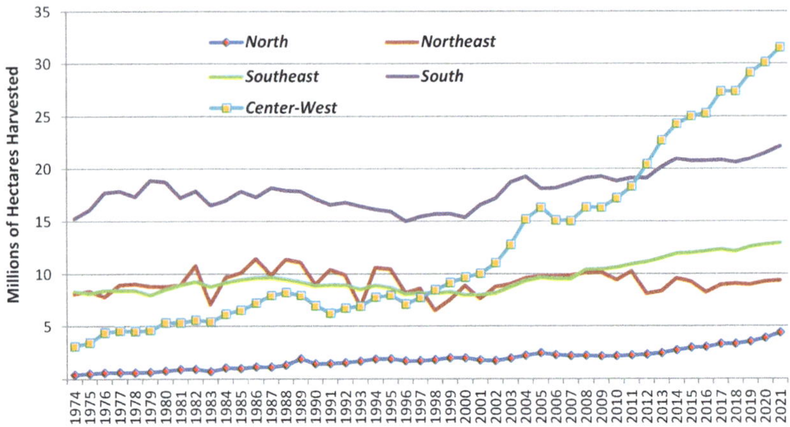

Graph 2.2 Area harvested in seasonal crops, by region, 1974–2021 (*Source* IBGE, Sidra, tabela 1612)

the opening of the previously abandoned Cerrado biome to agricultural production (see Map 2.1) and to a lesser extent to the exploitation of part of the Amazonian region as well.

Even with this incorporation of new lands, growth of production actually exceeded growth in land used for agriculture. While the production of all major grains grew at an impressive 3.9% per annum from the late 1970s to the end of the 2010s, land dedicated to their production only grew by 1.2% per annum (see Graph 2.3). This process can be explained by the extraordinary increase in productivity in the main commercial crops , as well as the ability to produce two crops in the same year, reaching even three crops in some regions. The case of maize is illustrative. The second crop, called the small harvest or "safrinha" due to its initially small output, is currently larger than the first corn harvest of the year. Moreover most of this growth was in previously unused scrub forested lands, especially in the Cerrado, which was only put into agricultural production in the past four decades. Although the legal Amazon has been invaded by illegal ranching and logging, the major commercial producing farms and ranches have been able to expand production mostly on non-forested lands.

The massive subsidies offered to producers enabled local agricultural production to supply most of domestic needs cheaply for the first time in modern times. Nevertheless, in this initial mid-twentieth-century period

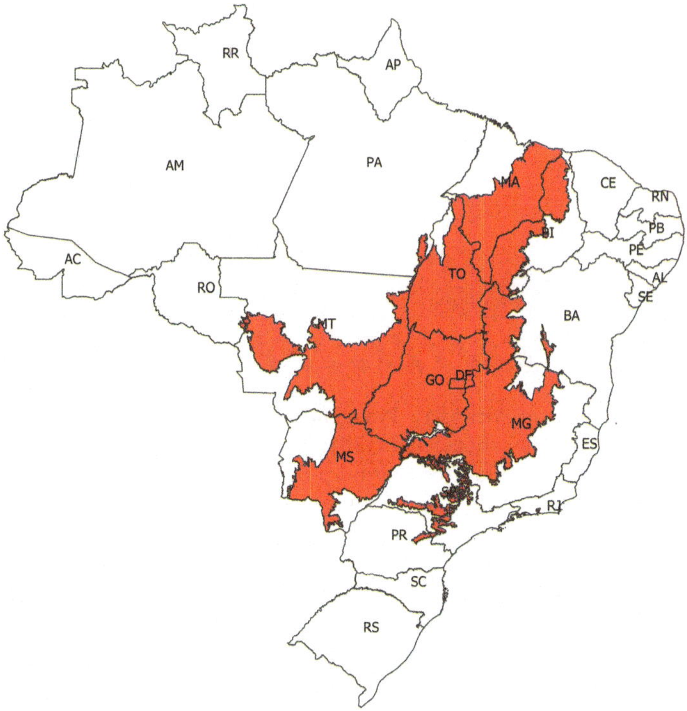

Map 2.1 Cerrado and states of Brazil (*Source* IBGE, Bases Cartográficas, Biomas Brasileiros)

some food products did not perform well. Maize, for example, which was a product which would become one of the crops with the best performance in the twenty-first century showed only a modest increase in productivity in this phase. The same happened with rice, beans, and cassava, essential items in the national diet, whose productivity did not grow significantly.

In general, however, the results of agriculture until the end of the military era in 1985 were positive, with a significant increase in production, major increases in the productivity of numerous crops and the formation of a complex agroindustrial sector. Between 1960 and 1980, the cultivated area nearly doubled, from 25 to 47 million hectares, and this was accompanied by increasing mechanization. In the same period,

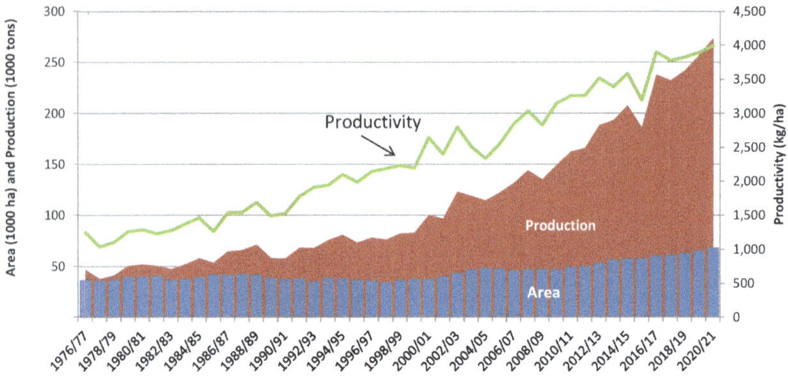

Graph 2.3 Changes in Area (ha), Production and Yield (kg/ha), 1976–2021 (*Note* Conab—séries históricas (safra 2017/2018 estimativa): https://www.conab.gov.br/info-agro/safras/serie-historica-das-safras and as of April 2021, at https://www.conab.gov.br/info-agro/safras/graos)

the number of hectares per tractor declined from 410 hectares to only 99 hectares, a ratio that remains stable to this day. Average fertilizer consumption per hectare increased from 8.3 kg in 1964 to 27.8 kg in 1970 and to 88 kg in 1980.[9]

Like all sectors of the economy, agriculture was affected by the oil induced national debt problems of the 1980s and 1990s. It began with the rise in oil prices in the 1970s and intensified with the Mexican debt crisis in 1982. This general world crisis was reflected in Brazil in the deterioration of public accounts, the acceleration of inflation, a dramatic crisis in the balance of payments, with the loss of reserves and of international credit. This resulted in a moratorium on foreign debt and a sharp decline in economic activity. The need for internal and external adjustments led to the adoption of recessive policies reinforced by agreements with the IMF, the effects of which extended for more than a decade. The supply of rural credit, based on large government subsidies and the use of resources from banking demand deposits, was dramatically reduced. In 1984, credit for agriculture was only 37% of the volume than had been available in 1979; in 1990, it fell to 23% of the 1979 rate. The share of credit in agricultural GDP declined sharply from 70 percent of agricultural GDP in the second half of the 1970s to just over 20 percent in the 1990s.[10] Equally from the mid-1980s, rural lending began to be readjusted by monetary correction.

Thus, the cost of credit, which had been negative in the early military period, turned positive and rose along with other financial market rates. Also reduced or eliminated were the policies of guaranteeing minimum prices and the formation of regulatory stocks. At the same time inflation was increasing dramatically. The succession of recessive policies and alternative heterodox plans were ineffective in containing the inflationary process, creating great uncertainty and negatively affecting agriculture with its long productive cycles.

But the crisis, which affected all sectors of the economy, also provided opportunities for agriculture. The international oil crisis and its impact on the foreign debt owed by Brazil which would culminate in the 1987 moratorium, gave agriculture a new role as the government promoted the replacement of oil with ethanol. In addition, in the face of external bottlenecks, the government intensified its stimulus to agricultural exports. Differentiated policies were established for products destined for the foreign market, such as coffee, sugar, soybeans, orange juice, cocoa, cotton, and tobacco.

On the other hand products for the domestic market suffered the impact of inflation and the reduction of government support. Wheat was the most emblematic case. Production quotas, external control, and producer and consumer subsidies made the product profitable to the producers, who increased supply and reduced the consumer price. The importance of wheat in the basic diet and the potential political impact of adopting real prices delayed the decision to end subsidies. But in 1987 wheat subsidies were finally eliminated; and in 1990 the free market was established for all stages of wheat production and marketing. With the end of these subsidies local production could not compete with imports. Whereas, in 1987, domestic production reached 6.2 million tons and accounted for 90% of domestic demand; in 1995, national production was just 1.4 million tons, and satisfied only 17% of the market. [11] Currently, Brazil has returned to producing six million tons, as the product has become competitive in the domestic market due to increased productivity, which has multiplied by four since the end of the 1980s.

Another state subsidized product which eventually became self-sufficient was ethanol production. The world oil price crises of the 1970s led the government to create the *Proálcool* program, which was an ambitious program of production and consumption of alcohol as automotive fuel. Launched in 1975, the program expanded in 1979 after the second oil shock. In addition to adding alcohol to gasoline sold in the country, the government encouraged the manufacture of cars powered exclusively with hydrated alcohol. Production targets were set at three billion liters per year for the first phase and rose to 7.7 billion liters in 1979. To promote the program, several tax incentives were made available along with public funding. The first cars powered by ethanol were adapted vehicles, but from the early 1980s appeared new and more efficient engines designed for the use of fuel alcohol. The government administered a policy that efficiently remunerated the alcohol producer and made that fuel competitive. Although very costly in terms of public resources, Proálcool proved to be effective and the market was geared almost exclusively to alcohol-powered vehicles. In 1984, for example, 95% of the cars made in Brazil were powered by this fuel. The program stimulated improvements in productivity of the refineries and in the growing of cane. But with the decline in international oil prices, alcohol became uncompetitive. Thus, in the mid-1980s the program went into crisis, with a rapid decline in sales of alcohol-powered vehicles, with such sales almost ceasing in the 1990s. Automotive consumption was limited to alcohol added to gasoline. But a new upward trend in oil prices and renewed government support revitalized the program in the early twenty-first century. This in turn was bolstered by the emergence of flex-fuel engines that run on ethanol and/or gasoline. Currently, Brazil is the second largest producer of ethanol and ethanol fuel (anhydrous and hydrated) in the world and by 2016 this fuel accounted for two thirds of the country's gasoline consumption.[12]

In the late 1980s and throughout the 1990s, most of the world was being swept by a neoliberal policy revolution, which was finally implanted in Brazil. The GATT Uruguay Round, which resulted in the creation of the World Trade Organization (WTO), when it was concluded in 1993, included a major agreement on agriculture. This agreement focused on three main points: open market access, reduction of export subsidies and government support for agriculture. This agreement effectively contributed to the liberalization of trade and the entry of large multinational groups into underdeveloped countries.[13] In 1991, through the Treaty of Asunción, a regional free market zone was created known as the Common Market of the South (Mercosur), which allowed the free circulation of goods, services, and productive factors among the signatory nations. In 1994, by the Ouro Preto Protocol, a Common External Tariff for Mercosur was defined.[14]

The opening of the market in the 1980s and 1990s reflected the weakening of the previously dominant import substitution model and the worldwide trend toward trade liberalization. The opening would be reinforced by the policy of broad liberalization adopted in the government of Fernando Collor (1990–1992). Initially this new liberal period had a negative impact on the agricultural sector due to the drastic reduction of subsidies. Between 1970 and 1986 these credit subsidies represented 11.4% of the agricultural GDP of the period.[15] In 1987, for example, $ 2 billion was spent on wheat subsidies alone, another US $ 1.5 billion was earmarked for guaranteeing minimum prices and regulatory stocks; and the sugar and alcohol segment consumed US $ 1 billion. Rural credit amounted to US $ 700 million. The total subsidy, which totaled $5.3 billion in 1987, two years later was reduced to just $ 1 billion.[16]

For agriculture, the removal of import restrictions took place in stages. In 1988, a major reduction in tariffs was adopted, reinforced in 1990, when all restrictions on imports of agricultural products were eliminated. The following year, a timetable was established for the process of tariff reductions and simplifications. Thus, the average tariff dropped from 32 to 14%; and the maximum rate, from 105 to 35%. When the system was fully deployed, most products went on to be taxed at only 10%. The extreme case was cotton, with zero tariffs due to the government's intention to support the textile industry with imports.

Fortunately for agriculture, the new tariff structure also focused on internationally produced machinery, equipment, fertilizers, and other agricultural inputs that now could be imported at reduced rates. Between 1991 and 1992 prior import and export licenses for agricultural products were eliminated, as well as taxes levied on exports of various agricultural products. Even the sugar and alcohol segment, regulated by a complex system of quotas, began to operate in the free market. The reforms did not eliminate all government agricultural programs, but many underwent major changes, such as the minimum price guarantee policy and regulatory stock operations. Until the 1980s, most of the cotton, rice, beans, maize, and soybean crops were financed by the Federal Government Loan Program (EGF) and later acquired through the Federal Government Acquisitions Program (AGF).[17] The government purchased the products, formed regulatory stocks, then placed them on the market when there was a need to control prices. In 1993, in order to reduce the amount of resources needed to regulate prices, the settlement price of the EGF was created. Once the financing was obtained, the product stock remained in the producer's possession. When the settlement price exceeded the market price, the farmer had the right to sell the product directly on the open market, and the differential value would be reimbursed by the federal government. The mechanism avoided mobilizing large amounts of resources for the housing of regulatory stocks, and avoided the onerous and inefficient administration of large stocks by the government.

But even in the turbulent 1980s and 1990s, agriculture recorded average annual growth of 3%, higher than the average national GDP growth in the period. However, performance was erratic, alternating positive and negative years, and exhibiting better results in production for export than in production destined for the domestic market. If we consider the crisis faced by agriculture in this period, with the acceleration of inflation, recessionary policies, fiscal crisis, elimination of subsidies, and reduction of official credit supply, we can consider the performance of agriculture as positive. In addition, structural transformations were occurring in Brazilian agriculture that would have great effect at the beginning of the twenty-first century.

The collapse of government support and the opening of the national economy to world trade forced a deep and painful reorganization of the entire Brazilian economy. Both industry and agriculture had been systematically supported by the government in previous decades, but agriculture alone was able to make the necessary changes to compete successfully in the international market due to its spectacular productivity growth. This is a surprising result and has innumerable internal and external causes, but above all it was government policies developed over the previous decades which were fundamental. Since the 1960s, government support allowed agriculture to play a key role in generating exports while at the same time supplying local markets efficiently and cheaply with raw materials and food. The rapid growth of Brazil's urban population provided an important and expanding market that allowed the continued growth of agriculture. Brazil's urban population went from 31 million persons in 1950 to 111 million in 1991, and by then accounted for 84% of the national population.[18]

But the loss of substantial government credit did create a temporary crisis affecting many producers and cooperatives and resulted in significant defaults of farmers. Under the pre 1990 governments there was a comprehensive system of subsidies. The system worked relatively well while there was economic stability. With the state's fiscal crisis and the unchecked inflation of the late 1980s and early 1990s, however, the abundant and subsidized credit system, public or offered through bank liabilities, collapsed and had to be replaced by alternative forms of credit.

With the need to obtain new sources of rural credit, alternative credit mechanisms began to be adopted in the early 1990s. Although foreign direct investments went mostly into mining, infrastructure and industry, a modest amount of such investments were made in agriculture. But agriculture, in contrast to industry, remained overwhelmingly dominated by national capital. Nevertheless foreign and national capital now was made available to replace government support. These new sources of agricultural credit came in the form of international trading companies. This type of credit essentially benefited commodity producers, who were less vulnerable to the risk of dollar-denominated financial transactions.[19]

The government also did not totally abandon agriculture in the new period of globalization and created public and private mechanisms to increase the supply of agricultural credit, even when the previous programs were exhausted. It would also provide new support for family farms. Thus, in 1986, when the Movement Account (which supplied monetary resources to agriculture) was closed, the Rural Savings Account was created, whose resources would be applied exclusively to agriculture. Savings Account applications represent a traditional form of long-term, risk-free deposits, the funds of which banks were required to invest in real estate sector for housing. A new alternative for raising funds for agriculture was opened with this type of account. In 1987 this so-called *Caderneta de Poupança* quickly represented more than a fifth of the resources destined for agriculture and since then it has been an important source of credit resources for the sector. In the Constitution of 1988, the Constitutional Financing Funds were created, whose resources should be directed to the North, Northeast and Central-West regions, with priority being given to the financing of small rural and industrial producers.[20] Also from the mid-1980s, monetary correction was introduced gradually in rural loans, reducing their impact somewhat.[21]

The government has also tried to protect producers against relative price fluctuations. In 1991, the so-called Agricultural Law created the payment mechanism for credit operations by product equivalence.[22] As agricultural credit contracts were corrected for inflation, correcting the federal government purchase guarantee prices by the same correction index applied to the respective loan eliminated the risk of the disparity of indicators, which increased when inflation reached exceptional levels.[23] In the same year, BNDES (National Bank for Economic and Social Development) intensified its activities in the agricultural area, especially in investment financing. In 1994, the government created the Rural Producer Certificate (CPR), an instrument representative of the promise of future delivery of agricultural products that could be issued in dollars.[24] The CPR represented an important instrument for the integration of Brazilian agriculture with the international market, since it allowed the direct and anticipated sale of products. In 2001, the law was supplemented allowing the financial settlement of the certificate, complementing the original law that required liquidation in products. In 1998, a resolution created the so-called "63 caipira," which represents the ability to provide foreign loans in *reais*, but with indexation in dollars. This type of loan, traditional in the Brazilian financial market, was now applied to agriculture and was another step toward the internationalization of agribusiness activities in Brazil.

In 1996, the government also developed major programs to aid small farmers, through *Pronaf* (the Family Agriculture Strengthening Program), establishing a long-term program to support such farmers. It aimed at the sustainable development of family farmers by increasing their productive capacity, by generating jobs, and improving their income. In the same year, the government authorized the use of funds from the Worker Support Fund to finance small and medium-sized farmers through *Pronaf*. These support measures for small farmers addressed the social and political demands of political movements related to small farmers and advocates for land reform, particularly the MST (Landless Rural Workers Movement).

These new private and public financial instruments gave the agricultural sector a flexibility similar to the other economic sectors, and expanded credit options for the financing of inputs and for commercialization of production. These were necessary for the new stage of Brazilian agriculture, which began to operate through large value chains with the participation of agents in Brazil and abroad. This is an industry that has become fully integrated with the international market, with technology and instruments of commercialization and financing comparable to those available to its leading competitors. Nevertheless farmers still depend on official sources of financing or credit directed by the Brazilian private banking sector and part of these public funds although now positive, are given at interest rates below free market credit rates.[25] The amount of rural credit reached R$ 236 billion [or approximately1.2 trillion US dollars) in the 2020/21 harvest. The so-called business or commercial agriculture absorbed 86% of the credit granted, and family farming (PRONAF) the other 14%. Of the total resources, R$ 154 billion was to be invested with controlled interest and R$ 82 billion at regular market rates. Of the total amount of resources, a quarter will be directed to investments and three quarters for costs of production.

Even with this continued government support, since the 1980s the private sector has come to play an ever increasing role in providing for agricultural credit. The suppliers and distributors of inputs, such as companies selling seeds, fertilizers, or pesticides; national and international trading companies and producer cooperatives; and finally agro-processors of all types are now significant credit suppliers to farmers. The system works in several ways. One is through the advance of resources for the anticipated purchase of the crop by suppliers and distributors of inputs under a contract system. This credit is only repaid after the respective harvest. In addition, there are exchange operations that involve the possibility of delivering the harvested product, as a form of payment of purchased inputs at a predefined parity. Agricultural production has thus became deeply integrated with private suppliers of agricultural inputs (such as seed, pesticide, and fertilizer venders); processors of agricultural products (such as soybeans crushers, juice producers, and meatpackers); distributors in general (such as supermarket chains); and private companies (such as the international trading companies). It was these various sources in complex "value chains" with crop contracts that replaced a large part of the previously available state supported credit. It also led to a significant part of the agricultural sales no longer being made in the spot market.

According to one study, the share of bank credit is higher in the South of the country, while there is greater use of credit from suppliers of inputs and commercial companies in the financing of production in the Center-West.[26] The decline in the government's financing model encouraged the integration of agribusiness into these value chains. The farmer had to become an entrepreneur to survive and grow in the new business environment where the producer can buy and sell his inputs and products in the open global market, but he also has to compete in this sophisticated market. It is the international market that now sets agricultural prices, which generates the dynamics of production, its viability, and profitability. If there are advantages, there are also risks. It's not an amateur environment.[27]

Although it has a variety of credit instruments, Brazilian agriculture has suffered like the other economic sectors with the high interest rates practiced in Brazil. Although controlled-interest operations still exist in some agricultural segments, commercial farmers are still burdened with high interest rates, which were often higher than those practiced in agriculture in the rich countries who were their competitors in the international market. Even international credit is burdened by the high risk of Brazil. Although Brazil has for some years practiced interest rates more compatible with the international market, since 2021 the resurgence of inflation has seen interest rates again rise above those of its competitors. This has added to the so-called "Brazilian costs" of production, which include taxes and higher logistic costs due to poor infrastructure

The second factor enabling agribusiness to survive was the migration of experienced entrepreneurial farmers from the Southern states to the states of the Center-West in search of new larger production units. The third and vitally important factor was the arrival of a whole new set of modern inputs (such as new seeds and soil enrichment and crop preservation practices) created by *EMBRAPA* and other research centers, which finally came into full use by the end of the twentieth century.

Until the 1950s, there was limited public or private agricultural research and low coordination among the few existing centers in the country. There were some research and extension centers, state and private, founded in the nineteenth and early twentieth centuries. Several belonged to agricultural schools founded in Brazil at that time, which later were integrated into large universities, and by the end of the twentieth century, these university centers had modern teaching and research facilities. Among the earliest and most important such centers were the Agronomic Institute of Campinas, the Luiz de Queiroz College of Agronomy (ESALQ) of the University of São Paulo, the Lavras School of Agriculture, and the Viçosa Veterinary School. But without a national infrastructure, the dissemination of their research results was still limited.[28]

The creation of *Embrapa* besides intensifying agricultural research in general, would fill the gap in the national and regional dissemination of results. At its origin, *Embrapa* emphasized the need to adapt foreign technologies to Brazilian conditions. Research was to be directly related to well-defined programs by product or by region, with permanent evaluation of the results. Perhaps the most important factor in explaining Embrapa's success has been its human resources policy and training program. This training program allowed Brazil to expand the offer of researchers with a global vision of Brazilian development so that they could select their research projects within this model. Embrapa quickly hired and trained hundreds of researchers in educational institutions in Brazil and abroad, mainly the United States, with its own resources and financial support from numerous national and international entities such as FINEP, BIRD, BID, and USAID.[29] In 2016, Embrapa employed 2444 researchers, of whom 330 held master's degrees, 1,829 were PhDs, and 285 were postdoctoral fellows. Despite some fluctuations, there was a steady increase in budget allocations for Embrapa by the federal government.[30]

Brazil is among the countries that have one of the best-developed and financed agricultural research systems in the developing world, ranking third in public spending on agricultural R&D, after China and India. Aside from Embrapa almost every state has an agricultural research program or institute and several privately financed research organizations exist for individual crops. Among the important state organizations is the São Paulo Agribusiness Technology Agency (APTA), which involves numerous state entities, such as the Agronomic Institute of Campinas and the Biological Institute. with 498 full-time researchers, the Agricultural Research and Rural Extension Company of Santa Catarina (Epagri), with 263, and the Agricultural Research Company of Minas Gerais (Epamig), with 167 scientists. There are 96 federal and state universities in higher education institutions working in agricultural research, including colleges, research centers, and agricultural departments, in addition to research foundations and smaller agencies.[31]

Basic research is essential for productivity growth, especially in a tropical country, because it opens up possibilities for discoveries of new varieties, which are more resilient and productive; develops improved management techniques and new ways of planting; promotes improvements in the quality of inputs; and deals with conditions that are often unique to the tropics. The effects of the research are not immediate but cumulative, and also vary over time depending on the crop and soils. Together with the research, the results of the rural extension and guidance services provided by these public and private research centers are also significant. In this sense, the role of Embrapa and other public and private entities was crucial for this extraordinary Brazilian growth in productivity, since it provided the farmers with the means and knowledge to adopt technological changes and innovations modified to the specific conditions of the climate and local soils. According to the study of the results of total factor productivity, the strongest effect on productivity is related to research spending. A 1% increase in research spending results in an increase of 0.35% in TFP, followed by the importance of credit and exports.[32]

The survival of Brazilian agriculture in the post 1990 period required increased productivity, which the more entrepreneurial farmers were able to obtain through the use of new technologies, more efficient seeds, more systematic application of fertilizers, insecticides, and intensified use of machinery and equipment. Much of this adaptability resulted from years of this government-sponsored research. It was this research which provided Brazilian farmers with the seeds and the technology adapted to the soil and climate conditions of the country, and to its quite various regions and multiple products. This allowed the transformation of entire regions of Brazil into productive centers of modern agricultural production. This was the dynamic element that explains the revolution in Brazilian agriculture, which occurred even during the protracted crisis of the Brazilian economy.

The transformation of the Brazilian economy since the 1990s was also greatly influenced by the success of the *Real Plan*, which finally controlled the inflationary process. After almost half a century of economic instability, acceleration of inflation, and successive stabilization plans, the *Real Plan*, implemented in 1994, created a new pattern of economic relations, compatible with a country of the economic importance of Brazil. The stability achieved with the *Real Plan* was based on three fundamental points: a currency anchor, the maintenance of an overvalued currency—the *real*—and the broad opening of the economy. Unlike previous stabilization plans, it was possible to use the exchange rate anchor because Brazil had renegotiated its external debt, allowing free access to the international financial market, which offered abundant resources, high liquidity, and low interest rates. At the same time, in the domestic market, real interest rates were extremely high, attracting foreign capital and generating an abundance of dollars that overvalued the national currency.[33]

The deepening of the process of trade liberalization increased exposure to international competition, and the maintenance of an overvalued currency had a positive effect on price stability. Imported goods or Brazilian commodities had their prices controlled by the competition, which helped in the initial phase of the Real Plan. Unlike agriculture, which was completely exposed to international competition, important industrial sectors still maintained high levels of protection, limiting the progressive effect of market opening on industrial productivity.

The introduction of fertilizers and agricultural equipment would be of great importance in the process of modernization of Brazilian agriculture, but the sector would not have reached its current competitiveness in the world agribusiness market without the diffusion of this knowledge about new inputs and new technologies and practices. In this sense, *Embrapa* and other public and private research institutes, as well as multinational agricultural enterprises, played an important role in providing education of farmers in the latest techniques. In the past, government agricultural credit was associated with public and private technical assistance. The idea was to strengthen human capital to better utilize the investments made available for the acquisition of capital goods and modern inputs. Technical assistance was linked to rural credit and was mandatory until the 1990s.

In the early 2000s, the government once again became invested in technical agricultural assistance programs. In 2010, the General Law on Technical Assistance for Rural Extension (ATER) was approved, which establishes the National Policy for Technical Assistance and Rural Extension for Family Agriculture for Agrarian Reform (PNATER) and the National Program for Technical Assistance and Rural Extension in Family Agriculture and Agrarian Reform (PRONATER).[34] But this government technical assistance is limited to small family farms and specific groups of rural producers, as well as to minority groups such as indigenous communities.[35] Finally, in 2013, a federal entity was created to manage the program, the National Agency for Technical Assistance and Rural Extension (ANATER), which can also approve other public and private entities to carry out extension activities.[36] The public system of technical assistance and rural extension in Brazil now focuses on the small landholder, a trend that has occurred in other countries.

On the other hand commercial producers now obtain such services on the private market which has grown enormously in Brazil in recent years.[37] Several studies, sponsored by the FAO and the World Bank, have pointed out that the technological modernization of agriculture, the specialization of producers, and the expansion of the scale of production lead to the emergence of a private agricultural information market. This is what happened in Brazil, with the consolidation of a large and sophisticated specialized information market, offered by private entities, which include technical assistance companies, agricultural suppliers, and equipment manufacturers. This market consists of specialized firms, cooperatives, and a host of other organizations. Producers active in commercial agriculture often benefit from the vertical integration of cooperatives of producers, commercial enterprises, or industrial processors that provide technical knowledge, as well as credit through fixed-term contracts. Both large and small producers have responded actively to the crises of the 1980s and 1990s with complex private, commercial, and cooperative arrangements. These mechanisms allowed many producers to collectively reduce their costs, compensate for the lack of official agricultural extension programs, and quickly utilize the latest and most appropriate technology for their crops or breeding. The evolution of productive integration also involved the substantial cooperative sector. Many cooperatives and their members have created such value chains, disseminating and using the most modern agricultural and agroindustrial technology, and developing complex systems of financing and commercialization.[38] Although federal and state government agencies have intensified their efforts in rural extension in recent years, the provision of such services does not address the need for much of the small family farmer establishments. In contrast the modern commercial sector shows widespread use of modern technologies and inputs, including the so-called genetically modified crops, and thus is current with the latest technical information.

The magnitude of the agribusiness advances in Brazil is impressive. The area planted in grains grew from 40 million hectares in 1980/81 to 77 million hectares in the harvest of 2022/23 In contrast to this relatively modest increase in planted area, there was a massive increase in production, from approximately 52 million tons to 312 million tons of grains in the same period. This exceptional growth of output resulted from the extraordinary increase in productivity, which rose from 1293 kg per hectare in the harvest of 1980/81 to about 4059 kg in that of 2022/23.[39]

Although the indicators of production by area are a practical way of measuring and comparing agricultural productivity, the best way to analyze the dynamics of growth is through the analysis of Total Factor Productivity (TFP), which measures the relationship between production and the quantity of inputs used, such as land, labor, and capital. Several studies show that Brazil had an extraordinary performance in TFP comparable to the countries with the best agricultural performance.[40] One of these TFP studies, for the period 1970 to 2017, shows a high and persistent growth in labor and land productivity, above 3% per year (see Table

2.3). Part of this growth was the incorporation of new, highly productive land and the adoption of new farming practices, but the greatest effect was the result of investments in research, extension services, and use of new technologies.

In this period (1970–2017), Total Productivity of Factors increased by 2.03% per annum, with significant regional differences. The best performance occurred in the Center-West (3.87%), the main area of productive expansion in Brazil. The South and Southeast also showed significant growth, in the order of 2.43% and 1.91%, respectively. It is worth noting that in the more recent period, between the 2006 and 2017 census, growth rates remained high, except in the North and Northeast. In the case of the latter region, the indicators show a loss of dynamism in both land and labor productivity. The strong expansion and modernization of the northeastern savannah, was not able to compensate for the poor performance of the other northeastern agricultural areas.[41] On the other hand all other regions show that production continued to grow at an accelerated pace, although the amount of inputs remained practically stable. The high and increasing agricultural productivity makes Brazil highly competitive in the international agricultural market (see Table 2.4).

Brazil's agricultural performance as measured by its TFP is high compared to the main agricultural countries in the world, such as China, the United States, India, Australia, Canada, and Argentina. In the period from 2001 to 2009, for example, the TFP of Brazilian agriculture showed an average annual growth of 4%, against 2.8% in China, 2.3% in the United States and 2.1% in Canada and India. Argentina and Australia showed significantly lower growth rates. China and India are not competitors of Brazil and are in fact among its main markets. The Brazilian competition is with other major producers and exporters of meats and grains, such as the United States, Australia, and Canada.[42] Brazilian performance in this context has been exceptional since the 1980s (see Table 2.5).

This extraordinary performance of Brazilian agriculture occurred when the Brazilian economy as a whole did not have such good results. Overall productivity in Brazil is low even in comparison with similar countries, and has stagnated since the 1980s. Brazil's exceptional performance in terms of production and productivity in agriculture has allowed Brazil to play an important role in the international market for agribusiness products. Although the agricultural sector has a reduced participation in the composition of the national GDP, of the order of 7%, the so-called

Table 2.3 Sources for growth of Brazilian Agriculture, 1975–2011 (annual rates of growth)

Indicators	*1975–2011*	*1975–1979*	*1980–1989*	*1990–1999*	*2000–2009*	*2000–2011*
Index of production	3.77	4.37	3.38	3.01	5.18	4.85
Index of inputs	0.20	2.87	2.20	0.36	−0.51	−0.80
Total factor productivity	**3.56**	**1.46**	**1.16**	**2.64**	**5.72**	**5.69**
Productivity of labor	4.29	4.25	2.13	3.52	5.86	5.71
Productivity of land	3.77	3.15	2.91	3.25	5.61	5.32
Productivity of capital	3.05	2.77	2.87	1.89	4.62	4.35

Source Gasques et al. (2012), p. 89

Table 2.4 Total productivity of factors by Region and Brazil, 1970–2016

Brazil/Regions	*Total Productivity of Factors (FTP)*					
	Product		*Inputs*		*TFP*	
	1970–2017	*2006–2017*	*1970–2017*	*2006–2017*	*1970–2017*	*2006–2017*
Brazil	3.21	3.29	1.17	1.05	2.03	2.21
North	3.82	2.42	2.93	2.28	0.87	0.13
Northeast	2.09	−0.21	0.26	−0.30	1.83	0.08
Southeast	2.79	3.16	0.86	0.59	1.91	2.56
South	3.65	3.73	1.19	1.46	2.43	2.23
Center-West	5.91	5.79	1.96	1.90	3.87	3.82
	Productivity of Land, Labor and Capital					
	Productivity of land		*Productivity of labor*		*Productivity of capital*	
	1970–2017	*2006–2017*	*1970–2017*	*2006–2017*	*1970–2017*	*2006–2017*
Brazil	3.04	3.06	3.23	3.21	2.69	2.40
North	2.71	1.50	2.50	2.06	3.45	1.53
Northeast	2.21	0.82	1.99	−0.21	1.98	−0.69
Southeast	2.95	3.24	2.79	2.90	2.24	2.19
South	3.56	3.31	3.91	3.85	2.80	2.42
Center-West	5.46	4.97	5.71	5.54	5.48	5.23

Source Vieira Filho et al. (2018): 111

Table 2.5 Agricultural production by countries and groups of countries and value of production and total factor productivity, 1961–2009

		Agricultural output and productivity growth by country—annual change					*Agricultural TFP—annual change*				
Countries and groups	*Value produc-tion*	*1961–1970*	*1971–1980*	*1981–1990*	*1991–2000*	*2001–2009*	*1961–1970*	*1971–1980*	*1981–1990*	*1991–2000*	*2001–2009*
All developing countries		6.2	3.0	3.4	3.6	3.3	0.7	0.9	1.1	2.2	2.2
All developed countries		2.1	1.9	0.7	1.4	0.6	1.0	1.6	1.4	2.2	2.4
Transiion economies		3.3	1.3	0.9	−3.5	2.0	0.6	−0.1	0.6	0.8	2.3
Brazil	**127**	**3.6**	**3.9**	**3.4**	**3.7**	**4.5**	**0.2**	**0.5**	**3.0**	**2.6**	**4.0**
USA	229	2.0	2.3	0.6	1.9	1.4	1.2	1.8	1.2	2.2	2.3
China	487	4.9	3.3	4.5	5.3	3.4	0.9	0.6	1.7	4.2	2.8
Argentina	41	1.8	3.0	0.5	3.2	2.7	0.2	3.1	−1.0	1.5	1.2
Australia	23	3.0	1.8	1.7	3.6	−0.8	0.6	1.7	1.3	2.9	0.6
India	205	1.7	2.8	3.4	2.5	3.3	0.5	1.0	1.3	1.2	2.1
Canada	28	2.8	2.3	1.3	2.5	2.0	1.4	−0.4	2.7	2.6	2.1

Notes Value of Production—average period 2006–2009—US$-constant values of 2005
Source Fuglie (2012)

agribusiness, which includes agricultural production, industrial processing of agricultural products, distribution channels of production, supply chain of inputs for agriculture, including machinery and equipment, logistics, research, technical assistance, and financial services related to agriculture, currently accounts for more than 20% of national GDP. This productive segment has a great impact on the Brazilian economy, the value of production, jobs, and, above all, on exports.

The behavior of agribusiness represents a fundamental factor for balance of payments equilibrium. Agribusiness exports have grown steadily since the beginning of the twenty-first century. Starting from US $ 20 billion in 2000, these exports reached US $ 100 billion in 2013 and US $ 158 billion in 2022. The greatest importance of agribusiness performance in the external area is not only the quantity exported, but its representativeness in the total value exported by Brazil which was 49% in 2022. Also as Brazil exports a high ratio of its agricultural products and imports relatively few agricultural items, the country has the best net result in agribusiness exports in the world, surpassing the United States and the Netherlands. Since the Brazilian trade balance, excluding agribusiness, is usually negative, it is agricultural exports that allow the generation of positive balances in Brazilian international trade (see Table 2.6).

The performance of Brazilian agriculture has also benefited from changes in the international commodity market, particularly in the agricultural commodities. After a long period of relative stability in the 1980s and 1990s, agricultural commodity prices grew rapidly in the early twenty-first century, influenced by the expansion of the Chinese economy and its increasing share of the commodities market. The FAO Food Price Index, using as its 100 base the average for the years 2014 to 2016, peaked at 131 in 2011, representing an extraordinary growth of 130% in a decade. There was a significant drop after the peak of 2011, but the index has recovered since 2016 and reached 116 at the beginning of 2021.[43] Despite this decline, Brazilian agribusiness exports managed to remain relatively stable until 2014, showing significant decline in 2015 and 2016 and then a major recovery afterward.[44] The competitiveness of Brazilian agricultural exports allowed it to systematically grow as world demand increased. Thus its share of global world agricultural trade grew from an average of 3.1% in the 1960s to 5.8% in the 2010s (see Graph 2.4). This was only possible thanks to the extraordinary increase in agricultural productivity, and only through this productivity can Brazil be

Table 2.6 Value of exports and imports. Totals and agribusiness, Brazil 1990–2022

Anos	*Exports (US$ billion)*			*Imports (US$ billion)*			*Balance (US$ billion)*	
	Total Brazil (*a*)	*Agribusiness* (*b*)	*% b/a (%)*	*Total Brazil* (*a*)	*Agribusiness* (*b*)	*% b/a (%)*	*Total Brazil*	*Agribusiness*
1990	31.4	13.0	41	20.7	3.2	15	10.8	9.8
1995	46.5	20.9	45	50.0	8.6	17	−3.5	12.3
2000	55.1	20.6	37	55.9	5.8	10	−0.7	14.8
2005	118.6	43.6	37	73.6	5.1	7	45.0	38.5
2010	201.9	76.4	38	181.6	13.4	7	20.3	63.1
2015	191.1	88.2	46	171.5	13.1	8	19.7	75.2
2016	185.2	84.8	46	137.6	13.6	10	47.7	71.2
2017	217.7	96.0	44	150.7	14.2	9	67.0	81.8
2018	239.3	101.2	42	181.2	14.0	8	58.0	87.2
2019	225.4	96.8	43	177.3	13.8	8	48.0	83.0
2020	209.8	100.7	48	158.9	13.1	8	50.9	87.6
2021	280.6	120.5	43	219.5	15.5	7	61.1	105.0
2022	335.0	158.9	47	272.7	17.2	6	62.3	141.7

Source Elaborated from data found in AGROSTAT and Ipeadata

competitive in the international market in the long term, when it will have to face natural periods of price fluctuations.[45]

It was this opening up of the international market which also helps to explain the sustained and extraordinary productivity of commercial agricultural producers. This productivity compensates for the structural difficulties faced by agriculture in terms of poor infrastructure, exchange rate crises, complex tax systems, and high interest rates. But if it was the productivity that allowed the country to play a significant role in the international agricultural market, it was also the international market that allowed for the continuous increase of productivity, since the international agricultural market was almost unlimited for a competitive producer. A process of continuous increase in competitiveness would have been impossible in a closed local market, no matter how broad. In this case, the expansion of supply would have caused a fall in agricultural prices, preventing sequential increases in production through higher productivity.[46]

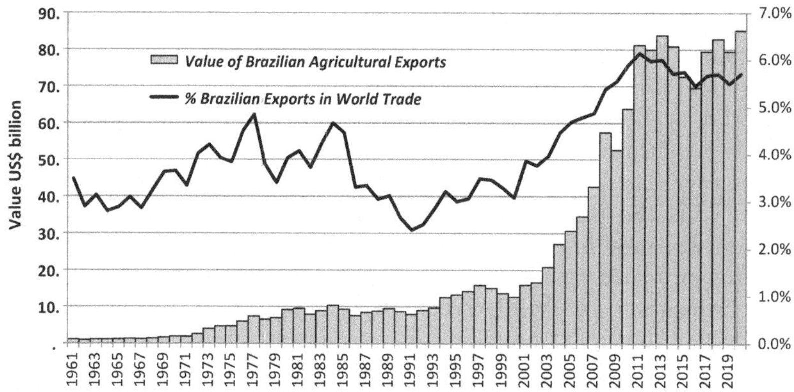

Graph 2.4 Total value of Brazilian Agricultural exports and its participation in total world agricultural trade, 1961–2020 *Source* Faostat

It is important to emphasize that the transformation of Brazil into a major exporter of agricultural products occurred simultaneously with the growth of production and productivity of traditional food crops. This allowed agriculture to adequately supply the domestic market, which in turn led to a systematic fall in domestic prices of local food. According to a study in 2013, between February 1976 and August 2006, the value of a basic food basket declined significantly at the rate of 3.13% per year. The authors conclude that the largest beneficiaries would have been the poorest consumers and that without this drop in food prices, the income transfer programs carried out by the Cardoso and Lula governments would have been less successful.[47]

Brazil still suffers from the so-called "Brazil cost," due to inefficiencies in infrastructure, high interest rates, and a perverse tax system. Even so, Brazilian agriculture has increased its production in an extraordinary way, explained essentially by a continuous increase in yields per hectare of almost all crops. Once entering the world market with its cooperatives, processing and trading companies, modern commercial agriculture in Brazil has taken advantage of the unique physical conditions of this tropical and semi-tropical country whose lands are greater than the combined lands of Western and Central Europe. It is now a fundamental part of the international commodities market and has the potential to expand production to meet world needs for its products for decades in the future.

With the continued improvement in productivity, as well as the incorporation of new land that is already deforested and/or degraded pasture lands which have still not been fully developed, Brazil still has potential growth in land utilization for agriculture. There is also a large traditional segment of national farmers who can be drawn into more advanced commercial production. These have begun to receive major government support in recent years and these small family farms have the potential to increase their participation in the international market. Growth of the agricultural sector is estimated to continue at a fast pace in the coming decade. The latest estimates from EMBRAPA are that grain production will grow from 262 million tons to 333 million tons in the next decade, increasing at an average annual rate of 2.4% between the harvests of 2020/21 to 2030/31. Land devoted to these grains will only increase by 1.6% from 69, million hectares to 81 million.[48] In turn the Total Factor Productivity which grew at an estimated 3.37% between 2010 and 2019 is expected to slow, but still grow by 1.55% per annum between 2020 and 2030.[49]

Notes

1. MAPA, *Brazilian Agricultural Foreign Trade* (2012):20; also see Constanza Valdes, Kim Hjort, and Ralph Seeley, "Brazil's Agricultural Competitiveness: Recent Growth and Future Impacts Under Currency Depreciation and Changing Macroeconomic Conditions" (USDA, Economic Research Report Number 276, September 2020) found at https://www.ers.usda.gov/webdocs/publications/99427/err-276.pdf?v=347.3.
2. Constanza Valdes, "Brazil's Momentum as a Global Agricultural Supplier Faces Headwinds," *Amber Waves* USDA, ERS (September 27,2022) found at https://www.ers.usda.gov/amber-waves/2022/september/brazil-s-momentum-as-a-global-agricultural-supplier-faces-headwinds/.
3. Thomas W. Merrick and Douglas H. Graham, *Population and Economic Development in Brazil, 1800 to the Present* (Baltimore: The Johns Hopkins University Press, 1979), pp. 170–171.
4. Herbert S. Klein and Francisco Vidal Luna. *Feeding the World: Brazil's Transformation into a Modern Agricultural Economy* (Cambridge: Cambridge University Press, 2019).
5. Herbert S. Klein and Francisco Vidal Luna, *Brazil, 1964–1985, The Military Regimes of Latin America in the Cold War* (New Haven: Yale University Press, 2017), cap. 3.
6. Crop financing and acquisitions for regulatory stocks operated basically through Federal Government Loans (EGF or Empréstimos do Governo

Federal) and Federal Government Acquisitions (AGF or Aquisições do Governo Federal).

7. Sistema Nacional de Crédito Rural (SNCR).
8. FAOSTAT accessed 5/19/2017, and CONAB. "Milho Total (1ªe 2ª safra), BRASIL, Safras 1976/77, accessed at http://www.conab.gov.br/conteudos.php?a=1252.
9. Ministério da Agricultura: www.agricultura.gov.br; IBGE. *Estatísticas do século XX*:; Banco Central: www.bcb.gov.br/?RELRURAL; and Ipeadata: http://ipeadata.gov.br/epeaweb.dll/epeadata?52305371.
10. Banco Central do Brasil—Departamento de Regulação, Supervisão e Controle das Operações do Crédito Rural e do Proagro-DEROP. Registro Comum de Operações Rurais—RECOR.
11. See Célio Alberto Cole, "A cadeia produtiva do trigo no Brasil: contribuição para geração de emprego e renda" (MA thesis, Porto Alegre: Iepe-UFRGS, 1998); J. F. Fernandes Filho, "A política brasileira de fomento à produção de trigo, 1930–1990," *Anais do XXXIII Congresso Brasileiro de Economia Rural* (Brasília: Sober, 1995), 1, 443–474.
12. *ANP. Anuário Estatístico Brasileiro do Petróleo, Gás Natural e Biocombustíveis, 2017* (Rio de Janeiro, 2018): 145 and 178.
13. Gleydson Pinheiro Albano. "Globalização da Agricultura: Multinacionais no Campo Brasileiro," *Terra Livre*, Ano 27, I, no 36 (jan-jun. 2001): 126–151.
14. On Mercosul see Luciana A. Bastos, "Avaliação do desempenho comercial do Mercosul: 1004–2005" (Phd thesis, FFLCH-USP, S. Paulo, 2008); Maria A. de Carvalho and Roberto L. da Silva, "Intensidade do Comércio Agrícola no Mercosul," *47º. Congresso da SOBER*, accessed at http://www.sober.org.br/palestra/13/447.pdf.
15. Carlos J. C. Bacha, Leonardo Danelon and Egmar Del Bel Filho. "Evolução da Taxa de Juros Real do Crédito Rural no Brasil,- período 1985 a 2003," *Teoria e Evidência Econômica* (Passo Fundo) 14, no.26 (maio 2006): 43–69; also see Carlos J. C. Bacha. *Economia e Política Agrícola no Brasil* (São Paulo: Atlas, 2004), p. 170.
16. José Graziano da Silva, *A nova dinâmica da agricultura brasileira* (Campinas: Instituto de Economia da Unicamp, 1996). These values represented the effective subsidies, not the total resources mobilized for the execution of these policies, which involved much higher sums.
17. In 1987, for example, 11% of cotton, 28% of rice, 43% of beans and 29% of corn produced was acquired through the AGF mechanism and in the same year 42% of cotton, 30% of rice, 5% beans, and 7% of maize benefited from EGF loans. World Bank, *Brazil the Management of Agriculture,* 1994: 48.
18. IBGE, *Estatística do Século XX*, tabela 2.3 found at https://seculoxx.ibge.gov.br/images/seculoxx/arquivos_download/populacao/2000/populacao2000aeb_s2_003a_a_003b.xls.

19. Steven M. Helfand e Gervazio Castro de Rezende, "Brazilian agriculture in the 1990s: Impact of the Policy Reforms" (Discussion Paper 98; Brasília e Rio de Janeiro, IPEA, 2001), pp. 4–5.
20. Paulo F. C. de Araújo, "Política de crédito rural: reflexões sobre a experiência brasileira" (Brasília, CEPAL/IPEA, 2001).
21. Maura M. D. Santiago and Valquíria da Silva, "A política de crédito rural brasileira e o endividamento do setor agrícola: antecedentes e desdobramentos recentes." *Agricultura em São Paulo*, 46, no.2 (1999): 47–70.
22. Artigo 4° of the Lei 8.174 of 30 janeiro de 1991.
23. On price volatility in situations of high inflation, see João Sayad and Francisco Vidal Luna, "Política Anti-inflacionaria y el Plan Cruzado," in *Neoliberalismo y Políticas Economicas Alternativas* (Quito: Corporacion de Estudios para el Desarrolo (CORDES), 1987): 189–204. On the theme of rural credit see Araújo. "Política de crédito rural," 29–30.
24. Lei 8929, of 22 de agosto de 1994 created the Cédula de Produto Rural (CRC). See Lucas Gonçalves Ruiz. *Uma Visão Geral sobre a Cédula de Produto Rural (CPR).* Accessed at http://www.migalhas.com.br/dePeso/16,MI227850,11049-Uma+Visao+Geral+Sobre+a+Cedula+de+Produto+Rural+CPR.
25. Carlos J. C. Bacha, Leonardo Danelon e Egmar Del Bel Filho. "Evolução da Taxa de Juros Real do Crédito Rural no Brasil,- período 1985 a 2003," *Teoria e Evidência Econômica* (Passo Fundo) 14, no.26 (maio 2006): 43–69.
26. Felipe P. Silva. "O Crédito Rural no Brasil," *Animal Business Brasil,* 2, no. 6, (2012): 61–66.
27. Antonio M. Buainain et al. "Sete Teses Sobre o Mundo Rural Brasileiro," in Antônio M. Buainain et al. *O mundo rural no Brasil do século 21. A formação de um novo padrão agrário e agrícola.* (Brasília: Embrapa, 2014), p. 1176.
28. According to the Agronomic Institute of Campinas (IAC), the improvement of coffee genetics began in 1932, and these various coffee cultivars were used in all regions of Brazil and in several countries in Latin America.
29. Alexandre Mengel, "Modernização da Agricultura e Pesquisa no Brasil: A Empresa Brasileira de Pesquisa Agropecuária, Embrapa" (Phd thesis, UFRRJ, 2015), pp. 127–140 and José Irineu Cabral, *Sol da manhã: memória da Embrapa* (Brasília: UNESCO, 2005), p. 142.
30. Embrapa Comunicações. *Embrapa em Números* (Brasília: Embrapa, 2016), p. 32. In 2015, the budget totaled US $ 870 million.
31. APTA, accessed at: http://www.apta.sp.gov.br/quem-somos; Embrapa accessed at https://www.embrapa.br/busca-de-noticias/-/noticia/13128392/brasil-lidera-investimentos-em-pesquisa-agricola-na-america-latina; and ASTI, accessed at https://www.asti.cgiar.org/brazil.

32. Gasques, Bastos, Valdes and Bacchi,"Produtividade da agricultura Brasileira," 83–92.
33. On the development of the *Plano Real* and the successive crises in the 1990s see Francisco Vidal Luna and Herbert S. Klein. *Brazil Since 1980* (Cambridge & New York: Cambridge University Press, 2006), chapter 2.
34. Lei 12.188, of 11 de janeiro de 2010.
35. Lei 11.326, of 24 julho 2006.
36. Lei 12.897 of 18/12/2013. Accessed at http://www.mda.gov.br/portal mda/sites/default/files/user_img_193/Anater.pdf.
37. See Geraldo B. Martha Jr, Elisio Contini and Eliseu Alves, "Embrapa: its origins and changes" in Werner Baer, ed., *The Regional Impact of National Policies: The Case of Brazil* (Edward Elgar Publishing, 2012), pp. 204–226; and Marcus Peixoto, *Extensão Rural no Brasil—uma abordagem histórica da legislação* (Textos Para Discussão no. 48; Brasília: Senado Federal, Coordenação de Estudos, 2008), p. 26.
38. Fabio Chaddad, *The Economics and organization of Brazilian Agriculture: Recente Evolution and Productivity Gains.* (Amsterdam: Academic Press, 2016), pp. 14–15.
39. CONAB, "Grãos por Unidade da Federação (13/04/23) at https://www.conab.gov.br/info-agro/safras/serie-historica-das-safras/itemlist/cat egory/907-graos-por-unidades-da-federacao
40. See José G. Gasques et al. "Produtividade Total dos Fatores e Transformações da Agricultura Brasileira: Análise dos Dados dos Censos Agropecuários," in José G. Gasques, José E. R.Vieira Filho and Zander Navarro, eds. *Agricultura Brasileira: desempenho, desafios e perspectivas* (Brasília, Ipea, 2010): 19–44; and José G. Gasques, Eliana T. Bastos, Constanza V. and Mirian R. P. Bacchi, "Produtividade da agricultura brasileira e os efeitos de algumas políticas," *Revista de Política Agrícola.* XXI, no. 3 (jul./ago./set. 2012): 83–92.
41. José Garcia Gasques, Miriam R. P. Bacchi, Eliana Teles Bastos and Constanza Valdes. "Crescimento e produtividade da agricultura brasileira: uma análise do censo agropecuário," in José Eustáquio Ribeiro Vieira Filho and José Garcia Gasques, eds., *Uma jornada pelos contrastes do Brasil. Cem anos de Censo Agropecuário* (Brasília: IPEA, IBGE, 2020), pp. 107–119. Also see Gasques, Bastos, Valdes and Bacchi, "Produtividade da agricultura Brasileira": 83–92.
42. Kleith O. Fuglie. "Productivity Growth and Technology Capital in the Global Agricultural Economy," in Keith O. Fuglie, Sun Ling Wang e V. Eldon Ball, eds., *Productivity growth in agriculture: an international perspective* (Oxfordshire: CAB International, 2012), Chap 16. Accessed at http://agecon.unl.edu/9280a86c-342e-4c5a-afab-d350503401b8.pdf.
43. *FAO Food Price Index*, accessed at http://www.fao.org/worldfoodsituat ion/foodpricesindex/en.

44. On the value of the current surplus see https://www.jornaldocomercio.com/_conteudo/2018/01/economia/606889-balanca-do-agronegocio-aumentou-13-em-2017.html.
45. Antonio M. Buainain et al. "Quais os riscos mais relevantes nas atividades agropecuárias?" in Buainain et al. *O mundo rural no Brasil do século 21*: 135–208.
46. Ruy Miller Paiva, Salomão Schattan and Claus F. Trench de Freitas. *Setor Agrícola do Brasil. Comportamento econômico, problemas e possibilidades.* (São Paulo: Secretaria da Agricultura, 1973), pp. 17–27.
47. Eliseu R. A. Alves, Geraldo da S. e Souza, Daniela de P. Rocha and Renner Marra "Fatos marcantes da agricultura brasileira," in Eliseu R. A. Alves, Geraldo da S. e Souza, and Eliane Gonçalves Gomes, eds., *Contribuição da Embrapa para o Desenvolvimento da Agricultura no Brasil* Brasília: Embrapa, 2013), p. 22.
48. MAPA, *Projeções do Agronegócio Brasil 2020/21 a 2030/31* (Brasília: MAPA, 2022),13, table 2. Grains are made up of 16 products which include: cotton, peanuts, rice, beans, sesame seeds, sunflowers, castor beans, maize, soybeans, sorghum, oats, canola, rye, barley, wheat, and triticale.
49. MAPA, *Projeções do Agronegócio Brasil 2020/21 a 2030/31*, 18.

CHAPTER 3

The Changing Structure of Brazilian Agriculture, 1920–2017

To understand the structure of Brazilian agriculture in both the pre and post modernization periods it is essential to examine the agricultural censuses carried out from 1920 until 2017, which was the latest one. It is evident from this review that there are major regional differences in all aspects of farming, from land ownership to the number of workers employed per hectare. Size and function also varied by region and even a supposed difference between commercial and family farms exhibits basic differences. While a family farm in some regions essentially means subsistence farming, in others it defines a thriving commercial-based agriculture. The use of machinery, modern farm practices, and even the employment of women and children differed by size of farm, the crops or animals it produced, and the region in which it was located. The same occurred for the educational attainment of farm owners and managers. Even the indices of concentration of land ownership differed by crop although for all farming, the indices of concentration of land ownership have remained high and stable over decades. This has occurred while the average size of farms has declined and their total numbers have grown over time. In many respects, there were two different farming worlds, one which became completely modern and accounts for most of the production and a larger group of mostly subsistence agriculturalists.

H. S. Klein and F. V. Luna, *Brazilian Crops in the Global Market*, Palgrave Studies in Economic History,
https://doi.org/10.1007/978-3-031-38589-6_3

Although farms of up to 100 hectares were just 72% of all establishments in 1920, since 1940 they have remained at a steady 86% to 91% of the properties, and have not exceeded one fifth of the lands in crops and livestock. On the other hand, establishments with more than 1000 hectares, which have remained around 1% of farms since 1940, control around 45% of lands dedicated to agriculture (see Table 3.1).[1]

But there are significant regional differences. In the 2017 agricultural census, establishments with up to 100 hectares were found in a greater proportion in the Northeast, South, and Southeast, representing about 90% of the farms. They also had a significant share of the agricultural land—from a quarter to almost a third in each of these three major regions (see Table 3.2). But in the North and even more in the Center-West they accounted for far fewer farms, and in the Center-West these under 100 hectare farms just owned 6% of the land, the lowest of any region.

Small farms were far more prevalent in the Northeast, where about 10% of establishments were less than 1 hectare and more than half owned 5 hectares or less, which is an insufficient area for the sustainability of a family (see Table 3.3). The most serious issue of poverty and small landowners occurs in the Northeast, particularly in the large semi-arid region with a high population density and low economic performance.[2] The other region of small farms, the Southern region and above all the state of Rio Grande do Sul, is quite different from the Northeast. This is an area that always was involved in commercial agriculture, with high yields by Brazilian standards. The South was occupied by European immigrants in the nineteenth and early twentieth centuries mostly in colonization projects, and these family farms systems led to increasing subdivision over generations through partible inheritance which resulted in ever smaller plots. The region also suffered from continued land exploitation over many generations without efforts to recover fertility and preserve the soil. It was these two factors which promoted the process of out-migration of the so-called *gauchos* to other regions, particularly the Center-West in search of larger more viable farms.

This distribution of farms can be seen more clearly at the state level by looking at the 81% of the agricultural units that were less than 50 hectares. These estates controlled only 13% of the land dedicated to agriculture nationally, and as could be expected, there were substantial differences among the states. Pernambuco and Sergipe in the Northeast, Espírito Santo in the Southeast and Rio Grande do Sul in the South are the states

Table 3.1 Distribution of land ownership in Brazil: establishments, total area and Gini Index, Agricultural censuses 1920 to 2017

	1920	*1940*	*1950*	*1960*	*1970*	*1975*	*1980*	*1985*	*1995*	*2006*	*2017*
Percentage of farms by size of farms											
Less than 10 ha		34%	34%	45%	51%	52%	50%	53%	49%	50%	51%
10–100 ha		51%	51%	45%	39%	38%	39%	37%	39%	40%	40%
Less than 100 ha	*72%*	*86%*	*85%*	*89%*	*90%*	*90%*	*89%*	*90%*	*89%*	*90%*	*91%*
100–1000 ha	24%	13%	13%	9%	8%	9%	9%	9%	10%	9%	8%
1000 ha+	4%	1%	2%	1%	1%	1%	1%	1%	1%	1%	1%
Total	100%	100%	100%	100%	100%	100%	100%	100%	100%	100%	100%
Total farms	648,153	1,904,589	2,064,642	3,337,769	4,924,019	4,993,252	5,159,851	5,801,809	4,859,865	5,175,636	5,073,324
Percentage of farms by their share of total farm lands											
Less than 10 ha		1%	1%	2%	3%	3%	2%	3%	2%	2%	2%
10–100 ha		17%	15%	19%	20%	19%	18%	19%	18%	19%	18%
Less than 100 ha	*9%*	*18%*	*17%*	*21%*	*24%*	*21%*	*20%*	*21%*	*20%*	*21%*	*20%*
100–1000 ha	28%	33%	33%	34%	37%	36%	35%	35%	35%	34%	32%
1000 ha+	63%	48%	51%	44%	40%	43%	45%	44%	45%	45%	48%
Total	100%	100%	100%	100%	100%	100%	100%	100%	100%	100%	100%
Total area	175,104,675	197,720,247	232,211,106	249,862,142	294,145,466	323,896,082	364,854,421	374,924,929	353,611,246	333,680,037	351,289,816
Average area ha.	270	104	112	75	60	65	71	65	73	64	69
Gini index	0.832	0.833	0.844	0.842	0.844	0.855	0.857	0.858	0.857	0.858	0.865

Source IBGE, SIDRA, tabelas 6880, 263. Gini: Hoffman (2020), p. 83; Szmrecsányi (2007), p. 241; Hoffman (2019), p. 9

Table 3.2 Distribution of farms by share of farms, and area by region of Brazil, Census 2017

	Brazil	*North*	*Northeast*	*Southeast*	*South*	*Center-West*
	Percentage of farms by size of farms					
Less than 10 ha	50.9%	35.3%	66.8%	43.7%	40.1%	19.9%
10–100 ha	39.6%	47.3%	28.5%	45.7%	52.3%	51.8%
Less than 100 ha	90.6%	82.5%	95.3%	89.4%	92.3%	71.7%
100–1.000 ha	8.4%	15.7%	4.4%	9.9%	7.0%	22.1%
1.000 ha+	1.0%	1.7%	0.3%	0.7%	0.7%	6.2%
Total	100.0%	100.0%	100.0%	100.0%	100.0%	100.0%
Total Farms	5,073,324	580,613	2,322,719	969,415	853,314	347,263
	Percentage of farms by their share of total farm lands					
Less than 10 ha	2.3%	0.9%	5.4%	2.9%	3.6%	0.3%
10–100 ha	18.2%	16.9%	27.4%	23.6%	28.8%	6.1%
Less than 100 ha	*20.4%*	*17.7%*	*32.8%*	*26.5%*	*32.4%*	*6.3%*
100–1000 ha	32.0%	33.8%	34.2%	40.8%	38.8%	22.1%
1000 ha+	47.6%	48.4%	33.0%	32.6%	28.9%	71.6%
Total	100.0%	100.0%	100.0%	100.0%	100.0%	100.0%
Total area	351,289,816	65,213,349	70,893,865	60,302,969	42,875,310	112,004,322
Average area ha.	69	112	31	62	50	323

Source IBGE, Sidra, tabela 6880

Table 3.3 Distribution of farms by share of farms, area and Gini by Region of Brazil, Census of 2017

	Brazil	*North*	*Northeast*	*Southeast*	*South*	*Center-West*
	Percentage of farms by size of farms					
Number of farms	5,073,324	580,613	2,322,719	969,415	853,314	347,263
>0–5	37.3%	27.0%	53.0%	28.0%	22.6%	11.6%
5–10 ha	12.8%	7.7%	12.0%	15.6%	17.3%	8.2%
10–20 ha	14.4%	9.4%	11.0%	17.6%	24.0%	13.1%
20–50 ha	16.9%	21.9%	11.9%	19.1%	21.3%	24.4%
50–100 ha	7.8%	15.2%	4.9%	8.8%	6.8%	14.2%
100–200 ha	4.3%	8.9%	2.4%	5.2%	3.4%	9.2%
200–500 ha	2.9%	4.9%	1.4%	3.5%	2.6%	8.4%
500–1,000 ha	1.1%	1.7%	0.4%	1.1%	1.0%	4.5%
1000–2500 ha	0.7%	1.1%	0.2%	0.5%	0.5%	3.8%
2,500–10,000 ha	0.3%	0.5%	0.1%	0.2%	0.1%	2.0%
10,000+	0.0%	0.1%	0.0%	0.0%	0.0%	0.4%
Producers without Lands	1.5%	1.6%	2.6%	0.4%	0.3%	0.2%
	Percentage of farms by their share of total farm lands					
Area in Hecatres	351,289,816	65,213,349	70,893,865	60,302,969	42,875,310	112,004,322
>0–5	1.0%	0.4%	2.8%	1.1%	1.1%	0.1%
5–10	1.3%	0.5%	2.7%	1.8%	2.5%	0.2%
10–20	2.9%	1.2%	4.9%	4.1%	6.7%	0.6%
20–50	7.6%	6.5%	11.9%	9.7%	12.8%	2.4%
50–100	7.7%	9.2%	10.7%	9.9%	9.3%	3.0%
100–200	8.4%	10.1%	10.4%	11.6%	9.4%	3.9%
200–500	12.8%	13.1%	13.9%	17.3%	15.8%	8.3%
500–1,000	10.8%	10.7%	9.8%	11.9%	13.6%	9.9%
1000–2500	14.8%	15.7%	10.4%	11.7%	15.5%	18.4%

(continued)

Table 3.3 (continued)

	Brazil	*North*	*Northeast*	*Southeast*	*South*	*Center-West*
2500–10,000	18.1%	19.6%	11.6%	12.4%	10.3%	27.5%
10,000+	14.7%	13.1%	11.0%	8.6%	3.1%	25.7%
Average	69	112	31	62	50	323
Gini Index	0.865	0.825	0.857	0.807	0.781	0.860

Note IBGE, Sidra, tabela 6880; Indice de Gini: Hoffmann (2020), p. 83

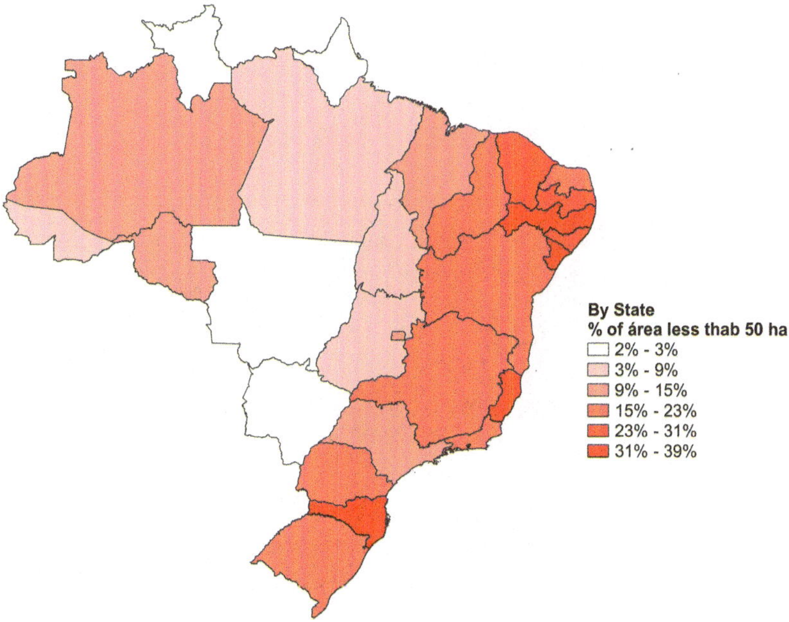

Map 3.1 Distribution of agricultural properties less than 50 Hectares by state, 2017 (*Source* IBGE, Bases Cartográficas Sidra table 6880, Census 2017)

with a high proportion of between 15 and 23% of their area dominated by these small units. These agricultural units were least important in the states of the North and Center-West regions (see Map 3.1)

The large estates, those containing 500 hectares or more of land, which represented only 2% of the farms but owned 58% of the cultivated lands nationally in 2017, were dominant in the three states of the Center-West: Mato Grosso and Mato Grosso do Sul, and to a lesser extent in Goiás. The three states of the North: Tocantins, Roraima and Amapá also have at least half the land area in these large estates. These large farms and estates are important as well in the southeastern state of São Paulo and the Southern states of Santa Catarina, and to a lesser extent, in the state of Rio Grande do Sul which were traditional ranching areas. As can be seen from this distribution, a good part of the Cerrado region (whose central zone encompasses Goiás and Tocantins) is dominated by these large estates (see Map 3.2).

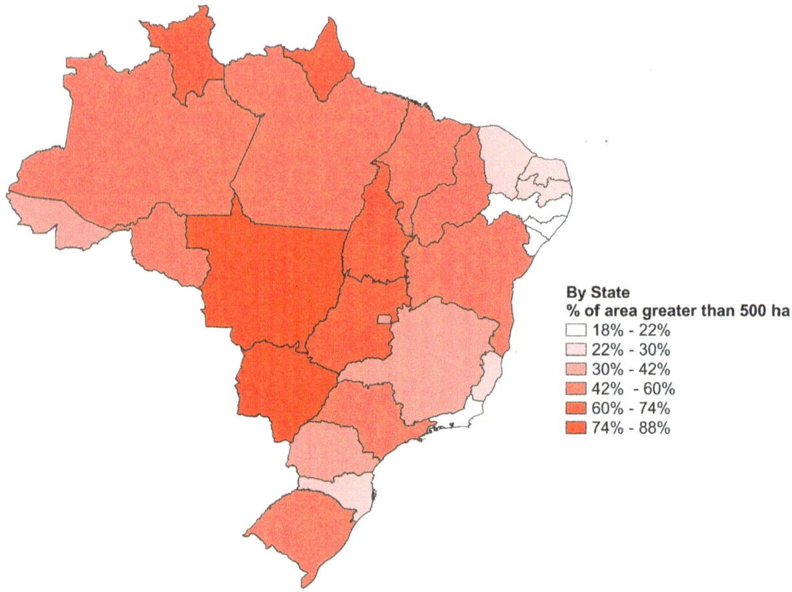

Map 3.2 Distribution of agricultural properties less than 50 hectares by state, 2017 (*Source* IBGE, Bases Cartográficas Sidra table 6880, Census 2017)

But in all regions, the concentration of land ownership, as expressed in the Gini Index, was quite high. The highest value in 2017 was obtained in the Center-West and the lowest in the South. These regional disparities in the distribution of property reflect different historical processes and particular physical conditions. In the case of the Northeast, the first area colonized with sugar was in the fertile coastal area known as the *zona da mata*. The arid hinterland of the Northeastern region was dedicated to marginal livestock production resulting in a low-income occupation and characterized by systematic division of the land. The most southern region of Brazil was dominated by both small commercial farms and large properties dedicated to pastoral activities. The Center-West was the most recent frontier region in Brazil and was occupied by *gaucho* entrepreneurs migrating from the South region. Here both traditional livestock production and modern agriculture are carried out in large-scale enterprises. But as more traditional small-scale agricultural units of the past survive in the regions, the resulting land distribution shows a very high rate of inequality. In this characteristic of land distribution, Brazil differs little from other major agricultural producers of the region, as Latin America in general has the highest level of land ownership inequality in the world.[3]

According to the 2017 census, the majority of farms are owner operator ones and only about 5% of the areas are exploited in the form of leasing. This is completely different from neighboring Argentina where leasing is a major factor in commercial agricultural production.[4] Areas occupied by groups of partners or squatter occupants are insignificant, and about 3% of the establishments are in the condition of "concessionaire or settler awaiting final title" (see Table 3.4).[5] Only 3% of farms and ranches did not possess title or usurped the land, though this reached as high as 8% in the North Region, and as low as 1% in the South region.[6]

Renting lands differ by crop and by region. In seasonal crops, leasing accounts for 11% of establishments, while it is limited to 2% in permanent crops and 3% in livestock. In the Southeast and the Center-West, the ratio of renters in seasonal crops is higher, being 16% and 14%, respectively.[7] Of these seasonal crops it is sugarcane which is the only major crop to use leasing systematically. Most of the lands occupied by the new cane fields in São Paulo were obtained through leasing rather than purchase and the leaser was usually a sugar mill.[8] In leasing for sugar cane planting, the mill is responsible for all the processes carried out on the land of the lessor (owner), from the preparation of the soil to the harvest and transportation of the cane to the mill. [9] The use of leased land is necessary due to the size of the sugar mills and their need for regular supplies of sugarcane in regions close to the processing units.

The farmers themselves also differed by region. Although males are predominant in all regions, the lowest ratio of male farm operators occurred in the northeast (77%) and their highest ratio in the south (88%). As for age, producers up to 45 years old represented 29% of all farm operators and those aged 65 years and over made up 23%. In relation to the national average, producers in the North represent the youngest group of farmers and the Southeast has the oldest ones. As for color, there were the same ratio of whites and brown farmers nationally, but regional differences were striking. Although just under half of the producers were identified as white, this percentage reached 88% in the South but only 23% in the North. In the Northeast, brown farmers predominated and in the North, unlike the other regions, there was a significant number of indigenous farmers who represented 5% of the total of local producers.

Table 3.4 Condition of farmer in relationship to his lands by Region, Census of 2017

Condition	*Brazil*	*North*	*Northeast*	*Southeast*	*South*	*Center-West*
	% of Establlishments					
Total	5,073,324	580,613	2,322,719	969,415	853,314	347,263
Owner	81%	84%	77%	83%	86%	81%
Without definitive Title (1)	5%	7%	5%	3%	3%	11%
Renter (1)	3%	1%	2%	5%	4%	4%
Partner (a)	2%	1%	3%	3%	2%	1%
Free Usage of Land (b)	5%	2%	7%	4%	3%	1%
Occupant	2%	3%	3%	1%	1%	1%
Producer without Lands	2%	2%	3%	0%	0%	0%
	% of Area					
Total	351,289,816	65,213,349	70,893,865	60,302,969	42,875,310	112,004,322
Owner	90%	93%	90%	86%	89%	91%
Renter (1)	2%	3%	3%	1%	1%	1%
Partner (a)	5%	2%	2%	7%	7%	6%
Free Usage of Land (b)	1%	0%	1%	4%	2%	1%
Occupant	1%	0%	3%	1%	1%	1%
Producer without Lands	1%	2%	1%	0%	0%	1%
	Average size of property					
Owner	77	124	36	64	52	362
Renter	106	313	26	89	77	486
Occupant	27	56	11	35	19	151

Note (1) Concessionaire or settler (a) awaiting final title (b) known as Commodate
Source IBGE, Sidra, tabela 6878

Table 3.5 Age, sex, color and education of the farm owner/producer by region, census of 2017

	Brazil	*North*	*Northeast*	*Southeast*	*South*	*Center West*
Total	5,056,525	579,929	2,319,876	962,689	848,839	345,192
Can read and write	77%	80%	62%	90%	96%	91%
Cannot read and write	39%	37%	62%	19%	8%	17%
Never attended school	15.5%	16.4%	23.4%	8.6%	3.9%	8.5%
Some or complete primary	63.6%	64.4%	62.1%	62.6%	71.9%	54.9%
Complete secondary or technical school	15.0%	15.1%	11.7%	18.2%	17.2%	22.4%
University undergraduate degree	5.6%	4.0%	2.6%	10.1%	6.6%	13.5%
MA or Doctorate	0.3%	0.2%	0.1%	0.5%	0.3%	0.6%
Ratio of men	81%	81%	77%	86%	88%	84%
Farmers under 45 years of age	29%	39%	32%	23%	24%	23%
Farmers 65 years of age or older	23%	16%	23%	27%	23%	25%
White	45%	23%	27%	63%	88%	53%
Black	8%	10%	12%	6%	2%	7%
Brown	44%	61%	60%	30%	9%	38%

Source IBGE, SIDRA, tabelas 6756 e 6755

There were few Black farmers (or 8% nationally) and their most significant participation was in the Northeast, where they represented 12% of all heads of agricultural establishments. Asian farmers were just 1% of all farmers in all regions.[10]

Even as late as 2017 some 23% of producers were still listed as illiterate, a figure double the national average. Here as well there were significant regional differences, with illiterates reaching 38% of the farm owners and operators in the northeast and only 4% in the South region. But there was progress in the group of producers who completed high school and university. In both cases their percentages doubled between the agricultural census of 2006 and that of 2017.[11] It is the farmers and ranchers of the states of the Southeast and above all the Center-West who were the best educated (see Table 3.5).

In the first half of the twentieth century the agricultural population continued to expand at high levels. But as mechanization began to occur

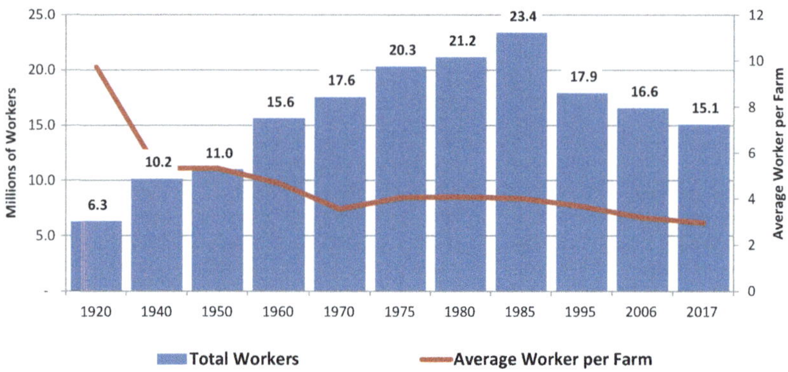

Graph 3.1 Total and average worker in agriculture 1920–2017

from the 1950s onward the pace of that growth slowed and would eventually reverse. This is well reflected in the successive agricultural censuses from 1920 to 1985, with the people employed in agriculture going from 6.3 million to 23.4 million persons in this period. Although total numbers were increasing, the proportion of the total population in agriculture after reaching its peak in 1940 gradually declined even as total numbers rose. By 1985, the percentage of persons in agriculture had declined to 17%, and by 2017 the agricultural labor force declined in actual numbers to 15.1 million people, by then representing only 7% of the national population.

This post 1985 decline is explained by the increasing mechanization and adoption of modern farming techniques throughout Brazil which reduced significantly the need for labor. Mechanization also had an impact on the number of workers per agricultural establishment. Even as the total number of workers rose steadily from 6 million to 21 million between 1920 and 1985, the average number of workers per farm kept declining from 10 workers per establishment in 1920 to half that by 1940 and to just 3 workers on average by 2017 (see Graph 3.1).

From 1950 onward, there were small relative changes regionally in workers employed in agriculture, with an increase in participation from the North and a retraction from the South. During this period, the Northeast maintained a prominent position, accounting for approximately 45% of the employed persons. The Center-West, despite being the largest agricultural exporter by value of any region in the country, employed only 6% of all farm workers nationally. This small share of workers in the Center-West is due to the extensive mechanization of the region's farms and also to their use of contracted machine operators from third parties (sees Table 3.6). Even small agricultural establishments lost workers. Between the 2006 and 2017 censuses, there was a reduction of 2.2 million workers in family establishments. Only in those rural establishments with more than 1000 hectares was there an increase in the number of employed persons between these two censuses.[12]

Of the 15.1 million people employed in agriculture in 2017, almost three quarters were men and just 4% were children under the age of 14. In general, the smaller the farm the fewer men and the greater number of children under 14 years old. The census also shows a significant difference in the number of workers by size of farm. Thus, establishments with less than 10 hectares represented half of the farms and ranches, and controlled just 2% of the total agricultural area, but used 42% of the persons employed in agriculture. If we expand our range to establishments of less than 100 hectares, this would include 90% of establishments, 20% of the agricultural area, and 80% of the agricultural workers employed. As could be expected, establishments with more than 1000 hectares accounted for only 7% of the farm and ranch workers nationally even though they controlled almost half of the farm lands. Everywhere a large share of the labor force was made up of family members. Thus in family farms 87% of the workers were related to each other, and even in the commercial establishments other half the workers were relatives. (see Table 3.7).

There were also differences in farm labor by the three major categories of agricultural production, which were seasonal crops, permanent crops and livestock. The high value seasonal crops were mainly sugar cane, soybeans, corn, and cotton, which used less labor, while the high value permanent crops were represented by coffee and oranges, used more labor. Seasonal crops and livestock absorbed approximately 80% of agricultural workers. The average worker per farm was highest in permanent crops and lowest for livestock. Ranching used the fewest workers on average, although the ranching in the Center-West, the largest region for such production, had a very high average worker per ranch compared to all other crops and activities. The predominant use of farm land was for the planting of seasonal crops and for livestock. Two thirds of the agricultural lands were used in animal ranching; a quarter was dedicated to seasonal crops and just 4% to permanent crops.

Table 3.6 Number of workers in agriculture by region, 1950–2017

	1950	*1960*	*1970*	*1975*	*1980*	*1985*	*1995*	*2006*	*2017*
Brazil	10,996,834	15,633,985	17,582,089	20,345,692	21,163,735	23,394,919	17,930,890	16,568,205	15,105,125
North	3%	3%	5%	7%	8%	11%	10%	10%	13%
Northeast	39%	43%	43%	43%	44%	45%	46%	46%	42%
Southeast	36%	29%	23%	20%	20%	20%	19%	20%	21%
South	18%	20%	24%	24%	21%	19%	19%	18%	15%
Center-West	4%	4%	5%	6%	6%	5%	6%	6%	8%
Total	100%	100%	100%	100%	100%	100%	100%	100%	100%

Source IBGE, Agricultural censuses

Table 3.7 Number of workers and the share of farms, area, children and women in farm labor, census of 2017

	% Farms (1)	*% Total area (1)*	*% Persons occupied*	*% Men*	*% Under 14 years of age*
N	5,030,721	351,289,816	15,105,125	10,726,106	580,052
Farm Size in Hectares	100%	100.0%	100%	71%	4%
>0 and <10 ha	51%	2%	42%	66%	4%
10–20	15%	2.9%	13%	69%	4%
20–50	17%	7.6%	17%	71%	4%
50–100	8%	7.7%	9%	74%	4%
100–200	4%	8.4%	6%	78%	4%
200–500	3%	12.8%	5%	82%	3%
500–1,000	1%	10.8%	2%	83%	2%
1000–2500	1%	14.8%	2%	85%	2%
2500–10,000	0%	18.1%	2%	88%	1%
10,000+	0%	14.7%	2%	90%	1%
Producers without Land	1%		0%	62%	6%

Note (1) The establishments are those with employed personnel. The area pertains to all establishments
Source IBGE, SIDRA, tabela 1885

In total agriculture uses less than a third of the nation's lands. Some two thirds of its territory is dedicated to the protection, conservation, and preservation of vegetation (of which a fifth of these preserved areas are found within rural properties). The entire production of grains (maize, rice, soybeans, beans etc.), of fibers (cotton, cellulose), and agroenergy products (sugarcane, energy forests) occupies just 9% of the country, while Indian land reservations occupy another 14%.[13]

But given the differences in soil, climate, and historical development, here as in all other features of Brazilian agriculture, there were important regional variations. Seasonal crops were the most important in the South where they absorbed half the lands and almost half the workforce. The prime area for permanent crops was the Southeastern states, but even in this region, the value of the seasonal crops corresponds to twice the value of permanent crops.[14] The Center-West represents the region that proportionally uses more land and personnel employed in livestock and less in permanent crops than any other region (Table 3.8).

Table 3.8 Type of agricultural production by region, census of 2017

	Brazil	*North*	*Northeast*	*Southeast*	*South*	*Center-West*
	Establishments					
N	5,073,210	580,610	2,322,699	969,380	853,293	347,228
Total	100%	100%	100%	100%	100%	100%
Seasonal crops	33%	31%	37%	16%	47%	15%
Permanent crops	11%	13%	9%	22%	5%	2%
Livestock	49%	44%	47%	53%	40%	80%
Forestry products, etc.(1)	7%	13%	6%	9%	7%	4%
	Area in hectares					
N	351,289,816	65,213,349	70,893,865	60,302,969	42,875,310	112,004,322
Total	100%	100%	100%	100%	100%	100%
Seasonal Crops	26%	14%	25%	24%	50%	26%
Permanent Crops	4%	5%	5%	10%	2%	0%
Livestock	64%	76%	64%	56%	38%	70%
Forestry products, etc.(1)	6%	6%	6%	10%	10%	3%
	Personnel employed					
N	17,549,443	2,253,310	7,699,744	3,761,817	2,535,549	1,299,023
Total	100%	100%	100%	100%	100%	100%
Seasonal Crops	34%	33%	37%	20%	48%	27%
Permanent Crops	14%	13%	10%	30%	8%	2%
Livestock	44%	41%	46%	40%	37%	66%
Forestry products, etc.(1)	8%	13%	6%	9%	7%	5%
	Average worker per establishment					
Total	3.5	3.9	3.3	3.9	3.0	3.7
Seasonal crops	3.6	4.1	3.3	5.1	3.0	6.9
Permanent crops	4.3	3.9	3.6	5.1	4.4	3.6
Livestock	3.1	3.7	3.3	3.0	2.7	3.1

Note (1) This includes Horticulture and floriculture, production of certified seeds and seedlings, forestry production, fisheries and aquaculture
Source IBGE, SIDRA, tabelas 6888 e 6879

As more non-traditional products entered the international market, there has been a shift in land use, with a systematic increase in the proportion of land dedicated to seasonal crops due to the accelerated growth in the production of grains and a corresponding decline in land used for traditional crops. In 1950, for example, coffee occupied an area larger than corn and represented 12% of the total area of temporary and permanent crops. Today it occupies half of the previous area and only 7% of the area dedicated to maize production and 4% of the area occupied by soybeans. In turn seasonal crops went from 9% of agricultural land use in 1970 to 16% in 2017. Also there has been a systematic increase in planted pastures, which in 2017 corresponded to 32% of the total area used for livestock, as the sector invested more heavily in modern ranching practices.[15]

There was an increasing use of machines in agriculture in the past half century. This drive toward mechanization became important in the mid-twentieth century when the automobile industry was established in Brazil under the government of Juscelino Kubistschek (1956–1961). The farm machinery industry then intensified under the subsequent military regime (1964–1985). Thus the ratio of hectares per tractor declined rapidly, going from one tractor per 2200 hectares in 1960 to one tractor per 52 hectares in the 2017 census. As with the other indicators, the use of tractors is least intense in the Northeast and most used in the South and Southeast. Only 5% of establishments with less than 10 hectares had a tractor, but half of the farms and ranches of 100 to 1000 hectares had them, and they were to be found on all properties with more than 1000 hectares. In the largest establishments there was obviously a greater number of specialized agricultural machines, but there was also far more use of outside services which provided machines and workers for planting, cleaning, and harvesting their crops. The Brazilian market is well supplied by a sophisticated national industry producing tractors and agricultural equipment, with the participation of most of the important global companies in this field, who are even able to export part of their production (see Tables 3.9 and 3.10).[16]

Although attempts were made to develop a national and even state farm assistance program in the 1970s and 1980s, technical assistance has been the least developed sector of modern Brazilian agriculture. The national agricultural research center Embrapa has worked systematically in all crops in all regions providing help with seeds, soils, and inputs. But despite the government's effort to develop technical assistance programs,

Table 3.9 Number of tractors by cultivated area, 1920–2006 and by region 2017

Anos	*Number of tractors*	*Average hectares of cultivated land by tractor (1)*
1920	1,706	3,893
1940	3,380	5,573
1950	8,372	2,281
1960	61,345	468
1970	165,870	205
1975	323,113	131
1980	545,205	106
1985	665,280	94
1995	803,742	63
2006	820,718	74
Region	Agricultural Census of 2017	
Total	1,229,907	52
North	58,436	65
Northeast	83,866	129
Southeast	373,952	39
South	517,042	30
Center-West	196,611	94

Note (1) This includes all types of plantings
Source IBGE, SIDRA, tabelas 1033, 6869 e 1112

it has never achieved results in the poorest, subsistence-oriented agricultural areas. Market-oriented farmers, who participate in productive integration processes and use modern inputs, usually receive assistance either from processing companies who have created complex value chains, from producer coops, or from a mix of government agencies and increasingly from private firms. Even despite this complex set of institutions and agencies, 80% of establishments did not receive any technical assistance in 2017. As could be expected the larger the farm or ranch the more likely it was to obtain this assistance. Thus only 13% of the farms under 10 hectares received such technical assistance support compared to 80% of the agricultural units over 10,000 hectares which obtained them.

Among those who received technical support, there were also important differences in the source of such assistance. As size of property increased, so did the likelihood that they obtained their assistance through

Table 3.10 Establishments with tractors, number of tractors, by region and size of property, Census of 2017

	By Region				
Regions	*Establishments*	*With tractors*	*Number of tractors*	*% With tractors*	*Trators by region*
Brazil	5,073,324	734,280	1,229,907	14%	100%
North	580,613	35,092	58,436	6%	5%
Northeast	2,322,719	53,284	83,866	2%	7%
Southeast	969,415	208,791	373,952	22%	30%
South	853,314	347,476	517,042	41%	42%
Center-West	347,263	89,637	196,611	26%	16%
	Tractors by size of property				
Hectares	*Establishments*	*With tractors*	*Number of tractors*	*% With tractors*	*Distribution of trators by size of farm*
>0 and <10	2,396,887	127,593	141,862	5%	12%
10–50	1,480,363	300,628	379,939	20%	31%
50–100	365,564	90,852	140,736	25%	11%
100–1000	388,584	174,690	367,563	45%	30%
1000+	46,634	40,288	199,284	86%	16%

Source IBGE, SIDRA, tabelas 6778, 6871 and 6898

private resources. Also the reverse was the case with government assistance, with the largest establishments using this source the least. Membership in a cooperative was important for producers, though again ratios increased with size of holding. In the properties of less than 10 hectares, for example, one third received guidance when they were members of a cooperative, whereas in the largest units of over 10,000 hectares, 89% who were coop members got assistance. Coops were especially important in the mid size establishments such as those in the 100–200 hectare range, where 45% of coop members received support.[17] Finally, the fact that only 320 thousand properties out of these 2.2 million farms of less than 10 hectares obtained technical assistance helps explain the low economic performance of this segment of the rural world (Table 3.11).

The regional variation noted in most other aspects also appears when we examine agricultural practices. It was the states of the South region which practiced more of what were considered good farming practices than any other region. This was due to their long history of soil erosion and their early realization of the need to adjust their practices.[18] In contrast, the Center-West, the zone of most recent settlement, was the zone which least practiced such activities given that these were mostly

Table 3.11 Technical assistance received by farms, by origin and size of establishments, census 2017

	None	*Obtained (1)*	*% Received from each source for those with technical support*				
			From government	*Self obtained*	*Coop*	*From processors*	*Others*
Brazil	4,047,881	1,025,443	388,077	316,394	251,520	134,950	96,761
Total	80%	20%	38%	31%	25%	13%	9%
>0 and <10 ha	87%	13%	48%	19%	17%	15%	10%
10–20	73%	27%	42%	22%	28%	18%	9%
20–50	74%	26%	39%	27%	31%	15%	9%
50–100	74%	26%	32%	38%	31%	9%	9%
100–200	70%	30%	24%	49%	28%	7%	9%
200–500	62%	38%	16%	61%	24%	5%	9%
500–1000	52%	48%	10%	73%	18%	5%	9%
1000–2500	42%	58%	7%	81%	12%	5%	10%
2500–10,000	33%	67%	5%	87%	6%	5%	12%
10,000+	20%	80%	5%	91%	4%	5%	16%
Producer without Land	95%	5%	59%	15%	15%	4%	16%
Commercial Farmers	73%	27%	26%	51%	22%	7%	9%
Family farmers	82%	18%	43%	22%	26%	16%	10%

Notes 1. Given that some farms or ranches obtained their techical assistance from more than one source, the total percentage is greater than 100% (2) Other consists of Private Companies, NGOs, and System S associatons (private institutions run with government support-.e.g. SENI and SENAR)
Source IBGE, SIDRA, tabela 6780

virgin lands only recently exploited. Even among the largest of these Center-West establishments there was a relatively low level of adoption of standard practices. The educational level of the owners does not seem to have had a marked influence on these practices, but belonging to a cooperative does show significant influence (see Table 3.12).

In terms of use of soil enhancements, such as the use of limestone and other soil pH amendments, the Southeast region used such application in about one third of the establishments, the South in just over a quarter and the Center-West in a fifth. The North and Northeastern agricultural units had very low usage of such practices. There is also a variation by size and place of establishment. Overall only 14% of farms used these inputs whereas 44% of those of 1000 or more hectares applied them. Regionally it was the South, Southeast and Center-West regions which most used them.[19]

These differences by size, access to resources, and use of modern farming practices help to explain the differential among farms in economic yield. Not only is there a perverse property distribution, but there are very significant differences in productivity and in the capacity to generate value in agricultural production among these establishments by size. Close to half of the farms are incapable of generating an adequate standard of living with their agricultural earnings. Thus, the 2.4 million establishments which farmed less than 10 hectares received only 8% of the value of agricultural production.

The poverty of the small farmers (those using less than 10 hectares) is evident when computing the value of production in minimum wages. This clearly identifies the social problem of the rural world in Brazil. Almost thirty percent of establishments generate an annual value of up to 1 minimum monthly wage (or US$ 296 in 2017 exchange value); if we consider the establishments up to 10 hectares, the average income of the establishments, adjusted by the number of workers in these properties, results in a value lower than 1 minimum wage per month over the course of the year per person employed (Table 3.13).

Region also explains the difference in the average worker income. In the Northeast the average farm worker earns only 9 minimum annual wages per person compared to 48 minimum wages in the Southeast and 59 minimum wages in the South. The value of the Center-West is much higher due to the use of professional and highly trained personnel through contractors. In the semi-arid region, which covers parts of several

Table 3.12 Agricultural practices of Establishments by region, education and Membership in a Coop, Census of 2017

	Agricultural Practices by Region (1)						*Level of Education*			*Coop Member*	
	Brazil	*North*	*Northeast*	*Southeast*	*South*	*Center-West*	*Primary*	*Secondary*	*Superior*	*Yes*	*No*
N	5,073,324	580,613	2,322,719	969,415	853,314	347,263	4,000,209	758,521	297,795	1,996,422	3,076,902
Total	100%	100%	100%	100%	100%	100%	100%	100%	100%	100%	100%
Level planting	9%	2%	2%	23%	19%	9%	8%	13%	20%	31%	13%
Crop rotation	19%	9%	13%	17%	46%	10%	18%	20%	19%	11%	5%
Fallow or resting soil	14%	10%	16%	13%	13%	7%	14%	13%	14%	8%	5%
Slopes protection	4%	3%	1%	6%	11%	5%	3%	5%	10%	11%	1%
Riparian forest recovery	2%	2%	1%	4%	6%	3%	2%	3%	8%	4%	2%
Protection of springs	2%	1%	0%	5%	5%	3%	2%	3%	7%	1%	0%
Stabilization of gullies	1%	0%	0%	2%	2%	1%	1%	1%	3%	0%	0%
Forest management	2%	6%	0%	1%	3%	1%	2%	2%	3%	0%	0%
Another	25%	27%	34%	12%	17%	11%	26%	21%	17%	1%	1%
None	44%	51%	42%	48%	28%	68%	43%	45%	46%	69%	87%

Note IBGE, SIDRA, tabela 6845

Note (1) when computing by area not by establishment, the proportion of the segment of "No agricultural practice would be: Brazil 43%; North 56%, Northeast 40%; Southeast 35%; South 23% and Midwest 49%

Table 3.13 Value of Agricultural Production and Personnel Employed by Size of Farm, Census of 2017

Size of establishments	*Number of farms*	*In mil Reais Value of production*	*In Reais Average value of production*	*Average value of annual production expressed in mimimum wages (1)*	*Average number of persons employed*	*Average annual salary per worker employed in minimum wages*
Total	4,751,193	462,361,551	97,315	104	3.0	35
>0–5	38%	5%	11,910	13	2.4	5
5–10	13%	3%	25,756	27	2.6	10
10–20	14%	6%	39,123	42	2.7	15
20–50	17%	10%	57,903	62	2.9	21
50–100	8%	7%	92,428	99	3.3	30
100–200	4%	7%	165,513	177	3.8	46
200–500	3%	11%	377,890	403	4.9	83
500–1000	1%	9%	860,551	918	6.6	139
1000–2500	1%	13%	1,893,821	2,021	10.3	196
2500–10.000	0.3%	16%	5,620,886	5,999	25.2	238
De 10,000+	0.05%	12%	25,882,839	27,623	131.0	211
Producer without lands	2%	0%	11,332	12	1.7	7
>0 and <100 ha	89%	31%	33,857	36	2.7	13
100–1000 ha	8%	28%	329,937	352	4.5	78
1000 ha+	1%	41%	4,067,317	4341	20.2	215

Source IBGE, SIDRA, tabela 6898 and 6885

northeastern states and northern Minas Gerais, the average was only 7 minimum annual wages per year per person employed (see Table 3.14).

This dichotomy between an advanced and backward agriculture identified in the 2017 agricultural census has been pointed out in several studies related to Brazilian agriculture, as they are long-term patterns.[20] The profound changes that occurred in Brazilian agriculture in terms of its modernization and expansion into the world market did not transform all of Brazilian agriculture. Only 469 thousand producers, corresponding to one tenth of all agricultural producers, accounted for 86% of the total value of agricultural production. In fact, 70% of the production value came from just 108 thousand producers. On the other hand, about

Table 3.14 Agricultural establishments by value of production, area and workers employed, by region and selected states, census of 2017

Regions	*No of farms*	*In mil Reais Value of production*	*In Reais Average value of production*	*Average value in minimum wages*	*Average area (ha) per farm*	*Average number of workers employed*	*Worker income per year in minimum wage (2)*
Brazil	4,751,193	462,361,551	97,315	104	69	3.0	35
North	12%	7%	56,797	61	112	3.5	17
Northeast	46%	12%	24,261	26	31	2.8	9
Southeast	18%	28%	148,915	159	62	3.3	48
South	17%	26%	150,771	161	50	2.7	59
Center-West	7%	27%	402,048	429	323	3.4	125
Semiarid Region	1,744,526	29,736,779	17,046	18	29	2.7	7
São Paulo	161,011	60,124,002	373,415	399	88	4.4	90
Mato Grosso	103,439	58,643,756	566,940	605	463	3.6	170
Rio Grande do Sul	353,039	54,250,540	153,667	164	59	2.7	60

Nota (1) The minimum wage in September of 2017 was R$ 937.00
Nota (2) Average annual value of production by average of employed persons, in minimum wages per year
Source IBGE, SIDRA, tabela 6898, 6769 e 6885

4 million producers accounted for only 8% of the value of production (production value of up to 50,000 *reais* a year). These 4 million establishments generated an average annual value corresponding to just 10 minimum annual wages. This value is the total production value, not the net income earned. For the Northeast, the poorest region, there were more than 2 million establishments whose average value of production reached only 6 minimum annual wages per annum (see Table 3.15).

This sharp variation explains why agrarian reform and the plight of agricultural labor represented one of the most important political issues in the mid-twentieth century and is a cause for intense demands and conflicts in the countryside even today. Land reform was the crux of the debate. The military when it came to power in 1964 rejected agrarian reform as a solution, but agreed on the need to make profound changes in Brazilian agriculture. [21] Its solution to the powerful demand for land was a colonization program which left the traditional agricultural establishments intact but which benefited one million landless families with land. This program was enacted in the so-called Land Statute of 1964.[22] The settlement program was based on the acquisition of land by immediate payment or through bonds, in the so-called "just indemnity." It also involved settlement of unclaimed public lands. This was a program that would be maintained and even intensified after the return of democratic governments in 1985.[23] The average area given per family was 91 hectares, with significant regional differences, being higher in the North, and lower in states with more developed agriculture, such as São Paulo and Paraná.

These settlements by 2020 involved one million families and 88 million hectares. This means that the colonies accounted for a quarter of the land and a quarter of the farms recorded in the census of 2017. But the national averages disguised important regional differences. In the northern region it appears that almost all the lands were owned by the colonies, and they were also of great importance in the Center-West (see Table 3.16). In all the other regions, however, the density of traditional farm ownership meant that these colonies were far less important.[24]

The history of the settlements cannot be considered a success from the point of view of the sustainability of the settlement projects or of the settled families. Distributed areas were abandoned, sold, fractioned, or integrated, changing over time the original profile of each establishment. It should be noted that in the 1996 census, 4.9 million agricultural establishments were counted and despite the fact that approximately

Table 3.15 Establishments and value of production by range of value classes and region (2017 Census)

Value (reais)	*Brazil*	*North*	*Northeast*	*Southeast*	*South*	*Center-West*
	Percentage of establishments by value of production					
>0 and <5000	43%	28%	66%	26%	17%	19%
5000–10,000	13%	17%	14%	12%	10%	11%
10,000–25,000	17%	26%	12%	20%	17%	20%
25,000–50,000	10%	14%	5%	15%	16%	16%
50,000–100,000	8%	8%	2%	11%	16%	12%
100,000– 500,000	8%	5%	2%	12%	19%	14%
500,000 or more	2%	1%	0%	3%	5%	8%
N	4,751,193	546,857	2,206,767	876,352	809,953	311,264
Total	100%	100%	100%	100%	100%	100%
	Participation in the total value of production by value produced					
>0 and <5000	1%	1%	4%	0%	0%	0%
5000–10,000	1%	2%	4%	1%	0%	0%
10,000–25,000	3%	7%	8%	2%	2%	1%
25,000–50,000	4%	9%	7%	4%	4%	1%
50,000–100,000	5%	10%	6%	5%	8%	2%
100,000– 500,000	16%	18%	12%	16%	26%	7%
500,000 or more	70%	53%	59%	72%	60%	88%
N	462,361,551	31,059,756	53,539,135	130,501,985	122,117,647	125,143,027
Total	100%	100%	100%	100%	100%	100%

Note IBGE, SIDRA, tabela 6898

Table 3.16 Settlement projects, settlement families and land granted Up to November 2020 (area in hectares)

States/regions	*Projects (number)*	*Total area (hectares)*	*Families settled*	*Families by project*	*Area by project*	*Area by family*
North	2,167	66,254,183	427,697	197	30,574	155
Pará	1,139	22,985,512	246,210	216	20,180	93
Amazonas	144	26,743,021	56,945	395	185,715	470
Rondônia	222	6,194,667	38,856	175	27,904	159
Tocantins	379	1,253,686	23,137	61	3,308	54
Northeast	4,351	10,860,366	323,956	74	2,496	34
Maranhão	1,029	4,739,716	131,917	128	4,606	36
Bahia	710	2,057,563	49,058	69	2,898	42
Southeast	776	1,386,229	42,034	54	1,786	33
Minas Gerais	317	791,897	14,155	45	2,498	56
São Paulo	285	365,394	17,927	63	1,282	20
South	837	829,618	35,729	43	991	23
Paraná	330	429,869	18,447	56	1,303	23
Center-West	1,297	8,333,408	139,019	107	6425	60
Mato Grosso	551	6,012,165	82,921	150	10,911	73
TOTAL	9,428	87,663,804	968,435	476	42,273	305

Source INCRA: http://www.incra.gov.br/media/docs/reforma-agraria/assentamentos-geral.pdf

900 thousand colonized families were settled since then, the number of agricultural establishments remained practically the same in 2017. This means that during this period the number of landowners who abandoned the countryside resembled the flow of new settlers.[25] There is thus a serious question about how many of these colonists survived and how many entered into successful commercial agriculture. Thus, even with the exceptional performance of commercial agriculture in recent years, a large portion of farms are at the margin of these advances, despite this massive settlement program.

Starting in the mid-1990s, small farmers, which include those from the settlements, were given support with the creation of PRONAF, the National Program for the Strengthening of Family Farming whose purpose was to promote the sustainable development of family farmers. This program has continued to grow and today represents the main support program for small and medium farmers in Brazil, particularly through credit and privileges in the sale of production to certain sectors, such as the biodiesel program and in supplying food for school meals. [26]

The existence of PRONAF explains the decision of the 2017 agricultural census to breakdown all variables by non-family or commercial farms, and family farms. These family farms are defined as a small establishment (up to 4 fiscal modules), with half of the workforce being family members, whose agricultural activity represents at least half of the family income and is strictly family managed.[27] Of the 5.7 million registered establishments, 77% were classified as family farms, holding 23% of the total farming area. The average size of these family farms is 21 hectares, against the 230 hectares for the commercial farmers. Of these family farms, about 40% had less than 5 hectares, and approximately half of them had less than 10 hectares.

Family farmers are more significant in the north, northeast and south, with little significance in the Center-West. In the semi-arid region of the Northeast and parts of Minas Gerais, 41% of the total area belongs to farmers with this classification. When comparing the three typical states of their region: Rio Grande do Sul (South Region), São Paulo (Southeastern Region), and Mato Grosso (West-Central Region), the disparities are more evident. In Rio Grande do Sul a quarter of the area belongs to family farmers, against 13% in São Paulo and only 9% in the state of Mato Grosso (Table 3.17).

The differences in commercial and family agriculture can be seen in the value of rural production and employment. Of the 17.6 million people employed in agriculture in 2017, two thirds worked on family establishments. This means that while in the commercial segment a value of 60 thousand *reais* was generated per person, or 64 minimum wages per year, in family farming the value of production was just 9 thousand *reais*, which corresponds to 10 minimum wages per year, less than one monthly wage per employed person. This value is not the surplus generated, but the production value, from which there is a need to exclude costs involved in production. The situation is even more perverse in the Northeast, and consequently in the semi-arid region in general, with a production value of only 3 minimum annual wages per employed person (see Table 3.18).

It is thus not surprising that the income earned from the activities of the farm families is on average lower than income earned by workers on commercial farms. In commercial establishments, 87% of income came from the sale of agricultural products, whereas the figure for family farms was 69%. In commercial establishments, other revenues were explained by rents obtained outside the farm. In the family farms, the main component of extra farm income was public funds: pensions, and government support

Table 3.17 Commercial and family agricultural establishments by area in hectares, census 2017

Regiões/estados	*Establishments*		*Total Area ha.*		*Commercial*			*Family*		
	Commercial	*Family*	*Commercial*	*Family*	*% estab.*	*% Area*	*Average Area in ha*	*% estab.*	*% Area*	*Average Area in ha*
Brazil	1,175,916	3,897,408	270,398,732	80,891,084	23%	77%	230	77%	23%	21
North	100,038	480,575	45,446,150	19,767,199	17%	70%	454	83%	30%	41
Northeast	483,873	1,838,846	44,968,122	25,925,743	21%	63%	93	79%	37%	14
Southeast	280,470	688,945	46,567,098	13,735,871	29%	77%	166	71%	23%	20
South	187,547	665,767	31,382,790	11,492,520	22%	73%	167	78%	27%	17
Center-West	123,988	223,275	102,034,572	9,969,750	36%	91%	823	64%	9%	45
Semi-Arid Region	388,693	1,446,842	31,080,298	21,844,922	21%	59%	80	79%	41%	15
São Paulo	66,065	122,555	14,357,761	2,154,384	35%	87%	217	65%	13%	18
Rio Grande do Sul	71,202	293,892	16,208,095	5,476,463	20%	75%	228	80%	25%	19
Mato Grosso	37,044	81,635	49,791,746	5,131,104	31%	91%	1,344	69%	9%	63

Source IBGE, SIDRA, tabela 6878

Table 3.18 Commercial and family establishments by total value of production and by average of unit and worker, census of 2017

	Establishments		*Value of production (R$ 1000)*		*Workers employed*		*Commercial (R$)*		*Family (R$)*	
Regions/ states	*Commercial*	*Family*	*Commercial*	*Family*	*Commercial*	*Family*	*Average value*	*Value per worker*	*Average value*	*Value per worker*
Brazil	1,175,916	3,897,408	355,889,076	106,472,475	5,905,918	11,643,525	302,648	60,260	27,319	9,144
North	100,038	480,575	19,815,977	11,243,780	515,875	1,737,435	198,084	38,412	23,397	6,471
Northeast	483,873	1,838,846	37,672,156	15,866,979	2,066,220	5,633,524	77,855	18,232	8,629	2,817
Southeast	280,470	688,945	104,700,895	25,801,090	1,824,241	1,937,576	373,305	57,394	37,450	13,316
South	187,547	665,767	78,163,176	43,954,471	802,851	1,732,698	416,766	97,357	66,021	25,368
Center-West	123,988	223,275	115,536,872	9,606,155	696,731	602,292	931,839	165,827	43,024	15,949
Semi-Arid Region	388,693	1,446,842	18,174,707	11,562,072	1,479,792	4,346,103	46,759	12,282	7,991	2,660
São Paulo	66,065	122,555	53,469,521	6,654,481	642,981	306,016	809,347	83,159	54,298	21,746
Rio Grande do Sul	71,202	293,892	33,984,853	20,265,687	304,847	769,591	477,302	111,482	68,956	26,333
Mato Grosso	37,044	81,635	54,859,600	3,784,157	223,893	230,326	1,480,931	245,026	46,355	16,430

Source IBGE, SIDRA, tabela 6878

Table 3.19 producer income by type for commercial and family establishments census 2017 (value in thousand reais)

	Total	*Commercial*	*Family*
Total	493,160,288	364,641,394	128,518,894
Production revenue of the establishment	**82%**	**87%**	**69%**
Vegetable products	50%	57%	31%
Animals and their products	30%	28%	35%
Agribusiness products	2%	2%	3%
Other establishment revenue	**2%**	**1%**	**3%**
Total establishment revenue	84%	88%	72%
Other producer receipts	**16%**	**12%**	**28%**
Retirement and pensions	7%	2%	23%
Rents obtained outside the establishment	8%	10%	3%
Government programs	1%	0%	2%

Source IBGE, SIDRA, tabela 6901

programs. A quarter of the total income of family establishments came from these sources (see Table 3.19).

These farms suffer from basic defects. Most have insufficient land or capital, their human capital is low, their level of productive organization is incipient, and they also have difficulty meeting average levels of productivity. In addition a significant portion of them are located in areas or regions with poor soils and difficult logistics in terms of access to markets. This is especially the case in the Semi-arid Region. This results in low yield per hectare, low gross production value, and low agricultural income.

Depending on the region and the local resources, some small producers are able to become significant agricultural producers and obtain an adequate agricultural income. This is especially the case in the South and Southeastern regions. [28] Although PRONAF has clearly helped the small family farms that were potentially viable or already in commercial production, it seems not to have helped the low productivity of a large share of the small family farm sector. In this case the only alternative is public assistance.

Nevertheless there are some crops where family farms are significant. Most of the production of cassava comes from these establishments, a typical product of the subsistence economy. They also predominate in the production of tobacco, and are participating in the soybean bonanza. The most valuable product in family farming was soybeans, although these family farmers accounted for only 9% of Brazil's total production. Family farmers were also major producers of maize used for animal fodder and even produced rice, wheat, and potatoes. In the case of permanent crops, their weight in the total produced is greater, as many of these crops, although essentially commercial, are developed on small properties. These include such fruits as bananas, apples, grapes, and mangoes which are produced in small orchards. Even in coffee, their participation is significant, representing 38% of the quantity of coffee produced. In terms of production value, coffee and bananas are the most representative products in this productive segment (Table 3.20).

In the ranching industry, especially in the case of cattle, 76% of the establishments are characterized as family farms, owning about one third of the cattle, with an average of 28 animals per establishment. This compares to an average of 197 animals in the commercial breeders. Of the other products with representativeness in livestock, family establishments are important in pig farming, in the production of chickens and in the raising of goats and sheep (Table 3.21).

Despite the concentration of land tenure and the persistence of a large sector of national agriculture with low economic yield, the performance of Brazilian agriculture in the past several decades has been extraordinary in terms of production, productivity and participation in the international market. This current position is due to the extraordinary increase in productivity of the main agricultural products exported by Brazil. Since the 1960s Brazil has experienced one of the highest growth rates of Total Factors Productivity in the world (see Table 3.22)

Only through this productivity could Brazil become competitive on the world market, especially when we consider the deficient infrastructure that still prevails in Brazil and the concentration of a large part of Brazilian production far from its ports. This is particularly evident in the dominant role of Mato Grosso in grains and proteins, whose production areas are approximately two thousand kilometers from the port of Santos, the main outlet for Brazilian production. Nevertheless Brazil is still faced with an extraordinary dichotomy between a world class agricultural system coexisting with a large share of marginal farms incapable of providing a living wage from agriculture. This is the basic challenge of contemporary Brazilian agriculture.

Table 3.20 Quantity and value of crops produced by commercial and family farms, census 2017

	Establishments		*Quantity produced*		*Value of production (R$1000)*	
	Comercial	*Familiar*	*Comercial*	*Familiar*	*Comercial*	*Familiar*
Seasonal crops						
N	592,030	2,434,616			202,819,868	34,165,125
	Percentage		Percentage		Percentage	
Total	20%	80%			100%	100%
Soybeans	30%	70%	91%	9%	47%	28%
Sugar cane	21%	79%	98%	2%	23%	5%
Corn grain	19%	81%	88%	12%	14%	17%
Paddy rice	15%	85%	89%	11%	4%	3%
Herbaceous cotton	28%	72%	100%	0%	4%	0%
Manioc	15%	85%	30%	70%	1%	15%
Dry leaf tobacco	5%	95%	6%	94%	0%	14%
Beans	18%	82%	78%	22%	2%	3%
Fodder corn	19%	81%	44%	56%	1%	6%
Wheat in grain	36%	64%	82%	18%	1%	1%
English potato	13%	87%	88%	12%	1%	1%
Permanent crops						
N	169,811	644,999			24,912,932	12,683,516
Total	21%	79%			66%	34%
Coffee	22%	78%	62%	38%	64%	36%
Oranges	25%	75%	92%	8%	92%	8%
Banana	18%	82%	51%	49%	52%	48%

Source IBGE, SIDRA, tables 6957 and 6955

Table 3.21 Livestock establishments and herds by species. Commercial and family farming. Census of 2017

	Total establishments	*Estabelecimentos*		*Total animals*	*Number of animals*		*Animals per ranch*	
		Comercial Percentage	*Familiar*		*Commercial Percentage*	*Family*	*Commercial Average*	*Family*
Total	4,006,656	23%	77%					
Cattle	2,522,487	24%	76%	172,719,164	69%	31%	197	28
Bubalinos (1)	14,735	45%	55%	950,173	72%	28%	104	33
Horses	1,167,066	30%	70%	4,236,062	53%	47%	6	2
Donkeys	237,575	17%	83%	376,874	24%	76%	2	1
Mules	281,491	31%	69%	615,498	55%	45%	4	1
Goats	326,317	22%	78%	8,260,607	30%	70%	35	23
Sheep	512,093	27%	73%	13,789,345	43%	57%	44	21
Pigs	1,445,901	19%	81%	39,346,192	49%	51%	68	17
Hens and chicks (2)	2,847,570	20%	80%	1,362,253,509	54%	46%	1,312	272
Quail	17,632	26%	74%	15,281,681	84%	16%	2,796	184
Ducks, geese (3)	250,356	24%	76%	3,779,132	26%	74%	16	15
Turkeys	82,608	23%	77%	15,636,988	38%	62%	320	151
Ostriches	1,013	51%	49%	13,791	55%	45%	15	12
Rabbits	16,095	23%	77%	200,345	30%	70%	16	11

Note (1) Type of water buffalo (2) Chickens, roosters, pullets, chickens and chicks; (3) Ducks, geese, drakes, partridges and pheasants
Source IBGE, SIDRA, tabela 6908

Table 3.22 Agricultural production as measured by total factor productivity by countries and groups of countries, 1961–2009 (Average change)

	Value of production	*Valor of agricultural production (annual change)*					*TFP of agriculture (annual variation)*				
Countries and groups	*US$ millions*	*1961–1970*	*1971–1980*	*1981–1990*	*1991–2000*	*2001–2009*	*1961–1970*	*1971–1980*	*1981–1990*	*1991–2000*	*2001–2009*
All Developed Countries		6.2	3.0	3.4	3.6	3.3	0.7	0.9	1.1	2.2	2.2
All Developing Countries		2.1	1.9	0.7	1.4	0.6	1.0	1.6	1.4	2.2	2.4
Economies in Transition		3.3	1.3	0.9	−3.5	2.0	0.6	−0.1	0.6	0.8	2.3
Brazil	**127**	**3.6**	**3.9**	**3.4**	**3.7**	**4.5**	**0.2**	**0.5**	**3.0**	**2.6**	**4.0**
USA	229	2.0	2.3	0.6	1.9	1.4	1.2	1.8	1.2	2.2	2.3
China	487	4.9	3.3	4.5	5.3	3.4	0.9	0.6	1.7	4.2	2.8
Argentina	41	1.8	3.0	0.5	3.2	2.7	0.2	3.1	−1.0	1.5	1.2
Australia	23	3.0	1.8	1.7	3.6	−0.8	0.6	1.7	1.3	2.9	0.6
India	205	1.7	2.8	3.4	2.5	3.3	0.5	1.0	1.3	1.2	2.1
Canada	28	2.8	2.3	1.3	2.5	2.0	1.4	−0.4	2.7	2.6	2.1

Source Fuglie, "Productivity growth and Tecnology Capital" Table A 16.2 (2012)
Note The Value of Production—average for the period 2006–2009—is in constant US$ of 2005

Notes

1. The unusual importance of large estates in the census of 1920 reflects the lingering importance of unproductive latifundia.
2. See Eric Sabourin and Patrick Caron, "Origem e evolução da agricultura familiar no Nordeste semi-árido," in Eric Sabourin and Patrick Caron, eds., *Camponeses do sertão: mutação das agriculturas familiares no Nordeste do Brasil* (Brasília, DF: Embrapa Informação Tecnológica, 2003), pp. 29–45.
3. See Luis Bauluz, Yajna Govind, and Filip Novokmet, *Global Land Inequality* WID.world Working Paper no 2020/10 (June 2020), found at https://halshs.archives-ouvertes.fr/halshs-03022360/document.
4. See Herbert S. Klein and Francisco Vidal Luna, "The Growth of the Soybean Frontier in South America: The Case of Brazil and Argentina" *Revista de Historia Económica*, 38: 3 (Fall 2020) pp. 1–42.
5. Some have suggested that the IBGE's data collection system underestimates leasing, as its practice is often hidden by the fear of farmers losing access to certain public resources. In addition, by inserting the "owner," it masks when the producer is both owner and tenant at the same time. See Ana Cecília Guedes, Ademir Antonio Cazella and Adinor José Capellesso. "O Arrendamento de terras no Brasil: subsídios para políticas públicas," *Revista Grifos*, no.44 (2018): 105–125; Patrícia José de Almeida. "Arrendamento e acesso à terra no Brasil" (MA thesis, Campinas, Unicamp, 2002); Luís Felipe Perdigão de Castro, "Dimensões e lógicas do arrendamento rural na agricultura familiar: um estudo de caso" *Revista em Agronegócio e Meio Ambiente*, p. (abr./jun. 2017) pp. 437–457; Ana Cecília Guedes and Ademir Antonio Cazella. "Arrendamento de terras e agricultura familiar na região do meio oeste de Santa Catarina" *INTERAÇÕES* (Campo Grande, MS), 20: 4 (out./dez. 2019), pp. 1249–1261.
6. IBGE, Sidra, Tabela 6774
7. IBGE, SIDRA, tabela 6878. The average farm being rented or leased is 106 hectares for the nation, though reaching 486 hectares in the Center-West.
8. On the special nature of sugar in São Paulo see Thomas Ribeiro de Aquino Ficarelli and Helena Ribeiro, "Dinâmica do arrendamento de terras para o setor sucroalcooleiro: estudo de casos no Estado de São Paulo," *Informações Econômicas, SP*, 40:1 (jan. 2010).
9. Rafael R. de Lima Filho, Alex S. L. da Silva and Gustavo A. M. Aguiar. "Cenário favorável para o arrendamento," *Agroanalisys*, 37, no.4 (2017): 25–26.
10. IBGE, Sidra, tabela 6776

11. In the 2006 census, the percentage of producers who completed the secondary school average degree was 7% and reached 15% in 2017; in the case of those completing post secondary school, the increase was 3% to 6%.IBGE, SIDRA, tabela 6756
12. IBGE, SIDRA, tabelas 805, 1109, 6778, 6884, 6885 e 6886. In the case of personnel employed by area, there was a great loss in establishments characterized as landless. In 2006, there were 687 thousand people and only 62 thousand were left in 2017. Probably some change in methodology accounts for this. But if this is correct there was a loss of approximately 10% in personnel employed in the farm size ranges from 0–10, 10–100, and 100–1,000.
13. Embrapa, "Ocupação e uso de terras no Brasil a partir do Cadastro Ambiental Rural—CAR," found at https://www.embrapa.br/en/busca-de-publicacoes/-/publicacao/1082917/ocupacao-e-uso-de-terras-no-brasil-a-partir-do-cadastro-ambiental-rural---car. For the maps associated with this report see https://www.embrapa.br/en/car/sintese
14. IBGE, SIDRA, tabelas 6955 and 6957. The Southeast represents two thirds of the value of permanent crops in Brazil. Coffee and oranges explain this greater representation of permanent crops in the Southeast.
15. IBGE, SIDRA, tabelas 6881 and 264. In 2017, there is a distinction between against pastures planted in good or bad conditions. Pastures planted in poor condition correspond to only a tenth of the pastures planted.
16. In 2019 the Brazilian tractor industry produced 53 thousand units, of which 12% were exported. Bradesco. *Monitor Setorial: Automotivo*, São Paulo, julho 2020. Also see Valdeson Amaro Lima, Isabel Cristina dos Santos and João Amato Neto. "Indústria de máquinas agrícolas no Brasil. Uma Análise evolucionária no período 1985–2015", Cidade do México. *ALTEE,* (2017), 16pp.; Luis Gustavo Baricelo. "A evolução diferenciada da indústria de máquinas agrícolas: um estudo sobre os casos norte-americano e brasileiro," (MA thesis, Piracicaba. ESALQ/USP, 2015).
17. IBGE, SIDRA tabela 6846
18. The World Bank has financed an important soil recovery program in Rio Grande do Sul since the 1980s, later accompanied by programs to intensify no-till planting with the support of Embrapa. Secretaria da Agricultura, Pecuária e Irrigação, Governo Rio Grande do Sul. *Conservar para produzir melhor. Programa Estadual de Conservação do Solo e da Água.* Accessed at https://www.soloeagua.rs.gov.br/upload/arquivos/201701/18083910-programa-conservacao-solo-e-agua.pdf.
19. IBGE, SIDRA, tabela 6850
20. Eliseu Alves, Geraldo da Silva e Souza and Daniela de Paula Rocha. "Lucratividade da agricultura", *Revista de Política Agrícola*, 21: 2 (abr./

mai./jun. 2012), pp. 45–63; and the essays in Silvia Kanadani Campos and Zander Navarro, eds., *A pequena produção rural e as tendências do desenvolvimento agrário brasileiro: ganhar tempo é possível?* (Brasília: CGEE, 2013); Steven M. Helfand, Vanessa da Fonseca Pereira and Wagner Lopes Soares, "Pequenos e médios produtores na agricultura brasileira: situação atual e perspectivas," in Buainain et al., *O mundo rural no Brasil do século 21*, pp. 533–558; Ajax Reynaldo Bello Moreira, Steven M. Helfand, Adriano Marcos Rodrigues Figueiredo, "Explicando as diferenças de pobreza entre produtores agrícolas no brasil", *48º. Congresso Sober*, Julho 2010, accessed at http://www.sober.org.br/palestra/15/156.pdf.

21. Other economists published studies contradicting the idea of the rigidity of the Brazilian agricultural economy and argued that the domestic market was sufficiently supplied even under traditional conditions and that agricultural production in Brazil responded adequately to price stimuli. These authors sought to demonstrate that if Brazilian agriculture could modernize it would free labor for the expanding urban sector without harming agricultural production, creating a market for the industrial sector and also generating exportable surpluses. See Afonso Celso Pastore, *A resposta da produção agrícola aos preços no Brasil,* (São Paulo: APEC, 1973); Antônio Delfim Netto, *Problemas econômicos da agricultura brasileira*, (São Paulo: Faculdade de Ciências Econômicas e Administrativas da USP 1966); Antônio Delfim Netto, *Agricultura e desenvolvimento no Brasil* (São Paulo: Estudo Anpes, 1969). This was the model adopted by the military in which was called "conservative modernization."
22. Lei n. 4504 of 30 de novembro de 1964.
23. Colonization declined drastically in the post 2010 period. See Ipea. *Avaliação da Situação de Assentamentos da Reforma Agrária no Estado de São Paulo. Fatores de sucesso e Insucesso* (Brasília: Ipea, 2013); Renato Ribeiro Fleury. "Reforma agrária e estrutura fundiária no Brasil: uma análise a partir do I Plano Nacional de Reforma Agrária," (MA thesis, FCL/Unesp, Araraquara, 2015); Sérgio Leite et al., eds., *Impactos dos Assentamentos. Um estudo sobre o meio rural brasileiro* (Brasília: Instituto Interamericano de Cooperação para Agricultura, IICA, São Paulo, Unesp, 2004); Lauro Francisco Mattei. "A reforma agrária brasileira: evolução do número de famílias assentadas no período pós-redemocratização no país". Estud. Soc. e Agric., Rio de Janeiro, vol. 20, n. 1, 2012 pp. 301–325. This author estimates that only twenty thousand companies would have benefited until 1985, out of a total that reaches around one million families.
24. The colonies established in the Amazonian region have been severely criticized from the point of view of the environment. See François-Michel le Tourneau e Marcel Bursztyn. "Assentamentos rurais na Amazônia: Contradições entre a política agrária e a política ambiental." *Ambiente & Sociedade*, Campinas v. XIII, n. 1: 111–130, jan.–jun. 2010; Monique

H.C. Sorares, Norme E. S. Beltrão, Cleber A. Santos e Yvens E. M. Cordeiro. "Impacto dos Assentamentos Rurais no Desmatamento da Amazônia". Mercator, Fortaleza, v. 17, e17009, 2018; Amy E. Duchelle et al. "Linking Forest Tenure Reform, Environmental Compliance, and Incentives: Lessons from REDD+ Iniatives in the Brazilian Amazon. *World Development*, vol. 55, pp. 53–77, 2014; Cinthya Martins Jardim. "Modos de vida em Assentamentos Rurais no Amazonas: Projeto de Assentamento Sustentável Paquequer—Nova Olinda do Norte (AM)." *Somanlu*, ano 13, n. 2, jul./dez. 2013, 21p; Olympio Barbanti Jr. "Ciclos Econômicos, Desflorestamento e Impactos Sociais na Amazônia Brasileira," in Artur Zimerman (Org.) *Novos rumos da questão agrária no Brasil* (Santo André, SP: Universidade Federal do ABC, 2017), pp. 10–39.

25. Foram contados 4.859.865 estabelecimentos agropecuários em 1995; em 2017 eram 5.073.324. IBGE, Sidra, tabelas 263 e 6879.
26. Producers of biodiesel (which is mandated for all diesel sold in Brazil) have advantages if they purchase their products from family producers. In many locations, school lunches must be purchased from family farms. In the 2020/21 Harvest Plan, which represents the budget for agricultural credit available for agriculture, family farming has lower interest rates than other agricultural producers. The *Plano de Safra de 2020/21* is available at: https://www.gov.br/agricultura/pt-br/assuntos/noticias/com-mais-recursos-e-melhores-condicoes-de-financiamento-plano-safra-2020-2021-tera-236-bilhoes/copy_of_ApresentacaoPlanoSafra202021.pdf.
27. IBGE, accessed at: https://censos.ibge.gov.br/agro/2017/2012-agencia-de-noticias/noticias/25786-em-11-anos-agricultura-familiar-perde-9-5-dos-estabelecimentos-e-2-2-milhoes-de-postos-de-trabalho.html.
28. Buainain and Garcia. "Os pequenos produtores rurais mais pobres," pp. 67–68.

CHAPTER 4

Soybeans

There is little question that one crop started the new era of Brazil's entrance into a leadership role in world agriculture, fully competitive with the classic temperate nations such as the United States, Canada, Australia, and Argentina. It was soybeans which created a new agricultural revival in the Southern States and helped open up the Center-West and parts of the Northeast to modern agricultural growth. It was no accident that maize, a rotation crop associated with Soybeans plantings would also have a major growth spurt and allow Brazil to quite suddenly become the world's leading exporter of maize as well as soybeans and a host of other products in this new period in Brazilian agricultural growth. How soybeans developed in Brazil is the fundamental issue explored in this chapter. Here we examine the historical evolution of soybean production and show how it became a crucial part of the larger agricultural development in the recent period.

Soybeans represent one of humanity's oldest staples, being domesticated in China probably 5,000 years ago. However, the details of where, when and under what circumstances soy developed are poorly understood.[1] From China soybean cultivation spread to Japan and other Asian countries, becoming an essential source of food in the region.[2] Although the West got to know the product from the first European navigations that arrived from Asia, it was not until the eighteenth century that the

H. S. Klein and F. V. Luna, *Brazilian Crops in the Global Market*, Palgrave Studies in Economic History,
https://doi.org/10.1007/978-3-031-38589-6_4

Asian legume began to receive attention for its properties in terms of oil extraction potential and for animal and human feed and it was not until the twentieth century that its large-scale cultivation began in the West.[3] Yet it is now recognized that soybeans "produce more edible protein per hectare of arable land than any other major annual crop or through animal grazing."[4] Meal produced from soybeans "has the highest level of crude protein in comparison to other sources of vegetable protein, and its amino acid balance nearly provides the essential amino acid nutritional requirements of swine and poultry."[5] Though only very recently used for human consumption in the west, it is a basic part of food consumption in Asia for several centuries and today is by far and away the largest oilseed produced in the world. Moreover in many countries, including Brazil, soybean oil has become the leading cooking oil and now accounts for 60% of oilseed oils produced in the world.[6]

Although there were attempts to grow soy in America as early as the late nineteenth century, it was not until the 1920s that the product effectively gained commercial importance in the West. The initial advances were in the United States. Beginning in 1898 the US Department of Agriculture began to breed new seed varieties. By 1925 some 809 thousand hectares (or 2 million acres) were being cultivated for soybeans and this expanded to 6 million hectares (or 15 million acres) by 1943. Initially they were grown mostly in the South and East mainly for forage. By the late 1940s the plants were being used primarily for their seeds and production became concentrated in the Middle West corn producing states. Soon there were crushing plants to produce meal and oil.[7] This in turn fed into the pastoral industry and finally the increasing trade with Asia after World War II led to expanding production and by the 1960s, the United States was exporting 3.6 million tons of soybeans, or 87% of total world exports of this product.[8]

In Brazil, soybeans were also tried in various plantings in the late nineteenth century. The plant was first introduced in the state of Bahia in 1882 and by the late 1880s several agricultural research centers in São Paulo were experimenting with the plant and by 1900 the state was offering seeds to potential producers. The first mention of the plant in Rio Grande do Sul was in 1901, and after 1908 Japanese immigrants began cultivating the plant on their small farms in São Paulo state. Despite all these experiments and small farm activity it was not until the 1940s that systematic production began which at first was concentrated in the southern state of Rio Grande do Sul and to a lesser extent in São Paulo.[9]

The reason for the concentration was that temperate zone Rio Grande do Sul was the center of wheat production and soybeans became the standard alternative crop to wheat. By the crop year 1949–1950 some 25 thousand hectares were planted with soybeans, producing almost 26 thousand tons of the beans for a yield of 1,368 kilos per hectare. By 1959/1960 soybeans were planted on 171 thousand hectares and production reached some 206 thousand metric tons, and ten years later 1.3 million hectares were planted and 1.5 million tons produced, though yields remained low. Until the early 1950s production was confined to the three southern states and São Paulo. Thereafter production slowly began in the Center-West region and parts of the North and Northeast though initially with yields below those obtained in the Southeastern and Southern region. By 1984/1985 the southern area cultivated 6.7 million hectares and produced 11.6 million tons, and the Center-West and Northeastern regions of production were now using 3.4 million hectares and producing 6.6 million tons of beans, with yields now finally above those in the southern area.[10] As of the crop year 1990/1991 the Northeastern and Northern states only accounted for 4% of the 15.4 million tons produced. Ten years later, at the turn of the century, their share had risen to 6% of the 38.4 million tons of soybeans grown.

The basic reason for the low initial yields is that the northern area was in the tropical zone and thus cultivars developed for temperate climates were not adequate for these temperatures and soils. It was at this point that the investments in research of the Brazilian national agricultural research center Embrapa [*Empresa Brasileira de Pesquisa Agropecuária*], led to the "tropicalization" of soybeans which would open up the Center-West region to largescale soybean farming. This was a new variety of soybean cultivar designed for tropical climates. For the first time in history the beans could now be successfully planted in the low latitude regions between Capricorn and the Equator.[11] Breeding programs began in the 1970s with state agricultural research centers and was coordinated by Embrapa when it created a national research center Embrapa/CNP Soja in 1977/1978. By 1980 a "tropical" cultivator was launched by Embrapa for "regions of low latitude."[12] In the early 1990s new cultivars were developed for the far northern producers of soybeans in Piauí and Maranhão.[13] Then in 1997, Brazil passed a Variety Protection law and the number of foreign cultivars developed by multinational companies increased significantly in the country, some of which were then developed jointly with Embrapa and other local research groups.[14] Crucial was

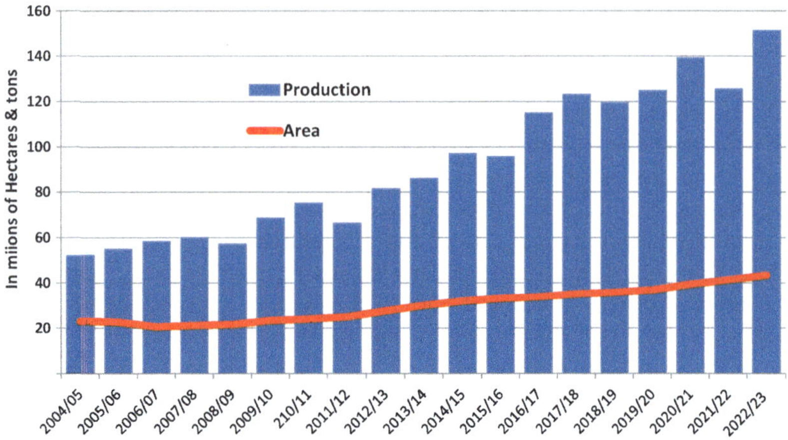

Graph 4.1 Area planted in soybeans (hectares) and soybean production (in tons), 1976/1977–2022/2023 (*Source* CONAD, Série histórica Soja 2023)

Roundup Ready Soybean cultivars developed by Monsanto and first used in the United States in 1996 which made the plants resistant to herbicides containing Glyphosate.[15]

Increasing use of these improved and GMO cultivars, plus the adoption of no-till plantings, the use of machinery, and the systematic use of fertilizers, herbicides, and insecticides, meant that production increased faster than the need for new lands. Whereas area went from 7 to 44 million hectares in this period, or a per annum growth of 4.0%, while production went from 12 million metric tons to 151 million metric tons, for a growth of 5.5% (see Graph 4.1).

The evolution of soybean production in Brazil is part of the history of the modernization of Brazilian agriculture in general in the past half century. [16] Initially soybeans proved to be an ideal product for wheat rotation. [17] But in 1987 government wheat support was eliminated, and the result led to declining wheat production. Soybean production, however, was not affected due to exceptional rise in prices for this product that occurred since the 1970s. The average price of soybeans in the 1970s was more than twice the average price from the previous decade and by the 2010s increased again (see Graph 4.2).

In this first phase of soybean expansion in the south of the country, cultivars developed in the United States were used. But the high price of

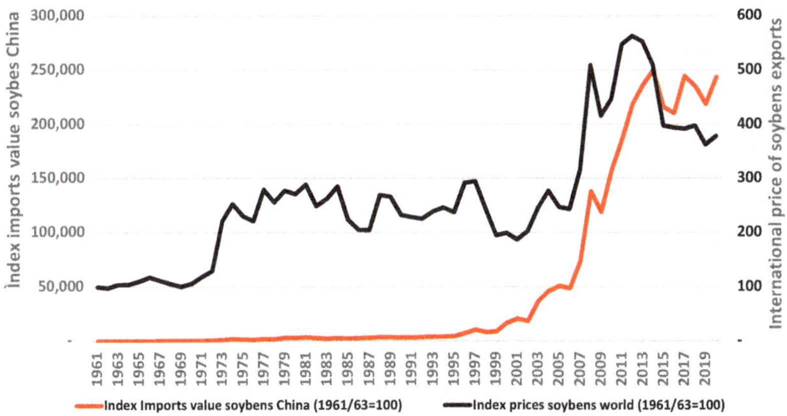

Graph 4.2 International price of soybens and imports value of soybeans by China (index 1961–1963 = 100) (*Source* FAOSTAT)

land in the Southern states restricted its potential expansion. Thus local farmers (known as *gauchos*) began to look for cheaper land in agricultural frontier areas such as the *cerrado* region in the Center-West region of the country. The exploration of the Center-West not only required new cultivars but also innovative soil management given the quality of local soils. Embrapa helped to resolve the problem of low fertility and high natural acidity of the Center-West soils, which made the use of the region commercially viable. The conquest of the so-called *Cerrado* biome is one of the most important achievements of the Brazilian agrarian sciences. In the Cerrado area, new technologies such as crop "tropicalization," soil correction, nitrogen fixation in legumes, fertilization, and crop management allowed Brazil to transform this very acidic and nutrient-poor land into 139 million hectares of arable land which has become one of the largest grain production regions in the world.[18]

Just as these innovations were being applied in the tropical regions, the temperate regional producers also adopted the latest technology, so that the regional disparities in yield began to disappear and a uniform increase occurred everywhere. This can be seen in the two principal producing states, Mato Grosso in the Center-West and Paraná in the South region, with their sharp differences in the crop year 1990/1991 disappearing ten years later. This was the reality for all producers, from the producers in

North and Northeastern states in what is called the "Matopiba" region which share the Cerrado biome, to all those in the far South. By the second decade of the current century almost all achieved the same level of beans per hectare (see Table 4.1).

Another feature of Brazilian soybean production is that size of unit has little impact on yield. Unlike the pattern of most food crops which exhibit high productivity in large farms and lower productivity in smaller units, is not evident in soybean cultivation.[19] Thus the thousand hectare farms of Mato Grosso producing soybeans had the same yield as the 50 hectare farms producing soybeans in Paraná. Of course soybeans, like all the other major commercial crops, were concentrated on large farms. In the agricultural census of 2017 farms of over 500 hectares produced 65% of the soybeans, but constituted only 5% of the producers. But there was room for smaller properties. Producers of up to 100 hectares accounted for 13% of production and brought together 83% of the producers. What is impressive about this distribution of soybean farms is that the average productivity of the largest and the smallest producers were almost identical suggesting a common use of seeds and modern technology from the largest to the smallest producer (see Table 4.2).

The other major issue facing soybean producers in the North/ Northeast and Center-West is the question of deforestation and the Amazon biome. Despite the extraordinary expansion of soybean production in Brazil, actual volume of land needed to produce soybeans has grown more slowly than output due to productivity increasing at a very fast pace. The expansion of soybean production in the Center-West mostly has been in areas not previously cultivated or in often degraded pasture areas. But it appears that the expansion of soybean cultivation may have pushed cattle ranchers further north into the forested area of the Amazon. In July 2006 under pressure from international organizations ABIOVE (The Brazilian Vegetable Oil Industries Association) and ANEC (the National Grain Exporters Association) agreed to the so-called Soy Moratorium, which guaranteed that its members would not purchase any soybeans produced on deforested Amazonian lands after July 2008. Almost all the satellite monitoring of this agreement finds a high level of compliance and relatively little expansion into the Amazon itself, though major expansion has occurred in the Cerrado region of low scrub plains.[20] One recent satellite survey estimated that 13% of the soybean crop may have come from the legal Amazon area. [21] Illegal loggers, ranchers, and miners are the main groups destroying the Amazon.

Table 4.1 Brazilian soybean production by region and principal producing states—1990/1991 to 2022/2023

	Production—Thousands tons			*Area—Thousands hectares*			*Productivity—ton/hec*		
Region/state	*1990/1991*	*2000/2001*	*2022/2023*	*1990/1991*	*2000/2001*	*2022/2023*	*1990/1991*	*2000/2001*	*2022/2023*
Principal producers as of 2019/2020									
Mato Grosso (CW)	2,607	9,641	43,903	1,100	3,120	11,808	2,370	3,090	3,718
Paraná (S)	3,617	8,623	21,293	1,966	2,818	5,788	1,840	3,060	3,679
Goiás (CW)	1,659	4,158	17,280	790	1,540	4,547	2,100	2,700	3,800
Rio Grande do Sul (S)	2,354	7,113	15,188	3,269	2,970	6,551	720	2,395	2,318
Mato Grosso do Sul (CW)	2,300	3,130	13,764	1,013	1,065	3,761	2,270	2,940	3,660
Bahia (NE)	556	1,450	7,489	278	691	1,920	2,000	2,100	3,901
Minas Gerais (SE)	963	1,496	8,321	472	642	2,165	2,040	2,330	3,843
São Paulo (SE)	968	1,378	4,792	500	530	1,268	1,935	2,600	3,779
Tocatins (N)	7	139	4,404	4	66	1,270	1,667	2,100	3,468
Maranhão (NE)	8	483	3,744	5	210	1,112	1,804	2,300	3,367
Piauí (NE)	–	143	3,310	–	62	926	–	2,300	3,575
Pará (N)	–	2	2,878	–	1	940	–	2,143	3,062
Santa Catarina (S)	250	527	2,589	300	196	738	833	2,690	3,508
Rondônia (N)	5	77	1,682	2	25	497	2,500	3,060	3,384
Regional producton									
Norte (N)	12	217	9,410	6	92	2,851	1,825	2,362	3,301
Nordeste (NE)	564	2,076	14,559	283	963	3,963	1,997	2,157	3,674

(continued)

Table 4.1 (continued)

Region/state	*Production—Thousands tons*			*Area—Thousands hectares*			*Productivity—ton/hec*		
	1990/1991	*2000/2001*	*2022/2023*	*1990/1991*	*2000/2001*	*2022/2023*	*1990/1991*	*2000/2001*	*2022/2023*
Centro-Oeste (CW)	6,667	17,002	75,266	2,946	5,760	20,203	2,263	2,952	3,725
Sudeste (SE)	1,930	2,874	13,114	972	1,172	3,433	1,986	2,452	3,820
Sul (S)	6,221	16,264	39,070	5,535	5,984	13,081	1,124	2,718	2,987
Brasil	15,395	38,432	151,419	9,743	13,970	43,531	1,580	2,751	3,478

Source CONAB "SOJA - BRASIL...0.1976/77–2010/22" with estimates for 2022/2023—created 3 September 2023 at https://www.conab.gov.br/info-agro/safras/serie-historica-das-safras?start=30

Table 4.2 Brazil: production of soybeans, number of producers, production and area

Census 2017 (area in hectares and production in tons)				
Farms grouped by size (hectares)	*Farms*	*Production*	*Area harvested*	*kilos/ha*
Total	236,245	103,156,255	30,722,657	3,358
Less then 10 ha	80,937	1,414,153	425,773	3,321
More than 10 and less than 100	113,051	12,182,441	3,575,928	3,407
More than 100 and less than 500	29,697	22,308,269	6,613,458	3,373
Over 500	12,560	67,251,391	20,107,499	3,345
Percentage by size of farm				
Grupos de Area Total (hectares)	Farms	Production	Area harvested	kilos/ha
Total	100%	100%	100%	100%
Less then 10	34%	1%	1%	99%
More than 10 and less than 100	48%	12%	12%	101%
More than 100 and less than 500	13%	22%	22%	100%
Over 500	5%	65%	65%	100%

Source IBGE, SIDRA, table 6958

Brazil has also become a major producer of the two leading products generated from soybeans, soy meal (*farelo de soja*) and soy oil (*óleo de soja*). Prior to 1970 the majority of crushing factories were small and located primarily in São Paulo and Rio Grande do Sul. At that time the crushing capacity of Brazilian mills was 40 tons per day and the majority were small units with simple machines primarily geared to the internal market. But this changed with the arrival of major multinational companies such as Cargill, Sanbra, Unilever, and Continental Grain which set up highly capitalized processing factories. These also set up plants in the new Center-West regions and also dedicated some of their output to exports. Several local meat processing groups such as Sadia entered this market, but the majority were foreign multinationals who were also grain processors. This foreign capitalization resulted in capacity doubling by the early 1980s and reaching 116 thousand tons per diem by the early 1990s.[22] Many of these plants also were integrated into the growing Value chains for chicken and swine producers being developed in the Southern States. As the industry grew there were new buyouts as more foreign companies entered so that by the twenty-first century there was only one major Brazilian firm remaining (Agroeliane), while ADM, Bunge, and Dreyfus entered the market. Four firms accounted for 44% of the market, and mostly coops and Brazilian firms for the rest. The four largest were Bunge, Cargill, ADM, and Dreyfus.[23]

While meal was both exported and consumed locally, the refined soybean oil became the major cooking oil in Brazil. By 2019 there were soybean oil producing factories in most of the Brazilian states with a capacity to crush 191 thousand tons per day, producing 21 thousand tons per day of refined soybean oil, and 14 thousand tons of packaged oil. Mato Grosso and Goiás factories accounted for 36% of this output and the plants of Rio Grande do Sul, Paraná, and São Paulo for 42%. Cargill was the chief producer of this refined oil with its brand "Liza" having a large share of the market.[24] All this production finally led to the internal market shifting from previous vegetable oils to consuming this refined soybean oil.

By 2023 it is expected that 34% of the soybeans grown in Brazil will be crushed, or some 53.5 million tons. Of these processed beans, over three quarters will be turned into meal and the rest into oil, or 11 million tons of oils. This pattern is the norm for the past three harvests, with consistently 77% of the crush being turned into meal.[25] These figures mean that Brazil ranks as the third largest world processor of soybeans behind China (131 million tons) and the United States (65 million tons) and correspondingly the third largest producer of this protein meal or cake (farelo).[26] As Brazil's pastoral industry has expanded in the past seventy-five years to become a major world producer and exporter of beef, chickens, and pork, nationally produced soybean meal has been an important factor in promoting that growth.

In the first decades of Brazilian exportation soybean meal was often more important than the unprocessed grain. But by 2000, the volume of beans exported finally exceeded that of soybean meal, and since then it has expanded at an even faster pace. Exports of soy meal, on the other hand, have remained relatively stable since that period even as local production has grown.[27] This has meant that the share of these two soybean products has declined as a share of total exports (see Graph 4.3) For the 2022/2023 harvest it is estimated that 61% of the 153 million tons of soybeans produced were exported and the rest were crushed for meal and oil. Although Brazil is one of the world's top producers of soybean oil and meal, it only exports 23% of its oil and 52% of its meal. The soy oil has now become the main edible oil in Brazil and thus soy exports have progressively declined to modest levels as ever more oil is consumed

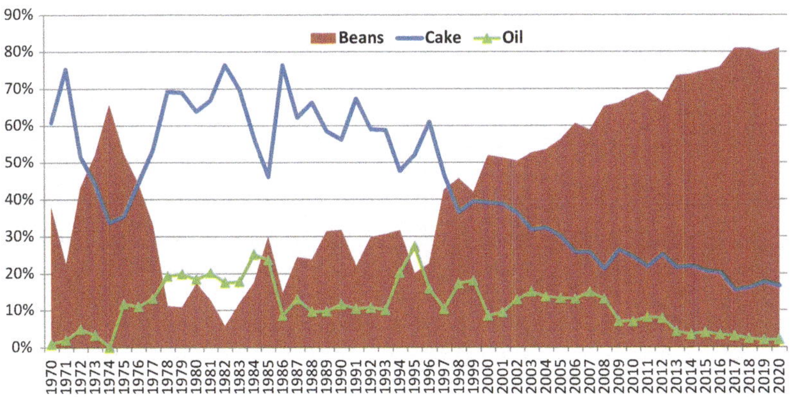

Graph 4.3 Relative share of soybean cake, oil and beans in the value of soybean exports, 1970–2020 (*Source* FAOSTAT, at http://www.fao.org/faostat/en/#data/TP)

nationally, soy meal is widely used as animal feed in the country, and Brazil is one of the largest producers and exporters of animal protein. But production has been more than sufficient for Brazil to export ever larger quantities of meal.

In this century soybeans have emerged as the fourth largest grain or oilseed in the world, behind corn, wheat, and rice.[28] Most of this importance has been due to the growth of Asian and American production. In terms of world production, the United States alone in the 1960s averaged some 70% of world production. Then with the development of Brazilian and Argentine production in the 1970s, American producers increased their share to an average of 80% of world production in that decade, with the importance of the United States slowly declining. Although the Americas to this day still account for 80% of world production, the role of the United States has steadily declined reaching just a third of world production in the 2010s, while Brazil now has replaced it as the leader with an average of 34% of world production in that decade.

Not only has the leadership in production changed, but so too has leadership in world exports of soybeans. Whereas the United States averaged 90% of world exports in the 1960s and 1970s, that share of world exports has progressively declined even faster than its share in world production. In the past five years from 2017 to 2021 US share of

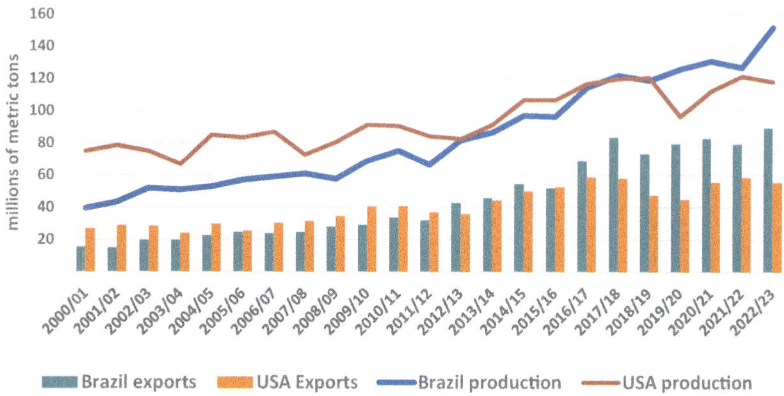

Graph 4.4 Soybean production and exports of Brazil and the USA, 2000/2001–2022/2023 (*Source* USDA, FAS, Oilseeds World Markets & Trade, December 2004, table 2; December 2017, table 21; March 2023, tables 8 and 9)

world exports has fallen to 34% while that of Brazil has risen to 50% of world exports, effectively reversing the role between the two American producers (see Graph 4.4). In the crop year 2022/2023 Brazil is expected to export a record 97.2 million tons accounting for an impressive 55% of world exports, compared to only 33 million tons exported by the United States.[29] As late as the crop year 2018/2019, Brazil produced the same 120.5 million tons as the United States, but in contrast to the United States has continued to grow whereas the United States production has remained relatively stagnant.[30]

As Brazilian production grew it slowly replaced the United States and has taken an ever larger share of the export market. Although Argentina independently developed its own soybean sector to add to its traditional exports of wheat, corn and meat, it has never really challenged the supremacy of Brazil as the dominant producer (see Graph 4.5).

Over time the soybean expansion of Brazil spread to its neighbors. In the case of Paraguay and Uruguay, it was often Brazilians who started the soybean farms, while in Bolivia it was local producers who slowly integrated themselves into the Brazilian soybean sector and shipped most of their beans through the port of Santos (see Graph 4.5). The Argentine case was a late but independent starter in producing soybeans. The

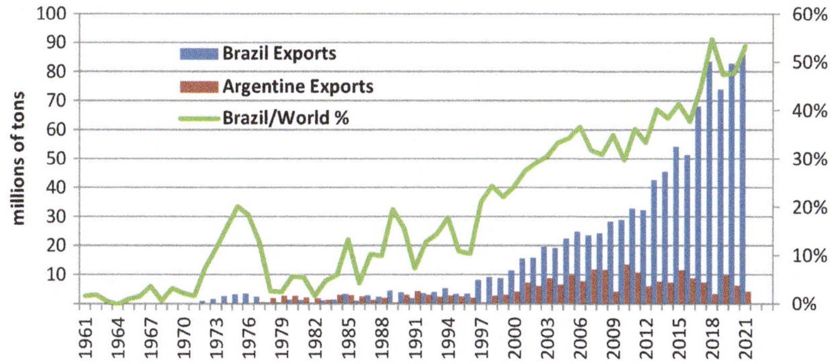

Graph 4.5 Volume of exports of Brazil and Argentina, and Brazilian share of world exports (%), 1961–2021 (*Source* FAOSTAT)

steady growth of this soybean frontier, centered in Brazil, has become the world's largest producer and exporter of soybeans and their by-products. By the late 2010s and early 2020s, these five American producers (Brazil, Argentina, Paraguay, Bolivia, and Uruguay) accounted well over half of the world production and of world exports.

There have also been significant shifts among these other South American producers. In the past several years Argentine production has declined and Paraguayan and Bolivian production has expanded. Although Argentina will produce 33 million tons and Paraguay 10 million tons of beans by the crop year 2022/2023, Paraguay is expected to export 6.4 million tons while Argentina will export only 3.4 million tons. While this reflects the lack of consumption of any crush products in Paraguay, it also reflects the declining importance of Argentina as both a producer and exporter. Argentine production peaked at some 61 million tons in 2015 and has been declining most years since, reaching just 33 million tons production in the 2022/2023 harvest (see Graph 4.6).

These countries also produced meal or cake and oil. In this Argentina was the leader in both oil and cake or meal production. It clearly dedicated a far higher share of its production toward the internal market. But here as well the South American countries have emerged in this century as the largest world producers of these products (see Table 4.3).

Although production of soybeans products initially have come primarily from the countries which were growing the soybeans, recently there have been changes in oil and meal supplies as non-producers or

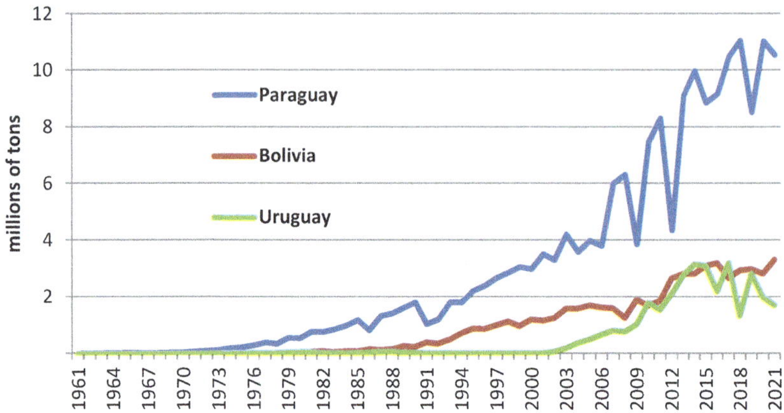

Graph 4.6 Soybean production of Paraguay, Bolivia and Uruguay, 1961–2021 (*Source* FAOSTAT)

major importers have begun or increased their output of processed beans (see Table 4.4). Some countries in Europe (mainly the Netherlands, Spain, and Germany) and China have increasing installed capacity for soybean processing. Most of them are non-soybean producing countries that purchase soybeans for processing and re-export meal and oil. This is the case of the Netherlands, the European Union's largest producer, which in 2022/2023 was the fourth largest exporter of soybean oil and soybean cake.[31]

Not only have Brazilian produced soybeans become a major factor in world trade, but they have become one of the most valuable of Brazilian exports in the current century. In the past few years soybeans have represented the first or second most valuable export, changing places with iron ore or petroleum in the current decade. With the exports of soy cake and soy oil added to the total, their value alone accounts for 16–18% of total exports in the most recent years (see Graph 4.7). The next most important products were petroleum at 13% and Iron ore at 9% of total value of all exports in 2022. Nor does any other agricultural product comes close to this importance. Maize the next most important agricultural product currently accounts for about 3–4% of the total value of exports.

Table 4.3 Soybean complex exports (cake, oils and grain—1961 to 2022/2023—in tons)

Countries/regions	*1961*	*1970*	*1980*	*1990*	*2000*	*2010*	*2022/2023*[a]
Cake, soybeans							
Argentina	–	–	289,756	5,208,961	12,930,671	24,952,347	27,600,000
Bolivia	–	–	24,153	58,398	628,560	1,000,051	1,675,000
Brazil	33,000	525,365	6,581,925	8,744,750	9,389,189	13,668,599	19,500,000
Paraguay	–	27,972	72,795	93,499	410,757	1,004,097	2,050,000
Uruguay	–	–	9,579	1,000	–	–	
Total Southern Cone	33,000	553,337	6,978,208	14,106,608	23,359,177	40,625,094	50,825,000
United States of America	614,390	3,660,351	7,024,495	4,565,054	5,936,337	8,354,882	12,428,000
Other countries	541,889	1,209,960	3,822,207	7,580,387	7,981,236	16,007,524	6,694,000
World	1,189,279	5,423,648	17,824,910	26,252,049	37,276,750	64,987,500	69,947,000
% Total Southern Cone	3%	10%	39%	54%	63%	63%	73%
Oil, soybean							
Argentina	–	–	91,756	1,003,215	2,979,696	4,899,817	5,500,000
Bolivia	–	–	39	8,771	154,998	213,558	390,000
Brazil	–	2,654	743,922	794,325	1,072,994	1,559,776	2,100,000
Paraguay	–	1,209	4,600	9,005	98,199	252,642	600,000
Uruguay	–	–	17	–	–	1,172	
Total Southern Cone	–	3,863	840,334	1,815,316	4,305,887	6,926,965	8,590,000
United States of America	273,261	674,450	1,067,097	533,737	587,750	1,656,734	590,000
Other countries	117,331	442,197	1,288,635	1,389,832	2,312,241	2,284,527	1,777,000
World	390,592	1,120,510	3,196,066	3,738,885	7,205,878	10,868,226	12,657,000
% Total Southern Cone	–	0%	26%	49%	60%	64%	68%
Soybeans							
Argentina	–	–	2,699,858	3,214,440	4,122,890	13,616,013	7,200,000
Bolivia	–	–	–	67,557	215,955	51,228	3,100,000
Brazil	73,270	289,623	1,548,883	4,076,804	11,517,260	29,073,200	89,500,000

(continued)

Table 4.3 (continued)

Countries/regions	*1961*	*1970*	*1980*	*1990*	*2000*	*2010*	*2022/2023*[a]
Paraguay	265	–	235,307	1,410,500	1,795,768	4,658,608	5,750,000
Uruguay	–	–	8,964	26,568	–	1,968,195	2,425,000
Total Southern Cone	73,535	289,623	4,493,012	8,795,869	17,651,873	49,367,244	107,975,000
United States of America	3,634,190	11,839,087	21,786,448	15,466,663	27,192,220	42,350,556	55,656,000
Other countries	465,708	498,154	597,861	1,614,248	2,533,688	5,598,062	5,511,000
World	4,173,433	12,626,864	26,877,321	25,876,780	47,377,781	97,315,862	169,142,000
% Total Southern Cone	2%	2%	17%	34%	37%	51%	64%

Note [a]2022/2023 are estimates
Source FAOSTAT and for 2022/2023 USDA Oilseeds World Markets and Trade, November 2022; USDA, FAS, IPAD, Crop Explorer November 2022

Table 4.4 Soybean oil and meal: production, imports, exports and consumption, 2022/2023 (thousands metric tons)

	Soyabeans oil				*Soyabeans meal**			
Country	*Production*	*Imports*	*Exports*	*Domestic consumption*	*Production*	*Imports*	*Exports*	*Domestic consumption*
China	16,486	1,000		17,100	72,864			72,514
United States	11,882		590	11,816	47,663		12,428	35,743
Brazil	10,160		2,350	7,900	40,867		21,100	19,850
Argentina	6,965		4,750	4,940	27,495		24,900	3,400
European Union	2,784	450	1,075	2,280	11,574	15,400		27,392
India	1,750	3,150		4,940	7,760			6,725

Source USDA—Oilseds: World Markets and Trade, March 2023, tables 8 and 9

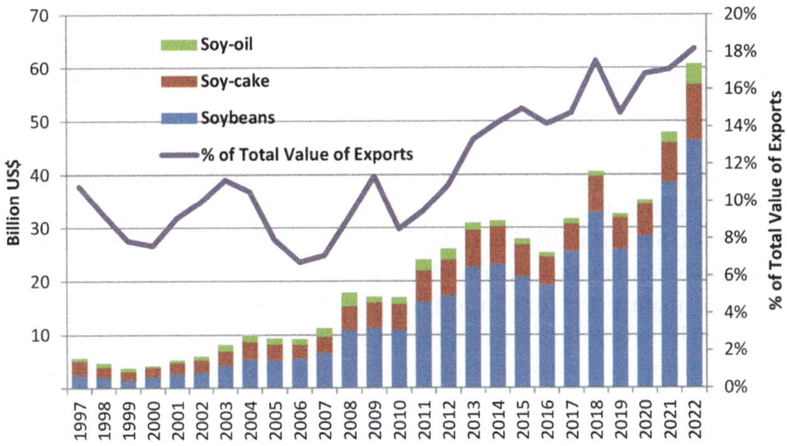

Graph 4.7 Value of soybean, soy cake and soy oil, and ratio of these to total value of exports, 1998–2022 (*Source* COMESTAT using SH4 categories at http://comexstat.mdic.gov.br/pt/geral)

Whereas some of Brazil's agricultural exports were controlled by national companies, some of which would turn themselves into multinational ones, in soybeans, the prime exporters were the multinational trading companies. These companies created complex value chains which distribute soybeans and their products throughout the world. There is currently an international division of labor, where nations specialize in one or a few stages, depending on their natural, human, and technological resources endowments and their geopolitical relations with other countries. Geographic flexibility and the ability to relocate its resources and operations on a global scale are critical to minimizing total costs and taking advantage of different factors of production across countries. For the model of globally distributed production chains to work, in addition to the processes of economic liberalization and deregulation, the presence of transnational corporations, which constitute links between geographically dispersed spaces is fundamental.[32]

The inputs of these global products, including genetically modified seeds and fertilizers and insecticides, are the main focus of attention of the large multinationals in the sector, which control the supply of these inputs in virtually every major agricultural country in the world, including the Southern Cone countries. The use of GMOs and the patenting laws on products provided by these large multinationals have been fundamental in the cultivation of soybeans. Such penetration has taken place under heated debate and permanent questioning from entities that defend biodiversity and sustainability

The export of soybeans is also affected by the logistic limitations in Brazil and the failure in recent decades of improving the transport infrastructure. Thus the extraordinary growth in soybean exports has occurred despite the logistical disadvantages that the country presents, as the main productive centers, particularly those in the Center-West, are located far from the main ports and local transport is both inefficient and expensive. Slowly new routes have opened for exporting via the Amazon river system, although Santos remains the main port of exit (see Maps 4.1 and 4.2).

Although initially Brazilian logistics costs were greater than other major soybean producers, Brazil productivity was sufficiently high so that it was able to compete in the international market even despite these so-called "Brazil costs." Nevertheless the wealth being generated by this primary export and the magnitude of its exports have stimulated public and private investments in support systems, processing, and logistics Even transportation costs, usually inefficient and therefore expensive in Brazil, are no different from the costs of American producer and have been systematically declining as a share of final costs of soybeans delivered to China. This can especially be seen in the shipments from Mato Grosso and

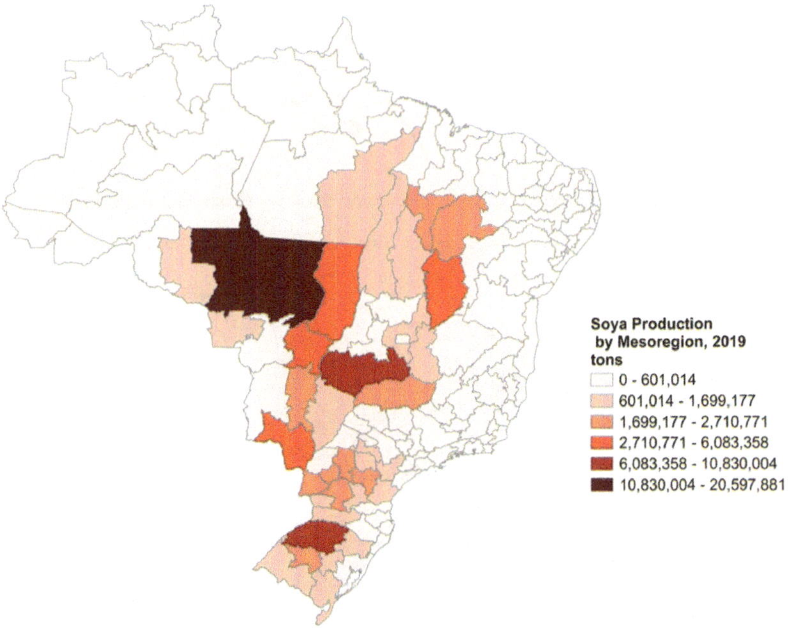

Map 4.1 Distribution of soybean production in Brazil in 2019 (*Source* IBGE Bases Cartográficas Sidra, table 1612)

Goiás to the port of Santos (see Table 4.5). In 2021 Santos accounted for 21% of all soybean exports, Rio Grande for 14%, Paranaguá for 13%, and São Luís for 8%.[33] The longer run histories from the Center-West show a systematic decline, while the newer routes to the Northern ports are more recent and have only reached the Santos percentages in the last year (see Graph 4.8a, b). These costs are now competitive with the United States.

Soybeans, unlike other major agricultural exports, have been concentrated mostly on one market. It was China which has become the prime market for Brazilian soybeans. While China took only 4% of the exported beans in 1997, by 2009 it was taking half of Brazil's exports and since then has accounted for between 70 and 80% of these exports (see Graph 4.9). But in the last year or two other countries have begun to increase their share of imports. In 2022 Spain and Thailand each took 4% of total exports, Iran reached 3%, and the Netherlands and Turkey each accounted for 2%, thus reducing China's share to 68% of the total.

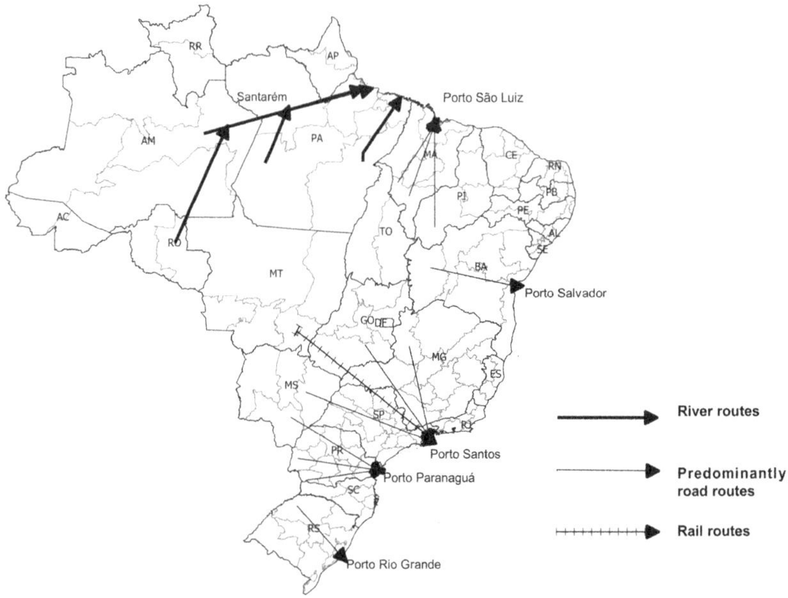

Map 4.2 Major routes for soybean exports

In contrast, the export of cake, which is becoming increasingly important, has a much more diverse set of destinations than do the soybean exports. It went from around 2 billion dollars in exports in the 1990s to a 10 billion dollar year in 2020 (see Graph 4.10) At the same time these exports go all over the world, and include both leading agricultural countries of Europe as well as the major Asian countries (see Graph 4.11). China is absent as an importer, since its own industries created cake from American bean imports from all sources.

Along with opening up some of the poorer frontier regions of Brazil to modern farming, soybean development in Brazil has also had a major impact in propelling Brazil into being a world class producer and exporter of maize. Maize became the main alternative crop planted in soybean fields. By the end of the second decade of the twenty-first century, Brazil passed Argentina to become the world's third largest producer of maize and the second largest exporter of this product and it most recently replaced the United States as the leading world exporter. It has done so by adopting no-till planting and developing two annual crops per year—with

Table 4.5 Comparative costs of transport from US and Brazilian Soybean Regions to Shanghai and Hamburg, 2021 (US$/ton)

	Truck	*Rail*	*Barge*	*Ocean*	*Total transport cost*	*Farm Value*	*Total*[a]	*% transport*
Transport to Shanghai								
Miniapolis, MN	13.66	36.38	12.49	50.88	113.41	465.42	578.83	19.6%
Davenport, Iowa	13.66	33.33	12.49	50.88	110.36	456.85	567.21	19.5%
North MT—Santos	60.94			37.00	97.94	463.10	561.04	17.5%
South Go—Paranaguá	36.83			38.75	75.58	466.39	541.97	13.9%
Transport to Hamburg								
Miniapolis, MN	13.66	36.38	12.49	19.75	82.28	465.42	547.70	15.0%
Davenport, Iowa	13.66	33.33	12.49	19.75	79.23	456.85	536.08	14.8%
North MT—Santos	60.94			31.25	92.19	463.10	555.29	16.6%
South Go—Paranaguá	36.83			31.00	67.83	466.39	534.22	12.7%

Note [a]Total is the Farm Value plus all Transport Costs
Source USDA—Grain Transportation Report, June 3, 2021, 2–3, tables 1 and 2

the second planting becoming the largest crop in any year. In 2022/2023 it is estimated that Brazil exported 40 million tons. The second "safrinha" of corn is primarily produced in the Center-West[34]

Brazil entered soybean production late by American standards. It was first associated as a rotation crop for wheat and then became an oil staple for Brazilian consumption by the end of the last decades of the twentieth century. But it has become a world dominant producer only in the last two decades. This growth is due to the extraordinary productivity achieved by national producers, despite the high costs of production. There has also been a steady shift of production from the temperate lands of the South region to the more tropical soils of the Center-West region. This migration was due to commercial farmers from the South bringing with them modern commercial agricultural practices. It was also made possible by the massive state investments in agricultural research, which through the efforts of Embrapa produced the adopted seeds which could

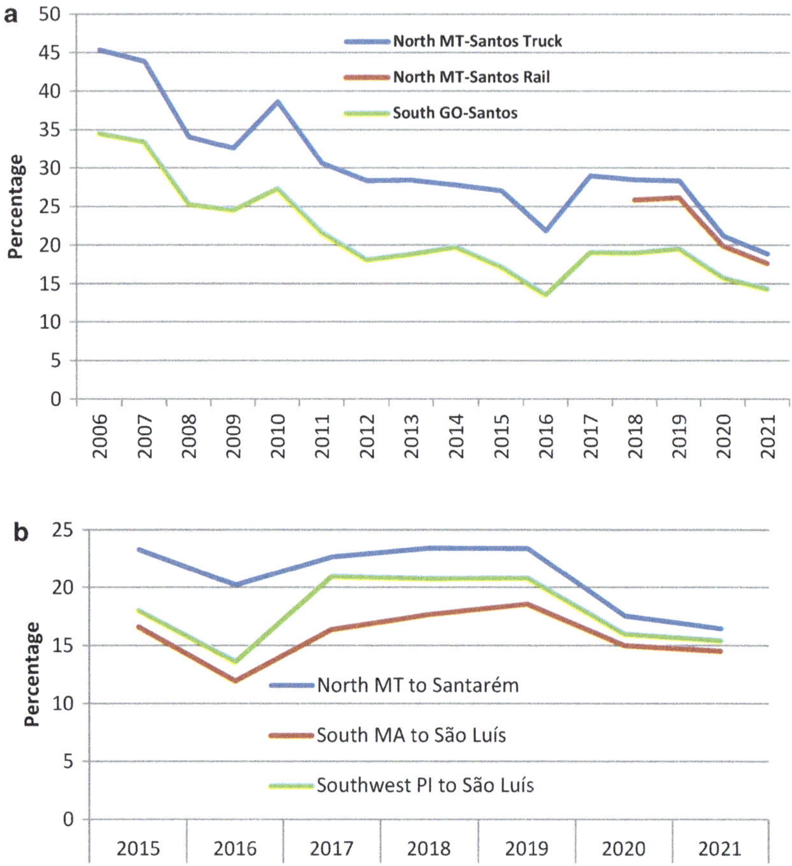

Graph 4.8 **a** Transport as % of landed cost by Origin via Port of Santos to Shanghai, 2006–2021. **b** Transport as % of landed cost by Origin via Northern ports to Shanghai, 2015–2021 (*Source* USDA, Soybean Transportation Guide, Brazil, 2021 at https://www.ams.usda.gov/services/transportation-analysis/soybean-datasets)

be used in these new more tropical soils, just as it adopted the chemicals needed to improve its fertility. Although it was behind the United States for most of the past half century, it has now taken the lead as not

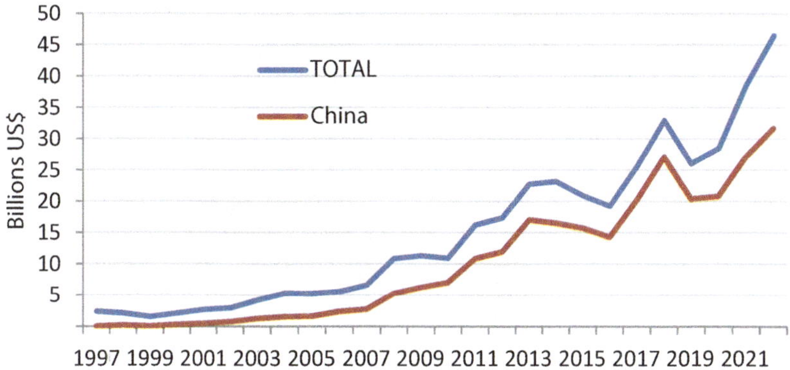

Graph 4.9 Total exports of Brazilian soybeans and Chinese imports of Brazilian beans, 1997–2022 (*Source* Comestat, using SH 1201)

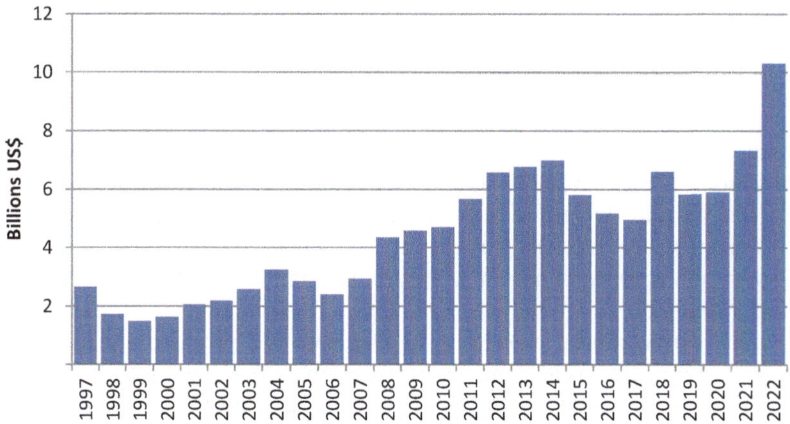

Graph 4.10 Growth of soy cake exports of Brazil 1979–2022 (*Source* Comestat, using sh4 2304)

only America's major producer, but the largest grower and exporter of soybeans in the world.

Productivity and area dedicated to soybeans has steadily increased in the past decade. What is impressive is that the yield per hectare has grown considerably in this period and in any given year, depending on

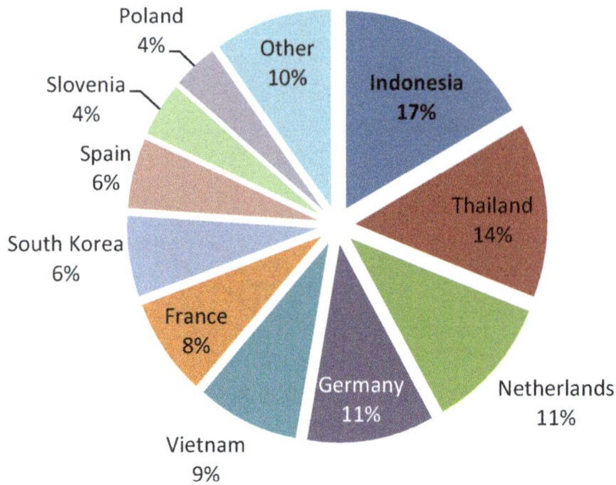

Graph 4.11 Percentage share of the value of total Brazilian soy cake exports by leading importers in 2022 (*Source* Comestat, using sh4 2304)

climactic conditions, can equal or exceed US productivity. Brazil moreover has increased area planted at a much higher average annual rate than the United States. Even Argentina and the three smaller regional producers (Paraguay, Bolivia, and Uruguay) have expanded at this pace. In this decade Argentina and Brazil increased their lands dedicated to this crop by around 10% per annum, and even Paraguay grew at 5% per annum, compared to only a 1.2% annual increase of the United States (see Table 4.6).

This extraordinary growth in production and productivity has been spurred by rising world demand and attractive prices, and has been made possible by increasing productivity, stemming from the introduction of innovative production processes such as biotechnology, modern agricultural training, massive introduction of machines, and chemicals and the creation of complex value chains that integrate various stages of the productive, financial, and commercial processes in both countries.[35] As in the case of the other major grains and oilseeds, there have been profound technological transformations in soybean cultivation since the late twentieth century, through the introduction of precision agriculture, new fertilizers and pesticides, and new cultivars, in particular genetically modified organisms (GMOs), which together represented a revolution in agricultural productivity in the major exporting countries.[36]

Table 4.6 Area planted in soybeans and yields for the major American producers, 2000/2001–2020/2021

Country	*Yield (ton per hectare)*			*Area (million hectares)*		
	2000/2001	*2010/2011*	*2020/2021*	*2000/2001*	*2010/2011*	*2020/2021*
Brazil	2.8	2.8	3.4	13.9	23.5	38.3
United States	2.6	2.9	3.4	29.3	31.2	33.5
Argentina	2.7	2.8	3.1	10.4	18.0	17.3
Paraguay	2.6	2.4	2.8	1.4	2.8	3.7
Bolívia	2.1	1.9	2.0	0.6	0.9	1.4
Uruguay[a]	2.3	1.9	2.4	0.01	0.9	1.0
World	2.3	2.5	2.9	75.3	101.5	126.9

Note [a]Given that 2000 was an exceptionally severe year for Uruguay we have used the more normal year of 2001 for comparisons
Source USDA, World Agriculture Production May 2020, table 11
USDA, *World Agriculture Production* May 2010, table 11
USDA, World Agriculture Production August 2002, table 11
FAOSTAT for Bolivian and Uruguayan numbers in 2000/2001

In Brazil as in the other South American producers, export agricultural production, particularly soybeans, is made by producers fully integrated into the international market using modern agriculture techniques and totally dependent on international prices. International companies have developed complex value chains and arranged contract sales for a large part of the soybean production. Finally Brazilian producers are agricultural entrepreneurs, capitalized and seeking areas able to expand their production. Many of these producers are not bound by political borders and have expanded into the neighboring states of Uruguay, Paraguay and Bolivia to create a modern soybean frontier whose center of gravity is Brazil. This Soybean Frontier now accounts for over half of the world production and dominates the world market.

Notes

1. Gyoung-Ah Lee et al. "Archaelogical Soyabean (Glyne max) in East Asia: Does Size Matter?" *PLoS ONE*, 6, no. 11: e26720. https://doi.org/10.1371/journal.pone.0026720, at: https://www.ncbi.nlm.nih.gov/pmc/articles/PMC3208558/

2. On the history of soybean production in Asia see William Shutheff and Akiko Aoyagi. *History of Soyabens and Soyfoos in Southeast Asia (13th Century to 2010)* (Lafayette, Ind, Soyinfo Center, 2010).
3. Tadayoshi Masuda and Peter D. Goldsmith, "World Soyabean Production: Area Harvested, Yield, and Long-Term Projections," *International Food and Agrobusiness Management Review*, 12, no. 4 (2009): 143–162.
4. Edmund W. Lusas, *Soybean Processing and Utilization* in H. Roger Boerma and James E. Specht, eds., *Soybeans: Improvement, Production, and Uses* (3rd ed; Madison, Wisconsin: American Society of Agronomy, Inc. Crop Science Society of America, Inc. Soil Science Society of America,2004), 949.
5. Richard F. Wilson, "Seed composition," in Boerma and Specht, *Soybeans: Improvement, Production, and Uses*, 629.
6. USDA, FAS, *Oilseeds: World Market and Trade, March 2023*, 10, table 1.
7. Edwin G. Strand, *Soybeans in American Farming* (Technical Report no 966; Washington DC, USDA, 1948), 1–8.
8. FAOSTAT, Trade.
9. Emidio Rizzo Bonato and Ana Lidia Variani Bonato, *A soja no Brasil: história e estatística*. (Londrina, PR, Embrapa, 1987), 1–10.
10. Bonato and Bonato, *A soja no Brasil*, 13 table 2, 14, table 3.
11. Embrapa Soja, "Historia" at https://www.embrapa.br/en/soja/cultivos/soja1/historia).
12. Gilson Jesus de Azevedo Campelo, Romeu Alfonso de Souza Kiihl, and Leones Alves de Almeida, "Características agronômicas e morfológicas das cultivares de soja desenvolvidas para as regiões de baixas latitudes,"in M. A. de Queiroz, C. O. Goedert, and S. R. R. Ramos, eds, *Recursos Genéticos e Melhoramento de Plantas para o Nordeste Brasileiro* (Petrolina-PE, Embrapa, 1999), found at http://www.cpatsa.embrapa.br/; Amélio Dall' Agnol *A Embrapa soja no contexto do desenvolvimento da soja no Brasil. Histórico e Contribuições.* (Brasília: Embrapa. 2016); Klein and Luna, *Feeding the World*, chapter 6.
13. Antonio Boris Frota and Gilson Jesus de Azevedo Campelo, "Evolução e perspectivas da produção de soja na região Meio Norte do Brasil," in M. A. de Queiroz, et al., ed., *Recursos Genéticos e Melhoramento de Plantas para o Nordeste Brasileiro* (Petrolina: Embrapa Semi-árido; Brasília, DF: Embrapa Recursos Genéticos e Biotecnologia, 1999), 143–151.
14. Anderson Simionato Milioli, Daniela Meira, Maiara Cecília Panho, Laura Alexandra Madella, Leomar Guilherme Woyann, Matheus Henrique Todeschini, Andrei Daniel Zdziarski et al., "Genetic Improvement of Soybeans in Brazil: South and Midwest Regions." *Crop Science* 62, no. 6 (2022): 2277.

15. Steven T. Sonka, Karen L. Bender, and Donna K. Fisher, "Economics and Marketing," in Boerma and Specht, *Soybeans: Improvement, Production, and Uses*, 919.
16. Herbert S. Klein and Francisco Vidal Luna, *Feeding the World: Brazil's Transformation into a Modern Agricultural Economy* (New York: Cambridge University Press, 2018).
17. CONAB, Série Histórica das Safras, Trigo. https://www.conab.gov.br/info-agro/safras/serie-historica-das-safras?start=30.
18. Eliseu Alves and Geraldo da Silva e Souza "A pesquisa agrícola numa agricultura integrada ao mercado internacional. O caso da Embrapa e do Cerrado," *Revista Política Agrícola.*, XVI, no. 2 (2007): 56–67; Embrapa Comunicações, *Embrapa em Números* (Brasília: Embrapa, 2016); Fábio Gelape Faleiro and Austeclinio Lopes de Farias Neto Savanas. *Desafios e estratégias para o equilíbrio entre sociedade, agronegócio e recursos naturais* (Planaltina, DF: Embrapa, 2008); and Klein and Luna, *Feeding the World*, chapter 4.
19. In contrast corn production differs in whether produced on modern commercial farms or family farms. Thus, the difference in productivity varies considerably by size of farm especially as the low tech small family farms produces part of their corn for self-consumption. Soybeans are a commercial crop even on small family farms.
20. Bernardo Friedrich Theodor Rudorff et al., "Remote Sensing Images to Detect Soy Plantations in the Amazon Biome—The Soy Moratorium Initiative," *Sustainability*, 4, no. 5(2012): 1074; Bernardo Friedrich Theodor Rudorff et al., "The Soy Moratorium in the Amazon Biome Monitored by Remote Sensing Images," *Remote Sensing*, 3, no. 1 (2011): 185–202. Even recent challenges to the agreement agree that it has most been successful, but argue that it needs additional reforms. Mendelson Lima et al., "Demystifying Sustainable Soy in Brazil," *Land Use Policy*, 82 (2019): 349–352.
21. Aline C. Soterroni et al., "Expanding the Soy Moratorium to Brazil's Cerrado," *Science Advances* 5, no. 7 (2019): eaav7336, 1–9.
22. Aline Fumie Sediyama, Luiz Gonzaga de Castro Júnior, Cristina Lelis Leal Calegario, and Paulo Henrique de Lima Siqueira, "Análise da estrutura, conduta e desempenho da indústria processadora de soja no Brasil no período de 2003 a 2010," *Revista de Economia e Sociologia Rural*, 51 (2013): 164.
23. Lucineia Hipólito Carvalho, "Poder de mercado na indústria brasileira de esmagamento de soja," (Phd thesis, Universidade Federal de Viçosa, 2004), 8–17.
24. Severino Morib Barbosa Camelo, and Isabel Lausanne Fontgalland, "Análise da produção e comercialização de óleo vegetal no Brasil: o

estudo de caso da empresa Cargill," *E-Acadêmica*, 2, no. 2 (2021): e062229–e062229.
25. ABIOVE, Monthly Statistics as of January 2023 found at https://abiove.org.br/en/statistics/
26. USDA, *Oilseeds: World Markets and Trade, March 2023*, 13–14 tables 4, 5.
27. IPEADATA, "Exportações – farelo de soja – qde.," "Exportações – soja em grão – qde.," e "Área colhida – soja – Hectare," at http://www.ipeadata.gov.br/
28. FAOSTAT.
29. USDA, IPAD, Soybean Explorer, March, 2023, at https://ipad.fas.usda.gov/cropexplorer/cropview/commodityView.aspx?startrow=11&cropid=2222000&sel_year=2022&rankby=Production.
30. USDA, *Oilseeds: World Markets and Trade, March 2023*:15, table 7.
31. FAOSTAT. In 2020 the Netherlands imported soybeans in grain and processed it as cake and oil and then exported the same products. It exported a total 615 thousand tons, of cake and 3.3 million tons of cake.
32. Valdemar João Wesz Junior, "O mercado da soja e as relações de troca entre produtores rurais e empresas no Sudeste do Mato Grosso (Brasil)" (Phd Thesis, Rio de Janeiro, Universidade Federal Rural do Rio de Janeiro, 2014), chapter 1; According to ABIOVE [Associação Brasileira das Indústrias de Óleos Vegetais] of the 121 existing processing units at the end of 2018, ABIOVE census of December 2018, accessed at http://www.abiove.org.br/site/index.php?page=estatistica&area=NC0yLTE=.
33. USDA, Agricultural Marketing Service, *Soybean Transportation Guide: Brazil 202*, 47.
34. USDA, *Grain: World Markets and Trade, November 2022*, 27.
35. Rocha, Pedro, and V. Villalobos Arámbula (2012): *Estudio comparativo entre el cultivo de soja genéticamente modificada y el convencional en Argentina, Brasil, Paraguay y Uruguay* (No. IICA F30 53. San José Costa Rica and Buenos Aires, 2012), chapter 1.
36. Bernard Hategekiman and Michael Trant "Adoption and Diffusion of New Technology in Agriculture: Genetically Modified Corn and Soyabens," *Canadian Journal of Agricultural Economics* 50 (2002):. 357–371; Brian D. Wright and Tiffany M. Shih, "Agricultural Innovation," (Boston: National Bureau of Economic Research, 2010; Working Paper 15793); and Greg Traxler, "The Economic Impacts of Biotechnology-Based Technological Innovations' (ESA Working Paper No. 04-08; UN, FAO, May 2004), 6–8.

CHAPTER 5

Maize

In the past two decades, the spectacular growth of maize exports by Brazil combined with continued exports of maize by Argentina has turned the South American countries into the primary world production zone for maize exports as well as soybeans. In both nations corn has expanded with soy production and in both cases it has been tied to major changes in meat production. In Brazil the availability of abundant supplies of soy and maize provided the underpinnings of the extraordinary surge in meat exports in this very same period. In this chapter we examine how this transformation of maize production occurred, how it evolved, and how it relates to the auxiliary agricultural production, both of soybeans and meat.

America, the continent where maize was domesticated and is universally grown, accounts for half of world production. Maize in turn is the largest cereal produced in the world, surpassing such other cereals as wheat, rice and soybeans in world importance. Yet it is only in recent years that Brazil has emerged, along with Argentina, as the leading source of maize exports for the world market. In the harvest of 2022/2023 it is estimated that Argentina and Brazil together produced some 181 million tons of maize and exported 86,000 tons which represented respectively 15% of world production and 47% of world exports.[1] While Argentina has a long history of exporting maize and other grains into the world

H. S. Klein and F. V. Luna, *Brazilian Crops in the Global Market*, Palgrave Studies in Economic History,
https://doi.org/10.1007/978-3-031-38589-6_5

market, this is a new development for Brazil. In both cases the revolution in genetically modified seeds, the adoption of no-till farming and the association of maize with the new South American crop of soybeans, led to major change in the yield and importance of maize within their agricultural economies. It also fostered significant change in their respective cattle and chicken industries due to the increasing abundance of maize for animal feed.

In Brazil maize was a largely small farming product with a limited internal market from colonial times until well into the twentieth century. It was the dramatic expansion of soybean production which began in the late twentieth century which soon incorporated maize as the major rotating crop to be used to balance soil nutrients. This led to an explosion of maize production and its association with commercial large-scale agriculture, especially of soybeans. This sudden expansion of maize, which only occurred in the past two decades, allowed Brazil for the first time to export a substantial amount of the maize it produced. It also provided the nation with an ever increasing amount of maize for animal feed, the primary domestic use of maize. This in turn permitted Brazil not only to supply the domestic market, but it allowed for the major growth of cattle and chicken production in this same period as these two products were important in animal feeds. By the second decade of the twenty-first century Brazil's maize exports finally equaled or surpassed those of Argentina. At the same time this newly abundant maize and soybean production allowed Brazil for the first time to become a major exporter of bovine and chicken meats, which grew so rapidly that Brazil became the world's largest meat and chicken exporter in this same period as the expansion of maize production.[2]

In view of its enormous adaptability to physical conditions and easy planting, maize is produced by 170 different countries. Among the twenty largest producers there are countries with totally different climate and geographical characteristics, such as India, South Africa, Canada, France, and Egypt. Currently the largest producers are the United States, China, Brazil, Argentina, and India in that order. What is impressive is that since 1980 the two South American countries have increased their production at a higher rate than all the other major producers, with the most recent period from 2000 to 2020 showing Brazil growing at almost twice the rate of the world increase in maize production (see Table 5.1).

Most maize producing countries are self-sufficient or produce a significant portion of domestic demand.[3] Thus, only some 10–15% of world

Table 5.1 World production of maize in selected countries, 1980–2020 (1000 tons)

				% annual growth	
Coountry	*1980*	*2000*	*2020/2021*	*1980–2020 (%)*	*2000–2020 (%)*
United States	168,647	251,854	373,949	2.0	2.0
China	62,715	106,178	260,000	3.6	4.6
Brazil	20,372	32,321	110,000	4.3	6.3
Argentina	6,400	16,781	50,000	5.3	5.6
India	6,957	12,043	28,000	3.5	4.3
Mexico	12,374	17,557	28,000	2.1	2.4
Canada	5,753	6,954	14,000	2.2	3.6
South Africa	11,040	11,431	14,000	0.6	1.0
Others	102,365	136,920	640,867	4.7	8.0
World	396,623	592,039	1,518,816	3.4	4.8
% Argentina + Brazil	7%	8%	11%		

Note The European Union is a major producer, but is not listed as such in FAOSTAT
Source FAOSTAT and USDA 2020: 29

production enters international trade. In the harvest of 2022/2023. The United States, Brazil, and Argentina are currently the leading exporters. Two of the largest exporters, the United States and Brazil are also the largest consumers, along with China and the European Union (see Table 5.2).

Brazil is unusual among world maize producers in the high percentage of national production which it exported and the high ratio of domestic supplies which went into animal feed. Whereas in the Quinquenium of 2014–2018, Brazil exported almost a third of its production, the world as a whole managed to export an average of only 15% of domestic production in this same period, as did the United States. Brazil, like Argentina devoted an extraordinarily high ratio of their domestic supply to animal feed—averaging three quarters of that national consumption. In contrast the United States used just 43% on average in this five year period from 2014 to 2018 for its domestic consumption for feed and the world in general applied just 56% of corn production to this end (see Table 5.3).

Maize is a traditional product of the Brazilian farmer since early colonial times and was cultivated with low productivity. For example in one of the first agricultural censuses carried out in Brazil, that of São Paulo in 1905, some 77% of the farms produced maize, though they used only

Table 5.2 World supply and distribution of maize 2022/2023 (estimated—1000 metric tons)

Countries/regions	*Production*	*Consumption*	*Imports*	*Exports*	*Ending stocks*
United States	353,836	305,448	1,250	57,000	30,020
China	274,000	295,000	18,000		206,117
Brazil	126,000	77,000	1,300	46,500	8,253
European Union	54,800	74,700	20,000	2,700	7,359
Argentina	55,000	14,000		40,000	
India	32,000	30,100		2,800	
Mexico	27,600	44,500	17,700		3,363
Canada	14,500	15,000	1,500	1,600	2,146
Others	230,649	319,555	123,727	32,877	43,501
Total	1,168,385	1,175,303	183,477	183,477	300,759
Brazil + Argentina	181,000	91,000	1,300	86,500	8,253
%Brasil + Argentina	15%	8%	1%	47%	3%

Source USDA, Grain: World Markets and Trade, November 2022: 27–28

Table 5.3 Usage of maize in the domestic market of Argentina, Brazil, and the United States, 2014–2018 (in thousand metric tons)

Element	*Brazil*	*Argentina*	*USA*
Production	82,288	43,462	364,262
Import quantity	941	9	1,193
Stock variation	–4,704	1,000	2,043
Export quantity	23,760	23,234	70,534
Domestic supply	64,173	19,237	292,878
Feed	49,378	14,203	133,991
Seed	469	427	838
Losses	8,321	633	17,864
Processing	45	811	25,310
Other uses (non-food)	0	2,647	110,955
Food	5,960	517	3,920

Source FAOSTAT at http://www.fao.org/faostat/en/#data/FBS

27% of their cultivated lands to do so. Coffee of course was the major crop and accounted for 64% of total agricultural production, but maize was second, valued at 16% of total output.[4] In the 1920 national agricultural census some 37% of the cultivated lands were dedicated to maize production. This made it the largest single crop in terms of land usage, with

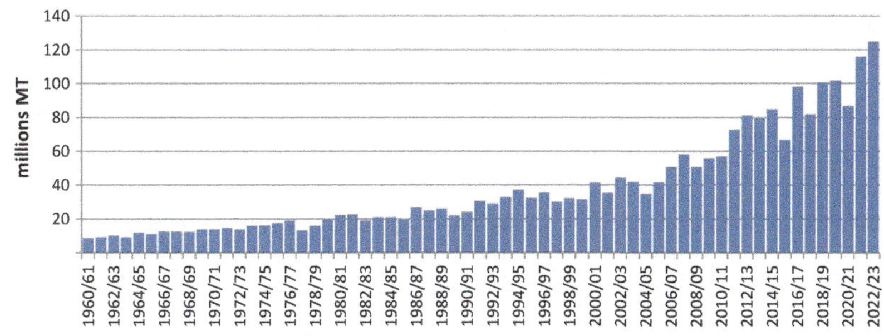

Graph 5.1 Growth of Brazilian maize production, 1960/1961–2022/2023 (*Source* USDA at https://apps.fas.usda.gov/psdonline/app/index.html#/app/advQuery)

coffee second. It accounted for 24% of the value of agricultural production, just behind coffee which represented 25% of total crop value in that year.[5] From 1919 to 1959 maize production went from 5 million tons to 9 million tons, growing at a rate of 2% per annum, with the greatest production coming from the Southeast and Southern Regions, with the states of Minas Gerais, São Paulo, Paraná and Rio Grande do Sul each producing well over a million tons.[6] It then increased to 41 million tons by 2000, for a more rapid growth of 3.9% per annum from 1960 to the end of the century. It then increased at a rate of 5.1% in the next 22 years, reaching 125 million tons by the harvest of 2022/2023 (see Graph 5.1).

But for all its importance in national consumption, Brazilian productivity in maize was quite low. In 1961 the yields per hectare of maize in Brazil were only 29% of the yields obtained in Canada and only a third of what farmers in the United States obtained. While the leading American producers continued to improve productivity throughout the last half of the twentieth century, Brazil remained at a relatively stagnant level of yield. It did not pass the 2 tons per hectare level until 2000 whereas Argentina passed that yield thirty years earlier and even Mexico reached that level by 1991. As late as 1991 Brazil was at only 27% of Canadian and US productivity in maize output (see Table 5.4). Although average productivity was low until the end of the twentieth century, the universality of its planting meant that production was usually sufficient to cover national needs, with imports only needed to meet production crises or supply imbalances in the off-season.

Table 5.4 Yield per hectare of maize in tons in selected American countries in 1961–2018

	Canada	*USA*	*Argentina*	*Brazil*	*Mexico*
1961	4.6	3.9	1.8	1.3	1.0
1971	5.2	5.5	2.4	1.3	1.3
1981	5.9	6.8	3.8	1.8	1.8
1991	6.7	6.8	4.0	1.8	2.1
2001	6.6	8.7	5.5	3.4	2.6
2011	9.5	9.2	6.4	4.2	2.9
2018	9.7	11.9	6.1	5.1	3.8
2019	9.2	10.5	7.9	5.8	4.1

Source FAOSTAT at http://www.fao.org/faostat/en/#data/QC

Table 5.5 Production, area planted and yield of maize and soybeans by size of farms, census 2017

Size of farm	*Maize*	*Soybeans*
Total	5.6	3.36
>0 and <1 ha	1.3	3.27
1–2 ha	2.0	3.28
2–5 ha	3.2	3.30
5–10 ha	4.7	3.33
10–20 ha	5.6	3.38
20–50 ha	5.8	3.42
50–100 ha	5.8	3.41
100–200 ha	6.0	3.39
200–500 ha	6.0	3.36
500+	6.0	3.34

Source IBGE, Censo Agropecuário de 2017

At the beginning of the twenty-first century there was a major increase in productivity, although it varied by region. The traditional southern Brazilian small farm producers continued having low yields, while new planting areas with their large farms in the Center-West had yields close to those of Canada and the United States. This can be seen in the agricultural census of 2017. In contrast to soybeans, which has had the same yields no matter what the size of the farm might be, there is major variation in productivity by size of farm (see Table 5.5).

This is well reflected as well in the geographically diverse patterns in yields over time. Comparing the best performing state of Mato Grosso

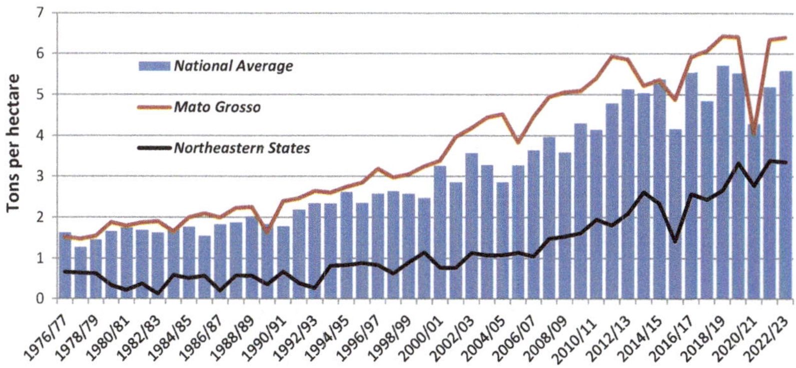

Graph 5.2 Maize yields by hectare for Mato Grosso and the Northeastern states, 1976–2022 (*Source* CONAB)

with all the states which made up the Northeastern region, the differences were profound. Of the 103 million tons Brazil produced in the harvest of 2019/2020, Mato Grosso was the largest producing state with 35 million tons, while all the Northeast states produced just 9 million tons of maize. Mato Grosso already had reached a yield of 2 tons per hectare by the harvest of 1984/1954 whereas the Northeastern region did not reach that level until 1991/1992. By the late 1990s Mato Grosso was up to 3 tons per hectare and reached 6.4 tons per hectare by 2019/2020 or double what was achieved by the Northeastern region in that crop year (see Graph 5.2).

Although major regional difference persists, over time there has been a slow but steady tendency to reduce this gap between regions. Some formerly marginal areas in the North and Northeast are now highly productive, such as the area called "Matopiba."[7] In general, among all farmers, even family farms producing for the national market, there is a slow but steady increase in yields in such basic crops as rice and beans as well as maize. Thus most states producing over 500,000 tons per annum of maize were now achieving between 4 and 6 tons per hectare. Only the insignificant producing states are still at minimally productive levels (see Table 5.6 and Map 5.1).

From 24 million tons in 1991/1992, Brazilian maize production reached 126 million in the harvest of 2022/2023. This massive growth of output permitted Brazil to satisfy all its needs and begin to export

Table 5.6 Area cultivated, production and productivity of maize by states and regions, 2022/2023

Region/states	*Area (1000 há)*	*Production (1000 tons)*	*Produtivity (kg/há)*
North	1,213.6	5,229.4	4,309
Roraima	15.0	90.0	6,000
Rondonia	286.2	1,480.5	5,173
Acre	50.6	170.0	3,359
Amazonas	4.8	13.5	2,803
Amapá	2.8	2.6	940
Pará	422.9	1,359.8	3,216
Tocantins	431.3	2,113.0	4,899
Northeast	3,252.8	11,675.2	3,589
Maranhão	608.5	3,013.6	4,953
Piauí	608.3	2,846.5	4,679
Ceará	528.8	498.7	943
Rio Grande do Norte	52.4	29.1	555
Paraíba	117.7	73.2	622
Pernambuco	239.6	126.5	528
Alagoas	40.2	83.9	2,088
Sergipe	182.2	949.1	5,209
Bahia	875.1	4,054.6	4,633
Center-West	11,143.7	69,208.7	6,211
Mato Grosso	6,955.0	44,582.8	6,410
Mato Grosso do Sul	2,210.3	11,277.6	5,102
Goiás	1,907.2	12,843.9	6,734
Distrito Federal	71.20	504.40	7,085
Southeast	2,246.9	13,030.1	5,799
Minas Gerais	1,403.0	8,785.2	6,262
Espiríto Santo	13.1	41.6	3,179
Rio de Janeiro	1.8	7.1	3,918
São Paulo	829.0	4,196.2	5,062
South	4,175.1	24,600.4	5,892
Paraná	3,028.1	17,794.8	5,877
Santa Catarina	315.5	2,493.4	7,903
Rio Grande do Sul	831.5	4,312.2	5,186
North + Northeast	4,466.4	16,904.6	3,785
CW + SE + South	17,565.7	106,839.2	6,082
Brazil	22,032.1	123,743.8	5,617

Source CONAB, Séries históricas das Safras, Milho Total (1ª, 2ª e 3ª Safras), estimate at https://www.conab.gov.br/info-agro/safras/serie-historica-das-safras/itemlist/category/910-Milho

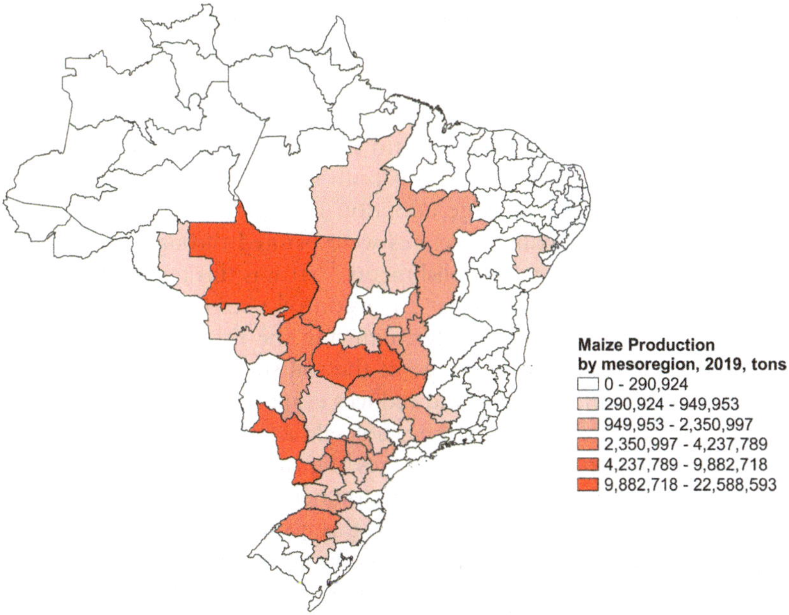

Map 5.1 Maize production by mesoregion, 2019 (*Source* IBGE Bases Cartográficas Sidra, table 1612)

maize by the twenty-first century. This very recent emergence of Brazil as a world class exporter is due to several significant developments. Since the 1960s there have been major improvements in Brazilian agriculture in general, including the improvement of crop treatments, new seeds, both hybrid or genetically modified ones, and the ability to occupy new territories, such as Cerrado thanks to the work of Embrapa which played a fundamental role in how to treat these previously unproductive soils. Finally the expansion of soybean crops into the tropical Center-West region was fundamental as maize became the major alternative crop to soybeans. Alternate cropping was fundamental in the tropical agriculture of the Center-West region to prevent plagues, as the repetition of the same crop increases the chances of crop infestation. Thus as the Center-West become the world's largest producer of soybeans, maize production expanded there as well on commercial large size farms, especially as Brazil was able to develop two and eventually three crops a year.

The adoption of no-till, or Direct Planting Agriculture, especially as it applied to maize in these new regions was also a crucial development.[8] Brazil was one of the pioneering countries in the adoption of this technology. Today the United States, Brazil, and Argentina respectively are the leading countries in the world in terms of cultivated area which uses this cultivation process which is both economically and ecologically beneficial and justified its wide adoption in Brazil.[9] By the 2017 agricultural census 32.8 million hectares were planted through this process, involving 557 agricultural establishments.[10] It was this technology which contributed to the extraordinary expansion of a second crop in the dry season. The no-till system is faster, reducing the risk of water deficit, in addition, it maintains the coverage of the soil surface and allows greater water infiltration into the soil and reduces evaporation.[11]

Another major change was the wholesale adoption of what has been called double cropping or tropical soybean-maize succession cropping which was fundamental for the development of the second corn (or *safrinha*), or the little harvest in which this no-till planting was crucial.[12] The traditional maize harvest was produced in the wet season from September to December. This new second harvest was planted in the dry season directly over the harvested crop of the wet season and without irrigation from January to April, using the no-till planting technique (*Plantio Direto*). The first crop was most often quick growing soybeans (or *soja precoce*). Although there were early experiments of this type of double planting in the Southern states in the 1980s and 1990s, they were less ecologically adopted for this production than zones closer to the equator. The adoption of this system on a large scale came after 2000 and was most fully developed in the hotter Center West region.[13] Suddenly Brazil was producing two harvests of maize every year , with the *safrinha* becoming ever more important over time and finally dominating national production. In 2000 only 15% of the maize came from the *safrinha*. By 2011/2012 it was over half the total production and by harvest of 2019/2020 this second harvest accounted for 73% of the crop (see Graph 5.2). Then beginning in the harvest of 2018/2019 was the first production from a third *safrinha* planted in April to June which is still quite modest, averaging just 1.7 million tons (see Graph 5.3).

The expansion of maize would not have occurred without the use of new hybrid GM seeds. Both on family farms and on non-family farms, these certified or transgenic GM seeds were fundamental in maize production. Although the majority of farms producing maize were family farms,

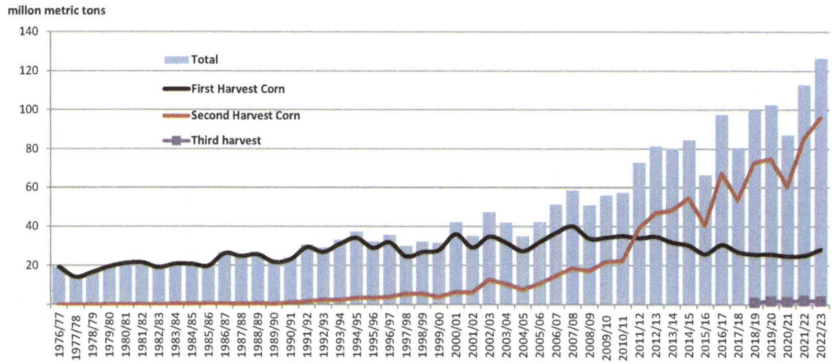

Graph 5.3 Total output of first and second harvest maize, 1976/1977–2022/2023 (*Source* CONAB)

in the case of seeds used, there was little difference between the two types of farms. Both family farms and non-family farms used certified or transgenic seeds in approximately a quarter of both these two types of establishments. Moreover in both cases those using these seeds produced the bulk of maize harvested. In the case of family farms, those using these seeds accounted for 81% of family farm maize production and among the non-family farms the ratio was 90% (see Table 5.7). As of 2017 GM maize was planted on 15.6 million hectares and GM soybeans on 33.7 million hectares. By this year Brazil was the world's second largest consumer of GM seeds in the world after the United States.[14]

This recent growth of a second maize harvest increased production and productivity and has enabled Brazil to become a significant exporter of maize in the world market and the second largest exporter after the United States. Even as recently as the 1980s and 1990s there was a recurring deficit in the maize trade with national production insufficient for domestic needs and with the country taking in annual imports of corn. It was only in the harvest of 2000/2001 that Brazil produced enough maize to begin to seriously export its surplus and at the same time satisfy the internal market. Thereafter both internal consumption and production began to expand at an ever rapid place. In the quinquennium of 1996/1997 both consumption and production averaged 34.2 million tons and by the quinquennium of 2016/2017–2020/2021 average consumption had almost doubled to 65.9 million tons, but national production had more than tripled to 98.4 million tons.[15]

Table 5.7 Types of seeds used in maize production in Brazil by type of farming unit, 2017

Seeds used	*All farms*	*Non-family farm*	*Family farm*
Total	1,655,450	312,495	1,342,955
Common, self-produced	910,449	159,178	751,271
Common, aquired	336,735	67,285	269,450
Certified	195,334	41,281	154,053
Transgenic	212,932	44,751	168,181
Cultivated area			
Total	15,783,895	13,038,855	2,745,039
Common, self-produced	1,026,910	368,506	658,403
Common, aquired	1,715,398	1,275,764	439,634
Certified	5,019,183	4,441,876	577,307
Transgenic	8,022,405	6,952,709	1,069,695
Quantity produced (tons)			
Total	88,099,622	77,127,610	10,972,012
Common, self-produced	2,157,531	1,350,772	806,759
Common, aquired	7,977,022	6,685,691	1,291,330
Certified	28,633,312	25,960,236	2,673,076
Transgenic	49,331,758	43,130,912	6,200,846

Source IBGE Sidra, tabela 6958

This growth of production provided for an ever increasing usage of maize in the internal market. Given the small consumption of maize as a human food in Brazil, most of the growing demand came from the animal feed market. In the seven year period from 2001 to 2007 animal feed accounted for over two thirds of domestic demand, and of this animal feed, 58% went for poultry consumption, some 15% for swine feed and 7% for feeding cattle.[16] Over time this pattern slowly changed as exports and production increased. Thus in the period from 2010/2011 to 2019/2020 period, exports went from 18 to 35% of annual production. In turn the percentage of maize going to animal feed declined from 72% to just 56% of total production. Consumption of animal feed actually increased from 39 million tons to 51 million tons in the same period, but exports and production increased even faster. There was however little change in the share of animal feed as poultry in this ten year period averaged 58% of the total feed consumed, swine increased to 28% and the cattle feed to 8%. Of the feed consumed by poultry, most (on average 85%) went to feed boiler or meat chickens and 15% for egg laying hens (see Table 5.8). It is estimated that 60% of the cost of producing chicken and pigs is made up of the cost of feed, which is essentially composed of soybeans and maize.[17]

This consumption of feed for chickens, and for a lesser extent for cattle, supported the explosive growth of the stock of these animals. Brazil's chicken stocks went from 690 million birds in the decade of the 1990s to 1.3 billion in the decade of the 2010s. In the same period the stock of cattle went from 141 million head to 242 million head.[18] This growth of stocks in turn permitted Brazil to greatly expand chicken and beef exports. Total beef exports, which only began to be significant in the 1980s, went from 188 thousand tons to 2.9 million tons from 2000 to 2022, with chicken export volume going from 907 thousand tons in 2000 to almost 4.7 million tons in 2022. It only began exporting pig meat in the late 1990s, and went from exporting 97 thousand tons in 200 to 1.4 million tons of exports in 2022, and is now the fourth largest exporter of swine in the world.[19] These meat exports took off in the new century thanks to the availability of national produced soybeans and maize. This explains the high correlations between maize production and the chicken meat exports in the period 2000–2022, while production of these two crops, fundamental for animal feeding, were very strongly correlated with each other (see Graph 5.4).[20]

These meat and chicken to exports only began to be significant after 2000 when production finally outpaced the growth of national corn consumption. Once started, these corn exports have been on a secular trend of growth, reaching 29 million tons in 2017 and 47 million tons in 2022/2023, second to the United States and just ahead of the 41 million tons which Argentina will export. Thus the two South American nations together were exporting 33 million tons more than the United States, the world's leading exporter. In turn the estimate of Brazilian maize production for the harvest year 2022/2023 is expected to produce 126 million tons of maize, and the national market will now consume an estimated 77 million tons, up from just 34.5 million tons in 2000. Of this 77 domestic consumption, 85% or 65.5 million tons will go for animal feed.[21]

This exceptional increase in production occurred with relative stability of the planted area, thanks to the extraordinary growth in productivity, which doubled in the twenty-first century, from 2.7 tons per hectare to 5.6 tons. This type of stability of land usage was found in all grains,

Table 5.8 Categories of consumption of total maize available in Brazil, 2010–2022 (in metric tons)

Category	*2010/2011*	*2011/2012*	*2012/2013*	*2013/2014*	*2014/2015*	*2015/2016*	*2016/2017*	*2017/2018*	*2018/2019*	*2019/2020*	*2020/2021*	*2021/2022*
Initial stock	11,547	9,212	11,223	14,078	17,881	14,201	8,074	8,074	17,017	10,500	10,700	6,900
Total production	53,749	70,907	83,462	82,760	87,153	73,887	100,687	100,687	95,748	102,586	87,097	112,832
Production 1st Safra	33,023	35,208	37,126	33,417	30,948	28,851	33,782	33,782	27,682	25,690	24,727	25,027
Production 2nd Safra	20,725	35,699	46,336	49,343	56,205	45,037	66,905	66,905	66,847	75,053	60,742	85,614
Production 3rd Safra									1,219	1,844	1,629	2,192
Imports	656	830	911	791	370	2,903	1,400	900	1,600	1,500	3,500	1,500
Substitute consumption	2,400	2,500	2,000	2,000	2,000	1,000	700	700	300	300	0	0
Total offer	68,352	83,450	97,597	99,628	107,403	91,990	110,861	98,300	116,300	115,200	100,500	130,100
Total demand												
Animal consumption	38,828	40,298	43,453	47,177	49,454	48,067	49,720	47,200	48,700	50,800	52,100	54,700
Industrial consumption	4,636	4,868	5,209	5,990	6,589	6,523	6,653	6,400	7,900	10,600	12,800	14,500
Human consumption	1,873	1,892	1,882	1,873	1,863	1,845	1,882	1,900	1,900	2,000	1,800	1,900
Other uses	2,849	3,545	4,257	4,014	4,227	3,584	3,876	3,500	4,000	4,100	3,900	4,000
Losses	1,075	1,418	1,669	1,655	1,743	1,582	2,014	1,700	1,700	1,700	1,400	2,000
Seeds	393	404	425	381	403	443	439	400	451	429	600	600
Exports	9,486	19,802	26,625	20,655	28,924	21,873	29,261	23,800	41,000	34,700	21,000	42,000
Total demand	59,139	72,226	83,519	81,744	93,203	83,917	93,844	84,900	105,800	104,500	93,600	119,700
Final stock	9,213	11,224	14,078	17,884	14,200	8,073	17,017	13,400	10,500	10,700	6,900	10,400

Source CONAB & Associação Brasileira das Industrias do Milho, "Estatística" accessed 22 March 2021 and November 2022 at http://www.abimilho.com.br/estatisticas

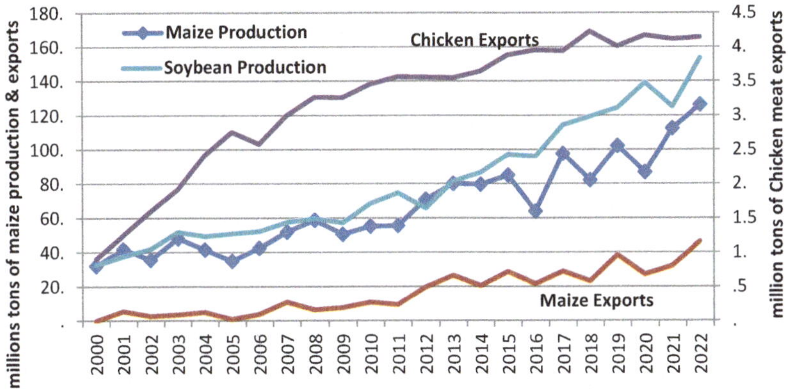

Graph 5.4 Brazilian production and exportation of maize, and total exports of chicken meat, 2000–2022 (*Source* FAOSTAT, CONAB and USDA)

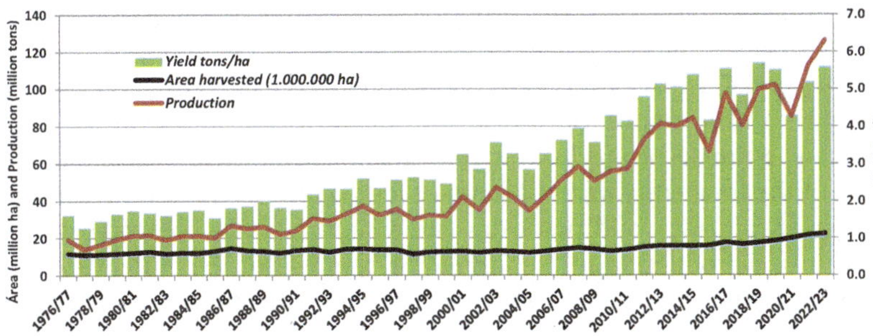

Graph 5.5 Maize in Brazil: area, production and yied, 1976–2022 (*Source* CONAB)

including soybeans.[22] Thus increasing productivity led to higher output with little expansion in land use (see Graph 5.5).

The structure of maize production is rather complex. According to the agricultural census of 2017, a total of 1.3 million family farms planted maize using 2.7 million hectares, and produced 11 million tons in the harvest. These family farms represent 81% of all farming units producing maize, accounted for 17% of the total land planted in maize crops and produced 12% of total maize crop. In other words, maize was spread throughout Brazilian agriculture, but its production was concentrated in the 312 thousand non-family producers, who occupied 83% of the land dedicated to corn production and accounted for 88% of maize produced.[23]

In other words, maize represents a crop open to all types of agricultural producers, unrelated to the size of the property, or whether it was a family or non-family farming unit. The vast majority of producers in fact are made up of small farmers, but today maize production is overwhelmingly produced by large farms with extensive cultivated areas. These productive farms are modern and competitive, explaining Brazil's ability to participate aggressively in the world maize market. Except for the production of soybeans, in which even small family farms achieve close to international levels of productivity,[24] this pattern of large, middle, and marginal farms is the norm in much of Brazilian agriculture. In general it is the middle and larger farms which are using modern agricultural technology, the latest in modified seeds and are fully integrated with international value chains, competing on equal terms with the major participants in world agribusiness. It is the small units, the majority of the farms, which in most cases are subsistence units only marginally producing for the domestic market.

The special nature of the tropical production is seen in the heavy use of fertilizers and chemicals for the land and the protection of the maize crop. A recent estimate of production costs for maize farmers suggests that a third of the total costs were made up of fertilizers and defensive chemicals such as insecticides, and pesticides (see Graph 5.6). In comparable data from maize production in the United States also for the year 2019, the costs of both fertilizers (16% of total costs) and chemicals (5%) were just half of the Brazilian costs for these two inputs.[25] In both cases seeds and labor were comparable between the two countries.

In Brazil it is large commercial producers, mostly producing soybeans as well as corn, who are the primary movers in this market. Their extraordinary increase in maize output has led to profound changes in both national and international markets for Brazilian meat production as maize has been, along with soybeans, the primary input into animal feed. This has allowed Brazil to become a leading world exporter of both beef and boiler chicken meat as well as satisfying a national population that was growing at over 2% per annum through most of this period.[26] The efficiency of Brazilian maize producers has also allowed the nation to become a major world exporter, despite the increased costs of production in a tropical country.

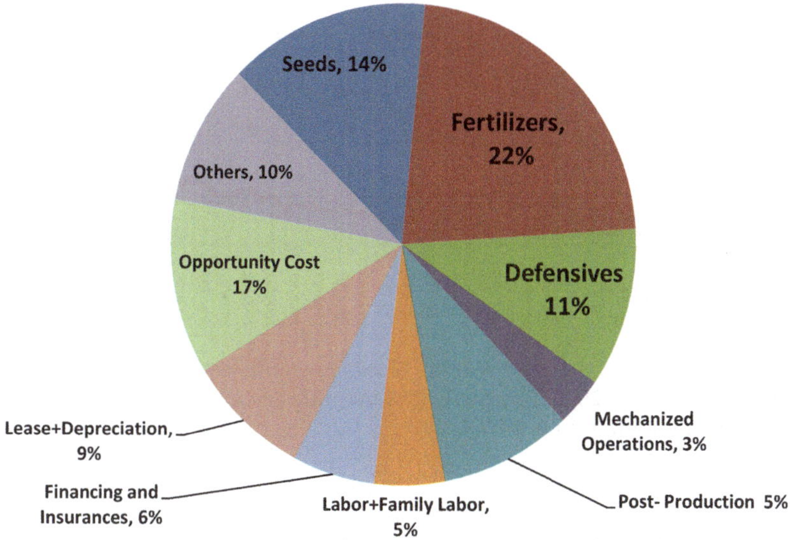

Graph 5.6 Costs of producing maize in Brazil in 2019

Much of this recent growth in production and productivity is due to the adoption of new cultivars and seeds. Although advances in seed development began in the 1930s, particularly in the United States, little was changed in Brazil seeds usage until the second half of the century.[27] It was Embrapa and the local research groups and Agricultural Faculties which began to produce cultivars of corn in the 1980s. The first Brazilian double hybrid of corn with high tolerance to acid soils, BR 201, was developed by Embrapa and made possible the cultivation of corn in extensive areas of the Cerrado. Embrapa has registered in the RNC/MAPA with 81 different corn cultivars, which are manipulated plants selected for desirable characteristics that can be maintained by propagation. In the harvest of 2015/2016 there were more than 477 different cultivars of corn available to plant, of which 284 were genetically modified and the other 193 were conventionally bred. While Brazil led the advance in cultivars, it was the multinational companies who mostly developed the genetically modified seeds.[28]

Gradually the hybrid seed market was consolidated, with the growing participation of multinationals in the sector and from the 1990s, GM

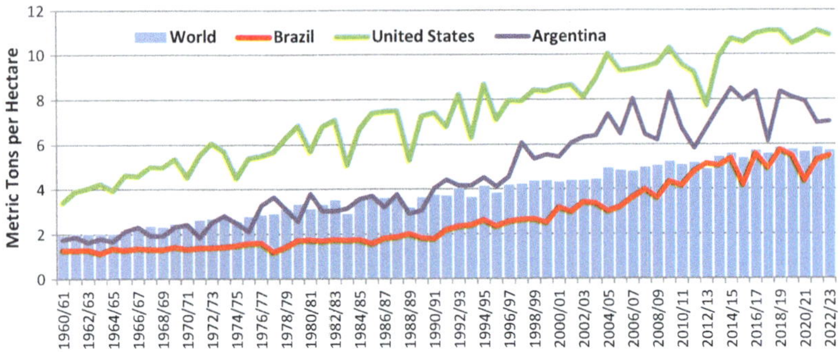

Graph 5.7 Maize yields for World, Brazil, Argentina and the United States, 1960/1961–2022/2023 (*Source* USDA AT https://apps.fas.usda.gov/psdonline/app/index.html#/app/advQuery)

hybrids were imported which had a tolerance to herbicides as well as protections against worms, caterpillars, corn borers, and other insects.[29] By the harvest of 2016/2017 some 70% of the seeds used for corn production were genetically modified ones, most of which were resistant to the herbicide glyphosate.[30] Although there was significant growth in maize productivity in Brazil, particularly since the 1990s, reaching average world levels, Argentine yields have always been above those achieved by Brazil, and both are well below those achieved in the United States which reached 11.9 tons in 2022/2023 harvest (see Graph 5.7).[31]

As in Brazil, the no-tillage planting (called *Siembra Directa* in Argentina) and new seeds led to the growth of the first and second harvest maize plantings. The first was called the *siembra temprana* and the second the *siembra tardia*. Throughout the harvests of the 2010s, there was a relative balance between the two harvests. In 2017/2018 for example, the early harvest produced 54% of total maize production and the second harvest 46%, little different from earlier years or later years. In that same year 99% of the maize produced was from hybrids and 55% of the farms were considered to be operating at a high technical level and most of the rest at a medium technical level.[32]

In maize as in soybeans, Argentina has had a different form of land utility and production than Brazil. In Argentina, just as with soybeans, a significant group of maize producers are non-landowners. As with soybeans, many maize producers are corporations which rent land to produce the crop, contracting out to specialized firms to plant, maintain, and harvest the crop. The owner of the land is often not the producer of the crop. This unusual renting system is of minor importance in Brazil were almost all producers are farm land owners, although contracting services are sometimes used for planting and harvesting. By the agricultural census of 1969, the larger the farm size, the greater was the importance of renters, and by the end of the twentieth-century renter-producer produced half the crops in the province of Buenos Aires.[33] This was both a response to increasing land costs and the uncertainties of government policies

By the beginning of the third decade of the twenty-first century Brazil had reached a new level of production and exports. Although Brazilian maize production has fluctuated depending on climatic condition, the secular trend of growth has been clearly increasing decade by decade. This growth and the recent declined in US production has reached the point that in the crop year 2022/2023 Brazil for the first time exceeded the maize exports of the United States which until then had been unquestionably the world leader in maize exports. While the leadership role will probably fluctuate in the coming years, it is now evident that Brazil, now accounting for 28% of world exports, will share with the United States the primacy in maize world exports. Again, all of these changes are quite recent. Brazil only passed Argentina in the 2010s and equaled the United States only in the 2020s (see Graph 5.8).

What is impressive is that Brazil's maize exports go to all regions of the world. This is quite different from the soybean exports which were concentrated primarily in supplying mainland China. The biggest maize importers were Egypt, Iran, and Spain which accounted for just 42% of all exported Brazilian maize in 2021, while the leading 25 countries accounted for 97% of these exports. These countries importing Brazilian wheat were found in all the world's regions including Europe (see Graph 5.9).

It is estimated that by the harvest of 2031 Brazil will export 65 million tons of maize exports and Argentina 43 million tons, and together they will account for 43% of world exports.[34] This major growth of a modern maize agriculture was based on the adoption of new cultivars developed in Brazil and adopted for local soils and conditions. It was then helped by the adoption of GMO maize seeds, both associated maize with the booming soybean expansion, and both adopted direct or no-till planting and double cropping. Thus maize in Brazil went from being a traditional

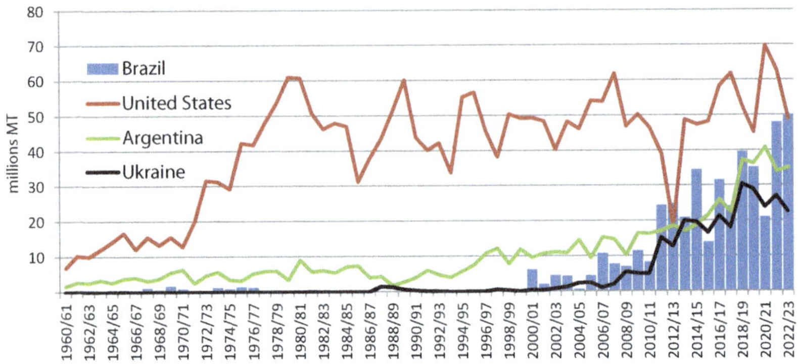

Graph 5.8 Maize exports by current leading exporters, 1960/1961–2022/2023 (*Source* USDA at https://apps.fas.usda.gov/psdonline/app/index.html#/app/advQuery)

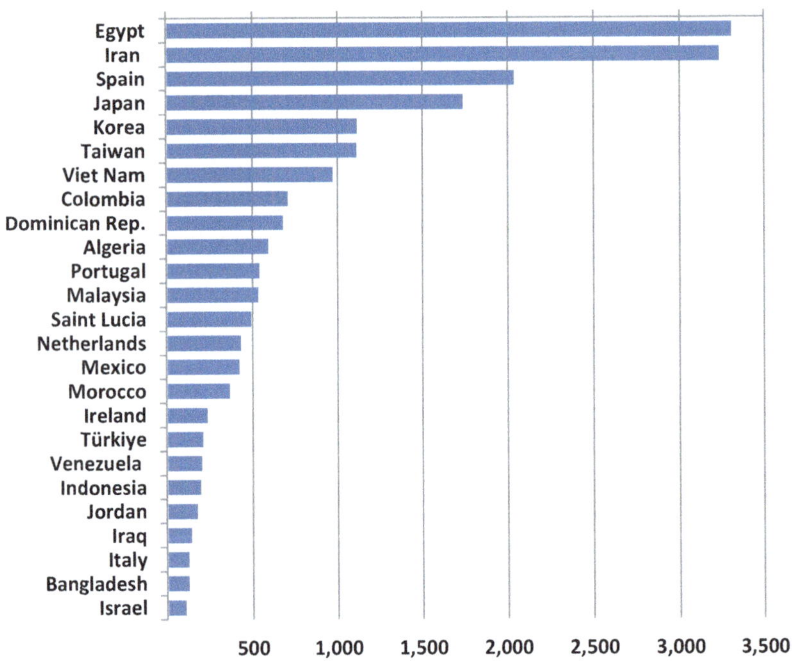

Graph 5.9 Major consumers of Brazilian maize exports in 2021 (thousand MT) (*Source* FAOSTAT, Trade Matrix data)

crop produced with yields well below world standard to a highly commercialized product capable of competition in the world market. In turn this boom in maize production would have a major impact internally. In the case of Brazil it lead not only to corn exports, but also to the successful emergence of abrand new export product, that of chicken meat.

Notes

1. USDA, *Grain: World Markets and Trade*, November 2021: 28, 29.
2. USDA, *Livestock and Poultry: World Markets and Trade*, January, 2021.
3. Ripusudan L. Paliwal, "Origen, evolución y difusión del maíz," in Ripusudan L. Paliwal et al., *El maíz en los trópicos. Mejoramientos y producción* (Roma, FAO, 2001), p. 18.
4. Francisco Vidal Luna, Herbert S. Klein and William Summerhill, "The Characteristics of Coffee Production and Agriculture in the State of São Paulo in 1905," *Agricultural History* 90, no. 1 (2016), table 1.
5. DGE [Directoria Geral de Estatística] (1920) *Recenseamento realizado em 1 setembro de 1920*, vol. 3, part 2, "Agricultura," p. xix, tabela 6.
6. IBGE, *Recenseamento Geral de 1960*, vol. 2, part 2, p. 124, table xii.
7. Matopiba is a region that comprises the Cerrado biome in the states of Maranhão, Tocantins, Piauí, and Bahia, and accounts for a large part of the Brazilian production of grains and fiber.
8. Silas Maciel de Oliveira, Rodrigo Estevam Munhoz de Almeida, Rafaela Alenbrant Migliavacca and José Laércio Favarin, "Importância do Sistema de plantio direto (SPD) para a cultura do milho," *Visão Agrícola*, no. 13 (2015): 41.
9. Paulino Motter and Herlon Goelzer de Almeida eds., *Plantio Direto. A tecnologia que revolucionou a agricultura brasileira* (Foz de Iguaçu: Parque Itaipu, 2015); Oliveira et al., "Importância do Sistema de plantio direto," 40–44; Felipe Pires Camargo, José Alberto Angelo, and Mario Pires de Almeida Oliveira, "Expansão do plantio direto nas principais culturas no Estado de São Paulo, 2011–2015," *Informações Econômicas*, 46, no. 6 (2016); A. Kassam, T. Friedrich, R. Derpsch and J. Kienzle, "Overview of the Worldwide Spread of Conservation Agriculture," *Field Actions Science Reports*, 8, no. 1–11 (2015): 3, found at https://journals.openedition.org/factsreports/3966.
10. IBGE, Sidra, Tabela 6640.
11. José Carlos Cruz et al., "Manejo da cultura do milho em Sistema de Plantio Direto," *Informe Agropecuário*, 27, no. 233 (2006): 42–53; José Carlos Cruz et al., *Cultivo do milho. Sistema de Plantio direto* (Embrapa Milho e Sorgo-Comunicado Técnico, INFOTECA-E, 2002), p. 7; José

Carlos Cruz et al., "Sistema de produção de milho safrinha de alta produtividade," *XXVIII Congresso Nacional de Milho e Sorgo, 2010*, Goiânia: Associação Brasileira de Milho e Sorgo, at https://ainfo.cnptia.embrapa.br/digital/bitstream/item/25232/1/0593.pdf.

12. Eduardo de Paula Simão, "Características agronômicas e nutrição do milho safrinha em função da época de semeadura e adubação" (MA thesis, Sete Lagoas, Universidade Federal de São João del Rei, 2016): 4.
13. Krystal Maria Montesdeoca, "Total Factor Productivity of Tropical Soybean-Maize Systems: The Case of the Safrinha Crop System in Mato Grosso, Brazil" (MA thesis University of Illinois, 2014); EMBRAPA, AGITEC (2020). Milho Safrina, at https://www.agencia.cnptia.embrapa.br/gestor/milho/arvore/CONT000fya0krse02wx5ok0pvo4k3mp7ztkf.html.
14. ISAAA. (2017). Global Status of Commercialized Biotech/GM Crops in 2017. Briefs, brief 53: 6, 15.
15. USDA, *Grain: World Markets and Trade*, January for years 2001–2021.
16. Cruz, Juliana Victorino da Silva, "Ocorrência de aflatoxinas e fumonisinas em produtos à base de milho e milho utilizado como ingrediente de ração para animais de companhia, comercializados na região de Pirassununga, Estado de São Paulo" (PhD thesis., Universidade de São Paulo, 2010): 21, tabela 2.
17. *Jornal de Comércio RS*, 2021 (22 março) "Alta dos grãos eleva custos de produção e frigoríficos reduzem abates em 2021," at https://www.jornaldocomercio.com/_conteudo/agro/2021/03/783834-alta-dos-graos-eleva-custos-de-producao-e-frigorificos-reduzem-abates-em-2021.html.
18. FAOSTAT at http://www.fao.org/faostat/en/#data/QA.
19. FAOSTAT and USDA, FAS [Foreign Agricultural Service], PS&D [Production, Supply & Distribution], at https://apps.fas.usda.gov/psdonline/app/index.html#/app/advQuery.
20. In the period 2000–2022 the correlation of maize production with soybean production was 0.94, and with chicken meat production it was 0.79.
21. USDA, FAS, PS&D, accessed December 2022.
22. Herbert S. Klein and Francisco Vidal Luna, "The Growth of the Soybean Frontier in South America: The Case of Brazil and Argentina," *Revista de Historia Económica*, 38, no. 3 (Fall 2020): 1–42.
23. IBGE Sidra, tabela 6959.
24. Klein and Luna, "The Growth of the Soybean Frontier in South America," table 6.
25. The US data comes from USDA found at https://www.ers.usda.gov/data-products/commodity-costs-and-returns/commodity-costs-and-returns/#Historical%20Costs%20and%20Returns:%20Corn.
26. Klein and Luna, *Feeding the World*, chapter 3.

27. Hebe Vessuri, “El hombre del maiz de la Argentina: Salómon Horovitz y la tecnología de la investigación en la fitotecnia sudamericana,” *Estudios interdisciplinarios de América Latina y el Caribe*, 14, no. 1 (2003): 89–118.
28. Embrapa Comunicações, *Embrapa em Números*, Brasília, Embrapa, 2016.
29. See Gutman, and Lavarello, “Biotecnología y desarrollo”.
30. Israel Alexandre Pereira Filho and Emerson Borghi, *Mercado de Sementes de Milho no Brasil Safra 2016/2017* (Sete Lagoas, MG: Embrapa Milho e Sorgo, 2016), pp. 11–12.
31. The highest yields in this crop year were found in Turkey which had yields of 12.4 metric tons per hectare.
32. Ayelén Gago, Juan. P. Gianatiempo and Martín Lópes, *La cadena de maíz en la Argentina: Evolución del cultivo durante las últimas campañas* (Buenos Aires: Bolsa Cereales, 9 November 2018), at https://www.bolsadecereales.com/imagenes/retaa/2018-12/161-lacadenademaizenargentinaretaapaseeee09.11.2018.pdf.
33. Ignacio Llovet, “Tenencia de la tierra y estructura social en la provincia de Buenos Aires,” in Oswaald Barsky et al., *La Agricultura pampeana: transformaciones productivas y sociales* (Buenos Aires: Fondo de Cultura Económica, 1988), pp. 249–294.
34. USDA, *Agricultural Projections to 2031* (February 2022), 89, table 28.

CHAPTER 6

Cotton

In the twenty-first century Brazil has emerged as the world's second largest exporter of cotton. This sudden expansion of national production represents the third distinct cycle in the history of cotton cultivation in Brazil. At the end of the eighteenth century Brazil was the world's largest exporter of Gossypium barbadense (also known as arboreal or bush cotton) and production was concentrated in just two northeastern states. Brazil's importance in international exports went into relative decline as United States production of Gossypium hirsutum, (also known as herbáceo or upland cotton), entered the market in the late eighteenth and early nineteenth centuries. But during the "cotton famine" crisis of the 1860s, Brazil re-emerged again as a major world producer as exports doubled. Thereafter the northeastern producers maintained a relatively stable volume of exports with a final boom in exports occurring before World War I.

The next phase of cotton production would occur after World War I. As early as the 1870s upland cotton began to be grown in São Paulo, but that state would not become the dominant producer until the 1930s. This shift in centers of production and in the type of cotton produced was also reflected in changes in consumption. By the 1930s the primary consumer of cotton was the internal market driven by Brazil's expanding textile and clothing industries, although the country still maintained modest exports.

H. S. Klein and F. V. Luna, *Brazilian Crops in the Global Market*, Palgrave Studies in Economic History,
https://doi.org/10.1007/978-3-031-38589-6_6

But this period ended in the 1980s as disease and the end of tariff protection reduced national production to such an extent that Brazil could no longer supply even its internal market and became instead a major importer of cotton in the 1990s. At the same time significant production of arboreal or bush cotton in the northeast came to an end and even the small southern and southeastern farms producing upland cotton began to decline. In the decade of the 1990s Brazil, for the first time in its history, became a significant importer of cotton.

The final period in this history of Brazilian cotton production occurred at the beginning of the twenty-first century when Brazilian farms again began to grow cotton on large estates in the region of the Center-West where thousand hectare cotton farms became the norm. Today Brazil is now the second leading world exporter of the product, shipping about 8 million bales, against 12 million bales sent into the world market by the United States.[1] Brazil is currently the fourth largest grower of cotton in the world, surpassed only by India, China and the United States and is also a major consumer of the product for its extensive textile sector. How this recent expansion occurred and how it relates to earlier periods of growth is the central theme of this chapter.

The first phase of this history can be said to have begun before the arrival of Portuguese colonists who adopted the native American Gossypium barbadense plant as their source for cotton. Wild cotton plants pre-date modern man, with several varieties scattered around the world, and there were several different continental centers where the plant was domesticated.[2] Both in the American continent and in Asia there is evidence of domesticated cotton since at least 6,000 years ago and complete textiles date from at least 3,000 years BC. In coastal Peru cotton of the Gossypium barbadense variety, sometimes called kidney cotton for the shape of its pods, or bush cotton for its growth on small trees or bushes, was cultivated as early as 2500 BC.[3] In Brazil there is evidence of its use by the Native Americans in South America prior to the arrival of the Portuguese.[4] In turn East Indian produced cotton cloths were to be found throughout Eurasia since the beginning of the Christian era, and already by the fifteenth-century expansion of the Portuguese overseas, East Indian cotton was well known in Europe and would became a staple in Portuguese world trade.[5]

Thus cotton was cultivated by the Portuguese from the earliest period of colonization. In this first phase the dominant plant was the Gossypium barbadense which in the Guianas and Brazil obtained two crops per annum and whose bushes usually remained productive for 5 to 6 years.[6] It produced extra-long staple cotton and was initially highly desired in the first cotton weaving looms.[7] Already in the sixteenth century Brazilian cotton lint was being imported into northern European markets.[8] But its major growth came in the eighteenth century with the direct support of the Portuguese government. To settle the northern frontier of its Brazilian colony the Portuguese government under the Marquis de Pombal established two merchant monopoly companies, one in 1755 to develop Maranhão [the Companhia Geral do Comércio do Grão-Pará e Maranhão] and the other to further expand production in Pernambuco [Companhia Geral de Pernambuco e Paraíba] with these private companies being given monopolies over slave imports and cotton exports. While cotton produced by African slave labor dominated in Maranhão and began with the merchant company support, in the case of Pernambuco cotton was already being produced by small free farmers well before the establishment of the company.[9] It would appear that Maranhão began exporting cotton before Pernambuco, and that this began in the 1770s on an annual basis, whereas Pernambuco did not enter the trade on a serious basis until the 1790s.[10] Maranhão remained the primary exporter and over two thirds of its exports went to England throughout most of the nineteenth century.[11]

Brazil, of course, was not the only American region producing cotton and until the 1780s the British imported most of their cotton from the French West Indies. But the growing conflict with France and the slave uprisings in Saint Domingue in 1791 led the British to seek new American imports and they turned to Brazil as a major supplier.[12] The first Brazilian cotton imported into England seems to have occurred in 1781.[13] Already in the year 1786 some 2 million out of the 20 million tons of cotton imported into England came from Brazil.[14] By the next year Brazil exported some 2.5 million tons.[15] The first cotton from the United States also appeared to have been first imported in the 1780s and it became significant quite rapidly by the 1790s.[16] Both the United States and Brazil thereafter were the principal American suppliers for cotton for the British textile industry for most of the nineteenth century.[17] Initially Brazil's production of long-fiber cotton was considered of better quality than the short fiber *herbaceous* or upland cotton that was being produced in the United States, and was initially more suitable for the production processes then adopted in English manufactures.[18] This allowed Brazil to maintain a prominent position in cotton exports to the English market for many years.[19] In the period 1785 to 1815, Brazil represented a fifth of cotton imports to Liverpool, and the United States only started to take the lead in the next few decades.[20] By 1820 England was importing 152 million pounds of cotton, of which Brazil accounted for 19%. Despite the fact that England had obtained preferential treatment in Brazil and was a major market for British exports in this period, the value of raw cotton exports of Brazil to England exceeded the value of British cotton goods imported into Brazil until 1825.[21]

The intrinsic quality of northeastern cotton and its adaptability to the technical conditions required by the market did not mean that the exported product was of good quality. Fraud and poor packaging were a constant complaint from importers and from Brazilian government officials.[22] Although Brazilian imports remained the second most important American cotton for British producers in the period from 1820 to 1833, its volume remained relatively stable, while imports from the United States in this period more than doubled (see Table 6.1).

Brazilian production in that period was primarily arboreal or tree cotton, which required little investments to enter into production, and the profitability of its export attracted both small and large farmers in the northeastern region. Although there were large landowners using slave and wage labor cultivating the crop, there was a significant participation of small landowners, renters, and even squatters. In addition, it was far cheaper to produce than sugar cane, and the processing of cotton was in the hands of small traders who bought cotton from producers and sold it to exporters.[23]

However, at the beginning of the nineteenth century new technological transformations occurred in cotton processing and fabric production which allowed the use of other cotton varieties in the English textile industry. This stimulated the demand for North American production of herbaceous cotton.[24] North American production expanded both in terms of land utilization, but also in terms of new seeds introduced, leading North American production to grow exponentially. The United States now became the main source of cotton supply to England.[25] Although Brazilian exports also grew in this period, they now fell below 5% of total English cotton imports even though their exports to England had doubled by mid-century. Thus by the 1850s Brazil was averaging exports to England of around 124 thousand bales per annum, or around 51 million tons of cotton, but it was well behind cotton imports from the East Indies and the United States (see Table 6.2).

Table 6.1 Imports of raw cotton into England 1820–1833

Origin	*USA*	*Brazil*	*Turkey & Egypt*	*Other Foreign*	*Sub Total All Foreign*	*British Colonies*	*Total*
1820	89,999,174	29,198,155	285,350	2,045,147	121,527,826	30,144,829	151,672,655
1821	93,470,745	19,535,786	856,868	2,504,180	116,367,579	16,169,041	132,536,620
1822	101,031,766	24,705,206	395,077	1,534,483	127,666,532	15,171,096	142,837,628
1823	142,532,112	23,514,641	1,334,547	1,988,773	169,370,073	22,032,430	191,402,503
1824	92,187,622	24,849,552	7,719,368	1,278,720	126,035,262	23,344,820	149,380,082
1825	139,908,699	33,180,491	8,938,246	7,245,229	199,272,665	28,732,626	228,005,291
1826	130,858,203	9,871,092	10,032,400	755,153	151,516,848	26,090,553	177,607,401
1827	216,924,872	20,716,162	5,071,519	1,279,873	243,992,426	28,456,483	272,448,909
1828	151,752,289	29,143,279	6,926,288	1,579,711	189,401,567	38,359,075	227,760,642
1829	157,187,396	28,878,386	5,986,385	1,070,800	193,122,967	29,644,444	222,767,411
1830	210,885,358	33,092,072	3,401,710	639,823	248,018,963	15,942,489	263,961,452
1831	219,333,628	31,695,761	8,081,024	697,691	259,808,104	28,866,749	288,674,853
1832	219,756,753	20,109,560	9,113,890	598,048	249,578,251	37,254,274	286,832,525
1833	237,506,758	28,463,821	987,262	1,696,108	268,653,949	35,002,888	303,656,837

Source Donnell (1872): 79–177

Table 6.2 Imports of raw cotton into Great Britain, 1852–1861 (in Bales)

	USA	*Brazil*	*West Indies*	*Egypt*	*East India*	*TOTAL*	*Average Weight per bale*	*Total in Pounds*
1852	1,794,698	142,839	9,468	189,230	221,379	2,357,614	418	785,482,600
1853	1,531,709	132,174	7,710	106,522	485,385	2,263,500	426	901,987,600
1854	1,667,902	107,037	8,252	81,218	308,184	2,172,593	408	886,417,900
1856	1,626,086	134,528	6,708	113,961	396,027	2,277,310	396	901,814,700
1856	1,758,295	121,521	11,323	113,111	469,508	2,463,768	414	1,019,999,900
1867	1,481,717	168,340	11,467	75,528	680,466	2,417,588	403	974,287,900
1858	1,855,340	108,886	6,897	101,405	350,218	2,422,746	419	1,018,130,000
1869	2,086,341	124,867	8,338	99,876	509,688	2,829,110	421	1,191,065,300
1860	2,580,843	103,050	9,956	109,985	562,852	3,366,686	421	1,417,374,800
1861	1,842,610	99,120	10,390	97,280	987,530	3,036,930	415	1,260,326,900

Source: Williams (1868), p. 8

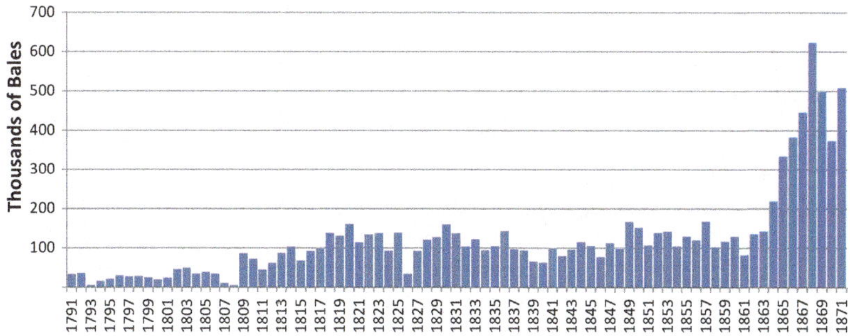

Graph 6.1 Brazilian raw cotton imports into Great Britain, 1791–1871 (in thousands of bales) (*Source* Smithers (1825), table 1, p. 147; and Donelle (1872))

This pattern of cotton imports to England was broken with the closure of North American ports to cotton exports during the Civil War in the United States. The result was a massive increase of Brazilian exports to England, as England encouraged alternative sources to expand production to meet its needs. Brazil succeeded in tripling its exports in a short period of time, reaching 384 thousand bales by 1865 and 624 thousand bales by 1868, and increased its share to 19% of all cotton imports into England (see Graph 6.1).

Except at the beginning and middle of the nineteenth century, and in the early twentieth century the share of cotton exports in the total value Brazilian exports was quite limited. Throughout the years 1821 to 1860, exports remained practically stable, but their share in Brazilian exports fell from a quarter to 5% of the total, as coffee came to dominate Brazilian exports (see Graph 6.2). In this period, production and exports were concentrated in the Northeast. In the middle of the nineteenth century, in some provinces such as Maranhão, Paraíba, Ceará, and Alagoas, cotton represented about 80% of the value of exports, but they were a reduced percentage in Bahia and Pernambuco due to their high sugar exports. Of these cotton exports, 80% went to England, 10% to Spain, and 5% to France (see Table 6.3).

Given the small investments required to produce cotton and its adaptability to the region's semi-arid conditions, cotton growing in the Northeast was carried out on both small and large farms. It involved family labor

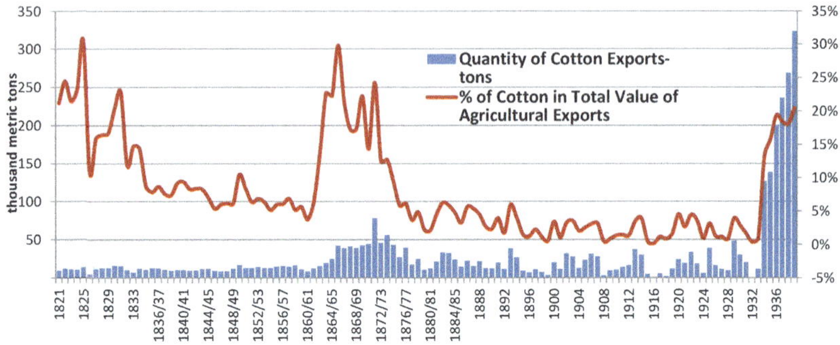

Graph 6.2 Quantity of Brazilian cotton exports (in tons) and their importance in the value of total agricultural exports of Brazil 1821–1939 (*Source* IBGE Anuario Estatístico 1939/1940)

Table 6.3 Brazilian exports of cotton by Province, 1849–1850

Province	*Arrobas*	*Value (mil réis)*	*% Value of Cotton in total Provincial Exports*
Maranhão	409,378	1,954,637	22
Pernambuco	203,178	1,048,271	14
Alagoas	177,968	1,121,317	49
Paraíba	176,078	864,869	58
Bahia	95,913	466,398	41
Ceará	43,043	204,553	88
Pará	3,544	13,877	1

Source Colleção dos Mappas Estatísticos do Commercio e Navegação do Imperio do Brasil, com suas províncias e paizes estrangeiros 1849–1850 (Rio de Janeiro, 1855):311
Rio de Janeiro, Typographia Nacional, 1855 p. 311

as well as African slave labor. It also became a crop associated with livestock, as cotton residues could be used to feed animals.[26] In Maranhão the cultivation was carried out on large farms by slave labor, while in other areas of the Northeast, production by small non-slave producers was important. In Pernambuco and neighboring regions cultivation methods were rudimentary differing little from traditional Amerindian practices. The plow was almost unknown, plant diseases were not treated and seeds were not selected.[27] Not only was the agriculture rudimentary, but so

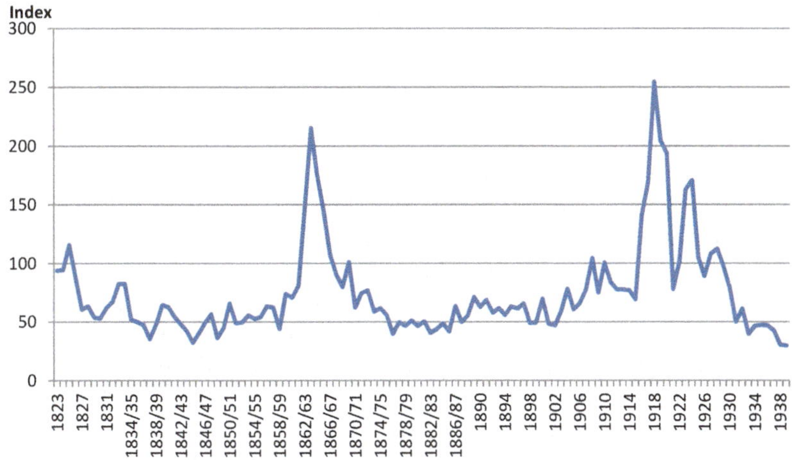

Graph 6.3 Average value of Brazilian exports of cotton in gold pounds 1823–1938 (1821–1823 = 100) (*Source* IBGE, *Anúario Estatístico 1939–40)*

were the ginning and packaging processes. Usually, the farmer sold his production to the ginner, who marketed it to exporters.[28]

The causes of the loss of Brazilian competitiveness over the years 1820 to 1860 are multiple. On the one hand, there was a significant drop in prices as expressed by the average value received in gold pounds for Brazilian exports. Compared to the average price of the period 1821–1823, the average value of Brazilian cotton exports fell by half until the US Civil War. Several memoirs and studies also point out the problems related to the baling and commercialization process, even accusing shippers of fraudulent practices. Although the Brazilian fiber was of high quality, the bales arrived mixed with low quality cotton. Finally, recent studies have also emphasized the high tax burden on cotton exported by Brazil.[29] These multiple causes reduced Brazil's competitiveness, which remained a relatively minor supplier in the growing world cotton market (see Graph 6.3).

The American Civil War disrupted North American cotton production and exports. Since the United States was by mid-century the main supplier of the product to England, which in turn was now the center of the world production of cotton fabrics, a crisis in cotton supplies occurred.[30] This "cotton famine" led England to seek alternative supplies for its raw cotton, preferably sources that had similarities with the North American product, since the production processes were adapted to the American standard. In order to supply their needs, the English authorities started to stimulate the expansion of production in several countries, including Brazil.

As early as 1857 the Cotton Supply Association was established to develop alternative supplies outside the United States. India was the principal area of initial activity.[31] Watts, writing in 1871, affirmed that this was the best area for growing cotton.[32] According to the same author, Brazil also had exceptional conditions for production, but the country ranked among the minor sources of supply. Although several northeastern provinces produced cotton for export, it would be in the province of São Paulo that the upland cotton would be planted, a region of the Southeast which had no production before 1861. The British Association began its experiments with the New Orleans seed, using the São Paulo Railway as a promoter.[33] Prices and demand were high and this drew small producers to concentrate on cotton and British merchants provided advances to farmers plant these cotton cultivators.[34] In contrast to the northeastern farmers, cotton producers in São Paulo used the *parceria* or sharecropping system to produce cotton. Cotton farmers used the land of others to produce the crop and paid the owners with a certain percentage of their output. This proved to be a highly efficient system beneficial to both farmers and landowners.[35]

The average price obtained by Brazilian cotton exports doubled between 1860/61 and 1865/66. This increase in prices and greater participation of foreign merchants led to Brazilian exports tripling between 1850 and 1860 and its share of the Liverpool market increased from approximately 5 to 12% of all cotton imports. At the same time the share of cotton in total Brazilian agricultural exports increased in value from 6 to 18% in the same period. But with the end of the US Civil War, the price gradually decreased. In 1870/71 prices returned to pre-war levels, putting an end to the euphoria of the cotton market in Brazil.

Although the Northeast continued to be the main cotton-producing region, São Paulo, now became an important producer and exporter, representing about a fifth of production in 1873/1874. Moreira in his survey of agriculture in 1875 provides more detail on cotton production by region. According to the author, Pernambuco cotton could be of quality and could substitute for the Louisiana product. The arboreal type was mainly cultivated here, but the herbáceo was growing rapidly.[36] In Alagoas cotton was cultivated by free labor and there was already a weaving factory in the province.[37] In the case of Bahia, cotton production served both the export market and local consumption for the seven textile factories in the province.[38] In the province of Rio de Janeiro herbaceous cotton was produced, and there were six cotton fabric factories, some with more than two hundred workers.[39] When analyzing São Paulo, he points out that even with a routine cultivation system, the product yielded extraordinary profits. Cultivation was done by free farmers and there were five textile factories in operation in the Province and two more were being constructed.[40]

In the development of cotton in São Paulo, the role of English representatives was decisive. They brought the knowledge of cotton planting and made seeds available which were adapted to the needs of English manufacturers. But the chief agricultural activity of the state was coffee production. Thus cotton farming only existed on coffee or cane farms and was seen as a temporary product which could take advantage of market conditions. Off the large estates it was essentially a "commercial crop of the poor." With the fall in prices local production declined, but did not disappear as there was growing demand for cotton by the expanding national textile industry.[41] The region of Sorocaba, would become the principal center of cotton production in the state in this period. This was due not only to the quality of its soil, but also because of its crucial location on the new Sorocabana railroad.[42] Thus by the 1870s São Paulo was the second most important state in terms of cotton exports (see Table 6.4).

Maranhão province also benefited from the extraordinary price increase that occurred during the 1860s, and increased its cotton production by 16%. But at the same time there was a massive shift locally into sugar production which began in 1848 and quickly surpassed cotton exports. It would appear that sugar drew resources from cotton production, but also opened up new lands that were not viable for cotton. Even as late as 1882 the province was producing cotton of a high quality, though bailing and shipping still were not up to world standards and so the Maranhão cotton sold for lower prices.[43]

The boom in cotton lint exports occurred along with ever increasing imports of finished cotton products. Thus in 1871/72, at the height of mid-nineteenth-century cotton production, the value of the cotton exported was almost the same as the value of imported cotton cloth,

Table 6.4 Volume and value of Brazilian cotton exports by province, 1873/1874

Province	*Quantity (ton)*	*Value (mil réis)*
Pernambuco	12,283	6,035,917
São Paulo (1)	9,897	4,750,791
Alagoas	5,964	2,809,730
Ceará	4,878	2,608,324
Paraiba	4,405	2,162,192
Maranhão	3,987	2,279,288
Rio Grande do Norte	2,007	344,933
Bahia	1,574	800,920
Sergipe	1,428	572,144
Rio de Janeiro	1,284	816,590
Piauí	170	88,850
Espírito Santo	3	9,983

Note (1) Value estimated from average of other provinces
Source Dr. Nicolau Joaquim Moreira. Indicações Agricolas para Imigrantes que se dirigem ao Brazil, R.J, 1875, p. 44 a 89

which came mostly from England and France.[44] Although Brazil remained a producer and exporter of cotton well into the twentieth century, it had only a modest international role except in special times, such as the run up to WWI. Nor did traditional bush cotton go out of production in the Northeast, which as late as 1920 still accounted for 63% of total cotton output. However short strand upland cotton also became increasingly important especially for local industry. Thus by the late nineteenth and early twentieth centuries both São Paulo and the traditional Northeastern producing states now primarily serviced the rapidly expanding national textile industry.

By the time of the 1920 industrial census there were 266 cotton spinning and weaving factories in Brazil, employing 92,000 workers.[45] Considering all fabric manufacturing establishments, there were 319 that year, of which 112 were in São Paulo. Cotton was the dominant cloth produced, with wool and linen fabrics of lesser importance.[46] As for agricultural production, the 1920 census shows the existence of 92 thousand cotton farmers, with a planted area of 379 thousand hectares, representing 6% of the cultivated area that year. Total production was 332 thousand tons of cotton seed and the average was 878 kilograms of cotton lint produced per hectare and the average area cultivated was just 4.1 hectares.

Cotton represented 16% of the value of the production of agricultural crops, against 25% for coffee and 24% for corn.[47]

By now the state of São Paulo led in national cotton production, with 20 thousand farmers growing cotton on 102 thousand hectares producing 105 thousand tons of cottonseed. This represented about one third of national production, with average productivity per hectare similar to the Brazilian average. The second state in terms of production was Pernambuco, followed by Paraíba and Ceará. Together, the northeast was still the most important region, representing two thirds of production with an average cultivated area of 5.7 hectares.[48]

By 1920 there was a recovery of exports after a strong decline during the First World War. Some 24 thousand tons of cotton were exported, corresponding to 5% of Brazilian exports. Nevertheless in that same year the local market consumed a large share of national cotton production. It has been estimated that from 1900 to 1925 the national cotton textile industry doubled every decade. National cotton textile production went from 33 million meters of cloth in 1900, to 75 million meters in 1910 and 186 million by 1920. The 17 factories in 1900 increased to 54 factories in 1920 and 64 in 1925. In this same period workers in these factories went from 4,570 in 1900 to 38 thousand in 1925, and the looms increased from 2,838 to 20,560.[49] In 1920 the production of 332 thousand tons of cottonseed would produce about 113 thousand tons of cotton lint, of which only 24 thousand tons were exported, and the rest was destined for the internal market.[50] São Paulo was by this date the unquestioned dominant producer of cotton, followed by Pernambuco (see Table 6.5).

A major transformation in cotton cultivation would occur after the crisis of the 1930s, which would be carried out mainly in São Paulo. The crisis of coffee production in the 1930s would result in the coffee economy losing its dynamism and displacement of production within the state and to other states. At the same time, there were major changes in land ownership and use in the state, with an important process of subdivision of properties.[51] From the point of view of the technical developments, there were also important advances in the production process. Since the early years of the twentieth century, studies were developed to improve cotton cultivation, particularly at the Instituto Agronômico de Campinas (IAC), a research institution in the State of São Paulo which had been created in 1887. It soon became one of the most important centers of research in Brazil, with a fundamental role in the development of crops in general, but especially with coffee and cotton. The

Table 6.5 Production of cotton by state by number of cotton farms, their size and output in 1920

States	*No of Farms*	*Hectares cultivated*	*Quantity Produced (tons)*	*Kilos of Cotton per Hectare*	*Average Area of Cotton Farms*	*Average Production (kg)*
São Paulo	19,764	109,788	104,584	953	5.6	5,292
Pernambuco	10,406	70,013	61,978	885	6.7	5,956
Paraíba	9,944	49,007	35,797	730	4.9	3,600
Ceará	2,811	30,762	29,426	957	10.9	10,468
Rio Grande do Norte	2,062	15,798	18,344	1,161	7.7	8,896
Bahia	3,886	18,508	15,910	860	4.8	4,094
Alagoas	5,225	16,474	15,634	949	3.2	2,992
Sergipe	4,021	16,053	14,593	909	4.0	3,629
Maranhão	2,401	2,633	13,616	602	9.4	5,671
Minas Gerais	11,690	10,429	8,667	831	0.9	741
Piauí	2,486	5,902	5,315	901	2.4	2,138
Pará	8,380	6,870	4,036	588	0.8	482
Paraná	482	2,165	1,782	823	4.5	3,696
Goiás	5,117	1,023	925	904	0.2	181
Rio Grande do Sul	422	1,222	610	499	2.9	1,445
Santa Catarina	2,068	727	372	511	0.4	180
Rio de Janeiro	45	501	302	602	11.1	6,707
Espírito Santo	339	437	263	601	1.3	775
Mato Grosso	162	132	80	604	0.8	492
Amazonas	42	86	52	602	2.0	1,233
Território do Acre	31	63	51	810	2.0	1,645
Distrito Federal	1	6	4	600	6.0	3,600
Total Brasil	91,785	378,599	332,338	878	4.1	3,621
Nordeste total	43,242	245,150	210,613	859	5.7	4,871

Source *Recenseamento do Brasil, 1920,* vol. III, 2ª. parte, Agricultura, p. XXVII

institute began working on cotton in 1907 and its work intensified after the creation of the Cotton Section in 1922.[52] In the earliest period the Institute concentrated on questions of fertilization and soil correction techniques, and after 1922 it dedicated its work to genetic seed development.[53] In other parts of Brazil research was also carried out to improve cotton and by 1930 there was already a national network of cotton research. There was also greater public action in the dissemination of agricultural knowledge and the distribution of seeds.[54]

This new productive cycle of Brazilian cotton would have different characteristics in relation to the previous phase of national production. In this post 1930 period in São Paulo there occurred an integration of agronomic research, seed production and distribution services, technical assistance and the fiber market, with the catalyst being the Mercantile Exchange. Research programs until 1970 were aimed at improving fibers, increasing productivity and resisting diseases. Thus, all seed varieties launched since 1970 were resistant to many of the diseases that attacked cotton in São Paulo. There was also the improvement of the maturity of the fiber and an increase in its productivity. Thus, for example, the launch of the improved seeds known as IAC-17 and IAC-18 by the Instituto Agronômico de Campinas allowed an average increase in productivity on the order of 30%. But research now expanded to other centers. In the neighboring state of Paraná, cotton production had strong support from the Paraná Agronomic Institute and encouragement from the state government. The Northeast also received greater attention in the development of cotton technology adapted to the region after the installation of the National Cotton Research Center of *Embrapa* in Campinas Grande in Paraíba in 1975.[55]

In addition to the use of cotton to produce the fiber used for yarn production, cotton seed in the twentieth century began to be used industrially in Brazil for the production of vegetable oil. The use of the cotton seed oil started only after the 1914/18 war, and before that the country exported the seed and it imported cotton oil in a volume of one million kilograms per annum, mainly from the United States. But from 1930 onward, Brazilian production of cotton and other vegetable oils was soon satisfying national needs and even began to export some quantities. [56]

By 1960, it was clear that São Paulo had emerged as the most efficient and largest producer of cotton. Of the 453 thousand cotton producers, 75% were located in the northeast, but accounted for only 37% of production. In that year, São Paulo accounted for 12% of all cotton farmers but almost half of all production. The productivity per hectare was 230 kg per hectare in the Northeast, against 1,082 kg per hectare in São Paulo. There was also a shift in Southern production as Paraná replaced São Paulo as the largest Brazilian cotton producer in 1980, accounting for 38% of production. That year, the Center-West still represented less than a tenth of production. The decline of Northeastern production in this period meant the loss of participation of tree cotton, which was only produced in that region. Arboreal production systematically declined from 35% in 1956, to 24% of national production in 1973 and 14% in the 1980 census. Its production would practically disappear as of the 1990s (see Table 6.6).

Even as Brazil turned more inward in its cotton production, it still remained a significant world producer and exporter. In the 1960s and 1970s, Brazil was the fifth largest cotton producer in the world and also the fifth largest exporter of cotton lint. At that time, the country had 3.6 million hectares planted in cotton, or more than 12% of the world area planted in cotton. Almost half of the population of the Northeast, directly or indirectly, lived off cotton and its by-products. Not only in the semi-arid Northeast, but also in all other producing regions, cotton farming was the least risky agricultural activity. The culture of cotton, depending on the farming practiced, whether rain fed or irrigated, single or intercropped, used between 0.3 to 2.0 employees per hectare, and in the northeastern semi-arid, areas, cotton was the only crop capable of generating income.[57]

The 1980 General Census showed there were more than 500 thousand producers, distributed in a relatively equal way among those dedicated to tree and herbaceous cotton. Although the area dedicated to tree cotton accounted for two thirds of the total area cultivated with cotton, its production represented only 12% of the total crop. Given the low costs of entry even for herbaceous cotton production, in São Paulo and Paraná a third of cotton farmers were tenants and sharecroppers, a percentage higher than in the Northeastern states.[58] In the Northeastern states arboreal cotton production was intercropped with livestock in about a third of farms, compared to only one fifth of the herbaceous cotton growers who also produced livestock. In both types of cotton there were a large proportion of small farms, but there was a great difference between the arboreal and herbaceous cotton crops in output. The average production per producer was 8 times higher in herbaceous; and twelve times higher production per hectare (see Table 6.7).

Table 6.6 Cotton production by state, and region, for area and output, 1920–1996

	1920	*1940*	*1950*	*1960*	*1970*	*1980*	*1996*
Number of Farms							
BRAZIL	91,785	442,407	351,432	453,481	358,156	260,422	93,688
Northeast	43,242	286,753	245,532	342,645	205,120	193,425	54,089
Center-West	5,279	16,053	9,306	13,497	16,951	6,508	5,455
São Paulo	19,754	100,700	72,934	54,418	49,144	14,419	5,934
Paraná	482	17,220	4,439	22,822	68,675	34,898	20,527
Cultivated Area (hectares)							
BRAZIL	378,599	2,412,484	2,037,411	2,180,800	1,485,280	1,044,457	640,124
Northeast	245,150	885,127	1,213,764	1,546,399	425,569	422,056	182,918
Center-West	1,155	5,107	10,430	32,022	86,442	61,662	152,103
São Paulo	109,788	1,416,482	719,623	408,297	531,099	236,687	91,315
Paraná	2,165	24,884	27,222	131,131	373,287	263,731	171,039
Production (in tons)							
BRAZIL	332,238	1,284,895	769,528	956,249	1,261,704	1,170,597	816,743
Northeast	210,613	392,059	295,377	356,209	100,923	124,634	78,763
Center-West	1,005	2,637	4,026	18,139	114,540	106,385	269,439
São Paulo	104,564	840,598	445,559	442,046	610,222	433,388	150,967
Paraná	1,782	27,785	18,695	112,903	397,063	452,490	267,433
Share of State in Total Production							
Northeast	63%	31%	38%	37%	8%	11%	10%
Center-West	0%	0%	1%	2%	9%	9%	33%
São Paulo	31%	65%	58%	46%	48%	37%	18%
Paraná	1%	2%	2%	12%	31%	39%	33%

Source IBGE, Censos Demográficos, Censos Agrícolas e Anuários Estatísticos do Brasil

Table 6.7 Characteristics of Herbaceo and Arbóreo cotton farms in 1980

	Arbóreo Cotton			*Herbáceo Cotton*		
	Farms 271,371	Production 156,156	Area 1,655,595	Farms 260,422	Production 1,170,597	Area 1,044,457
Status of Producer						
Owner	71%	83%	85%	60%	63%	67%
Renter	6%	4%	3%	19%	23%	19%
Sharecropper	7%	5%	5%	6%	10%	8%
Squatter	16%	8%	7%	15%	3%	6%
Destiny of Production						
For Coop	5%	14%	14%	4%	13%	11%
For Industry	4%	14%	15%	10%	46%	32%
For Intermediary	84%	70%	69%	82%	40%	55%
Economic Activity of Producer						
Agriculture	69%	77%	67%	80%	95%	88%
Ranching	24%	14%	23%	15%	2%	8%
Agriculture & Ranching	5%	8%	8%	4%	2%	4%
Size of Farms Producing Cotton						
Less than 10 ha	40%	15%	10%	59%	15%	22%
10–100 ha	49%	47%	44%	35%	50%	47%
100–1000 ha	11%	33%	38%	6%	28%	26%
1000–10.000 ha	1%	5%	8%	0%	6%	6%
10.000 ha or more	0.0%	0.1%	0.2%	0.0%	0.1%	0.1%
Area Cultivated in Cotton						
Less than 1 hectare	16%	4%	1%	38%	1%	4%
1–2	20%	7%	4%	21%	3%	7%
2–5	31%	19%	15%	24%	13%	19%
5–10	14%	18%	15%	9%	15%	16%
Less than 10 hectarers	**81%**	**48%**	**36%**	**92%**	**32%**	**45%**
10–100 ha	14%	43%	48%	7%	48%	41%
100–500 ha	0%	8%	13%	0%	15%	11%
500 + ha	0%	1%	3%	0%	5%	3%

Source IBGE, IX Recenseamento Geral, 1980. Vol. 2, tomo 3, número. Censo Agropecuário

The evolution of the harvested area in cotton in the state of São Paulo is impressive. Modest at the beginning of the 1930s, it rose to above one million hectares in the 1940s and 1950s and accounted for almost a third of all cultivated lands in the state, and gradually decreased thereafter reaching under 400,000 hectares by the late 1980s and absorbing only

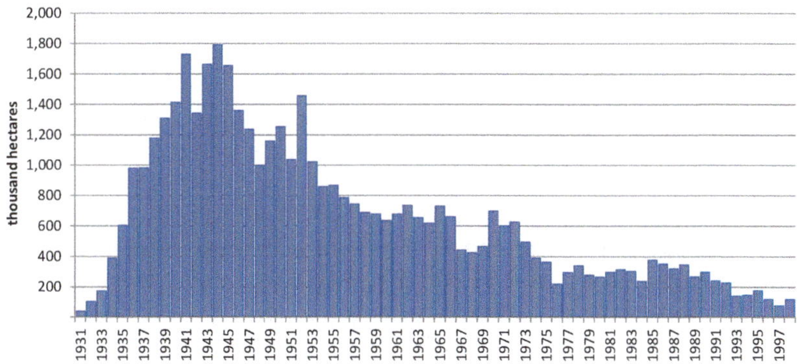

Graph 6.4 Cultivated cotton area of São Paulo, 1931–1998 (in Hectares) (*Source* Araújo et al. [2002])

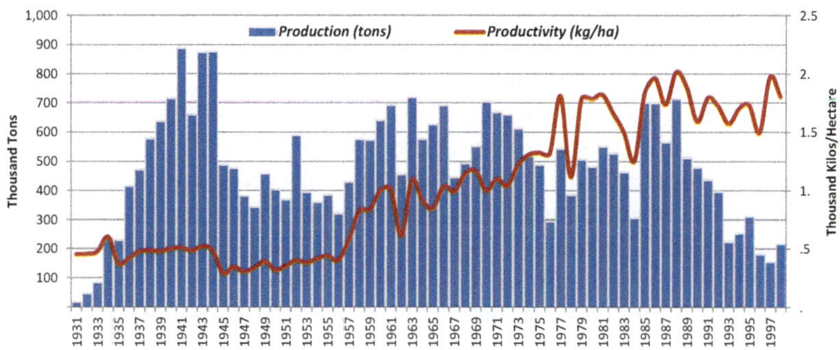

Graph 6.5 Cotton production and productivity in São Paulo, 1931–1998 (*Source* Araújo et al. [2002])

around 5% of cultivated state lands (see Graph 6.4). However significant increases in productivity allowed the state to maintain an average annual production on the order of 500 thousand tons throughout the decades of the 1940s to the 1980s, even with the impact of the boll weevil after 1983 (see Graph 6.5).

During the second half of the 1980s and the decade of the 1990s there occurred an acute crisis in national cotton production. First was the boll weevil plague, which began in São Paulo and Paraíba in 1983, and spread to Paraná the following year. Two harvests after its first appearance, the insect appeared in all the main cotton producing areas. As it was a well-known pest, and with control methods already developed in other countries, containment or even eradication plans were developed, but the operational limitations and the social and economic consequences of a radical plan made its execution unfeasible.[59] By the 1983/84 harvest, the cotton planted area in the Campinas and Sorocaba regions saw a 20% to 30% drop in areas planted and there was a sharp drop in productivity.[60] Although the boll weevil represented an extraordinary event in the trajectory of cotton cultivation, it had a limited effect on Brazilian production. Thus, if we compare the average production of the five years before 1983 and the five years after, there was an increase in the average annual production by 30%.

Yet in the following years there would be a profound crisis in Brazilian cotton culture, which lasted until the end of the twentieth century. This would be due directly to a decline in world prices and government policies liberating imports. Not only did production decline, but exports virtually disappeared in the 1970s and again in the 1990s, such that Brazil was forced to import cotton to satisfy national consumption Thus from the decade of the 1980s to the decade of the 1990s Brazil went from being a net exporter to a major importer of cotton (see Graph 6.6). This occurred when the world stocks of cotton were elevated and world prices were low. In 1988 there was a reduction in the tariff on imported cotton which went from 50 to 10%, and in 1990, the tariff was eliminated altogether as a stimulus for the national textile industry. This abruptly exposed the domestic production of cotton to foreign competition, which at the time was abundant and even subsidized by the government of the United States. Finally the terms of credit offered for financing cotton imports were better than those available for financing national production.[61] The prices received by the farmers, which were already declined, fell even further. At deflated prices there was a 50% drop between the average price paid for cotton between the 1980s and the 1990s.

The result of these changes was a dramatic decline in Brazilian cotton production. Cultivated area went from over two million hectares in the last five years of the 1980s, to just 800 thousand hectares between 1995 and 1999. The same occurred with the production of cotton seed which declined in half in the same period (see Graph 6.7).[62] Although the effects were felt in all regions, the Northeast was particularly affected. By the end of the decade of the 1990s average production was only a quarter of

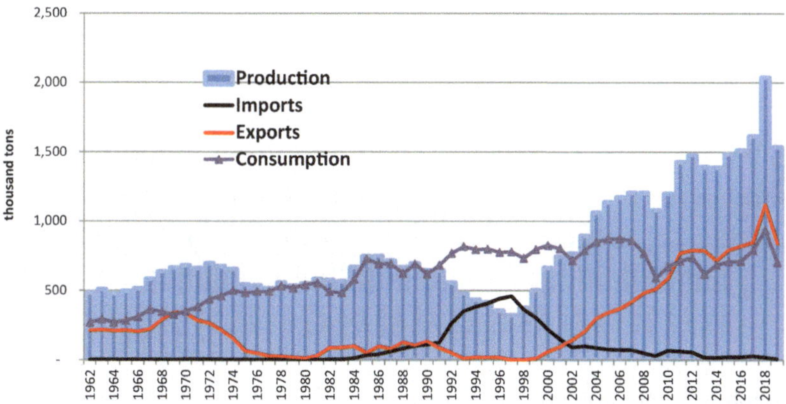

Graph 6.6 Brazilian production, importation, exportation and apparent consumption of cotton lint, 1961–2019 (3 year moving average) (*Source* http://www.fao.org/faostat/en/#data/TCL; and http://www.fao.org/faostat/en/#data/QCL)

the average of the 1980s. It has been estimated between 1985 and 1989 cotton farming generated about 2.1 million jobs; ten years later employment in the sector would be just 736,000 workers, of which 278,000 were in the northeast. Thus around 1.4 million jobs were lost to cotton, of which the Northeast lost about one million. Unlike the Southern states, there was no alternative economic activity to replace it in the states of the Northeast. The effects on the countryside, cities, personal income, and public finances of the Northeastern region were dramatic.[63]

Nevertheless the crisis of the 1990s, which seemed to mark the end of significant production in Brazil, was followed by an extraordinary revival of production in the twenty-first century. This involved both technical advances and the movement of production into a new region. As with soybeans, corn and a host of other crops, new seeds, new soils, and new farming practices were adopted. From the beginning of this century, Brazil has significantly increased its production, productivity and competitiveness. Thus, the Brazilian productivity of cotton cultivation, which in 1980 was only 40% of that obtained in the United States, is currently about 50% higher than that of the United States.[64] In fact, productivity is the key element to explain the current performance of Brazilian cotton. By the second decade of the century cotton would play a fundamental

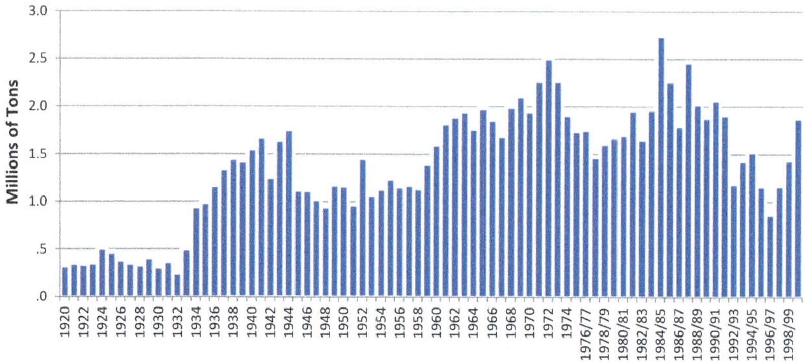

Graph 6.7 Brazilian production of cotton seed, 1920–1998/99 (*Source* IBGE (Séries Históricas Retrospectivas) e Conab)

role not only in international exports, but also in servicing the national textile and vegetable oil needs of Brazil.

Cotton farming now moved to the Cerrado region where it became a crop produced in predominantly large properties. Average productivity per hectare in the Cerrado has multiplied by four compared to the early 1990s. The Cerrado region includes several states. Cotton farming within the Cerrado was predominantly developed in the state of Mato Grosso and in the northeastern savanna areas in Bahia. Today, these two states grow 90% of the cotton, 73% in the state of Mato Grosso and 17% in western Bahia.[65] The states of São Paulo and Paraná, previously important producing centers, currently have a marginal position in the market. Even with the two leading states of Mato Grosso and Bahia, there is also a high concentration of production in just a few municipalities. Some two dozen municipalities account for 70% of total production (see Table 6.8 and Map 6.1).

Total production of cotton seed, which in the last five harvests of the twentieth century was around one million tons, in the following two decades rose to more than 3 million tons in the 2000s and to 4.8 million tons in the following decade. The harvest for the year 2020/21 was 7 million tons. Although there was an increase in planted area, from approximately 823 thousand hectares in the 2000/01 harvest to 1.6 million hectares in the 2019/20 harvest, it was the exceptional increase in productivity that explains this increase in volume of production. In these

Table 6.8 Average production in tons of the principal cotton municipalities in Mato Grosso and Bahia, 2019–2021 (> 70,000 tons average)

Mato Grosso		*Bahia*	
State Total	**4,515,607.67**	**State Total**	**1,382,319.67**
Sapezal	931,769	São Desidério	539,912
Campo Novo do Parecis	449,820	Formosa do Rio Preto	215,649
Campo Verde	368,913	Correntina	164,518
Diamantino	264,221	Barreiras	122,355
Campos de Júlio	256,185	Riachão das Neves	119,653
Primavera do Leste	188,258	Jaborandi	81,268
Lucas do Rio Verde	187,898	Luís Eduardo Magalhães	74,735
Sorriso	165,834		
Tapurah	134,454		
Nova Mutum	102,642		
Santo Antônio do Leste	99,274		
Nova Ubiratã	94,571		
Dom Aquino	86,538		
Ipiranga do Norte	83,033		
Pedra Preta	80,244		
Paranatinga	77,952		
São José do Rio Claro	73,766		
Santa Rita do Trivelato	71,128		

Source IBGE, Sidra tabela 1612. Brazilian Production averaged = 6,558,594 tons

two different harvest years average production of cotton seed per hectare went from 2,472 kilos per hectare to 4,329 kilos per hectare which was a yield 1 and a half times larger than that achieved by United States producers (see Graph 6.8).

In addition to its regional concentration, cotton cultivation has become the activity of large producers because they are in areas of the Cerrado suitable for the intense mechanization of production. In the 2017 census, only 3,211 cotton producers in Brazil were registered, compared to 1.6 million corn producers, 315 thousand bean producers, 236 thousand soybean producers, and 35 thousand wheat farmers. Cotton farms with less than 100 hectares are a negligible group among producers. In fact, if we consider only the 95 establishments with more than 10,000 hectares, their production accounts for 62% of total cotton output, clearly demonstrating the large-scale organization of the typical cotton producer in Brazil (see Table 6.9).

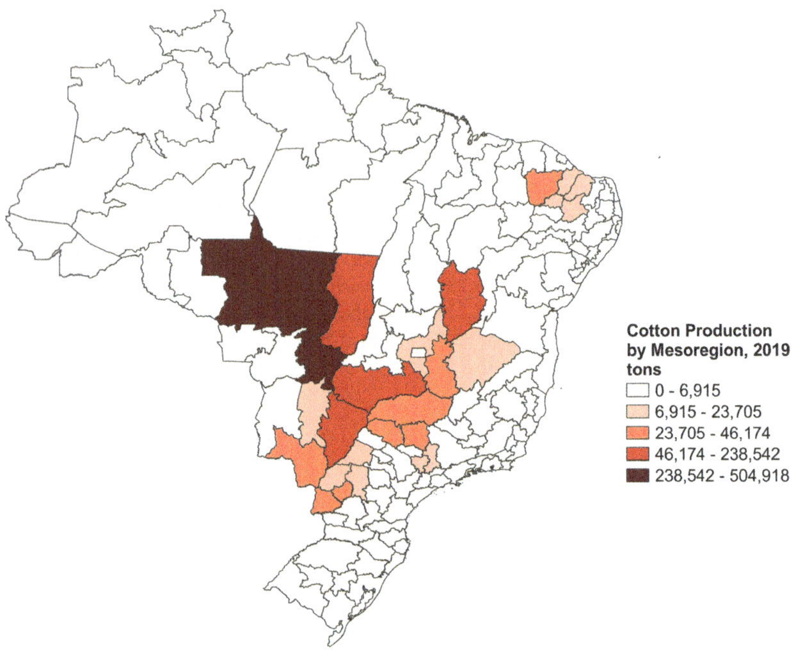

Map 6.1 Cotton production by Mesoregion, 2019 *Source* Bases cartográficas Sidra, table 1613

The causes of this exceptional performance can be credited to the advances in production methods, such as no-tillage farming practices and the introduction of genetically modified seeds. The *Embrapa* Cotton Research Center, played a fundamental role in developing cotton production in the Cerrado. It provided farmers with the latest in technical and scientific resources.[66] Cotton is one of the crops with the highest incidence of pests, so a fundamental issue to face in modernizing cultivation, productivity, and profitability is the management of pest control, with several of these plagues, such as the boll weevil, endemic. Pest control can represent 30% of the total production cost, due to the need for numerous sprayings.[67] This explains why the first genetically modified organisms introduced in Brazil were aimed at resistance to pests or resistance to the main pesticides used in cotton cultivation. [68] Although previously introduced in other countries, the first approval of genetically modified seeds

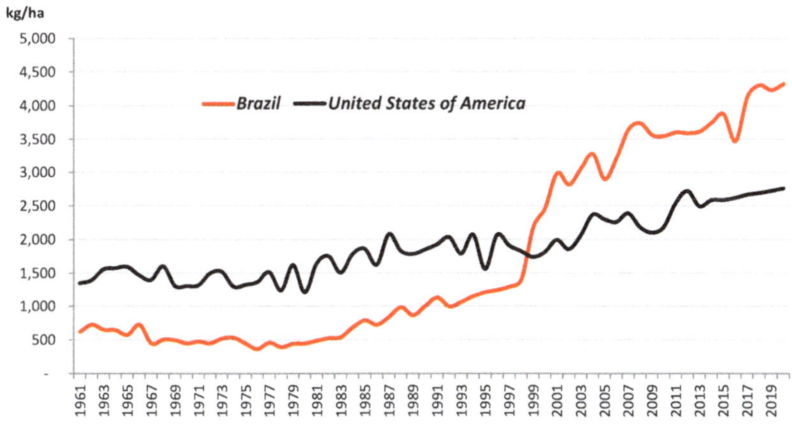

Graph 6.8 Productivity of cotton production Brazil and the USA, 1961–2020 (kgs/hectare) (*Source* Faostat)

for commercial use in Brazil occurred in 2005. By 2019 there were 22 transgenic cotton seeds approved for sale in Brazil, the majority resistant to insects and tolerant of herbicides.[69] In the latest harvest, the area planted with transgenic cotton, represented about 90% of the area planted in cotton, a ratio similar to the corn and soybean crops. Here as well multinationals dominate the market for genetically modified seeds.[70]

The dominance of multinationals did not eliminate the role played by public Research Centers in the country, which are fundamental for the development of the best field production methods.[71] An example of this is the agreement signed between Embrapa and Monsanto, through which the multinational allows Embrapa to carry out genetic improvements of cotton lines and cultivars containing Monsanto's technology using Embrapa's germplasm. This agreement allowed Embrapa to launch cotton cultivars on the market through multipliers, paying royalties to Monsanto.[72]

Currently, Mato Grosso accounts for more than two thirds of both the cultivated area and of cotton production in Brazil. In this state cotton is usually grown as a second crop, with millet or soybeans as the first crop in about 85% of the farms producing cotton.[73] The use of GM varieties in Mato Grosso started around 2008, with Monsanto's RR (Roundup Ready) and BG (Bollgad) technologies. Then in the 2010/2011 crop

Table 6.9 Main factors of cotton production in Brazil, Mato Grosso and Bahia, Census 2017

	Brasil				*Mato Grosso*				*Bahia*			
Size of Cotton Farms	Farms	Production in tons	Value in 1000 Réis	Area Cultivated ha	Farms	Production in tons	Value in 1000 Réis	Area Cultivated ha	Farms	Production in tons	Value in 1000 Réis	Area Cultivated ha
Less than 10 ha	1,597	710	1,192	1,300					872	411	668	859
10–20 ha	490	369	602	603					268	184	292	356
20–50 ha	460	743	1,487	763					208	416	755	427
50–100 ha	156	845	1,352	807					58	327	584	484
100–200 ha	60	2,933	11,414	1,150	3	1,350	7,257	300	21	195	360	295
200–500 ha	42	10,180	36,769	2,833	7	4,926	17,293	1,148	6	379	731	323
500–1,000 ha	46	81,026	318,691	21,010	27	71,421	281,374	18,158	1	-	-	-
1,000–2,5000 ha	106	267,735	867,202	70,103	70	214,723	686,829	53,687	9	17,228	56,047	5,340
2,500–10,000 ha	159	1,041,086	2,122,574	268,891	85	641,554	1,228,479	168,665	44	237,389	532,327	59,638
10,000 + ha	95	2,341,478	4,116,704	544,942	51	1,463,702	2,610,155	354,617	28	647,621	1,080,654	135,918
TOTAL	3,211	3,747,105	7,477,987	912,402	243	2,397,676	4,831,387	596,575	1,515	904,150	1,672,418	203,640

Source IBGE, Sidra tabela 6959, Censo Agrícola de 2017

were used the Liberty Link varieties, resistant to the herbicide glufosinate ammonium, widely applied in the control of weeds resistant to conventional herbicides. But this technology has been replaced by WideStrike and RF (Roundup Ready Flex), resistant to glufosinate and glyphosate. Currently, with the appearance of the Helicoverpa armigera caterpillar in the last years, second generation biotechnologies have been introduced.[74]

The correct technological package is essential for cotton production, as seeds, fertilizers, and pesticides represent more than 80% of the crop expenses.[75] Another key issue is soil management. Second cycle cotton is increasingly practiced after early soybean plantings. To ensure the long-term sustainability of the activity, it is important to use more alternative crops as well as no-till plantings, which favor crop rotations and the use of cover crops.[76] That Brazil has so far succeeded in this enterprise is seen in the fact that in the harvest of 2019/2020 producers generated 5 times more cotton plum on less than half the hectares than they did in 1976.[77]

According to USDA estimates, Brazilian exports of 1.7 million tons of cotton from the 2022/23 harvest will represent 20% of world exports, second to the United States, the largest exporter which will export 2.7 million tons and account for 30% of the world market.[78] Moreover the USDA estimates that Brazil will increase its share of world cotton exports to 27% of the world market by 2031, though still second to the United States which is estimated to keep its 32% of share of world exports in 2031.[79] Although Brazil has become the world's second largest exporter of cotton, this product represents a relatively small percentage of the Brazilian export basket, given the country's representativeness in the world agribusiness market. CONAB estimated that in the 2020/21 harvest which produced 2.7 million tons of cotton lint, 690 thousand tons were consumed locally, 2 million tons were exported and only modest change occurred in inventories (see Table 6.10).

In addition to representing an agricultural product which uses lots of inputs and technology, cotton is an essential raw material for the textile sector, and there thus exists a complex Value Chain for this product. ABRAPA, the Brazilian Association of Cotton Producers has estimated that the GDP of the cotton chain would represent a value in the order of US $ 74 billion, largely composed of the processing of cotton plume in the textile chain for the retail of cotton clothing and accessories.[80] Of the inputs used in the production process, the most significant items were estimated to be pesticides (34.7%), fertilizers (25.7%), seeds (12.5%), fuels and lubricants (14.0%). In the 2016/2017 crop, inputs totaled US $ 1.3

Table 6.10 Apparent world consumption of raw cotton, 2013/14–2020/21, in tons

Areas	*2013/14*	*2014/15*	*2015/16*	*2016/17*	*2017/18*	*2018/19*	*2019/20*	*2020/21 (1)*
Initial Stock	445.5	652.3	712.9	585.1	629.1	1,020.9	1,487.7	2,000.3
Production	1,734.0	1,562.8	1,289.2	1,529.5	2,005.8	2,778.8	3,001.6	2,737.9
Importation	31.5	2.1	27.0	33.6	30.0	1.7	1.0	1.0
Supply	**2,211.0**	**2,217.2**	**2,029.1**	**2,148.2**	**2,664.9**	**3,801.4**	**4,490.3**	**4,739.2**
Consumption	810.0	670.0	640.0	685.0	670.0	700.0	570.0	690.0
Exportation	748.6	834.3	804.0	834.1	974.0	1,613.7	1,920.0	2,010.0
Final Stock	652.3	712.9	585.1	629.1	1,020.9	1,487.7	2,000.3	2,039.2

Note (1): Estimate of November 2020
Source Conab, Análise mensal Algodão out./nov. 2020

billion.[81] It was estimated that in this highly mechanized crop, approximately 10 thousand people were employed in its cultivation. Another 170 thousand were involved in the preparation and spinning of cotton fibers and in other textile industries, 655 thousand in the clothing industry and another 384 thousand workers in retail activities, for a total of 1.2 million people across the chain.[82]

Another major area which has been part of the new phase of cotton production is a more active foreign policy of the Brazilian government in defense of its agricultural exports. This was first developed by the Brazilian government against government subsidization of cotton exports by the United States. These cotton subsidies and incentives became the subject of a long-standing dispute between the Brazilian and United States governments from the time of the founding of the World Trade Organization. In 2002, Brazil with other producing countries challenged US cotton subsidies. The dispute, which lasted for years, was concluded in 2014, with the commitment of the United States to make adjustments to its program to support cotton exports, thus providing better conditions of competitiveness for Brazilian cotton exports in the international market. The bilateral understanding included an additional payment of US $ 300 million to all the countries, which, like Brazil, were affected by the cotton support policies of the United States.[83]

Thus over six centuries after Portuguese colonists first exported American originated cotton on to the world market, Brazilian cotton has again become an even more important component of international trade. This has been a long and complex history with shifting production zones and alternative products which satisfied both the international and internal markets. For most of its history Brazilian produced cotton primarily satisfied the needs of the internal market. But Brazilian cotton of both arboreal and herbáceo varieties never disappeared from the world market. Although arboreal cotton dominated production until well into the twentieth century, the Northeastern producers could not compete against the short strand cotton which was introduced into the fields of São Paulo in the 1870s. In this long second phase of Brazilian cotton development it was the Southeastern and Southern states which grew to be competitive to the Northeastern producers. The crisis of the 1990s resulted in a decade of major cotton imports and the elimination of exports. The move of cotton production to the Center West opened up a new phase in national production. The adaptation of crop rotation and no-till agriculture along with genetically modified seed ushered in a new age in cotton production. In the space of just two decades Brazil went from being an importer of cotton to becoming the second largest exporter of cotton in the world, a position it had temporarily attained two centuries before.

Notes

1. USDA, FAS [Foreign Agricultural Service], IPAD [International Production Assessment Division], Cotton Explorer, accessed February 24, 2023 at https://ipad.fas.usda.gov/cropexplorer/cropview/commodityView.aspx?cropid=2631000
2. Jonathan F. Wendel, Curt Brubaker, Ines Alvarez, Richard Cronn, and James McD. Stewart, "Evolution and Natural History of the Cotton Genus," in A.H. Paterson, ed., *Genomics of Cotton, Plant Genetics and Genomics* (New York: Springer, 2009): pp. 3–22.
3. S. G. Stephens and M. Edward Moseley, "Early domesticated cottons from archaeological sites in central coastal Peru." *American Antiquity,* 39, no.1 (1974): p. 110.
4. Gabriel Soares de Souza. *Tratado Descritivo do Brasil* (Rio de Janeiro, Typographia Universal de Laemmert, 1851), p. 126.
5. Giorgio Riello, *Cotton: the Fabric that made the Modern World.* (New York: Cambridge UP, 2013), Chapter 2.
6. Edward Baines, *History of the Cotton Manufacture in Great Britain*, (London: Fisher, Firsher and Jackson, 1835), pp. 290–291.
7. The European water frame permitted the production of a cotton yarn strong enough to be used as warp, a longer longitudinal thread. Warps allowed cloth to be made entirely with cotton but required a longer cotton fiber than a fiber imported from Eastern Europe and Asia." Thales Augusto Zamberlan Pereira, "The cotton trade and Brazilian foreign commerce during the industrial Revolution," (Phd. thesis, São Paulo, FEA-USP, 2017), pp. 11–12.
8. The chronicler Gabriel Soares de Souza, mentioned a shipment of sugar and cotton leaving from Bahia in the sixteenth century. Gabriel Soares de Souza. *Tratado Descritivo do Brasil* [1587] (reprinted Rio de Janeiro: Typographia Universal de Laemmert. 1851), p. 126. On early Brazilian cotton imports into Europe see Alfred P. Wadsworth and Julia de Lacy Mann, *The Cotton Trade and Industrial Lancashire 1600–1780* (Manchester University Press,1931), p. 23.
9. António Carreira. *A Companhia Geral do Grão-Pará e Maranhão.* São Paulo, Editora Nacional, 1988, 2v. (Brasiliana); and Miguel Diegues Junior, "As Companhias Privilegiadas no comércio colonial,". *Revista de História*, 3, no. 3 (1950): pp. 309–336; Diego de Cambraia Martins e

Felipe Souza Melo. "O algodão do Brasil e a economia atlântica: comparações entre o Maranhão e Pernambuco (c.1750–1810)," 7ª Conferência Internacional de História Econômica e IX Encontro de Pós Graduação em História Econômica.

10. It was estimated that cotton exports from Maranhão began in 1760 and by 1807 had reached a total of 3.4 million tons, and that Pernambuco cotton exports began in the 1790s and totaled 2.3 million tons by 1807. Dauril Alden, "Late Colonial Brazil, 1750–1808,"in Leslie Bethel, ed., *The Cambridge History of Latin America* (11 vols; Cambridge: Cambridge University Press, 1984), II, table 8, pp. 636–37.
11. Pereira, "The cotton trade," p. 14. Although cotton was dominant in Maranhão, the primary export from Pernambuco remained sugar, followed by cotton, see José Jobson de A. Arruda, *O Brasil no comércio colonial* (São Paulo, Atica, 1980), p. 228. On the pre and post company slave trade to Pernambuco see Gustavo Acili Lopes, *A Fênix e o Atlântico. A Capitania de Pernambuco e a economia-mundo europeia (1654–1750)* (São Paulo: Alameda, 2017), Chapter 2.
12. Alexey Krichal. "Liverpool and the raw cotton trade: a study of the port and its merchant community, 1770–1815," (MA thesis Victoria University of Wellington, 2013): 17, 20; and Sven Beckert, *Empire of Cotton, A Global History* (New York: A Knopf, 2014), Chapter 4.
13. As reported in the 1830s, Pernambuco cotton was in high demand and its price was only exceeded by that of Sea Island George cotton. Moreover, "the supply of cotton received in this country from Brazil is considerable, and tolerably regular." Baines, *History of Cotton,* p. 305.
14. Baines, *History of Cotton*, p. 304.
15. E.J. Donnell. *Chronological and Statistical History of Cotton* (New York, James Sutton & Co. Printers, 1872), p. 43.
16. Baines, *History of Cotton*, p. 302.
17. On methods of cotton production in late eighteenth-century northeastern Brazil, see: Manuel Arruda Camara. *Memória sobre a cultura dos algodoeiros, e sobre o methodo de o escolher e ensacar, e* etc. (Lisboa: Oficina Literária da Casa do Arco do Cego, 1797). On the methods of production in Maranhão in the mid-nineteenth century see A. Turner. *Manual do Plantador d'algodão.* (Maranhão: Officina Typographica do Frias, 1859).
18. Pereira, "The cotton trade," pp. 11–12.
19. In the 1810s Brazilian cotton exports to England alone averaged over two thirds of the value of all these exports in the period from 1814–1821. José Jobson de Andrade Arruda. "O Algodão brasileiro na época da revolução industrial" *América Latina en la historia económica* 23, no. 2 (2016), p. 179, table 1.
20. Already in the period 1806–1815, US cotton imports represented 57% of all foreign cotton entering England, compared to 19% for Brazil. Alexey

Krichal. "Liverpool and the raw cotton trade: a study of the port and its merchant community, 1770–1815." (MA thesis, Victoria University of Wellington, 2013), p. 22; and, E.J. Donnel. *Chronological and Statistical History of Cotton,* New York, James Sutton & Co. Printers, 1872.

21. This is impressive given the fact that Brazil accounted for 8% of British cotton goods exports to 1850 compared to 11% to the United States, its largest market. Pereira, "The cotton trade," p. 14. There were three major treaties enabling special tariffs for England, that of 1808 opening all ports, 1810 giving England preferential treatment and the 1827 treaty which limited tariffs to 15%. See Stephen Haber and Herbert S. Klein, "The Economic Consequences of Brazilian Independence," in Stephen Haber, ed., *How Latin America Fell Behind* (Stanford: Stanford University Press, 1997), p. 245.
22. ee Ildefonso Albano, *A Cultura Algodoeira no Ceará.* Rio de Janeiro, Typ. do Jornal do Commercio, 1918, p. 23; and Sebastião Ferreira Soares, *Notas Estatísticas sobre a Produção Agrícola e Carestia dos Generos Alimenticios no Imperio do Brazil* (Rio de Janeiro: J.Villeneuve e Comp. 1860), pp. 47–53.
23. Manuel Correia de Andrade. *A terra e o homem no Nordeste: contribuição ao estudo da questão agrária,* (São Paulo: Cortez, 2011), pp. 158–159.
24. On the causes for the growth of cotton exports in the United States in the nineteenth century see Alan L. Olmstead and Paul W. Rhode, " Biological Innovation and Productivity Growth in the Antebellum Cotton Economy," *The Journal of Economic History*, 68, mo. 4 (Dec. 2008), pp.1123–1171; and Gavin Wright, *The Political Economy of the Cotton South, Households, Markets and Wealth in the Nineteenth Century* (New York: W.W. Norton, 1978), chapter 4.
25. Isaac Watts. *The Cotton Supply Association: Its Origin and Progress.* Manchester, Tubbs & Brook, 1871, p. 5.
26. Lúcia Ferreira Lirbório, "O Circuíto espacial de produção do algodão naturalmente colorido na Paraíba-Brasil,". (Phd. Thesis, FFLCH-USP, 2017), p. 104; Henry Koster. *Viagens ao Nordeste do Brasil.* ([1816] São Paulo: Cia Editora Nacional, 1941), p. 452; and Francisco R.B. Nogueira e Sara V.D. Simões. "Uma abordagem sistêmica para a agropecuária e a dinâmica evolutiva dos sistemas de produção do nordeste semi-árido". *Revista Caatinga,* Mossoró, 22, no.2, (abril/junho 2009), p. 4.
27. For the late nineteenth century practices see Ildefonso Albano. *A Cultura Algodoeira no Ceará.* Rio de Janeiro, Typ. do Jornal do Commercio, 1918, p. 33.
28. Koster. *Viagens ao Nordeste do Brasil.* p. 452.
29. Pereira, "The cotton trade and Brazilian foreign commerce." loc.cit.
30. Watts, *The Cotton Supply*, p. 7.

31. According to the second author, who wrote in 1871, "Here the cotton plant had been naturalised for ages, whilst the soil and climate were found to be well suited to its cultivation." Watts. *The Cotton Supply*, pp. 12–13.
32. Watts, *The Cotton Supply*, p. 85.
33. Watts, *The Cotton Supply*, p. 85. On the development of cotton in São Paulo see Alice P. Canabrava. *O Algodão em São Paulo 1861–1875* (São Paulo: T.A.Queiroz, Editor, 1984); and Alice Piffer Canabrava, "Uma fazenda-modelo na Província de São Paulo (1863)," *Anais do IX Simpósio da ANPUH, O Homem e a Técnica*, volume IV. São Paulo, 1979, pp. 1173–1219.
34. Sven Beckert "Emancipation and Empire: Reconstruction the World Web of Cotton Production in the Age of the American Civil War," *American Historical Review* 109, no. 5 (2004): p. 1414.
35. See Caio Prado Jr. *A Revolução Brasileira*. São Paulo, Brasiliense, 1966. O autor cita a maior importância da parceria na produção de algodão, relativamente a outros cultivos, pp. 52–54; and Christian Brannstrom, "Forests for cotton: Institutions and organizations in Brazil's mid-twentieth-century cotton boom," *Journal of Historical Geography*, 36, no. 2 (April 2010), pp. 169–182.
36. The arbóreos of the *crioulo, caiena, and quebradiço* type supposedly lasted for 12 years. Nicolau Joaquim Moreira. *Indicações agrícolas para os imigrantes que se dirigem ao Brazil* '(Rio de Janeiro: Imperial Instituto Artístico, 1875), p. 60.
37. Moreira. *Indicações agrícolas*, p. 64.
38. Moreira. *Indicações agrícolas,* pp. 69–70. The seven fabric factories consumed 728 tons of cotton; exports that year were 1,574 tons. Several types of cotton were grown in Bahia, with white and yellow fibers. In the case of Rio de Janeiro herbaceous cotton was grown and Moreira estimates that one hectare of land produced 1,200 kilograms of raw cotton or 900 kilograms of clean cotton (p. 78).
39. In Rio de Janeiro, he also estimated that 1 hectare produced 1.200 kilos of raw cotton or 900 kilos of cleaned cotton. Moreira. *Indicações agrícolas* pp. 78–80.
40. According to Moreira um *alqueire* of seed (36.72 liters) generated 240 arrobas of the product (or 3,524 kilos) worth 1:200$000 milreis, with production costs of only 300$ 000 milreis. Large green, small green, white, and black seeds were used in the Province. The proportion of raw and ginned cotton was 7%. Moreira. *Indicações agrícolas,* pp. 81–85.
41. Canabrava. *O Algodão em São Paulo*, pp. XI–XIV.
42. Canabrava. *O Algodão em São Paulo*, Chapter 3.
43. Jerônimo de Viveiros. *História do Comércio do Maranhão, 1612–1895* (São Luis:. Associação Comercial do Maranhão, 1954), Vol. 2, p. 460; and *Breve Notícia sobre a Província do Maranhão, encaminhada a Sua Alteza*

Real o Senhor Conde D'Eu, e aos Exmos Membros da Comissão Superior na Exposição Nacional. (Rio de Janeiro, 1875), pp. 46–61.

44. Of the value of Brazilian exports, 81% went to England and 9% to France. In turn 85% of imports into Brazil came from England and 7% from France. "Estatística do Commercio Maritimo do Brazil do exercício de 1871–1872;" 2ª. parte, Commercio Geral, Organizada pela Commissão dirigida pelo Dr. Sebastião Ferreira Soares, vol. II.
45. Ministerio da Agricultura, Indústria e Commercio, Directoria Geral de Estatística. *Recenseamento do Brasil, 1920,* volume V, 1ª. parte, Industria, pp. xvi a xxii, xxiv,lxxii, lxxiii.
46. *Recenseamento do Brasil, 1920,* volume V, 1ª. parte, Industria, p. XXXVIII. According to the 1920 excise tax data, 535,433,927 meters of cotton fabrics would have been "consumed", against 2,097,818 meters of linen fabrics and 3,613,826 meters of wool fabrics.
47. *Recenseamento do Brasil, 1920,* volume III, 2ª. parte, Agricultura, p. XIX.
48. Ildefonso Albano. "A crise do Algodão". Discurso pronunciado na Câmara dos Deputados em 11 de dezembro de 1915. Rio de Janeiro, Typ. Do Jornal do Commercio, 1918, p. 13.
49. Paulo Pestana. "A indústria de tecidos de algodão". *Boletim da Directoria de Industria e Commercio,* São Paulo, Secretaria a Agricultura, Commercio e Obras Públicas do Estado de São Paulo, 17ª Série, abril, no. 4, (1926): pp. 63–65, 89–90.
50. This estimate is based on the 1920 census. It stated that São Paulo produced 11 million arrobas of cotton seed, equivalent to 55 thousand tons of raw cotton, which gives a return of 34%. This is close to the 35% estimate given in Ruy Miller Paiva, "Fatores que afetam a produção de algodão no sul do Brasil,"*Agricultura em São Paulo,* SP, 43, no. 3, (1996): p. 167.
51. Rui H.P.L. de Albuquerque. "Capital comercial, indústria têxtil e relações de produção na cotonicultura paulista (1920–1950)," (MA thesis, Unicamp, 1981), p. 180; and José Sidnei Gonçalves and Soraia de Fatima Ramos, "Da origem à hegemonia e crise do algodão meridional brasileiro no século XX," *Informações Econômicas,* SP, 38, no.2, (fev. 2008), pp. 28–29.
52. Albuquerque. "Capital comercial, indústria têxtil," pp. 120–124; and Arthur Botelho Junqueira. *O algodão.* (São Paulo: Est. De Artes Gráficas C. Mendes Junior, 1936), pp. 8–9.
53. Albuquerque. "Capital comercial, indústria têxtil,"pp. 137–138; and Rui Henrique de Albuquerque, Antonio Cesar Ortega and Baastian Philip Reydon, "O setor público de pesquisa agrícola do estado de São Paulo" (parte 1). *Cad.Dif.Tecnol.,* Brasília, 3, no. 1(jan./abril. 1986), pp.79–132,; and Lúcia Ferreira Lirbório, "O circuito espacial de produção

do algodão naturalmente colorido na Paraíba-Brasil," (Phd. Thesis, São Paulo, FFLCH-USP, 2017), p. 152.

54. Francisco das Chagas Vidal Neto and Eleusio Curvelo Freire, "Melhoramento genético do algodoeiro," in Francisco das Chagas Vidal Neto and J.J.V. Cavalcanti, eds.; *Melhoramento genético de plantas no Nordeste* (Brasília: Embrapa, 2013), pp. 49–83; and Eleusio Curvelo Freire, Joaquim Nunes da Costa and Francisco Pereira de Andrade, "Recursos genéticos e melhoramentos do algodão no Nordeste do Brasil," Palestra apresentada no Simpósio sobre recursos genéticos no Nordeste. Petrolina. Setembro de 1997. Found at: http://www.cpatsa.embrapa.br:8080/catalogo/livrorg/algodao.pdf
55. Eleusio Curvêlo Freire, José de Alencar Nunes Moreira and Luís Carlos Medeiros. "Contribuição das Ciências Agrárias para o Desenvolvimento o caso do Algodão," *Revista Economia Rural*, 18, no.3 (jul./set. 1980), pp. 383–413; and Napoleão Esberard de Macedo Beltrão. *Breve História do Algodão no Nordeste do Brasil* ((Documentos 117; Campina Grande, Embrapa, 2003), p. 14.
56. Ministério das Relações Exteriores, *Relações das condições geográficas, econômicas e sociais, 1940–1941,* (Rio de Janeiro, 1941), pp. 189–194. According to Bunge Brasil, em 1929, Sanbra launched its cotton oil *Salada, the first such product on the market,*in 1929. Found at: http://alhe.mora.edu.mx/index.php/ALHE/article/view/e1002/1556#:~:text=%E2%80%9CEm%201929%20a%20Sanbra%20lan%C3%A7a,banha%20de%20porco%E2%80%9D%20(Bunge
57. Beltrão. *Breve História do Algodão no Nordeste do Brasil*, pp. 14–15.
58. Patrícia José de Almeida Salinas, "Arrendamento e parceria na agricultura brasileira: condicionantes, contratos e funcionamento," (Phd thesis, Campinas: Unicamp, 2009).
59. José Ednilson Miranda and Sandra Maria Morais Rodrigues. "História do bicudo no Brasil," in Jean Louis Belot, ed., *O bicudo-do-algodoeiro (Antohonomus grandis BOH., 1843) nos cerrados brasileiros: biologia e medidas de controle* (Cuiabá: Instituto Mato-grossense do Algodão, 2015), pp. 9–46; Raimundo Braga Sobrinho and Maurice James Lukefahr, *Bicudo (Anthonomus grandis BOHEMAN): nova ameaça à cotonicultura brasileira. Biologia e Controle.* (Documentos 22; Campina Grande, Embrapa, 1983); and Pimentel et al. *Bicudo uma grave ameaça à cotonicultura nordestina.* (Documentos 24; Campina Grande, Embrapa, 1983).
60. Rosalia Azambuja and Paulo Eduardo Degrande, "Trinta anos de bicudo-do-algodoeiro no Brasil" (São Paulo: Arq. Inst. Biol., https://doi.org/10.1590/1808-1657000012013), pp. 377–410; and Clayton Campanhola, Dial Franklin Martin and Salomão Schattan, "Algumas consequências da presença do bicudo-do-algodoeiro na região infestada de Campinas e

Sorocaba, Estado de São Paulo, na safa 83/84," *Pesquisa Agropecuaria. Brasileira*, 23 no. 8 (ago. 1988), pp. 811–823.

61. Gonçalves and Ramos, "Da origem à hegemonia e crise do algodão," p. 37.
62. José Sidnei Gonçalves, "Crise do Algodão brasileiro pós-abertura dos anos 90 e as condicionantes da retomada da expansão em bases competitivas," *Informações Econômicas*, SP, 27, no.3 (mar. 1997); Aluísio G. de Lima Campo. "A crise internacional do algodão". *Revista de Política Agrícola*, XI, no. 3 (jul./ago./set. 2002); Andrew Macdonald, "A crise do algodão tem solução," *Revista de Politica Agrícola*, VI, no.2 (Abr./Mai./Jun. 1997): Alexandre Bragança Coelho, "A cultura do algodão e a questão de integração entre preços internos e externos" (MA thesis, São Paulo, USP, 2002). The question of price integration is addressed by José Sidnei Gonçalves and Simone Pereira Gonçalves, "Transformações da produção do algodão brasileiro e os impactos nas paridades de preços no mercado interno," *Revista Economia Ensaios*, 23 no. 1 (2008), pp. 1–34, Maria Zeferino Barbosa, Maria Antonio Margarido and Sebastião Nogueira Junior, "Análise da elasticidade de transmissão de preços no mercado brasileiro de algodão," *Nova Economia*, Belo Horizonte, 12, no.2 (Jul./dez. 2002), pp. 79–108.
63. Hugo Biehl and Renato Zandonadi, "Implicações sócio-econômicas do abandono da cultura do algodão no Brasil," *Revista de Politica Agrícola*, VII, no. 3 (Jul/Ago/Set.1998), p. 12; Robério Ferreira dos Santos. "Aspectos Econômicos e Sociais da Cotonicultura no Nordeste do Brasil," (Circular Técnica 31;Campina Grande, Embrapa, 2000).
64. FAOSTAT, found at: http://www.fao.org/faostat/en/#data
65. Conab, *Análise Mensal Algodão*, out./nov. 2020.
66. Lúcia Ferreira Lirbório, "O circuito espacial de produção do algodão naturalmente colorido na Paraíba-Brasil." (Phd thesis, São Paulo, FFLCH-USP, 2017), pp. 152–153.
67. Thaise Dantas de Almeida Xavier, "Avaliação do modelo de negócio para o desenvolvimento das cultivares de algodão transgênico na Embrapa," (MA thesis. Recife, Universidade Federal de Pernambuco, 2018), p. 21.
68. David Goodman, Bernardo Sorj and Jonh Wilkinson. *Da lavoura às biotecnologias*. (Rio de Janeiro: Centro Edelstein de Pesquisas Sociais, 1990), p. 33.
69. "Informativo de biotecnologia Céleres, novembro de 2019." The OGM Roundup Ready, of Monsanto, was approved in Brazil in 2008. Found at: https://apps.agr.br/wp-content/uploads/2019/07/eventos_aprovados_algod%C3%A3o.pdf
70. Xavier, "Avaliação do modelo de negócio," p. 49.
71. Lirbório. "O circuito espacial de produção do algodão," p. 151.
72. Xavier, "Avaliação do modelo de negócio," p. 58.

73. Jean-Louis Bélot e Patrícia M.C.A. Vilela (ed.). *Manual de Boas Práticas de Manejo do algodoeiro em Mato Grosso.* Cuiabá, IMA/MT e AMPA, 2020 (safra 2019/2020), p. 13.
74. Bollgard II e TwinLink—GLT, ocupam o mercado nos últimos 3 a 4 anos. Jean-Louis Bélot and Patrícia M.C.A. Vilela, eds., *Manual de Boas Práticas de Manejo do algodoeiro em Mato Grosso.* Cuiabá, IMA/MT e AMPA, 2020 (safra 2019/2020), pp. 15–16.
75. Conab, acesso em: https://www.conab.gov.br/info-agro/custos-de-producao
76. Bélot and Vilela, *Manual de Boas* Práticas, pp. 56–57; and Edna Santos. *Aumento da produção de algodão no Brasil traz novos desafios para a pesquisa"* (Campina Grande: Embrapa Algodão, 2019).
77. CONAB [Companhia Nacional de Abastecimento], "Algadão, Série histórica," found at https://www.conab.gov.br/info-agro/safras/serie-historica-das-safras
78. USDA, *Cotton: World Markets and Trade, February 2023*, table 1.
79. USDA *Agricultural Projections, February 2022*, 97, table 36.
80. Marcos Fava Neves e Mairun Junqueira Alves Pinto, eds., *A cadeia do Algodão Brasileiro. Desafios e estratégias, safra 2010/2011.* (Brasilia: ABRAP, 2011); Marcos Fava Neves and Mairun Junqueira Alves Pinto, eds., *A cadeia do algodão brasileiro. Safra 2016/2017. Desafios e Estratégias.*(Brasília, ABRAPA, 2017), p. 19, Tabela A.1; and Antonio Márcio Buainain and Mario Otávio Batalha, eds., *Cadeia Produtiva do Algodão,* (Brasília, MAPA, 2007).
81. Neves and Pinto, *A cadeia do algodão brasileiro. Safra 2016/*2017, graph A.1.
82. Neves and Pinto, *A cadeia do algodão brasileiro*, Tabela A.3.
83. Camex. Ministério da Economia. "Brasil e EUA assinam memorando que encerra contencioso do algodão". Found at: http://www.camex.gov.br/noticias-da-camex/211-brasil-e-eua-assinam-memorando-que-encerra-contencioso-do-algodao. SeeWorld Trade Organization. "DS267 United States–Subsidies on Upland Cotton". Found at: https://www.wto.org/english/tratop_e/dispu_e/cases_e/ds267_e.htm. For studies of this debate see Sérgio Rodrigues Costa and Miguel Garcia Bueno. *A saga do Algodão: das primeiras lavouras à ação na OMC.* (Rio de Janeiro: Insight Engenharia, 2004); Alexandre Magno Ramos Paiva, "A contenda sobre o algodão entre o Brasil e os Estados Unidos na Organização Mundial do Comércio: considerações acerca do efeito para a inserção do Brasil no Mundo,". (MA thesis, João Pessoa: Universidade Estadual da Paraíba, 2013).

CHAPTER 7

São Paulo, Florida, and the World Orange Juice Market

Brazil is currently the world's leading orange grower and the leading world exporter of all types of processed orange juice. It grows 35% of world oranges and accounts for 72% of the orange juice production. Three of every five glasses of orange juice consumed in the world today are produced at Brazilian factories and Brazilian juice makes up three quarters of orange juice exports in the world market.[1] While the size of Brazil and its semi-tropical condition makes it ideal for orange production, its dominance in the orange juice market is surprising since the local market has traditionally involved only the consumption of fresh fruit. Although the local market is still dominated by fresh fruit consumption, Brazil was the country which would become the principal world juce producer. But it was the United States which created the modern orange juice processing industry and it was Florida which first dominated world consumption. How and why Brazil, and above all São Paulo, replaced Florida as the world's leading producer and exporter of orange juice is the basic theme of this study.

Although oranges have been grown in Brazil since the earliest colonial period it is only in the twentieth century that it became the world's largest producer and it was only at the end of that century that it would come to dominate juice production. Oranges originated in Asia and were brought to the Iberian Peninsula during Islamic rule. Columbus brought them

H. S. Klein and F. V. Luna, *Brazilian Crops in the Global Market*, Palgrave Studies in Economic History,
https://doi.org/10.1007/978-3-031-38589-6_7

to the Caribbean, Pizarro carried them to Peru,[2] and the Portuguese brought them to be planted in Brazil in the sixteenth century.[3] By the 1540s orchids of oranges were established in the Portuguese colony and the Jesuits in particular were active in planting citrus groves.[4] Already in the 1810s Brazilian growers had developed a unique local variety of navel orange known as Laranja Bahia in the town of Salvador de Bahia. It was this variety that soon spread throughout Brazil and eventually the world. In 1870 the US Department of Agriculture imported Bahian orange seedlings to Washington and these Bahian orange trees were soon growing in California and from there quickly spread throughout the world, now being called the Washington Navel.[5]

In the late nineteenth century the orange groves of Rio de Janeiro, then Brazil's principal producers, began to export fresh oranges to Argentina and Uruguay. The first shipments were in 1886 and by 1909 the Brazilian government was proposing a tariff free trade of fresh fruits to these Rio de la Plata countries.[6] At the time, Rio de Janeiro was still the predominant producer of oranges, but in the decade of the 1920s this dominance shifted to São Paulo as overproduction and climatic events reduced coffee trees in the state, opening up space for the development of alternative crops. In 1927 the state of São Paulo sought to promote oranges as replacement for coffee and established a state Citrus Service (*Serviço de Citricultura*) with several experimental stations to promote orange production.[7] The classic case of the shift from coffee to oranges in the state of São Paulo was the municipality of Bebedouro, the region which would become the leading producer of oranges in the state. As early as 1924 the São Paulo Secretary of Agriculture introduced orange seedlings and offered technical assistance to potential growers. The good local soils and climate and the direct access that the region had to railroads were considered fundamental to the success of the enterprise. By 1932 one of the larger local coffee fazendas converted into orange production planting 40,000 orange trees to replace its coffee trees. With state support, several other fazendas followed this leadership and growth thereafter was quite rapid.[8] Growth of area dedicated to oranges grew quickly. In the 1930s orange groves averaged about 37 thousand hectares, reaching 41 thousand in the three-year period 1940–1942. But World War II saw a decline in production and land use and it was not until the late 1950s that the area in production passed pre-war levels. But by 1970–1972 orange groves were occupying 105 thousand hectare of state lands

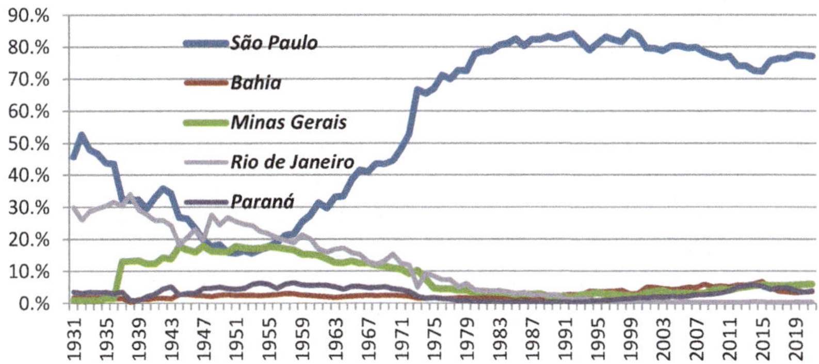

Graph 7.1 Ratio of principal producing states in total Brazilian orange production, 1931–2021 (*Source* IPEADATA and IBGE, Sidra, tab 1613)

and steadily grew to 397 thousand hectares by 1978–1981 and to 472 thousand hectares, or 8% of all crop lands in the state by 1982–1984.[9]

In 1939 the state was already exporting almost three million boxes of oranges.[10] In a 1935 survey, there were listed some 19 million orange trees in Brazil, of which 8.9 million were in São Paulo and some 6.5 million in Rio de Janeiro, 1.5 million in Minas Gerais, with Bahia and Espírito Santo each with 400 thousand trees and with lesser numbers in other states. In this decade as well began the first exports of boxes of oranges to Europe. In São Paulo in the 1940s the Bahiana naval variety was grown on 80% of the trees and the Bahiana and the Pêra variety were then most used in exports. The Valencia variety had just been introduced in this decade and it would eventually become the dominant variety.[11]

The leadership of São Paulo in Brazilian orange production was well established by the 1930s, but its dominant position collapsed in the period 1948 to 1956 due to a devastating Asian plague that destroyed a large portion of its trees. At this point, Rio de Janeiro temporarily became the leading state producer. But local producers replanted new trees and applied insecticides, and by 1957 São Paulo growers were again the nation's leading producers. By 1972 the state accounted for over half of the national production. After that date its dominance only increased and by the current century it was averaging 80% of national production (see Graph 7.1).

Although oranges were grown throughout Brazil, most of the commercial production was concentrated in just a few states, most especially in Bahia and Sergipe in the Northeast and Minas Gerais, São Paulo and Paraná in the Southeast. But productivity in the Northeastern states is low and output has been declining.[12] Moreover over three quarters of production in Bahia and Sergipe goes toward fresh fruit consumption for the local market.[13] The key state in both the growth of production and in the development of an export market has been the state of São Paulo. Orange production in the state was increasingly concentrated in what has been called the Citrus belt (cinturão citrícola brasileiro) which contains 331 municípios in São Paulo, as well as 16 municípios in the adjacent region in Minas Gerais (in the so-called Triângulo Mineiro region). The citrus belt began in the regions of Campinas, Ribeirão Preto, and São José do Rio Preto. Then Sorocaba and the Triângulo Minero were included in the citrus belt area in the decade of the 1990s.[14] These orange-producing municipalities are concentrated in the North, Center, and Southern parts of the state in some 11 key areas dominated by a major municipality. These include what are considered greater regions centered on their leading municipalities, These larger units include Bebedouro, Altinópolis, Votuporanga, São José do Rio Preto, Duartina, Matão, Brotas, Porto Ferreira, Limeira, Avaré, and Itapetininga in a Northwest to Southwest line as seen in Map 7.1.

These districts currently include some 387,000 hectares of orchards with 199 million trees. The distribution of these trees among producers is quite skewed, with those owning over 200,000 trees accounting for only 3% of the orchards, but owning over half of the trees (see Table 7.1). This results in a high GINI of 0.790 which suggests a significantly unequal distribution, but not that different from all other major agricultural crops in Brazil where the average concentration level has been a steady 0.83 to 0.87 over several decades.[15]

Already by the mid-1930s Brazil had become the third largest grower of oranges after the United States and Spain and ahead of China.[16] Three decades later it surpassed Spain and by 1981 it finally passed the United States, which until then had been the world's leading producer. Even with this recent expansion of orange production in India and China, Brazil remains the world's leading producer of oranges accounting for 22% of world production and it is only in 2018 that the combined Chinese and Indian production reached total Brazilian output (see Graph 7.2).

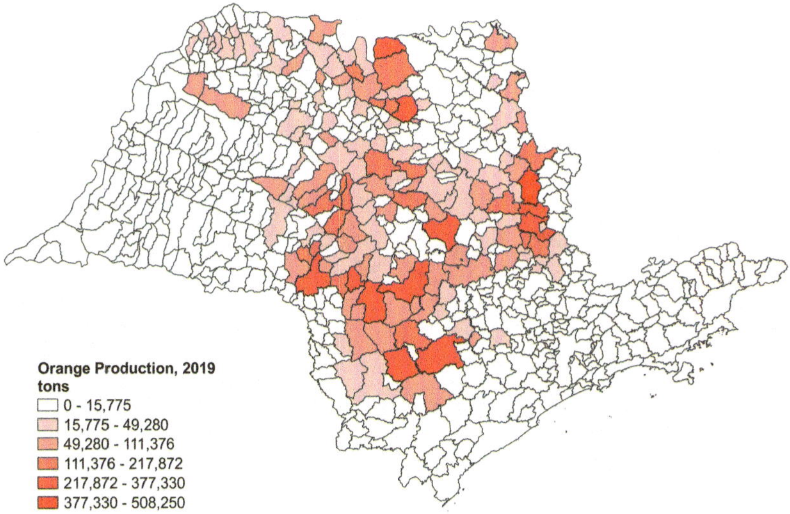

Map 7.1 Orange Production in the Municipalities of the State of São Paulo, 2019 (*Source* IBGE Bases Cartográficas Sidra, table 1613)

Table 7.1 Structure of the Orange Orchards in the Citrus Belt of São Paulo and Minas Gerais in 2022

Number of trees	*Owners*	*%*	*Trees (000)*	*%*
<10 thousand	3,056	60%	11,217	6%
10–19 thousand	681	13%	9,191	5%
20–29 thousand	317	6%	7,522	4%
30–49 thousand	333	6%	12,260	6%
50–99 thousand	348	7%	23,469	12%
100–199 thousand	198	4%	26,638	13%
>200 thousand	201	4%	109,015	55%
Total	5,134	100%	199,312	100%

Note This includes both producing and non-producing trees, the non-bearing trees represented 15% of the total
Source Fundecitrus, *Inventario 2022–2023* tabela 4 found at https://www.fundecitrus.com.br/pes/estimativa

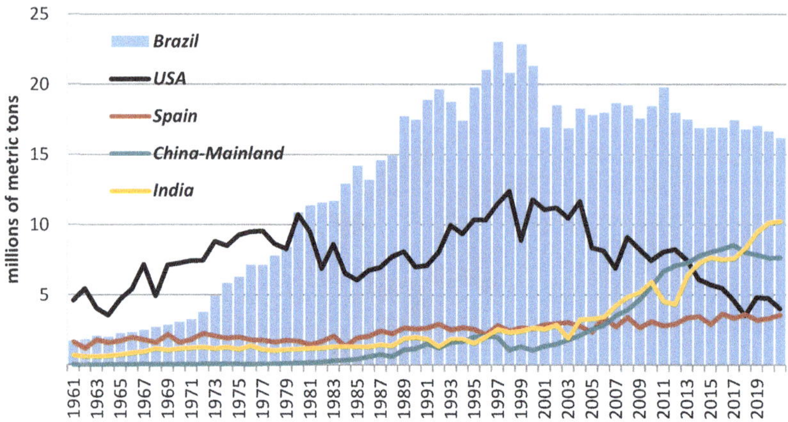

Graph 7.2 Production of oranges by current world's leading producers, 1961–2021 (*Source* FAOSTAT at http://www.fao.org/faostat/en/#data/QC)

Along with increasing volume, there was also increased productivity with yield per hectare. This has resulted in declining use of land (see Graph 7.3), although oranges are still the most produced fruit in Brazil and used the most arable land, far outpacing the hectares dedicated to bananas. Improved trees from protected nurseries have enabled Brazilian producers to go from a density of 250 trees per hectare in 1980 to 357 trees per hectare in 1990 to an average of 476 trees per hectare in 2000.[17] By the harvest of 2022/2023 the São Paulo growers were averaging 515 trees per hectare.[18] Thus the average number of boxes of oranges went from 380 boxes per hectare in 1990 to 475 boxes in 2010.[19] Productivity has continued to expand since then. As expressed in tons per hectare, productivity increased steadily from an average of 15 tons/ha in the ten-year period from 1962–1971, to an average of 27 tons/ha in the period from 2012–2021.[20]

Not only were these new yields impressive by Brazilian standards, but it was evident by the 2010s that Brazil was the world's highest yielding orange producer per hectare among the leading world producers of oranges (see Graph 7.4). It should be stressed that there is a difference in productivity among types of oranges. Earlier maturing oranges such as the Hamlin, Westin, and Rubi were producing 859 oranges per tree as of December 2022, while Pêra Rio (which were grown on the largest

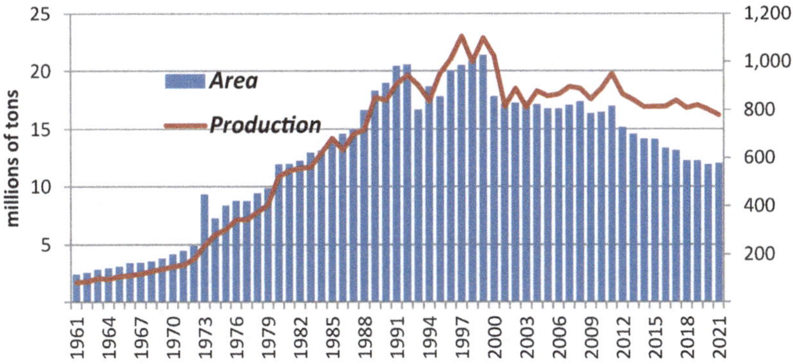

Graph 7.3 Brazilian production of oranges and area of producing orchards, 1961–2021 (*Source* FAOSTAT at http://www.fao.org/faostat/en/#data/QC)

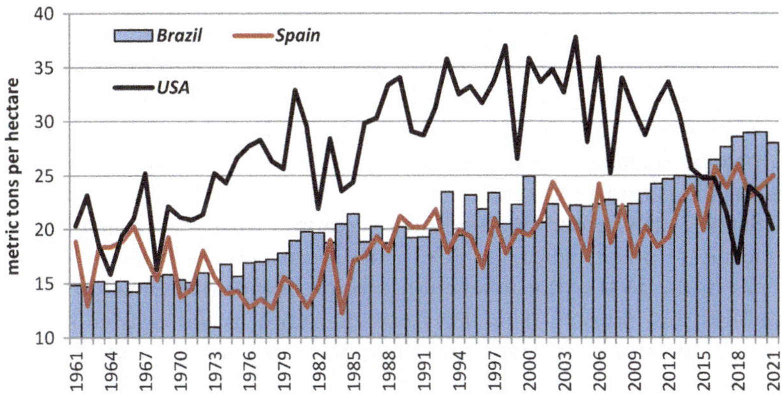

Graph 7.4 Comparative yield of oranges per hectare by leading producers, 1961–2021 (*Source* FAOSTAT at http://www.fao.org/faostat/en/#data/QC)

number of trees, were at 560 oranges per tree, and Valências at 680 per tree, for an overall average of 668 oranges per tree.[21]

Currently in all of Brazil the major orange varieties being grown are the Pêra Rio, the Valência varieties, and the Natal, with smaller production of Hamlin, Lima and the navel oranges: the Bahia and the Bahiana.[22] But in the core region of São Paulo and Southwest Minas Gerais in the crop year 2019/2020, the predominant variety of the 174 million trees were the Pêra Rio and the Valência varieties (accounting for 70% of the trees), the Hamlin varieties for 15%, 11% are navel producing trees and a diverse group of other varieties make up 5%.[23] The choice of variety is determined by the season. Thus 23% of the crop are early season varieties (Hamlin, Westin, Rubi) which are harvested May–August, some 22% are midseason (the Pêra variety) which occurs roughly from September to October and 55% are late season (Natal and Valência) which are harvested October to January. The late season varieties are prized for making juice while the midseason varieties go both to the fresh fruit market and to processing.[24]

At the same time as yield increased so did the use of oranges change. While fresh orange exports continued to evolve to neighboring countries and Europe, most of this fresh fruit was directed toward the expanding internal market, as the Brazilian population in the last half of the century was growing at an impressive 2.4% per annum.[25] All of these changes in volume and productivity were due to several factors. From the 1960s there was a generalized mechanization and modernization of Brazilian agriculture with massive inputs of chemicals and new seed varieties in almost all major crops much of this subsidized by government research and capital.[26] Soon production outstripped national consumption and growers sought alternative sources of income. The obvious solution was to process oranges into juices even though there was little demand for this in the national market.

Such a new processing industry, creating what was called frozen concentrate orange juice, or FCOJ, had been developed in the United States in the 1940s. But it was not until the 1960s that Brazil began to establish this industry. This delay was due both to the early monopoly position of the United States and the initial disinterest of producers who primarily served a fresh fruit market. This industry might have remained a relatively small part of the citrus sector of Brazilian agriculture had the US' orange juice industry not entered a series of crises and ultimately long-term secular decline which finally opened up international markets for a Brazilian FCOJ.

The idea for this new system was developed by the US and Florida governments in World War II as an effort to provide sources of vitamin C for the military, but it only came to fruition after the war. In 1945 a private company (which eventually became Minute Maid Corporation) was granted the right to use the process in its own new factory. By 1948 there were three factories in production, one of which was owned by Tropicana. Already by the 1950s orange concentrate was absorbing almost half of the Florida orange crop.[27] The introduction of frozen concentrate orange juice created a new national and export industry of world importance. This process involved the extraction of water from the juice, and the addition of some juice or essence to retain flavor before it was pasteurized, frozen, and then packaged for shipping. The resulting product could last a long time and could be shipped long distances. Once arriving at its destination it could be defrosted and water added, and the result was a drinkable orange juice with a shelf life of several weeks.

Although Florida would begin to export this new product on a modest scale to Europe, most was shipped into the domestic market.[28] In the 1960s for example, on average only 4% of the frozen concentrate was exported and this only increased to 10% of total Florida production by the 1970s.[29] Thus the greater portion of US frozen juice ended up being consumed nationally thanks to an active marketing campaign by Minute Maid and Tropicana, which companies in turn became part of the Coca Cola and Pepsi Cola conglomerates respectively.[30] As US production of oranges grew steadily from 1930 to 1962 it was able to more than satisfy the local market, peaking in 1962 at 109 million boxes or 4.4 million metric tons (at 40.8 kg per box).[31]

But after this initial expansion, Florida's orange producers experienced a series of freezes in the 1960s which severely cut orange production and thus also orange juice processing.[32] The freeze of December 1962 had a profound impact and production steadily declined to just 55 million boxes in the crop year 1963/64. Growers however steadily recovered and another peak of 207 million boxes was reached in 1979/1980. But in the next decade Florida's groves were struck both with a series tree diseases and freezes which cut production significantly and it was not until 1996/1997 that production returned to the levels of the 1970s. From the late 1990s production grew steadily until a final peak production of 242 boxes was reached in 2003/2004. But unlike previous periods of crises, there was no recover after that date as Florida production went into a long term decline due to climactic conditions and above all to the citrus greening disease becoming endemic in its orchards in the current century and to hurricane winds, all causing high fruit drop rates. Production today has declined to just 41 million boxes (see Graph 7.5). It is also estimated that productivity per tree has systematically declined since the 2003/2004 peak due to greening disease and.[33] Finally in the season of 2022–2023 California orange production for the first time passed Florida output at an estimated 46,100 boxes to just 18,000 boxes from Florida.[34] Although

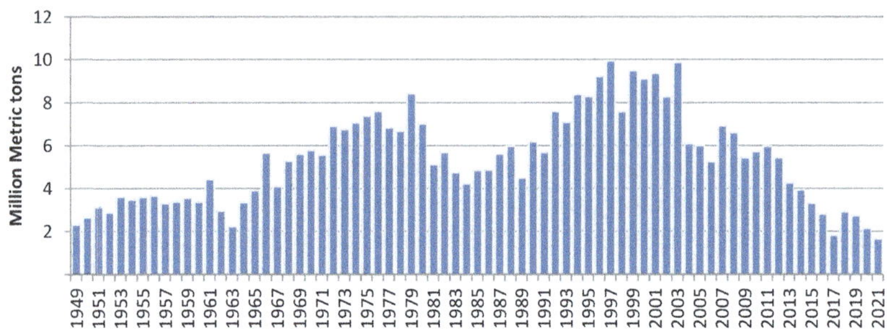

Graph 7.5 Florida orange production 1949–2021 in metric tons (*Source* USDA, Florida Citrus Statistics, 2019–2020, p. 14; and USDA, Cirtus Summary 2022)

California was always the second largest national orange producer until the current season, most of its output went into fresh fruit sales due to their low juice content, whereas almost all of Florida orange production went into the production of juice.[35]

The United States juice producers also created the second major type of juice exports. Like the United States, Brazilian juice production was initially dominated by frozen concentrated orange juice (FCOJ). But in the 1970s Tropicana, then still an independent processing company, began to use "flash pasteurization" to treat orange juice. This process enabled the company to extend the shelf life of fresh orange juice for up to three months. Although it was cheaper to produce since the juice was only pasteurized and no water was extracted, this new processed juice known as NFC (not from concentrate, also called chilled or single source orange juice SSOJ, or SSJ) was more costly to ship because of its greater bulk than the frozen concentrate, which was also pasteurized but in which all the water was extracted. Initially, the NSF juice sold at a 30% price differential from the FCOJ, but it eventually declined in price as it became the dominant form of orange juice consumption in the US and eventually in Europe. By the 2004/2005 crop year, Florida was using more boxes of oranges to produce the newer NFC juice than the traditional FCOJ. Once introduced, NFC thereafter dominated national juice production in the United States (see Graph 7.6). Much of the success of NFC juice was the ability of Tropicana to use the extensive milk delivery infrastructure to bring the product to market. But it also used aseptic storage to

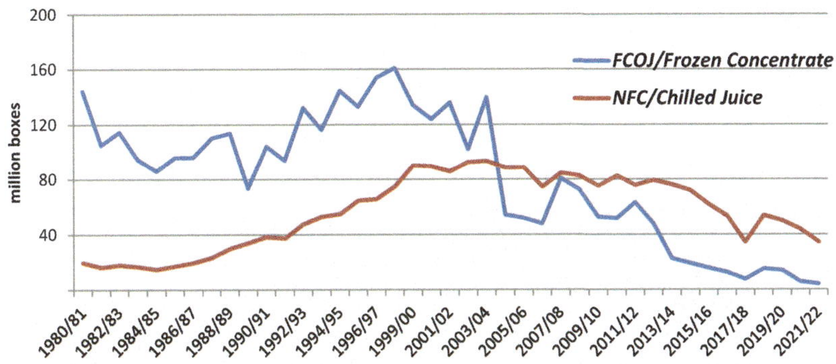

Graph 7.6 Florida production of Frozen Concentrate and Chilled Juice in boxes, 1980–2022 (*Source* USDA Fruit and Nut Yearbook, 2022, table c-28 [box = 40.8 kg/90 US pounds])

store non-concentrated juices over a longer period, which involved stripping the juice of oxygen, so it does not oxidize, in the enormous tanks in which it could be stored for up to a year. Soon all the other producers were dedicating a share of their output to producing the NFC variety which had better flavor than the FCOJ.[36]

But despite the creation of two new juice processing industries, as Florida orange production experienced these boom and bust cycles so did its production of orange juice which peaked in last years of the twentieth century and the first years of the current century only to go into a long period of secular decline paralleling the decline in output of oranges (see Graph 7.7).

All these changes in the then-world leader in orange juice production slowly opened the way for Brazilian processors to enter the world market, first with frozen concentrated juice and then in the current century with NFC single-source juices. In turn it was to fill the gap in US consumption of these products that US producers turned to Brazilian orange growers and processors and thus helped to stimulate Brazilian production. Thus a combination of severely declining juice production and exports and a deficit of national producers in satisfying consumption even for the US market opened up a space for Brazilian participation in the world orange juice market.

That Brazil could replace the United States in this market had a lot to do with the extraordinary growth of Brazilian orange production at the

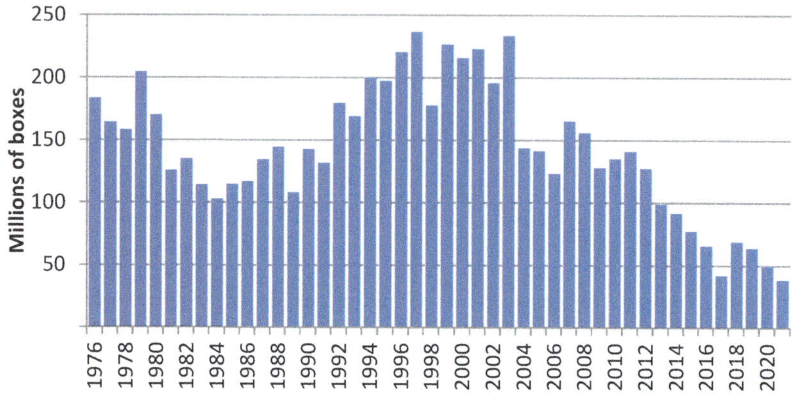

Graph 7.7 Florida production of all types of orange juice, 1980–2021 (*Source* USDA,ERS, Fruit and Tree Nut Yarbook tables, C-29 [1997] and C28 [2022])

end of the twentieth century and the modernization of Brazilian agriculture in this period. By the end of the second decade of the twenty-first century, Brazilian producers became the world's most efficient producers in terms of yields per hectare. At the same time the concentration of the industry in the highly developed state of São Paulo with its railroads and easy access to the international port of Santos, all part of the old coffee system, made transport costs sufficiently low as to make exporting profitable.

Just as Florida played a dominant role in the US orange industry, so did São Paulo play that same role in Brazil. São Paulo, like Florida, had the same climactic conditions for orange production. It has high seasonal and diurnal variations in temperature and a lot of rainfall. Also like Florida it has seen periods of rapid growth, disease, and some episodes of frost, but it has been able to grow steadily in a secular manner since the mid-twentieth century. But just like other permanent crops in Brazil, its fixed costs were high. Newly planted orange trees took two years to produce and often lasted up to 20 years. This made for a delayed response to price changes, so that overproduction was a constant problem. To this were added world trade crises and the introduction of new diseases which reduced tree production. The arrival of a new Asian originated disease had a dramatic impact in reducing orange production, especially in the state of São Paulo which temporarily lost its lead position. It also led to the shift in the 1970s from growing the Bahiana orange to the Pêra variety (Pêra IC clone) which was more resistant to diseases.[37]

For most of the second half of the twentieth century and until recently, Florida and São Paulo were the largest producing regions of oranges. But the relationship of the two changed over time with São Paulo in long-term expansion and Florida in long-term decline. Florida reached 80 million bearing trees in 2000/2001 and declined to 49 million such trees in production by December 2021. Whereas in 2000/2001 its total production in metric tons was the same as São Paulo—or roughly between 10 and 12 million metric tons of oranges,[38] output declined to some 2.2 million metric tons in 2020/2021, compared to 15.9 million tons produced by the Citrus Complex of São Paulo/Minas Gerais in the same crop year. By this time the São Paulo/Minas Gerais district had 197 million orange-bearing trees, almost four times as many as in Florida's orchards.[39]

Even before the 1962 freeze the first simple frozen orange juice factory was established in Brazil in 1959, but growth was slow. [40] The delayed Brazilian transition to the new technology was due to the limited demand for the product in the national market. Moreover, the US market was well protected with tariffs and thus the world's most important consumer market at this time was relatively closed to outside producers. But the freeze of 1962 suddenly created a demand for imports to make up for the dramatic fall in Florida production just as home consumption was rising.[41]

A Brazilian orange wholesaler, José Cutrale bought a small processing plant in 1963 and offered to supply the Minute Maid division of Coca Cola with Brazilian juice. The American company sent technicians to Brazil to help Cutrale develop a modern production system and he began to supply juice to the North American market. Other processors soon followed as Florida production was again badly affected by the winter freezes of 1983 and 1985. Already by 1981 Brazilian production had definitively passed orange production in the United States and this difference in output became even more pronounced over the next several decades.

Thus the crisis of production in the US market opened the possibility of Brazil to export first frozen concentrated orange juice, or FCOJ, and then the new single source NFC processed juice in the current century. It gave an incentive to local capital to develop a completely new industry to take advantage of the abundant national production of

oranges to be sold as fresh fruit on the internal market.[49] Most of the sales of oranges to processors by independent growers were by contract for three years. But there was also a spot market for sales of fresh fruit both to provide fresh oranges to the national market and also to the 50 to 100 small independent crushers known as barracões (or shacks) that created fresh juice for the local market and were distributed throughout the Citrus belt.[50]

The drive for ever greater concentration was due to the high costs of the new processing plants, the special port facilities, and the tankers which were used to ship the condensed juice overseas. There were also problems of oversupply in periods of world economic crises such as the second oil shock and the Depression of 2008, which drove many smaller producers out of production and at the same time, led the processors to start buying land and produce their own oranges.[51] An estimate of the costs of producing a box of oranges on orchards owned by processors in 2010/2011 found that the most important production costs were for wages (53%), 12% for pesticides and herbicides, and 10% for fertilizers.[52] Although there were significant final price differences for NFC versus FCOJ, the price paid for the oranges to the growers were the same in both cases so the growers thus received more of the final price of FCOJ than NFC. An estimate for Florida producers in the same crop year of 2010/2011 suggests that the farmer's share of the final price of a gallon of FCOJ juice was 22%, compared to 15% for NFC.[53]

Unlike coffee, the other major permanent crop, most of the oranges are handpicked. The oranges are then put in large bags of up to 700 oranges and then driven to the nearby processing plant where the oranges are cleaned and sorted and juice is produced and pasteurized. The complexity of the processing companies can be seen in Brazilian-owned Citrosuco, which is the largest of the national packing houses and has the world's largest orange juice factory located in the heart of the Citrus belt in Matão with a capacity of grading more than a thousand truckloads of oranges per diem. It also has two other processing plants in São Paulo and one in Florida. The company owns 25 orange farms and uses an estimated 6,500 workers to harvest its oranges. It owns 5 ships that exclusively carry juice and has five terminals, one in Santos, and four others in the US, Belgium, Japan, and Australia.[54] Cutrale the other Brazilian giant has 5 processing plants in the Cirtus belt, and two terminals, one in Santos and the other in Guarujá.[55] Defeyfuss (known as LDC) is a French-Swiss origin company that began its Brazilian operations in 1942 and has three juice factories in São Paulo and manages 38 Orange farms. It is the most diversified of the three and operates in most areas of Brazilian agriculture.[56]

Once in production, Brazilian exports of FCOJ developed quickly first to the United States and then to the rest of the world, and above all to Europe. Brazil only began exporting in 1963 but had passed the United States in the volume of FCOJ exports by 1971. In the next year, it took half of the world exports and by 1980 it accounted for over 70% of the value of international juice exports. In this same period, the share of United States FCOJ exports in the world market kept declining. In just a few years Brazil dominated world markets for this product, even as other producing countries from Israel to Korea entered the market.

Given the long distance Brazil from its major market, there was a need to develop complex port storage facilities, specialized shipping and end terminal storage and processing infrastructure to deal with this new type of juice product. This explains the relatively long delay in Brazilian producers entering this market. After heavy capital investments in terminals, ports, and shipping, Brazil in 2002 finally began to export non-concentrated juice (NFC) along with traditional FCOJ. This new product because of the higher shipping and storage costs than FCOJ is estimated to cost three times more to produce than an equivalent quantity of frozen concentrated juice.[57] But NFC is better accepted in the traditional North American and European international markets for its quality and taste and by the end of the first decade of the twenty-first-century NFC juice had become a significant export.

Brazil also now took an increasing share of Chilled orange juice (Single strength or NFC) which had come to dominate the US and European Market. Brazil averaged 67% of the value of total world exports by the decade of 2000–2009, and still accounted for 51% on average in the following decade. In contrast, the United States averaged just 12% of the market in 2000–2009 and only averaged 8% in the latest period. Many of the new juice exporting countries that entered the market in the last decade, such as the Netherlands, and Belgium, grow no oranges and in fact obtained their juice from Brazilian orange producers via Brazilian processors.[58] Thus they import most of their juice from Brazil and reprocess it.[59] Also, declining Florida production has led to an increasing mixture of Brazilian imported juice in United States juice production.[60] After several periods of boom and bust, the United States entered a new period of long-term secular decline in 2005 and production fell to just 4.1

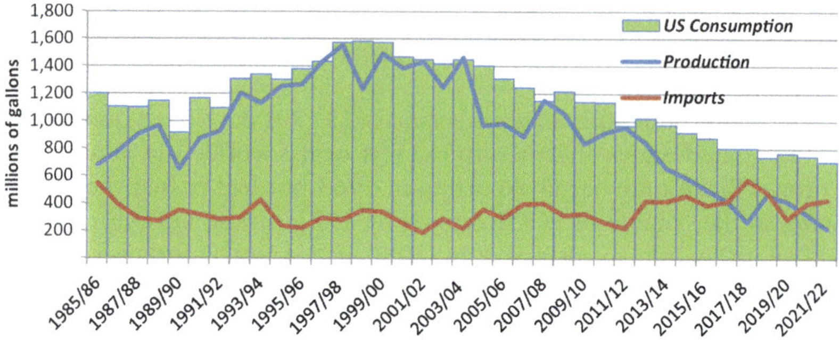

Graph 7.8 U.S. production, consumption, and importation of NFC orange juice, 1985–2022 (*Source* USDA Fruit and Tree Nut Yearbook, 2022, table g-32)

million metric tons in the harvest year 2021/2022, this compared to 16 million tons produced in Brazil in the same harvest year.[61] Although US per capita consumption of orange juice has slowly declined in the current century, Florida producers could no longer supply the national market. Brazil's exports thus supplied the US market, and even today Brazilian juice still accounts for over half of US imports and in turn imports account for an average of 51% of national orange juice consumption in the past five years (see Graph 7.8).[62]

But tariff and anti-dumping constraints enacted by the US government, eventually forced Brazilian producers to locate in the United States and to become major processors in the Florida market. Thus by 2020, the largest orange processor in Florida was Citrosuco, with Cutrale the third largest and Dreyfuss the fourth, out of six major producers by 2020. Altogether these Brazilian-based firms account for over 60% of Florida orange juice processing, and in turn Florida accounts for 98% of US juice production. Brazil also is the leading importer of orange juice to the United States supplementing North American production.[63] Brazil has thus become a major external supplier for the US orange juice market as well as the principal processor of US national production. It has also competed with the United States in exports of orange juice to Canada, though NAFTA shifted the market in favor of US imports.[64] Although a decade behind Florida in production and exports, by the 1970s Brazil completely dominated the world markets for frozen orange concentrate (see Graph 7.9).

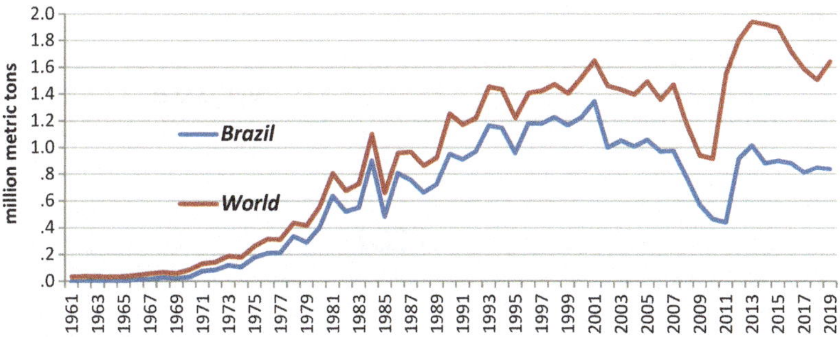

Graph 7.9 Volume of Brazilian and world exports of concentrated orange juice, 1961–2019 (*Source* FAOSTAT, at http://www.fao.org/faostat/en/#data/TP)

But it took longer to develop the NFC market because of the high cost of entry. Between the land, port and sea containers and ships needed to be developed it was not until the season of 2001/2002 that Brazil finally began to export the new style of chilled orange drink.[65] It nevertheless slowly increased its share both in the value and volume of Brazilian exports, but still accounts for only 30% of both types of juices by the third decade of the twenty-first century (see Graph 7.10a and b).

The bulk of the exports of Brazilian Juice was made up of NFC juice, which retained all its water, but the majority of the income came from the Frozen concentrate exports. In the harvest seasons from 2016–2022 Frozen concentrate made up on average 59% of the value of total exports, but only 22% of the total volume. Thus the average price per ton of FCOJ was US$1.66, as opposed to NFC which was 34 cents per ton (see Table 7.2).

By the harvest of 2021/22, Brazil turned 301 million boxes of oranges into orange juice (or 1.02 million tons of juice). Of these oranges, two thirds will be made into frozen concentrate FCOJ and one third into NFC orange juice—which has become the more or less normal ratio in the modern period. São Paulo growers account for over 90% of the oranges crushed for juice in the past three seasons as well as 90% of the juice exported.[66] While as expected the US, Belgium, and the Netherlands took 98% of the quantity of Brazilian NFC juice exported, what is surprising is that the Netherlands and Belgium took 41% of the quantity

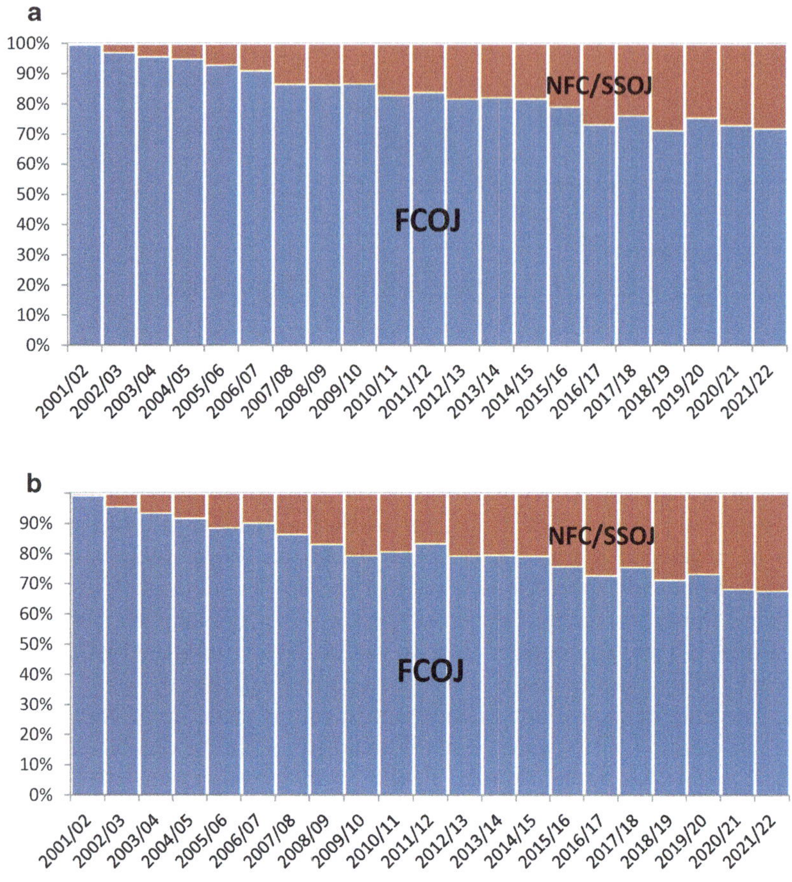

Graph 7.10 (**a**) Share of the volume of total Brazilian orange juice exports by type of orange juice 2001–2021. (**b**) Share of the value of total Brazilian orange juice exports by type of orange juice 2001–2021 (*Source* CITRUSBR at https://citrusbr.com/estatisticas/exportacoes/)

of FCOJ, with the rest going to the Asian and Middle Eastern countries, with China taking 21% of such exports.[67] This suggests that while the United States almost exclusively imported NFC for the American market, and while Asian producers were now a major market for FCOJ,

Table 7.2 Brazilian exports in volume (tons) and value (USD) by type of juice, 2016–2022

Crop Year	*FCOJ*		*NFC*	
July/June	*Value*	*Qty*	*Value*	*Qty*
2016/2017	$749,521,000	420,017,000	$444,292,000	1,317,745,000
2017/2018	$1,045,330,000	581,423,000	$514,710,000	1,505,009,000
2018/2019	$620,164,000	320,671,000	$487,754,000	1,484,426,000
2019/2020	$683,149,000	433,537,000	$464,936,000	1,371,151,000
2020/2021	$520,121,000	382,033,000	$474,657,000	1,485,030,000
2021/2022	$556,675,000	368,471,000	$528,732,000	1,502,924,000
Average	$695,826,667	417,692,000	$485,846,833	1,444,380,833

Source Annual December issues of USDA, FAS, *Citrus Annual Brazil*

that Europe remained an important market for that older FCOJ product much of which went into mixed fruit drinks.

Given the better quality of the NSF product, it is surprising that frozen concentrate has maintained its dominance in Brazilian exports. Thus NFC is the primarily consumed orange juice bought in Europe and North America.[68] But the growth of new consuming classes in the BRICS and other developing countries which have acquired a taste for orange juice, accept FCOJ juice because of their cheaper cost and longer shelf life than NFC juices.[69] Also, these cheaper FCOJ juices were used in all mixed fruit drinks and sodas which have been expanding in developing and advanced country markets. Thus after an initial abrupt shift in European and US consumer demand for NFC juice, which initially depressed FCOJ production, in the late 2010s frozen concentrate exports have continued to grow and even still remained an important part of the European market.

Although international trade data appears to suggest that Brazil is not as dominant in NFC or Single Strength Juice exports as in FCOJ, in fact, it is even more dominant since the leading countries in terms of export competition are Belgium, the Netherlands and Germany, none of which produce oranges and thus get all their juice from Brazil. Brazil's two major rivals in terms of volume of juice production were Mexico and the United States who equally are consumers and exporters of this product. But most of their production is consumed in the United States and Canada.[70] Also, their total exports are relatively minor, accounting for only 12% of the volume of NFC exports in 2019 (see Graph 7.11).

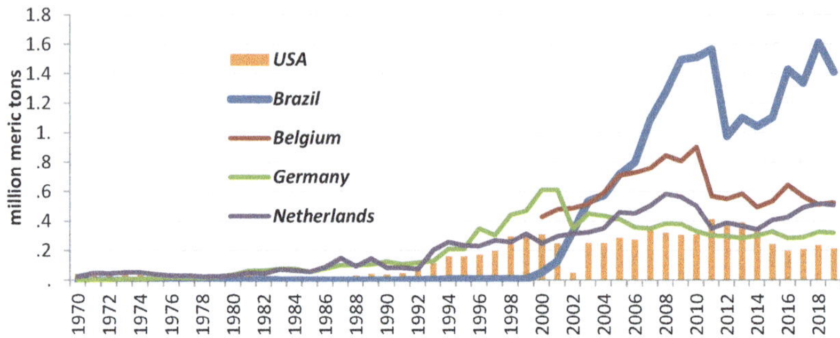

Graph 7.11 Volume of NFC/SSOJ exports by major exporting countries, 1970–2019 (*Source* FAOSTAT at http://www.fao.org/faostat/en/#data/TP)

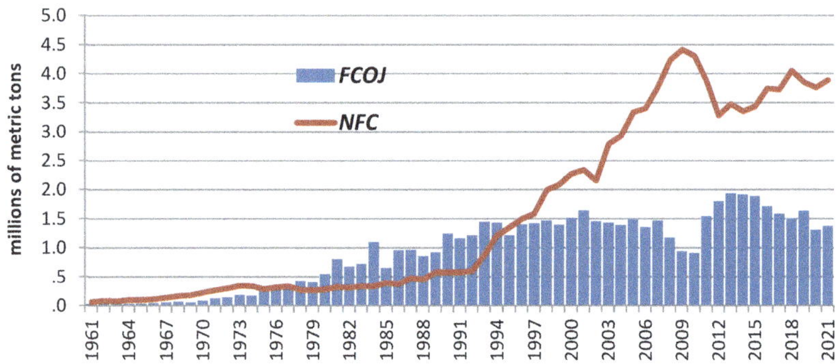

Graph 7.12 Comparisons of volume of world exports of Frozen Concentrate and Chilled (NFC) orange juice, 1961–2019 (*Source* FAOSTAT at http://www.fao.org/faostat/en/#data/TP)

This change in the balance of both types of juices was also reflected in the volume of world exports in this period. From the mid-1990s frozen concentrate dominated the market, but that changed in the first years of the century as non-frozen juice took an ever-increasing share of international markets.[71] But the rapid growth of NFC slowed in the last years of the decade of the 2010s and frozen concentrate has slowly stabilized in export volume (see Graph 7.12).

In terms of world volume, Brazil accounted for 2 million metric tons of the two types of orange juice in 2020, or 40% of the world output of

Table 7.3 Major producers of single strength and concentrate orange juice in 2020 (metric tons)

Producers	*NFC*	*FCOJ*
Brazil	1,323,301	720,595
Belgium	605,618	152,802
Netherlands	481,883	147,270
Germany	309,175	3,774
Spain	266,477	12,403
USA	219,135	38,855
Mexico	173,259	898
Other	380,146	234,069
World	3,758,994	1,310,666

Source FAOSTAT at https://www.fao.org/faostat/en/#data/TCL

NFC in that year and 55% of frozen juice concentrate in the same period (see Table 7.3). Although such countries as Spain, the US, and Mexico mostly processed their own oranges, such major producers as Belgium, Germany and the Netherlands, derived much of the juice they processed from Brazilian oranges.

Even significant producers of NFC/SSOJ obtained most of their juice from Brazil. This can be seen when examining the production and trade of the major European producers. In the European market single strength juice has become the major product produced and exported by these EU producers. But except for Spain, there is little relation between their production and exports. In fact most of the exports are made possible by Brazilian imports. Evidently the major exporters and producers in the European Union could not satisfy both their internal demand and their exports based on their own production of either type of juice Thus these European exporters are really packagers of Brazilian juice (see Table 7.4).[72] In the most recent season for which data is available (2021/2022 July–June) Brazil exported 1.871 million tons of orange juice valued at USD$1.085 billion dollars. FCOJ made up 51% of the value of these exports, but accounted for only 20% of the volume. Thus the value of FCOJ was 66 cents per ton, compared to 35 cents per ton for the far more voluminous NFC juice. Belgium, the US, and the Netherlands took 51% of the FCOJ and China and Japan another 27%. The United States alone took 42% of the Brazilian NFC exports and Belgium and the Netherlands took 55% of the total.[73]

In this question of consumption and trade, Brazil is rather unique in using very little of its orange juice production for its domestic market. Brazil on average exported 100% of its NFC, but kept 3% of its FCOJ for the home market in the five-year period from 2015–2019. In this period its exports of all these types of juices amounted to 76% of world exports. This can clearly be seen in the destination of oranges in the past decade. On average the home market consumed 30% of the national production of oranges and juice processing plants consumed 70%, of which over 97% was exported (see Table 7.5).[74]

Why Brazil and above all why São Paulo should have become the leading center both of oranges and then of orange juice production in the world of course had to do with local climate and soils. But its citrus industry also benefited from governmental financial support and the well-integrated logistics structure that existed for the state's exports of coffee, rather than from its initial productivity, which was quite low. Until 1980 its orchards were no more productive than the world average, and overall it differed little from Spain. It was only after that date that it passed the world average yield of oranges per ton, and only became more productive than any other producer including the United States in the past few years.

Table 7.4 Average annual production and trade of orange juice in Europe and Brazil, 2014–2018 (in metric tons)

Country/ Product	*Produced*	*Imported*	*Exported*
Belgium			
FCOJ	14,416	281,346	180,577
NFC	11,505	756,367	550,078
Germany			
FCOJ	0	114,693	8,091
NFC	58,414	324,409	306,608
Netherlands			
FCOJ	0	286,627	159,121
NFC	8,569	452,180	437,648
Spain			
FCOJ	48,914	40,433	15,955
NFC	232,561	38,141	224,594
BRAZIL			
FCOJ	918,838	22	867,806
NFC	1,304,766	3,900	1,304,593

Soruce FAOSTAT at http://www.fao.org/faostat/en/#data/SD

All this was due to active government intervention in the state and national governments which promoted the modernization of São Paulo agriculture. The first was the desire of the state government in the twentieth century to find an alternative to the coffee fazendas which were in a permanent state of crisis due to periodic overproduction and the move of coffee producers to other states. State research and government financing helped to replace coffee trees with orange trees. This production soon met the needs of a growing national market, but like coffee, soon outpaced the ability of that market to absorb production. Second was the existence of a complex credit and transport infrastructure which already existed for coffee, the other principal São Paulo permanent crop. Not only was credit readily available, but also in contrast to other agricultural centers in Brazil, the costs of transport were modest for São Paulo producers. Finally of great importance was major federal funding which under the federal agricultural research center Embrapa provided basic research on trees, crops and diseases, but was also crucial in constructing all the earliest juice factories, just as it would be with the first cellulose factories as well.[75] Government industrial policies, as elaborated by the BNDES development bank, were thus a key component in explaining the development of São Paulo into a world leading orange and juice

Table 7.5 Fresh orange production and use in Brazil, 2011/2012–2022/2023

Crop year	*Production metric tons*	*Processing into juice*	*Fresh domestic consumption*
2011/2012	20,482,000	65%	35%
2012/2013	16,361,000	67%	33%
2013/2014	17,870,000	66%	34%
2014/2015	16,716,000	69%	31%
2015/2016	14,414,000	66%	34%
2016/2017	20,890,000	77%	23%
2017/2018	15,953,000	69%	31%
2018/2019	19,298,000	74%	26%
2019/2020	14,870,000	68%	32%
2020/2021	14,676,000	69%	31%
2021/2022	16,932,000	73%	28%
2022/2023[a]	16,542,000	72%	28%
Average	17,083,667	70%	31%

Notes [a]Estimate
Source USDA *Citrus: World Markets and Trade*, July 2016, January 2021 & January 2023

producer. Finally the long-term trade relations between the United States and Brazil through the coffee trade, allowed Brazil to become the chief importer of orange juice to the United States, with a US company even providing technical assistance to Brazilian producers in the earliest phase of the Brazilian orange juice industry.

Once developed, the orange juice industry had unusual characteristics compared to most other agricultural products. The structure of the Brazilian and international markets for orange juice of all kinds has become highly monopolistic, especially after the introduction of NFC juices in the current century. Three firms dominate juice production in Brazil and even had a significant share of orange-producing orchards. This has led to constant conflicts between producers and the three major processors.[76] But it has also led these highly capitalized national and trading companies to dominate the specialized world shipping of juice and even participate in the processing of it in European, North American, and Asian ports. Even in the final delivery of juice to market, there is a very monopolistic situation. It is estimated that 35 Bottling companies account for 80% of orange juice sales—and the 10 largest accounted for 52% of sales.[77]

While monopoly conditions may affect prices and profits, even more important is the question of overproduction. Orange crops are highly variable in terms of production, but consumption of juice and oranges is moderately stable. This explains the high volatility of prices since they depend on production and non-sold stock, which can vary dramatically yearly due to climatic conditions or periodic problems of overproduction due to planting decisions several years in the past. This is a classic problem unique to permanent crop production, and was a constant theme in the history of Brazilian coffee production. Especially in the past decade, bumper national crops and world consumption of juice that is flat or declining have led to ever-higher stocks and lower prices. There also have been important changes recently in consumption with European and North American consumers not only shifting to new NSF products but also reducing their intake of orange juice in general, while developing countries and Asia have been slowly increasing their consumption initially with FCOJ produced juice.

This history of the orange production and juice processing industry in Brazil is a complex story of shifting local production, government and private investments and fortuitous market changes due to changing climate conditions. Without the frosts which systematically attacked and reduced Florida production, and then the tree diseases, there would have been no way for Brazil to have become such a significant producer and competitor. At the same time once it had replaced Florida, Brazilian producers were able to rapidly increase productivity. This productivity increase was found in almost all the major seasonal and other permanent crops as well. This was a generalized pattern in Brazilian agriculture since the 1960s and was based on major government and private research initiatives, as well as the systematic support of the government for both producers and the construction of processing plants. This systematic support from the 1960s until well into the current century meant that Brazil was able to modernize all aspects of juice production, from better producing and disease resistant trees to the development of a complex world transport infrastructure for processed juice to be shipped throughout the world.

Notes

1. Marcos Fava Neves and Vinícius Gustavo Trombin, eds., *The Orange Juice Business: A Brazilian Perspective* (Netherlands: Wageningen Academic Publishers, 2012), 12; USDA, *Citrus: World Markets and Trade*, January, 2022, 10–12.
2. John McPhee, *Oranges* (New York: Macmillan, 1967), 6.
3. J. Barbosa Rodriques, *Hortus fluminensis; ou, Breve noticia sobre as plantas cultivadas no Jardim Botanico do Rio de Janeiro para servir de guia aos visitantes* (Rio de Janeiro: Typ. Leuzinger, 1894), 51.
4. Herbert John Webber and Leon Dexter Batchelor, *The Citrus Industry: History, World Distribution, Botany and Varieties* (2 vols, Berkeley: University of California Press, 1967), I, 23.
5. Webber and Batchelor, *The Citrus Industry*, I, 529–530.
6. Ana Claudia Giannini Borges and Vera Mariza H. de Miranda Costa, "A evolução do agronegócio citrícola paulista e o perfil da intervenção do estado," *Revista Uniara*, no. 17/18 (2005/2006): 103.
7. Borges and Costa, "A evolução do agronegócio citrícola paulista," 104.
8. Maria Ann Najm Chalita, "Cultura, Política e Agricultura Familiar: a identidade sócio-profissional de empresário rural como referencial das estratégias de desenvolvimento da citricultura paulista" (PhD thesis, Porto Alegre, Universidade Federal de Rio Grande do Sul, 2004): 106–110.
9. Orlando Martinelli Júnior, "A Agroindustria Citrícola no Estado de Sao Paulo," *Estudos Economicos*, 19, no. 2 (1989), 285, table 2.
10. Orlando Martinelli Jr., "O complexo agroindustrial no Brasil: um estudo sobre a agroindústria citrícola no Estado de São Paulo" (MA thesis, FEA/USP, 1987).

11. Webber and Batchelor, *The Citrus Industry*, I, 88–91.
12. See for example, Airan Miguel Dos Santos Pantal and Valter Rubens Alcantara Santos Sobrinho, "Agronegócio da citricultura sergipana entre 2010 a 2017," *Citrus Research & Technology*, 40 (2019): 1–9.
13. Marcos Fava Neves, Vinicius Gustavo Trombin, Lourival Carmo Monaco Neto, and Rafael Bordonal Kalaki, *Orange Juice Chain Past, Present and Future* (Western Cape, SA: KAAP-AGRI, 2019), 56, found at https://www.fruit-processing.com/wp-content/uploads/2019/04/OJC_Neves_et_al_2019.pdf.
14. Luiz Fernando Paulillo and Ana Claudia Vieira, *Agroindústria e citricultura no Brasil: diferenças e dominâncias* (Editora E-papers, 2006), 20–21. The regions and municípios defined by the association of Citrus growers as the principal orange producers of Brazil are found in Fundecitrus, *Inventário de árvores e estimativa da safra de laranja 2019/20*, 23, quadro 1.
15. Herbert S. Klein and Francisco Vidal Luna, *Feeding the World: Brazil's Transformation into a Modern Agricultural Economy* (New York: Cambridge University Press, 2018), 54.
16. Webber and Batchelor, *The Citrus Industry*, I, 121, table 18.
17. Marcos Fava Neves and Vinícius Gustavo Trombin, eds., *The Orange Juice Business, A Brazilian Perspective* (Netherlands: Wagenigen Academic Publishers, 2011), 13.
18. This includes bearing and non-bearing (new) trees. USDA, FAS, *Citrus Annual Brazil*, December 16, 2022 (BR2022-0061), table 1.
19. Marcos Fava Neves, Vinícius Gustavo Trombin, and Rafael Bordonal Kalaki, "Peeling Back the Citrus in Brazil: Mapping and Quantification of the Brazilian Citrus Chain," *Citrus Research & Technology*, 35, no. 2 (2017): 22.
20. CONAB, *Laranja - Análise Mensal - Abril-Maio-2020*, gráfico 2, found at https://www.conab.gov.br/info-agro/analises-do-mercado-agropecuario-e-extrativista/analises-do-mercado/historico-mensal-de-laranja/item/13587-laranja-analise-mensal-abril-maio-2020.
21. Citrusbr, "Reestimativa da safra de laranja 2022/23 do Cinturão Citrícola de São Paulo e Triângulo/Sudoeste mineiro – cenário em dezembro/2022," at https://www.fundecitrus.com.br/pdf/pes_relatorios/1222_Reestimativa_da_Safra_de_Laranja.pdf.
22. Ivar Antonio Sartori, Otto Carlos Koller, Sergio Francisco Schwarz, Renar João Bender, and Gilmar Schäfer, "Maturação de frutos de seis cultivares de laranjas-doces na depressão central do Rio Grande do sul," *Revista Brasileira de Fruticultura*, 24, no. 2 (2002): 364.
23. Fedecitrus, "Reestimativa da safra de laranja 2019/20 do cinturão citrícola de São Paulo e Triângulo/Sudoeste mineiro – fechamento em

abril/2020," found at https://www.fundecitrus.com.br/pdf/pes_relatorios/0420_Reestimativa_da_Safra_de_Laranja.pdf.

24. Neves, Trombin, and Kalaki, "Peeling Back the Citrus in Brazil," 55–56.
25. IBGE, *Sinopse do Censo Demográfico 2010*, table 2.
26. Klein & Luna, *Feeding the World*.
27. Alissa Hamilton, *Squeezed: What You Don't Know About Orange Juice* (New Haven: Yale University Press, 2009), chapter 2. Until 1942 California had been the leading producer of oranges, primarily using irrigation as their source for water. But Florida's heavy rains made it an idea state for this production and by 1942 it had passed California production to become the leading producer of oranges. McPhee, *Oranges*, 10–11.
28. USDA, NASS, *Agricultural Statistics 2000* (Washington, DC: GPO, 2000), v-14, tab 5–29.
29. USDA, NASS, *Agricultural Statistics 1970* (Washington, DC: GPO, 1970), 266, tables 325 and 326; USDA, NASS, *Agricultural Statistics 1980* (Washington, DC: GPO, 1980), 222–223, tables 323 and 325.
30. Hamilton, *Squeezed: What You Don't Know About Orange Juice*, chapter 3.
31. Susan L. Pollack, Biing-Hwan Lin, and Jane E. Allshouse, *Characteristics of US Orange Consumption* (US Department of Agriculture, Economic Research Service, 2003), 2 table 1 for data on consumption.
32. On the early post war history of the Florida orange production see Raymond E. Crist, "The Citrus Industry in Florida," *The American Journal of Economics and Sociology*, 15, no. 1 (October 1955): 1–12; for the pre-war period see James Padgett, "Rebuilt and Remade: The Florida Citrus Industry, 1909–1939" (MA thesis, University of Central Florida, 2018) found at https://stars.library.ucf.edu/cgi/viewcontent.cgi?article=7736&context=etd.
33. On the impact of greening disease, called Huanglongbing (or HLB), on Florida production, see Ariel Singerman and Pilar Useche, "Impact of Citrus Greening on Citrus Operations in Florida," *EDIS* [University of Florida, Institute of Food and Agricultural Sciences (IFAS)], no. 2 (2016): 1. Apparently Florida growers did not destroy the infected trees which meant that the disease could not be controlled and is still active in the state. See Jim Graham, Tim Gottwald, and Mamoudou Setamou, "Status of Huanglongbing (HLB) Outbreaks in Florida, California and Texas," *Tropical Plant Pathology*, 45 (2020): 265. The citrus canker disease has affected Florida groves since the early twentieth century, with a major new outbreak in 1984. See Tim S. Schubert, Shabbir A. Rizvi, Xiaoan Sun, Tim R. Gottwald, James H. Graham, and Wayne N. Dixon, "Meeting the Challenge of Eradicating Citrus Canker in Florida—Again," *Plant Disease*, 85, no. 4 (2001): 344.

34. USDA, *Citrus: January Forecast*, January 12, 2023, found at https://www.nass.usda.gov/Statistics_by_State/Florida/Publications/Citrus/Citrus_Forecast/index.php.
35. On the special climatic reasons for Florida dominance in juice production see Kathleen A. Miller and Michael H. Glantz, "Climate and Economic Competitiveness: Florida Freezes and the Global Citrus Processing Industry," *Climatic Change*, 12 (1988): 135; for the estimates of decline see Jeff Luckstead and Stephen Devadoss, "Trends and Issues Facing the U.S. Citrus Industry," *Choices*, 36, no. 2 (2021): 1–2.
36. Chris Foster, Andrew McMeekin, and Jospehine Mylan, "The Entanglement of Consumer Expectations and (Eco) Innovation Sequences: The Case of Orange Juice," *Technology Analysis & Strategic Management*, 24, no. 4 (2012): 396.
37. Orlando Martinelli Júnior, "O complexo agroindustrial no Brasil: Um estudo sobre a agroindústria citrícola do Estado de São Paulo" (MA thesis, FEA/USP, São Paulo, 1987): 104; Ary Apparecido Salibe, Teófilo Sobrinho, and G. W. Müller, "Sinopse de conhecimentos e pesquisas sobre a laranja 'Pêra'," *Laranja*, 23, no. 1 (2002): 231. The greening disease HLB only appeared in São Paulo in 2005, and has so far had a moderate impact despite lack of eradication programs. See José Belasque Jr., José Carlos Barbosa, Cícero Augusto Massari, and Antônio Juliano Ayre, "Incidência e distribuição do huanglongbing no estado de São Paulo, Brasil," *Citrus Research & Technology*, 31, no. 1 (2017): 1–9.
38. USDA, NASS [National Agricultural Statistics Service], Florida Field Office "10/07/11: Forecasting Florida's Citrus Production (Brochure)," and USDA, NASS, Florida Field Office, "Commercial Citrus Inventory Prelim. Report; 2020, October 26. 2020," found at https://www.nass.usda.gov/Statistics_by_State/Florida/Publications/Citrus/index.php. For the Brazilian data see IBGE, *Sidra*, table 1613.
39. USDA, *Cirtus Fruits Summary 2021* (September), p. 8; Fundecitrus, *Inventário de árvores e estimativa da safra de laranja 2020/21 do cinturão citrícola de são paulo e triângulo/sudoeste mineiro* (Araraquara: Fundecitrus, 2021), 32, table 4, found at https://www.fundecitrus.com.br/pdf/pes_relatorios/2020_06_25_Invent%C3%A1rio_e_Estimativa_do_Cinturao_Citricola_2020-20211.pdf.
40. Christian Lohbauer, "O Contencioso do Suco de Laranja entre Brasil e Estados Unidos na OMC," *Revista Política Externa*, 20, no. 2 (2011): 1.
41. Dhamodharan, Mahalingam, Stephen Devadoss, and Jeff Luckstead, "Imperfect Competition, Trade Policies, and Technological Changes in the Orange Juice Market," *Journal of Agricultural and Resource Economics* (2016): 190; Christian Lohbauer, "O Contencioso do Suco de Laranja entre Brasil e Estados Unidos na OMC," *Politica Externa*, 20 (Set. 2011): 113.

42. By the 1990s it was estimated that Brazil accounted up to 90% of US juice imports, and Mexico only 10% even after NAFTA. Manuel Angel Gómez Cruz and Rita Schwentesius Rindermann, *La Agroindustria de naranja en México* (Mexico, 1997): 36.
43. Jeff Luckstead, Stephen Devadoss, and Ron C. Mittelhammer, "Imperfect Competition Between Florida and São Paulo (Brazil) Orange Juice Producers in the U.S. and European Markets," *Journal of Agricultural and Resource Economics*, 40, no. 1 (January 2015): 164–178; Mark G. Brown, "European Demand for Orange Juice" (Research Paper 2010-5, Florida Department of Citrus): 1, found at https://ageconsearch.umn.edu/record/104349/files/RP%202010-3.pdf.
44. Brunna da Silva Santos, Natália Patto, and Thais Duarte Tavares, "Exportação de suco de laranja pelo porto de Santos," found at https://fateclog.com.br/anais/2019/EXPORTA%c3%87%c3%83O%20DE%20SUCO%20DE%20LARANJA%20PELO%20PORTO%20DE%20SANTOS.pdf.
45. For the creation of the "blockchain" id on Brazilian made juice (which shows the origins of the fruit to consumer) see https://www.aholddelhaize.com/en/sustainable-retailing/sustainability-strategy/our-healthy-and-sustainable-ambition-2025/product-safety-and-sustainability/albert-heijn-uses-blockchain-to-make-orange-juice-production-transparent/.
46. Marcos Fava Neves, *Food and Agribusiness in 2030: A Roadmap* (Netherlands: Wageningen Academic Publishers, 2020); for the details of the logistics see Tetra Pak, *The Orange Book* at https://orangebook.tetrapak.com/chapter/transport-and-handling-bulk-product.
47. Cutrale in associaton with the Safra family of Brazil bought Chiquito Brands, the US banana giant in 2015.
48. This concentration is registered in n a Herfindahl-Hirschman Index of concentration of 3,888.This index is the sum of the squares of the percentage of concentration of the leading firms in the industry. The figure calculated for Brazil is found in See Navin Yavapolkul, "Three Essays on the International Orange Juice Market" (PhD thesis, University of California, Davis, 2011), 0, table 2.1. Anything above a 2,500 level is considered by the US Justice Department to be a high concentrated industry. US Department of Justice, "Herfindahl-Hirschman-Index," found at https://www.justice.gov/atr/herfindahl-hirschman-index#:~:text=The%20HHI%20is%20calculated%20by,%2B%20202%20%3D%202%2C600.
49. Paulillo and Vieira, *Agroindústria e citricultura no Brasil*, 40.
50. Paulillo and Vieira, *Agroindústria e citricultura no Brasil*, 47–50; Fabiana Ortiz T. Mello and Luiz Fernando Paulillo, "Formas plurais de governança no Complexo Agroindustrial Citrícola: estudo de caso na microrregião de Bebedouro," *XLVI Congresso da [SOBER] Sociedade Brasileira de*

Economia, Administração e Sociología Rural, 2008 found at https://ageconsearch.umn.edu/record/108523/files/319.pdf.

51. The detailed history of foundings and acquisitions in this area is found in Ana Claudia Giannini Borges and Vera Mariza Henriques de Miranda Costa, "Fusões e aquisições no processo de evolução da indústria processadora de citros do estado de São Paulo," *XLV Congresso da SOBER*, 2007 found at https://docplayer.com.br/9248312-Fusoes-e-aquisicoes-no-processo-de-evolucao-da-industria-processadora-de-citros-do-estado-de-sao-paulo.html.
52. Neves, *The Orange Juice Business, A Brazilian Perspective*, 23, table 5.
53. USDA, Economic Research Service at https://www.ers.usda.gov/data-products/chart-gallery/gallery/chart-detail/?chartId=76267.
54. https://www.citrosuco.com.br/a-citrosuco/#do-brasil-para-o-mundo.
55. https://www.cutrale.com.br/institucional.xhtml.
56. https://www.ldc.com/br/en/who-we-are/heritage-in-brazil/; https://www.ldc.com/sustainability-report-2020/responsible-business/juice/.
57. Neves and Trombin, eds., *The Orange Juice Business*, 50–51.
58. For example Dreyfus has a major processor in Ghent. "After processing fruit at our facilities in Brazil, we transport the juice to our terminal in Santos for export. From there it sails on our own fleet of chartered ocean vessels to our terminal in Ghent, Belgium, for distribution to customers in Europe and beyond.... Upon arrival in Belgium, juice is stored in temperature-controlled silos at our storage facilities, which are among the largest in the world and capable of handling both frozen concentrate orange juice (FCOJ) and not from concentrate (NFC) orange juice in bulk and drums." https://www.ldc.com/be/en/ldc-in-belgium/.
59. Thus for example, in 2019 the Netherlands was the world's second largest exporter of FCOJ after Brazil, with exports valued at 347 million dollars, but it imported 479 million dollars of FCOJ. Even the US had a negative balance of imports over exports of 371 million dollars. Only Belgium which exported 308 billion dollars was the only one to make a profit, and then of only 38 million dollars after reducing the value of imports. Brazil of course had no imports and exported 1.4 billion dollars of FCOJ. Data from FAOSTAT at http://www.fao.org/faostat/en/#data/TP.
60. As a US government report noted: "There is a relatively high degree of substitutability between domestically produced certain orange juice and subject imports from Brazil. Four of five extractor/processors, six of seven importers, and 17 of 20 purchasers indicated that U.S.-produced FCOJM and imports of FCOJM from Brazil are either "always" or "frequently" used interchangeably. With respect to NFC, four of six extractor/processors, four of five responding importers, and eight of ten responding purchasers indicated that U.S.-produced NFC and subject imports of NFC from Brazil are either "always" or "frequently" used "interchangeably."

US International Trade Commission, *Certain Orange Juice from Brazil* (Investigation No. 731-TA-1089 (Review), April 2012, pub 4311), 13.
61. FAOSTAT at http://www.fao.org/faostat/en/#data/QC.
62. The USDA estimates that in the crop year 2022/2023, the US will produce just 125 thousand metric tons of orange juice, and import 410 thousand metric tons. USDA, *Citrus: World Markets and Trade*, January 2023, 12. In 2021/2022 Brazil supplied 50% of orange juice imports to the US and Mexico 37% Per capita US consumption declined from 5 US gallons per capital in 1985/1986 to just 2.12 gallons in this same year. USDA, Economic Research Service [ERS], *Fruit and Tree Nuts Outlook* (FTS-375 September 2022), 19; USDA, Fruit and Tree Nuts Yearbook Tables (as of November 2022), table G-40, found at https://www.ers.usda.gov/data-products/fruit-and-tree-nuts-data/fruit-and-tree-nuts-yearbook-tables/.
63. US International Trade Commission, *Certain Orange Juice from Brazil*, tables 1-5 and 1-6. Citrosuco took over processing of Tropicana Brand orange juice in the late 2010s. That means it produces 36% of all orange juice in Florida. Calculating the shares of each company, means that overall the Florida Orange processing industry is considered moderately concentrated at an HHI of 2,115 by US Department of Justice standards. These percentages calculated from table 2.1 with the Citrosuco output combined with Tropicana in Yavapolkul, "Three Essays on the International Orange Juice Market," 10.
64. Yan Liu, Richard L. Kilmer, and Jonq-Ying Lee, "Canadian Orange Juice Imports and Production Level Import Demand," *Journal of Agribusiness*, 25, no.1 (2007): 17–29.
65. Aline Zulian, Andréa Cristina Dörr, and Sabrina Cantarelli Almeida, "Citricultura e Agronegócio Cooperativo n Brasil," *Revista Elet. em Gestão, Educação e Tecnologia Ambiental*, 11, no. 11 (June 2013): 2298–2299. Also see Leda Coltro, Anna Lúcia Mourad, Rojane M. Kletecke, Taíssa A. Mendonça, and Sílvia P. M. Germer, "Assessing the Environmental Profile of Orange Production in Brazil," *International Journal of Life Cycle Assessment*, 14, no. 7 (November 2009): 656.
66. USDA, FAS, *Citrus Annual Brazil*, December 16, 2022 (BR2022-0061), table 10.
67. Calculated from USDA, FAS, *Citrus Annual Brazil*, December 16, 2022 (BR2022-0061), 14–15 tables 11, 13.
68. Neves and Trombin, eds., *The Orange Juice Business*, 29, table 6.
69. Both in production and transport, FHC is more costly than FCOJ. It is estimated that because water is still contained in NFC and removed in FCOJ, "in order to ship equivalent volumes of NFC and FCOJ, six times the volume of NFC must be shipped". See Yavapolkul, "Three Essays on the International Orange Juice Market," 3, 12.

70. Gómez Cruz and Schwentesius Rindermann, *La Agroindustria de naranja en México*, p. 41. In 2018/2019 crop year Mexico exported 89% of the juice it produced, most of it to the United States. USDA, *Citrus: World Markets and Trade*, January 2020, 10.
71. It should be noted that the FAO changed its nomenclature sometime in 2022. Thus "Juice, orange, concentrated" (FCOJ) became simply "Orange Juice concentrated" and "Juice, orange, single strength" (NFC) has become simply "Orange Juice".
72. As of the harvest year of 2021/2022 Brazil accounted for 63% of all world orange juice production. Its 970 thousand metric tons (at 65 Degrees Brix) output, compared to the 230 thousand tons produced by United States and 135 thousand produced by Mexico. The European Union was the third largest producer at 78 thousand tons. USDA, *Citrus: World Markets and Trade*, January 2022, 11.
73. USDA, FAS, *Citrus Annual Brazil*, December 16, 2022 (BR2022-0061), 14–15, table 10, 11, 13.
74. Marcos Fava Neves, Vinícius Gustavo Trombin, and Rafael Bordonal Kalaki, "Mercado brasileiro de suco de laranja: uma alternativa para mitigar os efeitos do declínio do consumo no mundo," *Citrus Research & Technology*, 35, no. 2 (2017): 62.
75. See Herbert S. Klein and Francisco Vidal Luna, "The Development of a Modern Cellulose Industry in South America," *Latin American Research Review*, 57, no. 4 (2022).
76. On the failure to pass on higher juice prices to farmers see Adriana Ferreira Silva, Geraldo Sant'Ana de Camargo Barros, and Margarete Boteon, "Price Analyses of the Brazilian Citrus Supply Chain," *Journal of Food Science and Engineering*, 7 (2017): 49–58. And on the monopolitic market see Luiz Fernando Paulillo and Marcelo Costa Neves, "Análise das estruturas de governança de compra de laranja dos maiores packing houses no estado de São Paulo," *Organizações Rurais & Agroindustriais*, 17, no. 4 (2015): 461–478; Nobuiuki Costa Ito and Decio Zylbersztajn, "Power and Selection of Contract Terms: The Case from the Brazilian Orange Juice Sector," *Revista de Administração* (São Paulo), 51, no. 1 (2016): 5–19. On the perception of growers see Fernanda Geraldini Palmieri and Margarete Boteon, "A percepção do citricultor sobre a indústria paulista de suco de laranja: parceria ou conflito?" *Citrus Research & Technology*, 39 (2018): 1–12.
77. Neves, Trombin, Neto, and Kalaki, *Orange Juice Chain*, 17, Fig. 1.

CHAPTER 8

Sugar and Ethanol

Although sugar production has been a constant in Brazilian history from the early days of the colonization, it is only in the second half of the twentieth century that Brazil has returned to being the world's largest producer and exporter of sugar along with emerging as the second largest world producer of ethanol. Although the country was a dominant producer of sugar for Europe in the sixteenth and seventeenth centuries, Brazilian exports went into relative decline in the following centuries and Brazil was virtually eliminated from the world market by the early twentieth century. It was late to adopt the centralized stream driven mills and even its production moved from region to region as it was more absorbed in satisfying its internal market than developing an export industry. It was only in the second half of the twentieth century that Brazil finally developed a modern sugar industry and it was only at the end of that century that it would become again a dominant world sugar producer.

Both the late growth of a modern sugar industry as well as its extraordinary development in the period since 1990 was due in large part to government policies. It took government support to belatedly introduce steam driven central mills in the late nineteenth and early twentieth century. But that same support led to the protection of less efficient Northeastern producers from the crisis of the 1930s to the 1990s, a period when Brazil created a regulated and protected home market and

H. S. Klein and F. V. Luna, *Brazilian Crops in the Global Market*, Palgrave Studies in Economic History,
https://doi.org/10.1007/978-3-031-38589-6_8

determined all levels of production and sale of sugar. But even in this period of protected markets, government policies of positive incentives to produce ethanol for local consumption to replace imported gasoline was a key factor in the emergence of a major ethanol industry and modernizing refineries. These government incentives began in the 1970s and returned with even greater force in the demand for flex engines in 2003. Finally the opening of the market after 1990 eliminated the regulated state structure and allowed São Paulo unlimited expansion at a time when the world sugar market itself was in transition. Thus when Cuba left the world sugar market, Brazil already had a modern milling industry, a modern cane-producing sector, and even the ability to construct its own mills. It also had the technical knowledge to create an industry capable of easily switching between sugar and ethanol production depending on market conditions.

There is no doubt that Brazil's relative position in the world sugar market changed with the growth of the West Indies producers in the early eighteenth century (see Graph 8.1). This suggested to many scholars that Brazilian sugar production had gone into a secular decline in the nineteenth century. The reality is that the Northeastern sugar economy continued to grow and expand over the next two centuries, even in terms of exports, especially after the British sugar law of 1845, which allowed for the import of non-British sugar into England. But most importantly it grew because of the internal market rather than from developing new or expanding older export markets. Its production grew steadily, though of course not as spectacularly as that of Cuba, which in the nineteenth century became the principal world producer of sugar (see Graph 8.2).

Also the growth of other agricultural exports from Brazil, first coffee, then cotton, and then natural rubber, reduced the relative importance of sugar in national agricultural exports despite the rising value of sugar exports until the end of the nineteenth century. During the nineteenth century sugar exports came primarily from Pernambuco, Bahia and Rio de Janeiro. Although exports from Rio de Janeiro began to decline after the 1830s, total sugar production continued to grow in the country for the rest of the century.[1] In addition to the traditional areas of the Northeast and the growing production that took place in Rio de Janeiro, a sugar activity also developed in São Paulo, concentrated in the so-called sugar quadrilateral area centered on Campinas. Even as coffee became dominant in the province, sugar activity was never abandoned in São Paulo. But these estates were small in comparison to Rio de Janeiro and never

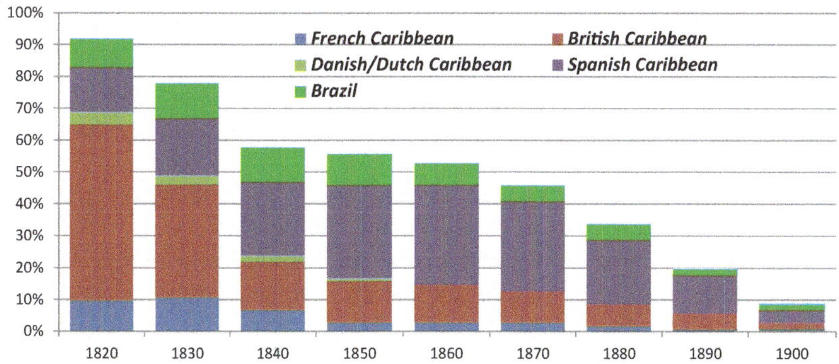

Graph 8.1 Share of world sugar export market, Brazil and selected countries, 1820–1900 (*Source* Absell, 2019, pp. 266–267)

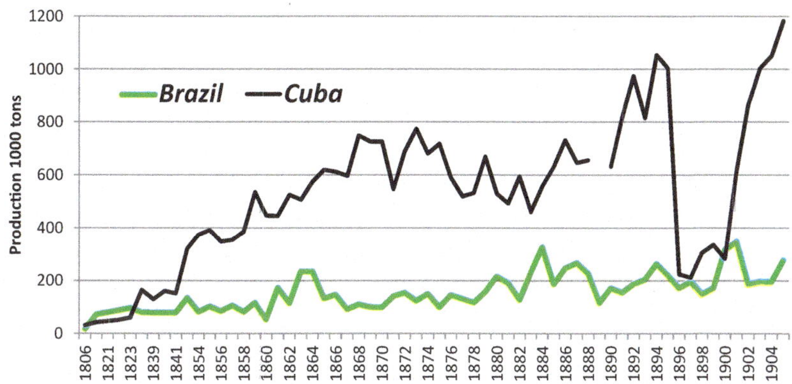

Graph 8.2 Brazilian and Cuban sugar production, 1806–1905 (*Source* Deerr, 1949, vol. 1, p. 122 e 131)

approached the size of the Northeastern plantations, and thus São Paulo remained a modest producer and exporter throughout this period.

The introduction of the so-called *usinas*, or large central mills driven by steam power, represented a revolution in the sugar production processes in the nineteenth century. By the middle of the nineteenth century these mills dominated Cuban sugar production. But Brazil was slow to adopt this new form of production. These central mills rationalized industrial production, increased productivity and maintained the competitiveness of sugar cane in the face of competition from sugar beet, whose production was spreading across Europe. Given the conditions of the international market, the survival of the Brazilian sugar industry depended on cost reduction, which, in turn, required better processing of sugar.[2]

Although numerous concessions were issued by the Brazilian government in the nineteenth century promoting the installation of central mills (called *usinas* in Portuguese), few were actually built in the period.[3] Brazil continued to produce poor quality sugar for the national and international markets until the end of the century.[4] The plantation owners continued to use their old equipment and there was no regular supply of sugarcane to the few central mills which were established. In contrast to the relationship developed in Cuba between cane producers (colonos) and the mills, which guaranteed a steady supply of cane to these large factories, in Brazil most producers could not be incorporated into a coherent system of supply.[5] The alternative was for the new modern mills themselves to produce their own cane.[6]

But in the twentieth century, the central mill soon began to dominate national production. By 1917 there were already 215 *usinas*, and they now accounted for half of the national sugar production.[7] That year, Pernambuco generated 40% of national production, Rio de Janeiro, 20%, and Alagoas, 10%. São Paulo, with only 8% of national production, was only able to supply 40% of what it needed to meet its domestic sugar demand, and had to import sugar from other parts of the country.[8] In 1939, there were 345 *usinas*, now accounting for 70% of the national sugar produced, and the rest was produced by the 18,000 *engenhos*, or traditional small mills. The survival of these old mills, despite the rapid growth of modern milling plants, shows how slow was the transition to new technology.

Because of this late transition and low international price, the systematic growth of production was stimulated by the expansion of the domestic market rather than the international market. The displacement of production to the domestic market reflected the lack of competitiveness of national production in the international market The First World War however would lead to a dramatic rise in international prices, stimulating exports and production and leading to expansion of installed modern mill capacity in the Northeast and in the Southeast. Although there was a decline in prices after 1917, exports were profitable until the mid-1920s. From 500 thousand bags in 1914, exports reached 4.2 million bags in 1922, representing 30% of national sugar production and 5% of the value of Brazilian exports. But exports in the second half of the 1920s returned to levels of ca. 500 thousand bags. As production had followed the growth of exports, with an increase from 6.6 million bags in 1914 to 15 million bags in 1914, a crisis of overproduction in the sector occurred. Once again sugar producers had only the domestic market, which grew the most in the Southeastern states (see Table 8.1).

In the first half of the twentieth century new zones that adopted modern mills gained prominence. By 1930, the Northeast's share of production had declined significantly, in favor of the Southeast states.[9] There are several reasons to explain the process of gradual transfer of production from the Northeast to the Southeast region, but perhaps easy access to the larger southeastern market was the determining factor. With the drop in the competitiveness of Brazilian sugar exports, most of the national production was newly oriented toward supplying the domestic market. The economic and demographic impacts of coffee production, especially in São Paulo, made this state the largest market for national sugar production. In 1910, for example, São Paulo produced 24 thousand tons of sugar, but needed to import another 50 thousand tons from the Northeast to satisfy local consumption.[10] As in that year national sugar production was 331 thousand tons, the state of São Paulo would have consumed about a quarter of the national sugar production,and this amount exceeded sugar exports, which totaled only 59 thousand tons.[11]

As late as 1920 the participation of the Northeast in sugar production, particularly Pernambuco, was still important. In that year São Paulo imported 83 thousand tons of northeastern sugar to supplement its own production of 56 thousand tons. The value of these sugar imports into the state was equal to the expenditures on wheat grain imported from abroad.[12] This demonstrated the opportunity to develop local production. But it is likely that the higher profitability provided by coffee initially discouraged investments in this sector.

What had been a free market until the late 1920s changed with the growing crisis of the world economy. In response to declining world and national prices the federal government in 1931 intervened to protect the sector. In addition to establishing production quotas and administered prices, it provided incentives for the production of fuel alcohol, which guaranteed use for the growing surplus of sugarcane and allowed reducing gasoline imports. The 1931 decree established the mandatory addition of 5% of anhydrous alcohol to gasoline sold in the country

Table 8.1 Production and exportation of sugar, 1900–1928

Year	*Production (sacks of 60 kg)*	*Exportation (sacks 60 kg)*	*% of production exported*	*Value of exports*	
				£1000 English pounds	*% of Brazilian exports*
1900	5,205,385	1,536,467	30%	1,431	4%
1901	5,899,587	3,119,435	53%	1,551	4%
1902	3,168,750	2,279,287	72%	936	3%
1903	3,309,300	364,816	11%	199	1%
1904	3,295,500	131,024	4%	93	0%
1905	4,647,500	629,108	14%	406	1%
1906		1,415,805		606	1%
1907		214,298		136	0%
1908		526,283		306	1%
1909		1,141,383		671	1%
1910	5,529,166	980,400	18%	679	1%
1911	5,039,500	603,467	12%	409	1%
1912	5,556,593	79,533	1%	56	0%
1913	5,964,783	88,523	1%	66	0%
1914	6,618,200	530,005	8%	373	1%
1915	6,672,216	986,170	15%	756	1%
1916	7,565,650	907,299	12%	1,306	2%
1917	8,025,364	2,302,649	29%	3,860	6%
1918	8,607,800	1,927,225	22%	5,459	9%
1919	11,587,698	1,007,147	9%	3,106	3%
1920	12,127,978	1,819,014	15%	4,973	6%
1921	14,340,872	2,868,231	20%	2,507	6%
1922	14,209,028	4,201,859	30%	3,030	5%
1923	14,371,862	2,552,910	18%	2,951	4%
1924	15,370,394	547,430	4%	680	1%
1925	12,489,362	53,031	0%	55	0%
1926	15,594,480	286,149	2%	226	0%
1927	13,986,433	807,683	6%	636	1%
1928	15,699,989	500,620	3%	571	1%

Source For production and exports: Gileno de Carli "O açúcar na Formação Econômica do Brasil"; and for value of exports: IBGE, 1986

and exempted those imports necessary for the construction of distilleries producing anhydrous alcohol from paying tariffs.[13] Like other economic sectors, the sugar and alcohol production was placed under strict control which would last until the 1990s.[14] To administer this system in 1933 it created the Institute of Sugar and Alcohol (IAA, or Instituto do Açúcar e do Álcool). The government now controlled all phases of the production, transformation, and commercialization process, even determining how much sugar cane could be produced.[15]

Another result of the world economic crisis was the negative impact it had on coffee production, which liberated land and resources from coffee to sugar and orange production within the Southeastern region. At the same time, the cost of transportation favored sugar mills being installed close to the major consumer markets and thus concentrated milling in São Paulo.[16] Thus even with the quotas of production the shift to the Southeast continued. Between the harvest of 1929/1930 and 1939/1940 São Paulo doubled its production, and now became the second largest producer after Pernambuco. At the same time, there was a decline in the share of production from the traditional *engenho* mills.[17] There was also a major increase in ethanol production (see Table 8.2); and at the end of the decade Pernambuco, São Paulo and Rio de Janeiro accounted for about 90% of its production.[18] The accelerated growth in production was caused both by incentives to mills and by direct investments by the IAA in the establishment of *usinas*. In turn anhydrous alcohol soon became the dominant form of alcohol production in the country.[19]

Public intervention in the market was undeniably effective, as production stabilized, allowing the recovery of prices.[20] The average price, which had fallen by around 40% in the first two years of the 1930s, recovered in the final years of the decade.[21] Thus by 1939 a balanced system had been established, which guaranteed profits for the Northeast producers and also provided a steady supply of sugar at reasonable prices to the richest and most dynamic states in the Southeast.

But this regulation actually favored the survival of the inefficient Northeastern producers and restrained the potential further expansion of the producers of São Paulo and Rio de Janeiro. There was a temporary boost for Paulista sugar producers during WWII due to the severe restriction of the coastal shipping industry which transported sugar from the Northeast to the Southeastern markets. This encouraged the expansion of sugar production in both Rio de Janeiro and São Paulo, to the detriment of the productive capacity of the Northeast.[22] As a consequence of these changes, Pernambuco was reduced to a 32% share of national production by the end of the 1940s, with São Paulo share now increasing to 23% and Rio de Janeiro to 16%. In this decade there had been an increase of 25% in the total national production. The domestic market continued to constitute the destination of almost all the sugar produced.

Table 8.2 Number of Usinas, and the production and export of sugar, 1929–1960

							Anhydrous alcohol	
Crop year	*Usinas*	*Production sugar (sacks)*	*Production Usinas (sacks)*	*Exports (sacks)*	*% of production exported*	*% of the value of agricultural exports*	*Prodution in liters (1000)*	*% of total Alcohol (1)*
1929/1930		19,601,272	10,804,034	1,407,302	13%			
1930/1931		16,996,145	8,256,153	184,937	2%	1%		
1931/1932		17,125,279	9,156,948	674,315	7%	0%		
1932/1933		16,269,907	8,745,779	424,500	5%	1%		
1933/1934		16,602,100	9,049,590	398,280	4%	0%	100	0%
1934/1935		16,554,703	11,136,010	1,448,197	13%	0%	3,256	7%
1935/1936	300	17,900,199	11,841,087	1,380,466	12%	1%	7,810	13%
1936/1937	302	14,996,654	9,550,214	4,960	0%	1%	14,098	25%
1937/1938	300	16,742,712	10,907,204	184,716	2%	0%	20,616	32%
1938/1939	291	18,339,728	12,702,719	805,913	6%	0%	36,505	40%
1939/1940	298	19,631,952	14,406,239	1,102,211	8%	0%	31,499	34%

Crop year	*Usinas*	*Production sugar (sacks)*	*Production Usinas (sacks)*	*Exports (sacks)*	*% of production exported*	*% of the value of agricultural exports*	*Anhydrous alcohol*	
							Prodution in liters (1000)	*% of total Alcohol (1)*
1940/ 1941	299	20,566,701	13,511,832	416,084	3%	0%	67,599	53%
1941/ 1942	297	20,881,919	13,839,083	769,248	6%	1%	70,654	55%
1942/ 1943	301	31,547,817	14,759,017	386,202	3%	0%	76,952	51%
1943/ 1944	299	21,658,742	15,314,442	963,148	6%	2%	46,660	37%
1944/ 1945	283	n.g	14,896,924	418,227	3%	0%	30,422	25%
1945/ 1946	287	n.g	15,417,553	340,515	2%	2%	26,120	25%
1946/ 1947	289	n.g	18,352,339	1,036,543	6%	1%	36,103	31%
1947/ 1948	319	n.g	22,622,512	5,698,306	25%	1%	61,517	43%
1948/ 1949	328	n.g	23,578,876	941,990	4%	2%	75,126	45%
1949/ 1950	319	n.g	21,139,508	400,433	2%	5%	30,600	23%
1950/ 1951	323	n.g	24,817,491	322,392	1%	1%	28,416	20%

(continued)

Table 8.2 (continued)

Crop year	*Usinas*	*Production sugar (sacks)*	*Production Usinas (sacks)*	*Exports (sacks)*	*% of production exported*	*% of the value of agricultural exports*	*Anhydrous alcohol*	
							Prodution in liters (1000)	*% of total Alcohol (1)*
1951/1952	319	n.g	26,595,636	741,537	3%	0%	47,997	28%
1952/1953	328	n.g	30,802,209	4,108,902	13%	2%	99,154	43%
1953/1954	326	n.g	33,375,565	2,508,678	8%	1%	144,506	53%
1954/1955	317	n.g	35,567,988	9,683,042	27%	4%	168,490	55%
1955/1956	311	n.g	35,463,770	389,691	1%	0%	165,837	59%
1956/1957	308	n.g	37,580,069	6,815,894	18%	4%	104,409	41%
1957/1958	312	n.g	44,377,638	12,936,964	29%	6%	245,098	61%
1958/1959	308	n.g	53,858,650	10,107,055	19%	5%	281,728	63%
1959/1960	307	n.g	50,864,051	14,278,663	28%	6%	302,160	64%

Note (1) share of anhydrous alcohol in relation to the total alcohol produced
Source *Anuário Açucareiro*, various years; IBGE, 2008

Even so, São Paulo could not satisfy the local market. In the 1950/1951 harvest the state of São Paulo, produced 5.7 million bags and imported 1.1 million bags. As for alcohol production, it increased by 40% over the decade, with São Paulo, Pernambuco, and Rio de Janeiro as the main producers. In addition, São Paulo by this time was the most populous state, with the largest urban population, accounting for more than half of the value of industrial production and more than a third of the national GDP.[23]

The central *usina* mills which could process their own or third-party sugarcane increased their share of national production throughout the twentieth century.[24] Although theoretically self-sufficient in sugarcane, the *usinas* usually needed to use cane supplied from independent growers. The IAA regulated these *usina* relations with cane farmers, requiring that the majority of mills use at least 40% of sugarcane from these independent farmers. It also controlled the labor relations and contracts whose terms were to be submitted to the IAA.[25]

In 1950, sugarcane was grown on 828 thousand hectares, with output fixed at 32 million tons, with an average yield of 41 tons per hectare (a relatively low productivity given that today output exceeds 70 tons per hectare). The four states of Pernambuco, São Paulo, Rio de Janeiro and Alagoas dominated cane production, while São Paulo, Pernambuco and Rio de Janeiro had the largest shares of alcohol distillers (see Table 8.3). The government's anhydrous alcohol program would be abandoned in the 1950s, due to low petroleum prices and the creation of the state petroleum company Petrobrás, which built numerous oil refineries.[26]

A new phase began slowly in the 1950s and would lead to major changes in national production and marketing in the 1990s. The 1950s began a new phase in the evolution of exports, which in the last three years of the decade absorbed a quarter of Brazilian production. The growth of the sector was reflected in the expansion of planted area, which between 1931 and 1960 grew at a rate of 4.8% per year and in production at an annual rate of 5.5%.[27] By 1960, São Paulo accounted for 27% of the planted area, 35% of the cane produced, 41% of the milled sugar, and 55% of alcohol generated. Despite the existence of production quotas, the need to meet the strong growth of the domestic market, and the resumption of exports, led the Instituto do Açúcar e do Álcool to increase the quotas of the São Paulo mills which reduced southeastern planter opposition to the quota system.[28] At the same time the crisis of overproduction of coffee, which led to a coffee plantation eradication program in the

Table 8.3 Sugar production by state in 1950

States	Production of sugar cane				Production of sugar		Usinas and enghos		Production of Alcohol		
	Area (ha)	*Production*	*ton/hec*	*% fornec*	*Production (t)*	*% usinas (1)*	*Usinas*	*Engenhos*	*Distilleries*	*Production*	*% Anidro*
Acre	1,405	56,510	40			0%		61			
Amazonas	396	10,193	26			0%		20			
Pará	4,927	120,603	24	3%	2,643	5%		37		50,476	0%
Maranhão	7,106	173,020	24	0%	3,831	9%	15	216	1	–	
Piauí	7,843	234,260	30	0%		3%	5	9	1	–	
Ceará	22,903	1,053,850	46	70%	19,410	2%	16	47	2	18,790	0%
Rio Grande do Norte	5,058	253,652	50	46%	138,185	34%	4	81	1	–	
Paraíba	31,133	1,450,740	47	52%	544,210	57%	10	50	6	1,857,744	0%
Pernambuco	151,804	5,422,832	36	47%	7,064,963	91%	65	553	41	36,310,008	44%
Alagoas	50,704	2,325,044	46	58%	1,852,179	84%	31	342	17	6,477,591	24%
Sergipe	12,235	574,157	47	36%	670,704	97%	65	95	6	394,890	0%
Bahia	43,655	2,239,564	51	28%	1,003,439	62%	21	638	3	266,522	0%
Minas Gerais	132,354	4,587,221	35	40%	896,377	17%	142	5,260	47	4,834,767	0%
Espiríto Santo	16,414	450,720	27	65%	85,904	18%	9	242	3	8,900	0%
Rio de Janeiro	80,162	3,688,276	46	64%	3,805,479	93%	46	899	16	26,451,532	19%
São Paulo	145,643	6,913,524	47	34%	6,728,348	88%	188	1,538	59	51,172,271	10%
Paraná	9,721	437,236	45	17%	346,574	9%	5	22	4	4,317,240	0%
Santa Catarina	39,573	1,012,905	26	89%	113,533	9%	6	5,362	6	836,900	0%
Rio Grande do Sul	37,692	623,448	17			0%		277	11	248,644	0%
Mato Grosso	6,623	315,930	48	32%	24,221	79%	15	37	7	49,104	0%

States	*Production of sugar cane*				*Production of sugar*		*Usinas and enghos*		*Production of Alcohol*		
	Area (ha)	*Production*	*ton/ hec*	*% fornec*	*Production (t)*	*% usinas (1)*	*Usinas*	*Engenhos*	*Distilleries*	*Production*	*% Anidro*
Goiás	20,803	726,652	35		23,483	0%	14	2,732	–	69,000	0%
BRASIL	828,162	32,670,814	39	45%	23,383,482	71%	680	18,530	241	140,094,856	20%
Norte/Nordeste	339,169	13,914,425	41	47%	11,299,564	79%	232	2,149	78	45,376,021	38%

Note (1) Data are from the crop year 1943/1944
Source Anúario Açucareiro, 1950/1951

1960s, made both skilled labor and good quality land available to the sugar sector in São Paulo.[29]

The leadership of São Paulo was reinforced by the early development of a local machinery and equipment industry housed in the state. The pioneer would be Oficina Dedini in Piracicaba, which started its activities in the 1920s, carrying out maintenance and repair of machine parts for the *usinas*. This small maintenance and repair shop soon was producing replacement parts that had previously come from abroad. In 1929, it was able to build its first complete plant and gradually incorporated new equipment in its production line, using technology developed in Europe and the United States to increase the scale of the equipment produced. It was soon able to build ever larger mills.[30] By the late 1940s the company was capable of producing all the necessary equipment for both sugar mills and alcohol distilleries, and was able to meet the needs of all national producers. The company adopted an aggressive and unusual commercial policy. To encourage the implementation or expansion of a plant, the company or its controller, sold its equipment in exchange for an equity interest in the plant, thus becoming a partner in numerous mills in São Paulo.[31] By the 1970s, competition already existed, not only from national companies but also from multinational companies. These new companies concentrated in the São Paulo municipalities of Piracicaba and Sertãozinho. Between 1970 and 1975 the turnover of companies in the sector multiplied by 6.5.[32]

There were also changes in the international sugar market which significantly affected Brazil. From the 1930s, attempts had been made to control the international market. The International Sugar Agreement of 1937 sought to define national export quotas, but there was still an expansion of world production and a new quota agreement was signed in 1953, which also had little effect, since several countries including Brazil, did not ratify the agreement.[33] The international market would also be affected in the late 1950s by the Treaty of Rome, which created the Common Agricultural Policy (CAP) in Europe, making the market more restricted for countries like Brazil.[34] In 1962, however, the sugar market would be shaken by the Cuban revolution and the breakdown of its preferential trade with the United States. Although Brazil did not obtain any US quotas, Cuban sugar was redirected to the Eastern European countries and these cheap imports progressively reduced their local beet production. Although this reorientation allowed Cuba to maintain output, the dissolution of the bloc in 1989 eventually led to a dramatic

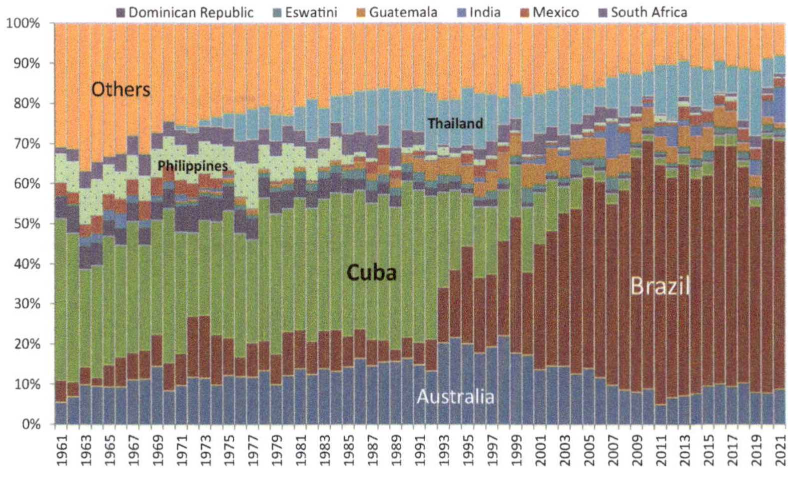

Graph 8.3 Share of volume of world exports by principal sugar producers, 1961–2021 (*Source* FAOSTAT)

fall of Cuban production which reached only 15% of its 1990 output in 2018. It was these fundamental changes in the world market which permitted Brazil to multiply its production by more than three times and devote most of that increase to exports (see Graph 8.3).

From the 1970s onward, Brazilian agricultural policy changed profoundly. The military regime restructured Brazilian agriculture, which directly affected sugar production. This included encouraging research on sugar and alcohol by Embrapa, the government agricultural research center which was established in this decade.[35] There was a wide-ranging reformulation of the IAA with greater public control and a new pro export policy, and with less concern for the preservation of the structure of the Northeastern sugar and alcohol sector. There would be greater incentives to productivity in order to reduce prices in the domestic market and generate competitiveness in the international market. Most of these new government and private investments were made in São Paulo, a region with the greatest potential for modernization and competitiveness. The programs affecting this change were the National Sugarcane Improvement Program (Planalsucar), the Sugar Industry Rationalization Program, and the Sugar Industry Support Programs. They were part of a new emphasis on the modernization of Brazilian agriculture which

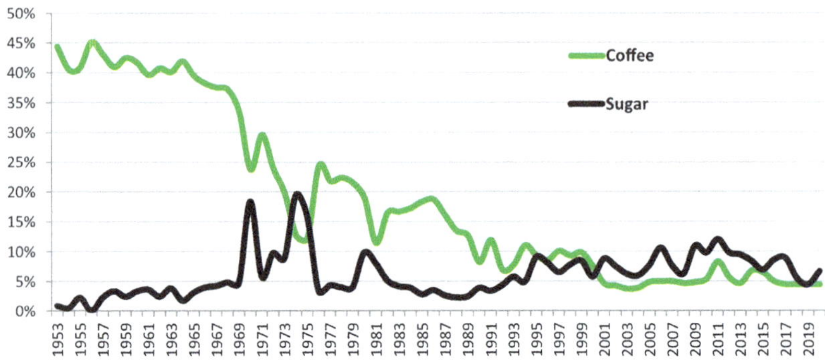

Graph 8.4 Percentage of coffee and sugar exports in total value of Brazilian agricultural exports, 1953–2020 (*Source* IBGE, Estatísticas do Século XX, 2007, and FAOSTAT)

began after 1964 as the military governments promoted rural production in order to reduce the prices of foods and promote agricultural exports to obtain divisas in its effort to develop a modern import substitution industry. This was done through subsidization of rural credit, price support, development of a government modern agricultural research program with the creation of Embrapa, and the expansion of agricultural research faculties in the universities.[36]

As a result of these policies, between 1960 and 1970 the quantity of sugar exported by Brazil more than doubled and in some years it exceeded the value of coffee exports, still the main product of the Brazilian export basket. Between 1973 and 1975, Brazilian sugar exports represented 15% of total world exports of the product and by then São Paulo represented 40% of the sugarcane planted in Brazil. By the first two decades of the twenty-first century, raw sugar exports (defined as sugar whose liquid has been eliminated by centrifugal process and is 97–99% sucrose) exceeded coffee exports as a percentage of agricultural exports (see Graph 8.4).

Government investments in agricultural research were evident in the response to the mosaic plague which attacked the Paulista sugar cane plantings in the 1960s and 1970s. The Sugar Experimental Station of Piracicaba developed new strains of cane resistant to this insect. The close relationship between a public research institution and companies in the sector was a new element in the sugar and alcohol industry. This initiative also led to a profound change in the organization of agricultural

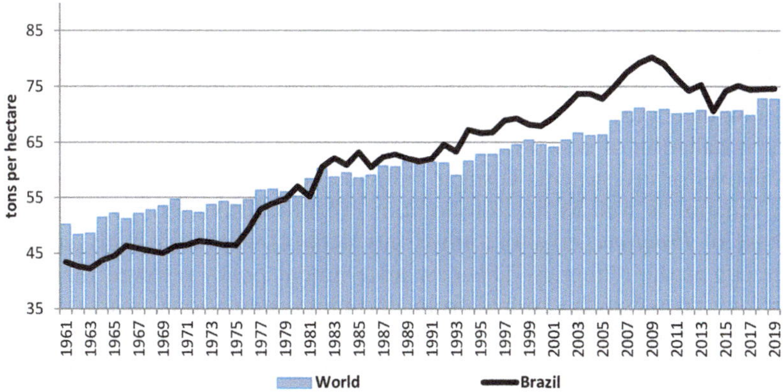

Graph 8.5 World and Brazilian rates of sugar cane productivity, 1961–2019 (*Source* Faostat)

research on sugarcane. The sugar research network created would include the Station at Piracicaba, the Instituto Agronômico de Campinas and the Copersucar Technology Center—CTC, a private institution created in 1970. The CTC worked closely with *Embrapa* and international research centers to create new varieties of sugarcane.[37] The result was that yields per hectare began to continuously increase (see Graph 8.5), and Brazil surpassed average world productivity by the 1970s. It also progressively increased yields per hectare even more rapidly in the 1990s.[38] Partnerships between the main sugar and alcohol machine industries, mainly Dedini and Zanini, with Copersucar Technological Center and the São Paulo State Institute of Technological Research (IPT) were also fundamental in creating the basis for expansion by providing the latest advances in machinery and equipment.[39]

In the second half of the 1970s the first shock in oil prices occurred, and made Brazil extremely vulnerable due to its heavy dependence on petroleum imports. Brazil imported almost 80% of its petroleum needs, and the 1973 price jump generated a deficit in the current account balance of the order of 6.8% of GDP.[40] The government responded by creating the so-called *Proálcool* program, which was to prove of fundamental importance in the transformation of the sugar and alcohol sector.[41]

The *Proálcool* program stressed the need for an automotive fuel policy. This meant that the production of alcohol from sugar cane, cassava or any other input would be encouraged through the expansion of the supply of raw materials, modernization and expansion of existing distilleries and the installation of new production and storage units. Financing was made available for investments in sugar mills able to alternatively produce sugar or ethanol as well as for autonomous ethanol distilleries.[42] In this first phase of *Proálcool*, ethanol (anhydrous alcohol) was mixed with gasoline directly at the refineries. This new government policy resolved the sugar sector's crisis which resulted from declining international market prices which had reduced the value of Brazilian sugar exports from US$1.2 billion in 1974 to US$200 million in 1976.[43] The program was initially successful, with massive investments in the sector, growth in production capacity, and increased production of sugarcane and alcohol, all made feasible thanks to technological developments in the sector since the 1960s.[44]

The success of the plan was achieved through abundant and subsidized credit. Between 1975 and 1979, projects were approved for 136 dual production units producing either ethanol or sugar, and 73 autonomous distilleries, most of which were in São Paulo.[45] Until 1979 the demand was essentially for anhydrous alcohol, used for mixing with gasoline sold to the market. Thus, between 1975/1976 and 1979/1980, production increased from 555 million liters to 3.4 billion liters. At the end of the decade, there was the second oil shock of 1979, further promoting an additional effort to replace imported fuels. Next, the government encouraged the automobile industry to produce automobiles powered exclusively by hydrated alcohol. Their success was extraordinary, and by 1983 three quarters of the cars and light commercial vehicles sold used this hydrated alcohol, a percentage that remained steady for several years. In addition to new motors, regular gasoline was required to contain 20% of anhydrous alcohol.[46] Thus by the harvest of 1985/1986 alcohol production reached 12 billion liters, having experienced a growth of 35% in ten years. Sugarcane production grew by 10% annually in that same period.[47] Much of this growth occurred in São Paulo, which accounted for two thirds of alcohol production. In that state, alcohol production multiplied by 21 between the mid-1970s and the mid-1980s. The program's costs to the government also came from the difference between the price paid for the two types of ethanol and the final subsidized price to the consumer. Also Proálcool was criticized for its high cost and for replacing crops essential to domestic supply by the use of land and resources for the production of sugarcane. If there were doubts in that period, the agricultural performance from the 1990s onward demonstrated that an energy program through alcohol could expand without affecting Brazilian production and exportation of other agricultural products. Increasing agricultural productivity and the economic occupation of the Center-West allowed for these results.

Given its high costs and changes in the international market for fuels, the program went into crisis by the late 1980s. The main cause was the dramatic drop in oil prices, which made the program extremely costly for the public sector which assumed the burden of the price differential. Since there is a power consumption differential between the two fuels (gasoline uses 25% less to go the same distance as ethanol fuel), alcohol was usually sold for a price around 75% of the price established for gasoline, which in turn was directly linked to the international price of oil. The country was simultaneously facing rampant inflation and a fiscal crisis making it impossible to support a program of such magnitude.[48] Moreover demand for alcohol was so high that in the harvest year 1986/1987, the consumption of anhydrous and hydrated alcohol surpassed national production, requiring their importation.[49] The demand for alcohol was maintained by the huge fleet that used only alcohol, by the government subsidies that sustained the price relation between gasoline and alcohol for the consumers, and by the payment to producers for their production costs. All this reflected the relatively low productivity of this government-regulated system. Although demand for alcohol-based automobiles slowly declined, the massive sale of such vehicles for a decade kept consumption high. Between 1980 and 1989 when 4.5 million alcohol cars were sold, and the majority of them were still in use a decade later. But by 1991 production of these cars declined to 150,000 units and was halted in 1996.[50]

A basic change began in 1990 when the government of Brazil adopted the Washington consensus and opened up its economy to the world market. This wrenching experience had a major impact on national industry and on agriculture. After the initial shock of the loss of subsidies, the agricultural sector experienced a spectacular recovery. Also the opening in the world market for new sugar exporters because of the collapse of Cuba and the rise of China now permitted a steady increase of Brazilian sugar exports. The *Proálcool* program now faced some temporary restraints, though ethanol kept being consumed in a mixture with petrol. But in the case of sugar all price and production controls were removed and the IAA and *Planalsucar* program were abolished in 1990. Also, the government freed the prices of anhydrous alcohol, sugar cane, crystal sugar, and molasses, all of which led to a new competitive phase in the industry resulting in consolidations of producers and the elimination of non-competitive ones, as well as a stimulus for increased productivity. It also resulted in increased private research. In 1997 the private sector founded *Única* an entity representing the main sugar, ethanol and bioelectricity producing companies in the Southeastern region of Brazil which were mainly located in the state of São Paulo. This organization not only defended the interests of its companies but also funded significant research and development efforts.[51]

At the beginning of the twenty-first century, the creation of flex engines, which allow the alternative use of gasoline and alcohol, represented a fundamental innovation that guaranteed a continual role for fuel alcohol.[52] The first vehicles were launched in Brazil in 2003 and allowed the use of gasoline and alcohol without any determined proportion. The consumer now had the choice of fuels based on the relative prices of the two products at each refueling. The success of these cars was enormous and by 2010 flex motors represents 90% of the automobiles and light commercial vehicles made in Brazil (Graph 8.6).

There are two types of fuel alcohol, anhydrous or "dry" ethanol, and hydrated or hydrous (also known as "wet") ethanol. The first is almost pure alcohol; the second contains about 5% water. Anhydrous or dry ethanol serves to form the mixture with gasoline in the refinery itself and was predominant in this first phase of pro-alcohol. It required a secondary process to reduce the water content. The production of hydrated, ethanol grew substantially thanks to the launch of cars powered by alcohol and then by flex-fuel engines. These two types of engines could use hydrated or "wet" alcohol. This can be seen in the changing importance of the two fuels in the current century (see Table 8.4).

Despite the years of crisis in demand for hydrated alcohol and the temporary freezing of gasoline prices after the 2008 crisis, there was a continuous growth in alcohol production due to the recovery that occurred in the production of hydrates from the second half of the 2010s. This was mainly caused by the expansion of hydrated alcohol, as well as the relative stability in the production of anhydrous alcohol. Thus, the hydrate that represented about half of the alcohol produced in the earlier period, accounted for about two thirds in the last three harvests. Although

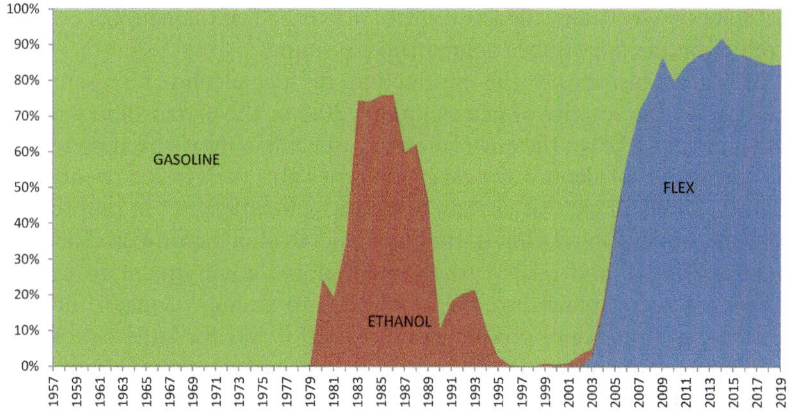

Graph 8.6 Participation of the type of engine produced in autos and light trucks, 1957–2019 (*Source* Associação Nacional dos Fabricantes de Veículos Automotores [Anfavea])

Table 8.4 Production of ethanol by type in Brazil, 2005–2021 (in thousand liters)

Harvest years	*Anhydrous*	*Hydrated*	*Total Brazil*	*% hydrated*
2005/2006	9,105,448	7,746,041	16,851,489	46%
2006/2007	8,220,716	9,211,462	17,432,178	53%
2007/2008	8,640,050	14,367,118	23,007,168	62%
2008/2009	10,063,711	16,619,714	26,683,425	62%
2009/2010	6,949,840	18,812,783	25,762,623	73%
2010/2011	8,016,983	19,578,500	27,595,483	71%
2011/2012	9,677,885	13,749,286	23,427,171	59%
2012/2013	9,852,373	13,788,092	23,640,465	58%
2013/2014	11,824,428	16,132,284	27,956,712	58%
2014/2015	11,728,042	16,931,881	28,659,924	59%
2015/2016	11,208,500	19,253,024	30,461,524	63%
2016/2017	11,072,845	16,734,678	27,807,523	60%
2017/2018	10,994,918	16,242,736	27,237,654	60%
2018/2019	9,324,469	23,027,174	32,351,643	71%
2019/2020	10,116,457	23,885,161	34,001,618	70%
2020/2021	9,321,812	20,424,611	29,746,423	69%
2021/2022 (1)	9,694,362	15,107,080	24,801,442	61%

Notes (1) Estimate
Source CONAB, "Cana-de-Açúcar – Agrícola" from November 23, 2021 at https://www.conab.gov.br/info-agro/safras/serie-historica-das-safras

the State of São Paulo still accounts for about half of the national ethanol production, its importance is gradually declining.

Although historically the production of fuel alcohol represented a response to the scarcity of petroleum (1930s) or the extraordinary rise in petrol prices (1970s), the environmental aspect has always been present in the advantages of alcohol as a clean and renewable fuel. In the twenty-first century, when Brazil was already achieving self-sufficiency in oil production, the strategy in relation to the sugar and alcohol sector would be even more ambitious and related to the new global commitment to carbon emission targets. Brazil had the conditions to become a major international player in ethanol production. By 2000 it was the largest producer and exporter of sugarcane in the world. It began significant production of ethanol in the 1970s and from 1980 to 2006 it was the world's largest producer of fuel alcohol, being replaced by the United States in that later year. Although production had continued to grow since then, it has been outpaced by the United States, and accounted for 31% of world production in 2019, and along with the United States produced 84% of the world's fuel ethanol despite over two dozen countries now producing it.[53]

But the sector soon faced one of the most serious crises in its recent history. In order to deal with the 2008 crisis, the government returned to control gasoline and diesel prices, completely distorting the relative prices of the economy and seriously affecting the production chains. Investments in the sector stopped, and companies faced serious financial problems, including the state-owned *Petrobras*.[54] By controlling gasoline prices, alcohol alone could no longer compete since it was costly to produce. The sector's crisis was profound. Flex vehicles continued to account for almost all car sales, but the preferred consumption was gasoline, mixed with ethanol, since the price of hydrated alcohol was not competitive. Thus, sales of hydrated alcohol, whose consumption grew from 4.5 billion liters in 2004 to 16.5 billion in 2009, started a downward process reaching less than 10 billion liters in 2012, replaced by gasoline mixed with ethanol. This had a major impact on prices and productivity of the industry.

Although the country maintained its leadership in sugar exports, many of the companies in the sector did not recover from the crisis. Thus in 2019, of the 444 Brazilian mills, 79 went bankrupt, 12 more than in 2018. Although there has been a process of concentration and entry of large foreign groups in the sector since the 1990s, the situation is

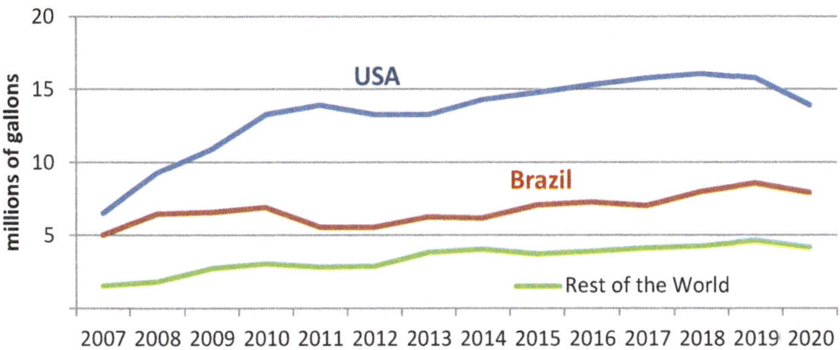

Graph 8.7 Principal world ethanol producing nations, 2007–2020 (*Source* US Dept. of Energy, AFDC, at https://afdc.energy.gov/data/search?q=production)

still relatively precarious due to the potential government intervention in prices of sugar and alcohol affecting the market. But despite this long crisis that affected the business side of the sugar and alcohol sector, this sector has maintained high rates of growth and invested in technological development throughout this century. Moreover, Brazil has steadily maintained its production of ethanol in the current century even as the United States entered the market in a major way with its corn derived ethanol. From 2007 to 2020 Brazil averaged 29% of world production, being the second in production and consistently produced more than all other world producers together (the US excluded) (see Graph 8.7).

This technical investment allowed the sector not only to produce greater quantities of sugar and alcohol through mechanization and modernization, but also to generate clean energy through the burning of sugarcane bagasse.[55] This is part of a long-term process of the industry overcoming the negative environmental aspects with which it was associated, from the discharge of *vinasse*, to the burning of sugarcane before the harvest. The *vinasse* is a residue from the distillation of the fermented sugarcane juice. For each liter of alcohol produced, 10 to 15 liters of vinasse are generated and when released in rivers was highly polluting. Since the 1970s, when the alcohol program intensified, *vinasse* has become a concern for environmental authorities. The State of São Paulo in 2005 regulated the storage, transportation, and use of *vinasse*.[56] It is now used to irrigate the cane fields, taking advantage of its potassium and other nutrients, thus reducing the consumption of fertilizers.[57]

A second negative aspect of the cultivation was the burning of the cane before the harvest, a practice to facilitate the manual work in the harvest. Its perverse effects included the emission of greenhouse gases, as well as pollution of the atmospheric air by smoke and soot, and its impact on the biological activity of the soil, altering its fertility. In addition, burning destroys part of the raw material that could be used in the production of biomass energy, which is currently becoming one of the main products of sugarcane activity.

Harvest mechanization has emerged as the alternative to burning cane. The mechanization process, which was still timid at the beginning of the twenty-first century, would be streamlined and expanded due to the contract signed in 2007 between the government of the State of São Paulo and local sugar cane producers who agreed to end the firing of the fields in all regions by 2017.[58] The resulting mechanization process was intense. The percentage of the harvest mechanized in Brazil, which was 24% in the 2007/2008 harvest, reached 92% in the 2019/2020 harvest and even 98% among the Southeastern Region producers.[59] The mechanization revolutionized labor in this industry, reducing its numbers to a small cadre of skilled and semi-skilled workers and effectively ending the use of temporary workers, the so-called "bóias-frias." The number of people employed in sugarcane farming in Brazil fell from 727 thousand in 2008 to approximately 300 thousand a decade later.[60]

Mechanization also favored the use of biomass for energy production, which today represents an important business for the sector. In 2019, sugarcane derivatives, essentially ethanol and bagasse biomass, represented 18% of the total energy generated in Brazil and 39% of the energy supply from renewable sources. Sugarcane bagasse also represented 5% of the domestic supply of electricity and of the 36.8 GWh generated from this source, 22.5 GWh were sold to the market, while the remainder was consumed in the sector's production process (see Table 8.5).

In sugar as in many of the other crops, the opening up of a major new commercial agricultural region in the current century in the Center-West region has created a new zone of sugar production. In the harvest of 2005/2006 the Center-West accounted for only 9% of the 431 million tons of sugar cane harvested in Brazil. By the harvest of 2022/2023, it made up 22% of the 637 million tons harvested and was systematically increasing its production. The role of the Northeast changed little, averaging over this same period just 9% of total production (see Graph 8.8). Of the states of the Center-West it was Goiás and Mato Grosso do Sul

Table 8.5 Internal offer of electrical energy, 2019 in thousand Tep (1)

Non-renuable	**158,395**
Renuable	**135,642**
Hydraulics and electricity	36,364
Firewood and charcoal	25,725
Sugarcane derivatives	52,841
Other Renewables	20,712
Total	294,036
Internal Offer of Electricity (GWh)	
Hydraulic	397,877
Bagasse (2)	36,827
Wind	55,986
Solar	6,655
Other Renewable	18,094
Other	110,890
Total without Imports	626,329
Imports	24,957
Total	651,285

Notes (1) TPE: toneladas equivalentes de Petróleo
(2) 22.5 TWh were surplus to the market
Source Resenha Energética Brasileira, 2019, MME, 30 May 2020

which experienced the most dramatic growth. The former went from producing 16 million tons in 2005/2006 to 72 million tons in 2022/2023, and Mato Grosso do Sul went from 10 to 45 million in the same period, while the Northeastern state of Alagoas produced a relatively stable 16 to 19 million tons in this period, replacing the former dominant Northeastern state of Pernambuco which had lower productivity and smaller sugar producing farms. Essentially sugar plantations of these new zones of the Center-West have the same productivity as those of São Paulo.[61]

Already by the harvest of 2015/2016 the Center-West had 39 sugar mills producing sugar and ethanol and 20 distilleries just producing ethanol and in contrast to São Paulo some 80% of the milled sugar cane went for ethanol production, compared to only 53% in São Paulo. Also these new mills of the Center-West owned more sugar lands, since 77% of their cane came from their own fields, whereas in São Paulo private landowners provided 38% of the cane milled.[62] If these trends continue it would appear that the Center-West will soon challenge the dominance of São Paulo not only in cane growing but also in the milling of sugar and alcohol (see Map 8.1).

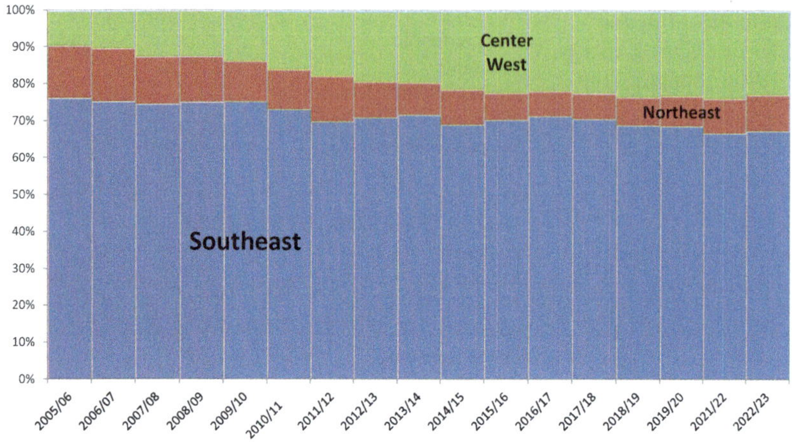

Graph 8.8 Changing regional importance in the production of sugar, 2005/2006–2021/2022 (*Source* Conab, https://www.conab.gov.br/info-agro/safras/serie-historica-das-safras)

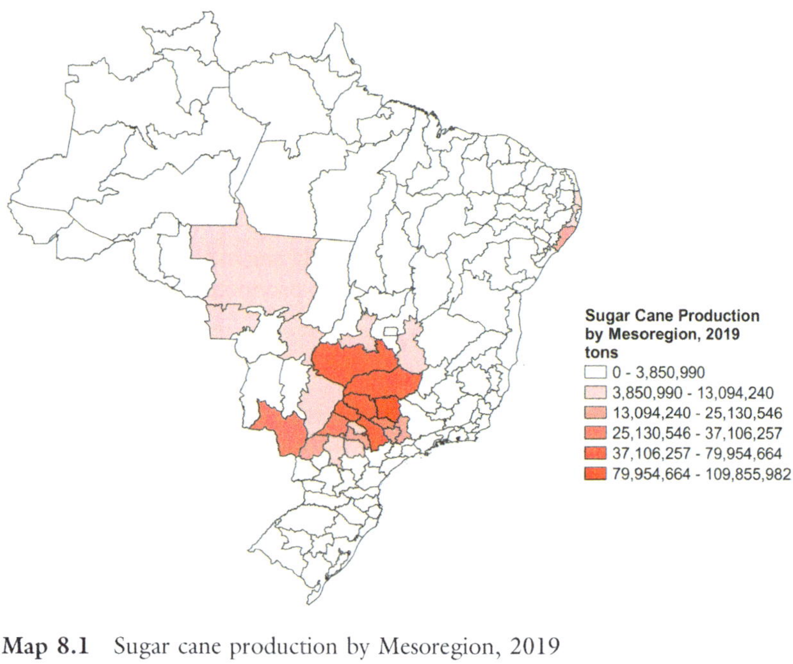

Map 8.1 Sugar cane production by Mesoregion, 2019

Not only has the Brazilian sugar-alcohol industry changed in terms of product and location, but since the 1970s, there have also been changes in the sector's business structure. Traditional family ownership has given way to corporate ownership, much of it with the control or participation of former families. There has also been the entry of major multinational groups in the sector. Although the sector is not highly concentrated, there are currently large business groups participating in the industry, concentrating numerous plants and operating in broad segments of the sector or in parallel or complementary segments. The four largest business groups in sugarcane processing are currently Raizen, operating 24 mills; BP Bunge, operating 11 mills, Atvos (ex-Odebrecht), with 8 plants and Bioserv with another 8 plants. Raizen, for example, has two plants producing second-generation ethanol, and has a network of gas stations that previously operated under the Shell brand and generates 26.9 TWh of electrical energy. BP Bunge is an association between British BP and Bunge, and produces 1.4 tons of sugar and 1.8 billion liters of ethanol. Atvos, a company currently undergoing judicial reorganization, will have a production capacity of 3 billion liters of alcohol and 700 thousand tons of sugar. Bioserv, of the Louis Dreyfus group, also produces sugar, alcohol and electricity in its 8 operating mills.[63]

By the second decade of the twentieth century Brazilian exports of centrifugal sugar represented half the value of the world exports. Especially in the second decade of the century Brazil became the dominant exporter of refined centrifugal sugar. In the decade of 2010–2020 world exports averaged US$15 billion, and those of Brazil averaged US$8 billion, which represented over half of world production (see Graph 8.9). Moreover, no other country came even close to Brazil, with Australia the second most important exporter accounting for only 8% on average in this decade.

Although China was the predominant importer of refined centrifugal sugar from Brazil, importing an average annual US$782 million worth of sugar, it was not as important for Brazilian sugar exports, as it was in the case of of beef and soybeans. A significant share of exports went to Russia, the Middle Eastern countries, other Asian countries and Nigeria (see Table 8.6). The relative weight of the importing countries can be seen in the year 2020. China accounted for just 17% of refined sugar exports from Brazil, and this appears the norm for most years in this decade. As with broiler chicken exports, a lot of the sugar exported by

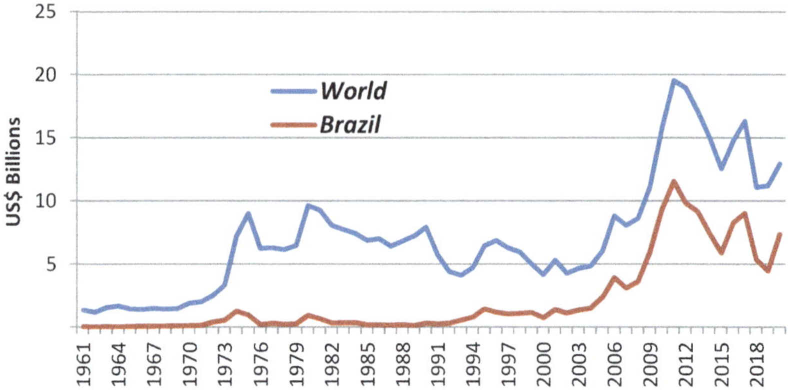

Graph 8.9 Value of centrifugal sugar exports for the world and Brazil, 1961–2020 (*Source* FAOSTAT)

Brazil went to North Africa and the Middle Eastern countries, but there were also substantial exports to North American countries and Europe.

Even though in the past few years India has emerged as a leading refined sugar exporter, it in turn is a major importer of Brazilian refined centrifugal sugar in the same period. From 2010–2020, the value of Brazilian refined centrifugal cane exports averaged US$8 billion, and these sugar exports represented 53% of the value of total world refined cane sugar exports in this period.[64]

The history of sugar and alcohol production in Brazil has gone through several distinct phases. Starting from a free market dynamic slave sugar plantation economy in the colonial and early nineteenth century, it became a relatively stagnant industry in the late nineteenth and early twentieth century. Though capable of supplying an expanding national market in the late nineteenth and early twentieth century it lost its dynamism in the international market because of its low productivity. Complete government control of the industry from production to marketing from the 1930s to the 1990s preserved less efficient Northeastern producers but at the same time was also instrumental in creating a modern ethanol refining industry. For all its high costs to the government and in terms of maintenance of inefficient regional producers, when the Brazilian market was opened to competition and government subsidization ended in the 1990s, sugar planters and mill owners were able to

Table 8.6 Average importation of Brazilian centrifugal sugar, 2010–2020 by principal importing countries (in millions US$)

Country	*Average annual value*
China	782.1
Algeria	669.9
Bangladesh	632.9
Russian Federation	570.7
India	551.0
Egypt	440.2
Malaysia	422.5
Nigeria	408.4
Indonesia	383.2
Saudi Arabia	347.9
United Arab Emirates	332.0
Canada	327.1
Iraq[a]	272.9
Iran	260.7
Venezuela	203.1
United States of America	120.6
Georgia	102.4

Notes [a]Only for period 2014–2020
Source FAOSTAT

successfully compete in the world market, quickly becoming the largest exporter in the world. By 2009 it accounted for roughly half of all world sugar exports and had also become the leading country exporter of centrifugal sugar. It has only been in the second decade of the current century that the newly energized zones in São Paulo and the states of the Center-West region finally came into full production using the most modern technology and planting practices.

Although São Paulo is facing new competition from other growing areas, it has been at the forefront of all the latest scientific and technical changes and effectively responded to fundamental environmental concerns which have been associated with the production of sugar and ethanol. Mechanized harvesting, no-till planting and the use of bagasse as a source of fuel all have reduced the environmental impact of the industry. Just as the expansion of sugar production did not impact the growth of other crops it also had little if any impact on Amazonian developments. Just 6% of all lands dedicated to seasonal crops in the Center-West region were dedicated to sugar production in 2021, and this production was mostly in abandoned pasture lands in the Cerrado region.[65] Government action was also fundamental in Brazil becoming the world nation with the highest presence of flex motors and thus basically committed to the ethanol revolution. There is little question that Brazil today has established itself as a dominant player in the world market for sugar and the second most important for ethanol production and will probably still be a major player in years to come.

Notes

1. Christopher David Absell, "The Bittersweet Century: Slavery, Tariffs and Brazilian Export Growth During the Nineteenth Century" (PhD thesis, Universidad Carlos III, 2020): 312–313.
2. *Relatório da Comissão encarregada de estudar a difusão applicada a cana de assucar, apresentado ao Exmo. Sr. Conselheiro Rodrigo Augusto da Silva, Ministro e Secretario de Estado dos Negocios da Agricultura* (Rio de Janeiro: Imprensa Nacional, 1887), 30.
3. Alice P. Canabrava, "A grande lavoura," in Sérgio Buarque de Holanda, ed., *História da civilização brasileira* (São Paulo: Difusão Europeia do Livro, 1971), 85–137; Roberta Barros Meira, "Banguês, Engenhos Centrais e Usinas" (MA thesis, FFLCH-USP, 2007); Gileno de Carli, *Gênese e evolução da indústria açucareira de São Paulo* (Rio de Janeiro: Pongetti, 1943); Peter Eisenberg, *The Sugar Industry In Pernambuco: Modernization Without Change, 1840–1910* (Berkeley: University of California Press, 1974); Jonas Soares de Souza, "O Engenho Central de Porto Feliz: subsídios para o estudo dos engenhos centrais do Brasil no século XIX," *Anais do Museu Paulista*, tomo XXV (1971–1974): 25–43; Alcides Ribeiro Soares, "A experiência dos engenhos centrais," in Nilo Odália and João Ricardo de Castro Caldeira, eds., *História do Estado de São Paulo: A Formação da Unidade Paulista* (São Paulo: Imprensa Oficial, I, 2010), 161–187.
4. Eisenberg, *The Sugar Industry in Pernambuco*, 111–124.
5. Manuel Moreno Fraginals, *El ingenio: complejo económico social cubano del azúcar* (3 vols; Havana: Editorial de Ciencias Sociales, 1978); Alan Dye, *Cuban Sugar in the Age of Mass Production: Technology, and the Economics of the Sugar Central, 1899–1929* (Stanford: Stanford University Press, 1998).
6. Carli, *Gênese e evolução da indústria açucareira de São Paulo*, 57.
7. Gileno de Carli, "O açúcar na formação econômica do Brasil," *Annuário Açucareiro* (1937): 32–33.
8. Ministério da Agricultura, Indústria e Comércio, *Indústria Assucareira no Brasil* (Rio de Janeiro: Directoria Geral de Estatística, 1919), 44, 68.

9. In 1939/1940, the Northeast still represented 55% of the national sugar production, with Pernambuco the largest producer (*Anuário Estatístico do Brasil, 1939–40*, 198–203).
10. Paulo Pestana, "Produção agrícola em 1910–11," *Boletim Directoria de Industria e commercio* (Secretaria da Agricultura Commercio e Obras Publicas do Estado de São Paulo), 3ª. série, fevereiro, (2) (1912): 40.
11. Noel Deerr, *The History of Sugar*, 2 vols. (London: Chapman and Hall, 1949), I: 113; IBGE, *Estatísticas Históricas*, tabela 6_38ab_agro1921_99.xls.
12. In 1920, expenditure on wheat imports by São Paulo was in the order of £2.5 million. In the same year, imports and sugar by cabotage totaled valor was equivalent to £2 million. *Anuário Estatístico de São Paulo*, 1921, II: 231, 275.
13. Carlos Gabriel Guimarães, "O Instituto do Açúcar e do Álcool e a indústria do álcool-motor no primeiro governo Vargas (1930–1945)," *História Econômica & História de Empresas*, XV, no. 1 (2012).
14. Tamás, Szmrecsányi, "1914–1939 crescimento e crise da agroindústria açucareira do Brasil. São Paulo," *Revista Brasileira de Ciência Social*, 3, no. 7 (1988): 12, found at: http://anpocs.com/images/stories/RBCS/07/rbcs07_02.pdf.
15. Tamás Szmrecsányi, *O planejamento da agroindústria canavieira do Brasil (1930–1975)* (São Paulo: Hucitec/Unicamp, 1979); Gileno de Carli, *História contemporânea do açúcar no Brasil* (Rio de Janeiro: Instituto do Açúcar e do Alcool, 1940); Pedro Ramos and Walter Belik, "Intervenção estatal e a agroindústria canavieira no Brasil," *Revista Econômica e Sociologia Rural*, 27, no. 2: 203; Tamás Szmrecsányi and Eduardo Pestana Moreira, "O desenvolvimento da Agroindústria Canavieira do Brasil desde a Segunda Guerra Mundial," *Estudos Avançados*, 11, no. 5 (1991).
16. Szmrecsányi, "1914–1939 crescimento e crise da agroindústria açucareira do Brasil. São Paulo"; Gileno de Carli, *Aspectos de Economia açucareira* (Rio de Janeiro, Irmãos Poncetti, Editores, 1942).
17. Only in Minas Gerais was there still a predominance of the engenhos, there representing 83% of sugar production. But this was due to their concentration on cachaça (drinking alcohol) production (Shimada, 1992).
18. *Anuário Açucareiro,* Instituto do Açúcar e do Álcool, various years.
19. Szmrecsányi and Moreira, "O desenvolvimento da Agroindústria Canavieira do Brasil desde a Segunda Guerra Mundial," 59.
20. Miguel Costa Filho, "Apresentação", *Anuário Açucareiro 1941*, 1941, XV–XXX.
21. *Anuário Açucareiro, Instituto do Açúcar e do Álcool*, vários exemplares.
22. Barbosa Lima Sobrinho, *A ação do Instituto do Açúcar e do Álcool* (Rio de Janeiro, Relatório do Sr. Barbosa Lima Sobrinho, como Presidente da Comissão Executiva, no Período de maio de 1938 a abril de 1946.

Instituto do Acucar e do Alcool; Producao de cana; Financiamento; Preco; Brasil, 1946).

23. IBGE, *Censo demográfico de 1960, Serie Nacional*, vol 1 and Ipeadata regional at http://www.ipeadata.gov.br/Default.aspx.
24. The relations between usinas and producers were regulated from 1941 onwards by the so-called Lavoura Canavieira Statute. Decreto-Lei 3.855, 21 novembro 1941.
25. Carli, *Gênese e evolução da indústria açucareira de São Paulo*, 85.
26. Szmrecsányi and Moreira, "O desenvolvimento da Agroindústria Canavieira do Brasil desde a Segunda Guerra Mundial," 61.
27. Ministério do Planejamento e Orçamento, Instituto de Pesquisa Econômica Aplicada, Ipeadata, série regional, found at http://www.ipeadata.gov.br/Default.aspx.
28. Szmrecsányi, *O planejamento da agroindústria canavieira do Brasil (1930–1975)*, 238–240.
29. Pedro Ramos, "Um estudo da evolução e da infraestrutura da agroindústria canavieira do Estado de São Paulo (1930–1982)" (MA thesis, São Paulo, FGV, 1983); Stahis Panagides, "Erradicação do café e diversificação da agricultura brasileira," Rio de Janeiro, IPEA, 1968, 8.
30. As these devices were not patented, they were in the public domain, Barjas Negri, "Estudo de caso da indústria nacional de equipamentos. Análise do grupo Dedini 1920–1975" (MA thesis, UNICAMP, 1977): 36.
31. Negri, "Estudo de caso da indústria nacional de equipamentos. Análise do grupo Dedini 1920–1975," 44–50.
32. Negri, "Estudo de caso da indústria nacional de equipamentos. Análise do grupo Dedini 1920–1975," 142, 172; Nascimento, Jeffeson Ferreira do Nascimento, "Formação industrial de Sertãozinho (1930–1980): as lições da história versus o mito empreendedorismo local," *Revista Iluminart*, IX, no. 15 (2017).
33. Ramos, "Um estudo da evolução e da infraestrutura da agroindústria canavieira do Estado de São Paulo (1930–1982)."
34. Patrícia Nasser de Carvalho, "A política agrícola comum da Europa: controvérsias e continuidade," TD 2258; Brasília, IPEA, 1990.
35. On research centers working on sugar before the 1980s, see Carlos Henrique de Brito Cruz et al., *Cultivo do milho. Sistema de Plantio direto* (Sete Lagoas, Mapa, Comunicado Técnico 51, 2002), 31–32; Eduardo Fernandes Pestana Moreira, "Expansão, concentração e concorrência na agroindústria canavieira em São Paulo: 1975 a 1987" (MA thesis, Campinas, Unicamp, 1989).
36. Herbert S. Klein and Francisco Vidal Luna, *Feeding the World: Brazil's Transformation into a Modern Agricultural Economy* (New York: Cambridge University Press, 2018).

37. Fabrício Brollo Durham, José Vitor Bomtempo, and Denise Lima Fleck, "A estruturação do Sistema de Produção e Inovação Sucroalcooleiro como Brasil para o Proálcool," *Revista Brasileira de Inovação*, Campinas (SP), 10, no. 1 (January/June 2011): 52–60; Carlos David Guevarra Abarca, "Inovações tecnológicas na agroindústria da cana-de-açúcar no Brasil," in *Encontro Nacional de Engenharia de produção* (Rio de Janeiro, ABEPRO, 1999), at: http://www.agencia.cnptia.embrapa.br/Repositorio/ENEGEP 1999_A0105_000fxgg417302wyiv80soht9h4yxjyhn.pdf.
38. Diego Nyko et al., *A evolução das tecnologias agrícolas do setor sucroenergético: estagnação passageira ou crise estrutural?* (Rio de Janeiro, BNDES, Setorial 37, 2013); Michelle Oliveira Silva, "Inovações institucionais e tecnológicas no setor sucroalcooleiro: arranjo de rede nas interações público/privado, de Planalsucar à Ridesa" (MA thesis, Universidade Federal de Goiás, 2013).
39. Carlos Henrique de Brito Cruz et al., *Cultivo do milho. Sistema de Plantio direto*; Luís Augusto Barbosa Cortez, ed., *Proálcool 40 anos. Universidades e empresas: 40 anos de ciência e tecnologia para o etanol brasileiro* (São Paulo: Blucher, 2016); Pery Francisco Assis Shimada, "A evolução diferenciada da agroindústria canavieira no Brasil de 1975 a 1995" (PhD thesis, Piracicaba, Escola Superior de Agricultura Luiz de Queiróz/USP, 1997).
40. Francisco Vidal Luna and Herbert S. Klein, *Brazil Since 1980* (New York: Cambridge University Press, 2006), chapter 2; Ipeadata, "Transações correntes - últimos 12 meses (Antiga metod. - BPM5) - (% PIB)".
41. Elton Alisson, "Proálcool: uma das maiores realizações do Brasil baseadas em ciência e tecnologia," *Agência Fapesp*, 2016, at https://agencia.fapesp.br/proalcool-uma-das-maiores-realizacoes-do-brasil-baseadas-em-ciencia-e-tecnologia/24432/.
42. Although inflation in 1976 was around 35% a year, investments would obtain funds at fixed rates between 15 and 17%, with a 12-year term and a 3-year grace period. Sugarcane would be financed at rates of 7% per year, with a term of 5 years.
43. Tamás Szmrecsányi, *O planejamento da agroindústria canavieira do Brasil (1930–1975)*, 307.
44. Rubismar Stolf and Ana Paula Rodrigues de Oliveira, "The success of Brazilian Alcohol Program (Proálcool)—A Decade-by-Decade Brief History of Ethanol in Brazil," *Engenharia Agrícola*, 40, no. 2 (2020): 244.
45. Sílvio Carlos Bray, Enéas Rente Ferreira, and Davi G. Gaspar Ruas, *As políticas da agroindústria canavieira e o Proálcool no Brasil* (Marília: UNESP, 2000), 60.
46. The percentage of alcohol in gasoline was periodically modified to meet oil price conditions and the availability of anhydrous alcohol, and also differed by regions. Since 1976 the percentage had varied from 10 to

25%. In 1984, for example, it was 22% for Brazil. MAPA, acesso: https://www.gov.br/agricultura/pt-br/assuntos/sustentabilidade/agroenergia/arquivos/cronologia-da-mistura-carburante-etanol-anidro-gasolina-no-brasil.pdf.

47. Pery Francisco Assis Shimada, "A evolução da agroindústria canavieira em Minas Gerais de 1705 a 1955" (MA thesis, Piracicaba, Escola Superior de Agricultura Luiz de Queiroz/USP, 1992): 88.
48. Part of the loss with the alcohol operation, was borne by Petrobrás, as it was required to buy fuel alcohol at a higher price than that established for sale to distributors (Shimada, 1992: 98).
49. Pery Francisco Assis Shimada, "A evolução da agroindústria canavieira em Minas Gerais de 1705 a 1955," 94–95.
50. *Anuário da Indústria Automobilística Brasileira* (São Paulo, Brasília, ANFAVEA, 2020).
51. Únicas's producers represented more than 50% of the national cane production, 60% of the ethanol production and 70% of the bioelectricity offered by the system. *Unica*. Acesso: https://unica.com.br/sobre-a-unica.
52. Sérgio Figueiredo, "O carro a álcool: uma experiência de política pública para a inovação no Brasil" (MA thesis, Universidade de Brasília, 2006); Paulo Cesár Ribeiro Pinheiro, *Os carros flex fuel no Brasil* (Brasília: Câmara dos Deputados, Consultoria Legislativa, Nota Técnica, 2009).
53. US Energy Information Administration [EIA]. 2023.
54. Ministério Público Federal. Acesso: http://www.mpf.mp.br/grandes-casos/lava-jato.
55. Decreto 3.546, 17 julho 2000, for example, created CIMA (Conselho Interministerial do Açúcar e Álcool) within the Ministério da Agricultura e do Abastecimento, whose main objective would be to adapt sugarcane products for the National Energy Matrix.
56. Cetesb, norma técnica P4.231/2005.
57. Raffaella Rosetto and Antonio Dias Santiago, "Adubação, resíduos alternativos," Brasília: Embrapa, 2007; Melissa A.S. da Silva, Nori P. Griebeler and Lino C. Borges, "Uso de vinhaça e impactos nas propriedades do solo e lençol freático," *Revista Brasileira de Engenharia Agrícola e Ambiental*, 11, no. 1 (2007): 108–114; Alline A. Freitas Silvestre et al., "Utilização da vinhaça na agricultura," *Journal of Agronomic Sciences,* Umuarama, 3, no. Especial (2014): 47–62; Manuel Moreno Ruiz Poveda, "Análise econômica e ambiental do processamento da vinhaça com aproveitamento energético" (MA thesis, Universidade de São Paulo, 2014).
58. State law 11.241 of 19 setembro 2002, determined that in the State of São Paulo burning in mechanized areas would be gradually eliminated by 2021; in non-mechanized areas, by 2031.

59. CONAB, Acompanhamento da Safra Brasileira, Cana-de-açúcar. V.6, safra 2019/20, no.1, maio, 2019:44.
60. Carolina Rocha Batista and Italo do Nascimento Mendonça, "Avaliação da mecanização sobre o mercado de trabalho na lavoura da cana-de-açúcar," *Revista de Economia Regional, Urbana e do Trabalho*, 8, no. 2 (2019): 50–86.
61. CONAB, "Cana-de-Açúcar – Agrícola," April 25, 2023, found at https://www.conab.gov.br/info-agro/safras/serie-historica-das-safras/itemlist/category/891-cana-de-acucar-agricola.
62. CONAB. *Perfil do Setor do Açúcar e do Etanol no Brasil edição para a safra 2015/16*, Brasília, 2019: 45–46, 2019: 55.
63. Junior Ruiz Garcia, Divina Aparecida Leonel Lunas Lima, and Adriana Carvalho Pinto Vieira, "A nova configuração da estrutura produtiva do setor sucroenergético brasileiro: panorama e perspectivas," *Revista de Economia Contemporânea*, 19 (2015): 162–185; Caio César Barbosa and Sérgio Rangel Fernandes Figueira, "Avaliação da concentração de crédito BNDES para empresas do setor sucroalcooleiro brasileira entre 2002 e 2018," *Economia e Sociedade*. Campinas, 30 (2021): 141–161.
64. FAOSTAT, TRADE.
65. IBGE, Sidra, tabela 1612.

CHAPTER 9

Coffee

Coffee long dominated Brazil's development, beginning with its commercial cultivation at the beginning of the nineteenth century until the end of the twentieth century. It was a dynamic element of the Brazilian economy, representing more than half of Brazilian exports for most of this period. It was coffee that paid for the importation of several million slaves in the first half of the nineteenth century and supported the massive migration of several million Europeans and Asians in the late nineteenth and early twentieth century. Even the early industrialization was linked to the coffee economy and gave economic and political hegemony to the states of southeast.

Despite the late twentieth century reduction in the relative importance of coffee in the national economy and the loss of its dominant position in the international market, Brazil remains the world's leading producer and exporter of green coffee beans. It accounts for 30% of world coffee production, followed by Vietnam (17%) and Colombia (9%) and represents 28% of the amount of green coffee exported, followed also by Vietnam and Colombia. Unlike these competitors, Brazil is also a large consumer, and the local market absorbs more than a third of national production.[1] As there is an important added value in the coffee production chain, which is largely done by countries that do not produce beans, there are large exporters, such as Switzerland, Italy, Germany, and France,

H. S. Klein and F. V. Luna, *Brazilian Crops in the Global Market*, Palgrave Studies in Economic History,
https://doi.org/10.1007/978-3-031-38589-6_9

processing and exporting coffee products, such as roasted coffee and extracts of coffee.[2] Coffee is thus one of the most important agricultural products, ranking second in international trade after crude oil.[3]

World production is based on two species. C. Arabica, or Arabica coffee, is a softer drink, with a more pronounced aroma and flavor, which can be sold pure or mixed with C. Canephora, known as Conilon or Robusta. Robusta is characterized as a more rustic coffee tree with greater production potential, and has a more pronounced bitterness, higher caffeine content, and soluble solids. It is mainly used in blends with arabica or in the manufacture of soluble coffee.[4] Until recently Brazil was primarily a producer of arabica coffee, but today robusta coffee now accounts for around a third of the total of coffee beans produced.[5]

By 2022 Brazil produced 50 million bags of coffee and used 1.8 million hectares to do this, with an average productivity of 27.4 bags per hectare. Production has moved due to changing climate and soil conditions over time. For most of the nineteenth and twentieth century São Paulo was the leading producer. Currently the leading zones of coffee production are Minas Gerais with 44% of output, and Espírito Santo with 33%. São Paulo is now down to only 8% of national production just ahead of Bahia with 7%.[6] Coffee by the 2017 agricultural census represented 5% of the total value of agricultural production, compared to soybeans (at 38%), sugarcane (at 18%), and corn (at 12%). Coffee exports by the end of the second decade of the current century represented on average just 2% of the value of all Brazilian exports. Despite the decline of coffee's relative importance in the value of production and exports, it is still the agricultural crop that employs the most workers. In the third quarter of 2020, some 706 thousand persons were working in coffee.[7]

The history of coffee in Brazil dates back to the early years of the nineteenth century, when coffee plantations penetrated the Paraíba Valley of Rio. From there coffee spread into São Paulo and Minas Gerais. In the decade of 1821–1830, it represented 18% of Brazilian exports; in the following decade it exceeded sugar, accounting for 44% of the exported value. Although initially a small farmer crop planted with food crops in the first decade of the nineteenth century, the primary labor force in coffee quickly became African and African Brazilian slaves. All of these fazendas were organized in the classic gang organization with no sexual division among the field hands.[8]

By the time of the São Paulo provincial census of 1854 coffee production had reached a new level of importance in the province.[9] In that year the coffee crop was 3.4 million arrobas, the equivalent of 50,000 metric tons, or 847,000 sacks of coffee at 60 kilos per sack.[10] This was seven times greater than the crop reported in 1836. In 1829 there were 10,000 slaves found on coffee estates, and by 1854 such estates contained 50,000 slaves. By 1881 there were 146 coffee fazendas in São Paulo with 12.9 million trees. In Rio de Janeiro there were 569 coffee farms with 81 million trees. The average size of the Rio de Janeiro coffee plantations was 628 hectares with an average of 56 slaves per unit.[11] The center of the coffee zone for both provinces was the Paraíba Valley which they both shared.

But planters faced two fundamental problems, the increasing scarcity of slave labor after the end of the Atlantic slave trade in 1850, and the precarious internal transport infrastructure. Although the province already had a large slave population by this time, and there would be internal transfers of slaves from less developed centers within Brazil, the end of the trade put into question the future of slave labor. This explains the first attempts to import free immigrant labor into the coffee estates as early as the decade of the 1850s. But these two forms of labor were ultimately incompatible and attempts to exploit the free wage laborers more systematically led to intense conflict.[12] Though these early efforts failed, from the middle of the nineteenth century there were systematic attempts made by paulista planters to find a solution to the labor question, but that would require a revolutionary change in labor organization that planters initially could not accept.[13] By the time of abolition it was agreed that a new labor system had to be implemented. At the same time the only available source of labor were European immigrants, as the slaves abandoned the plantations. But Brazil could not compete with the other leading American importing countries, Argentina and the United States. The solution was some type of subsidization of the immigrant flow. The creation in 1881 of the state-supported Worker Exchange and Residence called the *Hospedaria dos Imigrantes*, was a major new advance in this effort to foment immigration.[14] The law which established the exchange stipulated that immigrants would both have their railroad fares paid from Santos to the capital, and would also be paid the difference in cost between the passage from Europe to Brazil and Europe to the United States.

But this was still insufficient to compete with other American states. Finally in 1884, under pressure from the coffee growers, the government of the province of São Paulo assumed the entire cost of the passage of European immigrants who came to work in paulista agriculture. This financial aid was paid directly to the immigrant as long as he was married or with children. With this law, the state established the basis for a massive migration of Europeans to São Paulo. Between 1827 and 1887, only 85,000 European immigrants entered São Paulo, but in the next ten years 823,000 Europeans came to the state. Of these immigrants, almost two thirds were Italians, with the Spaniards and the Portuguese each contributing ten percent.[15] These immigrants primarily moved to the new western areas of coffee production, which were the most profitable in the state.

Along with subsidization of passage from Europe to the farm gate, planters also had to move from gang labor under strict managerial supervision to a system of individual family workers paid for output per region in a type of sharecropping arrangement. All this required a complete reorganization of management and operations. The free labor immigrants who worked on the coffee fazendas were known as *colonos*, and their remuneration could be either arranged as sharecroppers or in the form of a fixed income for the care of a given number of coffee trees. Under sharecropping arrangements, the coffee planters and the colonos both assumed the risks associated with the production and sale of coffee. In the other form of remuneration, the colono received income for caring for a fixed number of coffee trees under his responsibility and also was paid for a quantity of coffee which these trees produced in a given year. Normally the colono was also authorized to plant subsistence crops among the coffee trees or in areas of the fazenda not occupied by coffee. For the colonos this second payment option was the most desirable and offered the best returns for their labor.[16] After all these experiments the new system of labor was in full function by 1888, on the eve of emancipation. Thus despite the impact of the progressive destruction of slavery during the decade of the 1880s there was no collapse of coffee production. The end of slave labor and the successful establishment of free wage labor signified the consolidation of the West Paulista and other pioneer regions of the state as the new hegemonic areas of paulista agriculture.

A second problem that was finally resolved in this second half of the century, was the financing of the railroads into the interior of São Paulo. Since productivity in coffee depended on continuous incorporation of virgin lands, there was a systematic push to open up the western and northern frontier lands. Thus by the end of the century, the Paraiba Valley planters had exhausted local soils and the move was then on to expand coffee plantation into the West Paulista planes. This could only be viable if railroads replaced the dominant mule transport system.[17] Thus with both planter and foreign capital and government subsidies a dense railroad network was finally established by the 1880s which permitted the opening up of the frontier to coffee production.[18] Railroads would be identified as primarily related to coffee, but once established these railroads also moved people and non-coffee products throughout the state and across state borders, and thus were crucial in expanding the domestic market as well as the export market.[19]

During the nineteenth century, the coffee market operated freely, without government interference, despite several intense price fluctuations. As the coffee tree begins to produce in four years, price stimulus had a lagged effect on production; on the other hand, the coffee tree remains productive for two or three decades. This characteristic of what is called permanent cultivation crops, as opposed to annually planted seasonal crops, tends to periodically produce imbalances in output. This is due to the fact that supply does not adjust quickly to market signals, as occurs with seasonal crops. In addition, in the regions where production was initially consolidated, that is the states of Rio de Janeiro, São Paulo and Minas Gerais, frosts periodically occurred which, depending on their intensity, would hinder current production or even affect output for several years. The coffee tree also has a biennial production cycle, usually alternating one year with a higher and one with a lower output.[20]

At the beginning of the twentieth century, a crisis of overproduction materialized which was so severe that for the first time, producers demanded public government intervention in the market. In 1900, for example, Brazil produced 13.8 million sacks of coffee (of 60 kilos per sack), of which 8.9 million came from São Paulo. In that same year, there were 5.8 million sacks of unsold coffee being held off the market, of which 3.6 million were of Brazilian origin. At the same time the world was consuming 14.3 million sacks per annum. In 1906, the most critical year, Brazil produced 20.6 million sacks, of which 15.4 million were from São Paulo. Unsold stocks then reached 8.6 million sacks (7.5 million of which was Brazilian coffee), while world consumption reached just 17.5 million sacks. Clearly coffee planters in Brazil were now producing more than the world market could consume.[21] This led to the first short-term intervention in the market by the local governments. New plantings were prohibited, part of the production was removed from the market, stocks were formed, and then sold when market conditions allowed. Two other market interventions by the state took place in 1917 and 1921, with similar characteristics, but without planting bans. On these three occasions, the government withdrew from the market as soon as the price rebalancing occurred. However, the success of these interventions stimulated the government to adopt a permanent intervention in the coffee market in 1922.[22] This government intervention would have completely different characteristics. The idea was to restrict the supply of coffee to the market to keep prices high. The excess production would be stockpiled in the interior and would only be sent to the ports for sale overseas when world prices permitted.

Since competitors did not engage in market control, this meant that they were able to benefit from Brazilian controls and also were able to increase their share of world markets. But such a policy also kept prices high and stimulated an increase in plantations in Brazil and in competing countries. The consequence was the overproduction that materialized at the end of the decade. The 1929 crisis occurred when the coffee market faced one of its most severe periods of overproduction. Thus, the average annual production increased from 24 million bags between 1921–1925, then to 33 million bags in the 1926–1930 period, and finally to 39 million bags in 1931–1935 in the midst of the international crisis. In the fifteen years between 1921 and 1935 the average annual world consumption was only 23 million bags. In 1930, the existing world stockpile (then 31 million bags) already exceeded that year's consumption.[23]

As a response to the world depression of the late 1920s and early 1930s, the government forgave part of the debts of the coffee farmers, and withdrew a large portion of production from the market, which was then destroyed. In the 1930s, some 78.2 million bags would be burned, equivalent to three times the world consumption of one year. Despite this effort, prices remained depressed throughout the 1930s. The destruction of coffee was only halted in 1944 and new plantings were finally allowed in 1943. These policies reduced Brazilian productive capacity by a third, and also reduced Brazil's participation in the international market.[24] Then in 1952, the federal government created the Brazilian Coffee Institute (IBC) with broad powers in all aspects of production, consumption, and marketing of coffee in Brazil and abroad.[25]

But at the end of the decade, the new plantations arrived on the market and resulted in the exceptional harvest of 1959, on the order of 44 million bags, double the average obtained in the previous ten years. World production totaled 79 million bags, well above the international market's

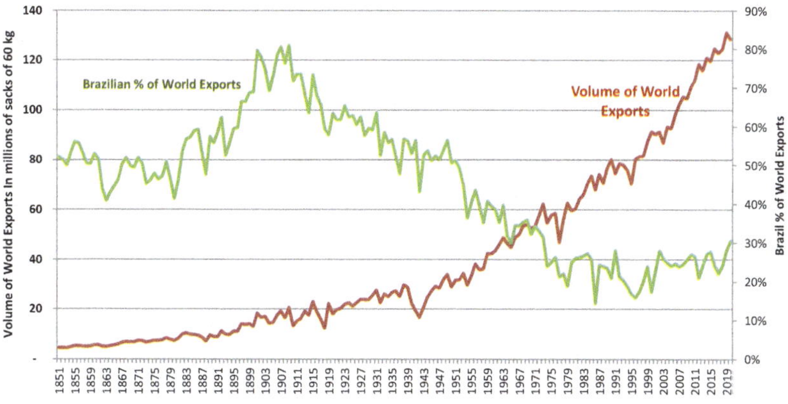

Graph 9.1 World coffee exports in volume and Brazilian coffee exports as a share of world exports, 1851–2020 (*Source* IBGE, Estatisticas Históricas; Bacha and Greenhill [1992]; and FAOSTAT)

absorption capacity. In 1962, a wide-ranging coffee eradication program was initiated, which would be of fundamental importance not only in reducing coffee growing but also in stimulating other crops in former coffee areas, especially in the state of São Paulo. The program lasted until 1967, with the elimination of approximately half of the existing coffee plantations.[26]

Over the years, mainly due to the intervention policies practiced by Brazil, the country increasingly lost its share in the international market. In the years between 1910 and 1920, Brazil on average accounted for about 2/3 of world exports, which then declined to just over 50% in the following two decades; to 43% in the 1950s and then to 36% in the 1960s. It fell below 30% in the mid-1970s and averaged 25% in the period from 2000–2019 (see Graph 9.1).[27]

In turn the share of coffee in the value of Brazilian exports after reaching a peak in the 1920s, steadily declined throughout the 1930s and 1940s, when they reached, on average of one third of the value of national exports. The market recovery in the immediate post-war period, with consequently high prices, allowed for a sharp increase in the value of coffee exports and in their share of the total value of exports. As late as 1964 coffee still represented half the value of Brazilian exports, but in the following year, a long-term decline in its role in exports occurred.

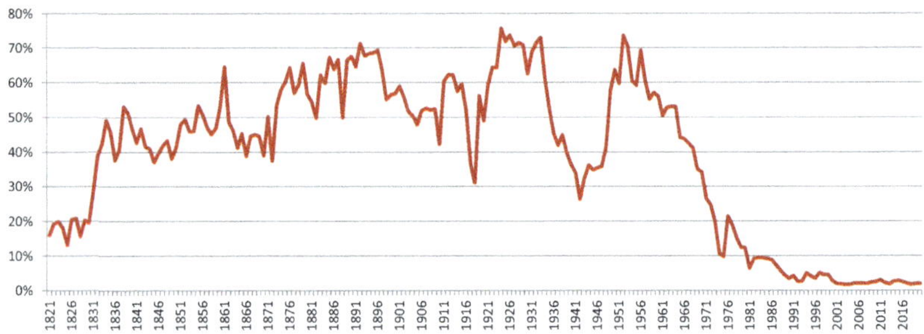

Graph 9.2 Percentage of coffee exports in the total value of Brazilian exports, 1821–2020 (*Source* IBGE, Estatísticas Históricas Brasileiras; Ipeadata)

This was due to the massive growth of other agricultural products in the twenty-first century has meant that in the twenty years from 2000–2020, although coffee exports have increased significantly, they now represent just 2% of the value of all Brazilian exports (Graph 9.2).

In the 1920s São Paulo represented the main center of coffee production in Brazil and in the world.[28] But gradually there was a shift in production to the state of Paraná, which surpassed São Paulo in the early 1960s. This situation continued until 1975 when a devastating frost practically destroyed the coffee plantations in Paraná. This experience finally brought a rapid shift toward the warmer northern states, especially toward Minas Gerais and Espírito Santo, which soon were accounting for 45% and 27%, respectively of national production. Most recently coffee has also become important in Bahia a state even closer to the equator. Thus by 2020 São Paulo accounted for only 9% of national coffee production and Paraná's production was quite limited (see Graph 9.3 and Map 9.1).

Coffee, like most other agricultural products was controlled by government agencies, but in this case control went back to the crises of overproduction in the early twentieth century. First, the states and then the Federal government was forced to control production, eliminate trees, and eventually in the 1930s burn large stocks of coffee. The federal government created the Brazilian Coffee Institute (IBC) in 1952 which controlled exports and tried to deal with overproduction and signing of international coffee agreements. Even so, there were signs of overproduction in this period. In 1959, Brazilian coffee production reached 44 million bags and total world production reached 79 million bags but world consumption was only 42 million bags. By 1963 the world had

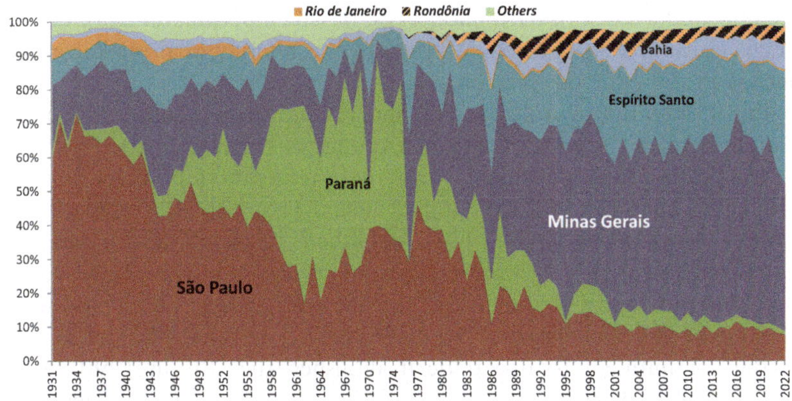

Graph 9.3 Relative importance of Brazilian states in coffee production, 1931–2022 (*Source* Ipeadata & Conab)

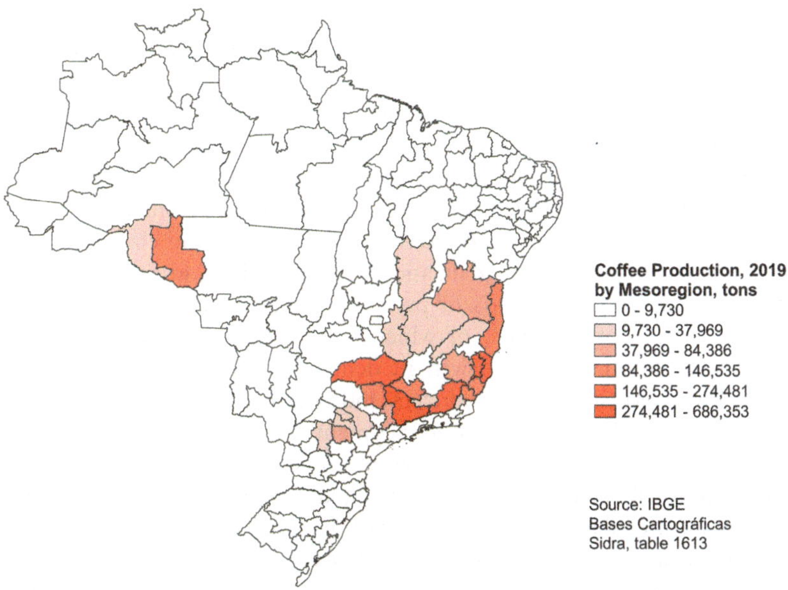

Map 9.1 Coffee Production by Mesoregion, 2019 (*Source* IBGE Bases Cartográficas Sidra, table 1612)

accumulated a stock of 81 million bags, of which 63 million belonged to Brazil, causing a sharp drop in prices in the international market and a decline in the value of coffee exports

In 1959 an international agreement was signed between Latin American and African producers, defining quotas of coffee exports. In 1962, a new agreement was signed, with the participation of practically all producing countries and the United States. That year the International Coffee Organization (ICO) was established and in 1963 an international agreement led to the eradication of coffee trees around the world. Between 1962 and 1967 almost half of the coffee trees in the world were eradicated. Brazil abandoned the ICO agreements in 1989, and as part of the commitment to free trade it abolished the IBC in 1990 which had controlled domestic prices and also in quotas for exports. Thereafter Brazil was forced to face free market competition with no support from the government.[29]

The result of this opening up of the coffee producers was positive, in the sense that in order to compete in an ever more complex world coffee market, Brazilian growers had to increase productivity and also begin to specialize and distinguish their coffee products. There was a continued dispersion of coffee to new zones, and the adoption of mechanization and other modern farming practices and the introduction of variable prices for different quality of the products. In this sense, the opening was a true shock for producers and led to important changes in production.[30]

The coffee market since 1990 has undergone profound changes due to an intense process of industrialization of the product, greater differentiation of international brands of processed coffee, and the international emergence of coffee shops, of which Starbucks is the most successful case. In addition to the growth in demand for coffee, new opportunities for artisanal coffee producers and roasters have also opened up the international market. Another segment that grew exceptionally fast was that of coffee capsules for home machine coffee makers. Numerous non-traditional products were also launched, mainly beverages containing coffee or coffee flavor. Brazil, as the world's largest producer and second largest consumer in the world, second only to the United States, was also influenced by these new trends as seen in the rise of organic coffee producers in Minas Gerais. In turn, Brazil recovered its position in the international market due to the greater competitiveness of national production, and to problems that occurred with several competitive producers. Many of these have suffered the effects of rust, a disease that has historically attacked coffee plantations and which has been particularly serious in several Central American countries since 2012.[31]

Changes in the organization of the coffee market have intensified the blending processes of various types of coffee, and have increased the relative demand for robusta coffees. Brazil and Colombia, two of the most important coffee producers, historically produced arabica coffee, and this coffee initially dominated the world market. The two countries basically produce the same products, but the harvesting and post-harvest treatment of the beans is totally different, producing coffee of different quality. Harvesting in Colombia is done two or three times, making the products homogeneous in terms of fruit ripeness, a system called selective harvesting. In Brazil, the harvest is traditionally done only once, mixing coffee with different levels of maturity. In the post-harvest process, Colombia adopts the wet or pulping process. In Brazil, the dry procedure is predominantly used, in which the fruit is dried on cement terraces, without removing the peel. Thus, the Colombian product is able to differentiate itself, with advantages in relation to the Brazilian product.[32] Although niche crops are developed in Brazil, including gourmet coffee, Brazil maintains its traditional practices both because of lower costs and a national acceptance of this product. Nevertheless new harvesting techniques and modification of trees are beginning to create more uniform beans. Together Brazil and Colombia dominate the world production of Arabica coffee (see Graph 9.4).

In general, there has been an improvement in coffee productivity in the last twenty years.[33] The increase in productivity in the period 2004–2015 involved mechanization and automation of planting and harvesting, changes in handling techniques and application of pesticides with more appropriate tools, plus investments in tree varieties resistant to diseases via genetic improvement. A study on productivity in coffee in the six main producing states of Brazil, found an increase in the average yield nationally of 34% in the period, but with a much higher rate of 50% in Espírito Santo and Bahia.[34] It found that labor productivity surpassed land productivity, going from 2.8 tons per worker to 4.8 tons per worker, an increase of 72%. There was also a significant increase in land productivity that would have saved 769 thousand hectares for other uses in the period.[35]

In order to understand regional production and coffee productivity in Brazil, it is necessary to segment the market into its two basic products arabica and robusta coffee. Brazil only began producing robusta coffee

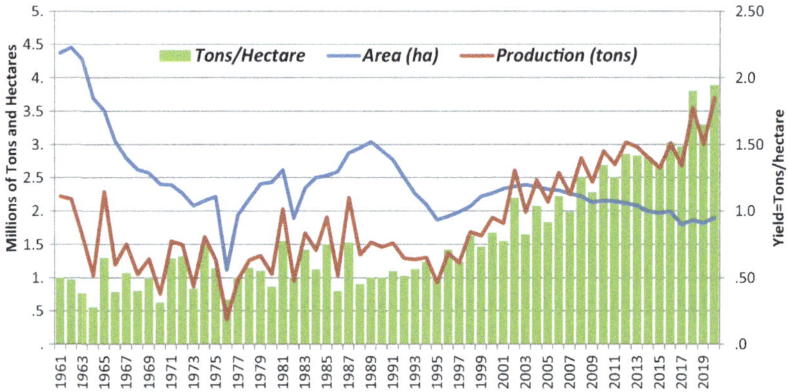

Graph 9.4 Brazilian coffee production in tons, area harvested and yield per hectare, 1961–2020 (*Source* Faostat)

in the late 1970s, but today about a third of Brazilian coffee production is made up of these robusta beans, which has doubled in the last twenty years from 31 million bags to 63 million bags and is today the world's second largest producer. Whereas Minas Gerais accounts for more than two thirds of arabica production, followed by São Paulo and Espírito Santo, Espírito Santo has become the major producer of Robusta coffee along its coastal zone, accounting for two thirds of this type of coffee, with smaller output in the Northern state of Rondônia as well as lowland Bahia which also produces arabica.

Despite the current absolute predominance of Minas Gerais and Espírito Santo in coffee production, there has been a surge of new producing areas, such as in the Northeastern state of Bahia and the Northern state of Rondônia, located in the extreme west of Brazil, on the border with Bolivia and within the Amazon biome. In the case of Rondônia, production is concentrated in the so-called Matas de Rondônia, involving 15 municipalities and over 10,000 producers.[36] In the last twenty years, production in Rondônia has remained relatively stable, with output of around two million bags, but productivity has increased from 12 bags per hectare in 2008 to over 35 in the last four harvests due to the cultivation of new species, improvement in cultural treatments and support from the regional Embrapa Rondônia office.[37] In the case of Bahia these new areas are both on the Atlantic coast producing Robusta and the more highland areas producing traditional Arabica coffee. In the 2022 harvest, a harvest of 2.3 million bags of Robusta was obtained, with productivity higher than the national average. As for arabica, the estimated production results in 1.2 million bags with productivity similar to the national average (see Table 9.1).[38]

In 2020, coffee trees occupied a total area of 1.9 million hectares, of which 1.5 million were planted with arabica and 370 thousand with robusta. Between 2008 and 2020 there was a significant increase in the productivity of the two types of coffee, particularly robusta, which went from 20 bags per hectare in 2008 to 47 bags per hectare in 2020, higher than the average production of Arabica coffee that went from 21 bags per hectare to 32 bags per hectare in the same period. In the case of arabica, Minas Gerais, the largest producer maintains a productivity higher than the national average in the period; in the case of robusta coffee, the productivity achieved in recent years in Bahia stands out, much higher than Espírito Santo, the largest producer.[39]

This increase in coffee productivity in Brazil began in the final years of the twentieth century, just as it did for many of the main agricultural products in Brazil, as a result of the long and successful process of modernization of Brazilian agriculture.[40] In the case of coffee there was, like in many other crops, an average increase in production on fewer hectares. In the case of coffee, production increased 70% between the period 1995/2000 and 2015/2019 at the same time as there was a reduction of about 25% in the planted area. Moreover this Brazilian yield per hectare after 1995 was superior to the evolution of the world average. This explains why Brazil planted area has declined at the same time as its share of production has increased in terms of world land use and production of coffee (see Graph 9.5).

According to the 2017 census, there were 264 thousand establishments in Brazil that were coffee farms, defined as establishments that had 50 or more trees. Some 188 thousand farms produced Arabica coffee and 76 thousand farms with robusta, and together these two coffee trees occupied a total of 1.6 million hectares. Total production was 2.3 million tons from 4.4 billion coffee trees. Of the total production value, Minas Gerais represents two thirds, followed by Espírito Santo, and São Paulo was third. Some 83% of the value of production was made up of arabica coffee. Unlike the large plantations of the nineteenth and early twentieth centuries, the typical coffee farm now is relatively small, with an average of 7 hectares of harvested area of Arabica and only 4 of robusta. In São

Table 9.1 Production of Arabica and Robusta Coffee by Principal State Producers, 2001–2022 (1,000 bags @ 60 kgs)

	Arabica coffee										*Robusta coffee*				
Years	*Total*	*Bahia Cerrado*	*Bahia Planalto*	*Goiás*	*Minas Gerais*	*Espírito Santo*	*São Paulo*	*Paraná*	*Others*	*BRAZIL*	*Rondônia*	*Bahia Atlân-tico*	*Espírito Santo*	*Others*	*Brazil*
2001	1,700				14,650	1,900	3,520	540	240	22,550	1,910	490	5,650	700	8,750
2002	1,750				25,100	2,500	5,800	2,340	460	37,950	2,100	550	6,825	1,055	10,530
2003	1,410				12,020	1,600	2,810	1,970	270	20,080	2,500	370	5,010	860	8,740
2004	1,877				18,747	2,295	5,870	2,526	400	31,715	1,760	402	4,500	895	7,557
2005	1,407				15,189	2,056	3,223	1,435	508	23,818	1,772	405	6,014	935	9,126
2006	1,725				21,957	2,128	4,470	2,248	487	33,015	1,263	526	6,881	827	9,497
2007	1,686				16,437	2,167	2,632	1,732	442	25,096	1,482	656	8,139	697	10,974
2008	1,566				23,545	2,867	4,420	2,608	478	35,484	1,876	576	7,363	694	10,509
2009	1,332	436	896		19,598	2,603	3,423	1,467	443	28,866	1,547	542	7,602	913	10,604
2010	1,728	486	1,242		24,903	2,792	4,662	2,284	455	36,824	2,369	565	7,355	982	11,271
2011	1,549	429	1,120		21,882	3,079	3,112	1,842	725	32,189	1,428	741	8,494	632	11,296
2012	1,337	528	809	247	26,644	2,789	5,357	1,580	638	38,344	1,367	813	9,713	589	12,482
2013	1,080	399	681	266	27,380	3,486	4,010	1,650	680	38,286	1,357	723	8,211	574	10,866
2014	1,331	435	896	237	22,347	2,857	4,589	559	624	32,306	1,477	1,040	9,949	570	13,036
2015	1,162	338	824	226	21,966	2,939	4,064	1,290	628	32,049	1,724	1,184	7,761	518	11,187
2016	1,267	346	922	227	30,428	3,932	6,031	1,047	677	43,382	1,627	826	5,035	499	7,987
2017	978	288	690	190	24,102	2,950	4,412	1,210	598	34,249	1,938	2,380	5,915	488	10,721

Years	*Arabica coffee*										*Robusta coffee*				
	Total	*Bahia Cerrado*	*Bahia Planalto*	*Goiás*	*Minas Gerais*	*Espírito Santo*	*São Paulo*	*Paraná*	*Others*	*BRAZIL*	*Rondônia*	*Bahia Atlân-tico*	*Espírito Santo*	*Others*	*Brazil*
2018	1,880	497	1,383	195	32,970	4,751	6,302	1,000	580	47,484	1,978	2,670	8,988	537	14,174
2019	1,200	300	900	249	24,235	3,002	4,340	953	566	34,296	2,199	1,800	10,496	518	15,013
2020	1,867	350	1,517	248	34,337	4,765	6,181	942	676	48,737	2,445	2,120	9,193	553	14,311
2021	1,229	250	979	235	21,859	2,945	4,007	876	273	31,424	2,263	2,240	11,221	568	16,293
2022	1,232	276	956	280	21,750	4,341	3,903	558	346	32,410	2,801	2,333	12,234	603	17,970

Source Conab, accessed at: https://www.conab.gov.br/info-agro/safras/serie-historica-das-safras

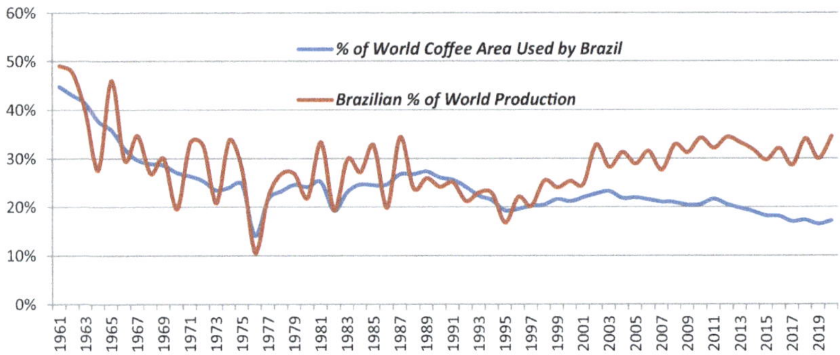

Graph 9.5 Ratio of Brazilian production and area planted in total world production and area planted, 1961–2020 (*Source* FAOSTAT)

Paulo arabica producing farms are an average of 12 hectares, and Bahia, the robusta producer with the largest average size farm, was 10 hectares (see Table 9.2).

This domination of the small cultivated farms is due to the intense use of labor in coffee production. This makes it more conducive to the participation of family farmers. Thus, of the 264 thousand producers of coffee, more than three quarters were family farmers. They accounted for one third of the production of arabica and half of the production of robusta. In terms of the value of production, family farming accounts for just over a third of the value generated by coffee farming. The production of coffee, segmented by the size of the total area of the establishments, shows that 75% of the Arabica producing farms were smaller than 10 hectares and 95% less than 100 hectares. As for production, a quarter came from establishments of up to 10 hectares and half from establishments of up to 100 hectares. In the case of robusta, production took place in smaller establishments, as 32% came from units of up to 10 hectares and 72% from units of up to 100 hectares (Table 9.3).

Because of the change in the size and distribution of coffee farms from previous eras of coffee production, control of coffee growing is far less concentrated than in most Brazilian agricultural crops and is fundamentally different from its historical condition under slavery. Thus the GINI distribution of farms and production for Arabica coffee was 0.65, which is a very low rate in modern Brazilian crops. While the Robusta GINI was even more egalitarian at 0.45 (see Table 9.4).

Table 9.2 Basic structure of coffee production by type, census 2017

State/ Nation	*Farms > 50 trees*	*Area in hectares*	*Production in tons*	*Coffee trees (000)*	*Production value (reais)*
	Arábica Coffee				
Brazil	188,392	1,283,999	1,880,438	3,665,630	13,454,201
Rondônia	524	954	869	1,136	4,365
Bahia	18,219	53,971	52,151	130,980	361,481
Minas Gerais	119,742	931,270	1,423,184	2,778,445	10,480,767
Espírito Santo	26,320	119,956	113,511	261,389	747,755
São Paulo	10,418	129,307	206,752	373,103	1,423,677
Paraná	9,865	32,144	61,358	73,038	280,171
Others	3,304	16,397	22,613	47,539	155,985
	Robusta Coffee				
Brazil	75,969	333,294	476,373	685,740	2,853,507
Rondônia	16,812	40,588	34,602	46,390	186,258
Bahia	3,016	31,358	65,418	65,148	394,335
Minas Gerais	3,277	9,632	12,403	21,088	76,512
Espírito Santo	49,005	240,690	353,753	539,305	2,139,387
São Paulo	299	2,708	2,846	3,932	17,977
Paraná	222	1,067	1,228	1,803	7,427
Others	3,338	7,251	6,123	8,074	31,611
	Total				
Brazil	264,361	1,617,293	2,356,811	4,351,370	16,307,708
Rondônia	17,336	41,542	35,471	47,526	190,623
Bahia	21,235	85,329	117,569	196,128	755,816
Minas Gerais	123,019	940,902	1,435,587	2,799,533	10,557,279
Espírito Santo	75,325	360,646	467,264	800,694	2,887,142
São Paulo	10,717	132,015	209,598	377,035	1,441,654
Paraná	10,087	33,211	62,586	74,841	287,598
Others	6,642	23,648	28,736	55,613	187,596
% Arábica	71%	79%	80%	84%	83%
% Robusta	29%	21%	20%	16%	17%

Source IBGE, Sidra, Censo 2017, tabela 6955

Table 9.3 Family and non family farms producing coffee, census 2017

Type of farm	*Farms > 50 trees*	*Area in hectares*	*Production in tons*	*Coffee trees (000)*	*Production value (reais)*
	Arábica coffee				
Non-family	43,883	785,353	1,225,251	3,246,145	9,015,164
Family	144,509	498,647	655,188	1,606,328	4,439,037
Total	188,392	1,283,999	1,880,438	4,852,474	13,454,201
	Robusta coffee				
Non-family	14,858	139,449	239,585	400,676	1,461,642
Family	61,111	193,845	236,788	448,350	1,391,865
Total	75,969	333,294	476,373	849,026	2,853,507
	Total all coffee				
Non-family	58,741	924,802	1,464,836	3,646,821	10,476,806
Family	205,620	692,492	891,976	2,054,678	5,830,902
Total	264,361	1,617,293	2,356,811	5,701,500	16,307,708

Source IBGE, Sidra, Censo 2017, tabela 6955

Table 9.4 Farms, area cultivated and production of coffee by type, census of 2017

	Arabic coffee			*Robusta coffee*		
Size of farms in hectares	*Farms > 50 trees*	*Area in hectares*	*Production in tons*	*Farms > 50 trees*	*Area in hectares*	*Production in tons*
0–5	69,092	98,684	129,787	19,385	32,744	34,139
5–10	39,192	114,310	148,674	15,409	40,098	50,173
10–20	32,912	146,232	194,002	14,895	54,209	69,958
20–50	27,286	211,751	286,235	15,424	81,385	111,589
50–100	10,362	158,312	226,706	7,080	50,033	76,069
100–200	5,305	163,991	242,835	2,535	31,446	54,626
200–500	3,079	189,924	308,673	923	21,869	39,526
500–1,000	767	93,762	152,664	211	11,240	22,107
1,000–2,500	291	65,997	111,913	72	7,579	12,004
2,500–10,000	88	36,831	68,615	17	2,665	6,154
10,000+s	8	4,141	10,049			
Total	188,382	1,283,935	1,880,153	75,951	333,268	476,345
Percentage 0–10 ha	75%	28%	25%	65%	38%	32%
Percentage 0–100 ha	95%	57%	52%	95%	78%	72%

Source IBGE, Sidra, Censo 2017, tabela 6955

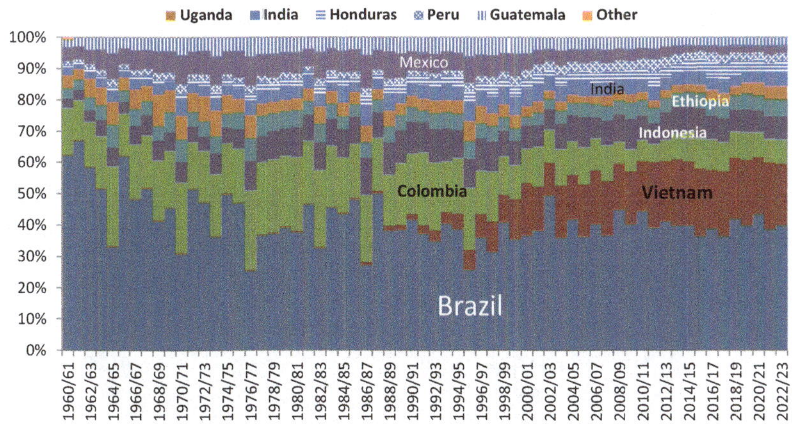

Graph 9.6 Ten principal producers of coffee in the world, 1961–2020 (*Source* FAOSTAT)

The relative decline of Brazil during this period has been matched by increasing participation of new and older national producers. A major group of new producers is Asians and among them the leader is Vietnam, which has quite recently become the second largest producer in the world, replacing Colombia in that role. There has been a relative stagnation of Central American producers and a constant production of many smaller nations which make up a significant portion of total world production (see Graph 9.6).

In the harvest of 2020/2021 Brazil produced a total of some 68 million sacks of coffee out of a total of 176 million produced worldwide. Brazil was the largest producer of arabica coffee, totaling 35 million sacks of the 88 million bags produced in the world, and is the second largest producer of robusta after Vietnam, with 21.3 million bags out of the world total of 77 million (Graph 9.7a and b).

The international coffee market also consists of important processed products. According to the USDA, in the 2020/2021 harvest some 115.5 million coffee bags were exported in the form of beans, 4,665 bags in the form of roasted and ground beans and 16 million in the form of soluble coffee. Brazil was the leader in the export of beans followed by Vietnam and Colombia. Some products, such as roast and

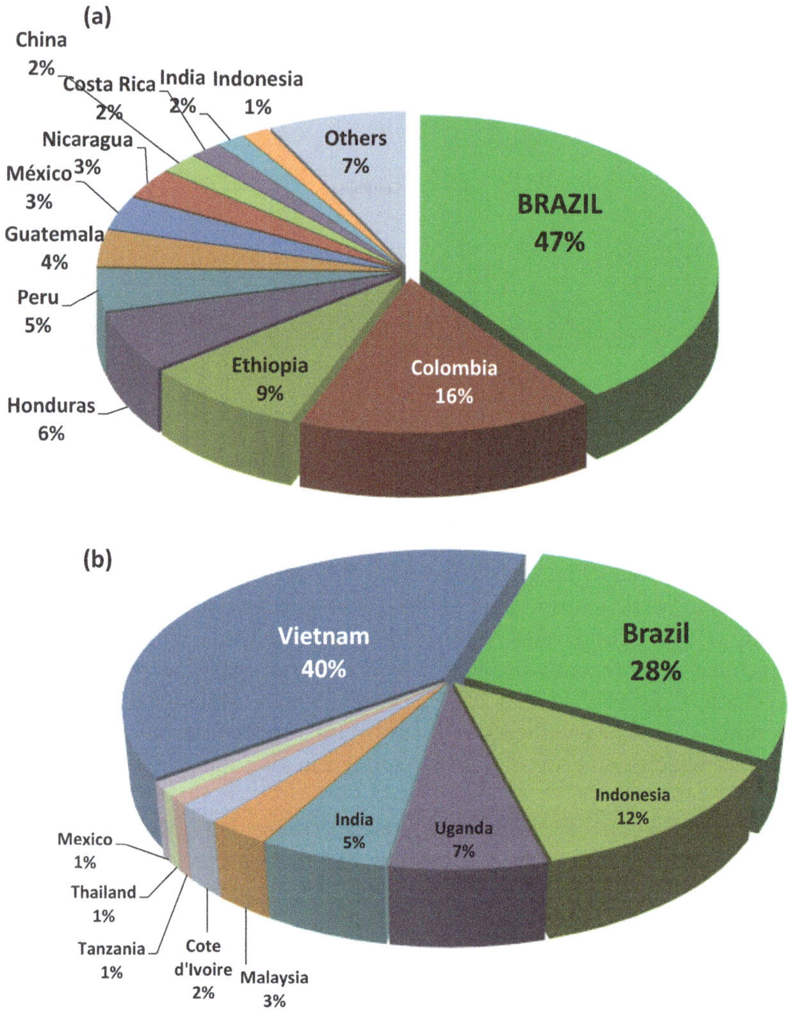

Graph 9.7 (**a**) Share of the production of Arabica coffee by country, 2020/2021 (88 million sacks). (**b**) Share of the production of Robusta coffee by country, 2020/2021 (46 million sacks)

Table 9.5 Quantity of coffee beans and products by principal exporting countries, 2020/2021 (1,000 sacks)

Country/ Region	*Bean exports*	*Roast and ground exports*	*Soluble exports*	*Total*
Brazil	32,000	20	3,200	35,220
Vietnam	26,000	550	2,300	28,850
Colombia	12,400	200	900	13,500
Indonesia	6,500	60	1,200	7,760
Uganda	5,800			5,800
Honduras	5,200			5,200
Ethiopia	4,100			4,100
Peru	3,850			3,850
India	3,680		2,000	5,680
Guatemala	3,150			3,150
Maylasia			2,900	2,900
Mexico		200	950	1,150
Costa Rica		10		10
Swtzerland		1,450		1,450
European Union		2,100	1,100	3,200
Others	12,770	75	1,671	14,516
Total	115,450	4,665	16,221	136,336

Source USDA, Coffee: World Markets and Trade, June 2021, p. 8

ground coffee, have significant exports from Switzerland and the European Union, through the processing of green coffee imported from the Americas and Asia (Table 9.5).

Brazil is the world's largest exporter of coffee in terms of value, although it is not an important exporter of the other principal coffee products, which is dominated by industrialized and non-growing countries that process imported green coffee beans. Nevertheless, it has the largest trade balance in coffee, since it imports little coffee or coffee products. This compares to the negative coffee balance of most of the European countries and the United States, which imports more coffee than it exports (see Table 9.6).[41]

Brazil is also the second largest world consumer of coffee (using 22 million sacks), just behind the United States which consumes some 27 million sacks of coffee. In contrast to Brazil, the other countries are not major consumers of the coffee they produce. Vietnam consumes just 3 million bags, Colombia 2 million, and Indonesia 5 million, despite

Table 9.6 Value of exports and imports of coffee and their products by producing country, 2019 (US$ 1000)

Countries	*Coffee, green*	*Coffee, roasted*	*Coffee, extracts*	*Other*	*Total*	*Total imports*	*Trade balance*
Brazil	4,575,024	9,765	582,539	58	5,167,386	81,714	**5,085,672**
Germany	928,580	1,421,441	826,389	683	3,177,093	3,643,420	–466,327
Switzerland	5,953	2,499,859	179,517	254	2,685,583	780,198	**1,905,385**
Viet Nam	2,183,204	35,075	455,303	542	2,674,124	100,013	**2,574,111**
Colombia	2,282,170	80,790	246,220	210	2,609,390	101,538	**2,507,852**
Italy	47,032	1,647,018	70,614	4,411	1,769,075	1,679,741	**89,334**
Indonesia	872,727	9,258	600,559	1,138	1,483,682	169,282	**1,314,400**
France	23,509	1,190,964	207,579	2,078	1,424,130	2,915,060	–1,490,930
USA	134,508	683,324	221,854	4,666	1,044,352	6,258,231	–5,213,879
Netherlands	87,762	683,539	260,755	6,043	1,038,099	1,290,641	–252,542
Honduras	954,728	366	58	467	955,619	2,309	**953,310**
Belgium	552,181	263,892	115,044	6,941	938,058	1,128,808	–190,750
India	499,702	1,667	299,872	1,376	802,617	131,759	**670,858**
Ethiopia	731,766	7,760	79	18,910	758,515	881	**757,634**
Guatemala	663,017	1,058	557	225	664,857	20,946	**643,911**
Peru	635,156	1,598	68	81	636,903	55,375	**581,528**
Malaysia	2,325	23,941	493,569	193	520,028	374,414	**145,614**
Nicaragua	458,282	1,891	18,007	51	478,231	2,879	**475,352**
World	18,198,838	11,086,973	7,197,219	112,453	36,595,483		

Source FAOSTAT

Table 9.7 Major producers of coffee and their internal consumption, 2019/2020 (1,000 sacks)

Country	*Production*	*Consumption*	*Surplus*
Total	165,053	49,982	115,071
Brazil	58,211	22,000	36,211
Viet Nam	30,487	2,650	27,837
Colombia	14,100	2,025	12,075
Indonesia	11,433	4,806	6,627
Ethiopia	7,343	3,781	3,562
Honduras	5,931	350	5,581
Uganda	5,509	254	5,255
India	4,988	1,450	3,538
Mexico	3,985	2,425	1,560
Peru	3,836	250	3,586
Guatemala	3,606	393	3,213
Nicaragua	2,882	210	2,672
Côte d'Ivoire	1,929	317	1,612
Costa Rica	1,472	352	1,120
Tanzania	926	95	831
Kenya	844	72	772
Papua New Guinea	752	2	750
El Salvador	661	292	369
Venezuela	650	1,275	−625
Laos	622	157	465
Ecuador	559	149	410
Thailand	517	1,400	−883
Others	3,811	5,277	−1,467

Source International Coffee Organization, found at: http://www.ico.org/new_historical.asp

their large populations (Table 9.7). Regionally, coffee consumption is concentrated in Europe, with 54 million bags, Asia & Oceania with 36 million bags and North America with 31 million bags. Outside the European Union, the largest consumers are the United States, Brazil, Japan, Indonesia, and Russia.[42] As for the largest importers, the United States, Germany, Italy, and Japan stand out. The first three have high consumption in the domestic market, but also are coffee processors and exporters of higher added value products (see Graph 9.8).

Thus the contemporary history of coffee in Brazil is one of revival and a major increase in productivity along with the progressive importance of a new type of coffee being introduced to the traditional production. What is impressive is that despite the growing importance of Asian producers, Brazil has actually been able to increase its exports and its share of world

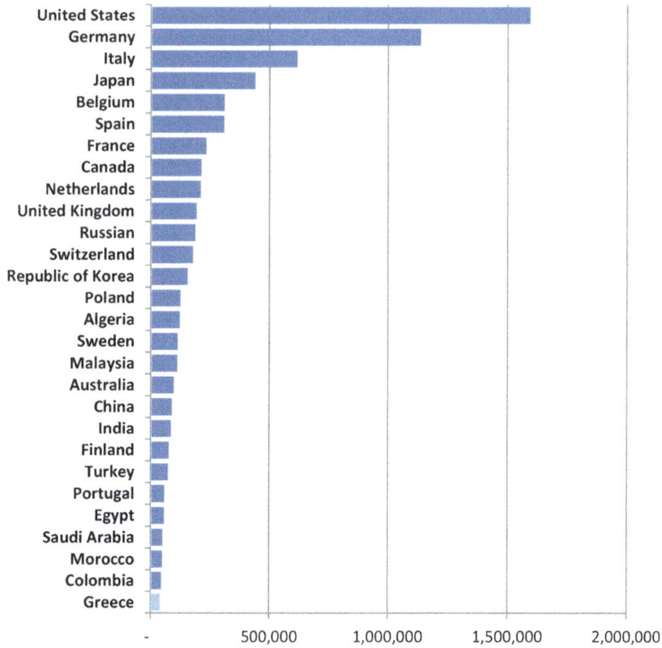

Graph 9.8 Principal countries importing green coffee beans, 2020/2021 (in tons) (*Source* Faostat)

production in the past 20 years. But this is really a new system of production compared to the nineteenth and early twentieth century. First, it is now produced in different regions than where the old plantation system was installed. It also is no longer based on large plantations of thousands of hectares and millions of trees. Now it has a strong component of family farms and the biggest producers are relatively small by traditional standards. It is also a system using the latest in inputs, from machinery to fertilizers, to modified trees which grow more uniformly and often permit mechanized harvesting.

Finally, compared to all the other major agricultural export products, it is one that has a huge internal market. Even so, Brazil is able to satisfy the domestic market and export into the world market a major share of its production and have the highest positive trade balance of this product in the world. But despite all these changes it has not moved into the more lucrative processing part of the industry. It produces a mixed quality product which mostly goes into general low-grade coffee products such as soluble or instant coffee and leaves others to produce the higher value products. The cost of producing high-grade handpicked coffee is one that the current producers are unwilling to make, except for a select few farms in Minas Gerais. They have also not been willing to get into high-grade coffee roasting, another labor-intensive product.

Notes

1. International Coffee Organization, accessed at: http://www.ico.org/new_historical.asp. In the 2019/2020 harvest, the United States consumed 26 million bags and Brazil 24 million. The European Union block consumed 45 million bags. USDA, *Coffee: World Markets and Trade*, December 2020.
2. FAOEST, accessed at: http://www.fao.org/faostat/en/#data.
3. "Coffee is one of the most important agricultural commodities, ranking second in international trade after crude oil. The total global production of green coffee is above 134.16 million bags (60 kg capacity) with a retail sales value in excess of $22.7 billion during 2010–2011 in the world Market". M. K. Mishra and A. Slater, "Recent Advances in the Genetic Transformation of Coffee," *Biotechnology Research International*, 2012, Article ID 580857, 17 pages, https://doi.org/10.1155/2012/580857.
4. Romário Gava Ferrão et al., eds., *Café Conillon* (Vitória, Incaper, 2017), 39. *Bureau de Inteligência competitiva do Café*, 4, no. 9 (17 novembro 2015), 2; USDA, *Coffee: World Markets and Trade*, December 2020. Arabica coffee is best adapted to mountainous regions with altitudes between one thousand and two thousand meters, with humid climate, mild temperatures and its cultivation is more suitable in regions with average temperatures between 18 °C and 23 °C. Robusta coffee is widely distributed in the African and Asian continents, as it adapts to the most varied climatic conditions and low altitudes. It is a plant originating from low, hot and humid equatorial regions, being adapted to much higher temperature conditions, with annual averages between 22 °C and 26 °C. José G. P. Ormond, Sérgio R. L. de Paula, and Paulo Faveret Filho, *Café: (re)conquista dos mercados* (Rio de Janeiro, BNDES Setorial, n.10, set., 1999), 10–11.
5. CONAB, Série Histórica de Produção tables "Café Conilon," and "Café Arábica" for 2001–2021, found at https://www.conab.gov.br/info-agro/safras/serie-historica-das-safras. The growth of robusta coffee production can be attributed to several factors, its use in soluble coffee production which has been increasing, growth of its utilization in blends in

order to reduce costs due to its lower costs than arabica, and the use of a new steaming process which reduces the harshness of its taste. Niraldo José Ponciano, Paulo Marcelo de Souza, and Marlon Gomes Ney, "Ajustamentos na cadeia agroindustrial do café brasileiro após a desregulamentação," *Revista Ideas* 3, no. 2 (2009): 266.

6. CONAB, acesso em: https://www.conab.gov.br/info-agro/safras/cafe.
7. CEPEA, "Mercado de trabalho no agronegócio brasileiro, 3°. Trim. 2020," accessed at: https://www.cepea.esalq.usp.br/upload/kceditor/files/3tri2020_Relatorio%20MERCADO%20DE%20TRABALHO_CEPEA.pdf.
8. See Pedro Carvalho de Mello, "The Economics of Labor in Brazilian Coffee Plantations, 1850–1888" (PhD thesis, Department of Economics, University of Chicago, 1977).
9. José Antonio Saraiva, "Quadro estatístico de alguns estabelecimentos rurais da Província de São Paulo (1855)," in *Documentos com que o Illustríssimo e Excelentíssimo Senhor Dr. José Antonio Saraiva, presidente da Província de São Paulo, instruiu o relatório da Abertura da Assembleia Legislativa Provincial no dia 15 de fevereiro de 1855* (São Paulo, 1855).
10. The *arroba*, a unit of weight, corresponds to 14.688 kilograms. Francisco Vidal Luna and Herbert S. Klein, "Nota a respeito de medidas para grãos utilizados no período colonial e as dificuldades para sua conversão ao sistema métrico," *Boletim de História Demográfica*, VIII, no. 21 (março 2001), found at http://historia_demografica.tripod.com/bhds/bhd24/fvl.pdf.
11. Van Delden Laerne, *Brazil and Java: Report on Coffee-Culture in America, Asia, and Africa (1885)* (London & The Hague: Martinus Nijhoff, 1885).
12. On the conflict with these first immigrants into the West Paulista region see Thomaz Davatz, *Memória de um colono no Brasil (1850)* (Belo Horizonte: Itatiaia; S.Paulo, EDUSP, 1980).
13. On the theme of immigration see Pierre Monbeig, *Pioneiros e Fazendeiros de São Paulo* (São Paulo: Hucitec-Polis, 1984); Thomas H. Holloway, *Immigrants on the Land: Coffee and Society in Sao Paulo, 1886–1934* (Chapel Hill: University of North Carolina Press, 1980); Warren Dean, *Rio Claro: A Brazilian Plantation System, 1820–1920* (Stanford: Stanford University Press, 1976).
14. The Hospedaria dos imigrantes do Brás was constructed between 1886 and 1888, and was the largest center for receiving immigrants than in existence in Brazil. Between 1887 and 1978 more than two million persons passed through its doors. Arquivo de Estado de São Paulo at http://www.arquivoestado.sp.gov.br/livros_estrangeiros.php; see Rosa Guadalupe Soares Udaeta, "As hospedarias de imigrantes em São Paulo:

o caso da Maçan D´Oro," *Anais do XX Encontro Regional de História ANPUH/SP* – UNESP-Franca (06 a 10 de setembro de 2010).

15. The Japanese immigration only began in 1908 when 3,200 Japanese immigrants arrived. This was marked a change from the earlier anti-Asian and anti-African sentiments and was made possible by a law no. 97 de 5 October 1892 which opened the country to Asian immigrants.
16. Rogério Naqués Faleiros, *Fronteiras do Café* (Baurú: Edusc, 2010), 1–37.
17. "The Supply of Mules to Central Brazil: The Sorocaba Market, 1825–1880," *Agricultural History*, 64, no. 4 (Fall 1990): 1–25; Carlos Eduardo Suprinyak, "Comércio de animais de carga no Brasil imperial: uma análise quantitativa das tropas negociadas nas províncias do Paraná e São Paulo" (MA thesis UNESP, Araraquara, 2006).
18. On the railroads see William R. Summerhill, *Order Against Progress: Government, Foreign Investment, and Railroads in Brazil, 1854–1913* (Stanford: Stanford University Press, 2003); Flávio Azevedo Marques de Saes, *As ferrovias de São Paulo, 1870–1940* (São Paulo: Hucitec-INL-MEC, 1981).
19. According to Summerhill, the gains to the Brazilian economy with the introduction of the railroad was greater than in most other nations. Summerhill, *Order Against Progress*, 189.
20. On the nineteenth century coffee economy see Antônio Delfim Netto, *O problema do café o Brasil* (São Paulo: IPE-USP, Ensaios Econômicos 16, 1981); Marcelino Martins and E. Johnston. *150 anos de café* (Marcelino Martins & Johnston Exportadores Ltda., 1992). On the government policies of the 1930s see Eugênio Lefevre, *A administração do Estado de São Paulo na República Velha* (São Paulo: Typografia Cupolo, 1937).
21. In 1906 Brazil produced 20.6 million bags, of which 15.4 million came from São Paulo. Unsold stocks on the international market reached 9.6 million bags (of which 7.5 million were Brazilian coffee), while world consumption was only 17.5 million bags.
22. Antônio Delfim Netto, *O problema do café o Brasil* (São Paulo: IPE-USP, Ensaios Econômicos 16, 1981), Capítulo 3.
23. Martins and Johnston, *150 anos de café*. Apêndice Estatístico, Tabela 1.1 e 1.2.
24. Edmar Lisboa Bacha, "Política Brasileira do café. Uma avaliação centenária," in Marcelino Martins and E. Johnston. *150 anos de café*: 65.
25. Bacha, "Política Brasileira do café": 73. Edmar L. Bacha, "Análise econométrica do mercado internacional do café e da política brasileira de preços," EPGE, *Ensaios Econômicos*, no. 2, 1970, p. 5.
26. On the erradication program see Stahis Panagides, *Erradicação do café e diversificação da agricultura brasileira. IPEA, outubro 1968*; Bacha, "Política Brasileira do café. Uma avaliação centenária," 80–81.

27. In that year of 1961, Brazil accounted for 37% of the total value of exports of green coffee and other coffee products (roasted and extracts), see FAOSTAT.
28. Martins and Johnston, *150 anos de café*, Apêndice Estatístico, Tabela 1.3.
29. On the world coffee market in this period see Steven Topic, "The Integration of the World Coffee Market," in William Gervase Clarence-Smith, and Steven Topik, *The Global Coffee Economy in Africa, Asia, and Latin America, 1500–1989* (New York: Cambridge University Press, 2003), 21–49.
30. Fernando Tadeu Pongelupe Nogueira and Danilo R. D. Aguiar, "Efeitos da desregulamentação na extensão e no grau de integração do mercado brasileiro de café," *Revista de Economia*, 37, no. 3 (2011): 21–46; Ponciano, Souza, and Ney, "Ajustamentos na cadeia agroindustrial do café brasileiro após a desregulamentação," 256–287.
31. About a third of the coffee plantations in Central America were renewed or required severe pruning, strongly affecting the 2013/2014 and 2014/2015 crops. Valeria Piñero, Samuel Morley and Pablo Elverdin, *Los efectos de la Roya en las economias Centroamericanas* (Stanford: International Food Policy Research Institute, Documento de Discusión 01457SP, 2015); Stuart Mccook, "Cronica de uma praga anunciada. Epidemias agrícolas e história ambiental do café nas Américas," *Varia Historia*, 24, no. 39 (January/June 2008): 87–111; Maryn McKenna, "Coffee Rust Is Going to Ruin Your Morning," *Atlantic*, September 16, 2020; Eugenio Schieber, *Impacto economico de la Roya del cafeto e America Latina.* Guatemala, 1973.
32. José G. P. Ormond, Sérgio R. L. de Paula, and Paulo Faveret Filho, *Café: (re)conquista dos mercados* (Rio de Janeiro, BNDES Setorial, n.10, set./1999), 17–18; also see Lucio Garcia Caldeira et al., "Café da Colômbia: o posicionamento da marca como instrumento para agregação de valor," *XII SEGET. Simpósio sobre excelência em gestão e tecnologia*, outubro 2015; Alexander Macias Calderón, "Estratégias de diferenciação do café: os casos do Brasil e da Colômbia" (MA thesis, Universidade Federal da Bahia, 2003).
33. After the extinction of the IBC in 1990, several research support bodies were created, with an essential role for *Embrapa Café*. In 1996, the Deliberative Council on Coffee Policy (CDPC) linked to the Ministry of Agriculture was created. Under the management of the CDPC and with coordination of Embrapa, the National Coffee Research and Development Program was established in partnership with the institutions of the National Agricultural Research System, known as the Coffee Research Program. *Embrapa Café, História*. Accessed at: https://www.embrapa.br/cafe/historia.

34. Priscila C. Moreira, Gustavo C. Moreira, Nicole R. Castro, and Rodrigo P. da Silva, "Produtividade e economia de fatores de produção na cafeicultura brasileira," *Revista de Política Agrícola*, 28, no. 2 (abr/maio/jun. 2019): 6–21; Samuel Frederico, "Globalização, competitividade e regionalização: a cafeicultura científica globalizada no território brasileiro," *GEOUSP- Espaço e tempo (online)*, São Paulo, 18, no. 1 (2014): 55–57, accessed at http://www.revistas.usp.br/geousp/article/view/81077.
35. See Rodrigo Peixoto da Silva, "Efeitos poupa-terra e poupa-trabalho na agricultura brasileira," *Revista de Política Agrícola*, 27, no. 3 (jul./ago./set. 2018): 69–81; J. E. R. Vieira Filho, "A fronteira agropecuária brasileira: redistribuição produtiva, efeito poupa-terra e desafios estruturais logísticos," in J. E. R. Vieira Filho; J. G. Gasques (Org.), *Agricultura, transformação produtiva e sustentabilidade* (Brasília: Ipea, 2016), 89–108.
36. Alisson A. V. Campos, Mauro M. L. Faria, and Túlio Pires, *Expansão da Cafeicultura em Rondônia*, 8/9/2022. Acesso: https://revistacampoenegocios.com.br/expansao-da-cafeicultura-em-rondonia/; Wilson Veneziano, Cafeicultura em Rondônia, Situação Atual e Perspectivas. Porto Velho, Embrapa Rondônia, 1996.
37. Segundo estimativas da Conab, a safra 2022 de café robusta em Rondônia alcancou a produtividade de 43 sacas por hectare, pouco abaixo da mèdia nacional, que resultou em 47 sacas por hectare. CONAB, Série Histórica de Produção table "Café Conilon".
38. CONAB, Série Histórica de Produção table "Café Arábica".
39. CONAB, Série Histórica de Produção tables "Café Conilon,"and "Café Arábica" for 2001–2021, found at https://www.conab.gov.br/info-agro/safras/serie-historica-das-safras.
40. See Herbert S. Klein and Francisco Vidal Luna, *Feeding the World: Brazil's Transformation into a Modern Agricultural Economy* (Cambridge: Cambridge University Press, 2018).
41. The country with the highest per capita coffee consumption is Finland (12 kg per annum), followed by Norway (9.9 kg), Iceland (9 kg), Denmark (8.7 kg), Holland (8.4 kg), and Sweden (8.2 kg). Germans consume (5.5 kg), and the French (5.4 kg), with Brazil itself listed as consuming 5.8 kg per annum per person. Surprisingly the United States is a low consumer, at just 4.2 kg per annum consumption, lower than Brazil. See COOPERCAM, acesso: http://coopercam.com.br/noticias/selecionada/mapa_paises_cafe.
42. IOC, http://www.ico.org/prices/new-consumption-table.pdf.

CHAPTER 10

Cellulose

Although lumbering was a part of the Brazilian economy from earliest settlement, the development of a modern pulp and paper industry only occurred in the late twentieth century. It was only in the 1960s that Brazil had sufficient production to begin exporting small quantities of chemical wood pulp and yet today is the second largest producer of chemical wood pulp or cellulose in the world, and the leading exporter of cellulose. As late as 2000 the United States and Canada accounted for over 50% of world production of cellulose while Brazil only accounted for 5%. But Brazil, China, and Indonesia quickly emerged as the next most important producers in the twenty-first century, with Brazil second only to the United States by 2021 (see Graph 10.1). There was also a fundamental change in exports as China and the United States absorbed ever larger share of their production and Canada production began to stagnate. By 2021 the combined Canadian and US exports were down to 22% of the volume of world exports and Brazil alone now accounted for 27% of this export market (see Graph 10.2).[1] Nor is this dominance about to change as the FAO estimates that production in Brazil will increase to 29 million tons by 2026, compared to the United States which will remain at about 44 million tons.[2] Equally Brazil has emerged as the 8th largest producer of paper roughly equal to such classic producers as Canada and Finland.

H. S. Klein and F. V. Luna, *Brazilian Crops in the Global Market*, Palgrave Studies in Economic History,
https://doi.org/10.1007/978-3-031-38589-6_10

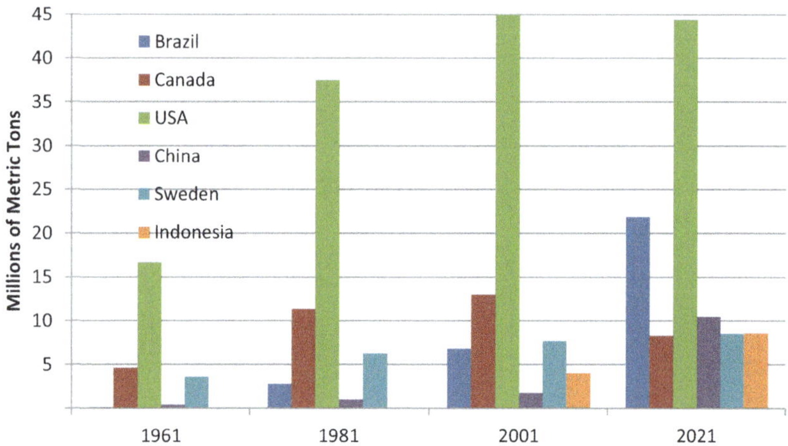

Graph 10.1 Volume of chemical wood pulp production by leading producers in select years, 1968–2021 (*Source* FAOSTAT at https://www.fao.org/faostat/en/#data/FO)

How and why Brazil emerged so quickly as a world leader in cellulose and a significant producer of paper and paper products is the basic theme developed in this chapter.

Despite the late start of Brazil as a chemical wood pulp producer, forestry production was actually one of the oldest of Brazil's agricultural activities. The fine woods of the continent have been exported to Europe for decades. Shipbuilding yards in colonial times were to be found in the ports of the Atlantic and wood for construction was produced everywhere. There were even specialty woods, such as Brazilwood (pau brasil) which were exported to Europe from the sixteenth century and used to create the famous red dyes in much demand in Europe.[3]

But the modern industry of planted forests and pulp and paper mills is a quite recent development going back only to the mid-twentieth century. It is an industry which has only been developed with major support of government subsidies, as well as national and foreign capital. This industry and government labs also created new tree types from imported species and new planting techniques to be used in both tropical and semi-tropical areas as well as the temperate regions of the country. Planted forests of modified pines and eucalyptus trees have formed the basis for this industry in Brazil, with eucalyptus hardwood short fiber bleached kraft paper the major product.

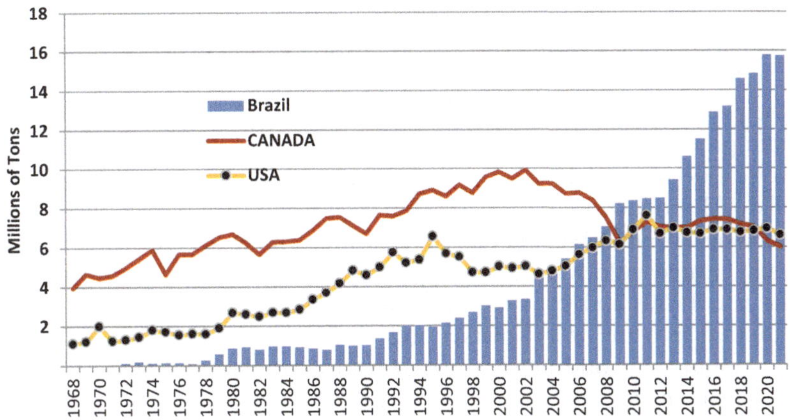

Graph 10.2 Volume of chemical wood pulp exports by Brazil, Canada and the USA, 1968–2021 (*Source* FAOSTAT, Forestry)

By the time that Brazilian producers entered the world market, mechanical grinding of wood pulp was in decline as was the application of sulfite. World producers were instead turning to sulfate to produce wood pulp which was increasingly gaining market share. The sulfite processes led to poor quality cellulose with weaker fibers and mechanical pulping processes left most of the lignin with the fibers, whereas the new kraft process using sulfate removed the lignin in the original wood and created stronger and more long lasting fibers.[4] The new South American pulp and paper industries quickly concentrated their efforts on producing two types of kraft papers. While the initial product was unbleached, Brazilian mills concentrated their production on bleached cellulose which would go to make white papers. The bleaching process increases the "brightness" of the resulting paper from 70% up to a brightness of about 92%. Newsprint is about 60% bright, white tablet paper 75%, and high grade bond 85% brightness.[5] In the Brazilian industry there were two types of bleached cellulose produced, depending on whether the trees used were hardwoods or softwoods. The softwood pine trees produced long fibers and the bleaching process was known as BSKP (or Bleached Softwood Kraft Pulp). The second process was based on hardwood trees, above all eucalyptus, and was knowns as BEKP (Bleached Eucalyptus Kraft Pulp) which produced short fiber cellulose.[6] In three countries studied here, each produced a different mix of BSKP and BEKP depending on climactic conditions in each country.

Why the new Brazilian producers concentrated on these bleach cellulose products can be seen in the changes which occurred at this time in both production and sales into the international market. The production worldwide of mechanically produced pulp, which accounted for a third of world production in 1961 steadily declined in each decade thereafter, reaching 20% in 2010 and just 1% of world production by 2019. Chemically created pulp was already appearing on the international market in the late 1960s and by 1970 accounted for over two thirds of all pulp exported into the world market and by 2019 it represented 99% of all the volume of world pulp exports. Of this chemically created cellulose, bleached sulfate pulp in turn dominated the world market. By 2019 it accounted for 96% of the volume and the value of chemically produced wood pulp.[7]

Given its late start the modern cellulose industry in Brazil local producers quickly concentrated on bleached sulfate which produced cellulose as its primary product. This in turn would be based on two trees non-native to the region, which were various types of pines and eucalyptus. Thanks to their late entry they were able, often with massive government support, to quickly become a major factor in the international market. Currently there are only eleven countries that are able to export over 1 million metric tons of chemical pulp and Brazil is the leader, shipping 15.8 million tons in 2022 which represented 27% of the world export market. Unlike other major producers, Brazil consumed much less of its output and was able to export more. Thus the US exports only 30% of its national production, whereas Brazil exported 65% of its national production (see Tables 10.1 and 10.2).

Given the unusual productivity of the trees they adapted to their climatic conditions, and the local development of leading research on hardwood chemical pulp production by Brazil, the pulp and paper industry of Brazil and other leading South American countries have become the most profitable in the world.[8] Of the three leading South American nations, Brazil was the first of the countries to develop a sophisticated pulp and paper industry. Small paper production began in Brazil in the late nineteenth century. One of the earliest was the *Companhia Melhoramentos de São Paulo* which was founded in 1883 and used rags as the primary material. The first major wood based paper production factory was the *Fábrica de Papel Paulista* founded in 1889. Then in

Table 10.1 Average annual chemical wood pulp production by major producers, 2016–2020

Country	*Average annual volume (tons)*	*% of total production*
USA	44,361,139	30
Brazil	19,457,000	13
Canada	8,946,097	6
China, Mainland	8,882,000	6
Sweden	8,271,617	6
Finland	7,590,400	5
Indonesia	7,550,600	5
Russian Federation	5,993,000	4
Chile	4,953,740	3
Uruguay	2,640,490	2
Portugal	2,634,740	2
India	2,434,800	2
Germany	1,612,670	1
France	1,565,440	1
Austria	1,298,361	1
Spain	1,232,570	1
Other	16,324,898	11
World	145,749,562	100

Source FOASTAT at https://www.fao.org/faostat/en/#data/FO

Table 10.2 Average annual chemical wood pulp exports by major world producers, 2016–2020 (in metric tons)

Country	*Average annual volume*	*Share of total (%)*
Brazil	14,280,693	25
Canada	7,114,578	13
United States of America	6,873,663	12
Chile	4,556,714	8
Indonesia	4,353,192	8
Finland	3,548,482	6
Sweden	3,063,294	5
Uruguay	2,625,774	5
All Other Exporters	10,398,126	18
World Annual Average	56,814,515	100

Source FAOSTAT

1908 the Klabin brothers imported modern machinery to produce paper based on imported pulp. Finally in 1912 came the *Anglo Brazilian Pulp and Paper Mills Co* which used pine wood from Paraná to create cellulose. Up to WWI the principal products produced were non-bleached wrapping paper and cartons, and until the late 1920s most of the pulp was imported. By the end of that decade chemical wood pulp was being produced nationally on a significant scale and more refined paper was being manufactured as well. But well into the 1930s the industry still relied primarily on imported cellulose. At the end of the decade just over half of the 128,000 tons of cellulose used in local paper was imported, but this share soon declined as paper production expanded rapidly so that imports were down to a quarter of cellulose needs in the next decade.

Directly supported by the Vargas government the Klabin Company established a new factory in 1934 which used its vast Paraná plantation of softwood araucaria trees to create long fibers as the source for cellulose. Kubitcheck in his industrialization plan put great emphasis on creating a national paper industry. The use of softwood and the sulphite process, common to the Northern Hemisphere countries, however, limited the potential of Brazil. But the big change came with the shift to the use of sulphates to extract the pulp and the milling of hardwood short fiber trees like the modified eucalyptus trees being developed in Brazil. Already by the late 1960s Brazil was self-sufficient in cellulose production and eucalyptus was beginning to replace bagasse, straw, grasses, and even the pines woods of Paraná as the primary national source for cellulose.[9]

It was also in this decade that Brazil adopted a modern forestry law which promoted tree plantations as part of a reforestation project. The new Forestry Code of 1965 became a major stimulus for forestry replanting aided by a 1966 tax code which permitted investments in forest plantations receiving tax exemptions. This led to the progressive decline in cutting native woods and the transition to forest plantations both for cellulose production as well as carbon for the steel industry. Both these industries were behind the growth of major plantations. Even sawmill lumber for furniture and other uses now became ever more dependent on tree plantations rather than native forests.[10] This reforestation to replace the trees used to make cellulose was accompanied by the progressive reorganization of the industry into ever fewer and larger units of production tied closely to these new tree farms. Initially only Klabin (with 22 thousand hectares of replanted trees) and the US owned Champion Paper

Company (with 17 thousand hectares) had integrated reforested plantations close to their pulp and paper production. Tree plantations went from half a million hectares in 1965 to 4.5 million hectares by 1985, and reached 9 million hectares of all types of trees by 2019, a figure which has remained stable to 2023.[11] On these totals a quarter was planted in American pine and three fourths were in eucalyptus trees, a species originated in Oceana and first planted in Brazil in the 1860s by the railroads, which used these hardwoods for railroad cross tie sleepers.[12]

It was these planted forests that enabled the industry to integrate tree plantations with pulp and paper mills everywhere after 1970, with major capital support from the Brazilian Development Bank (BNDES).[13] The 1970s and 1980s saw construction of numerous modern mills in joint public/private enterprises.[14] There was also a major push to produce modern technicians and scientists in this field and to carry out of basic research on cloning and hybridization of the trees used by the industry. In the 1960s at the federal universities of Viçosa and Paraná, the first forestry schools were established, and in 1968 was created a major research institute IPEF (Instituto de Pesquisas Florestais) supported by Universidade de São Paulo and the major production companies to help develop both new tree varieties and new industrial methods to produce cellulose from short fiber trees, primarily eucalyptus trees.[15] Companies also invested heavily in R&D and soon Brazil became a technological world leader, rather than a follower, in short fiber production.[16]

Significant deforestation of Brazilian softwoods and the needs to develop fast growing trees adapted to local climate conditions led to this major government and private sponsored research. Constant experimentation and adaptation by researchers led to the creation of new species of pine and especially of eucalyptus trees adapted to tropical and semi-tropical climates. In the late 1970s IPEF sent an expedition to Australia to collect seeds from all the varieties of eucalyptus then extant and carried out extensive modifications of the original seeds.[17] Brazilian eucalyptuses adopted from the original Australian varieties reached a productivity of 39 m^3 (cubic meters) per hectare per year by 2019, the highest in the world. This compared to Sweden at 6 m^3 per hectare and 4 m^3 per hectare per annum in Finland. Even Chile had better results with eucalyptus trees, which achieved 20 m^3 per annum. Brazil also led the world in productivity of output in pines, being 31 m^3 with Chile at 18 m^3 and Sweden and Finland at 4 m^3 per hectare per year.[18] This extraordinary productivity was due to both the adaption of new species by EMBRAPA, which now heavily invested in forestry research, and to climate. By 2019 Brazilian eucalyptus trees could be cut in 7 years and an average tree could be cut three times.[19] This compared to 12–15 years needed for the first cut in the Iberian Peninsula for the same tree. Even with pines Brazil could begin cutting in 15 years, compared to 25 years in Chile and 70–80 for the first cut in the two Scandinavian counties.[20]

This unusual productivity explains the comparative advantage of Brazil as a cellulose producer compared to the other major world exporters of this product.[21] In 2000–2002 it was estimated that Brazilian costs of production was US$ 157 per ton of cellulose, compared to an average cost of the two North American and two Iberian producer costs of $US 283 per ton. Labor of course was the cheapest among these five producers, but what was exceptional was the cost of wood input, which was $63 per ton in Brazil compared to the others which averaged US$ 130 per ton. Even chemical inputs were the lowest in Brazil.[22]

The best method for extracting pulp from these eucalyptus trees proved to be a chemical extraction using sulfate in a process similar to the so-called Kraft system of extraction [BHKP]. This process used larger amounts of caustic soda and a longer cooking time for this short fiber hardwood.[23] These technological and biotechnological advances using eucalyptus based pulp and the sulfate system were combined with major structural, ecological, and power usage changes. Almost all pulp and paper produced in Brazil now comes from planted forests. There is a close integration of forest plantations and the mills, with mills located close to their forest sources because of the high cost of transport.

There are also major efforts to control the environmental impact of cellulose production. The chemicals used in extracting the fiber and bleaching the pulp are recycled, the resulting black water is treated and all waste products are used to produce energy for the plant. Finally there has been a major effort to control gas emissions and convert waste water to useful products and the self-generation of electricity.[24] But despite all the efforts to control negative effects of the milling process, there still remain some environmental concerns in terms of plantations. Obviously native forests have a more diverse habitat than planted ones. Moreover Eucalyptus plantations are considered among the least favorable to other flora and fauna than other types of tree plantations. These trees lack broad leaves and tend to suppress ground vegetation. Their oil is insect repellant and they are highly flammable. But most plantations leave about 20% of the area unplanted, and in early stages of growth there is more fauna activity. Finally like all trees they play a key role in carbon gas reduction and are usually planted in areas which had been already deforested long before and thus tend to revive depleted soils.[25]

With government and private support a massive tree plantation regime began in this period following the Forest Code adopted in 1968. With these government incentives tree plantations grew rapidly and by 1990 Brazil had the third largest area of planted trees in any tropical area in the world, just behind China and India.[26] Initially there were more plantations of pines than of eucalyptus, but by 2000 some 62% of the 4.8 million planted forests trees were Eucalyptus and 38% were in Pines. Already in 1973 two thirds of the close to million tons of cellulose being produced now came from eucalyptus trees.[27] By 2013 eucalyptus trees accounted for three quarters of the 8.3 million hectares planted trees and by 2019 these plantations reached 10 million hectares, with 7.2 million hectares planted in Eucalyptuses and 2 million hectares in pines, with other tree varieties planted on 387 thousand hectares.[28] Almost all of the pine plantations were located in the states of the Southern region, while the eucalyptus trees were better spread throughout the country, though half of these planted forests were in the states of the Southeastern region (see Map 10.1).[29] These plantations of *Eucalytpus grandis* trees, the most common variety used, would run to 1,111 trees planted per hectare with 9 m^2 growing space between trees. This was the norm in the Aracruz planted forests. The Jari River plantation in the Amazon Basin which was established in the late 1960s currently uses 75,000 hectares of planted forest of Pines, the *Pinus caribaea* variety. Here the space around trees is 6 m^2 and 1,667 trees per hectare are planted.[30] By 2019 almost all the trees used to produce cellulose in Brazil came from these plantations and sawmills, which produced everything from sawn lumber to chips, obtained 72% of their wood from forest plantations and only 18% from native trees.[31]

Another key element in the industry was the growth of a national chemical sector which began to be implanted in Brazil in the 1960s. This allowed producers to reduce costs by using national chemical inputs. Klabin introduced the first sulfate processing mill in 1958. Another major producer of cellulose in this period was *Suzano Papel e Celulose* which was led by Leon Feffer who had established his first paper producing factory in 1939. His son Max Feffer was the leader in introducing eucalyptus wood into Brazil and the company began using this wood to produce cellulose in 1958.[32] It was thus Suzano which was the first to heavily invest

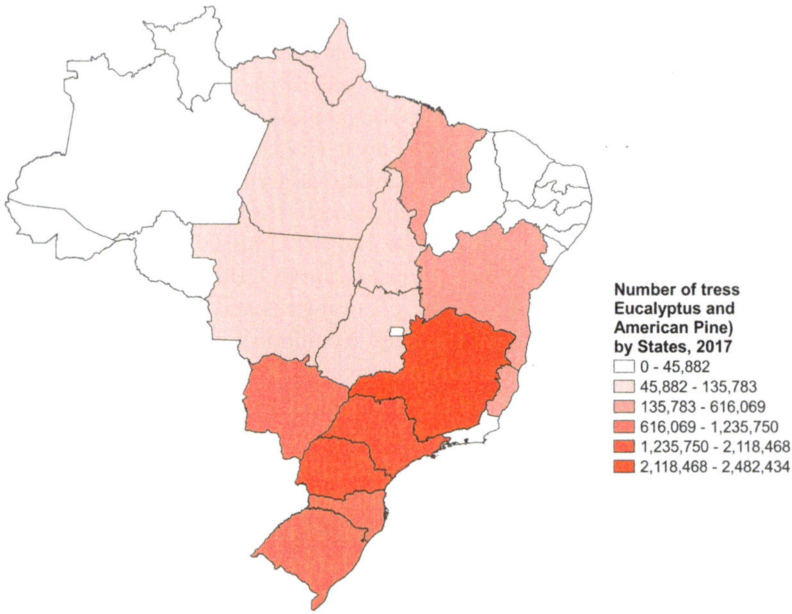

Map 10.1 Number of tress (eucalyptus and American pine) by state, 2017 (*Source* IBGE Bases cartográficas Sidra, table 540)

in short fiber hardwood eucalyptus trees using the sulfate process as the basic input for generating cellulose. By the end of the decade several other major producers had entered the market and the era of the plantations of eucalyptus had begun. While both sulphate bleached and unbleached chemical wood pulp was almost equally produced to the early 1980s, in that decade most of the industry moved toward producing bleached sulfate pulp which has dominated the market ever since. By the late 2010s sulphate bleached cellulose accounted for 90% of output.[33]

The 1990s for the forest industry, like the rest of Brazilian agriculture, was a period of crisis due to the end of tariff protection, of government funding and poor world prices. But the extraordinary productivity of Brazilian production due to new eucalyptus adaptations meant that the producers could compete on the world market, and in 1999 prices again grew as Chinese demand increased. It was also in this context that in Brazil, as in most other producing countries, there was an ever greater concentration of the industry. Thus from the 148 companies producing cellulose in 1980, most were integrated into ever larger companies and by 2008 there were only 38 companies left in cellulose production.[34]

In the current century the BNDES again returned to financing the industry. It also promoted amalgamations, with special emphasis on the paper and pulp industries, as well as on meatpacking companies. Mill construction was quite expensive and returns were slow due to the time it took trees to mature. A mill to be competitive needed to produce at least 2 million tons of pulp per year. This required at a minimum some 150 thousand hectares of planted trees, or some 300 thousand hectares if renewable programs were enacted.[35] The great advantage of Brazil was that its climate provided a good environment for new types of eucalyptus which reached maturity in just seven years—half the time of wood growth in most temperate climates.

As late as 2015 there were numerous producers and there was little difference in output among the leaders. Many of these smaller companies and groups had Chilean, Finnish, Japanese, North American, and Brazilian capital invested.[36] But the government thought this division among relative equals weakened the industry in terms of its export potential and in 2018–2019 the BNDE provided the funding for Suzano to take over *Fibria Celulose* the world's largest eucalyptus pulp producing mill. Fibria had been established as an amalgam of the mills owned by Votorantim, a major Brazilian industrial group, and the traditional Brazilian company Aracruz which had entered in crisis in 2008. With this purchase of Fibria by the Brazilian owned company, Suzano became the largest Brazilian paper and pulp company and one of the largest in the world.[37] But both Brazilian and foreign investments have continued to reshape the field. Currently Suzano and Klabin dominate production, but two Chilean companies have recently entered production or are planning major mills. CPMC Celulose Riograndense acquired a cellulose factory in 1972 from the Chilean company Arauco. Arauco remained in Brazil generating various wood based products in its other mills, but in January 2022 it announced a project to return to cellulose production by creating a new 2.5 million tons per annum factory to produce short fiber cellulose in Mato Grosso do Sul. To this end it had acquired 285,000 hectares to plant trees which should be ready to harvest when the mill opens in 2028.[38] Finally a Japanese paper company CENIBRA with production in Minas Gerais, initially launched with the support of the Vale do Rio

Table 10.3 Brazil's position in world production of paper products, 2021

	Printing & writing papers		*Household and sanitary papers*		*Cartonboard*
China	23,600,000	China	10,800,000	China	15,250,000
USA	7,926,075	USA	7,281,000	USA	8,482,180
Japan	6,128,000	Japan	1,836,000	Sweden	3,045,000
Germany	5,770,333	Italy	1,622,580	India	2,835,000
India	5,120,000	Germany	1,514,476	Finland	2,394,787
Indonesia	4,809,000	**Brazil**	1,330,000	Indonesia	2,350,000
Finland	3,070,574	Mexico	1,258,300	Germany	1,830,530
Canada	2,419,000	Canada	1,123,000	S Korea	1,469,000
Brazil	2,303,000	Indonesia	970,712	Japan	1,375,000
Sweden	2,018,130	France	832,000	Russia	886,575
Austria	1,982,686	Spain	802,500	Poland	840,000
Italy	1,884,000	UK	742,000	**Brazil**	784,000
Others	14,996,552	Others	7,520,702	Others	8,800,047
World	82,027,350	World	37,633,270	World	50,342,119

Source FOASTAT at https://www.fao.org/faostat/en/#data/FO

Doce mining company, is also a significant producer. Growth of production has been rapid in recent years and an increasing volume of foreign and domestic capital is being invested in forests and cellulose production.

Brazil has also emerged as a major producer of paper and paper products. It is the ninth largest producer of printing and writing paper and the 6th largest in the production of Household and Sanitary Papers, the sixth largest producer of tissue paper (or Household and Sanitary papers) and twelfth largest world producer of multilayered cartonboard (see Table 10.3).

The evolution of Brazilian cellulose production and exports has been extraordinary. Production went from 165 thousand tons in 1961 of chemical wood pulp to some 19 million tons by 2019. Once national needs were supplied there was also a major effort to increase exports. Already by 2000 the local market took only 14% of total production.[39] Results were impressive. Between 1999 and 2019 national production of cellulose was increasing at an extraordinary rate of 9% per annum.[40] Although Brazil only began to export in 1968, by 2005 it exported half of the cellulose that it produced in that year and by 2021 was exporting 74% of the 21.8 million tons national production (see Graph 10.3). At the same time the value of these exports grew from around US$ 3 million in 1961 to a

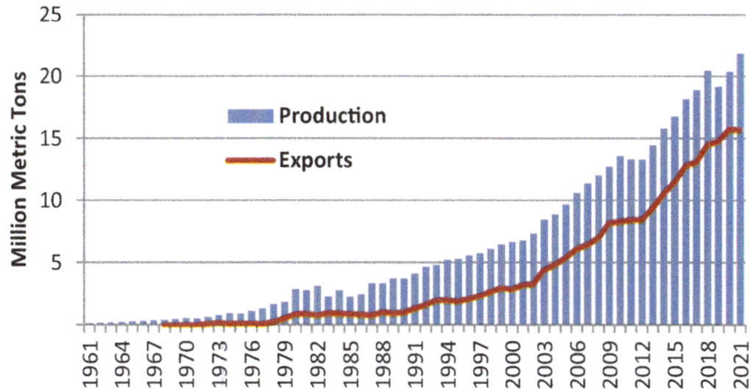

Graph 10.3 Volume of Brazilian chemical wood pulp production and exports, 1968–2021 (*Source* FAOSTAT at https://www.fao.org/faostat/en/#data/FO)

recent high of US$ 7.2 billion by 2019.[41] It was only in 2007 that Brazil finally passed Canada in total production to become the world's second largest producer, and only in 2009 that Brazil passed the volume of US exports to become the largest world producer of cellulose. By 2021 Brazil was the world's leading exporter of chemical wood pulps, accounting for 27% of world exports, and it ranked second in the world for the production of both chemical wood pulp and for the bleached variety, accounting for 13% of world production of the first and 16% of the second pulp.[42] By this time some 90% of production nationally was the bleached variety.

Brazil's primary export markets were Europe and China.[43] In 2020 China consumed just under half of all exports, the United States 15%, Italy (8%), and Holland next at 6%—these four accounting for over three quarters of Brazilian cellulose exports.[44] Cellulose, although a major income producer, accounted for only approximately 3% of all national exports on average between 1997 and 2020. Nevertheless cellulose earned more than sugar or coffee exports and just under half of what was obtained by meat exports in 2020.[45]

But cellulose was not the only forestry product which entered the world market. Another major area of growth in the Brazilian forestry industry has been paper production which eventually lead to Brazil becoming the 10th largest producer in the world and the 11th largest exporter behind Portugal and Korea in 2019, accounting for 3.4% of world paper exports in that year (see Graph 10.4). While its current national production is a tenth of China, the leading producer, its 1.3

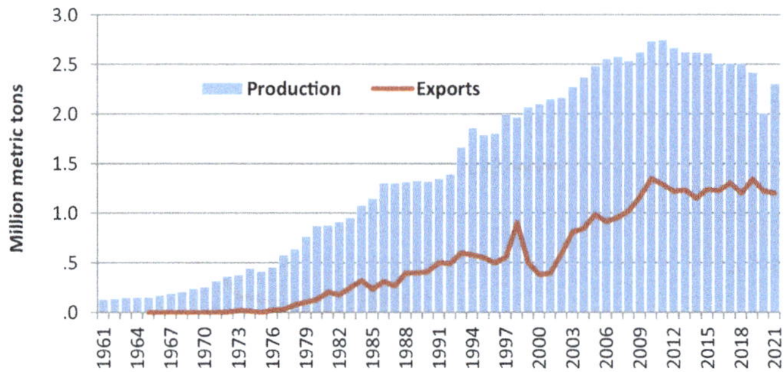

Graph 10.4 Volume of Brazilian production and export of printing and writing paper, 1961–2021 (*Source* FAOSTAT at http://www.fao.org/faostat/en/#data/FO)

million tons of paper exports in 2019 compare favorably to the 4.8 million tons exported by Germany, the world's leading exporter.[46] Paper producing companies in Brazil were smaller and less capitalized than in cellulose industry and dedicated far more of their output to national consumption. But even here there was continual concentration to fewer firms, going from 294 companies in 1975 to 211 in 2008. Initially paper sales went primarily to the local market which still absorbed 80% of production in 2000, but by 2019 the local market absorbed less than half of total output and by that year total exports of printing and writing paper were worth US$ 1.1 billion.[47] Brazil was the only South American country to significantly export of printing and writing paper, accounting for 91% of Latin American production.

Brazil also produced another US$ 3 billion in a large number of wood by-products as of 2019. The most significant were Sawnwoods, about equally divided by pine and eucalyptus, and printing and writing paper. It also exported significant amounts of plywood, cartonboard, and miscellaneous paper products (see Table 10.4). But many of these products were more absorbed in the national markets than were exported. Although 51% of paper production went into exports and lesser amounts for cardboard, almost all the tissue paper (known as Sanitary and Household Paper) was absorbed in the home market. Of all the Paper and Paper products exported in 2021 some 18% went to Canada, 15% to China, and 11% to Finland. In contrast only two countries accounted for over two thirds of

Table 10.4 Volume of cellulose and paper products produced and exported in 2020 (in metric tons)

	Production	*Exports*	*% Exported*
Cellulose	20,953,000	15,628,000	75
Packaging & Wrapping	5,515,000	662,000	12
Printing and Writing Paper	2,061,000	856,000	42
Newsprint	80,000	26,000	33
Tissue	1,339,000	52,000	4
Carboard	792,000	212,000	27
Others	453,000	283,000	62
Total	31,193,000	17,719,000	57

Source Revista O Papel (December, 2022): 36

cellulose exports—with the United States absorbing 44% of these exports and Argentina 35%.[48]

But these were not the only products generated from the planted forests of Brazil. Some 40% of the wood logs from 2010–2019 were used for non-cellulose or paper production.[49] This sector, which accounted for 29% of the total value of forestry products in 2019 includes the production of wood for shipbuilding, the furniture industry, civil construction, the manufacture of pallets, wooden panels, laminate floors, and posts among other items. This sector was equal in value for log woods destined for cellulose and paper in 2019, though the latter sector had been higher in previous years, both now accounted for 29% of the value produced by forestry.[50] Some of this sector went as unprocessed sawed lumber or log exports which in 2019 earned Brazil US$ 1.5 billion compared to the US$ 7.4 billion obtained from the processed pulp, and US$ 2 billion from paper (see Table 10.5). Another US$ 1.3 billion went into woods that were manufactured.[51] Still other timber went for products that had little export value, since they were primarily destined to the local market, among the largest of which were the 6.3 million tons of charcoal that was produced in Brazil in 2019.[52] A large share of this charcoal was used in making steel from iron ore. Brazil is the world's leading user of charcoal as a reducing agent for iron ore, whereas most steel making countries use coke obtained from coal.[53] Roughly 15% of the pig iron produced in 2021 for example was made using charcoal. In that year the Brazilian

Table 10.5 Value of major categories of forestry exports of Brazil in 2020 (in 1000 US$)

Category	*Value*	*%*
Chemical wood pulp	5,788,315	51
Printing and writing paper	900,819	8
Sawnwood (pine & eucalyptus)	707,347	6
Plywood	644,625	6
Other paper and paperboard	614,665	5
Dissolving wood pulp	299,178	3
Cartonboard	256,327	2
Case materials	159,976	1
Industrial roundwood (Pine etc.)	148,933	1
Miscl others	1,731,676	15
Total	11,251,861	100

Source FOASTAT at https://www.fao.org/faostat/en/#data/FO

steel industry consumed 1,700,000 tons of charcoal and 9,644,000 tons of coking coal to produce pig iron.[54]

Brazil was the leader in the evolution of this industry in South America. It entered the international market for cellulose in the mature period of its evolution and was thus able to adopt the latest in sulfate chemical bleached paper production. There were early attempts to develop a national pulp and paper industry using many of the early sources and methods, from rags to machine produced pulp. This was probably similar to many other such developing countries in the world. But like the other South American producers it all started to develop a more modern chemical industry with significant government support. First were enacted forestry laws which supported reforestation in these countries, and then government research proved important in developing the woods needed to produce cellulose. This was followed by domestic and foreign direct investment in the industry. Forest plantations were established in almost all regions, but most especially in poorer regions or those with soils unproductive for agriculture. New tree types were imported and they were modified by private and public research groups to fit a tropical climate. Everywhere cellulose mills developed close to their own tree plantations.[55] The result was that when the modern mills were finally created in the last decades of the twentieth century there already existed abundant and sustainable wood resources to make pulp. This may explain the very rapid increase in exports once the modern mills were constructed. It should also be stressed that these changes in forestry industries were parallel to changes in other agricultural activities. Thus the value chains, market skills, and the adaptation of modern farming technology developed in other areas as well as in the paper and pulp industries.

Brazil was not the only South American nation to develop a pulp and paper industry. The evolution of the paper and pulp industries in Chile, like that of Uruguay, got a much later start than in Brazil, but together the three South American countries had become the largest exporters of cellulose in the world. In 2021 these three countries produced 29.4 million tons of cellulose, or 19% of world production, but they exported 22.3 million tons, which accounted for 39% of the world market.[56]

Of the three Chile was second in importance in South American production and like Brazil had its own natively developed companies and production. It too was also dependent on two major imported tree species for its cellulose production, which are pines (called *pina radiate*) that were imported from California in the late nineteenth century and the Eucalyptus (primarily the *Eucaliptus globulus*) whose origin was Australia. By 2018 Chile had 2.3 million hectares of planted forest.[57] Although Chile like other countries raised tariffs on imported papers and encouraged a local industry to develop from the late nineteenth century, Chile still imported most of its pulp and paper needs until well into the twentieth century. But with massive government support, two companies would dominate production. The first, founded in 1920 to produce paper, was the *Compania Manufacturera de Papeles y Cartones* S.A. (or CMPC) would become a giant multinational company and primarily a pulp and paper exporter.[58] Between forestry developments, the creation of forestry university programs and the promotion of new forestry industries, the Chilean government like that of Brazil played a crucial role in developing the industry. The first cellulose plant of the CMPC was established in the mid-twentieth century and it and the mills that followed were developed with government capital. The biggest of the state owned plants were the Arauco mill built in 1972, and the Constitución mill in 1975, which were eventually privatized in the following decades and these two were amalgamated into one company under the name of Arauco (also known as Celco or Celulosa Arauco y Constitución). It is Arauco and CMPC which dominate cellulose production and have also become significant players in Brazil and Uruguay.[59]

As had happened in Brazil, cellulose production took off in Chile in the 1990s, quickly satisfied local demand and was quickly able to concentrate on exports of cellulose. The success of these exports was due to the low costs of production compared to other producing countries. It was estimated in 1990, that Chile produced softwood Kraft pulp at US$ 473 per ton, compared to US$ 517 in the US south, and US$ 708 in Finland.[60] But Chile also engaged in a modest export of semi-finished wood products which were mostly destined for American markets and it was only in 2007 that cellulose finally passed other forestry products in value of exports. Whereas Chile stressed the growing of pines and the resulting long-fiber pulp, Brazil concentrated on the short fiber producing eucalyptus wood. Forestry products made up on average 7% of Chilean exports between 2012 and 2021 a figure slightly higher than that of Brazil.[61] In contrast to the other major exporters, Chile also had a significant export of furniture and wood manufactured products, which made up a significant share of these forestry exports. Like Brazil the biggest consumer of Chilean cellulose products was China, which was already consuming almost half of Chilean output by 2015. In contrast paper and paperboard exports of Chile went primarily to the Americas and Europe with no particularly dominant country.[62]

Like the other two countries, the cellulose industry in Uruguay began with government support of forestry laws designed to reforest the country. Thus for decades before the creation of the first cellulose mills, investors had already been developing pine and eucalyptus wood plantations in Uruguay, but especially after the forestry law of 1987 which provided all types of support for a potential forestry industry.[63] The government promoted the development of plantations of both major types of trees now common in Chile and Brazil, which were pines and various species of eucalyptus trees which had been introduced into Uruguay in the mid-nineteenth century.[64] Planting proceeded at a rapid pace and by 2019 Uruguay had 1 million hectares in planted trees, some 80% in Eucalyptus and 18% in Pines and 2% in other species.[65] Of the 42.2 million cubic meters of woods cut from all trees that year in 2019, three quarters went into making of sawlogs, panels, and veneers and only a quarter were used to produce pulp.[66] All of the woods processed were turned into kraft bleached sulphate produced cellulose.[67] Uruguay was the last of the major South American exporting states to become a significant forestry product exporter and with a different history from the other producers in terms of the ownership of the milling industry and the role it would play in the national economy. Unlike Brazil and Chile, the wood prepared for the cellulose factories by national saw mills is shipped to mills outside normal national boundaries. The only two major pulp producing mills processing Uruguayan woods are situated in tax free zones and are completely foreign owned and pay no taxes to the national government. Thus national tree producers export the major part of their output of their cut wood to free zones to be processed into cellulose.[68] Of course the mills have also invested in national forests in preparation for their own development and these too were tax exempt.[69] Uruguay's pulp and paper mills primarily concentrated on producing only chemically sulfate bleached wood pulp when it entered the international market in a significant way in 2008.[70] This of course was long after both Brazil and Chile had become major producers and exporters and unlike the two other countries, the Uruguayan industry was completely foreign owned.[71] It also started as a concentrated industry with just two giant foreign owned mills operating. The first mill, which opened in 2007, was the UPM Fray Bentos mill, jointly owned by two Finnish companies, UPM-Kymmene and the Metsä group, and the second, a joint project of the Swedish-Finish company Stora Enso and Arauco of Chile which began operations in 2009.[72] Over ten years after its introduction, wood products for the first time became the principal export of the country, surpassing meat exports, until then the classic leader. In 2020 the value of cellulose reached US$ 1.1 billion just behind the US$ 1.5 meat exports and accounted for 14% of the value of all Uruguayan exports in this year.[73] Of all wood exports, cellulose made up 77% of the total value of all forest products in 2020, the highest of any of the three exporting South American countries.[74] Some 64% of woods produced by the national sawmills went to produce cellulose in this same year.[75] As in the case of Brazilian and Chilean exports, China consumed 35% of its cellulose production.[76] The value of these exports went from half a billion dollars in the first year to US$ 1.4 billion in 2019.[77]

In all three cases, many of the developments are similar. They all entered the international market for cellulose late and were thus able to adopt the latest in sulfate chemical bleached paper production. In the case of Brazil and to a lesser extent in Chile there were early attempts to develop a national pulp and paper industry using many of the early sources and methods, from rags to machine produced pulp. This was probably similar to many other such developing countries in the world. But they all started to develop a more modern chemical industry with significant government support. First these governments created new forestry laws which supported reforestation in these countries, and then government research proved important in integrating and modifying imported trees. This was followed by state support for domestic investments, at least in the case of Chile and Brazil and then finally foreign direct investment in the industry which was the case in Uruguay. Forest plantations were established in almost all regions, but most especially in poorer regions or those with soils unproductive for agriculture. New tree types were imported and they were modified by private and public research groups to fit a tropical climate. Everywhere cellulose mills developed their own tree plantations.[78] The result was that when the modern mills were finally created in the last decades of the twentieth century there already existed abundant and sustainable wood resources to make pulp. This may explain the very rapid increase in exports from all three countries once the modern mills were constructed. It should also be stressed that these changes in forestry industries were parallel to changes in other agricultural activities. In virtually the same period Brazil emerged as the world's largest producer of soybeans, of sugar and a host of other agricultural products as well as becoming the world leader in exports of meat products.[79] In turn Chile became a modern international exporter of fruits, wines, and farmed fish, while Uruguay also became a major exporter of soybeans along with its traditional meat exports. Thus the value chains, market skills, and the adaptation of modern farming technology developed in other areas as well as in the paper and pulp industries.

Notes

1. FAO, *Forest Products*, 2010: 144–145, 148; FAO, *Forest Products*, 2014: 260–261, 264 and FAO, *Forest Products*, 2018: 254–255, 259, 266, and for 2019 data see FAOSTAT accessed 9 April 2023 at http://www.fao.org/faostat/en/#data/FO.
2. FAO, *Pulp and Paper Capacities Survey 2021–2026* (Rome, 2022), 42, table 1.2.
3. Shawn William Miller, *Fruitless Trees: Portuguese Conservation and Brazil's Colonial Timber* (Stanford: Stanford University Press, 2000).
4. On the evolution of paper making in Europe and South America see Juha-Antti Lamberg, Jari Ojala, Mirva Peltoniemi, and Timo Särkkä, eds., *The Evolution of Global Paper Industry 1800–2050: A Comparative Analysis* (Springer Science & Business Media, 2012). On the processes of making cellulose see Christopher J. Biermann, *Handbook of Pulping and Papermaking* (Elsevier, 1996).
5. Biermann, *Handbook*: 123, 128.

6. Marco Luraschi, *Análisis de la cadena productiva de la celulosa y el papel a la luz de los objetivos de desarrollo sostenible: Estudio de Caso Chile* (CEPAL, Naciones Unidas. M. 2005): 17.
7. FAOSTAT at http://www.fao.org/faostat/en/#data/FO.
8. Wieland Gurlit, Eduardo Mencarini, and Ricardo Montealto, "Weighing the Risks in South American Basic Materials," *McKinsey Quarterly*, 2, no. 1 (2007): 4.
9. Emerson Martins Hilgemberg and Carlos José Caetano Bacha, "A evolução da indústria brasileira de celulose e sua atuação no mercado mundial," *Análise Econômica*, 19, no. 36 (2001): 145–164; Hannes Toivanen, and Maria Barbosa Lima Toivanen, "Innovation and the Emergence of Brazilian Pulp and Paper Sector," *O Papel*, 72, no. 4 (April 2011): 65–71, found at http://www.revistaopapel.org.br/edicoes_impressas/41.pdf#page=65.
10. Mauricio Mendonça, "El complejo forestal en Brasil," in Jorge Katz and Néstor Bercovich, eds, *El desarrollo de complejos forestales en América Latina* (Bogotá: CEPAL/Alfaomega, 2003): 83–88; Carlos José Caetano Bacha, "Análise da evolução do reflorestamento no Brasil," *Revista de economia agrícola*, 55, no. 2 (2008): 5–24.
11. See the IBA [*Indústria Brasileira de Arvores*] data as of March 2023 at https://www.iba.org/dados-estatisticos.
12. Edison da Silva Campos and Celso Foelkel, *A evolução tecnológica do setor de celulose e papel no Brasil* (São Paulo:—ABTCP—Associação Brasileira Técnica de Celulose e Papel, 2016), 112.
13. Campos and Foelkel, *A evolução tecnológica do setor*: 113–114.
14. Thais Linhares Juvenal and René Luiz Grion Mattos, "O setor de celulose e papel," in Jorge Kalache Filho, ed., *Banco Nacional de Desenvolvimento Econômico e Social 50 anos: histórias setoriais* (Rio de Janeiro, 2002): 49–75 and found at https://web.bndes.gov.br/bib/jspui/handle/1408/12975?mode=full.
15. Nilma de Oliveira Morator, *A história do IPEF na Silvicultura Brasileira* (Piracicaba SP: IPEF, 2008); and Campos and Celso Foelkel, *A evolução tecnológica do setor*: 114.
16. Paulo N. Figueiredo, "Evolution of the Short-Fiber Technological Trajectory in Brazil's Pulp and Paper Industry: The Role of Firm-Level Innovative Capability-Building and Indigenous Institutions," *Forest Policy and Economics*, 64 (2016): 1–14.
17. Katia Regina Pichelli, ed., *Embrapa Florestas: 30 anos* (Embrapa Florestas, Colombo RS, 2008), found at https://ainfo.cnptia.embrapa.br/digital/bitstream/item/51443/1/Livro-30anos.pdf.
18. Bradesco, DEPEC, *Monitor Setorial, Papel e Celulose*, Setembro 2019, n.p. table "Produtividade por tipo de fibra, Comparação internacional,"

found at https://www.economiaemdia.com.br/BradescoEconomiaEmDia/static_files/pdf/pt/monitores/setorial/infset_papel_e_celulose.pdf.

19. See Milton Geraldo Ramos, Pedro Nicolau Serpa, Constâncio Bernardo dos Santos and José Antônio Cardoso Farias, *Manual de Silvicultura, I—Cultivo e manejo de florestas plantadas* (Boletim Didático No 61; Florianópolis: Epagri, Santa Catarina, 2006), chapters 9 and 10; and EMBRAPA, Florestal, Eucalipto, found at https://www.embrapa.br/en/florestas/transferencia-de-tecnologia/eucalipto/perguntas-e-respostas.
20. BRADESCO, "Produtividade por tipo de fibra, Comparação internacional," p. 52.
21. Fabrícia Gladys FS Rossato, Andres Susaeta, Damian C. Adams, Ieda Geriberto Hidalgo, Thais Duekc de Araujo, and Adriana de Queiroz, "Comparison of Revealed Comparative Advantage Indexes with Application to Trade Tendencies of Cellulose Production from Planted Forests in Brazil, Canada, China, Sweden, Finland and the United States," *Forest Policy and Economics*, 97 (2018): 63–64.
22. Caio César Radicchi, "Competitividade das exportações brasileiras de celulose: uma análise do Custo Brasil" (MA thesis, Universidade Federal de Viçosa, 2004):232, quadro 7;. Raphael Almeida Videira, "Uma análise da concorrência no setor brasileiro de celulose"(MA thesis, São Paulo, Fundação Getúlio Vargas, 2004): 9, table 3.
23. Felipe Santiago Montenegro, "Spread de crédito no setor de papel e celulose: um estudo da precificação de empresas brasileiras no mercado offshore"(MA thesis, FGV, 2018): 19.
24. See for example João Carlos de Almeida Mieli, "Sistemas de avaliação ambiental na indústria de celulose e papel" (Phd thesis, Universidade Federal de Viçosa, 2007); Antônio José Juliani, "Aplicação da modernização ecológica no setor de papel e celulose do Brasil" (Ph.d thesis Universidade Federal de Brasília, 2015); Debora Cristina Leite Nunes, "Conservação de água em máquina de fabricação de papel, O caso da Bahia Sul Papel e Celulose S.A." (MA thesis: Universidade Federal de Itajubá, 2007).
25. Julian Evans, *Plantation Forestry in the Tropics: Tree Planting for Industrial, Social, Environmental, and Agroforestry Purposes* (Oxford: Oxford University Press, 1992): 337–340.
26. Evans, *Plantation Forestry in the Tropics*: 33–35, table 3.1.
27. Jorge Maurício Mendonça, "Emergência e consolidação do padrão eucalipto na indústria brasileira de celulose de mercado," (MA thesis; Campinas: UNICAMP1992): chapter 1.
28. IBGE, *Produção da Extração Vegetal e da Silvicultura 2019* v. 34 (Rio de Janeiro, 2019): 1.
29. IBGE, Sidra, tabela 5930.

30. See Evans, *Plantation Forestry in the Tropics*, p. 183, table 11.3; also see Kenneth L. McNabb and Lineu H. Wadouski, "Multiple Rotation Yields for Intensively Managed Plantations in the Amazon Basin," *New Forests*, 18, no. 1 (1999), 365–366.
31. IBDE, Sidra, tabela 6945.
32. For a history of the company see http://www.suzano.com.br/suzanoholding/memoria/.
33. FAOSTAT found at http://www.fao.org/faostat/en/#data/FO.
34. Adriana Estela Sanjuan Montebello and Carlos José Caetano Bacha, "O setor de celulose e papel na economia brasileira," *O Papel*, 72, no. 4 (2011): 48, tabela 2.
35. André Barros da Horta, *Panoramas setoriais 2030: Papel e Celulose* (BNDES, 2017): 83 at https://web.bndes.gov.br/bib/jspui/bitstream/1408/14241/2/Panoramas%20Setoriais%202030%20-%20Papel%20e%20celulose_P.pdf.
36. Campos and Celso Foelkel, *A evolução tecnológica do setor*: 119.
37. See https://www.statista.com/statistics/815028/brazil-paper-cellulose-sector-company-net-revenue/.
38. *Revista O Papel* (February 2023): 45–47.
39. Montebello and Bacha, "O setor de celulose," p. 48 tabela 1.
40. Campos and Celso Foelkel, *A evolução tecnológica do setor*: 117–119.
41. FAOSTAT, found at http://www.fao.org/faostat/en/#data/FO.
42. FAOSTAT, found at http://www.fao.org/faostat/en/#data/FO.
43. https://www.celuloseonline.com.br/china-foi-o-maior-comprador-de-celulose-do-brasil-em-2018/.
44. MDIC, Secint/Sepec,Exportação: 2020/2019, "Principais produtos e países: acumulado," found at https://www.gov.br/produtividade-e-comercio-exterior/pt-br/assuntos/comercio-exterior/estatisticas/balanca-comercial-brasileira-acumulado-do-ano.
45. MDIC Secint/Sepec, Séries Históricas, "CUCI (Classificação Uniforme para o Comércio Internacional)" which covers Exports and Imports by-product from 1997–2020, found at https://www.gov.br/produtividade-e-comercio-exterior/pt-br/assuntos/comercio-exterior/estatisticas/balanca-comercial-brasileira-acumulado-do-ano.
46. FAOSTAT, found at http://www.fao.org/faostat/en/#data/FO.
47. Montebello and Bacha, "O setor de celulose," p. 48 tabelas 1 and 2.; and FAOSTAT for latest figures.
48. *Revista O Paper* (Junho, 2022), 18, Fig. 3.
49. IBGE, Sidra, tabela 291.
50. IBGE, *Produção da Extração Vegetal e da Silvicultura 2019*: 3.
51. MDIC Secint/Sepec, Séries Históricas, "CUCI (Classificação Uniforme para o Comércio Internacional)" found at https://www.gov.br/produtividade-e-comercio-exterior/pt-br/assuntos/comercio-exterior/estatisticas/balanca-comercial-brasileira-acumulado-do-ano.

52. FAOSTAT, found at http://www.fao.org/faostat/en/#data/FO.
53. Ibá at https://www.iba.org/carvao-vegetal-2.
54. Instituto Aço Brasil, *Anuário Estatístico 2022*, 65, table 25.
55. Lima-Toivanen, "The South American Pulp and Paper Industry," pp. 243–244.
56. FAOSTAT.
57. In 2019, for example another 127,000 hectares were planted in trees. See INFOR, *Anuario Forestal 2020* (Santiago: Ministerio de Agricultura, Instituto Forestal; Boletín Estadístico no. 174): 24, and 31, table 2.7 This and all other INFO studies are found at https://wef.infor.cl/publicaciones/publicaciones.php.
58. Maria Barbosa Lima-Toivanen, "The South American Pulp and Paper Industry: The Cases Brazil, Chile, and Uruguay." in Juha-Antti Lamberg, Jari Ojala, Mirva Peltoniemi, and Timo Särkkä, eds., *The Evolution of Global Paper Industry 1800–2050* (Dordrecht: Springer, 2012): 263–273: 246, 248.
59. Luraschi, "Análisis de la cadena productiva de la celulosa:" 11, 23. For more detailed analysis of Chilean developments see Herbert S. Klein and Francisco Vidal Luna, "The Development of a Modern Cellulose Industry in South America," *Latin American Research Review*, 57, no. 4 (December, 2022), 753–774.
60. Brent Herbert-Copley, "Innovation, Regulation and Environmental Management in the Chilean and Canadian Pulp and Paper Industries," (PhD diss., Carleton University, 1999): 198, table 6.2.
61. Chile Aduanas, at https://www.aduana.cl/exportacion-por-productos/aduana/2020-04-02/091449.html.
62. FAOSTAT.
63. For the law see http://www.sice.oas.org/investment/natleg/ury/l_forestal_s.pdf; and Horacio Martín Melo Pissón, "Estudo geoeconômico da cadeia produtiva de papel e celulose no Uruguai" (MA thesis, Universidade Federal de Santa Catarina, 2018): 30. For more details on the evolution of the industry in Uruguay see For more detailed analysis of Chilean developments see Klein and Luna, "The Development of a Modern Cellulose Industry in South America."
64. Pissón, "Estudo geoeconômico da cadeia produtiva de papel e celulose," p. 60.
65. Data found at SPF (Sociedad de Productores Forestales del Uruguay), *Contribución del complejo forestal a la economía uruguaya* (Informe ejecutivo–Diciembre 2020): 7, found at http://www.spf.com.uy/wp-content/uploads/2020/12/SPF-Impacto-Forestaci%C3%B3n_Diciembre 2020.pdf.
66. MGAP, *Anuario Estadístico Agropecuario 2020*: 154, cuadro 4.
67. FAOSTAT, found at http://www.fao.org/faostat/en/#data/FO.

68. Humberto Tommasino and Waldemar Annunziatto "¿Cómo mejorar la cadena forestal uruguaya? *Anuario 2014 OPYPA* (MGAP): 224–229, All these OPYPA *Anuarios* will be found at https://www.gub.uy/ministerio-ganaderia-agricultura-pesca/buscar?search_api_fulltext=Anuario+OPYPA&search-in-site=MGAP; also see Fernando Resquin Pérez, "Producción de biomasa en plantaciones intensivas de Eucaliptus spp. en Uruguay" (Phd thesis, Universidad de Córdoba, 2019).
69. Thus the Finnish company UPM-Kymmene as early as 1990 created the Compañia Oriental Forestal to create tree plantations. See UPM, *125 Años en Uruguay, Informe 2015*: 8, 10, found at https://cld.bz/bookdata/5IWy0Tu/basic-html/page-8.html#. Pissón, "Estudo geoeconômico da cadeia produtiva de papel e celulose," 98.
70. See exports for 2012–2019 at MGAP, "Exportaciones (Volumen con Zona Franca)" found at https://www.gub.uy/ministerio-ganaderia-agricultura-pesca/datos-y-estadisticas/microdatos/exportaciones-volumen-zona-franca-2012-2019.
71. See "Beneficios Tributarios para Zonas Francas," found at https://www.gub.uy/ministerio-economia-finanzas/politicas-y-gestion/beneficios-tributarios-para-zonas-francas.
72. https://www.montesdelplata.com.uy/english/our-company-2.
73. Uruguay XXI, *Informe de Comercio Exterior Uruguay 2018*: 4 cuadro 1.
74. MGAP, DGF [Dirección General Forestal]—, *Estadísticas Forestales 2020*: 38 cuadro January 5, 10 at https://www.gub.uy/ministerio-ganaderia-agricultura-pesca/sites/ministerio-ganaderia-agricultura-pesca/files/2020-07/DGF%20Boletin%20Estadistico%202020.pdf.
75. MAGP, DFG, *Estadísticas Forestales 2020*: 7, cuadro 1.2.
76. Banco Central, *Informe Annual de Comercio Exterior—2018*: 4–5 found at http://www.adau.com.uy/innovaportal/file/15997/1/informe-anual-de-comercio-exterior---2018.pdf. Also see Darío Fuletti and Cecilia Petraglia, "Evolución reciente y perspectivas del comercio exterior de productos forestales," MGAP, *Anuario 2018 OPYPA*: 241–252. The data on volume and values is found in FAOSTAT accessed March 29, 2019 at http://www.fao.org/faostat/en/#data/FO.
77. Uruguay XXI, *Informe de Perspectivas de Comercio Internacional2020*, cuadro 4, and following unnumbered pages found at https://www.uruguayxxi.gub.uy/es/centro-informacion/articulo/perspectivas-del-comercio/.
78. Lima-Toivanen, "The South American Pulp and Paper Industry," pp. 243–244.
79. See Herbert S. Klein and Francisco Vidal Luna, *Feeding the World: Brazil's Transformation into a Modern Agricultural Economy* (New York: Cambridge University Press, 2018).

CHAPTER 11

Cattle

Brazil is today one of the most important producers and exporters in the world of animal protein, involving cattle, pigs, and poultry. It has the largest cattle herd in the world and one of the largest stocks of chickens and swine. In turn it is the world's largest exporter of beef and veal, accounting for about a quarter of the world's exports, and is also the world's largest exporter of processed chicken meat and the third largest exporter of processed pork meat.[1] In 2022 Brazil exported US $ 25.6 billion of meat products, which corresponded to 14% of agribusiness exports, and was only surpassed in value by soybeans, which obtained US$ 60.8 billion and accounted for 45% of such exports. In turn Beef and its products alone accounted for US$ 12.9 billion in exports, which was the same as the value of all maize exports.[2]

Cattle, like pigs and chickens were introduced by the Portuguese as they settled Brazil. Given the vast expanse of territory extensive cattle breeding became the norm. This ranching economy was important both in the production of meat aimed at the domestic market and some of its products entered the export market. Thus dried beef and leather were a consistent part of Brazilian exports from early colonial times. Extensive, low-productivity livestock farming was traditionally practiced with immense herds occupying a large part of the Brazilian territory. Many of

H. S. Klein and F. V. Luna, *Brazilian Crops in the Global Market*, Palgrave Studies in Economic History,
https://doi.org/10.1007/978-3-031-38589-6_11

the colonial and republican latifundias were essentially large cattle ranches with limited agricultural activity.

From the beginnings of Brazilian colonization, livestock activity has played a fundamental role in the process of occupying Brazilian territory. As a counterpart to the growth of the sugar-producing coastal regions of the northeast, was the development of extensive livestock production in the hinterland. Throughout the sixteenth and seventeenth centuries there was a long process of territorial expansion through conquest of Indian lands in the interior of the northeast. Concurrently raising livestock in the sugar areas became too costly and ranching was expelled from areas under the direct influence of the sugar plantations.[3] Antonil, writing in the early years of the eighteenth century, estimates the existence of approximately 1.3 million head of cattle in the region of the São Francisco River, which included parts of Bahia, Pernambuco, and the current states of Maranhão and Ceará. On large ranches animals received only the necessary care for survival and to prevent them from becoming wild.[4] These large agricultural units were exploited directly and by leasing in areas forcefully appropriated from Indian tribes.[5] Nor was the process of incorporating the Indians into work on cattle ranches a peaceful process, since many of these workers were slaves.[6]

A large share of the cattle raised in the hinterlands (the *sertão* region) were shipped hundreds or thousands of kilometers to the sugar regions and there slaughtered for their meat or were used as work animals in sugar production.[7] The free population of the sugar regions supported themselves with beef and the slaves were given animal parts of lesser value and beef jerky for their consumption.[8] In the sertão itself, meat and milk were the basic food source. Another major product was salted meat which was initially produced in Ceará and later in other northeastern areas along the coast.[9] The availability of salt on the coast stimulated the formation of these jerked beef productive units, which shipped their output to other population areas by coastal shipping.[10] The other major export, leather, was used in a host of products. For example, tobacco shipped from Bahia was packaged in leather.[11] In addition, 90 thousand half soles were shipped from Bahia and Pernambuco each year to Portugal.[12]

Northeastern cattle ranching also benefited from the discovery and exploration of gold in the final years of the seventeenth century, in areas of the current states of Minas Gerais, Goiás, and Mato Grosso which opened up a new regional market. These mining regions were located in inhospitable areas far from the coast. The provisioning of these mining centers opened up new markets in the central and southern provinces of the colony.[13] Although the Crown attempted to prohibit trade between the mining regions and the northeastern colonies, it quickly abandoned the attempt given the food needs of the miners, and it also promoted cattle ranching in the mining regions of Minas Gerais, Goiás, and Mato Grosso.

Cattle ranching also expanded in the region of São Paulo and from there to the southern provinces. The region of the so-called Curitiba fields was initially exploited by the *paulistas* for cattle breeding. This occupation later extended to the region of Laguna, in the current state of Santa Catarina, which represented the limit of legal possession of Portugal determined by the Treaty of Tordesillas. There were already cattle in the natural pastures of the far southern colonies brought there by Spaniards settling in the Rio de la Plata region or by Jesuits who established missions along the Paraná and Paraguay Rivers.[14] Many of these cattle were abandoned and living in the wild, and were hunted for their leather.

Slowly the Portuguese established ranches in this southern region which by the late eighteenth century became known as *charqueadas*, or ranches which produced *charque* or sun dried jerked beef.[15] Most of this system was developed in the province of Rio Grande do Sul, which also produced hides, tallow, and grease. These products along with beef jerky accounted for more than three quarters of the province's exports, driving the regional economy and guaranteeing the continuous demand for cattle raised in the estates that occupied the southwestern border of the country.[16] In 1784 there were already 460 thousand head of cattle in Rio Grande do Sul, distributed among 1,540 ranches, of which close to 60% were in units with more than one thousand heads.[17] The growth of this economy was also stimulated by the decline in processed meats from the northeastern ranches due to massive droughts that occurred from the 1770s onward.[18]

The center of *charque* production was the Pelotas region in Rio Grande do Sul, but dried and salted meat was also produced in Montevideo and Buenos Aires.[19] In Pelotas, 300 to 400 thousand head of cattle would be slaughtered annually in the more than three dozen *charqueadas* existing on the banks of the São Gonçalo and Pelotas rivers. The fattening phase of the cattle would be in the pastures of the Rio Grande region or in the north of Uruguay, from there taken by land to Pelotas.[20] The *charqueadas* also produced greases, tallow, and salted hides, mostly destined

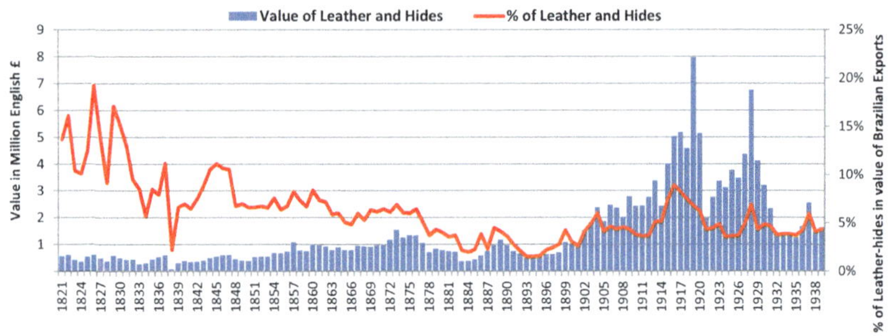

Graph 11.1 The relative share of exports of leather and hides, and sugar, 1821–1939 (*Source* IBGE, Estatísticas Históricas Retrospectivas)

for export. The grease and tallow were used for industrial purposes and in the manufacture of soap, candles, and waxes. Grease could also be used in cooking.[21] So successful was this ranching economy that it was able to import African slaves and by the early nineteenth century 30% of the provincial population were slaves, a ratio found in almost all the prosperous provinces.[22] The workforce in the *charqueadas* was essentially based on African slave labor. A study based on inventories in Pelotas shows an average of 55 to 65 slaves per owner, performing multiple activities in these *charqueadas*.[23]

The ranching economy from all regions was also involved in international trade. Throughout the nineteenth century, hides and skins represented around 10% of exports between 1821 and 1850, and 5% in the second half of the nineteenth century. In the first three decades of the twentieth century there was a significant increase in the value of exports of hides and skins, which reached a value similar to that obtained with sugar exports (see Graph 11.1).

The most valuable of these exports were unprocessed hides, since these were then tanned and cleaned in Europe. In a detailed analysis of the pastoral exports of Brazil in 1870/1871 these unprocessed hides represented 87% of the value of all pastoral products exported. At the same time the dominance of Rio Grande do Sul was evident, as it accounted for 82% of the nation's pastoral exports to Europe (see Table 11.1).

The Brazilian pastoral sector, as well as agriculture in general, was quite rudimentary during the first three centuries of colonization. The only concern for improvement occurred with sugar, the main agricultural

Table 11.1 Exports of livestock products, by main exporting provinces, 1870/1871 (mil réis)

Principal products	*Rio de Janeiro*	*Pernambuco*	*Bahia*	*Rio Grande do Sul*	*Total*
Animal hairs	4,943			461,517	466,460
Unprocessed leather hides	495,853	582,595	825,450	7,783,203	9,687,101
Wool				509,465	509,465
Bones				157,961	157,961
Others	24,298	4,169	33,836	193,516	255,819
Total	525,094	586,764	859,286	9,105,662	11,076,806

Source Estatísticas do Commercio Maritimo do Brazil, exercício de 1870–1871; 2a. Parte

export product until the beginning of the nineteenth century. Even in this case, Brazil lagged behind the advances that were occurring in milling in the Caribbean production centers. In the case of livestock, concerns about technical improvement began only in the nineteenth century, with the introduction of new breeds with greater milk capacity in Bahia and the import of the first batches of forage grass seeds of African origin. From 1870 onward, new breeds of European origin were imported into Rio Grande do Sul and the Zebu breed to other parts of Brazil.[24] In the twentieth century, there was an increase in zebu cattle importations as the adaptability of this breed to Brazilian tropical conditions became well known.[25]

The evolution of the livestock industry in Brazil by the mid-nineteenth century began to diverge from the neighboring Argentine experience even though they had shared a common history until then. Both colonies had developed dried beef production for regional and local consumption and were major exporters of hides. But from the second half of the nineteenth century Argentina, with the aid of British capital, began to improve herds and create a modern meatpacking industry which exported chilled and frozen beef to Europe.[26] In contrast the Brazilian cattle industry changed little from the colonial period until well into the twentieth century and only supplied meat to the domestic market. The Brazilian pastoral sector, as well as Brazilian agriculture in general, was quite rudimentary during most of these centuries and there was little incentive to export beef even after the introduction of refrigeration.

There were some changes. New breeds of European milk cows were introduced and forage grass seeds of African origin were imported to create planted pastures. From 1870 onward, breeds of European cattle were imported into Rio Grande do Sul and into other states, but in Mato Grosso and other tropical zones they did not survive. It was the Indian Zebu which by the early twentieth century was being bred by the Center-West ranchers and those of Minas Gerais, especially after the 1890s as the railroads reached this state from the coast.[27] In the twentieth century, there was an increase in zebu cattle importations in the 1930s and again in the 1950s and 1960s.[28] Although some zebu were introduced probably in the colonial period given Portuguese contact with India where these animals predominated, systematic importation came only in the twentieth century.

By 1960 the census registered the existence of 29 million hectares occupied by crops and 122 million hectares occupied by pastures. Of these pastures, 102 million were natural and only 20 million were planted. Most of the natural pastures were found in the Center-West and Southeast. About half of the planted pastures were concentrated in the Southeastern states, basically in Minas Gerais and São Paulo. In general, livestock was raised on new and uncultivated land or land depleted by exploitation in traditional farming regions, with little capital applied.[29] The census records the existence of 56 million cattle, with a greater concentration in Minas Gerais, Rio Grande do Sul, and São Paulo. The herds were made up predominantly of zebu and their crosses with the native breeds (Map 11.1).[30]

Ranching of course resulted in the largest farm units. The average size of the 339 thousand ranches that raised cattle averaged 313 hectares. About 40% of the cattle were in herds of up to 100 heads, which represented 93% of ranching units, and 60% of the animals were found on ranches housing more than 100 animals. Less than a third of the cattle belonged to establishments with less than 100 hectares even though these establishments accounted for 82% of all ranches. Those over 100 hectares, accounted for some 82% of all the animals.[31] Brazil at the time was estimated to have the 4th largest cattle herd in the world, behind India, the United States, and Russia, and fifth in terms of the stock of pigs.

In this period ranchers used traditional methods, and practiced extensive breeding with little concern for improving the herd, or adopting methods already available and practiced in many countries.[32] Furthermore, the modern slaughter, industrialization and commercialization of

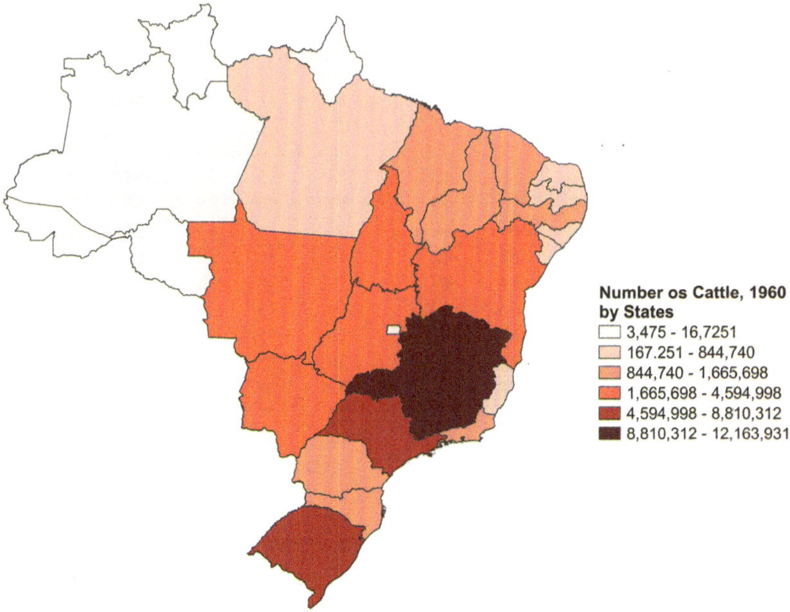

Map 11.1 Distribution of Cattle by State in 1960 (*Source* IBGE Bases Cartográficas Censo Agricola 1960)

beef meat, still had little impact in Brazilian ranching practices.[33] In 1960 of the 1.2 million tons of "prepared beef" generated by meatpackers, two thirds took place in local and unregistered slaughterhouses which existed throughout Brazil and only a fifth in registered *frigoríficos*. Three quarters of this "prepared beef" was *de natura* (unprocessed) and a fourth was cut and prepared by the *frigoríficos*. In this period a large part of the slaughtering took place on the ranches themselves rather than in slaughterhouses.[34]

Using the FAO's estimates of the size of the Brazilian herds at mid-century, the yield estimates of Brazilian producers were low compared to other countries with large stocks of animals, such as the United States, USSR, and Argentina. The data suggests that Brazil was still less efficient than these other countries. The Brazilian slaughter rate is even lower than the world average, as was its yield of kilos of carcasses produced per head. The Brazilian results are half of those obtained in Argentina and about a

Table 11.2 Cattle stock and yield indicators, Brazil, world and main countries, 1961–1971

	World	*USA*	*URSS*	*Brazil*	*Argentina*	*World*	*USA*	*URSS*	*Brazil*	*Argentina*
	Stocks (in millions)					*Slaughtered/stocks (%)*				
1961	942	98	76	56	43	18	35	34	13	24
1962	957	100	82	58	43	19	35	36	12	27
1963	970	104	87	60	40	20	34	41	12	32
1964	988	108	85	62	42	19	36	39	12	22
1965	1,009	109	87	64	47	19	38	36	12	20
1966	1,028	109	93	66	49	19	38	35	12	23
1967	1,050	109	97	68	51	19	37	38	11	24
1968	1,065	109	97	71	51	20	38	39	12	25
1969	1,070	110	96	73	48	20	37	37	13	29
1970	1,082	112	95	75	48	19	35	36	13	27
1971	1,097	115	99	79	50	19	35	33	12	19
	Yield kg/carcass					*Yield kg of carcass/heads of stock*				
1961	160	215	110	192	210	29	76	38	24	50
1962	158	213	111	194	202	31	74	40	23	55
1963	159	224	104	193	202	32	75	43	23	65
1964	163	225	108	191	216	32	82	42	23	48
1965	166	219	124	191	218	32	82	45	23	43
1966	171	228	135	191	210	33	86	47	22	48
1967	172	236	138	193	201	34	88	52	22	49
1968	175	239	146	194	200	35	90	57	24	50
1969	179	244	155	193	209	35	90	58	25	60
1970	182	255	156	193	203	35	90	57	24	54
1971	186	256	169	193	211	35	89	56	23	40

Source Calculated from data from FAOSTAT

quarter of the values of the United States. Only in kilograms per carcass is Brazil closer to leading country norms. But this was due to the fact that in Brazil the cattle were older at the time of slaughter, which resulted in heavy carcasses. All these factors indicated a ranching industry with the low levels of productivity (see Table 11.2).[35]

Gradually, in the second half of the twentieth century, the stock of animals was being improved by the introduction of different breeds, specialized both for beef and dairy production. In the southeastern states these animals were crossed with European dairy breeds, mainly with the black and white Dutch cattle which were exploited both for milk and meat. In the far south, with a colder climate, European beef breeds (Hereford, Polled Angus, and Devon) replaced the creole cattle and formed the majority of the herd in Rio Grande do Sul. In São Paulo, in addition to these breeds, there were others such as Canchim (Charolais x Zebu), Pitangueiras (Red Polled × Guerrer and Gir), and others of lesser importance.[36] This process of improving the quality of beef and dairy cattle relied on multiple public and private initiatives, which basically improved the levels of productivity of cattle breeding.[37]

In livestock, as well as in Brazilian agriculture as a whole, a major transformation phase began in the 1960s and 1970s which would result, forty years later, in the exceptional performance of Brazilian produced meat products in the international market. There was a revolution in government support for agriculture whose aim was to reduce food prices by mechanizing and modernizing the rural industries so as to provide new exports, reduce food prices, and thus support the development of an import substitution industry. This was highly successful and this "conservative modernization" without land reform, created a modern agricultural sector.[38]

In these two decades the government provided cheap and abundant credit, minimum price support and the establishment of regulatory stocks.[39] In addition, Embrapa, the government agricultural research institute, would strengthen the existing agricultural research system in relation to the pastoral sector which was also supported by experimental stations in several of the Agricultural Faculties in the federal and state universities. Embrapa contributed to advances in control of cattle diseases and pests; developed five forage cultivars responsible for about 80% of the national planted pastures and made Brazil the largest exporter of tropical forage seeds in the world. This research contributed to the increase of the average weight of beef cattle herds and significantly increased the productivity of milk cows.[40] In addition Embrapa had a fundamental role in the economic occupation of the Cerrado, today the Brazilian breadbasket and a major source of soybean meal and maize, essential for the development of competitive livestock on the international market, particularly for swine and poultry.

The next important development was the modernization of the meatpackers themselves. From the late colonial period major municipalities were already controlling fresh meat supplies by granting monopolies to producers. By the nineteenth century municipalities began to create their own slaughterhouses.[41] Nevertheless fresh meat still competed with *charque* in the diet of most Brazilians. Even as late as 1870 it was estimated that the population of the province of Rio de Janeiro probably consumed at least 35 kilos of *charque* per inhabitant per annum.[42] To guarantee supplies and for health considerations, municipal governments established regulated municipal slaughterhouses. These then dominated meat processing for the urban populations for the rest of the century until the arrival of foreign companies. Part of the industry finally began to modernize, thanks to foreign and domestic investments and the adoption of refrigeration and the availability of refrigerated vessels in the late nineteenth century. This process profoundly altered the meat market and eventually limited the market for dried or salted meat. In 1910 the government gave permits for the establishment of modern *frigorificos* to produce frozen meat in Brazil. In 1913 the first nationally owned frigorífico Cia. Frigorífico e Pastoril was established in Barretos São Paulo in the traditional area where cattle from Minas and the Center-West region were fattened before slaughter.[43] But the big growth came in the period of World War I as European demand encouraged the establishment of multinational companies. The Brazilian government provided incentives to the sector, which included customs exemptions on imports of machinery and equipment and reductions in railway freight on government lines. The crisis of the late 1920s directly affected the sector, which underwent a consolidation which resulted in foreign capital owning practically all the production capacity dedicated to the export of frozen and canned meat, though leaving the regulated and unregulated slaughter houses under Brazilian control for the local market. American companies such as Armor & Co, Sulzberger, Swift and Wilson & Co, and Anglo the later controlled by British capital, emerged as the dominant producers along with two national companies in Barretos, in the state of São Paulo and the Cia Frigorífico de Pelotas in Rio Grande do Sul both of which began to operate in the 1910s.[44] In 1940, in central Brazil, foreign slaughterhouses controlled about 420,000 hectares of pastures, between their own and leased land, and from 35 to 40% of the slaughtered cattle were their own. In the 1940s and 1950s, extensive areas of forest in western São Paulo were transformed into pastures that began to fatten lean cattle from Mato Grosso and Goiás for these foreign owned slaughterhouses in the state of São Paulo. But by the 1960s these foreign companies were being replaced almost totally by native companies, many of them founded after 1980. This was also accompanied by an increase in the number of beef processed in the late twentieth and early twenty-first century which doubled between 1989 and the second decade of the new century (see Graph 11.2).

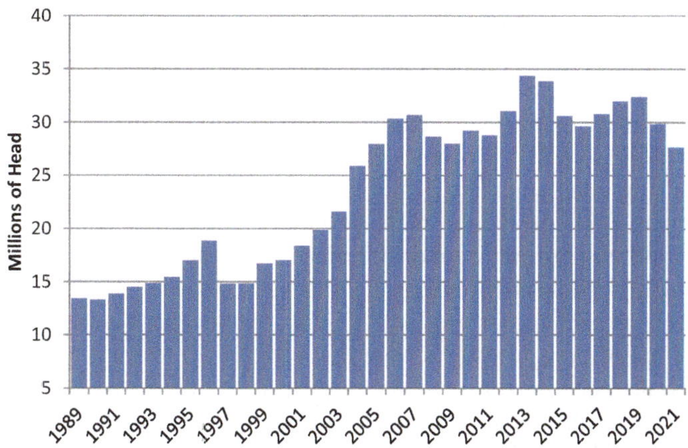

Graph 11.2 Number of beef slaughtered per year, 1989–2021 (*Source* 1989–1996 IBGE Sidra, Table 41; 1997–2021 at https://www.ibge.gov.br/estatisticas/economicas/agricultura-e-pecuaria/9203-pesquisas-trimestrais-do-abate-de-animais.html?=&t=series-historicas)

The emergence of the largest of the modern Brazilian meatpackers goes back to the foundation of two companies dedicated to the processing and packing of pork and chicken products in the state of Santa Catarina. These were Perdigão which was founded in 1934 by the brothers Ponzoni and Brandalise and Sadia founded by Attílio Fontana in 1944. Since these two companies first concentrated on chickens they eventually adopted in the 1960s the vertical integration model of the US poultry industry. This meant that these meatpackers provided all the imports (animals, rations, antibiotics, etc.) to the farmers who raised the animals and exclusively contracted to sell them to the meatpackers. Most of these inputs, rations and animals, would often be produced by the meatpackers themselves as they diversified into a host of other industries to supply their farmers. These two companies then moved into pork production, again providing guidance, and inputs to the pig farmers. By the last decades of the twentieth century they dominated the national markets for processed chicken, turkeys, ducks, and pork products.

Eventually these two companies followed the *gaucho* farmers to the Center-West and from the 1970s onward they bought or established processing plants dedicated exclusively to beef production. In this case, they did not create systems of vertical integration, but simply processed the beef sold by ranchers on the spot market. These two companies which had already created a joint trading company in 2001 to sell their goods in emerging markets overseas, finally merged in 2009 as the Brazilian Foods Corporation (or BRF) which eventually became one of the world's largest meatpacking companies.[45]

Whereas BRF produced meat products from both small and large animals and was primarily a world leader in chicken meat, the other major Brazilian meatpackers to emerge in this new era were dedicated almost exclusively to beef and its products. Unlike the Southern companies, some of these major new producers were first established in the Center-West in what would become the new leading cattle center of the country. This was the case with Friboi, a company founded by José Batista Sobrinho in 1953 as a small slaughterhouse in the town of Anápolis, Goiás. It slowly expanded by buying 12 other beef slaughterhouses in the region and by 2005 it was the leading producer of fresh, chilled, and processed beef in Brazil. In that year with the help of the state development bank, BNDES, it bought out Swift of Argentina, its first international acquisition, and then renamed the Company JBS after its founder. Two years later it bought all of the Swift company holdings, including in the United States and Australia. It thus became the third largest meatpacker in the United States behind Cargill and Tyson and the largest meatpacker in the world. In 2009 it bought out Bertin, Brazil's second largest beef producer, which was a far more diversified company. Thus JBS now expanded beyond beef and hides into a large number of allied companies. In the same year it bought Pilgrim's Pride of the United States and thus became the world's second largest chicken meat producer as well. It also purchased major meat packing companies in Europe and Australia during this period with the result that it is now the leading animal protein company in the world and its second largest food company.[46] By 2020 the company had 250,000 employees of which 57% were employed in Brazil and its 35 Brazilian beef processing plants were processing 33,450 head of cattle per day.[47]

But JBS and BRF were not the only companies which expanded. Two São Paulo companies appeared in the late 1980s and early 1990s as significant meatpackers. In 1986 Marfrig was founded to provide special meats for restaurants and eventually became a major meatpacker with its first major plant established in Mato Grosso do Sul, soon followed by others in Mato Grosso. By 2006 it expanded into neighboring countries by

Table 11.3 Number of plants and animals processed of leading companies in Brazil in 2014

Companies	*No. of units*	*Animals slaughtered*
JBS	48	11,143,000
Marfrig	17	2,756,430
Minerva	9	2,127,995
BRF	2	476,684
Subtotal	76	16,504,109
Total	230	26,883,614

Source Carvalho (2016), 49, table 5

buying local meatpackers. In 1992 the Minerva company was created in Baretos, São Paulo, by a family already working in ranching and transport. It expanded locally by purchasing other companies, and then in 2004 built a modern meatpacking plant in Goiás and a year later another one in Mato Grosso. Like Marfrig it also soon purchased other meatpackers in neighboring countries in the first decade of the new century. Thus by 2014, the major beef companies operating in Brazil were JBS, Marfrig, Minerva, and BRF.[48] These four companies accounted for half the beef processed in Brazil in that year, even though they owned only a third of the slaughterhouses (see Table 11.3).

The result was that these four national companies, JBS, Marfrig, Minerva, and BRF now control the national market for beef. In addition, the numerous barriers imposed by importing countries (tariffs, sanitary rules, and import quotas) led to some of the Brazilian meatpackers creating units or purchasing them in overseas markets from the earliest years as their production soon exceeded domestic demand.[49] JBS is the most emblematic case, as it currently is the largest beef company in the world, with operations in fifteen countries, operating with a multiplicity of brands in numerous countries.[50] In 2017, JBS in its 37 Brazilian plants, representing about 30% of the national production of processed beef. Marfrig in 14 plants slaughtered about 14.5 thousand cattle per day, with a 16% share of the market and Minerva, in its 11 plants slaughtered 11.8 thousand cattle per day, with 11% of the market.[51] By 2020 Marfrig had 20 beef slaughterhouses and was processing some 30,100 head of cattle per day.[52] This concentration is replicated in Brazilian beef exports. In 2017, JBS accounted for 34%, Marfrig 17%, Minerva for 16% of all exports and these three companies were responsible for more than two thirds of total Brazilian beef exports.

Slaughter and meat processing are thus currently carried out in large industrial complexes involving some of the largest meat packing companies in the world. By 2020, there were 1,039 slaughterhouses producing 7.3 million tons of meat. Of these slaughterhouses, the 195 under federal inspection accounted for three quarters of slaughtered cattle. The most significant plants were found in states with large animal herds. The final part of the modernization of the beef industry was the creation of a health inspection system. The sanitary inspection of animal products had its origin in the beginning of the twentieth century, but it was intensified in the period of WWI when several international meatpackers were installed in Brazil. In 1952 Brazil established a modern inspection system under local and federal control, and in 1971 these sanitary and industrial inspections were federalized after problems arose with state and municipal inspections.[53] This centralization of animal inspection and the growing demands both in the domestic and international markets led to the introduction of international standards in the slaughtering and processing of meat in Brazil. It even led to different slaughter and processing methods, such as those required for meats exported to religious communities in the Middle East and Asia.

The growth of the national beef herds, the production of meat, and the penetration of Brazil in the international market has been spectacular in recent decades. Since 1980 one third of the growth of world beef herds is explained by the growth of the Brazilian cattle herd, which became the world's largest in 2005 and by 2019 represented 14% of the world's total of cattle (see Graph 11.3).

Already by 2018, the country produced 9.9 million tons of meat from cattle, it exported 2.1 million tons and consumed 7.8 million tons and had negligible imports. This resulted in an internal consumption of 37.5 kg per inhabitant per year, similar to consumption per capita in the United States, and higher than Australia and Europe. But of course it was much lower than the world's highest consumer, Argentina which reached 55.4 kg per inhabitant per annum. The average world consumption in that year was only 9.1 kg (see Table 11.7). Among the countries with the largest cattle herds, only Argentina, with 1.2 cattle per inhabitant surpasses Brazil which has one beef cattle for every person, and is well above the rate for the United States (0.30) and countries with large non-exporting herds, such as India or China (Table 11.4).

As early as 1960 Beef exports represented only 2% of the value of Brazilian agricultural exports. The major regional exporter was still

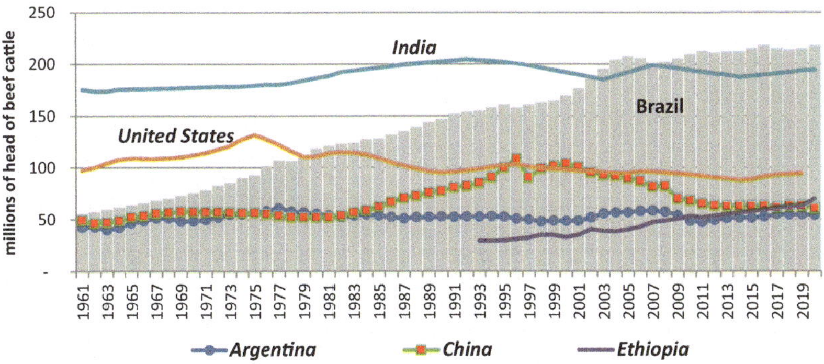

Graph 11.3 Growth of the cattle herds of the principal producing countries of the world, 1961–2020 (*Source* FAOSTAT at https://www.fao.org/faostat/en/#data/QCL)

Table 11.4 Bovine meat, new food balance (2018)

	Unit	*Brazil*	*World*	*% Brazil*
Production	1000 metric tons	9,900	71,343	14%
Import quantity	1000 metric tons	47	12,171	0.4%
Stock variation	1000 metric tons	5	1,358	0.4%
Export quantity	1000 metric tons	2,093	13,535	15%
Domestic supply quantity	1000 metric tons	7,849	68,621	11%
Food	1000 metric tons	7,849	67,739	12%
Food supply quantity (kg/capita/yr)	kg	37.5	9.1	
Food supply (kcal/capita/day)	kcal/capita/day	157.0	39	
Protein supply quantity (g/capita/day)	g/capita/day	14.0	3.48	
Fat supply quantity (g/capita/day)	g/capita/day	10.8	2.64	

Source Faostat

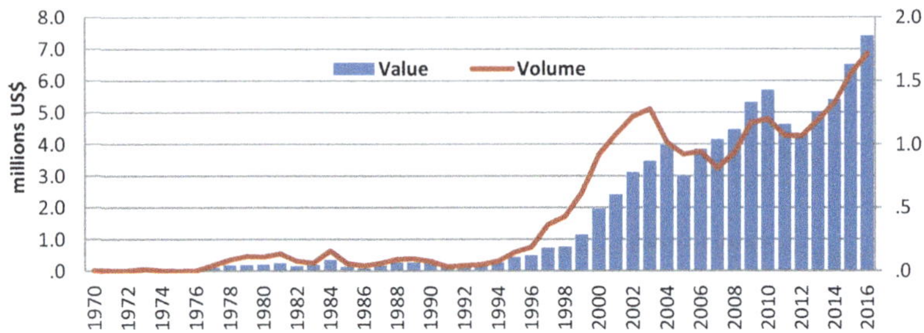

Graph 11.4 Value and volume of Brazilian boneless beef and veal exports, 1974–2020 (*Source* Faostat)

Argentina, which accounted for 23% of world beef exports compared to just 3% of such exports for Brazil.[54] But sixty years later Brazil leads in international beef exports, accounting for 22% of the international market. Brazilian international meat exports have grown in value from less than US$ 200 million in 1997 to US$ 12.9 billion in 2022. It was only in 2000 that Brazil's volume of beef exports finally surpassed those of Argentina. But since then the difference has become pronounced. By 2010–2015 it was exporting four times as much as Argentina and in the next quinquennium it increased to five times the Argentine average. By 2020 it was the world's leading exporter of Bovine Meat, accounting for 15% of the world market (see Graph 11.4).[55]

This exceptional growth of livestock in Brazil was due to a major increase in the productivity of Brazilian cattle ranching. The current raising of livestock is completely different from that which existed 40 years ago in Brazil, when production barely met domestic demand. The improvement in the weight of the animals, in their decreasing mortality and increasing birth rates led to the decreasing age of animals at slaughter.[56] There has also been a major improvement in planted pastures, which went from 14% of all pastures in 1950 to accounting for 70% of them in 2017.[57] This has permitted the increase in the number of cattle per hectare, which went from 0.41 in 1950 to 0.68 in 1980, reaching 1.29 in 2006 and 1.36 in 2017. Between 1950 and 2017, the number of cattle multiplied by 4.8 against 1.5 of the pastures. A recent study suggests that between 1990 and 2015 there was a land-saving effect which was estimated to be in the order of 324 thousand hectares in ranching. This increasing productivity has an impact on the economics of the industry, but also on its ecological impact as well.[58]

There has also emerged feedlot feeding, which has doubled to 14% of total grazing animals, a system which improves carcass weight and uses less pasture.[59] In addition, the percentage of cattle over 40 months of age that were slaughtered, went from 45% of in 1997, to just 6% in 2019, indicating a more rapid turnover of the bovine stock.[60] All these improvements led to a significant increase in the yield of kg per carcass per head, which went from 24 to 44 kg, between 1980 and 2017 and the yield of kg per hectare of pastures, which went from 16 to 60 kg, between 1980 and 2017. If we compare the yield of kg of carcass per head, this indicator, which was only 47% of that obtained by Argentina in 1980, in 2019 represented 86% of the result obtained by that country in 2017.

Over the past fifty years there has been a significant regional change in the cattle herds in Brazil. In 1974, the highest concentration occurred in the Southeast (33%) and Center-West (25%), with a negligible participation of the North region. But by 2019 the states of the North region, part of which encompasses the lands of the legal Amazon zone, accounted for 23% of the national herd, and the Center-West increased its share to 35%.[61] The expansion into the North region was stimulated by the post 1964 governments through incentives for settlement in the region. Thus it was government action which has been a major factor in the displacement of herds to the interior of Brazil (see Map 11.2).[62]

There are significant differences in the characteristics of cattle ranching by type of ranch and by region. Ranches classified as family farms are the vast majority of such units, and represented fewer than two million agricultural establishments in the 2017 agricultural census, against six hundred thousand of non-family or commercial ranches. But the majority of the animals, some two thirds of the herds, were concentrated in these commercial establishments. Thus, the average number of cattle per establishment was 197 in commercial farms, against 28 in family farms, resulting in an overall average of 68 heads per establishment. Large land holdings were especially significant in the states of the Center-West region, whereas in the South, almost half of the herds were in smaller units.[63]

But rather than use land as an indicator, the distribution of cattle by the size of the herds provides more accurate information on the structure of cattle ranching. In Brazil, about 40% of herds contained fewer than 10 animals, but these ranches were of little importance in their share of the

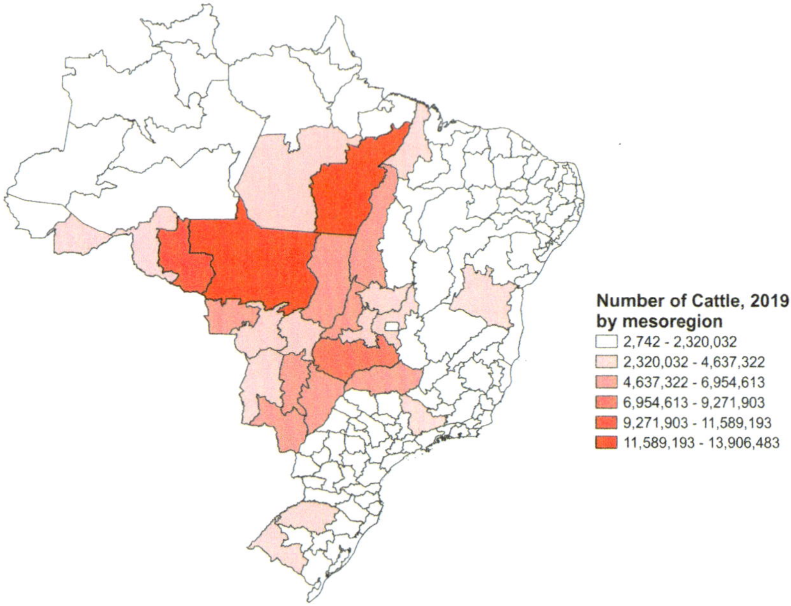

Map 11.2 Distribution of Cattle by Mesoregion in 2019 (*Source* IBGE Bases Cartográficas Sidra, table 3939)

total number of animals. Those ranches with more than 500 heads, about 50 thousand establishments, contained 44% of all animals. The Center-West region was the home to many of these larger ranches, with 60% of the ranches containing more than a thousand animals located there and another 21% of these large ranches were in the North region.

This distribution is also reflected in the average size of herds by state. The difference in herd size is striking, going from an average of 356 animals in Mato Grosso do Sul to an average of 44 in Rio Grande do Sul (see Table 11.5). The form of occupation and the cost of land explain these differences. In order to be competitive, the Center-West and North regions need scale to overcome the problems of distances from consumer centers or exporting ports, unlike their counterparts in Argentina who had easy access to railroads and ports.

Brazilian beef exports really only became substantial in volume and value in the late 1990s and exploded in the current century. The cause

Table 11.5 Distribution of ranches and cattle by type of unit by region and major state producers, census 2017

	commercial ranches		*Family ranches*		*Total*		*Herds*	*Average head per ranch*		
Regions and states	*Unit*	*Herd*	*Unit*	*Herd*	*Unit*	*Herd*	*% family*	*Commercial*	*Family*	*Total*
Brazil	604,273	119,111,570	1,918,214	53,607,594	2,522,487	172,719,164	31	197	28	68
North	58,990	21,893,798	205,388	12,870,481	264,378	34,764,279	37	371	63	131
Northeast	168,855	11,311,331	700,462	10,372,945	869,317	21,684,276	48	67	15	25
Southeast	166,989	20,853,093	386,022	10,687,289	553,011	31,540,382	34	125	28	57
South	113,019	14,401,601	448,876	9,178,752	561,895	23,580,353	39	127	20	42
Center-West	96,420	50,651,747	177,466	10,498,127	273,886	61,149,874	17	525	59	223
Mato Grosso	27,066	18,762,725	65,272	5,546,750	92,338	24,309,475	23	693	85	263
Goiás	46,028	13,700,184	79,379	3,592,104	125,407	17,292,288	21	298	45	138
Minas Gerais	107,194	12,426,006	274,572	7,149,833	381,766	19,575,839	37	116	26	51
Pará	21,828	9,836,708	75,190	4,512,845	97,018	14,349,553	31	451	60	148
Mato Grosso do Sul	22,416	18,133,166	32,303	1,352,035	54,719	19,485,201	7	809	42	356
Rondônia	13,117	4,964,883	59,738	4,862,134	72,855	9,827,017	49	379	81	135
Rio Grande do Sul	48,106	7,647,785	212,568	3,809,111	260,674	11,456,896	33	159	18	44
São Paulo	36,859	5,830,783	69,655	2,501,091	106,514	8,331,874	30	158	36	78
Bahia	61,305	4,695,992	230,752	3,481,769	292,057	8,177,761	43	77	15	28

Source IBGE, SIDRA, tabela 6907

for this basic change in the role of Brazilian beef exports was due to the pastoral industry adopting the latest modern developments and breeds. All of this occurred only in the last fifty years, and in some cases, only in the last decade or two. Finally the massive expansion in the production of basic elements of animal feed, corn and soybeans, and the adoption of the latest grasses for planted pastures, all contributed to falling costs of inputs. In each case the impetus for change was a combination of government support for agriculture with credit, price supports and modern meatpacking facilities, and the steady growth of a major urban national market. which pressured producers to expand. So productive were these ranchers that they were not only able to produce enough for the domestic market, but were able increasingly to expand exports to the international market.[64]

But without fundamental changes in the international market, none of these developments could have occurred. In 1960, when comparative world data become available from the FAO, the Brazilian herd was already twice the size of Argentine herds, then the world's leading exporter, and by 2020 it was four times larger. This was due to the expansion of the cattle frontier toward the north and Center-West, freeing the traditional areas of the south and southeast for farming areas which became the first centers of soybean production. The two southern Brazilian regions, which in 1974 had over half of the national herd, contained only 30% of national stock in 2019 due to the rise of the northern and center-western ranchers.

Brazil has positively responded to the insertion of Mainland China into the world beef market. This demand coincided with a major shift in supply as Brazil emerged as the major beef supplier in the twenty-first century. Between 1999 and 2020, the amount of beef exported by Brazil multiplied by six, while the total market multiplied by two. Thus Argentina and Brazil have reversed their relative position in the world beef market in the last 60 years. Argentina exports and share of the market fell systematically from 1980 onward and by 2004 Brazilian beef exports (defined here as Cattle and Buffalo meats) began replacing Australia as the world's leading exporter (see Graph 11.6). By 2020 Brazil had become the leading world exporter in both tonnage and value (see Table 11.6).

Moreover Brazilian beef exports, in contrast to its poultry and pork exports, was far more widely distributed throughout the world providing meat for all the major regions (see Table 11.7).

The explosive Brazilian rise in the last ten years also can be seen as a response to public policies and levels of state interventionism. In

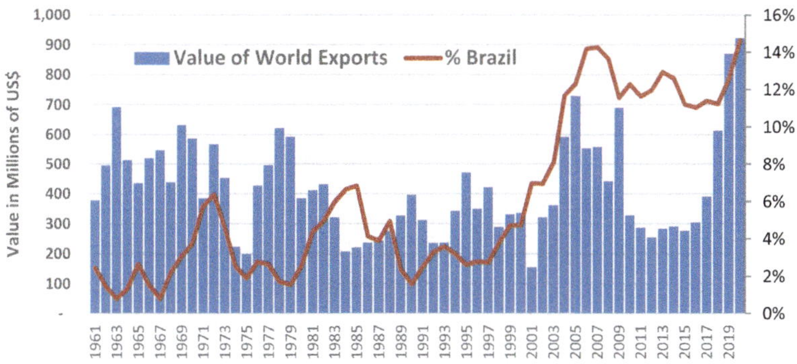

Graph 11.6 Value of world exports of beef and the share of those exports for Brazil, 1961–2020 (*Source* FAOSTAT)

Table 11.6 Value and volume of boneless beef and veal exports by leading exporters in 2020

Country	*US$ (000)*	*%*	*Country*	*Tons*	*%*
Brazil	7,428,848	19	Brazil	1,715,557	24
Australia	6,196,012	16	Australia	976,697	14
USA	5,747,237	15	USA	821,919	11
Argentina	2,576,998	7	Argentina	553,945	8
New Zealand	2,183,195	6	New Zealand	398,237	6
Netherlands	2,025,087	5	Canada	338,013	5
Ireland	1,972,866	5	Ireland	325,729	5
Canada	1,863,507	5	Netherlands	285,134	4
Uruguay	1,397,856	4	Paraguay	271,105	4
Paraguay	1,115,940	3	Uruguay	255,536	4
Mexico	1,012,761	3	Poland	176,929	2
Poland	831,898	2	Mexico	162,429	2
Others	4,718,825	12	Others	907,755	13
World	39,071,030	100	World	7,188,985	100

Source FAOSTAT, Trade

the 1960s and 1970s, the Brazilian government implemented efficient mechanisms of agricultural policy, such as minimum prices, regulatory stocks, credit, and strong support for agricultural research and education. With abundant and growing herds every effort was made to support exports and modernize production. Thus an opening of production to

Table 11.7 The top six importing countries of Brazilian beef, 2000, 2005, 2010, 2015, 2020 (1000 US$)

2000			*2005*			*2010*			*2015*			*2020*		
Country	*Value*	*%*	*Country*	*Value*	*%*	*Country*	*Value*	*%*	*Country*	*Value*	*%*	*Country*	*Value*	*%*
Netherlands	98,376	20	Russian Fed	555,273	23	Russian Fed	1,021,845	27	China, HK	653,279	14	China	4,037,361	54
Italy	60,106	12	Egypt	252,714	10	Iran	807,321	21	Egypt	623,925	13	China HK	802,943	11
Spain	54,095	11	Netherlands	191,478	8	Egypt	409,960	11	Russian Fed	552,133	12	Egypt	394,216	5
Chile	53,784	11	UK	181,661	8	China, HK	234,014	6	Venezuela	537,736	12	Chile	374,486	5
UK	49,315	10	Italy	152,685	6	Venezuela	186,133	5	China	476,391	10	Russian Fed	184,836	2
Germany	37,792	8	Chile	139,982	6	Italy	141,935	4	Iran	382,752	8	Saudi Arabia	157,789	2

Source FAOSTAT, Trade Matrix

foreign markets was encouraged by all governments. At no time were rules imposed that penalized exports through mechanisms that resulted in confiscation of exporters' revenue.

Equally important was the expansion of crops and livestock into new areas of the Center-West which had been unoccupied until the 1980s. It was only then that new lands were opened for ranching by the government which resulted in the arrival of an entrepreneurial class of southern ranchers. With that same government support modern production and slaughter methods were introduced. Also massive government credit allowed Brazilian meatpackers to purchase major producers abroad. Thus its companies are not only the leading producers of beef in Brazil but also in the world with branches in many other countries including the United States.

If there are no significant changes in South American climate and sanitary conditions, Brazilian producers should remain major sources of beef for many years to come. It is estimated that world consumption of beef will increase 5.9% by 2030 from a base of 2018–2020, and it is assumed that most of this expanded consumption will occur in Asia and in poorer and middle income countries that are steadily increasing their animal protein consumption.[65] Current estimates are that Brazil will export 3.6 million tons of carcass meat and account for 26% of world exports by 2031, compared to just 2.6 million tons of exports in 2022 which accounted for 22% of world.[66]

The challenges for Brazil are essentially in issues of sustainability and environment. There are millions of hectares of deteriorated land that require recovery to increase productivity per hectare. In the programs and goals for reduction of carbon gas, the recovery of pasture is one of the most important items. There is also the need to eliminate the relationship between deforestation and cattle ranching expansion. If there is no clear evidence that cattle raising is not related to deforestation, especially in the Amazon, Brazil will face barriers to export to various markets in the world. Thus this extraordinary expansion of the beef industry in Brazil faces continued challenges in everything from sanitary conditions to environmental controls. Fortunately the laws are well developed to handle these issues. Unfortunately enforcement of these laws has been a serious problem for the most recent governments.

Notes

1. USDA, *Livestock and Poultry: World Markets and Trade*, October 2022, 5, 10, 15.
2. MAPA, Agrostat, accessed at: https://indicadores.agricultura.gov.br/agrostat/index.htm.
3. Francisco Carlos Teixeira da Silva "Pecuária e formação do mercado interno no Brasil-colônia," *Estudos Sociedade e Agricultura*, 8 (abril 1997): 119–156, p. 119.
4. João Antônio Andreoni (André João Antonil), *Cultura e Opulência do Brasil,* São Paulo, Editora Nacional, s/d, p. 309. Sobre o tema, see Celso Furtado, *Formação Econômica do Brasil,* São Paulo, Editora Nacional, 1968, cap. XI; Caio Prado Jr. *História Econômica do Brasil.* São Paulo, Brasiliense, 1972, chap. 8; Roberto Simonsen. *História Econômica do Brasil (1500–1820)* (Brasília: Edições do Senado Federal, 2005), chaps. VII and VIII; Capistrano de Abreu, *Capítulos de História Colonial* (São Paulo, Civilização Brasileira/MEC, 1976), chap. IX; Tereza Schorer Petrone, "As áreas de criação de gado," in Sérgio Buarque de Holanda, ed., *História Geral da Civilização Brasileira* (Rio de Janeiro, Bertrand Brasil, Tomo I, A Época Colonial, vol. 2, 2008), chap 4.
5. Maria Yedda Leite Linhares, "Pecuária, alimentos e Sistemas agrários no Brasil (Séculos XVII e XVIII)". *Arquivos do Centro Cultural Calouste Gulbenkian, Le Portugal et l'Europe Atlantique, le Brésil et l'Amérique Latine. Mélanges offerts à Fréderic Mauro* (Lisboa and Paris, Dez., 1995). The theme of leasing as a practice used in the formation of large breeding farms is cited by Antonil. Antonil, *Cultura e Opulência do Brasil*: 309; Silva, "Pecuária e formação do mercado interno:" 119–156.
6. Luiz R.B. Mott, "Os índios e a pecuária nas fazendas de gado do Piauí colonial," *Revista de Antropologia* (1979): 61–78; Silva, "Pecuária e formação do mercado interno: 119–156." Sobre o tema veja Maria Yedda Leite Linhares, "Pecuária, alimentos e Sistemas agrários no Brasil (Séculos XVII e XVIII)". *Arquivos do Centro Cultural Calouste Gulbenkian, Le Portugal et l'Europe Atlantique, le Brésil et l'Amérique Latine. Mélanges offerts à Fréderic Mauro*, vol. XXXIV (Lisboa, Paris: Dez., 1995); Capistrano de Abreu, *Capítulos de História Colonial* (São Paulo, Civilização Brasileira/MEC, 1976): 106–1108. Also see Geronazzo Araujo, "O Muro do Demônio: economia e cultura na Guerra dos Bárbaros no nordeste colonial do Brasil. Séculos XVII e XVIII" (MA thesis, Universidade Federal do Ceará, 2007).
7. Maria Isaura Pereira de Queiroz, "Pecuária e vida pastoril: sua evolução em duas regiões brasileiras," *Revista do Instituto de Estudos Brasileiros*, 19 (1977): 55–78.

8. On the draughts of 1777 and 1791 see José Nilson B. Campos, "Secas e políticas públicas no semiárido: ideias, pensadores e períodos," *Estudos Avançados*, 28, no. 82 (2014): 68.
9. The *charqueadas* of Ceará date from the period prior to 1749. Raimundo Girão. *Evolução histórica cearense* (Fortaleza, Etene/BNB, 1986): 139.
10. Valdelice Carneiro Girão, "As Charqueadas," *Revista do Instituto do Ceará* (1996): 72–92; Leonardo Cândico Rolim, "O negócio das carnes secas do Siará Grande," *XXVII Simpósio Nacional de História, ANPUH*, Natal, 2013; Almir Leal de Oliveira, "As carnes secas do Ceará e o mercado Atlântico no século XVIII". Accessed at: http://www.humanas.ufpr.br/portal/cedope/files/2011/12/As-carnes-secas-do-Cear%C3%A1-e-o-mercado-Almir-Leal-de-Oliveira.pdf; Almir Leal de Oliveira "A força periférica da empresa comercial do charque" Accessed at: http://www.humanas.ufpr.br/portal/cedope/files/2011/12/A-for%C3%A7a-perif%C3%A9rica-da-empresa-comercial-do-charque-Almir-Leal-de-Oliveira.pdf.
11. Antonil, *Cultura e Opulência do Brasil*: 309.
12. According to Antonil these exports represented 8% of the value of sugar exports, and 60% of the value of tobacco exports. Antonil, *Cultura e Opulência do Brasil*: 310.
13. Simonsen. *História Econômica do Brasil*: 205.
14. Simonsen. *História Econômica do Brasil*: chap. VIII; and Carlos G.A. Mielitz Netto. "Modernização e diferenciação na Bovinocultura de corte Brasileira" (Phd thesis, Unicamp, Campinas, 1994): 20.
15. Queiroz dates the first ranches to 1715 in the zone of Viamão which were founded by paulistas for the domestication of horses and mules to be sold north. Queiroz. "Pecuária e vida pastoral," 66.
16. Jonas Vargas, "'A aristocracia do sebo' Riqueza, prestígio social e estilo de vida entre os charqueadores de Pelotas (Rio Grande do Sul, 1850–1890," *Revista Digital Estudios Historicos* [Uruguay], VIII, no. 17 (Diciembre 2016): 23 pp., 23 p.
17. Helen Osório. "Estancieiros d Rio de São Pedro: constituição de uma elite terratenente no século XVIII." *Actas do Congresso Internacional Espaço Atlântico de Antigo Regime: poderes e sociedades*, accessed at http://cvc.instituto-camoes.pt/eaar/coloquio/comunicacoes/helen_osorio.pdf.
18. Campos, "Secas e políticas públicas no semiárido": 65–88.
19. Jonas Moreira Vargas, "Abastecendo *plantations*: a inserção do charque fabricado em Pelotas (RS) no comércio atlântico das carnes e a sua concorrência com os produtores platinos (século XIX)," *História* (São Paulo), 33, no. 2, (jul./dez. 2014): 540–566, The author explains that in most sources, "carne-seca," "charque," and "tasajo" (the latter in the region of the River Plate) are treated as synonyms, while "salted meat" was a term intended for meat. prepared and preserved in barrels with brine.

20. Jonas Moreira Vargas, "'As mãos e os pés do charqueador': o processo de fabricação do charque e um perfil dos trabalhadores escravos nas charqueadas de Pelotas," Rio Grande do Sul (1830–1885)," *Sæculum Revista de História*, 36 (Jan./Jun. 2017): 155. Queiroz, "Pecuária e vida pastoral": 55–78.
21. Vargas, "'As mãos e os pés do charqueador'": 158.
22. Helen Osório, "Para além das charqueadas: estudo do padrão de posse de escravos no Rio Grande do Sul, segunda metade do século XVIII," *3º Encontro Escravidão e Liberdade no Brasil Meridional*, accessed at: http://www.escravidaoeliberdade.com.br/site/images/Textos3/helen%20osorio.pdf. Also see Helen Osório, "Fronteira, escravidão e pecuária: Rio Grande do Sul, no período colonial," Helen Osório, "Fronteira, escravidão e pecuária: Rio Grande do Sul no período colonial," *II Jornada de História Regional Comparada*, Porto Alegre: PUCRS (2005): 1–16. accessed at: http://cdn.fee.tche.br/jornadas/2/H4-09.pdf.
23. Vargas, "'As mãos e os pés do charqueador'": 159.
24. Mielitz Netto, "Modernização e diferenciação na Bovinocultura": 21.
25. Daniele Maria Machado Ribeiro Azevedo, "A pecuária de corte no Brasil: a introdução do gado zebu." Agrolink, December 12, 2007. Acesso em: https://www.agrolink.com.br/colunistas/coluna/a-pecuaria-de-corte-no-brasil--a-introducao-do-bovino-zebu_385142.html#:~:text=A%20entrada%20de%20gado%20zebu,de%20lavoura%20e%20para%20alimenta%C3%A7%C3%A3o.
26. Barsky and Gelman, *Historia del agro argentino*: 182–184; Sesto, *História del capitalismo agrário pampeano*; Martínez, Fernández, Género, and Rumiano, "El ganado bovino criollo en Argentina."
27. Carlos G.A. Mielitz Netto, "Modernização e diferenciação na Bovinocultura de corte Brasileira" (Phd thesis, Unicamp, Campinas, 1994): 21; and Wilcox, *Cattle in the Backlands*, chapter 7; and Wilcox, *Cattle in the Backland*, 204–208.
28. Daniele Maria Machado Ribeiro Azevedo, "A pecuária de corte no Brasil: a introdução do gado zebu." Agrolink, December 12, 2007. Acesso em: https://www.agrolink.com.br/colunistas/coluna/a-pecuaria-de-corte-no-brasil--a-introducao-do-bovino-zebu_385142.html#:~:text=A%20entrada%20de%20gado%20zebu,de%20lavoura%20e%20para%20alimenta%C3%A7%C3%A3o.
29. Afonso Simões Corrêa, *Pecuária de Corte – Problemas e Perspectivas de Desenvolvimento* (Campo Grande, Embrapa, 1986), 9.
30. Corrêa. *Pecuária*, p. 7.
31. IBGE, *Censo Agrícola 1960*, Série Nacional, vol. II, 1ª e 2ª partes.
32. On the history of cattle breeding from earliest times Marleen Felius, Marie-Louise Beerling, David S. Buchanan, Bert Theunissen, Peter A.

Koolmees, and Johannes A. Lenstra, "On the History of Cattle Genetic Resources," *Diversity*, 6, no. 4 (2014): 705–750.
33. Paiva, Schattan and Freitas. *Setor Agrícola*; and Mielitz Netto. "Modernização."
34. W.J. Yardley-Podolsky, "Um perfil da indústria de carnes e de seu futuro," *Revista de Administração de Empresas*, 21, no. 2 (1981): 49–58.
35. There is a divergence until 1976 between the FAO estimates and those of IBGE on the size of the herds. Thereafter they become identical.
36. The major cross breeding are Canchim (Charolais with Zebu), and Pitangueiras (Red Polled with Guzerat and Gir). Corrêa. *Pecuária*, p. 7.
37. Kepler Euclides Filho, *Melhoramento Genético Animal no Brasil: Fundamentos, História e Importância* (Campo Grande: Embrapa Gado de Corte, 1999); Kepler Euclides Filho, "Evolução do melhoramento genético de bobino de corte no Brasil," *Revista Ceres*, 56, no. 5 (set./out. 2009): 620–626; João Eustáquio Cabral de Miranda, and Ary Ferreira de Freitas, *Raças e tipo de cruzamentos para produção de leite* (Juiz de Fora: Embrapa, Circular Técnica 98, 2009).
38. Herbert S. Klein and Francisco Vidal Luna, *Feeding the World. Brazil's Transformation into a Modern Agricultural Economy* (Cambridge: Cambridge University Press, 2019).
39. Luis Otávio Bau Macedo, "Modernização da pecuária de corte bovina no Brasil e a importância do crédito rural," *Informações Econômicas* (São Paulo), 36, no. 7 (Jul. 2006): 83–95; Waldemiro A. Silva Neto, Carlos J.C. Bacha and Mirian R. P. Bacchi, "Evolução do financiamento rural para a pecuária e sua relação com a dinâmica regional dessa atividade no Brasil" (TD 24; Goiâna, *NEPEC/FACE/UFG*, maio 2011).
40. Eder Barbosa de Aguilar, "Inovação biotecnológica na pecuária de leite: o papel da Embrapa" (MA thesis, Vitória, Universidade Federal do Espírito Santo, 2007).
41. Larissa Virginia Brown, "Internal Commerce in a Colonial Economy: Rio de Janeiro and Its Hinterland, 1790–1822" (Phd Thesis, University of Virginia, 1986), chapter 8; and Lopes, *Rio de Janeiro in the Global Meat Market*, chapter 2.
42. Lopes, *Rio de Janeiro in the Global Meat Market*, 41.
43. Armen Mamigonian, "Notas sobre os frigoríficos do Brasil central pecuário," *Boletim Paulista de Geografia* 51 (1976): 9.
44. Wilson Suzigan, *Indústria brasileira. Origem e desenvolvimento* (São Paulo: Brasiliense, 1986), 331–344.
45. Angelo Brião Zanela, "Ensaios sobre business groups: Perdigão e Sadia e a consolidação de grupos econômicos no Brasil (1934–2009)" (Phd thesis, Universidade Federal do Paraná, 2019), chapters 2 and 3.
46. Ronald Jean Degen and K. Matthew Wong, "An Examination of the Resource-Based Horizontal Acquisition Strategy of JBS—The Biggest

Meat Packer in the World," *Proceedings of the New York State Economics Association*, Volume 5 (2013).
47. JBS, Sustainability Report 2020, p. 5; JBS, Institutional Presentation, 1Q22, p. 19. Both found at https://ri.jbs.com.br/en/financial-information/results-center/#.
48. Thiago Bernardino de Carvalho, "Estratégias de crescimento e reestruturação da indústria de carne bovina no Brasil: o papel de políticas públicas discricionárias"(Phd thesis, Universidade de São Paulo, 2016), 73–78.
49. Onofre Aurélio Neto, "A estratégia de internacionalização de empresas brasileiras do setor frigorífico: os casos da JBS e da Minerva," *Boletim Goiana. Geografica*, 39 (2019): 57226.
50. JBS, https://ri.jbs.com.br/a-jbs/unidades-de-negocios/#:~:text=A%20JBS%20USA%20Beef%20%C3%A9,(por%20meio%20da%20Primo).
51. A study on the livestock value chain presented in 2015 showed the following distribution: JBS 36%, Marfrig 9%, and Minerva 10%. Thiago Bernardino de Carvalho and Sérgio de Zen, "A cadeia de Pecuária de Corte no Brasil: Evolução e tendências," *Revista iPecege*, 3, no. 1 (2017): 94; Pamela Andrade, "Carta de Conjuntura – Mapeamentos e Características dos Frigoríficos Brasileiros," *Scot Consultoria*. Accessed at: https://www.scotconsultoria.com.br/noticias/cartas/48077/carta-conjuntura---mapeamento-e-caracteristicas-dos-frigorificos-brasileiros.htm#:~:text=Segundo%20levantamento%20da%20Scot%20Consultoria,16%2C6%25%20o%20SIF.
52. https://www.marfrig.com.br/en/Paginas/home.aspx. Accessed June 26, 2022.
53. Maria Fernanda Garnica, "Análise retrospectiva e tendências do serviço de inspeção do Estado de São Paulo" (Jaboticabal, SP: MA thesis, Unesp, 2014), 4–5.
54. FAOSTAT, considering the items listed as: "Meat, beef preparations," "Meat, cattle," and "Meat, cattle, boneless (beef & veal)."
55. Faostat.
56. Rodrigo da Costa Gomes, Gelson Luiz Dias Feijó and Lucimara Chiari, *Evolução e Qualidade da Pecuária Brasileira* (Nota Técnica; Campo Grande: Embrapa Gado de Corte, 2017). Of the beef herd in Brazil, about 85% are Zebu cattle, of which the Nellore breed predominates. Heitor de Paula Edson Júnior, and Merik Rocha Silva, "Melhoramento genético em bovinos de corte," in Amado de Oliveira Filho, ed., *Produção e Manejo de Bovinos de Corte* (Cuiabá-MT: KCM Editora, 2015), 45; José H. F. de Oliveira, Cláudio de U. Magnabosco and Arnaldo M. de S. M. Borges, *Nelore: Base Genética e Evolução Seletiva no Brasil* (Documentos 49, Planaltina: Embrapa Cerrados, 2002).
57. IBGE *Censo Agrícola, Brasil 1950* (Rio de Janeiro, 1956); *Censo Agrícola, Brasil 1960* (Rio de Janeiro, 1967); *Censo Agropecuário 2006* (Rio de

Janeiro, 2011); *Censo Agropecuário 2017* (Rio de Janeiro, 2019), and IBGE, Sidra table 3639.
58. José Eustáquio Ribeiro Vieira Filho,. *Efeito poupa-terra e ganhos de produção no setor agropecuário brasileiro* (TD 2386; Brasília, IPEA, 2018), 25; and. Geraldo B. Martha Jr, Eliseu Alves and Eliseu Contoni, "Land-Saving Approaches and Beef Production Growth in Brazil," *Agricultural Systems* 110 (July 2012): 173–177.
59. ABIEC, *Beef Report 2020.*
60. ABIEC, *Beef Report 2020.*
61. Moacyr Bernardino Dias-Filho and Monyck Jeane dos Santos Lopes, *Histórico e desafios da pecuária bovina na Amazônia* (Belém: Embrapa Amazônia Oriental, 2020); Mirlei Fachini Vicente Pereira, "A modernização recente da pecuária bovina em Rondônia: normas territoriais e a nova produtividade especial," *Revista do Departamento de Geografia UERJ*, 26 (2015): 95–112; Juliane Carneiro Martins and Ana Maria A. A. Attai, "Análise da pecuária Maranhense entre os anos de 1974 e 2017," *IV Congresso Internacional das Ciências Agrárias* (Virtual), 2019.
62. José Matias Pereira, "O processo de ocupação e de desenvolvimento da Amazônia," *Revista de Informação Legislativa*, 34, no. 134 (1997), 75–85; Rodolfo Coelho Prates, and Carlos José Caetano Bacha, "Os processo de desenvolvimento e desmatamento da Amazônia," *Economia e Sociedade* (Campinas), 20, no. 3 (43) (2011): 601–636.
63. IBGE, Censo 2017 and Sidra, tabela 6908.
64. Antonio Márcio Buainai and Mario Otávio Batalha, eds., *Cadeia produtiva da Carne Bovina* (Brasília, MAPA, 2007); Cacilda Borges do Valle, Liana Jank and Rosangela Maria Simeão Resende, "O melhoramento de forrageiras tropicais no Brasil," *Revista Ceres*, 56, no. 4 (2009): 460–472; and Luciano Eduardo Morello Polaquini, José Gilberto de Souza and José Jorge Gebara, "Transformações técnico-produtivas e comerciais na pecuária de corte brasileira a partir da década de 90," *Revista Brasileira de Zootecnia,* 35, no. 1(2006): 321–327.
65. OECD-FAO, *Agricultural Outlook 2021–2030* (Paris, 2021), 164–165.
66. USDA, *Agricultural Projections to 2031* (February 2022), 98, table 37.

CHAPTER 12

Chickens and Swine

Along with Beef, Brazil has recently become a major exporter of broiler or meat chickens (*carne de frango*) and pigs. From being an industry which essentially supplied the domestic market, the production of chicken and pig meat has outpaced that market and permitted Brazil to become a major exporter of these products. So successful has this industry become, that Brazil now is the world's leading exporter of broiler chicken meat and a significant exporter of pork, all of which occurred only in the past few decades. Razing these smaller animals for commercial consumption used a production structure quite different from that needed for raising beef. These two animals were mostly raised on smaller farm units rather than in large ranches with their extensive natural and planted pastures. Pasture was not an essential part of this system and modern farming methods allowed for very high concentration of animals on relative small units.

In many ways the evolution of chickens followed a pattern similar to other European animals imported into the New World. Chickens were introduced into the Americas by the Portuguese and Spanish colonizers, and were eventually ubiquitous in all rural and even urban areas from colonial times until the twentieth century.[1] Chicken meat was a locally consumed product everywhere and many households kept hens for their egg production. The stock of poultry was growing quite significantly even before the introduction of modern production methods. In 1920 the

H. S. Klein and F. V. Luna, *Brazilian Crops in the Global Market*, Palgrave Studies in Economic History,
https://doi.org/10.1007/978-3-031-38589-6_12

country counted some 53 million birds, which increased to 63 million in the census of 1940 and some 78 million in 1950 for a growth rate of 2.8% per annum between 1920 and 1960.[2]

At the same time the growing wealth of the world in the past seventy five years has led to an increasing demand for cheap animal protein. It was chicken meat that met this demand due to the creation of a modernized and industrial style industry. Although the modern poultry industry was first established in the United States and Western Europe in the mid-twentieth century, today over half of the world's chicken are produced in developing countries, of which Brazil, China, and India are the leading producers.[3] In the past six-year period (2017–2022) the United States accounted for 21% of world production, and Brazil was the second largest producer accounting for 17% of total would poultry flocks.[4] But the United States was also the largest consumer of chickens, which meant that only 11% of its production on average went for exports, whereas China was a net importer as the world's second largest consumer. Brazil, in contrast, despite being the third largest consumer of chicken meat in the world after the United States and China, was still able to export on average 24% of its production in this period and as early as 2004 replaced the United States as the world's largest chicken meat exporter.[5] By the year 2023, Mexico and China although big producers, still needed imports to satisfy their domestic market. In that same year Brazil was able to export 32% or 4.8 million tons of its broiler chickens, a record no other producer could match (see Graph 12.1).[6] China was always Brazil's primarily importer, and already by 2010 Brazil had replaced the United States chicken meat exports in the Chinese market.[7]

The success of the broiler chicken industry in Brazil owes much to direct government investment in the industry. Governments that needed to control industrial wages in order to promote local industry were willing to invest heavily in farming in general and in the chicken industry in particular though subsidized credit, state agricultural research, and the introduction of the latest techniques and machinery needed to develop this industry. An essential reason that the various Brazilian administrations were willing to provide substantial support for this industry was the impact meat prices had on the price index. Especially under the military governments (1964–1985) there was a basic policy of reducing consumer prices so as to contain worker wages. Chicken meat was the cheapest animal protein available, and its greater consumption compared to the more expensive beef had an important impact on the cost of living index,

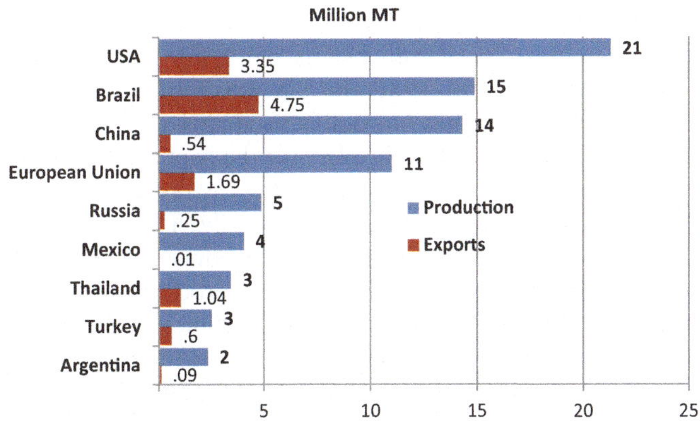

Graph 12.1 Production and exports for leading chicken meat producers in 2023 (*Source* USDA, PS&D at https://apps.fas.usda.gov/psdonline/app/index.html#/app/advQue)

which explains why this new industry was actively promoted by these governments.[8]

To develop this industry on a large scale there was also the need to adopt new business practices in housing and producing these animals, and the adoption of contract farming whereby processors of meat or feedstock companies provided the inputs for farmers to produce quality animals. The industry also needed government subsidized credit, the introduction of imported breeding stock, and construction of new specialized abattoirs to produce chicken parts. All of these factors would come together in the last quarter of the twentieth century. In turn Brazil's comparative advantage in this new industry was the concurrent growth of soybean and corn production, since soybean meal is the principal protein source and corn the principal grain used as an energy source for growing these animals. Only premixes, the third ingredient in this animal consumption, are imported. Together these three feeds account for half to 60% of the cost of raising broiler (or meat chickens).[9]

The broiler chicken industry was the first livestock industry to industrialize. This first occurred in the United States in the 1920s and was fully developed by the 1950s. At first broilers were male chickens that became redundant after the egg laying hens were produced and were sold for meat. The first exclusive broiler farm with 50,000 animals appeared in Maryland in the 1920s, and in 1937 Swift created the first broiler slaughter house. In 1926 vitamin D was synthesized permitting indoor growth of broilers. Then in 1933 the US government provided major support for the modernization of poultry production.

Initially the farmers sold their broilers on the spot market. Production grew quickly during WW II as chicken meat was not rationed nor price controlled, so production expanded dramatically. Then in the 1950s a new system based on vertical integration of producers began to emerge. This was initiated by the major animal feed producers who began to supply the feed, the day old birds and the technical expertise for local farmers who grew the birds and delivered them to the feed companies, who in turn sold them on to the meatpackers. The farmers usually were poor and small landowners and thus willing to abandon normal farming to concentrate on broiler meat production with these contracted sales. In the United States the Southern states were the poorest in the nation and thus the industry was concentrated in this region. Vertical integration meant that the feed companies expanded at both ends of the production chain, buying and creating both hatcheries and slaughterhouses. By the early 1960s some 90% of the broiler chickens were produced in this contract system. Breeds were improved and technology was applied to their housing and feeding. The result of these changes was that the final weight of broilers doubled and their period of growth was reduced from 70 to 50 days, enabling chicken meat to seriously compete in price to all other meats and become the lowest priced meat on the national market.[10] Finally there was a shift from providing whole chickens, to a sophisticated market for body parts which required an entirely new processing industry.

In this new system, the breeding of chickens for either egg or meat production became a highly specialized separate industry due to the development of new breeds through hybridization and genetic manipulation that was essentially controlled by North American and European producers. The birds created for specific characteristics were the great grandparents, their offspring (the grandparents) were called the multiplier flocks which in turn produced the birds sold to the hatcheries. It was these fourth generation birds that produced the eggs for the hatcheries. These flocks could produce the needed eggs for meat and egg production, but the quality of their offspring declined which each breeding. Thus breeders had a lock on production, as only pure breeds (the great grandparents and grandparents) could produce the desired animals grown for the specialized broilers and layers.[11] Given the constant genetic engineering involved, many of these breeding companies eventually were taken over by the big international biotechnology firms which franchised their animals throughout the world.[12]

The Brazilian broiler industry began in the 1940s. São Paulo farmers introduced the Leghorn race in 1940, and Hampshire breed was introduced in 1947. By the 1950s farmers with government support were importing breeding stock and chicks from the United States. In the next several decades international breeding companies from all over the world established branches in Brazil. Also Brazilian company research groups and universities established breeding and genetics programs. In 1960 the US breeding company Arbor Acres set up a branch in Brazil, with other European and Canadian companies quickly following. A key development occurred in 1965 when Brazil prohibited the importation of chicks and *matrizes* or parent breeders, thus guaranteeing local production of these two key groups of animals and encouraged the establishment of international breeders in Brazil.[13] In the 1970s the newly established Agricultural Faculties at state and federal universities and the national research foundation EMBAPA, set up special poultry breeding programs all financed by the Federal government. Finally in 1985 the innovative Granja Guanabara in Rio de Janeiro, which had been a leader in breeding since the 1950s, was purchased by the government and joined Embrapa. By 1980 there were 32 breeding companies in residence producing breeding stock (*matrizes*) for local farmers, of which only three were Brazilians. In this decade an average of 250,000 purebred birds (great grandparents) per annum were being imported. These imported birds in turn were mated for desired characteristics and produced grandparent purebreds with the desired traits. These in turn produced 12 million parents (*matrizes*) who produced on average of 1.2 million broiler or meat chicks.[14] The Embrapa, Suínos e Aves center in 1975 was able to create a new breed, and two other Brazilian developed breeds were the Chester (which the Brazilian company Perdigão created from a mixture seven imported purebred lines), and the Ag Ross which was developed jointly by an international company: Agroceres with Aviagen and Perdigão with Tyson.[15] Since these broiler chickens and those producing eggs were cross bred from pure genetic lines it was impossible for their descendants to maintain the quality of the original purebred lines, thus the original foreign breeder companies were protected from competition.[16] Most of these international companies aligned themselves with local producers. Arbor Acres was represented in Brazil by Sadia, the Scottish Breeder Ross by Agroceres, and the Tyson Cobb company from the

United States by Perdigão. While most of the great-grandparent birds were imported, Tyson Foods in 2001 appears to be the first to set up a local farm producing these purebred animals.[17]

Until the 1990s there were systematic investments by the national government in these breeding activities, but this ended with the liberal opening up of the national economy in that decade. At the same time local companies stopped their laboratory work and all the major international breeders established themselves in Brazil. Currently the two dominant breeds used in Brazil are the Cobb types which account for 60% and Ross chickens for 35% of these broiler chickens.[18] Today many of these breeding companies along with the processors have come under control of two Brazilian companies JBS and BRF. Both of these companies began in the beef industry. JBS bought Smithfield Farms in 2008 and the world's largest chicken processor Pilgrim's Pride in 2009. It eventually purchased leading Brazilian competitors, such as Seara, the French owned Frangosul, and the Tyson operation in Brazil. BRF, the amalgam of Sadia and Perdigão was already heavily involved in the poultry Industry since Sadia was the largest Brazilian poultry processor at the time of amalgamation. Today JBS and BRF account for 70% of Brazil's chicken exports and just under half of all the slaughtering.[19] Currently the only major breeders not owned by these companies are Aviagen (Arbor Acers and Ross) Hybro and Isa (Hubbard).[20] These breeding programs have produced a major change in these animals and it is estimated that since the mid-twentieth century the body mass of broilers has increased by a factor of 5.[21]

In the 1960s the first international companies providing animal feed arrived in Brazil. The US companies Purina establishing a center in São Paulo in 1967 and Cargill placed one in Campinas in 1970, and the Swiss Company Roche entered Brazil in 1972.[22] Another group of providers were Brazilian feed companies who were mostly granaries that processed cereals. It was Purina that started to provide free feed for contracted chickens, as it had done in the United States. By the end of the century the pattern was for the application of 2 kg of cereal feed to produce 1 kg of meat with the final chicken ready within 50 days of birth. Of this feed, made up of grains, medicines, and various vitamins, maize was the most important ingredient, accounting for almost two thirds of its cost. Another 20% was made up of soybean cake and thus the new industry was closely tied to maize and soybean production and its evolution in Brazil.[23] In fact most of the maize dedicated to animal feed went to chickens. International companies were also crucial in providing the chemical and biological inputs to guarantee the health of the broiler chickens. These included such international companies as Roche, Pfizer, Rhodia, Hoechst, and Bayer which established local branches in Brazil in the 1970s and 1980s, but also a local Brazilian company called Tortuga which ended by being the leading producer of vaccinations.[24]

The purebred birds were either produced locally or imported, and they in turn produced the breeding stock (*matrizes*). This second group of chickens produced the specific eggs, either for meat (broilers or *de corte*) or for egg production (laying hens or *de postura*). These parent eggs were then sent to a hatchery to be grown into day old chicks, which were then vaccinated and sold to chicken farmers who bred them until they reached a given weight, at which time they were given (under contract) to the packinghouses which slaughtered, cleaned, and cut the chickens into the desired parts. Under the vertical contract system, the Feeding Houses, the Slaughter/Packaging Companies, or a producer coop offered the chicken farmer a contract in which they would supply the feed, premixes, and medicines to the farmer who would in turn be required to give all his birds to the processing company. The feeding companies could also sometimes own the slaughterhouses, as was the case of the LAR Cooperativa Agroindustrial do Paraná which had several feed operations in the state, in Santa Catarina, in Mato Grosso, and in Paraguay and ran a slaughter house which processed 300 thousand chickens per day.[25]

As in the case of the United States, the growing of broiler chickens was primarily done on relatively small farm units. Production was organized into newly designed thousand bird sheds which used limited space, since these animals were less dependent on climate and soils given their feeds and medicines. The volume of birds produced could be substantial even on a relatively small farm in terms of the number of hectares it owned.

In the first phase of production live weight was more important than carcass yield. But with basic changes in the meatpacking sector in the 1980s which involved automation of poultry cuts and packaging and the introduction of electronic weighing, there was a shift to the weight of the bird being more important, which meant that carcass yield became more important and led to new breeds of birds adopted to these new production methods. Now meatpackers shifted from supplying whole animals to producing cut up parts of chickens both boned and deboned. This packaging of chicken parts began in Brazil in 1985 and soon dominated local production. This necessitated the introduction of new chick types with high meat yields of parts, higher weight, and better feed conversion ratios. It also led to modern machinery installation in slaughterhouses dedicated exclusively to broiler chickens.[26]

The social and economic transformation of the 1970s and 1980s was the driving force for the modernization of the chicken industry in Brazil. The massive migrations of rural populations to urban centers led to the rising demand for cheap meat to feed these expanding urban populations. Given its declining costs, this meant that chicken meat began replacing beef in national consumption. In 1970 beef consumption was 22.2 kgs per inhabitant and chicken consumption just 3.3 kgs per inhabitant, but by 1990 beef was down to 12.5 kgs per inhabitant and chicken was up to 13.4 kgs per inhabitant. By 2010 national consumption of chicken meat reached 44 kgs per inhabitant a figure roughly the norm to the present day. Prior to 1970 there were only 4 meatpacking plants devoted to processing chickens, in the 1970s this increased to 80 such companies and 32 more were added in the 1980s. By this later decade there were already 32 large *frigoríficos* that could process 3,000 birds per hour.[27] Also feed costs kept declining as national production of maize and soybeans kept increasing from the 1980s onward. Given their importance in the feeding of chickens, this was another major factor in promoting the recent development of the poultry meat industry. Along with the growth in volume, there was a growth in efficiency of production. Whereas in 1960 it took 2.2 kilos of food to produce a 1.6 kg broiler in 56 days, by 2010 it took 1.8 kilos of feed to produce a bird weighing 2.3 kilos in just 41 days from birth.[28] By 2019 birds were averaging 2.95 kilos. At the same time there was a long-term secular decline in chick mortality.[29]

As in the case of the United States, the increasing industrialization of chicken production would be based on a complex contract system between the suppliers of day old chicks, the farmers who grew chicken for meat consumption, the feed companies, and the slaughterhouses. In contrast to the North American experience, the initial prime movers in the creation of these vertical chains were the meatpacking companies who were supported by cheap government credit. Whereas the meatpacking plants throughout the first half of the twentieth century were owned by foreign multinationals, by the second half of the century most of these foreign owned companies had sold their plants to Brazilian companies. Among these Brazilian based companies, the key producers of chickens and of swine meat were Sadia, Perdigão, Chapecó, FrangoSul, and Seara (of the Grupo Hering).[30] The first of such totally vertically integrated chicken producing chains was modeled on the one established for pork by the meatpacking company Sadia in 1964 in the city of Concordia, Santa Catarina.[31] This system was soon applied both to swine and to chicken production from local farmers. As this system developed, these slaughtering companies supplied the producers with their animal stock, feed, chemicals and finally provided technical assistance. In turn the farmers delivered their entire stock of animals to Sadia, which processed, packaged, and sold the final product.

By the 1970s these vertical chains were established with strong government support in all regions and were organized both by cooperatives as well as private meatpacking companies. By 1977 it was estimated that 95% of the chickens slaughtered in Santa Catarina had been obtained via this vertical chain and only 5% were sold on the spot market.[32] Chicken farmers in the three southern provinces of Paraná, and Rio Grande do Sul and Santa Catarina used only these vertical chains. The big chicken producers in the state of São Paulo initially remained independent of these vertical production chains even though they contained some of the largest of meatpackers concentrated on chicken production.

The next phase in this evolution of the poultry industry in Brazil would occur in the late twentieth and beginning of the twenty-first century with the rise of the Center-West as the new heart of soybean and maize production. This in turn led to the migration of the major chicken producer companies to the Center-West states of the nation. In 2005 Sadia, established a major meatpacking plant in Lucas Rio Verde, a key center of soybean and corn production on the BR 163 highway in Mato Grosso, and another *gaucho* company, Perdigão opened up a plant in 2005 in nearby Nova Mutum off the same highway.

The growth of a highly specialized chicken production industry was evident by the agricultural census of 2006. Some two thirds of chickens were resident in farms that produced no other products, with the ratio being 90% in the state of São Paulo. The average chicken farm in the Southern state of Paraná, the largest producer, contained 466,000 birds, and those of São Paulo, the second most important state, held on average 229,000 birds. According to this census the 1.4 billion chickens being raised in Brazil represented 86% of all animals in the country's farms and ranches, whereas cattle accounted for only 11% of all these animals, despite the fact that Brazil by this date had the second largest cattle population in the world.[33] Chicken producing farms were averaging 478 animals per establishment nationally and those of the Southern region were averaging 1,265 chickens on its half a million chicken farms.[34] The most outstanding large producer was the Southeastern state of São Paulo which averaged over 3,404 chickens per establishment. Paraná was second with an average of 2,041 chickens of all types, and Santa Catarina with 1,455 animals. Unusual was the Federal District which had just over 2,000 chicken farms which averaged over 4,000 birds per farm.

Although private commercial companies would become important in this livestock sector, the family farms remained an important element. Family farms in the agricultural census of 2017 represented 80% of the farmers producing chickens and had a significant 46% of the stock of chickens. Of course the commercial producers were generally much larger and averaged 1,312 chickens per unit, while the family farmers averaged just 272 chickens per farm.[35] But it is worth noting that in the three southern states, and especially in Paraná, family farms were more important than they were nationally (see Table 12.1). Moreover in the three southern states family farms contained the majority of the chickens, even though the average size of their flocks was smaller than the commercial farms. In the Southeastern and Central-West states the commercial farms dominated production.

Table 12.1 Importance of family farms in the key producing states in the census of 2017

Region/State	*Farms*		*Chickens*	
Southern Region	*Commercial*	*Family Farms*	*Commercial*	*Family Farms*
Paraná	32,835	130,460	159,071,345	174,218,266
Santa Catarina	18,670	91,475	41,440,761	118,819,554
Rio Grande do Sul	33,888	205,269	32,753,050	122,088,721
Southeast Region				
Minas Gerais	79,134	262,494	78,712,708	33,939,776
São Paulo	14,441	37,719	123,962,357	53,607,710
Center-West Region				
Goiás	33,640	68,642	72,432,434	19,112,680
Mato Grosso	19,758	54,002	42,612,447	10,839,723
Brazil	565,614	2,281,956	742,187,294	620,066,215

Source IBGE, Sidra, tabela 6907

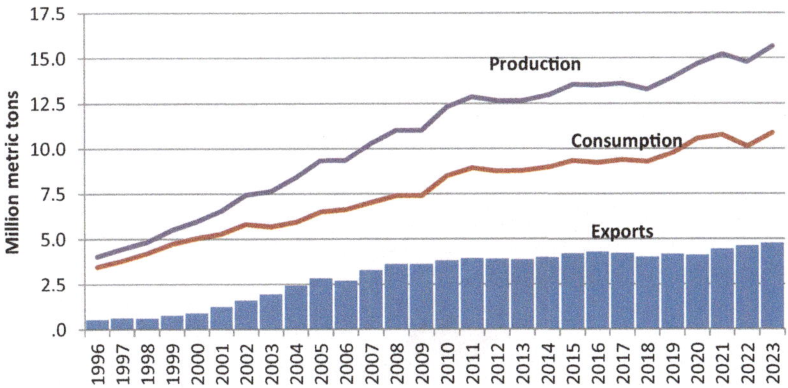

Graph 12.2 Production, export and internal consumption of poultry meat, 1996–2023 (*Source* CONAB, "Oferta e Demanda de Carnes—Fev 2023, found at https://www.conab.gov.br/info-agro/analises-do-mercado-agropecuario-e-extrativista/analises-do-mercado/oferta-e-demanda-de-carnes)

The production of poultry meat doubled from 4 million tons in 1996 to 8 million tons in 2004, and by the end of the second decade of the twenty-first century reached a steady 12 to 14 million tons. Although Brazil was the second largest consumer of chicken meat in the world, its per capita consumption put it in the middle range of countries in terms of consumption. In an estimate of per capita consumption in 2010, the world leaders were the countries of the Middle East, with Kuwait and the United Arab Emirates consuming over 60 kgs (of ready to cook) chicken meat per capita, with Hong Kong, the United States, Brazil, and Saudi Arabia in the 40 kg per capital range, most of the Latin American countries and Australia in the 30 kg range, the EU-27 at 18 kgs, and India the lowest at just 2.3 kgs per capita.[36] Thus of the almost 14 million tons of broiler production in Brazil in 2020, 69% were internally consumed and 31% exported.[37] This allowed for a very solid growth in exports and even a more spectacular growth in national consumption, which went from an estimated 22.1 kilos per person per year in 1997 to 49.7 kilos in 2021 (see Graph 12.2). By 2022 Brazil earned US$ 9.5 billion dollars for the 4.7 million metric tons of its poultry meat exports. This represented some 37% of the value of all meat exports for Brazil in that year.[38]

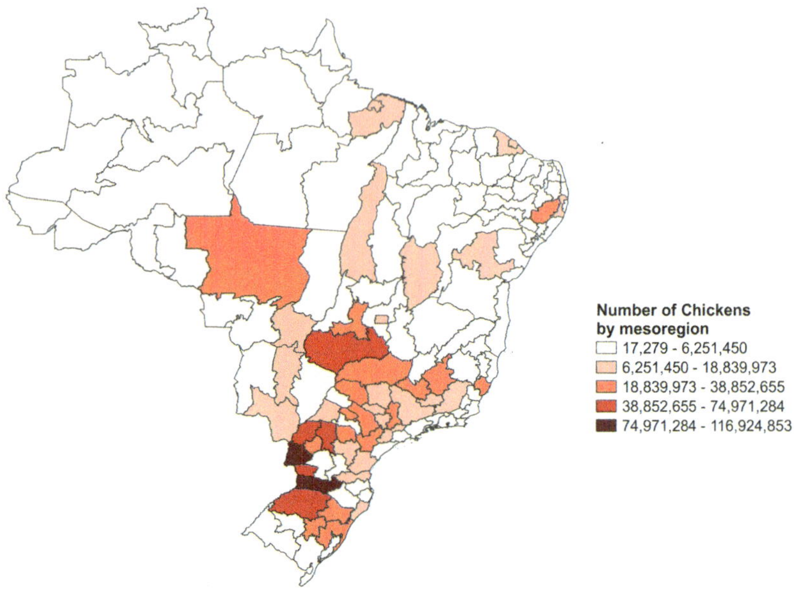

Map 12.1 Number of chickens by mesoregion in 2019 (*Source* IBGE Bases cartográficas Sidra, table 3939)

Although the three southern states and the two Southeastern states of São Paulo and Minas Gerais still dominated chicken meat production in the late 2010s, the second decade of the century saw the growth of chicken production in the Center-West states of Goiás and Mato Grosso (see Map 12.1). Moreover once these newer states had entered the market, production of broiler chicks (*pintos de corte*) averaged just over 6 billion birds per annum from 2016 to 2021 with only modest yearly variation.[39]

Just as there was relative stability in the production states by the third decade of the twenty-first century, there was also relative stability over time in the states exporting poultry meats. The three southern states remained the leading exporters, but São Paulo declined as exporter as much more of its output was domestically consumed. In turn the Center-West states of Goiás and Mato Grosso do Sul were slowly increasing in importance as exporters, though they still accounted for less than a fifth of the value of all exports in the latest period (see Graph 12.3). The

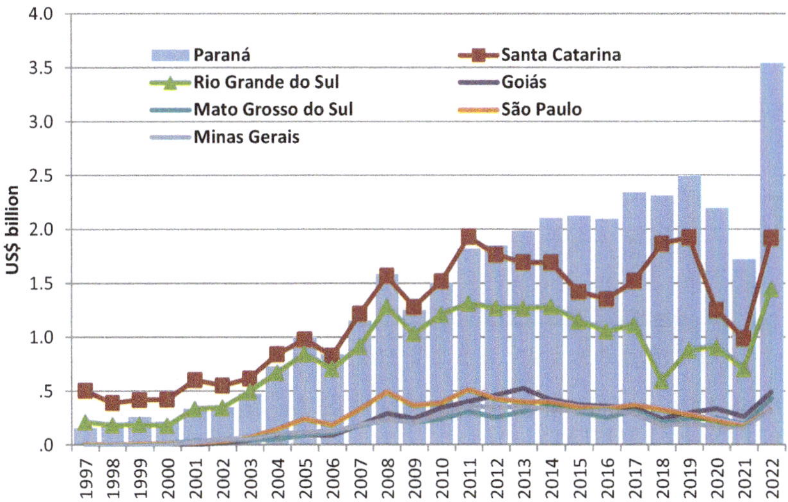

Graph 12.3 Growth of value of meat poulty exports by principal states, 1997–2022 (US$ FOB) (*Source* COMEXSTAT using SH4 Code found at http://comexstat.mdic.gov.br/en/geral)

three states of the Southwest region systematically accounted for four fifths or more of exports from 1997 to the present, averaging 80% in the quinquennium from 2017–2021.[40]

So successful was this new industry that it not only produced more than enough meat to satisfy the growing and increasingly wealthier national population, but it also would also replace the United States as the world's most important exporter of chicken meat. Brazil only began to export chicken meat in 1975, and only reached a million tons by 2001. But by 2004 it had surpassed United States exports for the first time, and since 2014 Brazil has led all world exporters averaging 28% of world exports from 2011–2021. In turn the four leading exporters account for two thirds of all world exports of chicken meat (see Graph 12.4).

These chicken exports were controlled by both private companies and cooperatives, most of which were in vertically integrated production systems. The dominant players were all Brazilian owned companies. The biggest companies were BRF, the world's largest meatpacker, SHB and SEARA. The four cooperatives were also significant and they exported almost as much as SEARA, the leading exporter (see Table 12.2).

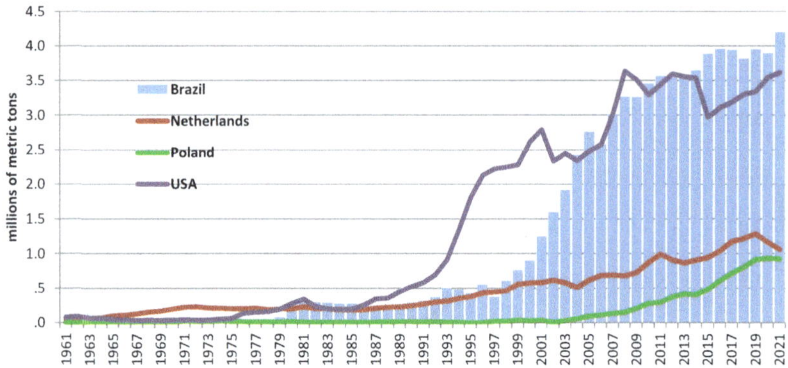

Graph 12.4 Volume of chicken exports by leading exporting countries, 1961–2021 (*Source* FAOSTAT)

Table 12.2 Volume of exports of leading companies exporting chickens from Brazil in 2018 (in metric tons)

Company	*Volume*
Seara Alimentos	823,831
SHB Comercio E Industria De Alimentos S.A	771,294
BRF	541,702
Cooperativa Central Aurora Alimentos	295,828
C.VALE—Cooperativa Agroindustrial	195,296
COPACOL-Cooperativa Agroindustrial Consolata	176,106
LAR Cooperativa Agroindustrial	138,865
JBS AVES LTDA	107,160
Vibra Agroindustrial S/A	106,545

Source data-view?selectedColumnsIds=0_14-1_22-2_9-3_16&toolLayout=1&countries=27&commodities=25

Paraná in 2020 was the single largest exporter, followed by Santa Catarina and Rio Grande do Sul and together they accounted for 81% of the volume of exports. São Paulo and Minas Gerais (the two major states of the Southeast region) though major producers of chickens accounted for only 8% of exports, devoting most of their production of chicken meat for the internal market, while the states of the Center-West (Goiás, Mato Grosso, and Mato Grosso do Sul) accounted for 12% of the volume of exports and had become the second most important region for exports.

Despite the growth of a major production center in the Center-West, a recent study found that the total costs of chicken production, no matter what the system used, was still cheaper in Santa Catarina than in Goiás.[41] In Paraná in the period January to November 2021 it was estimated that 76% of the average cost of raising broiler chickens was made up of food, another 17% for other general costs, and only 4% for labor and 2% for the cost of capital.[42]

The Brazilian chickens were exported all over the world. Initially Europe was a major importer along with Africa and the Middle East, but its purchase of Brazilian chickens systematically declined in the 2010s. In turn Asia expanded as did Africa, while the Middle East remained a steady purchaser. The exports to the Middle East and some African countries required special production under halal conditions which was carried out in Brazil by trusted Islamic Centers and Certification Companies in the country which trained and employed Muslim inspectors to work in the slaughterhouses. This entire process was supported by government regulation, the local Arab Brazilian Chamber of Commerce, the national association of chicken producers, and with a constant interaction with religious authorities from the major importing countries which guaranteed the validity of the certification and the correct training of Brazilian Muslim inspectors. The first halal certified chickens were exported in 1975 and by 2014 it was estimated that 44% of Brazilian chicken exports were certified Halal-labeled and by the second decade of the current century Brazil became the leading halal chicken meat exporter in the world.[43] Saudi Arabia was Brazil's second leading importer of chickens in terms of volume and the United Arab Emirates its fourth largest consumer in 2020. So effective was Brazil in this market that in the five year period 2015–2019 some 83% of the chicken imported into Saudi Arabia came from Brazil, in Oman it was 70%, in Yemen it was 60%, and in the United Arab Emirates it was 58% in this same period. Overall Middle Eastern countries took 31% of Brazil's chicken exports in 2022, Asian countries 38%, and African ones 9% of the total in that year (see Graph 12.5).[44]

Some two thirds of the exported meat was in parts (cortes), and a quarter was made up of whole chickens. The remaining 9% was made up of salted meat, industrialized products, and sausages. But there were regional differences in these exports. While most of the world concentrated on imports of Chicken meat parts, 64% of Middle East imports were whole chickens, and the European Union was the unique as the most diverse importer, with salted meats accounting for 52% of its Brazilian

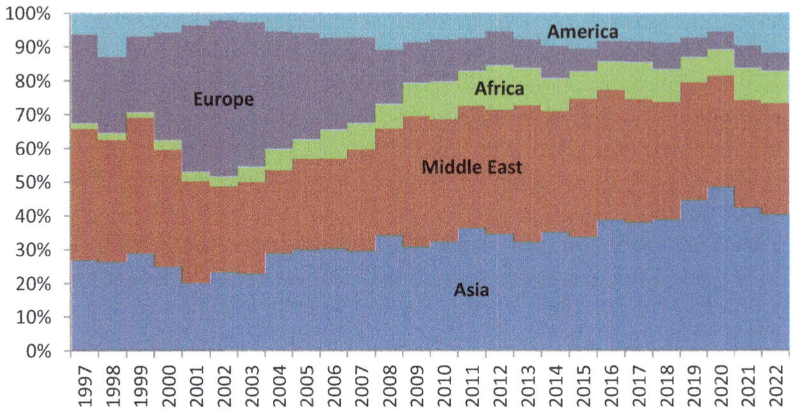

Graph 12.5 Regional share of imports of Brazilian broiler meat, 1997–2022 (*Source* COMEXSTAT using SH4 code 0207)

chicken imports.[45] This dominant position of Brazil whose 4.6 million tons poultry exports made up 31% of all poultry world exports in 2022, is estimated to increase another million tons by 2031.[46]

Given the fact that 64% of the exported chicken meat was processed in the three southeastern states of Paraná, Rio Grande do Sul, and Santa Catarina, it is no accident that 42% of chicken meat exports went through the port of Paranaguá in Paraná, and another 36% in the Santa Catarina port of Itajaí, while only 8% went through Santos, which otherwise was the primer agricultural port of Brazil.[47] As could be expected, the largest slaughterhouses were in the three southern states. In 2021 these states contained 40% of the 280 abattoirs specializing in chickens, and accounted for 59% of the 18 million tons of chicken meat processed.[48]

Supported by the government from the 1960s onward, the raising and processing of chickens has become a major sector in both the national market and in the export market as well. The per capita consumption of chickens in Brazil almost doubled between 1970 and today. It became the meat of choice for the majority of the population because of its low price compared to all other meats. At the same Brazil also found that its costs of feed and labor made its production of chickens competitive on the world market. It even used its resources from immigrant groups to create a modern halal sector of the industry. As the industry became more international establishing sanitary norms became ever more important and by 2006 the federal government implanted an effective sanitary inspection of all chicken slaughterhouses based on international standards in order to guarantee the viability of exports.[49] Although all sectors of the country produced chickens, it was the three southern states, and above all Paraná that dominated all aspects of the industry from the earliest period until today.

Until the middle of the last century, pig farming like chicken breeding was characterized by low technology, poor sanitary conditions, with little care taken in breeding or in the slaughtering of animals. Slaughtering was mostly done either on the farm which produced the pigs or in local makeshift slaughtering houses. Farms in general raised pigs for their own consumption, eventually selling the excess into the market. Even agricultural establishments not involved in commercial pig farming had some pigs for their own consumption. Pigs could be raised in open fields or in usually rustic facilities, the so-called *mangueirões* or pigsties.[50]

As with the other meat producing animals, pigs were introduced by the Portuguese colonists to Brazil and from the early days of colonization, pig farming has been practiced intensively in Brazil and national breeds were developed for the purpose of producing meat and lard for popular consumption. These creole breeds were characterized by their high proportion of fat, which was valued in the market.[51] From the 1950s, with both the growth of vegetable oils replacing lard, and the general modernization of national agriculture, the market in swine meat changed and the emphasis was now more on meat production alone and new breeds were imported so as to improve meat production.[52]

Even under traditional breeding practices, pig farming was an activity of great economic importance. According to the 1960 census, there were 26 million pigs in the country, distributed over 2 million establishments, with an average of 13 animals per establishment. Some 21% of these animals were located on farms of less than 10 hectares, and 37% of them on farms less than 20 hectares.[53] The largest herds were then located in the South (45%), Southeast (25%), and Northeast (20%). Rio Grande do Sul, Minas Gerais, and São Paulo concentrated the largest herds. This was approximately the same distribution as can be seen in the agricultural survey of 2019 (see Map 12.2). In that year Brazil slaughtered 8 million animals, producing 534 thousand tons of pork, all of which fed into the domestic market.

In the middle of the last century the Southern states of Brazil began the process of integration of farmers into a production chain, similar to the

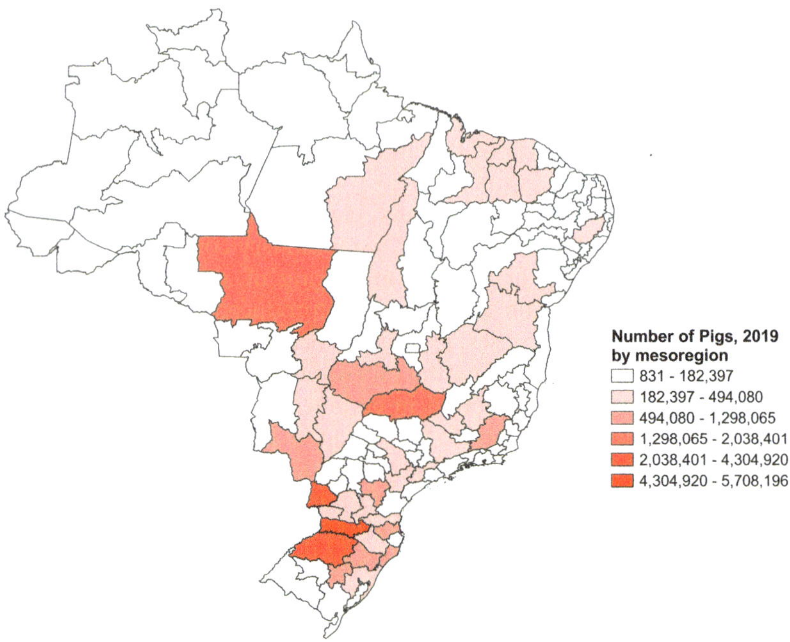

Map 12.2 Number of pigs by mesoregion, 2019 (*Source* IBGE Bases cartográficas Sidra, table 3939)

development that occurred in poultry farming. The meatpacking companies of Santa Catarina would be the first to adopt this system in both pig and poultry farming.[54] The core of the system was a slaughtering and or processing company, which vertically integrated various stages of the production process, such as genetic improvement, nutrition, slaughter of animals, and meat processing, in a contractual relationship with pig farmers, who provided the land, labor, and facilities to breed pigs.[55] The main agroindustrial and cooperative companies guaranteed the supply of raw materials in the desired quantity and quality to the farmers, as well as organizing the slaughtering and sale of the final products. This vertical integration enabled greater standardization and stabilization of the raw material and allowed for the transfer of risks and profits between the different segments.[56] These outside firms and coops started initially through technical assistance, and gradually integrated the activities of

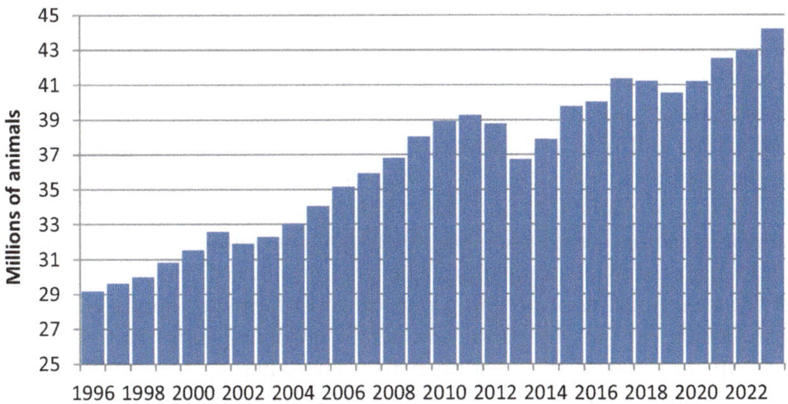

Graph 12.6 Size of the swine herd of Brazil, 1997–2022 (*Source* CONAB, "Oferta e Demanda de Carnes—Fev 2023)

creation and processing of the pigs.[57] In this early phase, the main concern was supplying the national market.[58] Eventually this model of an integrated system became the predominant system in the Southern states of the country, which was the largest pig-producing region in Brazil. In this vertical system the meat companies paid for the inputs required by the farmers to raise pigs in return for a guaranteed delivery of the grown pigs to the meatpackers at a fixed price[59] Production under this vertical system grew steadily in the next several decades, and from 1997 to 2015 the stock of pigs was growing at 1.4% per annum (see Graph 12.6).

In general, the southern swine producers were primarily smaller family size units and so were easily integrated into these value chains. In contrast, the Southeastern states were initially dominated by independent full-cycle producers selling their products on the spot market much like the poultry producers in this region. In the new zones of the Center-West the vertical integration system became important from the beginning with the lead taken by grain producers, rather than the meatpackers. Eventually in all regions the integration model become increasingly important as the sector's leading agroindustrial companies expanded their operations from their original base in the South to plants in the Southeast and Center-West regions.[60] The rapid growth of pig farming, as with poultry farming, was strongly influenced by the exceptional increase in grain production in

Brazil in the recent period, a fundamental component in the composition of costs in the sector.

In 2017, according to the agricultural census, there were 1.5 million farms raising some 39 million pigs, the third largest herd in the world.[61] Of this herd of pigs, the South region held 21 million heads, with herds in the Southeast and Center-West region each containing 6 million pigs. The states of Santa Catarina, Rio Grande do Sul, and Paraná were the largest breeding centers, and together they concentrated more than half of the national swine population. The large number of farms is a reflection of the commonality of breeding pigs on most farms for family consumption, which explains the large number of producing units but their low ratio in the total of the existing herds. Thus, herds of up to 20 heads, which probably had just two or three breeding stock, represented 92% of the establishments, but only 19% of the herds. On the other hand, 12 thousand establishments with more than 500 heads, less than 1% of the farms, held more than two thirds of the national stock of pigs. This result can be seen in the Southeast, South, and Midwest, but not in the North and Northeast, where large-scale commercial creation was less important. The large breeders, with more than 500 heads, had an average of 2,249 heads, but this figure was 8,069 thousand in the Center-West and reached 18,484 in Mato Grosso, where the grain supply was abundant, allowing a more adequate integration of intensive farming and livestock activities (Table 12.3). Nevertheless 80% of the farms were family run establishments, many in integrated systems, and they controlled half of the pig herds. But there were major regional differences, particularly if we compare the two great creative regions, the South and the Center-West. In the South, family farmers account for almost two thirds of the pig farms; in the Center-West this percentage drops to a quarter (Table 12.4).

The vertical chains are concentrated in a few companies. This is due to the consolidation process of the swine slaughterhouse sector in Brazil in the past two decades, which followed the trend in the cattle and poultry sectors. The BRF Group controls 28% of the market, followed by JBS with 14% of production, and Aurora, the former Cooperativa Central Catarinense with another 14%.[62] Their factories are found throughout Brazil in the main breeding regions. These three processing groups also would take the lead in swine exports from Brazil.[63]

Although there were significant improvements in Brazilian pig farming, both in terms of genetics and animal management, Brazil still is less

Table 12.3 Distribution of pigs by herd size, for regions and principal states, 2017 census

	Total	*1–20 (%)*	*21–50 (%)*	*51–100 (%)*	*101–250 (%)*	*251–500 (%)*	*501+ (%)*
	Establishments						
Brazil	1,471,279	92	5	1	0	0	1
North	159,402	89	9	1	0	0	0
Northeast	556,873	92	4	0	0	0	0
Southeast	235,775	94	3	0	0	0	0
South	375,844	92	3	0	0	1	3
Center-West	143,376	89	9	1	0	0	0
	Number of animals						
Brazil	39,346,192	19	5	2	1	5	68
North	1,758,908	53	26	9	4	3	4
Northeast	4,004,615	69	17	5	2	2	6
Southeast	6,343,331	16	4	1	1	1	76
South	21,101,886	8	2	0	1	9	80
Center-West	6,137,452	14	7	2	1	1	75

Source IBGE, Sidra, tabela 6926

Table 12.4 Swine establishments and herds, in Commercial and family farming, 2017 census

	Family Farms			*Commercial Farms*		
	Units	*Heads*	*Average*	*Units*	*Heads*	*Average*
Brazil	1,185,495	20,237,925	17	285,775	19,108,267	67
North	129,368	1,278,025	10	30,034	480,883	16
Northeast	456,484	3,024,240	7	100,389	980,375	10
Southeast	181,498	1,466,851	8	54,277	4,876,480	90
South	318,984	12,970,100	41	56,860	8,131,786	143
Center-West	99,161	1,498,709	15	44,215	4,638,743	105

Source IBGE, Sidra, tabela 6926

productive than producers in Europe and the United States, although the gap is less in 2021 than it was in 1980 (see Table 12.5). The genetic improvement of the herds has led to a higher percentage of lean meat in pig carcasses. This percentage, which was 46 to 48% in the 1980s, currently stands at 58%. In addition, in the last 15 years, the average

Table 12.5 Swine flocks and yield of pork meat production by regions and countries, 1980, 2000 and 2021

Country	*Stocks*	*Slaughtered*	*Meat Production (t.)*	*Yield*		
				slaughtered kg	*slaughtered/ stock*	*meat/ stock (kg)*
	1980					
World	797,698,062	755,958,071	52,674,296	697	0.95	66
Europe	248,639,429	305,976,643	24,479,997	800	1.23	98
U.S.A	67,318,000	97,174,000	7,536,440	776	1.44	112
Brazil	34,183,008	14,100,000	980,000	695	0.41	29
	2000					
World	898,679,637	1,098,910,474	89,757,721	817	1.22	100
Europe	200,406,363	295,343,073	25,282,953	856	1.47	126
U.S.A	59,110,300	98,105,900	8,596,946	876	1.66	145
Brazil	31,562,112	35,665,200	2,600,000	729	1.13	82
	2021					
World	975,409,675	1,400,092,105	120,372,127	860	1.44	123
Europe	187,195,085	332,672,391	30,788,805	925	1.78	164
China	454,807,281	609,593,203	53,907,071	884	1.34	119
U.S.A	74,146,100	129,062,400	12,559,966	973	1.74	169
Brazil	42,538,652	53,045,545	4,365,000	823	1.25	103

Source Faostat, http://www.fao.org/faostat/en/#data

carcass yield has increased from 75 to 90 kg.[64] These two indicators show that although Brazil has not yet achieved the results obtained in Europe and the United States, the evolution of productivity was significant. Despite this lower productivity, Brazil's abundant supply of grains, a crucial cost in swine breeding, allowed the country to effectively compete on the international market.

Exports of chilled and frozen pork were the last of the major Brazilian meat exports to develop an international market. They became significant only at the end of the twentieth and beginning of the twenty-first century. As with chickens most of the national production went for the internal market. But once begun Brazilian exports have expanded at an extraordinary rate. Exports went from a small quantity of 56 thousand tons of pork meat in 1997, to over a million tons by 2021, with the volume growing at extraordinary rate of over 10% per annum between 1998 and 2021 (see Graph 12.7).

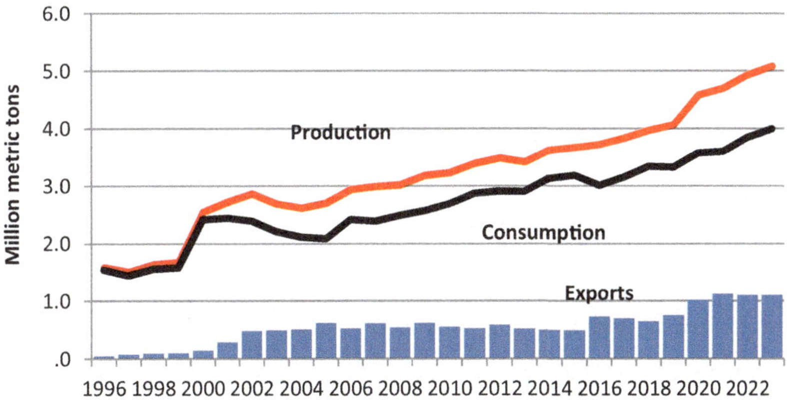

Graph 12.7 Production, export and internal consumption of swine meat, 1996–2022 (in metric tons) (*Source* CONAB, "Oferta e Demanda de Carnes—Fev 2023)

If anything, pork production and exports was even more dominated by the three southern states than was chicken production. The three southern states accounted for the overwhelming majority of exports, with Santa Catarina being the leading exporter for most of this period. In this respect the Central-Western states have only slowly begun to export, and are less significant than in chicken exports (see Graph 12.8).

In contrast to chicken meat exports, Brazilian pork exports go to different international markets. Europe initially was an important pork consumer, but has now been totally eclipsed by Asia, and the Americas (see Graph 12.9). The total value of pork meat exports in 2022 was US$ 2.5 billion, or a third of the US$ 9.5 billion earned by chicken exports.[65]

The importers of Brazilian pork exports have varied considerably over time. This is the case with the Russian Federation which was for a time was the principal importer of Brazilian pork. Recently Asian swine disease decimated pork stocks in China and led to an extraordinary growth of Chines port meat imports which will probably decline over time.[66] Otherwise Brazil is a major provider of pork meat to South American countries and the United States and even to Puerto Rico. It was also for a time a major exporter to Europe.

Whereas Brazil is the leading world exporter of poultry meat in all forms, its pork exports currently rank it as the fifth largest exporter in

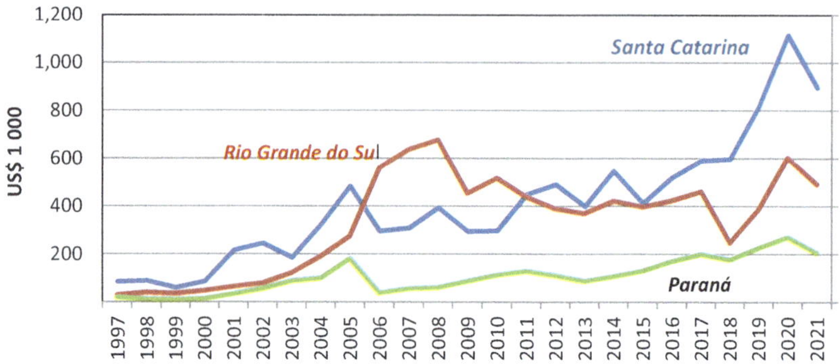

Graph 12.8 Value of pork meat exports by leading exporting states, 1997–2021 (*Source* COMEXSTAT using SH4 Code found at http://comexstat.mdic.gov.br/en/geral)

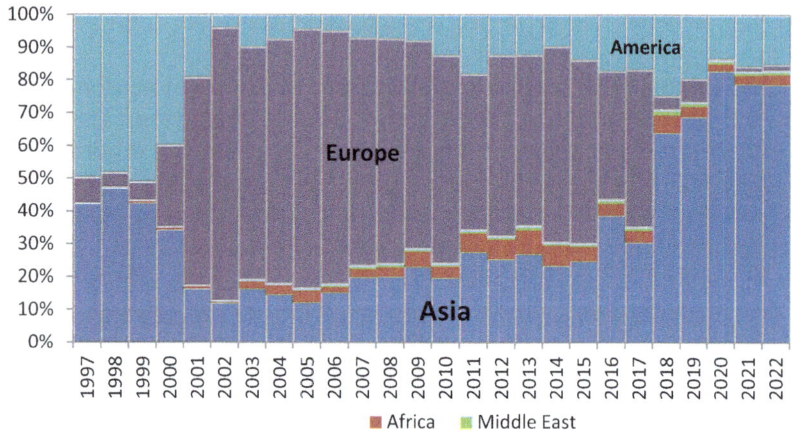

Graph 12.9 Relative share of Brazilian meat exports to world regions, 1997–2022 (*Source* COMESTAT)

the world, it was close to its other three competitors, Spain, Canada, and Germany all in the two billion dollar range (see Graph 12.10). By 2022 it accounted for 11% of the volume of world pork exports, and is expected to increase its share of world exports to 13% in 2031 when it is estimated to produce 1.8 million tons.[67] Whereas Brazil's primary export

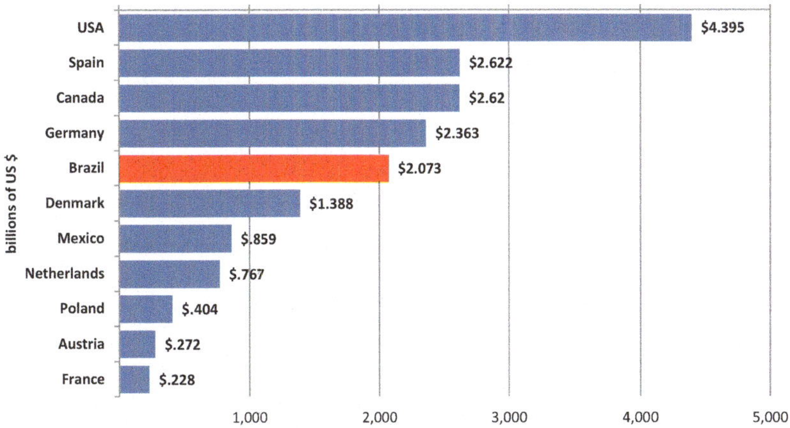

Graph 12.10 Major exporters of pork meat in 2020, by value FOB in US $ (*Source* Faostat)

was pork meat, this was not the case with the traditional European countries and the United States which exported a much higher ratio of their pork products as specialized categories such as sausages, casing, etc.[68]

Brazilians themselves are not major consumers of pork. Per capita consumption per year was 13.52 kg/year, below the world average consumption of 15.56 kg/year, and well below what was consumed in the United States and Europe. Nor has pork consumption varied much over the years and seems to be little affected by price differentials, in contrast to beef. It is less than half of the average consumption of beef (37.5 kg/capita/year) and well below that of chicken. This relatively stable consumption has allowed Brazil to export about a quarter of its pork production (Table 12.6).

The sector's value chain was estimated to be worth US $ 44 billion in 2015, with US $ 4 billion in inputs to the farm (food, medicine, etc.), US $ 5 billion on producing pork on the farms, and US $ 35 billion in processing and shipping to market. In that year pig production consumed 10.6 million tons of corn and more than 3.5 million tons of soybean meal in animal feed. The activity generated a total employment of 127 thousand direct jobs, of which 35 thousand in creation and 92 thousand in slaughter and processing.[69]

Table 12.6 Pork meat, new food balance (2018)

		Brasil	*World*	*% Brasil*
Production	1000 metric tons	3,763	120,607	3
Import Quantity	1000 metric tons	3	16,356	0
Stock Variation	1000 metric tons	–	2,884	0
Export Quantity	1000 metric tons	932	17,057	5
Domestic supply quantity	1000 metric tons	2,833	117,022	2
Food	1000 metric tons	2,833	115,869	2
Food supply quantity (kg/capita/yr)	kg	13.52	15.56	
Food supply (kcal/capita/day)	kcal/capita/day	103	123	
Protein supply quantity (g/capita/day)	g/capita/day	3.61	4.55	
Fat supply quantity (g/capita/day)	g/capita/day	9.69	11.42	

Fonte Faostat

In many ways the production of chickens and pigs share common features. In contrast to beef, both of these animals were produced on smaller properties with a significant role played by family farms. Most producers of these two animals were also slowly integrated into similar value chains by national meatpacking companies, and most of this commercial production of chickens and pigs had their origin in the southern and southeastern states of Brazil. Differences however emerge over time between these two animal industries. In the case of broiler chickens Brazil very quickly followed the lead of the more advanced countries in mass producing chickens as the alternative and cheaper meat compared to beef. This was systematically encouraged by the governments of the 1960s and 1970s as a means to reduce the cost of living and the problems related to inflation. Once production had satisfied national markets these producers were able to expand rapidly overseas and create a dominant role in the international market. In the case of pork, the evolution was slower. Pork production was primarily directed toward the internal market for a longer period. It entered the international market in a much later date than poultry meats and has only slowly became a major player in this field aided by crises of production in Asia. Whereas chicken exports of Brazil dominated the markets of the Middle East, as well as being important in Asia, pork after a first surge into Europe has now sent most of its production to Asia, with a modest but growing export to the Americas. But there is little doubt that by the second decade of the twenty-first century Brazil has created a modern pork and poultry industry capable of being a significant participant in world trade and together with chilled and frozen beef exports now plays a major role in the world animal protein market. At the same time these exports have become fundamental in Brazilian exports. In 2022 the chilled and frozen products of beef, chicken, and pork were worth US$ 25.6 billion, making it the second leading agricultural export after the complex of soybean products.[70]

Notes

1. Alice A. Storey, et al., "Investigating the Global Dispersal of Chickens in Prehistory Using Ancient Mitochondrial DNA Signatures," *PLoS One*, 7, no. 7 (2012): e39171.
2. Censo Agrícola 1960, Série Nacional, vol. II, 2a parte: 116, tabela IX.
3. The OECD-FAO estimates that in 2018–2020 some 60% of world chicken meat production and 62% of world consumption of this meat occurred in countries of the developing world. "Table C4 World Meat Projections 2021–2030," accessed January 1, 2022 and found at https://www.oecd-ilibrary.org/agriculture-and-food/data/oecd-agriculture-statistics_agr-data-en.
4. USDA,_*Livestock and Poultry, World Markets and Trade, October Oct 2021*: 4–5. The data for 2022 estimated production is from October 2021. In October 2021 the USDA shifted from reporting broiler chicken meat data in 1,000 Metric Tons (Ready to Cook Equivalent) to 1,000 metric tons carcas weight equivalent. The difference between these two rates varied by year between 39 to 43% in the years 2016–2020 when both figures are available making precise comparisons difficult between pre and post 2021 data. The ready to cook weight was defined as "dressed poultry, without feathers, head, feet, and most internal organs[and] includes neck and giblets." https://www.ers.usda.gov/data-products/food-availability-per-capita-data-system/glossary/#boneless. The carcass weight measures "the weight of skeletal muscle and bones after the other parts listed above have been removed. Also, for boneless meat products, the conversion factor "adds back" the weight of the bones removed from that portion

of the carcass." https://www.ers.usda.gov/data-products/livestock-and-meat-international-trade-data/documentation/.

5. USDA, *Livestock and Poultry, World Markets and Trade, October2006*, n.p.
6. The sources for Graph 11.1 are USDA, *Livestock and Poultry World Markets & Trade April 2023*, 14–15; USDA, *Poultry and Products Semi-annual, Mexico, Feb 2023*; USDA, *Poultry and Products Annual, Turkey Sept 2022.*
7. USDA, *Livestock and Poultry, World Markets and Trade, October 2017*, 24.
8. For a detailed analysis of this early period and the companies founded see Bernardo Sorj, Malori J. Pompermayer, and Odacir Luis Coradini, *Camponeses e agroindústria: transformação social e representação política na avicultura brasileira* (Rio de Janeiro: Centro Edelstein de Pesquisas Sociais, 2008), chap. 1.
9. Richard Henry and Graeme Rothwell, *The World Poultry Industry* (World Bank Publications, 1995), 10.
10. Douglas H. Constance, "The Southern Model of Broiler Production and Its Global Implications," *Culture & Agriculture*, 30, no. 1–2 (2008): 17–20. Constance claims that it was the first livestock sector to be vertically integrated; see Douglas H. Constance, Francisco Martinez-Gomez, Gilberto Aboites-Manrique, and Alessandro Bonanno, "The Problems with Poultry Production and Processing," in Harvey S. James, ed., *The Ethics and Economics of Agrifood Competition* (Springer, 2013), p. 155. Also see William Boyd, Making Meat: Science, Technology, and American Poultry Production," *Technology and Culture*, 42, no. 4 (Oct. 2001): 631–664.
11. For a detailed history of the evolution of this special industry see Glenn E. Bugos, "Intellectual Property Protection in the American Chicken-Breeding Industry," *The Business History Review*, 66, no. 1 (1992): 127–168.
12. Clare A. Narrod and Keith O. Fuglie, "Private Investment in Livestock Breeding with Implications for Public Research Policy," *Agribusiness: An International Journal*, 16, no. 4 (2000): 457–470; and Clare A. Narrod, Carl E. Pray, and Marites Tiongco, "Technology Transfer, Policies, and the Role of the Private Sector in the Global Poultry Revolution" (International Food Policy Research Institute, Discussion Paper 00,841, December 2008): 8.
13. By the 1960s Brazil was importing breeding stock and chicks from France as well as the United States. In 1970 the government prohibited the importation of chicks and parent breeding stock and only allowed the importation of primary breeders (the great grandparents). Celso de Jesus Junior, Sergio Roberto Lima de Paula, José Geraldo Pacheco Ormond, and Natália Mesquita Braga, *A cadeia da carne de frango: tensões, desafios*

e oportunidades (Brasília: BNDES, 2007), 196. It should be noted that the more advanced countries of Europe also adopted the US practices at around the same time as Brazil. See Andrew Godley, "The Emergence of Agribusiness in Europe and the Development of the Western European Broiler Chicken Industry, 1945 to 1973," *Agricultural History Review*, 62, no. 2 (2014): 315–336.

14. Aldair Tarcísio Rizzi, "Mudanças tecnológicas e reestruturação da indústria agroalimentar: o caso da indústria de frangos no Brasil" (Phd thesis, Universidade Estadual de Campinas, 1993), 86 table 16. The best analysis of these importations, local breeding efforts and dates of importation of major breeds is found in Carlos José Espindola, "Trajetórias do progresso técnico na cadeia produtiva de carne de frango do Brasil," *Geosul*, 27, no. 53 (2012): 94–98.
15. Jesus Junior, et al., *A cadeia da carne de frango*, 197, table 1. On the origin of the special Embrapa institute established in Santa Catarina to deal with chickens and pigs, see https://www.embrapa.br/en/suinos-e-aves/historia.
16. The great grandparents are created from a male and female of one pure stock (A). They give birth to a new bird which is crossed with a bird from another pure line (Male a x Female b) and these are the grandparents. They in turn produce a new male or female bird, the parent birds called a matriz which combines lines A & B. These parents are then bred with another crossed breed C & D of the opposite sex. These matriz birds produce the eggs which are the broiler chicks (or *pintos*) which thus have 4 purebred lines (ABCD) in their genetic makeup. See Jesus Junior, et al., *A cadeia da carne de frango*: 195 Fig. 1.
17. Rizzi, "Mudanças tecnológicas e reestruturação da indústria agroalimentar": 75 table 14.
18. Sumayya Goga and Teboho Bosiu, *Governance of Poultry Value Chains—A Comparative Perspective on Developing Capabilities in South Africa and Brazil* (Johannesburg: CREED, IDTT and SARChI Chair, 2019), 7, table 1.
19. For the history of JBS, https://jbs.com.br/sobre/nossa-historia/. On the history of the two companies that founded Brazilian Foods (BRF) see Angelo Brião Zanela, "Ensaios sobre business groups: Perdigão e Sadia e a consolidação de grupos econômicos no Brasil (1934–2009)" (Phd thesis, Universidade Federal do Paraná, 2019) and for the creation of BRF see https://www.brf-global.com/sobre/a-brf/nossa-historia/, both accessed January 3, 2022; and A. Campos, "Brazil's Poultry Industry (2016) Techreport," accessed January 3, 2022 at https://reporterbrasil.org.br/wp-content/uploads/2016/07/Monitor2_ENG.pdf.
20. Jesus Junior, *A Cadeia da Carne de Frango*, 197.

21. Carys E. Bennett, Richard Thomas, Mark Williams, Jan Zalasiewicz, Matt Edgeworth, Holly Miller, Ben Coles, Alison Foster, Emily J. Burton, and Upenyu Marume, "The Broiler Chicken as a Signal of a Human Reconfigured Biosphere," *Royal Society Open Science*, 5, no. 12 (2018): 180,325, 1.
22. For the growth of the feed industry in terms of companies and regulation see Espindola, "Trajetórias do progresso técnico na cadeia produtiva de carne de frango do Brasil": 99–101.
23. On the mix of elements which went to make up the feeding of chickens, see Jesus Junior, *A Cadeia da Carne de Frango*: 201 table 2. On the growth of these industries in Brazil see Herbert S. Klein and Francisco Vidal Luna, "The Growth of the Soybean Frontier in South America: The Case of Brazil and Argentina," *Revista de Historia Económica*, 39, no. 3 (Dec. 2021): 427–468.
24. Espindola, "Trajetórias do progresso técnico na cadeia produtiva de carne de frango do Brasil," 102–103.
25. Marilucia Ben and Carmen Rejane Flores Wizniewsky, "A territorialização e versatilidade da cooperativa agroindustrial Lar no Brasil e Paraguai," XI Econtro Nacional da ANPEGE, 2021, 1349–1350 found at http://www.enanpege.ggf.br/2015/anais/arquivos/4/138.pdf.
26. Inaldo Sales Patricio, Ariel Antonio Mendes, Alcides de Amorim Ramos, and Danilo Florentino Pereira, "Overview on the Performance of Brazilian Broilers (1990 to 2009)," *Brazilian Journal of Poultry Science*, 14, no. 4 (2012): 234; Aldair Tarcísio Rizzi, "Mudanças Tecnológicas e Reestruturação da Indústria Agroalimentar: o caso da indústria de frangos no Brasil"(Phd thesis, Campinas: Unicamp, 1993), 40.
27. Rizzi, "Mudanças Tecnológicas e Reestruturação da Indústria," 61, 63, tabelas 8 and 9. The consumption data from 2010 comes from ABPA [Associação Brasileira de Proteína Animal], Estatístico do Setor found at https://abpa-br.org/mercados/. From 2010 to 2019 average consumption was 43.2 kgs, see ABPA *Relatório Anual_2020*: 30.
28. Luciano de Souza Costa, Luis Alberto Ferreira Garcia, and Paulo Rogério Alves Brene, "A Indústria de frango de corte no mundo e no Brasil e a participação da indústria avícola paranaense neste complexo,"*Ciências Sociais em Perspectiva*, 14, no. 27 (2015): 322 table 1.
29. Goga and Bosiu, "Governance of poultry value chains": 13, table 2.
30. Walter Belik, "Agroindústria Processadora e Política Econômica"(Phd thesis, Campinas, UNICAMP, 1992): 44.
31. Luiz Antonio Rossi de Freitas and Oscar Bertoglio, "A evolução da avicultura de corte brasileira após 1980," *Economia e Desenvolvimento* 13 (2001): 102.
32. Sorj, Pompermayer, and Coradini, *Camponeses e agroindústria*: 26.

33. https://censos.ibge.gov.br/agro/2017/templates/censo_agro/resultadosagro/pecuaria.html; and USDA, *Livestock and Poultry, World Markets and Trade, Oct 2021*: 6.
34. Unfortunately the census does not break down the division between broilers, or meat birds, and layers, or egg producing ones.
35. IBGE, Sidra, tab 6624. The data in this table includes all farms, including those unknown as to their status as commercial or family farms.
36. USDA, *Livestock and Poultry: World Market and Trade, Oct 2010*: n.p.n.
37. ABPA, *Relatório Anual 2020*: 37, found at http://abpa-br.org/relatorios/.
38. MAPA, https://indicadores.agricultura.gov.br/agrostat/index.htm.; and https://balanca.economia.gov.br/balanca/publicacoes_dados_consolidados/pg.html#s%C3%A9ries-hist%C3%B3ricas-detalhadas. In comparative terms chicken exports were more valuable then cellulose exports in that year, though not in the level soybeans and their products which were valued at US$ 47 billion in exports in 2022.
39. Data by month as well, shows little variation. Statistics found June 1, 2022 at https://www.avisite.com.br/estatisticas-precos/.
40. COMEXSTAT using SH4 Code 0207, accessed December 29, 2021 and found at http://comexstat.mdic.gov.br/en/geral.
41. Ari Jabos Sandi and Marcelo Miele, "Análise comparativa dos custos de produção de frangos de corte em SC e GO,"*Guia Gessulli da Avicultura e Suinocultura Industrial*, 104, no. 9 (2012): 20–29, found at https://www.embrapa.br/en/suinos-e-aves/cias/estudos.
42. Embrapa Swine & Poultry, found at https://www.embrapa.br/en/suinos-e-aves/cias/custos/frango-uf.
43. Shadia Husseini de Araújo, "Assembling halal meat and poultry production in Brazil: Agents, practices, power and sites," *Geoforum*, 100 (2019): 220–228; and Flavio Romero Macau, Julio Araujo Carneiro da Cunha, Nawfal Assa Mossa Alssabak, and Januario Souza Leandro, "Food Value Chains: Social Networks and Knowledge Transfer in a Brazilian Halal Poultry Network," *International Food and Agribusiness Management Review*, 19, no. 3 (2016): 211–223. All these data are from partner trades at http://www.fao.org/faostat/en/#data/TM; and total import data in http://www.fao.org/faostat/en/#data/TP.
44. MAPA Agrostat at https://indicadores.agricultura.gov.br/agrostat/index.htm.
45. ABPA, *Relatório Anual 2021*: 38–43.
46. USDA, *Agricultural Projections to 2031* (February 2022), 100, table 39.
47. ABPA, *Relatório Anual 2021*: 43.
48. IBGE dataset found at https://sidra.ibge.gov.br/home/abate.
49. Priscilla Zygmantas Novelli, Daniela Cabral Paiva, Nadir Lopes Garcia, and Thiago Brava Izidoro, "Panorama sobre a regulamentação do sistema

APPCC em estabelecimentos de carne de aves sob inspeção federal," *Revista Higiene alimentar*, 30, no. 254/255 (2016): 139–145.

50. V.C. Souza, *História econômica da suinocultura no Paraná: tradição e modernização: depoimento [10 março, 2016]* (Nova Laranjeiras: Entrevista concedida a Odair José F. de Oliveira, 2016), p. 79.
51. These creole breeds were known as Piau, Tatu, Canastra, Nile, Caruncho, Pereira, and Pirapitinga.
52. These included the Landrace, Large White, Duroc, Hampshire, Wessen, and Pietrain breeds. Jerônimo Antônio Fávero e Elsio A. F. de Figueiredo, "Evolução do melhoramento genético de suínos no Brasil," *Ceres*, 56, no. 4 (2009): 420–427.
53. Censo Agrícola 1960, Série Nacional, vol. II, 2a parte: 13, tabela 11.
54. Sadia and Perdigão from 1990 were responsible for 64% of the chickens and 41% of the pigs slaughtered in Santa Catarina. Armando João Dalla Costa, "O grupo Sadia e a produção integrada. O lugar da agricultura no complexo agroindustrial" (MA thesis, Universidade Federal do Paraná, 1993), 28.
55. Denis Teixeira da Rocha, Altair Dias de Moura and Ademir Francisco Girotto. "Análise de risco de sistemas de produção de suínos, integrado e independente, em períodos de alta e baixa rentabilidade," *Revista de economia e agronegócio*, 5, no. 3 (2007): 402–424. For an excellent overview of pig farming, see *Produção de suínos: teoria e prática* (Brasília: Coordenação editorial: Associação Brasileira de Criadores de Suínos. Coordenação Técnica Integral Soluções em Produção Animal, 2014).
56. Josemar Xavier de Medeiros, "Sistemas de produção integrado, contratado, cooperado e independente," in *Produção de suínos: teoria e prática*: 39.
57. CEAG. *Análise do Sistema de Integração Agroindustrial em Suínos e Aves em Santa Catarina*. (Florianópolis: Centro de Assistência Gerencial de Santa Catarina—CEAG-SC, 1978); and Costa, "O grupo Sadia": 26–28.
58. Sadia's case is illustrative. To supply the domestic market, mainly São Paulo and Rio de Janeiro, the company started to use air transport and later created its own airline, Sadia SA Transportes Aéreos, which was transformed into Transbrasil in 1960. Costa. "O grupo Sadia".
59. Costa, "O grupo Sadia": 33.
60. Medeiros, "Sistemas de produção integrado": 40.
61. According to FAO data, in 2019 the world herd totaled 977 million heads. The largest herds were in China (447 million), the United States (73 million), and Brazil, which according to FAO data had 41 million animls. FAOSTAT, accessed at: http://www.fao.org/faostat/en/#data/QA.

62. Mapeamento da suinicultura brasileira, Brasília, Sebrae/Associação Brasileira de Criadores de Suínos, 2016: 85.
63. Mapeamento da suinicultura brasileira, Brasília, Sebrae/Associação Brasileira de Criadores de Suínos, 2016: 94.
64. Mapeamento da suinicultura brasileira, Brasília, Sebrae/Associação Brasileira de Criadores de Suínos, 2016: 86.
65. MAPA, Agrostat at https://indicadores.agricultura.gov.br/agrostat/index.htm.
66. Even despite this major growth, which continued throughout 2021, Brazil was only the third largest source of pork for the Chinese market, exceeded by the pork exports of Spain and the United States. *ABPA, Noticias* January 20, 2022 at abpa@abpa-br.org.br.
67. USDA, *Agricultural Projections to 2031* (February 2022), 99, table 38.
68. Comextat, accessed at: http://comexstat.mdic.gov.br/pt/geral.
69. Mapeamento da suinicultura brasileira, Brasília, Sebrae/Associação Brasileira de Criadores de Suínos, 2016: 39–54; Camila Goulart Arboite, et al., "Indicadores de desempenho da cadeia produtiva de suínos na região catarinense," SEGET, accessed at: https://www.aedb.br/seget/arquivos/artigos15/32322353.pdf; Karme Medeiros Anuciato, "Panorama da cadeia produtiva da suinicultura no Estado de Mato Grosso," *Revista Estudos Sociais*, 36, no. 19 (2016): 108–140; Diego Guimarães, et al., *Suinocultura: estrutura da cadeia produtiva, panorama do setor no Brasil e no mundo e o apoio do BNDES* (Rio de Janeiro:, Agroindústria, BNDES Setoria 45, 2017), Juliana Varchaki Porte, Viviane V. de Lacerda, Jose Braccini Neto and Ângela R. L. de Souza. "Análise dos custos da cadeia produtiva de suínos no Sul do Brasil," *Custos e Agronegócio on line*, v. 15, edição especial, abril, 2019. Accessed at: http://www.custoseagronegocioonline.com.br/especialv15/OK%202%20cadeia.pdf.
70. MAPA, at https://indicadores.agricultura.gov.br/agrostat/index.htm.

CHAPTER 13

Sustainability

The issue of the sustainability of Brazilian agriculture is crucial not only for Brazil, but for global sustainability. A large part of the Amazon rainforest, the largest tropical forest in the world, is in Brazilian territory. The future of this forest will play a crucial role in climate change, today a major concern linked to the future of the survival of the human species. In addition, Brazil occupies a prominent position in world food production and is one of the largest exporters of agricultural products. The country is considered an essential source to satisfy the expected increase in the world's need for food over the next thirty years due to growth in demand as world populations and income increase. Thus, understanding the sustainability of Brazilian agriculture, that is, the country's capacity to maintain its main biomes, especially the Amazon forest, is essential to understanding the future sustainability of the planet, particularly in the crucial issue of the greenhouse effect and climate change.

This is also an issue which initially seemed to becoming slowly resolved as international and national pressures created one of the world's most well developed governmental systems, with a very advanced legislation to protect the environment. From satellite monitoring to detailed farm restrictions on land usage, the government until 2019 seemed to be moving in a positive direction. Deforestation was significantly reduced every year, illegal mining was better controlled and Indian land areas

H. S. Klein and F. V. Luna, *Brazilian Crops in the Global Market*, Palgrave Studies in Economic History,
https://doi.org/10.1007/978-3-031-38589-6_13

were more systematically protected. But that all changed in January of that year when an anti-environmental president was elected. Since then many of the institutions such as *Ibama* have been weakened, key governmental experts dismissed, and the Minister for Environment was found to be shipping illegally Amazonian cut woods to the United States. Whether this change is permanent or temporary is still not resolved. There has been massive pushback nationally and an even greater international pressure has come from the consuming nations of Europe. Several EU countries have started boycotts of Brazilian products or are demanding certifications of non-Amazonian origin for those they do purchase. They have also delayed Brazil's attempt to have a free trade agreement with the European Union. Given these counter movements, nationally and internationally, and the recent change in government, it seems possible that this reversal is temporary. None of the laws have been reversed and the institutions and agencies still exist.

International concern with environmental preservation has been growing since the mid-twentieth century due to Brazil's increasingly expanding agriculture, livestock, and deforestation activities. This activity resulted in destruction of forests and the construction of highways and dams in fragile environments, all with the support of international credit institutions. Soon these international concerns were seconded by an important national environmental movement which emerged in Brazil in the 1970s and 1980s, being the first such movement in Latin America. The emergence of non-governmental organizations (NGOs) concerned with the environment and the rise of a new middle class in Brazil concerned about increasing urban pollution, in the last three decades of the twentieth century combined to create a powerful national ecological movement. One of the first formal ecological defense groups in Brazil was founded in June 1971, in Rio Grande do Sul. Other local groups were soon formed throughout the country and educational campaigns began to raise awareness of environmental preservation issues. As early as 1974 the government was forced to create the Special Secretariat for the Environment (SEMA). This body was created because international organizations made the approval of loans to Brazil conditional on the need to have a government agency here to produce environmental impact studies.

Another major cause was the 1974 and 1978 oil crises which made the public aware of serious issues related to the environment and led the national ecological movement to expand and become more political and more militant in Brazil. One of the most important of these movements was that of the rubber tappers in Pará, led by Chico Mendes, who organized a systematic opposition to deforestation in the mid- and late 1970s and became an international symbol of the ecological movement.[1] The growing strength of this movement was shown with the creation, in 1985 of a new pressure group—the Interstate Organization of Ecologists for the Constituent Assembly—whose aim was to influence the Constituent Assembly in the production of the new democratic constitution. This highly politicized organization promoted candidates concerned with ecology, and demanded to be heard on the ecological issue for the new constitution.[2] Its success was evident in the new Constitution of 1988, which was much advanced in terms of environmental preservation.[3] The environmental movement not only gradually influenced the main opposition parties and promoted candidates committed to the issue, but also founded a Green Party (PV) in early 1986. In 2010, the PV (Green Party), then led by Marina Silva, obtained 20% of the votes in the presidential election that year, coming in third place, after PT and PSDB.

In addition to its formal political involvement and educational campaigns, the ecological movement influenced federal and state laws. One of its first achievements was the creation in 1985 of a new Ministry of Urban Development and Environment, followed in 1989 by the creation of Ibama, the Brazilian Institute for the Environment and Renewable Natural Resources which, by the Constitution of 1988 was given control over all national forests. Slowly, these government agencies began to have an impact on the preservation of natural resources and to create systematic legislation for environmental protection.

At the same time, Brazilian and international environmental groups pressured the large international credit agencies to change their policies toward the Brazilian government, which became evident in the late 1970s when the World Bank began to grant its first loans for investments in the Amazon region. Of these loans, the most controversial was the *Polonoroeste* Program for the development of the Northwest region of Brazil. Although there were some attempts to control ecological conditions in the credit agreement, *Polonoroeste* was a failure both from an environmental and a social point of view. National and international criticism of the project forced the World Bank to temporarily suspend its financial support and change its environmental guidelines.[4] In the late 1980s, the World Bank, which was beginning to take a stronger stance on the environment, published two reports criticizing Brazil's tax laws for encouraging ecological degradation and deforestation in the Amazon.[5] Then in 1987 the World Bank created a Central Department of the Environment, as well as Environmental Divisions for the various regions where it operated and made their approval fundamental to all new loans.[6]

As a result of the 1992 United Nations Convention on Climate Change (Eco-92), the Brazilian government adopted a series of measures known as Agenda 21 to implement the decisions resulting from the event. The government committed itself to "sustainable development" through specific measures to reduce greenhouse gases in all areas and in all sectors of the economy, taking into account environmental protection, social justice, and economic efficiency. Brazil was the first country to sign the document and in 1994 it created an Inter-ministerial Commission for Sustainable Development (CIDES) to propose national strategies, policies, and programs related to Agenda 21. It was decided that the Ministry of Science and Technology would be responsible for coordinating actions related to climate change, and that the Ministry of the Environment would promote actions linked to the Convention on Biological Diversity, also signed in 1992.[7]

In 1997, the Kyoto Protocol was instituted, which stipulated numerical targets to reduce greenhouse gases and initially exempted developing countries from meeting these targets. Nevertheless in 1999 the federal government created the Inter-ministerial Commission on Global Climate Change (CIMGC) to coordinate actions related to the Kyoto Protocol. The Ministry of Science and Technology created the General Coordination of Global Climate Change to monitor estimates of greenhouse gas emissions in Brazil and define mitigation policies. In 2007, the Ministry of the Environment created the Secretariat for Climate Change and Environmental Quality and in 2008 the National Plan on Climate Change was approved, which established numerical targets for the reduction of greenhouse gases. The government also pledged to drastically reduce deforestation, particularly in the Amazon. Finally, in 2009 Brazil made a new effort in this area and defined targets to reduce greenhouse gases in various sectors of the economy. The commitment was to reduce emissions between 36 and 38% compared to projected levels for 2020 in the absence of mitigation measures. Also in that year, the Low Carbon Emission Agriculture Plan (ABC Plan) was adopted. With this voluntary plan, Brazil committed itself to reducing 1.2 billion tons of CO_2 and equivalents (CO_2eq).[8]

Brazilian sustainability programs have specified targets for forest control, agricultural practices, and the use of biofuels. The goals presented for land use were related to the control of two of the main Brazilian biomes: the Amazon and the Cerrado. In addition to these vast land areas, Brazil has other important biomes, such as the Atlantic Forest, Caatinga, Pantanal, and Pampa, which had less monitoring structure (Map 13.1). According to preliminary estimates, Brazil would have reached in 2018 a percentage of 73% of the goals established by the ABC Plan (Table 13.1).[9]

In 1988, the National Institute for Space Research (INPE) began monitoring the Amazon and developed a methodology that by the beginning of the twenty-first century was used to monitor other Brazilian biomes. In 2008, with support from the United Nations Development Program (UNDP), the Ministry of the Environment and *Ibama* signed an agreement to implement the Project for Monitoring the Deforestation of Brazilian Biomes by Satellite, whose objective was to permanently monitor the coverage of the main Brazilian biomes in order to quantify the deforestation of areas of native vegetation. This data in turn was to be used as a basis for actions to control and combat illegal deforestation in these biomes. Systematic monitoring improved the supervision of these biomes, allowing *Ibama* to apply the law more efficiently against predatory actors.[10]

Sustainability issues vary by region and biome in Brazil. Clearly the Amazon is the most essential biome being threatened, with the Cerrado and the Pantanal being among the other biomes that face serious environmental problems. The Amazon is today the largest tropical forest in the world, covering about 5.4 million square kilometers. Approximately 80% of this forest is in Brazil, and 60% of the protected part of the tropical forest is located in Brazilian territory. Due to its size and characteristics, the Amazon is a great reservoir of the planet's biodiversity, which is home to around 20% of the known species of plants and animals. It is also recognized as a reservoir for the ecological needs not only of indigenous peoples and local communities, but also the rest of the world. According to the NGO WWF-Brazil, of all the tropical forests on Earth, the Amazon is the only one that still has its size and diversity preserved.[11] Therefore, deforestation in the Amazon has a crucial impact on global warming. Furthermore, studies show that global warming could have drastic consequences on the forest, as it would reduce the period and volume of rain.[12] It has also been suggested that the Amazon influences weather and water

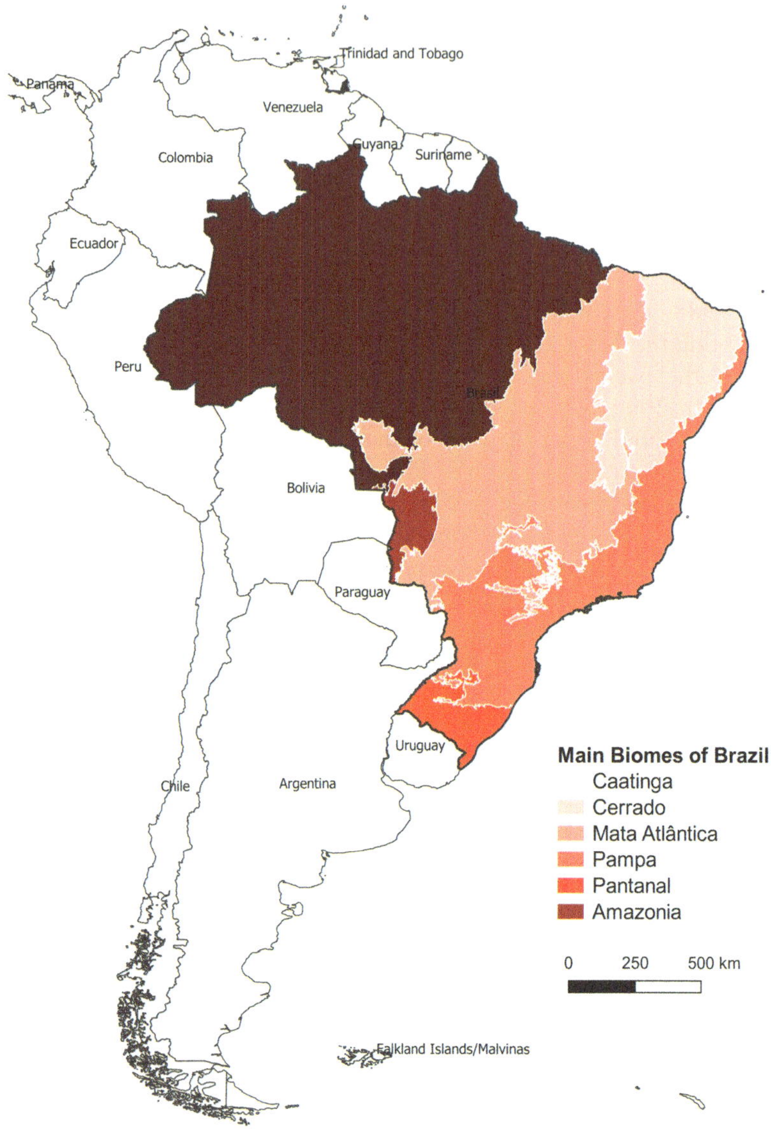

Map 13.1 Main Biomes of Brazil (*Source* Bases cartográficas Biomas do Brasil)

Table 13.1 Mitigation of Greenhouse Gas (GHG) emissions with ABC Plan technologies until 2018

	Increase in the area of adoption or intended use (1)	*Expected mitigation potential (2)*	*Increased area of adoption or use which occurred (1)*	*Estimated mitigation (2)*
Recovery of Degraded Pastures (RPD)	15	83 a 104	3.3	18
Crop-Livestock-Forest (iLPF) Integration	4	18 a 22	5.8	36.4
Direct Planting System (SPD)	8	16 a 20	12.7	23.2
Biological Nitrogen Fixation (FBN)	5.5	10	10.6	19.5
Planted Forests (FP)	3		10	89.1
Animal Waste Treatment (TDA) (3)		6.9		
Total (4)		133.9 to 162.9		98.1

Note (1) Millions of hectares (2) Millions of Mg CO_2 eq
(3) Target reached with volume of 4.3 million cubic meters of TODA: 100%
(4) Target Achieved for carbon fixation in the soil: (98.1/133.9)* 100 = 73%
Source Manzatto, Celso Vainer et al. "As tecnologias do plano ABC na mitigação de gases do efeitos estufa" (2019), *Agroanalysis,* FGV, vol. 39, no. 11, nov. 2019, pp. 30–31

conditions in all the major Brazilian agricultural regions, not only in the Northeast and North regions.

The Cerrado which has an area of approximately 2 million square kilometers, and only recently became a major grain producing region, is also included in the greenhouse gas emission targets. It is the second largest biome in South America and occupies about a quarter of the Brazilian territory in a zone running from North to South in the center of the nation. In the Cerrado biome are the headwaters of the three largest hydrographic basins in South America (Amazonas/Tocantins, São Francisco, and Plata), which results in great availability of water resources. From the perspective of biological biodiversity, the Cerrado is recognized as the richest savanna in the world. It houses a flora with more than 11,000 species of plants, 4,400 of which are native to the region. In 2018, the Cerrado had a native vegetation cover of approximately 1 million square kilometers, occupying 52% of the biome's area.[13]

The other eastern biomes, although they do not have specific protection programs, are also of crucial importance for greenhouse gases and global biodiversity. One example is the Atlantic Forest, where more than two thirds of the Brazilian population lives. This is the Brazilian biome with the smallest percentage of the original natural vegetation cover, but it still houses an important part of the country's biological diversity, with several endemic species and water resources that supply a population of more than 120 million people. Its remaining virgin area is restricted to fragmented stretches, which unfortunately continue to be destroyed for the extraction of exotic species and flora. Of the 1,103,961 km^2 of this biome, only 17% of the original area remains.[14]

The Pantanal, another important Brazilian biome, is one of the world's largest flood plains, recognized in Brazil and abroad for its biodiversity and for being one of the main wetlands in the world. The region has been declared a Biosphere Reserve and World Natural Heritage by UNESCO. It is spread over the two Center-West states of Mato Grosso and Mato Grosso do Sul and crosses the border into Bolivia. It occupies an area of 151,313 Km^2—about 2% of Brazil—and still preserves 88% of its biome.[15]

The Pampa biome is located in the extreme south of Brazil and also extends into Uruguay and Argentina. One of the largest of the Brazilian biomes, it occupies about two thirds of the area of Rio Grande do Sul. It is a rural ecosystem with predominantly herbaceous and low-lying vegetation. In the vicinity of water courses and on the plateau slopes, the vegetation becomes denser, with trees. The Banhados, or wetlands close to the coast, are also part of this biome. The Pampa landscape, although it appears monotonous and uniform, contains great biodiversity. Despite years of intense grazing and agricultural activity, this biome in 2018 still had an area of native vegetation cover of 45%.[16]

Finally, the Caatinga biome is a semiarid region of Brazil containing 20 million inhabitants and is the most populous semiarid region in the world. The Caatinga Biome includes several plant formations. The term "caatinga" denotes a dominant form of vegetation that extends over almost all the states of the Northeast and part of Minas Gerais. This ecosystem is very important from a biological point of view because it houses unique flora and fauna. It is estimated that at least 932 species have already been recorded in the region, of which 380 are endemic. Among the Brazilian biomes, this one is less known by science and has been treated with lower priority, despite being one of the most threatened due to the inadequate and unsustainable use of its soils. The Caatinga occupies 844,453 km^2, and in 2018 it had an area of native vegetation covering 546 thousand square kilometers, equivalent to 64% of the biome's area.[17] From an economic point of view, it represents one of the areas with the highest concentration of poverty in the country.

Monitoring these large Brazilian biomes began with the Amazon rainforest due to its importance and national and international pressure for its preservation. Data available from the 1980s onward show relatively stable but intense deforestation, generally exceeding 20,000 square kilometers annually. These numbers started to fall from 2006, maintaining levels around 6 thousand square kilometers from 2009 onward. The reduction in deforestation in the Amazon was made possible by intense monitoring. This led to a systematic reduction in the net emission of greenhouse gases by Brazilian forests, explaining a large part of the drop in greenhouse gas emissions observed since 2004.[18] In December 2010, the government established targets for greenhouse gas emissions and determined that there would be a need to reduce by eighty percent annual deforestation rates in the Legal Amazon (defined as all the states of the North, plus parts of Mato Grosso in the Center-West and Maranhão in the Northeastern region), using the period 1996 to 2005 as a base. It stipulated that there should be a 40% reduction in annual deforestation rates in the Cerrado Biome compared to the average recorded between 1999 and 2008.

The government also began to control activities related to agriculture and their effects on the emission of greenhouse gases began to be measured. This resulted in Brazil's plans to recover pastures and better integrate forests, crops, and animal husbandry, adopt non-till agriculture, and implement biological nitrogen fixation. It was proposed that the greatest reduction could occur in pasture recovery. The degradation of pastures leads to a progressive loss of soil productivity and its capacity for recovery with the consequent inability to sustain the levels of production and quality necessary for animals and also to overcome the harmful effects of pests, diseases, and invasive species. This process resulted from inadequate management and culminated in the deterioration of natural resources. The advance of the degradation process, the loss of vegetation cover, and the reduction of organic matter in the soil resulted in increased emission of CO_2 into the atmosphere. With the recovery of pastures it would be possible to reverse the process, the soil can start to accumulate carbon and CO_2 emissions can be significantly reduced. Although the government plan initially covered only 15 million hectares, there were approximately 60 million degraded hectares of pastures in Brazil.[19]

Another major area of reform in agriculture is the development of the so-called crop-livestock integration (ILP) and the crop-livestock-forest (ILPF) integration systems created to deal with the negative impact of a monoculture system that in many of these biomes causes loss of organic matter and compromises the quality of the soil. These integrated systems allow farms to produce grain, meat, milk, and wood year-round in the same rural property area through a rotation or succession system. The result of this combination is an increase in the rural producer's income, in addition to a reduction in deforestation and the emission of greenhouse gases. One of the main benefits of these integration systems is the increase in organic matter in the soil, which improves its physical, chemical, and biological condition and allows for better carbon fixation. The ILPF strategy is being adopted in Brazilian biomes with different levels of intensity. Preliminary results of research carried out by Embrapa in Mato Grosso demonstrated the efficiency of these crop-livestock-forest integration systems in reducing greenhouse gas emissions.[20]

No till, or direct planting without plowing is one of the most important technologies introduced in Brazilian agriculture, and today it is used in the production of cereals, vegetables, oilseeds, and cotton. The 2017 Agricultural Census indicates that 33 million hectares adopted the no-tillage system, practically half of the area occupied that year by seasonal crops in Brazil. This technology eliminates plowing and harrowing and allows for enormous fuel savings. The reduction in CO_2 emissions is around 40%. It also reduces soil erosion and the use of chemical fertilizers although it appears to use more insecticides.[21]

The biological fixation of nitrogen in the soil is another technological innovation widely used in Brazil. In this system, the N_2 gas present in the atmosphere is captured by microorganisms and converted into nitrogenous compounds available to plants. This new environment increases productivity, reduces the use of industrialized inputs, and contributes to the reduction of greenhouse gas emissions. Brazil maintains research and development programs with dozens of bacteria capable of supplying nitrogen to soybeans, rice, sugarcane, corn, wheat, beans, alfalfa, peanuts, and other crops. The inoculation of nitrogen-fixing bacteria in soybean seeds before sowing is a process that completely replaces the need to use nitrogen fertilizers in this crop. This system, in contrast to the use of nitrogen fertilizers, does not cause environmental pollution and was adopted by the government as a basic part of its ABC plan.[22]

Although not directly linked to agriculture, the bioenergy programs that Brazil has been developing for many years have achieved undeniable success in reducing greenhouse gas emissions. According to data from the sugarcane sector, the use of ethanol produced from sugarcane reduces the emission of greenhouse gases by 89%—such as carbon dioxide (CO_2), methane (CH_4), and nitric oxide (NO_2). There are also recent initiatives aimed at developing efficient processes for the use of bioenergy in the transport of cargo and passengers. The use of biodiesel is advancing in Brazil. In 2014 the government mandated an addition of 6% of biodiesel in all fuel sales. This percentage was gradually increased and reached 13% in March of 2021. Although biodiesel can be produced from numerous oils and fats of animal or from vegetables, soybeans are the most used raw material.[23] This is a measure of great importance in Brazil, since the nation is highly dependent on diesel fueled trucks in its cargo transport system, due to the country's insufficient railway network.[24]

In 2010 the government instituted a systematic process to monitor Brazil's greenhouse gas reduction targets. After a strong increase in the period 1990 to 2005, there was a significant drop in net emissions, and again a significant increase from 2020 onward. These movements are mainly explained by Land Use and Forest Use Change. In 2020, of the total gross emissions, 46% came from Land Use and Land and Forest Use Change, 27% from Agriculture and Livestock, and only 18% from Production of Energy (see Table 13.2 and Graph 13.1). Energy production in Brazil is relatively clean compared to most countries, as hydroelectricity is responsible for 58% of total energy generation, and 75% comes from renewable resources.[25]

Initially there were significant declines in land and deforestation between 2005 and 2010 but subsequently there was been some deterioration. The positive performance of this earlier period was largely based on the sharp and consistent drop in annual deforestation in both the Amazon and the Cerrado biomes that occurred after 2005. These two biomes represented around 90% of the total deforested area in the five main biomes in that year.[26] The long-term trend in deforestation was on a steady downward trend since 2004 in both the Amazon and the Cerrado (see Graph 13.2). However, from 2015 to 2022 this trend was reversed. Until then Brazil was considered a world leader in environmental protection. The international goals agreed to by the Brazilian government were

Table 13.2 Estimated GHG emissions in Brazil by sector and sub-sector 1990–2020 (TCO E-GWP AR5 in million tons)

Sector	*1990*	*1995*	*2000*	*2005*	*2010*	*2015*	*2020*	*Variation* *1990–2000 (%)*	*2000–2010 (%)*	*2010–2015 (%)*	*2015–2020 (%)*
Agriculture and Livestock	390	429	438	518	534	551	577	12	22	3	5
Production of energy	194	231	290	318	372	456	394	49	28	23	−14
Land use and land and forest use change	1391	1927	1536	1709	679	871	998	10	−56	28	15
Industrial processes	51	65	74	81	96	102	99	45	30	6	−3
Waste	28	37	49	62	72	83	92	75	47	15	11
Total - Gross Emissions	2055	2689	2387	2688	1753	2063	2160	16	−27	18	5
Removing	96	190	309	417	563	606	635	222	82	8	5
Total - Net Emissions	1959	2499	2077	2271	1189	1457	1524	6	−43	23	5
Agriculture and Livestock											
Cultivo de arroz	9	12	10	11	11	12	10	11	10	9	−17
Fermentação entérica	283	309	312	358	368	369	373	10	18	0	1
Manejo de Dejetos animais	17	19	18	21	23	26	27	6	28	13	4
Queima de residúos agrícolas	2	2	2	2	2	1	0	0	0	−50	−100
Solos manejados	79	87	96	116	130	143	167	22	35	10	17

Source Renata Fragoso Potenza, et. ***Análise das emissões brasileiras de Gases de efeito estufa*** e suas implicações para as metas Climáticas do Brasil, 1970–2020, 2021, SEEGE, pp. 49–51

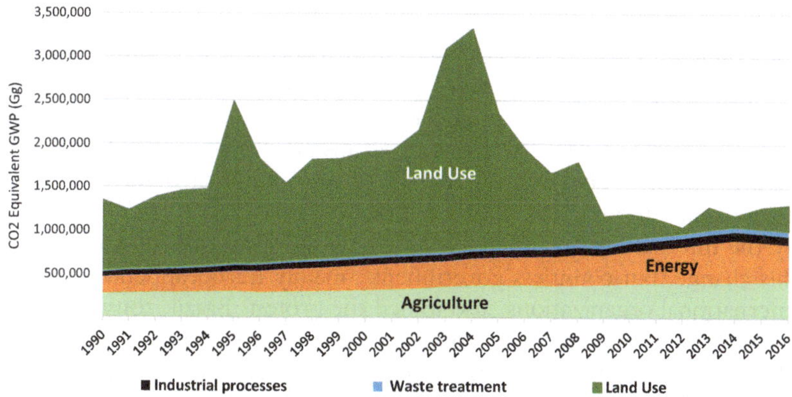

Graph 13.1 Net emissions in CO_2 equivalents by sector, 1990–2016 *Source* "Estimativas Anuais emissões gases de efeito estufa no Brasil" (MCTI, 2020, tab. 22)

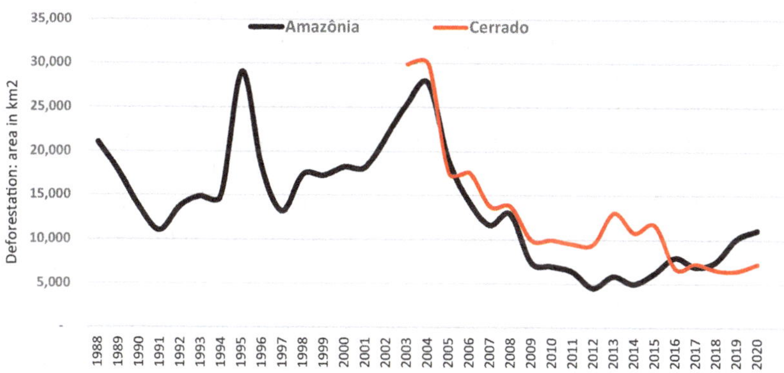

Graph 13.2 Annual deforestation in the Amazon and Cerrado, 1988–2020 (Prodes indicator, in km^2) (*Source* Prodes: http://www.obt.inpe.br/OBT/assuntos/programas/amazonia/prodes)

then actively pursued. The main government agencies supervising the environment in general were powerful and had freedom of action.

But the election of President Bolsonaro, from his inaugural speech in 2019 to his action in government, completely altered Brazil's posture in relation to the environment. Research and control bodies and their professionals were criticized, discredited, and gradually marginalized from the country's environmental management process. Faced with the difficulty of changing the legislation related to the subject, the government instead changed rules and regulations that make control difficult and in turn facilitated criminal activities against the environment, especially deforestation.[27] The lack of control allowed criminal deforestation to grow in the Amazon. This Brazilian policy was attacked internally, but also by the international community. Not only did environmentalists protest this change, but countless governments, mainly European, and the main international organizations, also joined the protest. Brazil, considered for a few years as an exemplary country in the environmental issue, particularly for the quality of its energy matrix, was now seen as a pariah and a global villain on the environment and has gradually been marginalized in the international debate.[28] The election of the Lula Ignácio da Silva government in 2022 has led to a complete change in government policies. The naming of Marina Silva, Brazil's leading environmentalist, was a promising start and his speeches in defense of the Indian communities, and the Amazon have led to European governments again funding Amazonian projects. It is hoped that the government can reverse the destructive policies of the Bolsonaro period.

Between 2010 and 2018 there was a decline in the natural areas of the Brazilian biomes and an expansion of anthropized or human affected areas, that is, areas occupied for economic and social activities. In terms of area, the Amazon was the biome that experienced the greatest change with a loss of 269 thousand km^2, corresponding to 7% of the extension of the biome in 2000. The Cerrado also lost a significant area (152 thousand km^2), which represents 13% of the biome in 2000. The Pampa, although in area represents a smaller portion of the total areas lost by the Brazilian biomes, still experienced greatest percentage loss of 17%. When the anthropized areas are considered, the largest change occurred in the Cerrado (see Table 13.3). But here the greatest period of loss of natural areas occurred between 2000 and 2010, totaling 323,000 km$_2$ (biennial average of 65,000 km^2) and fortunately that has been gradually reduced, being just 19,000 km^2 in the 2016–2018 biennium (see Graph 13.3). But what the current levels of change are is currently unavailable, so it is difficult to estimate long-term trends.

Considering the period 2004 to 2020, the state of Pará had the largest area deforested, representing 68 thousand km^2, followed by Mato Grosso with 45,000 km^2. Of the total deforestation in Amazonia, these two states

Table 13.3 Changes in natural and anthropogenic areas between 2000 and 2018 in the five main Brazilian biomes

	Amazônia	*Cerrado*	*Mata Atlântica*	*Caatinga*	*Pantanal*	*Pampa*	*Total*
	Natural Areas						
Extension of the Opening (year 2000)	3,684,512	1,185,192	195,614	581,581	134,205	96,194	5,877,298
Final Extension (2018)	3,414,711	1,032,486	181,781	546,314	132,096	80,033	5,387,421
Balance of Changes (Km^2)	269,801	152,706	13,833	35,267	2,109	16,161	489,877
Balance of Changes (%)	7%	13%	7%	6%	2%	17%	8%
	Anthropized Area						
Extension of the Opening (year 2000)	450,865	790,693	896,686	274,213	15,358	82,491	2,510,306
Final Extension (2018)	720,599	943,329	910,518	309,469	17,463	98,652	3,000,030
Balance of Changes (Km^2)	269,734	152,636	13,832	35,256	2,105	16,161	489,724
Balance of Changes (%)	60%	19%	2%	13%	14%	20%	20%

Source IBGE,Contas Econômicas Ambientais., accessed at https://www.ibge.gov.br/estatisticas/economicas/contas-nacionais/28920-contas-de-extensao-dos-biomas.html?edicao=28921&t=acesso-ao-produto

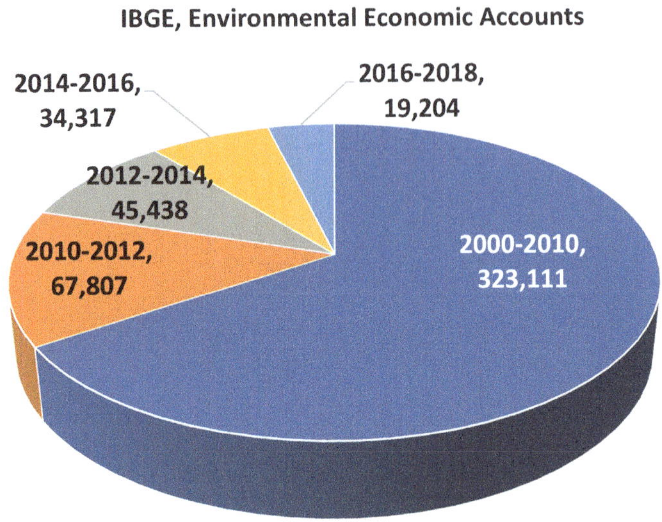

Graph 13.3 Balance of changes in Brazilian Biomes, 2000/2018 in square kilometers *Source* IBGE: Contas Econômicas Ambientais https://www.ibge.gov.br/estatisticas/economicas/contas-nacionais/28920-contas-de-extensao-dos-biomas.html?edicao=28921&t=acesso-ao-produto

accounted for two thirds of that deforestation. In the 2017 census they accounted for a quarter of the pasture areas in Brazil, more than a fifth of the cattle herds and 18% of the crop areas. Between 2006 and 2017, the area of pastures and crops in these two states grew by 7.6 million hectares, corresponding to 76 thousand km^2 (Graph 13.4).

As can be seen in this survey, Brazil has sought to address sustainability issues, for both ecological and economic reasons. With the tremendous expansion of commercial agriculture in recent years, important sectors of industry and renowned national research institutes have addressed these issues. Furthermore, given the phenomenal growth of Brazilian agriculture since the 1960s, these problems are of crucial importance even for the continued growth of agricultural productivity. There have been serious efforts to provide basic new procedures to reduce environmental destruction. The creation of a state-sponsored agronomy education and a modern research system has been a key factor in generating the crucial increase in productivity needed to maintain Brazil's world leadership in

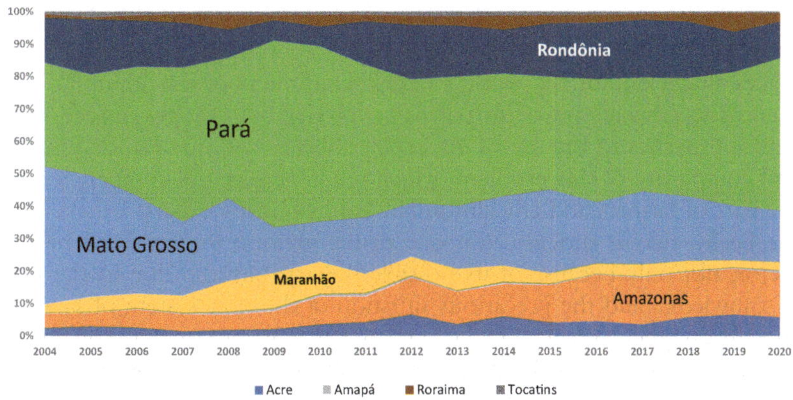

Graph 13.4 Participation in amazon deforestation by states, 2004–2020 *Source* Prodes: Accessed at: http://www.obt.inpe.br/OBT/assuntos/programas/amazonia/prodes

agriculture. It has also been crucial in making Brazilian farmers aware of these issues and teaching them the latest systems of control. Furthermore, the international community increasingly demands measures in favor of sustainability from Brazil. As a result of this world pressure, in order to maintain its leading position in the global food supply, Brazil must clearly demonstrate its commitment to sustainability and show results in this area.

However, in the area of sanitary control, which fundamentally depends on state action, Brazil has been less successful. The creation of the World Trade Organization (WTO) in 1995 defined rules and standards for international trade, including food quality. This led many of the participating countries, including Brazil, to modernize services related to animal health. Brazil has made significant progress in controlling its herds and processing its products. It has been very successful in controlling and eradicating diseases such as foot-and-mouth disease, swine fever, and Newcastle disease. The dairy sector, however, which exports little, has not shown an equivalent advance, and today it is the origin of the products with the greatest risk to national health. Furthermore, although Brazil now occupies a prominent position in the international meat market, periodic deficiencies in the control and inspection process for meat and other agricultural products continue to be an important problem nationally and internationally.[29]

Sanitary control also involves the need to limit pesticides which can harm human health, yet whose use is necessary in tropical agriculture and makes Brazil one of the world's largest consumers of this input.[30] This is an issue in which new efforts have involved both changes in seeds and new approaches to the use of insecticides. Given the importance, gravity, and complexity of this problem, which requires technical competence on the part of farmers and efficient public control, many experts believe that the health risk in agriculture is one of the greatest threats faced by the sector, not only because of its possible impact, but also due to the lack of knowledge and the precarious situation of the state system of sanitary control of agriculture.[31]

The arrival of biotechnology to agriculture through transgenic cultivars introduced a new period in the Brazilian seed industry, significantly altering the market dynamics and the relationship between cultivar users and seed producers. During the market restructuring movement, some of the largest agrochemical companies also started to work with biotechnology and seeds, which gave rise to an unprecedented movement toward convergence among important producers. Research that combines knowledge from the fields of genetic engineering, seeds, and agricultural chemicals has allowed these companies to create a unique environment for innovation and the development of new products.[32] At the end of 2016, there were 74 transgenic plants approved for commercialization in Brazil: 13 soybean, 46 corn, 13 cotton, 1 bean, and 1 eucalyptus cultivars. Today, the market is dominated by multinational companies such as Monsanto, with 26 transgenics, Syngeta and Dow with 11 each, DuPont with 12, and Bayer with 10. In 2007, Embrapa launched *Cultivance soy*, developed in partnership with BASF; a product with high tolerance to herbicides and adapted to various Brazilian regions. This was the first transgenic vegetable developed entirely in Brazil, the result of more than ten years of joint research between the two companies. In 2011, CTNBio approved the transgenic beans developed by Embrapa for commercial cultivation in Brazil. This bean is resistant to the golden mosaic virus, the worst enemy of this crop in Brazil and South America, and the result is a milestone in national science, as this was the first transgenic plant produced entirely by public Brazilian research institutions.[33] Brazil is among the countries that most use transgenic plants, along with the United States, Argentina, India, and Canada. According to estimates, in the 2015/2016 harvest, 44.2 million hectares were planted with transgenic seeds. The forecast is that 94% of the soybeans sown in Brazil, approximately 85% of the maize and 74% of the cotton will come from genetically modified material.[34]

It is in this area that the question of herbicide use has been most affected and potentially can lead to major changes in agricultural usage of these toxins. The use of genetically modified seeds fundamentally changes agricultural procedures. On the one hand it brings positive results, such as increased productivity and consequently less cultivated area and the lower intensity in the use of pesticides, since the seeds allow for defense against certain pests. But it introduces foreign elements into nature, and has been attacked by a large part of both international and Brazilian environmentalists. If the short-term results are known, the long-term consequences are totally unknown. What can be evaluated is the irreversibility of their use, in Brazil and worldwide. And the unique position of Brazilian production in the international market and its competitiveness is the result of the intense and widespread use of transgenic seeds and biological processes in agriculture.

Traditionally Brazilian crops have been affected by draught or excess precipitation. For this reason the government in 1999 decided to create a program to define agricultural zones in the country with planting calendars for all the major crops based on meteorological variables. These zones and times are updated annually according to the latest climate data and newer crops or cultivars. But the recent issue of global warming has created a new set of problems related to water and heat which will undoubtedly have a major impact in the future. Brazilian agronomists have in fact attempted to estimate this impact using the standard agricultural zones established by the government. For soybeans, by the end of this century, global warming will lead to a major decline in production as currently suitable areas for production will no longer be able to produce this grain and new areas that might come into production cannot compensate for their loss. Moreover there is no expectation of any new seed revolution being able to compensate for these problems. Depending on the intensity of global warming, total production could decline from 80,000 tons to over 300,000 tons from the lowest to the highest temperature change estimates. Coffee production, using the case of Minas Gerais, would suffer even heavier losses with just a 1 degree Celsius rise in temperature by 2099.[35] In contrast, it is suggested from quite local studies, that other crops, such as sorghum might survive and be only moderately affected by the need for new areas of production or declining yields.[36] Cowpea bean production in the Northeastern states, a staple food of the region, will also see reduced plantings and areas that will require new seed varieties to survive. This is a rain fed crop being produced in a large semi-arid region most of which will turn into a fully arid region if global warming persists.[37] Finally it is estimated that Brazilian maize yields will decline by mid-century due to global warming.[38]

Some recent developments in particular crops have improved local conditions considerably. Thus the end of burning of sugar cane has had a major impact on human health and gas emissions and the adoption of total mechanization of the harvest and no-till planting has been a fundamental factor in improving environment conditions in the last few decades. It has resulted in both the decline of greenhouse gases and black carbon emissions.[39] But it is unclear what global warming will do to the production of sugar cane in either São Paulo or Mato Grosso, the currently largest producers. What is clear from all these studies is that areas of production, yields and total volume of output will change for all crops over the century as the climate changes due to the rise of global temperatures.

Another issue related to sustainability is education. Brazil has invested heavily in research and teaching and, in many ways, is a leader in the adoption of modern technology and practice in commercial agriculture. It has already produced thousands of agronomists who are now working in commercial agriculture and applying the latest technology and sustainability practices. But this knowledge has not reached the majority of farmers, who in fact are subsistence producers with often a minimum level of education. In the commercial sector of Brazilian agriculture, however, there is a progressive commitment to sustainability and the protection of resources, as this commitment makes economic sense and has a fundamental impact on agricultural activity in the long term. But this may or may not be sufficient to overcome hostility to change and the need to adapt to a new reality.

Notes

1. Margaret E. Keck. "Social Equity and Environmental Politics in Brazil: Lessons from the Rubber Tappers of Acre," *Comparative Politics*, 27, no. 4 (July 1995): pp. 409–424.
2. For the origins of this movement see: Eduardo J. Viola. "The ecologist movement in Brazil (1974–1986): from environmentalism to ecopolitics,"

International Journal of Urban and Regional Research 12, no. 2 (June 1988): 211–228; Onil Banerjee, Alexander J. Macpherson, Janaki Alavalapati, "Toward a Policy of Sustainable Forest Management in Brazil: A Historical Analysis," *The Journal of Environment & Development* 18, no. 2 (June 2009), 130–153 and Wilson José Ferreira de Oliveira "Gênese e redefinições do militantismo ambientalista no Brasil," *DADOS Revista de Ciências Sociais*, 51, no. (2008): 751–777. On the evolution of policies and institutions in the States see: Barry Ames and Margaret E. Keck, "The Politics of Sustainable Development Environmental Policy Making in Four Brazilian States," *Journal of Interamerican Studies and World Affairs* 39, no. 4 (1998): 1–40.

3. Vladimir Passos de Freitas, "A Constituição Federal e a efetividade das normas ambientais," (Ph.d thesis, Faculdade de Direito da Universidade Federal. do Paraná, 1999) and Antonio H. de V. and Benjamin "O Meio Ambiente na Constituição Federal de 1988," *Informativo Jurídico da Biblioteca Ministro Oscar Saraiva*, 19, no. 1 (jan./jun. 2008). On the questions of conservation see Carlos José Saldanha Machado "Mudanças conceituais na administração pública do meio ambiente," *Ciência e Cultura*, 55, no. 4 (2003): 24–26.
4. On the problem related to ecology in all these joint projects of the World Bank with the Brazilian government in the Amazon, see: Sérgio Margulis, "O Desempenho ambiental do Governo Brasileiro e do Banco Mundial em Projetos Co-financiados pelo Banco." (Textos Para Discussão No. 194; Brasília IPEA, 1999).
5. See the studies of Hans Binswanger, "Brazilian Policies that Encourage Deforestation." (Environment Department Paper No. 16, World Bank, Washington, D.C 1988); and Dennis J. Mahar, *Government Policies and Deforestation in the Brazilian Amazon*, (Washington, DC: World Bank, 1989).
6. John Redwood II, "World Bank Approaches to the Brazilian Amazon: The Bumpy Road toward Sustainable Development," (LCR Sustainable Development Working Paper No. 13; Washington DC: World Bank, November 2002).
7. "ABC—Observatório—Agricultura de Baixo Carbono. A evolução de um novo paradigma" (Fundação Getúlio Vargas, Centro de Agronegócio da Escola de Economia de São Paulo). Accessed at www.observatorioabc.com.br.
8. See "ABC–Observatório–Agricultura de Baixo Carbono," and Eleneide Doff Sotta, Fernanda Garcia Sampaio and Juan Vicente Guadalupe Gallardo, eds., *Coletânea dos fatores de emissão e remoção de gases de efeito estufa da agricultura brasileira*. (Brasília, Mapa/Senar, 2020); Rodrigo C.A. Lima, Leila Harfuch and Gustavo R. Palouro, *Plano ABC: Evidência do período 2020-2020 e propostas para uma nova fase 2021-2030*,

Agroicone/Input, 2020; Brasil, Mapa, *Plano setorial de mitigação e de adaptação às mudanças climáticas para a consolidação de uma economia de baixa emissão decarbono na agricultura: plano ABC (Agricultura de Baixa Emissão de Carbono)* (Brasília, Mapa/ACS, 2012).

9. Celso Vainer et al. "As tecnologias do Plano ABC na mitigação de gases do efeito estufa," *Agroanalysis*, FGV, 39, no. 11 (nov. 2019): 30–31.
10. On this theme see http://siscom.ibama.gov.br/monitora_biomas/; Ministério do Meio Ambiente, Estratégia do Programa Nacional de Monitoramento Ambiental dos Biomas Brasileiros. Secretaria de Mudanças Climáticas e Qualidade Ambiental. Departamento de Políticas de Combate ao Desmatamento. Brasília: MMA, 2016.
11. Acessed at: https://www.wwf.org.br/natureza_brasileira/areas_prioritarias/amazonia1/bioma_amazonia/porque_amazonia_e_importante/.
12. Peter H. Raven, "Tropical floristic tomorrow," *Taxon*, 37 no. 3 (ago. 1988: 549–60; Yadvinder Malhi, J. Timmons Roberts, Richard A. Betts, Timothy J. Killeen,Wenhong Li, and Carlos A. Nobre. "Climate change, deforestation and the fate of the Amazon". *Science*, n. 319 (2008):169–72,; https://doi.org/10.1126/science.1146961. On the Amazon forest, see André de Arruda Lyra, "Estudo de Vulnerabilidade do Bioma Amazônia aos cenários de mudanças climáticas," (Phd thesis, Instituto Nacional de Pesquisas Espaciais, São José dos Campos, 2015). Governo do Estado da Amazônia. *A floresta amazônica e seu papel nas mudanças climáticas* (Manaus: Secretaria de Meio Ambiente e Desenvolvimento Sustentável, 2009); Maria Alice Dias Rolim Visentin. "A floresta Amazônica e as mudanças climáticas: proteção da biodiversidade." *Revista CEJ* (Brasília), v. XVII no. 60 (maio/ago. 2013): 96–102; Carlos A. Nobre, Gilvan Sampaio and Luis Salazar. "Mudanças climáticas e Amazônia". *Ciência e Cultura*, 59, no.3, (Julho/Set. 2007): 22–27; Ibama, accessed at http://siscom.ibama.gov.br/monitora_biomas/PMDBBS%20-%20AMAZONIA.html.
13. Accessed at: http://siscom.ibama.gov.br/monitora_biomas/PMDBBS%20-%20CERRADO.html.
14. Accessed at: http://siscom.ibama.gov.br/monitora_biomas/PMDBBS%20-%20MATA%20ATLANTICA.html.
15. Accessed at http://siscom.ibama.gov.br/monitora_biomas/PMDBBS%20-%20PANTANAL.html.
16. Accessed at http://siscom.ibama.gov.br/monitora_biomas/PMDBBS%20-%20PAMPA.html.
17. Accessed at http://siscom.ibama.gov.br/monitora_biomas/PMDBBS%20-%20CAATINGA.html.
18. According to the Ministério da Ciência e Tecnologia, Inovação e Comunicações, Brazil established the National Policy on Climate Change (PNMC)

with Law 12,187 of 2009, which defines the voluntary national commitment to adopt mitigation measures to reduce its greenhouse gas (GHG) emissions between 36.1% and 38.9% in relation to projected emissions for 2020. According to Decree No. 7,390/2010, which regulates the National Policy on Climate Change, the projection of greenhouse gas emissions for 2020 was estimated at 3,236 tons of CO_2eq. Therefore, the reduction corresponding to the established percentages is between 1,168 tons of CO_2eq and 1,259 tons of CO_2eq, respectively, for the year in question. On this subject, see: Ministério da Ciência e Tecnologia, Inovação e Comunicações, *Estimativas anuais de emissões de gases de efeito estufa no Brasi* (3a. ed. Brasília: MCT, 2016).

19. "ABC—Observatório—Agricultura de Baixo Carbono. A evolução de um novo paradigma." In calculating the balance of greenhouse gases, the emission of fertilizers applied to the soil and the emissions from cattle, excreta for example, are taken into account. On this topic, see the important study by Embrapa: Ademir H. Zimmer et al., *Degradação, recuperação e renovação de pastagens.* (Campo Grande: MS: Embrapa Gado de Corte, 2012), accessed at: www.embrapa.br/busca-de-publicacoes/-/publicacao/951322/degradacao-recuperacao-e-renovacao-de-pastagens.
20. Accessed at: https://www.embrapa.br/busca-de-noticias/-/noticia/2411761/estudo-comprova-mitigacao-de-gases-de-efeito-estufa-pela-ilpf. The research indicated that, in the conventional farming area, there is a greater flow of N2O emissions during the harvest, with intense peaks right after fertilization. However, when analyzing an area with integration between agriculture and forestry, it s observed that nitrous oxide emissions tend to remain in balance.
21. "ABC—Observatório—Agricultura de Baixo Carbono. A evolução de um novo paradigma."
22. Ana Lucia Ferreira. *Fixação biológica de nitrogênio pode reduzir as emissões de GEE na agricultura.* Accessed at https://www.embrapa.br/busca-de-noticias/-/noticia/8313328/fixacao-biologica-de-nitrogenio-pode-reduzir-as-emissoes-de-gee-na-agricultura; Ministério da Agricultura. *ABC Agricultura de Baixa Emissão de Carbono.* Acessado em 7/5/2021, em: https://www.gov.br/agricultura/pt-br/assuntos/sustentabilidade/plano-abc/plano-abc-agricultura-de-baixa-emissao-de-carbono; Embrapa. *Fixação Biológica de Nitrogênio.* Accessed at https://www.embrapa.br/tema-fixacao-biologica-de-nitrogenio/nota-tecnica.
23. In April 2021 there was a temporary reduction in the mixture from 13 to 10% due to issues related to the price of raw materials, mainly soybeans. But this mixture of 13% proved to be totally feasible from a technical point of view.

24. The program has a weakness in the majority use of soybeans in its production. In addition to competing with a food product, it suffers from the instability of the prices of this product on the international market.
25. In terms of energy, the insufficiency in the supply of electricity caused by delays in numerous projected works and by water scarcity in recent periods has recently required a more intensive use of fossil fuel power generation systems. But the completion of these new electric generation projects and the intensification of investments in renewable energy sources should reverse this process of relative deterioration in the Brazilian energy matrix.
26. In that year, 40,800 km^2 would have been deforested, of which 19.0 thousand km^2 in the Amazon, 17.6 thousand km^2 in the Cerrado, 2.7 thousand km^2 in the Caatinga, 713 km^2 in the Pantanal, 364 km^2 in the Pampa, and 350 km^2 in the Atlantic forest. Ministério da Ciência, Tecnologia, Inovação e Comunicações. *Estimativas Anuais de Emissões de Gases de Efeito Estufa no Brasil*, (Brasília, 5ª. Ed., 2020): 106, tabel 22.
27. The phrase by Environment Minister Ricardo Salles at the day's ministerial meeting was classic. According to the Minister, when press attention was focused on the Covid pandemic, the government would have the opportunity to pass the reforms of deregulation, simplification and all the reforms that can be made by ordinances and norms of the ministries, including that of *his own ministry. Globo (G1), accessed at:* https://g1.globo.com/politica/noticia/2020/05/22/veja-os-principais-pontos-da-reuniao-ministerial-que-teve-gravacao-divulgada-pelo-stf.ghtml.
28. Ascema, the National Association of Environmental workers held that "Since 2019, with the beginning of the current government, there has been an increase in the number and extent of forest fires, expansion of deforestation in the Amazon; an oil spill hit several points on the Brazilian coast without the government showing itself capable of providing a quick and competent response that would make it possible to discover those responsible for its origin; the attempts to incriminate and intimidate indigenous peoples, environmentalists and non-governmental organizations, in addition to intimidation and restriction of the actions of employees in the environmental area, resulting in a deliberate dismantling of public environmental institutions." *Cronologia de um desastre anunciado: Ações do governo Bolsonaro para desmontar as políticas de meio ambiente no Brasil* (Brasília: Ascema, 2020): 3.
29. In 2017, there was a scandal linked to the failure of sanitary inspections of meat produced in several Brazilian slaughterhouses, causing an immediate reaction in numerous importing countries. See: https://economia.uol.com.br/noticias/reuters/2017/03/17/escandalo-da-carne-impacta-industria-no-brasil-e-ameaca-exportacoes.htm.

30. According to Pereira, in Brazil many pathogens have an impact on agriculture and livestock. There are countless examples, such as traditional the fungal rust disease of coffee and soybeans; the boll weevil, foot-and-mouth disease, and more recet such as greening, and bacterial diseases in citriculture. Many of these diseases have wiped out crops. In 1989 the fungal disease known as witch's broom destroyed most of Bahian cocoa trees, which devastated production and led Brazil to become an importer of this product. Luciano Gomes de Carvalho Pereira. *Controle fitossanitário: Agrotóxicos e outros métodos* (Brasília: Câmara dos Deputados, Consultoria Legislativa, Estudo fevereiro de 2013). Also see Frederico Peres, Josino Costa Moreira e Gaetan Serge Dubois, "Agrotóxicos, saúde e ambiente. Uma introdução ao tema," in Frederico Peres, Josino Costa Moreira and Gaetan Serge Dubois, eds., *É veneno ou remédio? Agrotóxicos, saúde e ambiente* (Rio de Janeiro: Fiocruz, 2003): 21–41.
31. Antonio Márcio Buainain, Antônio Márcio, Maria Thereza Macedo Pedroso, Pedro Abel Vieira Junior, Rodrigo Lanna Franco da Silveira, and Zander Navarro, "Quais os riscos mais relevantes nas atividades agropecuárias?" Antônio Márcio Buainaim, Eliseu Alves, José Maria da Silveira e Zander Navarro. *O mundo rural no Brasil no século 21—a formação de um novo padrão agrário e agrícola* (Brasília Embrapa, 2014): 175–200.
32. *Associação brasileira de sementes e mudas, Anuário 2015.*: 11, accessed at: http://www.abrasem.com.br/wp-content/uploads/2013/09/Anuario_ABRASEM_2015_2.pdf.
33. Embrapa. *Os benefícios da biotecnologia para a sua qualidade de vida.* Accessed at https://www.embrapa.br/recursos-geneticos-e-biotecnologia/sala-de-imprensa/se-liga-na-ciencia/a-biotecnologia-e-voce.
34. *Associação brasileira de sementes e mudas, Anuário 2015*: 13. Accessed at: http://www.abrasem.com.br/wp-content/uploads/2013/09/Anuario_ABRASEM_2015_2.pdf.
35. J. Zullo Junior, Hilton Silveira Pinto, Eduardo Delgado Assad, and S. R. M. Evangelista, "Potential economic impacts of global warming on two brazilian commodities, according to IPCC prognostics," *TERRÆ* 3, no. 1 (2008): 28–39.
36. Marine Cirino Grossi, Flavio Justino, Camilo de Lelis Teixeira Andrade, Eduardo Alvarez Santos, Rafael Avila Rodrigues, and Luiz C. Costa, "Modeling the impact of global warming on the sorghum sowing window in distinct climates in Brazil," *European Journal of Agronomy* 51 (2013): 53–64.
37. Vicente de PR Silva, João HBC Campos, Madson T. Silva, and Pedro V. Azevedo, "Impact of global warming on cowpea bean cultivation in northeastern Brazil," *Agricultural Water Management*, 97, no. 11 (2010): 1760–1768.

38. Peter G. Jones and Philip K. Thornton, "The potential impacts of climate change on maize production in Africa and Latin America in 2055," *Global Environmental Change* 13, no. 1 (2003): 51–59.
39. Marcelo Galdos, Otávio Cavalett, Joaquim EA Seabra, Luiz Augusto Horta Nogueira, and Antonio Bonomi, "Trends in global warming and human health impacts related to Brazilian sugarcane ethanol production considering black carbon emissions," *Applied Energy* 104 (2013): 576–582.

CHAPTER 14

Conclusions

Brazil is today one of the most important countries in the world market of agribusiness products. Moreover, it is seen as the country that will probably contribute the most to the expansion of world consumption for the coming decades, a market increasing due to the growth of population and income in Asian countries and Africa. And this expansion of production in Brazil is possible by continuing to increase average productivity in Brazil and incorporating already deforested lands of low economic value, particularly degraded pastures. Nor will there be a need for expansion into the Amazonian biome to achieve this increased growth.

It is also seen as a country with great social and regional imbalances, poor infrastructure, a perverse tax system, and low rates of growth in the past thirty years. Despite these impediments, the bases of a modern agriculture implanted throughout the second half of the twentieth century, allowed Brazil from the beginning of the twenty-first century to create a highly competitive Brazilian agribusiness in the international market. As a result, Brazil has become one of the world's most important producers and exporters of numerous agricultural and livestock products, with leadership in many of them (see graphs 14.1a and b). Moreover, future projections about the world supply of food and raw materials from agriculture indicate increases in the Brazilian participation in the world market of essential products such as corn, soybeans, cotton, and meat in general.

H. S. Klein and F. V. Luna, *Brazilian Crops in the Global Market*, Palgrave Studies in Economic History,
https://doi.org/10.1007/978-3-031-38589-6_14

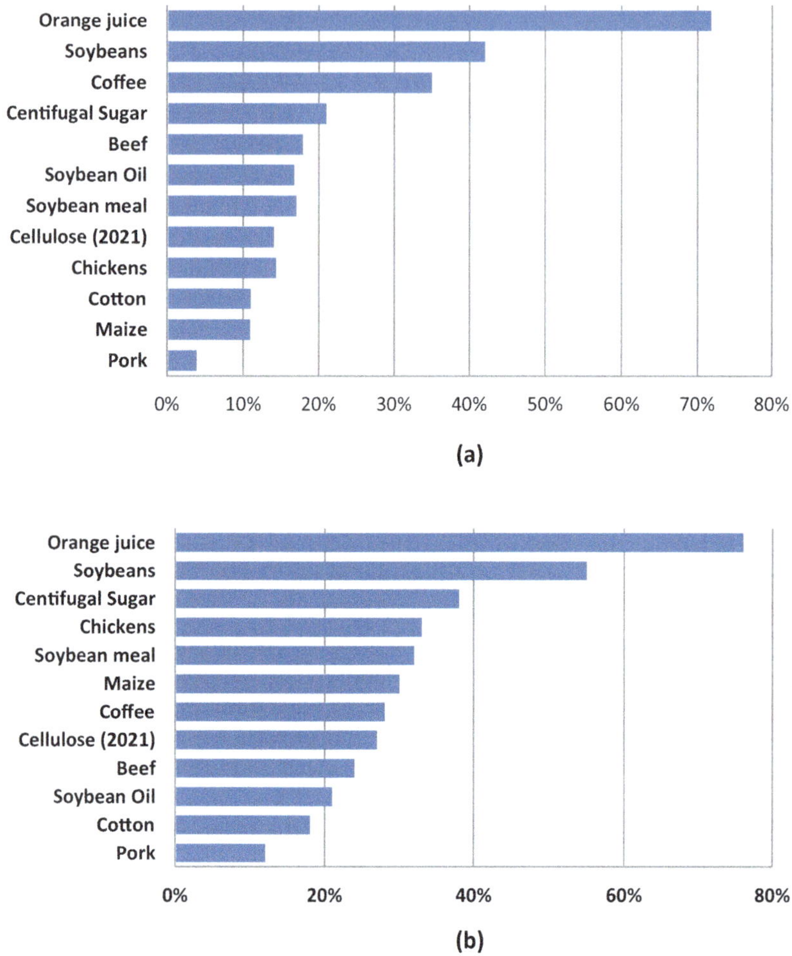

Graph 14.1 **a** Brazil's share of world production in selected agricultural products, 2022/23 (USDA): **b** Brazil's share of world exports in selected agricultural products, 2022/23 (USDA) (*Source* FAOSTAT and USDA, FAS, PS&D at https://apps.fas.usda.gov/psdonline/app/index.html#/app/advQuery)

Given its current state as one of the world's most important agricultural producers, the question remains as to why it took a century for Brazil to become a world agricultural exporter on the level of the United States, Canada, Argentina, and Australia all of which had emerged as significant world exporters a century earlier. The basic reason is geography. Brazilian production of most crops was confined to the temporal zone of the country—that is the Southeastern and Southern states, all of which shared geographical conditions similar to Uruguay, Paraguay, and Argentina. Although a small strip of the Northeastern coastal tropical zone permitted the growth of sugar and cotton, these crops eventually were not competitive on the world market as more efficient producers entered into production. It is only in the second half of the twentieth century that the tropical lands of the nation, which encompasses some 90% of the nation, became available for agricultural exploitation. It was only when these tropical lands were opened up for the production of temperate crops that Brazil could finally become a competitive world agricultural producer.

This opening of these previously non-producing frontier and abandoned lands was based on a massive investment in tropical agricultural research by the state, the universities, and private research groups. This permitted the seemingly arid soil to be treated so as to become productive along with the development of new seeds adopted to tropical conditions. The construction of a new road infrastructure to these frontier lands, and the migration of educated and skilled southern farmers now combined to create a new area of production, which quickly became the nation's most valuable agricultural zone. It was not until the mid-1970s that the famous Cerrado region, now one of the world's greatest grain producers, was finally farmed on a systematic basis. In this savanna was created "a modern, upland, rain-fed grain farming in a tropical region for the first time in human history." This was new even for Brazilian agriculture which saw temperate farm products produced in "a tropical region for the first time anywhere in the world, with high-levels of productivity."[1]

Until the mid-twentieth century Brazil was still a mono product agricultural exporter, with little presence in the world market outside coffee. In 1950 it still had an export profile similar in traditional products from the colonial period, such as coffee, sugar, cotton, tobacco, and cocoa, which made up 80% of total exports, of which 63% represented coffee. Exports of products such as soybeans, maize, orange juice, cellulose, or the meat complex were still non-existent or negligible in value. In the

Table 14.1 Productivity of selected crops for Brazil, the United States, Argentina and the World in 1961 (kg/ha)

Country & World	*Maize*	*Seed cotton*	*Soybeans*	*Rice*
Argentina	1,767	788	977	3,239
Brazil	1,312	631	1,127	1,699
United States	3,918	1,349	1,690	3,823
World	1,942	862	1,129	1,869

Source Faostat

nineteenth century there had been a boom in exports of natural rubber from the Amazon forest, but competition from Asian production soon eliminated Brazilian exports from the world market. There was of course a significant national production of traditional products such as corn, cassava, rice, beans, bananas, milk, cattle, and pig meat, all basic products of the Brazilian diet. But none of these crops had sufficient production or competitiveness to be exported in that period. In fact products such as maize, rice, and beans required sporadic imports to meet domestic demand. In the year 1950 the food import list was highly concentrated in four products wheat (58%), apples/pears/grapes, olive oil, and codfish. These products represented 81% of Brazil's agricultural imports (ft).

Moreover the characteristic production structure was little different from previous centuries whether aimed at the domestic or foreign market. This structure was defined by low productivity per hectare, was practiced with little mechanization and without the use of modern inputs such as fertilizers and insecticides. This can be demonstrated by comparing Brazil's productivity levels with the world average, Argentina and the United States (see Table 14.1). If we consider the year 1961, for which reliable and comparative data are available, Brazilian production of maize per hectare was lower than the world average, just 70% of Argentine productivity and a third of that obtained in the United States. In the case of cotton, the Brazilian average was also lower than the world average, 80% of the Argentinean average and less than half of United States output. Similar results were repeated with rice. Even with coffee, Brazilian average productivity was below that of Colombia, it's most direct competitor.

By the twenty-first-century Brazil, the whole structure and importance of Brazilian agriculture had changed. This radical transformation into an agribusiness which could easily satisfy the home market, and still produce significant volume for exports in dozens of old and new products, was not the work of chance. Crucial was decisive role of the public power. This modernization required huge public resources, particularly in the form of subsidized credit, which induced the introduction of mechanization processes and the use of modern inputs. But none of this would have had any effect without the support of public and private research entities, which allowed the domination of large areas of the Brazilian territory previously unsuitable for the modern practice of agriculture without the introduction of new technologies in crop care and seed varieties adapted to the adverse conditions of that region. Through more than half a century of continuous and successful research, Brazil is today the world leader in tropical agricultural technology.

The modernization of Brazilian agriculture which has occurred in the last sixty years has profoundly altered the nation's agrarian structure, the geographical configuration of its rural production, and the composition of its products. This change has involved the application of new technologies and machines on a major scale to all aspects of agricultural production. It has led to a massive decline of the rural population and the rise of a new more skilled rural labor force. The results have been both a major change in its impact on the domestic market as well as the dramatic insertion of Brazilian products in the international market.

These changes in Brazilian agriculture profoundly affected the nature of Brazil's international agricultural trade. Traditionally only a few products were exported. As late as the 1960s, coffee still represented about 60% of the value of all exports, with some modest exports of cotton, sugar, cocoa, and tobacco. It imported wheat on a major scale and sporadically needed to import maize, beans, or rice to complement shortfalls in supply. From the end of the 1960s onward, however, new Brazilian agricultural products began entering the international market. Thus soybeans and orange juice gained importance, to which were soon added significant exports of maize, cotton, and all types of meat. Forestry products and above all cellulose now became a significant export as well. At the same time all but wheat imports were eliminated, as local production now satisfied demand. The transformations that have taken place have allowed Brazil to stop being a food importer focused on exporting just one or two products, to becoming the largest net food exporter in the world and the third largest agricultural producer and exporter in the world (see Graph 14.2). The country ranks among the world's top five producers of 36 agricultural products and is the world's leading exporter of soybeans,

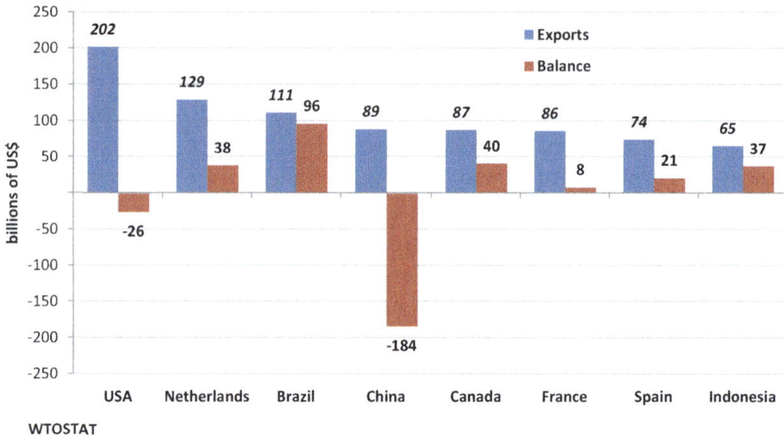

Graph 14.2 Agricultural balance of international trade by leading world exporters, 2021 (*Source* WTOSTAT)

maize, orange juice, sugar, meats, cotton, coffee, tobacco, ethanol, and cellulose. In addition, it is the world's third largest exporter of cotton. This unusual situation is due to the size of farm lands, the largest arable lands of any country in the world, and to its inclusion in both tropical and temperate zones, which means that it satisfies almost all of its agricultural needs and imports little in the way of agricultural products. Thus in 2021 Brazil exported US$ 129 billion of agricultural products, making it the third largest world exporter. But it imported only US$ 15 billion food and other agricultural products, leaving it with a trade surplus of over $96 billion dollars. This in turn allowed Brazil to show a positive trade balance in all its foreign trade, despite negative balances in manufactures and services. This was unique by world standards and even those countries that had a positive balance made less than half of what Brazil made (see Graph 14.2).

Along with its success in the international market, Brazilian agribusiness also greatly increased its capacity to serve the internal market with quality products at ever declining prices. Thus even non-exported traditional food crops have experienced major productivity increases. These included such products as rice, beans, and manioc/cassava all of which experienced increased production and much higher productivity than ever before. These production changes combined with the growth of a modern supermarket and retail system, permitted a steady decline in the costs of a basic basket of popular food items and the increasing consumption of food by the national population. Whereas hunger before 1960 was a significant issue in many parts of the country due to low stocks and poor distribution, this issue is no longer a basic concern.

This massive entrance into the international market has also led to an integration of national agriculture into the main international value chains, to new forms of financing, and to new roles of the state in relation to agriculture. Brazilian agriculture has become a modern capital intensive and competitive agriculture, operating simultaneously in the domestic and foreign markets. It has profoundly altered its business risks, and its relationship with other sectors of the Brazilian economy.

But at the same time the integration of Brazilian production into international markets has had effects on the behavior of the domestic market, which began to be directly influenced by the volatility of exchange rates and international commodity prices, including the main food items consumed by the Brazilian population. This was the case with the recent internal price rise that occurred in 2020 and 2021 due both to the recovery of commodity prices in the international market plus the impact of a 43% devaluation of the national currency between the beginning of 2020 and the end of March 2021. These developments had a direct effect on domestic food prices. Thus, part of the positive effect of the increase in agricultural productivity, which over the years has been transferred to consumers, was lost due to the recent acceleration in prices of the main commodities in the international market and to the effects of a declining value of the national currency. Even so, in the long-term, the variation in food prices has been less than other essential consumer items, such as housing, health, and education.

There is little question that the role of government was vital to this change in post 1960 Brazilian agriculture. The various administrations of the mid-twentieth century recognized the backwardness of national agriculture and decided to promote its change. The most important way to do this was to provide huge amounts of cheap credit, guarantee price stability, and promote new agricultural exports. All of this was done in the name of promoting industrial growth within the country by making cost of living cheap for industrial workers, providing more urban workers through rural mechanization which forced rural workers off the land, and providing foreign capital by generating agricultural exports in order to pay for industrial imports. It also used minimum prices and regulatory stocks to support producers. It even provided quotas of production through the action of such governmental entities as the Brazilian Coffee Institute and the Sugar and Alcohol Institute. In addition, the government directly managed the production, the importation, and processing of wheat in Brazil. The intensification of industrialization also allowed for an integration between agriculture and industry, benefiting the two productive segments as national producers now provided the machinery and chemical inputs needed by farmers, though at a cost above international prices. This system allowed farmers to experiment with new crops and new farming practices, it allowed them to purchase seeds, chemical, and biological inputs as never before and finally to purchase the machinery needed to expand production. The government also funded basic research in all areas of agriculture when it created Embrapa in 1974, which became one of the world's most advanced tropical agricultural research centers. Thus by the 1990s a large part of Brazilian agriculture had been modernized, new lands were opened up in the Center-West of the country and the entire Cerrado area which incorporated large parts of three regions, had been opened up to agricultural production.

When the government in the early 1990s was forced to abandon its protectionist policies, one of the sectors most affected was agriculture. Quotas on the import and export of agricultural products were abolished, the main government crop institutes were closed, wheat subsidies were slowly eliminated and production declined. Subsidized credit was eliminated and regulation of stocks and prices were adopted for an open economy. In some ways the transition to an unsubsidized market was a brutal shock and several major agricultural cooperatives and companies went bankrupt. But the so-called commodities boom of the late 1990s, driven by Chinese demand, provided a new stimulus to exports. At the same time value chains created by processors or trading companies which had evolved in previous years now replaced or supplemented producer cooperatives and state funding agencies. They began to supply inputs and credit for long-term sales contracts. Even supermarket chains provided credit to farmers. The government also slowly returned to agricultural credit through special bank savings investments. Thus the old government networks were replaced by private ones and after a short pause, agricultural exports expanded quickly. Nor did the government abandon its long-term commitment to agricultural education and research. Embrapa continued to influence soil improvement and seed selection in all national crops. Old agricultural schools were incorporated into new federal universities and the stock of professionally trained agronomists greatly expanded. In turn these new federal agricultural faculties became new centers of modern research in the field.

Agricultural production and productivity, already growing in the last decades of the twentieth century, would be accelerated by the maturation of new technologies, particularly in modified and genetically altered seeds, and by the rapid economic occupation of the Brazilian Cerrado, which was transformed into one of the most important centers of grain production in the world. This process also benefited from a period of strong demand for commodities, led by China, which made it possible to expand Brazilian production well above domestic demand. If the fundamental factor in this growth was the extraordinary productivity achieved by farmers, the competitiveness of Brazilian production also depended on countless other factors such as the integration of production into main value chains, which involved logistics, processing, and commercialization. Thus to understand Brazil's success in the international market, we need to consider not just agriculture, but also agribusiness which evolved along with the increased productivity and production. In this area Brazil succeeded in creating both national value chains as well as international business complexes, such as in the meat, orange juice, and cellulose sector. If Brazilian agriculture represents about 7% of GDP, estimates indicate that the GDP of agribusiness, involving inputs, industrial processing, services, logistics, and marketing, would come to represent another 21% of national GDP, bringing the total to 27%.

Currently, the domestic supply of most agricultural products is sufficient to meet domestic demand and generate exportable surpluses. This occurs in grains such as maize and soybeans, in meats (beef, pork, and poultry), sugar, coffee, cotton, etc. There are products whose production adequately meets consumption but do not generate exportable surpluses, such as rice and beans. These two products, basic in the Brazilian diet, show modest growth over time, basically accompanying the increase in domestic demand. Wheat is the only product which is dependent on large structural imports, which supply about half of the domestic demand. But even in this product, whose natural conditions are not the most suitable for its production in Brazil, domestic production, which reaches about 6 million tons, has doubled its productivity since the 1980s reaching about 85% of that obtained by Argentine growers.

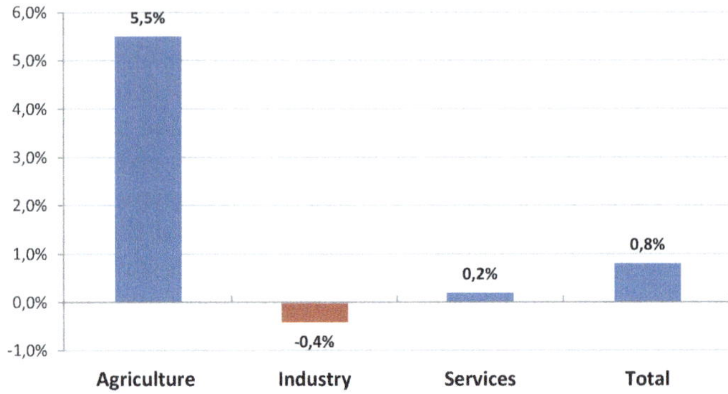

Graph 14.3 Average annual growth of productivity per hour worked, by Sector, Brazil, 1995–2022 (*Source* Veloso, et. al. 2003)

Throughout this work we have demonstrated the extraordinary increase in productivity, measured by production per hectare, as for example, Table 1.1 indicates that between 1976 and 2022 the area occupied as cereals multiplied by 2.1 against a production increase of 6.7. But the increase in productivity occurred not only in the production/area ratio but also in labor productivity, particularly due to the intense mechanization implemented in the commercial segment of Brazilian agriculture. A recent study shows that throughout the period 1995–2022 there was an exceptional increase in productivity per worker, on the order of 5.5% per year. This result is even more extraordinary if compared with the performance of productivity per worker in industry, negative by 0.4% per year, and productivity per worker in the services segment, of only 0.2% per year. That is, even in an environment not very prone to technological transformations that result in productivity increases, as has occurred in Brazil over the last three decades, agriculture has maintained its pace of modernization in all segments, providing continuous increases in land and labor productivity (see Graph 14.3).

Nevertheless the economic integration of Brazil and the wide opening of the domestic market for agricultural products means that even products not exported traditionally by Brazil have their domestic prices affected both by the international price and by the exchange rate variation. This pattern has emerged even for exportable foods, such as maize, whose local price has recently increased due to commodity prices rising on the world market and the impact of the devaluation of the Brazilian *real*. This is a recent pattern and it has had a major impact on the cost of living and consequent restraints on food consumption by the popular classes. For the first time in decades, the question of hunger has again emerged despite the extraordinary productivity and surplus of Brazilian agriculture. But it is a question of price and not of supply, which is more than sufficient to meet all national needs.

The economic crisis that Brazil is facing, first due to the decline in the economy which began in 2013, and which was exacerbated by the Covid epidemic (2020–2021), have resulted in a fall in employment and income, dramatically affecting the poorest strata of the population. Thus a significant portion of the population currently lives in a situation of hunger or food insecurity. It is not the structural famine of the 1950s. There is no shortage of supply; there is a lack of income to acquire the products of the basic food consumption basket, which have experienced a sharp rise in prices in the internal market. This lack of income is caused in part by the recent economic crisis, but also by the high level of inequality that still prevails in Brazil, which is one of the most unequal countries in the world. But otherwise the productivity of Brazilian agriculture has brought a falling price structure and increased consumption by all classes, and this should continue in the future, although with greater volatility than in the past.

Until the 1980s, there was a dichotomy between agricultural production for the domestic market and for the foreign market. The domestic food products such as rice, beans, meat, milk, wheat had their prices controlled and production quotas were established by the state. The opening of Brazil's economy and its transformation into a major exporter of agricultural commodities, affected many national food consumption items such as meat, soybeans, maize, sugar, and thus now directly or indirectly affects the population's cost of living. Thus, rising commodity prices benefit the trade balance, but can also directly affect the real income of local consumers. The same occurs with the depreciation of the exchange rate, in the past basically affecting imported products, but today directly affecting all commodities, imported or exported. The same is true today for fuels, although Brazil is currently a net exporter of oil and its derivatives.

But there is no doubt that the current position of Brazil in world agricultural products is so important that trends in consumption in the developing regions in Asia and Africa will be directly affected by the ability of Brazil to meet part of world demand. Studies on the trajectory of the international market for agricultural products show that few countries will be able to meet the additional demands expected by the increase in the world population and the increase in income of the poorest populations which will gradually be incorporated into the world market. Brazil is among the few countries able to offer additional surpluses in significant quantities, increasing its relative share in the agribusiness market. This process brings challenges.

At the same time that the world market needs a greater offer of agricultural products, it is becoming increasingly demanding in terms of product quality, of product health, and product sustainability. There is little question that Brazil can meet the necessary product quality on the goods it exports, but sanitary standards and environmental sustainability are fundamental issues which will require a major government response, which may or may not be forthcoming. Brazilian production currently meets international sanitary standards, which is the reason for the successful penetration of Brazilian products, including meat, in hundreds of countries. Brazilian meat producers are even successfully able to meet specific religious requirements of consumer countries. There are localized and temporary problems, but in general, the sanitary system has been able to meet the strict requirements of the most demanding markets. But this issue requires continuous care from producers and strict public control in order to maintain the current sanitary quality and follow the rules that will be increasingly stricter worldwide. In these markets, where credibility is fundamental, and competition is brutal, deviation from sanitary and ethical standards, even if temporary and localized, generates consequences which can be negative for an international supplier.

Undoubtedly the greatest risk for Brazilian agriculture is sustainability, which involves countless aspects such as the intensity and use of pesticides, the cultivation of genetically modified seeds and crops, the contamination of water, the quality of animal husbandry, and the question of greenhouse gasses. These are aspects that affect the majority of large agricultural producers. Brazil being a tropical producer is a heavy user both of insecticides and chemical fertilizers. Past practices have not always been up to international standards and sometimes local conditions can lead to debatable practices. But better education as well as more systematic government control can resolve some of these problems.

Also better education, systematic investments in roads and railroads, creation of more cooperatives of producers, and government-sponsored rural extension programs could open up new areas for production. The majority of the rural farms do not produce a surplus and depend on the continued support of government income transfer programs to survive. Part of this universe of poor agricultural units can be added to modern commercial agriculture. Rural poverty in Brazil is a complex issue that involves characteristics of the occupied land, infrastructure, access to the market, and the level of education of the farmers. Furthermore, there is a strong regional element in this poverty, which is more concentrated in the North and Northeast. However, even in this aspect, some areas of these two regions were integrated into commercial agriculture, with great success both from the point of view of production and individual income, as well as from the perspective of regional wealth generated by the new economic activity that is emerging in some specific centers. The revolution that has taken place in the Cerrado in the last thirty years is still expanding to other areas in the south and north of the Amazon and in the western part of the Northeast region, generating jobs and wealth and stimulating the implementation of the economic infrastructure necessary for its full integration into the productive complex of the agribusiness.

But perhaps the most sensitive sustainability issue at the moment is deforestation in general, and particularly deforestation in the Amazon. For a long time, especially in the era of the military regimes (1964–1985), the economic occupation of the Amazon was stimulated. The focus was on preserving sovereignty over that immense area, at that time little occupied and practically unexploited economically. Infrastructure works were carried out, land was distributed, and other incentives were offered to encourage occupation of the region. From the 1970s onward, the issue of deforestation in the Amazon became an important issue due to the loss of fauna and flora diversity, and to the negative impact occupation had on the native peoples of the region. In this century the issue of Amazonian deforestation gained greater dimension when global warming and the impact of greenhouse gases became an important theme. Brazil, which had an energy structure that was more "green" than most major countries, partly due to the intense use of hydroelectricity and the successful program for the use of fuel alcohol, was nevertheless severely criticized for the deforestation of the Amazon. Gradually, the government was able to control the levels of deforestation and assume a prominent position in the defense of the environment. Ambitious goals were established in international agreements and instruments for effective control were created. By the second decade of the century Brazil has satellite monitoring and major

Bibliography

Primary Sources

ABC–Observatório. "Agricultura de Baixo Carbono. A evolução de um novo paradigma," (Fundação Getúlio Vargas, Centro de Agronegócio da Escola de Economia de São Paulo). Found at: www.observatorioabc.com.br.

ABIEC [Associação Brasileira das Indústrias Exportadoras de Carnes], *Beef Report 2020*. Found at: http://abiec.com.br/publicacoes/beef-report-2020/ .

ABIOVE [Associação Brasileira das Indústras de Óleos Vegetais]. Found at: https://abiove.org.br/.

ABPA [Associação Brasileira de Proteína Animal], "Estatístico do Setor," found at https://abpa-br.org/mercados/.

ABPA [Associação Brasileira de Proteína Animal], *Relatório Anual 2020*, found at: https://abpa-br.org/wp-content/uploads/2020/05/abpa_relatorio_anual_2020_portugues_web.pdf.

ABPA, *Relatório Anual 2021*: 37 found at http://abpa-br.org/relatorios/.

AGROSITIO. "Nuevo aumento en derechos de exportación: atualización de impacto en campañas 2019/20 y 2020/2021". At: https://www.agrositio.com.ar/noticia/208984-nuevo-aumento-en-derechos-de-exportacion-actualizacion-de-impacto-en-campanas-201920-y-202021.

AGROVOZ (2020) Argentina, em el topo tem de los mayores produtores y exportadores de semillas. At: http://agrovoz.lavoz.com.ar/agricultura/argentina-en-el-top-ten-de-los-mayores-productores-y-exportadores-de-semillas.

H. S. Klein and F. V. Luna, *Brazilian Crops in the Global Market*, Palgrave Studies in Economic History, https://doi.org/10.1007/978-3-031-38589-6

Agrostat [MAPA—Ministério da Agricultura, Pecuária e Abastecimento]. Found at: http://indicadores.agricultura.gov.br/agrostat/index.htm.

Amazonia: Found at: https://www.wwf.org.br/natureza_brasileira/areas_prioritarias/amazonia1/bioma_amazonia/porque_amazonia_e_importante/.

Anuário Estatístico do Brasil. Found at: https://biblioteca.ibge.gov.br/index.php/biblioteca-catalogo?view=detalhes&id=720.

ANP. Anuário Estatístico Brasileiro do Petróleo, Gás Natural e Biocombustíveis, 2017 (Rio de Janeiro, 2018).

Anuário da Indústria Automobilística Brasileira, 2020 (São Paulo, Brasília: ANFAVEA, 2020).

Anuário Estatístico de São Paulo, vários exemplares.

APTA [Agência Paulista de Tecnologia dos Agronegócios], found at: http://www.apta.sp.gov.br/quem-somos.

ArgenBio, Consejo Argentino para la información y el Desarrollo de la Biotecnologia (2019). At http://www.argenbio.org/index.php?action=cultivos&opt=5.

ArgenBio, Consejo Argentino para la información y el Desarrollo de la Biotecnologia (2020). At: http://www.argenbio.org/index.php?action=novedades&note=712.

Ascema [Associação Nacional dos Servidores da Carreira de Especialista em Meio Ambiente]: *Cronologia de um desastre anunciado: Ações do governo Bolsonaro para desmontar as políticas de meio ambiente no Brasil.* (Brasília: Ascema, 2020).

ABRASEM, *Associação brasileira de sementes e mudas, Anuário 2015.* Found at: http://www.abrasem.com.br/wp-content/uploads/2013/09/Anuario_ABRASEM_2015_2.pdf.

ASA [Asociacion Semilleros Argentinos]. (2017). Estudio del sistema de Agronegócios de semillas Argentino: Uma visión sistémica desde la investigación y el conocimiento. *Buenos Aires*, 3 de abril de 2017. At: http://www.asa.org.ar/wp-content/uploads/2020/01/Impacto-del-sistema-de-semillas-en-Argentina-20170403.pdf.

ASTI [Agricultural Science and Tecnology Indicators]; found at: https://www.asti.cgiar.org/brazil.

Balanço Energético Nacional, 2020. EPE [Empresa de Pesquisa Energética], *Relatório Sintese* (Rio de Janeiro, 2020).

Banco Central do Brasil, found at: https://www.bcb.gov.br/.

Banco Central do Brasil (Crédito Rural): www.bcb.gov.br/?RELRURAL; "Beneficios Tributarios para Zonas Francas," found at https://www.gub.uy/ministerio-economia-finanzas/politicas-y-gestion/beneficios-tributarios-para-zonas-francas.

Banco Central [Uruguay], *Informe Annual de Comercio Exterior—2018*: 4–5 found at http://www.adau.com.uy/innovaportal/file/15997/1/informe-anual-de-comercio-exterior---2018.pdf.

BNDES, *O crescimento de grandes empresas nacionais e a contribuição do BNDES via renda variável. Os casos da JBS, Totvs e Tupy* (2014), acesso: https://web.bndes.gov.br/bib/jspui/handle/1408/9634?mode=full.

Bradesco, DEPEC, *Monitor Setorial, Papel e Celulose*, Setembro 2019, n.p. table "Produtividade por tipo de fibra, Comparação internacional," found at https://www.economiaemdia.com.br/BradescoEconomiaEmDia/static_files/pdf/pt/monitores/setorial/infset_papel_e_celulose.pdf.

Bradesco. *Monitor Setorial: Automotivo* (São Paulo, julho 2020).

BRF at https://www.brf-global.com/sobre/a-brf/nossa-historia/, *Breve Notícia sobre a Província do Maranhão, encaminhada a Sua Alteza Real o Senhor Conde D'Eu, e aos Exmos Membros da Comissão Superior na Exposição Nacional.* (Rio de Janeiro, 1875).

Briefs, I. S. A. A. A. "Global status of commercialized biotech/GM crops in 2017: Biotech crop adoption surges as economic benefits accumulate in 22 years." *ISAAA Brief*, 53 (2017): 25–26.

Bureau de Inteligência competitiva do Café. Vol. 4, no. 9, 17 novembro 2015.

Camara dos Deputados. Legislação: found at: https://www2.camara.leg.br/atividade-legislativa/legislacao.

Camex. "Brasil e EUA assinam memorando que encerra contencioso do algodão". Found at: http://www.camex.gov.br/noticias-da-camex/211-brasil-e-eua-assinam-memorando-que-encerra-contencioso-do-algodao.

CEAG. *Análise do Sistema de Integração Agroindustrial em Suínos e Aves em Santa Catarina.* (Florianópolis: Centro de Assistência Gerencial de Santa Catarina—CEAG-SC, 1978).

Celulose online: found at: https://www.celuloseonline.com.br/china-foi-o-maior-comprador-de-celulose-do-brasil-em-2018/.

CEPEA [Centro de Estudos Avançados em Economia Aplicada]; found at: https://cepea.esalq.usp.br/br.

CEPEA, Mercado de trabalho no agronegócio brasileiro, 3°. Trim. 2020, acesso em: https://www.cepea.esalq.usp.br/upload/kceditor/files/3tri2020_Relatorio%20MERCADO%20DE%20TRABALHO_CEPEA.pdf.

Cetesb [Cia Ambiental do Estado de São Paulo]; found at: https://cetesb.sp.gov.br/.

Cetesb [Cia Ambiental do Estado de São Paulo], Norma técnica P4.231/2005.

Chile Customs data, found at https://www.aduana.cl/exportacion-por-productos/aduana/2020-04-02/091449.html.

Comex Stat [Comex, MDIC], found at: http://comexstat.mdic.gov.br/pt/geral.

Comissão Executiva Têxtil, CETEX, *Indústria Têxtil Algodoeira.* (Rio de Janeiro: Ministério do Trabalho, Indústria e Comércio, 1946).

CONAB [Companhia Nacional de Abastecimento], found at: https://www.conab.gov.br/info-agro/safras

COOPERCAM [Cooperativa dos Cafeicultores de Campos Gerais e Campo do Meio Ltda], found at: http://coopercam.com.br/.

Embrapa [Empresa Brasileira de Pesquisa Agropecuária], found at: https://www.embrapa.br/.

Embrapa Café. *Embrapa Café, História*. Acesso: https://www.embrapa.br/cafe/historia.

Embrapa Comunicações. *Embrapa em Números* (Brasília: Embrapa, 2016).

Embrapa, Florestal; found at: https://www.embrapa.br/florestas.

Embrapa, Soja RR at: https://www.embrapa.br/soja/rr.

Embrapa. *Fixação Biológica de Nitrogênio*. Acessado em 19/4/2017, em: https://www.embrapa.br/tema-fixacao-biologica-de-nitrogenio/nota-tecnica.

Embrapa. *Os benefícios da biotecnologia para a sua qualidade de vida*. Acessado em 7/5/2021, em: https://www.embrapa.br/recursos-geneticos-e-biotecnologia/sala-de-imprensa/se-liga-na-ciencia/a-biotecnologia-e-voce.

"Estatísticas do Commercio Maritimo do Brazil, exercício de 1870–1871". Commercio Geral, Organizada pela Commissão dirigida pelo Dr. Sebastião Ferreira Soares,"Estatística do Commercio Maritimo do Brazil do exercício de 1871–1872;" 2ª. parte, Commercio Geral, Organizada pela Commissão dirigida pelo Dr. Sebastião Ferreira Soares, vol. II

FAOSTAT [Food and Agriculture Organization of the United Nations; Food and agricultura data], found at: http://www.fao.org/faostat/en/#data.

FAOSTAT [Food and Agriculture Organization of the United Nations, TRADE].

FAO Food Price Index, found at: http://www.fao.org/worldfoodsituation/foodpricesindex/en.

FAO, *Global Forest Resources Assessment 2015* (2nd ed., Rome: United Nations, 2016), appendix data tables 1.1 and 2.3 found at http://www.fao.org/forest-resources-assessment/past-assessments/fra-2015/en/.

FAO/ABC. *Algodão orgânico Colorido: Gerando renda e cidadania na agricultura familiar do semiárido brasileiro* (Série Estudos sobre a cadeia de valor do algodão na América Latina e no Caribe, Brasília, 2017).

Fedecitrus, "Reestimativa da safra de laranja 2019/20 do cinturão citrícola de São Paulo e Triângulo/Sudoeste mineiro—fechamento em abril/2020," found at https://www.fundecitrus.com.br/pdf/pes_relatorios/0420_Reestimativa_da_Safra_de_Laranja.pdf.

FIESP [Federação das Indústria do Estado de São Paulo], found at: https://www.fiesp.com.br/.

Instituto do Açúcar e do Álcool *Anuário Açucareiro*, vários exemplares.

ITAL [Instituto de Tecnologia de Alimentos]. Brasil Food Trends 2020. 2010.

Fundecitrus, Inventário de árvores e estimativa da safra de laranja 2019/20 do cinturão citrícola de são paulo e triângulo/sudoeste mineiro:

retrato dos pomares em março de 2019 (Araraquara: Fundecitrus, 2019) found at http://www.aenda.org.br/wp-content/uploads/2020/04/cir0581-anexo_relatorio-safra-2019-2020.pdf.

Fundecitrus, *Inventário de árvores e estimativa da safra de laranja 2019/20.*

Fundecitrus, *Inventário de árvores.*

Globo (G1), found at: https://g1.globo.com/politica/noticia/2020/05/22/veja-os-principais-pontos-da-reuniao-ministerial-que-teve-gravacao-divulgada-pelo-stf.ghtml.

Globo Rural, Found at: https://revistagloborural.globo.com/Noticias/Agricultura/Cana/noticia/2020/11/setor-sucroalcooleiro-passa-por-consolidacao-silenciosa-em-meio-previsao-de-safra-menor.html.

Governo do Estado da Amazônia. *A floresta amazônica e seu papel nas mudanças climáticas* (Manaus: Secretaria de Meio Ambiente e Desenvolvimento Sustentável, 2009).

Healthy and Sustainable: found at: https://www.aholddelhaize.com/en/sustainable-retailing/sustainability-strategy/our-healthy-and-sustainable-ambition-2025/product-safety-and-sustainability/albert-heijn-uses-blockchain-to-make-orange-juice-production-transparent/.

IBA [*Indústria Brasileira de Arvores*] data at https://www.iba.org/dados-estatisticos.

Ibama, Biomas: found at: http://siscom.ibama.gov.br/monitora_biomas/.

IBGE [Instituto Brasileiro de Geografia e Estatística]; found at: https://www.ibge.gov.br/.

IBGE, SIDRA [Sistema IBGE de Recuperação Automática]: várias tabelas. Found at: https://sidra.ibge.gov.br/home/ipca15/brasil.

IBGE, *Estatísticas do século XX:* found at: www.ibge.gov.br.

IBGE, *Censo Agrícola de 2017.* Found at: https://censos.ibge.gov.br/agro/2017/.

IBGE, *Produção da Extração Vegetal e da Silvicultura 2019* (vol. 34, Rio de Janeiro, 2019).

INFOR, *Anuario Forestal 2020* (Santiago: Ministerio de Agricultura, Instituto Forestal; Boletín Estadístico no.174). found at https://wef.infor.cl/publicaciones/publicaciones.php.

INFOR, *Anuario Forestal 2020*, "Resumen de indicadores/flujo de productos de madera 2019", found at: https://wef.infor.cl/publicaciones/anuario/2020/Anuario2020.pdf.

"Informativo de biotecnologia Céleres, novembro de 2019." The OGM Roundup Ready, of Monsanto, was approved in Brazil in 2008. Found at: https://apps.agr.br/wp-content/uploads/2019/07/eventos_aprovados_algod%C3%A3o.pdf.

INPE [Instituto Nacional de Pesquisa Espaciais]: found at: http://www.ccst.inpe.br/o-desmatamento-na-amazonia-aumenta-no-brasil-mas-permanece-baixo-com-relacao-ao-passado/.

ICO [International Coffee Organization], found at: http://www.ico.org/new_historical.asp.

IPEA [Instituto de Pesquisa Econômica Aplicada]: found at: https://www.ipea.gov.br/portal/.

IPEADATA, found at: http://www.ipeadata.gov.br/Default.aspx.

IPEA. *Avaliação da Situação de Assentamentos da Reforma Agrária no Estado de São Paulo. Fatores de sucesso e Insucesso.* (Brasília: IPEA, 2013).

IPEADATA Regional, found at: http://www.ipeadata.gov.br/Default.aspx.

JBS: found at: https://ri.jbs.com.br/a-jbs/unidades-de-negocios/#:~:text=A%20JBS%20USA%20Beef%20%C3%A9,(por%20meio%20da%20Primo).

Jornalismo Agropecuário, *Entendendo o Mercado de Soja*, 17–6–2015, p. 9. Found at: http://www.imea.com.br/upload/pdf/arquivos/2015_06_13_Paper_jornalistas_boletins_Soja_Versao_Final_AO.pdf.

LDC in Belgium: found at: https://www.ldc.com/be/en/ldc-in-belgium/.

MAGP, DFG, *Estadísticas Forestales 2020*, Brasil.

MAPA [Ministério da Agricultura, Pecuária e Abastecimento], found at: www.agricultura.gov.br.

MAPA, *Plano setorial de mitigação e de adaptação às mudanças climáticas para a consolidação de uma economia de baixa emissão decarbono na agricultura : plano ABC (Agricultura de Baixa Emissão de Carbono)* (Brasília: Mapa/ACS, 2012).

MAPA: Sustentabilidade: found at: https://www.gov.br/agricultura/pt-br/assuntos/sustentabilidade/agroenergia/arquivos/cronologia-da-mistura-carburante-etanol-anidro-gasolina-no-brasil.pdf.

MAPA, *Agrostat Indicators*. Found at: http://indicadores.agricultura.gov.br/agrostat/index.htm.

Mapeamento da suinicultura brasileira, Brasília, Sebrae/Associação Brasileira de Criadores de Suínos, 2016. Found at: https://abcs.org.br/wp-content/uploads/2020/06/01_Mapeamento_COMPLETO_bloq.pdf.

MDIC [Ministério da Indústria, Comercio Exterior e Serviços] Secint/Sepec, Séries Históricas, "CUCI (Classificação Uniforme para o Comércio Internacional)" found at https://www.gov.br/produtividade-e-comercio-exterior/pt-br/assuntos/comercio-exterior/estatisticas/balanca-comercial-brasileira-acumulado-do-ano.

MDIC, Secint/Sepec,Exportação: 2020/2019, "Principais produtos e países: acumulado," found at https://www.gov.br/produtividade-e-comercio-exterior/pt-br/assuntos/comercio-exterior/estatisticas/balanca-comercial-brasileira-acumulado-do-ano.

MDIC, Comex Stat at http://comexstat.mdic.gov.br/en/geral.

MGAP [Ministerio de Ganadería, Agricultura y Pesca, Uruguay], *Anuario Estadístico Agropecuario 2020*:156, cuadro 6, found at https://www.gub.uy/ministerio-ganaderia-agricultura-pesca/datos-y-estadisticas/estadisticas/anuario-estadistico-agropecuario-2020.

MGAP, "Exportaciones (Volumen con Zona Franca)," found at https://www.gub.uy/ministerio-ganaderia-agricultura-pesca/datos-y-estadisticas/microdatos/exportaciones-volumen-zona-franca-2012-2019.

MGAP, "Exportaciones del sector forestal de Uruguay crecieron casi 30 % en 2018," Abril 2019, found at http://www.mgap.gub.uy/noticia/unidad-organizativa/direccion-general-forestal/02-04-2019/exportaciones-del-sector-forestal.

MGAP, *Anuario Estadístico Agropecuario 2020.*

MGAP, DGF [Dirección General Forestal]. *Estadísticas Forestales 2020*:38 cuadro 5.1.10 at https://www.gub.uy/ministerio-ganaderia-agricultura-pesca/sites/ministerio-ganaderia-agricultura-pesca/files/2020-07/DGF%20Boletin%20Estadistico%202020.pdf.

MGAP, DGF, *Estadísticas Forestales 2020.*

MGAP, Dirección General Forestal, *Estadísticas Forestales 2020.*

Ministério da Agricultura, Indústria e Comércio, *Indústria Assucareira no Brasil* (Rio de Janeiro: Directoria Geral de Estatística, 1919).

Ministerio da Agricultura, Indústria e Commercio, Directoria Geral de Estatística. *Recenseamento do Brasil, 1920,* vol. V

Ministério da Agricultura. *ABC Agricultura de Baixa Emissão de Carbono.* Found at: https://www.gov.br/agricultura/pt-br/assuntos/sustentabilidade/plano-abc/plano-abc-agricultura-de-baixa-emissao-de-carbono.

Ministério da Ciência e Tecnologia, Inovação e Comunicações, *Estimativas anuais de emissões de gases de efeito estufa no Brasi.* (3a. ed. Brasília: MCT, 2016).

Ministério da Ciência, Tecnologia, Inovação e Comunicações. *Estimativas Anuais de Emissões de Gases de Efeito Estufa no Brasil* (5ª ed., Brasília, 2020).

Ministério das Relações Exteriores, *Relações das condições geográficas, econômicas e sociais, 1940–1941* (Rio de Janeiro, 1941).

Ministério do Meio Ambiente, Estratégia do Programa Nacional de Monitoramento Ambiental dos Biomas Brasileiros. Secretaria de Mudanças Climáticas e Qualidade Ambiental. Departamento de Políticas de Combate ao Desmatamento (Brasília: MMA, 2016).

Ministério Público Federal. Found at: http://www.mpf.mp.br/grandes-casos/lava-jato.

OECD-FAO, *World Meat Projections 2021–2030*, found at https://www.oecd-ilibrary.org/agriculture-and-food/data/oecd-agriculture-statistics_agr-data-en.

OECD-FAO, *Agricultural Outlook 2021–2030* (Paris, 2021).

OEC [The Observatory of Economic Complexity]. (2020). Cambridge, MIT. Found at: https://oec.world/en/profile/country/saarg.

Operações do Crédito Rural e do Proagro-DEROP. Registro Comum de Operações Rurais—RECOR.

OPYPA, *Anuarios* will be found at https://www.gub.uy/ministerio-ganaderia-agricultura-pesca/buscar?search_api_fulltext=Anuario+OPYPA&search-in-site=MGAP.

Plano de Safra de 2020/21 at : https://www.gov.br/agricultura/pt-br/assuntos/noticias/com-mais-recursos-e-melhores-condicoes-de-financiamento-plano-safra-2020-2021-tera-236-bilhoes/copy_of_ApresentacaoPlanoSafra202021.pdf.

Presidencia (Uruguay), "Evaluación financiera de ingresos y egresos del proyecto UPM 2," found at https://www.uruguayxxi.gub.uy/uploads/informacion/874bf57531e7df68884cf24a0bf49b5936bfadae.pdf.

Presidencia (Uruguay), "Impacto socioeconómico de las operaciones de UPM en Uruguay," prepared by CPA Ferrere, found at https://medios.presidencia.gub.uy/tav_portal/2019/noticias/AD_336/5.%20Impacto%20socioecon%C3%B3mico%20de%20las%20operaciones%20de%20UPM%20en%20Uruguay.pdf.

Proálcool 40 anos. Universidades e empresas: 40 anos de ciência e tecnologia para o etanol brasileiro (São Paulo, Blucher, 2016), pp. 25–26.

Produção de suínos: teoria e prática (Brasília: Coordenação editorial: Associação Brasileira de Criadores de Suínos. Coordenação Técnica Integral Soluções em Produção Animal, 2014).

Recenseamento do Brasil, 1920, vol. III.

Relatório apresentado ao chefe do Governo Provisório por Francisco Glicério, ministro e secretário de Estado da Agricultura, Comércio e Obras Públicas. (Rio de Janeiro: Imprensa Oficial, 1890)

Relatório da Comissão encarregada de estudar a difusão applicada a cana de assucar, apresentado ao Exmo. Sr. Conselheiro Rodrigo Augusto da Silva, Ministro e Secretario de Estado dos Negocios da Agricultura (Rio de Janeiro: Imprensa Nacional, 1887).

Relatório prospecção etanol de segunda geração—E2G 2030. Panorama analítico prospectivo dos biocombustíveis e bioprodutos (Projeto Agenda Positiva da Mudança do Clima e do Desenvolvimento Sustentável, Brasília: Centro de Gestão e Estudos Estratégicos, 2018).

Sanbra: Found at: http://alhe.mora.edu.mx/index.php/ALHE/article/view/e1002/1556#:~:text=%E2%80%9CEm%201929%20a%20Sanbra%20lan%C3%A7a,banha%20de%20porco%E2%80%9D%20(Bunge.

Secretaria da Agricultura, Pecuária e Irrigação, Governo Rio Grande do Sul. *Conservar para produzir melhor. Programa Estadual de Conservação do Solo e da Água*. Found at: https://www.soloeagua.rs.gov.br/upload/arquivos/201701/18083910-programa-conservacao-solo-e-agua.pdf.

SEEG *Observatório do Clima, Relatório Síntese*, 2019. Found at: https://www.oc.eco.br/wp-content/uploads/2019/11/OC_SEEG_Relatorio_2019pdf.pdf.

Sociedad de Productores Forestales, "Contribución de la Cadena Forestal a la Economía Uruguaya," November 2017, found at http://www.camaramercantil.com.uy/uploads/cms_news_docs/Informe%20Impacto%20Cadena%20Forestal%20CPA%20Ferrere%2022-11-17.pdf.

SPF [Sociedad de Productores Forestales del Uruguay], *Contribución del complejo forestal a la economía uruguaya* (Informe ejecutivo—Diciembre 2020):7, found at http://www.spf.com.uy/wp-content/uploads/2020/12/SPF-Impacto-Forestaci%C3%B3n_Diciembre2020.pdf.

Statista: found at: https://www.statista.com/statistics/815028/brazil-paper-cellulose-sector-company-net-revenue/.

Suzano: found at: http://www.suzano.com.br/suzanoholding/memoria/.

Única. Found at: https://unica.com.br/sobre-a-unica/UOL: See: https://economia.uol.com.br/noticias/reuters/2017/03/17/escandalo-da-carne-impacta-industria-no-brasil-e-ameaca-exportacoes.htm.

UPM, *125 Años en Uruguay, Informe 2015*:8, 10, found at https://cld.bz/bookdata/5IWy0Tu/basic-html/page-8.html. Pissón, "Estudo geoeconomico da cadeia produtiva de papel e celulose."

Uruguay XXI, *Exportaciones uruguayas de bienes por departamento*, Agosto 2020. Found at: https://www.uruguayxxi.gub.uy/uploads/informacion/494a3f71b4d4ca0a5258e931d3b117957cef373c.pdf.

Uruguay XXI, *Informe de Comercio Exterior Uruguay 2018*: Found at: https://www.uruguayxxi.gub.uy/es/centro-informacion/articulo/informe-de-comercio-exterior-de-uruguay-2018/.

Uruguay XXI, *Informe de Perspectivas de Comercio Internacional2020*, cuadro 4, and following unnumbered pages found at https://www.uruguayxxi.gub.uy/es/centro-informacion/articulo/perspectivas-del-comercio/.

US Department of Justice, "Herfindahl-Hirschman-Index," found at https://www.justice.gov/atr/herfindahl-hirschman-index#:~:text=The%20HHI%20is%20calculated%20by,%2B%20202%20%3D%202%2C600.

U.S. Energy Information Administration, found at: https://www.eia.gov/.

US International Trade Commission, *Certain Orange Juice from Brazil* (Investigation No. 731-TA-1089 (Review), April 2012, pub 4311). Found at https://www.usitc.gov/publications/701_731/pub4311.pdf.

US International Trade Commission, *Certain Orange Juice from Brazil* (No. 731-TA-1089 (Final). June 2007). Found at: https://www.usitc.gov/publications/701_731/pub3930.pdf.

USDA [US Department of Agriculture], Economic Research Service [ERS], *Fruit and Tree Nuts Outlook*, (FTS-371 September 2020).
USDA, ERS, *Fruit and Tree Nuts Yearbook Tables*, Table G-32 found at https://www.ers.usda.gov/data-products/fruit-and-tree-nuts-data/fruit-and-tree-nuts-yearbook-tables/.
USDA, *Oilseeds, World Market & Trade*, varios months and years.
USDA, *Citrus: World Markets and Trade*, varios months and years.
USDA, *Cotton: World Markets and Trade*, varios months and years.
USDA, FAS, *Brazil, Citrus Annual* (BR2020–0055), December 14, 2020.
USDA, *Florida Citrus Statistics 2017–2018,* May 2019.
USDA, *Grains: World Markets and Trade,* varios months and years.
USDA, *Livestock and Poultry: World Markets and Trade,* varios months and years.
USDA, *World Agricultural Production,* varios months and years.
USDA, *Coffee: World Markets and Trade.* varios months and years.
USDA, NASS [National Agricultural Statistics Service], Florida Field Office "10/07/11: Forecasting Florida's Citrus Production (Brochure)"
USDA, NASS, *Agricultural Statistics 2000* (Washington, DC: GPO, 2000).
USDA, NASS, *Agricultural Statistics1970* (Washington DC: GPO, 1970).
USDA, NASS, *Agricultural Statistics1980* (Washington DC: GPO, 1980).
USDA, NASS, Florida Field Office, "Commercial Citrus Inventory Prelim. Report; 2020, October 26. 2020," found at https://www.nass.usda.gov/Statistics_by_State/Florida/Publications/Citrus/index.php.
USDA,FAS, PS&D [Production, Supply and Distribution] at https://apps.fas.usda.gov/psdonline/app/index.html#/app/home.
Tetra Pak, *The Orange Book* at https://orangebook.tetrapak.com/chapter/transport-and-handling-bulk-product.
World Bank, *Brazil the Management of Agriculture,* 1994.
World Trade Organization. "DS267 United States—Subsidies on Upland Cotton". Found at: https://www.wto.org/english/tratop_e/dispu_e/cases_e/ds267_e.htm.

Secondary Sources

Abarca, Carlos David Guevarra. "Inovações tecnológicas na agroindústria dacana-de-açúcar no Brasil," in *Encontro Nacional de Engenharia de Produção* (Rio de Janeiro, ABEPRO, 1999). Found at: http://www.agencia.cnptia.embrapa.br/Repositorio/ENEGEP1999_A0105_000fxgg417302wyiv80soht9h4yxjyhn.pdf.
Abreu, Capistrano de, *Capítulos de História Colonial* (São Paulo: Civilização Brasileira/MEC, 1976).

Aguilar, Eder Barbosa de, "Inovação biotecnológica na pecuária de leite: o papel da Embrapa" (MA thesis, Vitória: Universidade Federal do Espírito Santo, 2007).

Albano, Gleydson Pinheiro, "Globalização da Agricultura: Multinacionais no Campo Brasileiro," *Terra Livre*, (São Paulo), (Ano 27), I, no. 36 (jan–jun. 2001): 126–151.

Albano, Ildefonso. "A crise do Algodão". Discurso pronunciado na Câmara dos Deputados em 11 de dezembro de 1915 (Rio de Janeiro: Typ. Do Jornal do Commercio, 1918).

Albano, Ildefonso. *A Cultura Algodoeira no Ceará* (Rio de Janeiro: Typ. do Jornal do Commercio, 1918).

Albuquerque, Rui H. P. L. de. "Capital comercial, indústria têxtil e relações de produção na cotonicultura paulista (1920–1950)," (MA thesis, Unicamp, 1981)

Albuquerque, Rui Henrique de, Antonio Cesar Ortega and Baastian Philip Reydon, "O setor público de pesquisa agrícola do estado de São Paulo" (parte 1). *Cad.Dif.Tecnol.*, Brasília, 3, no. 1 (jan./abril. 1986): 79–132.

Alden, Dauril, "Late Colonial Brazil, 1750–1808," in Leslie Bethel, ed., *The Cambridge History of Latin America* (11 vols, Cambridge: Cambridge University Press, 1984)

Alisson, Elton. "Proálcool: uma das maiores realizações do Brasil baseadas em ciência e tecnologia", Agência Fapesp, 5/12/2016, found at: https://agencia.fapesp.br/proalcool-uma-das-maiores-realizacoes-do-brasil-baseadas-em-ciencia-e-tecnologia/24432/.

Almeida, Patrícia José de. "Arrendamento e acesso à terra no Brasil," (MA thesis, Campinas, Unicamp, 2002).

Alves, Eliseu and Geraldo da Silva e Souza. "A pesquisa agrícola numa agricultura integrada ao mercado internacional. O caso da Embrapa e do Cerrado". *Revista Política Agrícola*, XVI, no. 2 (abr./mai./jun. 2007): 56–67.

Alves, Eliseu, Geraldo da Silva e Souza and Daniela de Paula Rocha. "Lucratividade da agricultura", *Revista de Política Agrícola*, 21: 2 (abr./mai./jun. 2012): 45–63.

Alves, E. R. A. G. S. Souza and E. G. Gomes, eds., *Contribuição da Embrapa para o desenvolvimento da agricultura no Brasil* (Brasília: Embrapa, 2013).

Ames, Barry and Margaret E. Keck, "The Politics of Sustainable Development Environmental Policy Making in Four Brazilian States," *Journal of Interamerican Studies and World Affairs,* 39, no. 4 (1998): 1–40.

Andrade, Manuel Correia de. *A terra e o homem no Nordeste: contribuição ao estudo da questão agrária* (São Paulo: Cortez, 2011)

Andrade, Pamela, "Carta de Conjuntura—Mapeamentos e Características dos Frigoriíficos Brasileiros," *Scot Consultoria*. Found at: https://www.scotconsultoria.com.br/noticias/cartas/48077/carta-conjuntura---mapeamento-e-caracteristicas-dos-frigorificos-brasileiros.htm#:~:text=Segundo%20levantamento%20da%20Scot%20Consultoria,16%2C6%25%20o%20SIF.

Andreoni, João Antônio (André João Antonil), *Cultura e Opulência do Brasil* (São Paulo: Editora Nacional, s/d).

Anuciato, Karme Medeiros, "Panorama da cadeia produtiva da suinicultura no Estado de Mato Grosso," *Revista Estudos Sociais,* 36, no. 19 (2016): 108–140.

Araujo, Geronazzo, "O Muro do Demônio: economia e cultura na Guerra dos Bárbaros no nordeste colonial do Brasil. Séculos XVII e XVIII," (MA thesis, Universidade Federal do Ceará, 2007).

Araújo, Paulo F. C. de, "Política de crédito rural: reflexões sobre a experiência brasileira," (Brasília: CEPAL/IPEA, 2001).

Araújo, Shadia Husseini de, "Assembling Halal Meat and Poultry Production in Brazil: Agents, Practices, Power and Sites," *Geoforum,* 100 (2019): 220–228.

Arboite, Camila Goulart, et al. "Indicadores de desempenho da cadeia produtiva de suínos na região catarinense," *SEGET*, found at: https://www.aedb.br/seget/arquivos/artigos15/32322353.pdf.

Arruda, José Jobson de Andrade, *O Brasil no comércio colonial* (São Paulo: Atica, 1980).

Arruda, José Jobson de Andrade. "O Algodão brasileiro na época da revolução industrial." *América Latina en la historia económica,* 23, no. 2 (2016).

Aurélio Neto, Onofre, "A estratégia de internacionalização de empresas brasileiras do setor frigorífico: os casos da JBS e da Minerva." *Boletim Goiana. Geografica,* 39 (2019): 57226.

Azambuja, Rosalia and Paulo Eduardo Degrande, "Trinta anos de bicudo-do-algodoeiro no Brasil," (São Paulo: Arquivos do Instituto Biologico) https://doi.org/10.1590/1808-1657000012013, pp. 377–410.

Azevedo, Daniele Maria Machado Ribeiro. "A pecuária de corte no Brasil: a introdução do gado zebu". Agrolink, 12–12–2007. Found at: https://www.agrolink.com.br/colunistas/coluna/a-pecuaria-de-corte-no-brasil--a-introducao-do-bovino-zebu_385142.html#:~:text=A%20entrada%20de%20gado%20zebu,de%20lavoura%20e%20para%20alimenta%C3%A7%C3%A3o.

Bacha, Carlos J. C. *Economia e Política Agrícola no Brasil* (São Paulo: Atlas, 2004).

Bacha, Carlos J. C., Leonardo Danelon e Egmar Del Bel Filho. "Evolução da Taxa de Juros Real do Crédito Rural no Brasil, período 1985 a 2003," *Teoria e Evidência Econômica* (Passo Fundo) 14, no. 26 (maio 2006): 43–69.

Bacha, Carlos José Caetano, "Análise da evolução do reflorestamento no Brasil," *Revista de economia agrícola* 55, no. 2 (2008): 5–24.

Bacha, Edmar Lisboa, "Análise econométrica do mercado internacional do café e da política brasileira de preços," (Rio de Janeiro: EPGE, Ensaios Econômicos n. 2, 1970).

Bacha, Edmar Lisboa. "Política Brasileira do café. Uma avaliação centenária," in Marcelino Martins e E. Johnston. *150 anos de café,* (Marcelino Martins & Johnston Exportadores Ltda., 1992), pp. 13–133.

Baines, Edward, *History of the Cotton Manufacture in Great Britain* (London: Fisher, Firsher and Jackson, 1835).

Banerjee, Onil, Alexander J. Macpherson, Janaki Alavalapati, "Toward a Policy of Sustainable Forest Management in Brazil: A Historical Analysis," *The Journal of Environment & Development* 18, no. 2 (Jun. 2009): 130–153.

Barbosa, Caio César and Sérgio Rangel Fernandes Figueira. "Avaliação da concentração de crédito BNDES para empresas do setor sucroalcooleiro brasileira entre 2002 e 2018" *Economia e Sociedade,* 30, no.1 (2021).

Barbanti Jr., Olympio. "Ciclos Econômicos, Desflorestamento e Impactos Sociais na Amazônia Brasileira". In Artur Zimerman (Org.) *Novos rumos da questão agrária no Brasil,* Santo André, SP: Universidade Federal do ABC, 2017, pp. 10–39

Barbosa, Maria Zeferino, Maria Antonio Margarido and Sebastião Nogueira Junior, "Análise da elasticidade de transmissão de preços no mercado brasileiro de algodão," *Nova Economia,* Belo Horizonte, 12, no. 2 (Jul./dez. 2002), pp. 79–108.

Baricelo, Luis Gustavo. "A evolução diferenciada da indústria de máquinas agrícolas: um estudo sobre os casos norte-americano e brasileiro," (MA thesis, Piracicaba: ESALQ/USP, 2015).

Barsky, Osvaldo, and Jorge Gelman, *Historia del agro argentino, desde la Conquista hasta fines del siglo XX* (Buenos Aires: Editorial Sudamericana, 2001).

Bastos, Luciana A, "Avaliação do desempenho comercial do Mercosul: 1004–2005" (Tese de Doutorado, FFLCH-USP, S. Paulo, 2008)

Batista, Carolina Rocha e Italo do Nascimento Mendonça. "Avaliação da mecanização sobre o mercado de trabalho na lavoura da cana-de-açúcar". *Revista de Economia Regional, Urbana e do Trabalho,* (vol. 8, no. 02, 2019).

Bauluz, Luis, Yajna Govind, and Filip Novokmet, *Global Land Inequality* WID.world Working Paper no 2020/10 (June 2020), found at https://hal shs.archives-ouvertes.fr/halshs-03022360/document.

Beckert, Sven, "Emancipation and Empire: Reconstruction the World Web of Cotton Production in the Age of the American Civil War," *American Historical Review,* 109, no. 5 (2004).

Beckert, Sven, *Empire of Cotton, A Global History* (New York: A Knopf, 2014)

Belasque Jr., José, José Carlos Barbosa , Cícero Augusto Massari and Antônio Juliano Ayre, “Incidência e distribuição do huanglongbing no estado de São Paulo, Brasil,” *Citrus Research & Technology* 31, no. 1 (2017): 1–9.

Belik, Walter, “Agroindústria Processadora e Política Econômica,” (Phd thesis, Campinas, UNICAMP, 1992)

Bélot, Jean-Louis e Patrícia M.C.A. Vilela (ed.). *Manual de Boas Práticas de Manejo do algodoeiro em Mato Grosso* (Cuiabá, IMA/MT e AMPA, 2020, safra 2019/2020).

Beltrão, Napoleão Esberard de Macedo. *Breve História do Algodão no Nordeste do Brasil* (Documentos 117; Campina Grande, Embrapa, 2003).

Beltrão, NE de M. “Breve história do algodão no Nordeste do Brasil.” *Embrapa Algodão-Documentos (INFOTECA-E)* (2004).

Ben, Marilucia and Carmen Rejane Flores Wizniewsky, “A territorialização e versatilidade da cooperativa agroindustrial Lar no Brasil e Paraguai,” XI Econtro Nacional da ANPEGE, 2021, 1349–1350 found at http://www.enanpege.ggf.br/2015/anais/arquivos/4/138.pdf.

Bennett, Carys E., Richard Thomas, Mark Williams, Jan Zalasiewicz, Matt Edgeworth, Holly Miller, Ben Coles, Alison Foster, Emily J. Burton, and Upenyu Marume, “The broiler chicken as a signal of a human reconfigured biosphere,” *Royal Society open science* 5, no. 12 (2018): 180325, 1.

Benjamin, Antônio Herman, “O Meio Ambiente na Constituição Federal de 1988,” *Informativo Jurídico da Biblioteca Ministro Oscar Saraiva*, 19, no. 1 (jan./jun. 2008).

Biehl, Hugo and Renato Zandonadi, “Implicações sócio-econômicas do abandono da cultura do algodão no Brasil,” *Revista de Politica Agrícola,* VII, no. 3 (Jul/Ago/Set. 1998).

Biermann, Christopher J., *Handbook of pulping and papermaking* (Elsevier, 1996).

Binswanger, Hans, “Brazilian Policies that Encourage Deforestation,” (Environment Department Paper No. 16, World Bank, Washington, D.C., 1988)

Bélot, Jean-Louis and Patrícia M.C.A. Vilela, eds., *Manual de Boas Práticas de Manejo do algodoeiro em Mato Grosso.* Cuiabá, IMA/MT e AMPA, 2020 (safra 2019/2020).

Bonato, Emidio Rizzo Bonato and Ana Lidia Variani Bonato,*A soja no Brasil: história e estatística.* (Londrina, PR, Embrapa, 1987).

Borges, Ana Claudia Giannini and Vera Mariza Henriques de Miranda Costa, “Fusões e aquisições no processo de evolução da indústria processadora de citros do estado de São Paulo,” XLV CONGRESSO DA SOBER “Conhecimentos para Agricultura do Futuro” (2008), found at: https://docplayer.com.br/9248312-Fusoes-e-aquisicoes-no-processo-de-evolucao-da-industria-processadora-de-citros-do-estado-de-sao-paulo.html.

Borges, Ana Claudia Giannini, and Vera Mariza H. de Miranda Costa. "A evolução do agronegócio citrícola paulista e o perfil da intervenção do estado." *Revista Brasileira Multidisciplinar*, 9, no. 2 (2005): 101–124.

Boyd, William, "Making Meat: Science, Technology, and American Poultry Production," *Technology and Culture*, 42, no. 4 (Oct., 2001): 631–664.

Bray, Sílvio Carlos, Enéas Rente Ferreira e Davi G. Gaspar Ruas. *As politicas da agroindústria canavieira e o Proálcool no Brasil* (Marília: Unesp, 2000).

Brown, Larissa Virginia, "Internal commerce in a colonial economy: Rio de Janeiro and its hinterland, 1790–1822," (Phd thesis, University of Virginia, 1986).

Brown, Mark G., "European Demand for Orange Juice" (Research Paaper 2010–5, Florida Department of Citrus), found at https://ageconsearch.umn.edu/record/104349/files/RP%202010-3.pdf.

Buainain, Antonio Márcio, and Junior Ruiz Garcia, "Os pequenos produtores rurais mais pobres ainda tem alguma chance como agricultores." *A pequena produção rural e as tendências do desenvolvimento agrário brasileiro: ganhar tempo é possível* 1 (2013): 29–70.

Buainain, Antonio M. et al. "Sete Teses Sobre o Mundo Rural Brasileiro," in Antônio M. Buainain et al. *O mundo rural no Brasil do século 21. A formação de um novo padrão agrário e agrícola* (Brasília: Embrapa, 2014)

Buainain, Antonio M. et al. "Quais os riscos mais relevantes nas atividades agropecuárias?" in Antônio Márcio Buainain et al. *O mundo rural no Brasil do século 21. A formação de um novo padrão agrário e agrícola* (Brasília: Embrapa, 2014): 135–208.

Buainain, Antonio Márcio and Mario Otávio Batalha, eds., *Cadeia Produtiva do Algodão* (Brasília: MAPA, 2007).

Buainain, Antonio Márcio, Antônio Márcio, Maria Thereza Macedo Pedroso, Pedro Abel Vieira Junior, Rodrigo Lanna Franco da Silveira, and Zander Navarro, "Quais os riscos mais relevantes nas atividades agropecuárias?" Antônio Márcio Buainaim, Eliseu Alves, José Maria da Silveira e Zander Navarro. *O mundo rural no Brasil no século 21—a formação de um novo padrão agrário e agrícola* (Brasília Embrapa, 2014): 175–200.

Bugos, Glenn E., "Intellectual Property Protection in the American Chicken-Breeding Industry," *The Business History Review*, 66, no. 1 (1992): 127–168

Cabral, José Irineu, *Sol da manhã: memória da Embrapa* (Brasília: UNESCO, 2005).

Caldeira, Lucio Garcia et al. "Café da Colômbia: o posicionamento da marca como instrumento para agregação de valor" XII SEGET. Simpósio sobre excelência em gestão e tecnologia, outubro 2015.

Calderón, Alexander Macias, "Estratégias de diferenciação do café: os casos do Brasil e da Colômbia" Dissertação de Mestrado, Universidade Federal da Bahia, 2003

Camara, Manuel Arruda, *Memória sobre a cultura dos algodoeiros, e sobre o methodo de o escolher e ensacar, e etc* (Lisboa: Oficina Literária da Casa do Arco do Cego, 1797).

Camargo, Felipe Pires, José Alberto Angelo, and Mario Pires de Almeida Oliveira, "Expansão do plantio direto nas principais culturas no Estado de São Paulo, 2011–2015." *Informações Econômicas,* 46, no. 6 (2016).

Camelo, Severino Morib Barbosa, and Isabel Lausanne Fontgalland, "Análise da produção e comercialização de óleo vegetal no Brasil: o estudo de caso da empresa Cargill," *E-Acadêmica,* 2, no. 2 (2021): e062229–e062229.

Campanhola, Clayton, Dial Franklin Martin and Salomão Schattan, "Algumas consequências da presença do bicudo-do-algodoeiro na região infestada de Campinas e Sorocaba, Estado de São Paulo, na safa 83/84," *Pesquisa Agropecuaria. Brasileira,* 23, no. 8 (ago. 1988): 811–823.

Campelo, Gilson Jesus de Azevedo, Romeu Alfonso de Souza Kiihl, and Leones Alves de Almeida, "Características agronômicas e morfológicas das cultivares de soja desenvolvidas para as regiões de baixas latitudes," in M. A. de Queiroz, C. O. Goedert, and S. R. R. Ramos, eds., *Recursos Genéticos e Melhoramento de Plantas para o Nordeste Brasileiro* (Petrolina-PE, Embrapa, 1999), found at http://www.cpatsa.embrapa.br/.

Campos, Alisson A. V., Mauro M. L. Faria and Túlio Pires. *Expansão da Cafeicultura em Rondônia.* 8/9/2022. Found at: https://revistacampoenegocios.com.br/expansao-da-cafeicultura-em-rondonia/.

Campos, André, "Brazil's Poultry Industry (2016)" accessed January 3, 2022 at https://reporterbrasil.org.br/wp-content/uploads/2016/07/Monitor2_ENG.pdf.

Campos, Edison da Silva and Celso Foelkel, *A evolução tecnológica do setor de celulose e papel no Brasil* (São Paulo: ABTCP—Associação Brasileira Técnica de Celulose e Papel, 2016)

Campos, José Nilson B. "Secas e políticas públicas no semiárido: ideias, pensadores e períodos". *Estudos Avançados,* 28, no. 82 (2014): 65–88.

Campos, Silvia Kanadani and Zander Navarro, eds., *A pequena produção rural e as tendências do desenvolvimento agrário brasileiro: ganhar tempo é possível?* (Brasília: CGEE, 2013)

Canabrava, Alice P., "A grande lavoura", in Sérgio Buarque de Hoilanda (org.), *História da civilização brasileira* (vol. 2, nol. 4, São Paulo: Difusão Europeia do Livro, 1971), pp. 85–140.

Canabrava, Alice P. *O Algodão em São Paulo 1861–1875* (São Paulo: T.A.Queiroz, Editor, 1984)

Canabrava, Alice Piffer, "Uma fazenda-modelo na Província de São Paulo (1863)," *Anais do IX Simpósio da ANPUH, O Homem e a Técnica* (volume IV, São Paulo, 1979), pp. 1173–1219.

Cap, Eugenio J. *Produtivity Increase+Sustentability: The case of No-Till in Argentina*. Berlin, 10 janeiro 2012. At: https://inta.gob.ar/sites/default/files/script-tmp-no_till_in_argentina_eugenio_cap_hffa_berln_2012.pdf

Carli, Gileno de, *História contemporânea do açúcar no Brasil* (Rio de Janeiro: IAA, 1940).

Carli, Gileno de, *O açúcar na formação econômica do Brasil* (Rio de Janeiro: Annuário Açucareiro, 1937).

Carli, Gileno de, *Aspectos de Economia açucareira* (Rio de Janeiro, Irmãos Poncetti, Editores, 1942).

Carli, Gileno de, *Gênese e evolução da indústria açucareira de São Paulo* (Rio de Janeiro, Pongetti, 1943).

Carreira, António, *A Companhia Geral do Grão-Pará e Maranhão* (São Paulo, Editora Nacional, 1988, 2v. (Brasiliana)).

Carter, Susan B, et al. *Historical statistics of the United States: Earliest Times to the Present* (5 vols.; New York: Cambridge University Press, 2006).

Carvalho, Lucineia Hipólito, "Poder de mercado na indústria brasileira de esmagamento de soja" (Phd thesis, Universidade Federal de Viçosa, 2004).

Carvalho, Maria A. de and Roberto L. da Silva, "Intensidade do Comércio Agrícola no Mercosul," 47°. *Congresso da SOBER*, found at: http://www.sober.org.br/palestra/13/447.pdf.

Carvalho, Patrícia Nasser de, *A política agrícola comum da Europa: controvérsias e continuidade* (Brasília: IPEA, TD 2258, 1990)

Carvalho. Thiago Bernardino de and Sérgio de Zen, "A cadeia de Pecuária de Corte no Brasil: Evolução e tendências," *Revista iPecege*, 3, no. 1 (2017).

Carvalho, Thiago Bernardino de, "Estratégias de crescimento e reestruturação da indústria de carne bovina no Brasil: o papel de políticas públicas discricionárias," (Phd thesis, Universidade de São Paulo, 2016)

Castro, Luís Felipe Perdigão de, "Dimensões e lógicas do arrendamento rural na agricultura familiar: um estudo de caso," *Revista em Agronegócio e Meio Ambiente*, (abr./jun. 2017), pp. 437–457

Chaddad, Fabio, *The Economics and Organization of Brazilian Agriculture: Recente Evolution and Produtivity Gains* (Amsterdam: Academic Press, 2016).

Chalita, Maria Ann Najm, "Cultura, Política e Agricultura Familiar: a identidade sócio-profissional de empresário rural como referencial das estratégias de desenvolvimento da citricultura paulista," (Phd thesis, Porto Alegre: Universidade Federal de Rio Grande do Sul, 2004).

Coelho, Alexandre Bragança, "A cultura do algodão e a questão de integração entre preços internos e externos" (MA thesis, São Paulo: USP, 2002).

Cole, Célio Alberto, "A cadeia produtiva do trigo no Brasil: contribuição para geração de emprego e renda" (Dissertação de Mestrado, Porto Alegre: Iepe-UFRGS, 1998).

Colombini Neto, Idelty, "Auge e declínio do "neodesarrollismo" argentino" *Economia e Sociedade*, Campinas, 25 (2/57) (2016): 401–428.

Coltro, Leda, Anna Lúcia Mourad, Rojane M. Kletecke,Taíssa A. Mendonça and Sílvia P. M. Germer, "Assessing the Environmental Profile of Orange Production in Brazil," *International Journal of Life Cycle Assessment*, 14, no. 7 (Nov. 2009)

Constance, Douglas H., "The Southern Model of Broiler Production and Its Global Implications," *Culture & Agriculture*, 30, no. 1–2 (2008): 17–31.

Constance, Douglas H., Francisco Martinez-Gomez, Gilberto Aboites-Manrique, and Alessandro Bonanno, "The Problems with Poultry Production and Processing," in Harvey S. James, ed. *The Ethics and Economics of Agrifood Competition* (Springer, 2013)

Corrêa, Afonso Simões. *Pecuária de Corte—Problemas e Perspectivas de Desenvolvimento* (Campo Grande, Embrapa, 1986).

Cortez, Luís Augusto Barbosa (Org.), *Proálcool 40 anos. Universidades e empresas: 40 anos de ciência e tecnologia para o etanol brasileiro* (São Paulo: Blucher, 2016).

Costa Filho, Miguel, "Apresentação", *Anuário Açucareiro 1941* (Rio de Janeiro: Instituto do Açúcar e do Álcool).

Costa, Armando João Dalla. "O grupo Sadia e a produção integrada. O lugar da agricultura no complexo agroindustrial" (Dissertação de mestrado, Curitiba, Universidade Federal do Paraná, 1993).

Costa, Luciano de Souza Costa, Luis Alberto Ferreira Garcia, and Paulo Rogério Alves Brene, "A Indústria de frango de corte no mundo e no Brasil e a participação da indústria avícola paranaense neste complexo," *Ciências Sociais em Perspectiva*, 14, no. 27 (2015), https://doi.org/10.48075/revistacsp.v14i27.13245.

Costa, Sérgio Rodrigues and Miguel Garcia Bueno, *A saga do Algodão: das primeiras lavouras à ação na OMC* (Rio de Janeiro: Insight Engenharia, 2004).

Crist, Raymond E. "The Citrus Industry in Florida," *The American Journal of Economics and Sociology*, 15, no. 1 (Oct., 1955): 1–12

Cruz, José Carlos, Cruz et al., *Cultivo do milho. Sistema de Plantio direto* (Sete Lagoas, Mapa, Comunicado Técnico 51, dez. 2002)

Cruz, José Carlos, et al., "Manejo da cultura do milho em Sistema de Plantio Direto" (Informe Agropecuário, Belo Horizonte, vol. 27, no. 233, pp. 42–53, jul./ago. 2006).

Cruz. José Carlos et al. "Sistema de produção de milho safrinha de alta produtividade". XXVIII Congresso Nacional de Milho e Sorgo, 2010, Goiânia: Associação Brasileira de Milho e Sorgo. Found at: https://ainfo.cnptia.embrapa.br/digital/bitstream/item/25232/1/0593.pdf.

Cruz, Juliana Victorino da Silva. "Ocorrência de aflatoxinas e fumonisinas em produtos à base de milho e milho utilizado como ingrediente de ração para animais de companhia, comercializados na região de Pirassununga, Estado de São Paulo" (PhD diss., Universidade de São Paulo, 2010).

Cruz, Manuel Angel Gómez and Rita Schwentesius Rindermann, *La Agroindustria de naranja en México* (Mexico, Clestaam,1997)

Dall'Agnol, Amélio, *A Embrapa soja no contexto do desenvolvimento da soja no Brasil. Histórico e Contribuições* (Brasília: Embrapa, 2016)

Davatz, Thomaz. *Memória de um colono no Brasil (1850)* (Belo Horizonte: Itatiaia; S. Paulo, EDUSP, 1980).

Dean, Warren, *Rio Claro: A Brazilian Plantation System, 1820–1920* (Stanford: Stanford University Press, 1976).

Deerr, Noel, *The history of sugar* (2 vols, London: Chapman and Hall, 1949–1950).

Degen, Ronald Jean and K. Matthew Wong, "An Examination of the Resource-Based Horizontal Acquisition Strategy of JBS—The Biggest Meat Packer in the World," *Proceedings of the New York State Economics Association*, V.5 (2013).

Delfim Netto, Antônio, *Agricultura e desenvolvimento no Brasil* (São Paulo: Estudo Anpes, 1969).

Delfim Netto, Antônio, *Problemas econômicos da agricultura brasileira* (São Paulo: Faculdade de Ciências Econômicas e Administrativas da USP 1966).

Delfim Netto, Antônio, *O problema do café o Brasil* (São Paulo, IPE-USP, Ensaios Econômicos 16, 1981).

Dhamodharan, Mahalingam, Stephen Devadoss, and Jeff Luckstead, "Imperfect competition, trade policies, and technological changes in the orange juice market," *Journal of Agricultural and Resource Economics* (2016).

Dias-Filho, Moacyr Bernardino and Monyck Jeane dos Santos Lopes, *Histórico e desafios da pecuária bovina na Amazônia* (Belém: Embrapa Amazônia Oriental, 2020).

Diegues Junior, Miguel, "As Companhias Privilegiadas no comércio colonial,". *Revista de História*, 3, no. 3 (1950): 309–336.

Donnell, E. J., *Chronological and Statistical History of Cotton* (New York: James Sutton & Co. Printers, 1872).

Duchele, Amy E. et al. "Linking Forest Tenure Reform, Environmental Compliance, and Incentives: Lessons from REDD+ Iniatives in the Brazilian Amazon." *World Development* (vol. 55, pp. 53–77, 2014)

Durham, Fabrício Brollo, José Vitor Bomtempo and Denise Lima Fleck, "A estruturação do Sistema de Produção e Inovação Sucroalcooleiro como Brasil para o Proálcool." *Revista Brasileira de Inovação, Campinas (SP), 10*(1): 35–72, jan./jun.2011, pp. 52–60.

Dye, Alan, *Cuban Sugar in the Age of Mass Production: Technology, and the Economics of the Sugar Central, 1899–1929* (Stanford: Stanford University Press, 1998).

Eisenberg, Peter. *The Sugar Industry In Pernambuco: Modernization without Change, 1840–1910* (Berkeley: University of California Press, 1974).

Eliseu R. A. Alves, Geraldo da S. e Souza, Daniela de P. Rocha and Renner Marra, "Fatos marcantes da agricultura brasileira," in Alves, Souza e Gomes, eds., *Contribuição da Embrapa para o Desenvolvimento da Agricultura no Brasil* (Brasília: Embrapa, 2013)

Espindola, Carlos José, "Trajetórias do progresso técnico na cadeia produtiva de carne de frango do Brasil," *Geosul*, 27, no. 53 (2012): 94–98

Euclides Filho, Kepler "Evolução do melhoramento genético de bobino de corte no Brasil," *Revista Ceres*, 56, no. 5 (set./out. 2009): 620–626

Euclides Filho, Kepler, *Melhoramento Genético Animal no Brasil: Fundamentos, História e Importância* (Campo Grande: Embrapa Gado de Corte, 1999).

Evans, Julian, *Plantation Forestry in the Tropics: Tree Planting for Industrial, Social, Environmental, and Agroforestry Purposes* (Oxford: Oxford University Press, 1992).

Faleiro, Fábio Gelape and Austeclinio Lopes de Farias Neto, *Savanas. Desafios e estratégias para o equilíbrio entre sociedade, agronegócio e recursos naturais* (Planaltina, DF: Embrapa, 2008).

Faleiros, Rogério Naqués, *Fronteiras do Café* (Baurú: Edusc, 2010).

Fávero, Jerônimo Antônio e Elsio A. F. de Figueiredo. "Evolução do melhoramento genético de suínos no Brasil." *Ceres*, 56, no. 4 (2009): 420–427

Felius, Marleen, Marie-Louise Beerling, David S. Buchanan, Bert Theunissen, Peter A. Koolmees, and Johannes A. Lenstra, "On the History of Cattle Genetic Resources," *Diversity*, 6, no. 4 (2014): 705–750.

Fernandes Filho, J. F., "A política brasileira de fomento à produção de trigo, 1930–1990," *Anais do XXXIII Congresso Brasileiro de Economia Rural* (Brasília: Sober, 1995), 1, 443–474.

Ferrão, Romário Gava et al. (editores técnicos). *Café Conillon* (Vitória: Incaper, 2017).

Ferreira, Ana Lucia. *Fixação biológica de nitrogênio pode reduzir as emissões de GEE na agricultura.* Found at: https://www.embrapa.br/busca-de-noticias/-/noticia/8313328/fixacao-biologica-de-nitrogenio-pode-reduzir-as-emissoes-de-gee-na-agricultura.

Ficarelli, Thomas Ribeiro de Aquino and Helena Ribeiro, "Dinâmica do arrendamento de terras para o setor sucroalcooleiro: estudo de casos no Estado de São Paulo," *Informações Econômicas, SP*, 40 (jan. 2010): 1.

Figueiredo, Paulo N., "Evolution of the Short-Fiber Technological Trajectory in Brazil's Pulp and Paper Industry: The Role of Firm-level Innovative

Capability-Building and Indigenous Institutions," *Forest Policy and Economics*, 64 (2016): 1–14.

Figueiredo, Sérgio. "O carro a álcool: uma experiência de política pública para a inovação no Brasil," (Dissertação de Mestrado, Brasília, Universidade de Brasília, 2006).

Fleury, Renato Ribeiro. "Reforma agrária e estrutura Fundiária no Brasil: uma análise a partir do I Plano Nacional de Reforma Agrária," (MA thesis, FCL/ Unesp, Araraquara, 2015).

Foster, Chris, Andrew McMeekin, and Jospehine Mylan, "The Entanglement of Consumer Expectations and (Eco) Innovation Sequences: The Case of Orange Juice," *Technology Analysis and Strategic Management,* 24, no. 4 (2012).

Frederico, Samuel. "Globalização, competitividade e regionalização: a cafeicultura científica globalizada no território brasileiro" *GEOUSP- Espaço e tempo (online)* (São Paulo, v. 18, n.1, 55–7, 2014), found at: http://www.revistas.usp.br/geousp/article/view/81077.

Freire, Eleusio Curvelo, Joaquim Nunes da Costa and Francisco Pereira de Andrade, "Recursos genéticos e melhoramentos do algodão no Nordeste do Brasil," Palestra apresentada no Simpósio sobre recursos genéticos no Nordeste. Petrolina. Setembro de 1997. Found at: http://www.cpatsa.embrapa.br:8080/catalogo/livrorg/algodao.pdf.

Freire, Eleusio Curvêlo, José de Alencar Nunes Moreira and Luís Carlos Medeiros. "Contribuição das Ciências Agrárias para o Desenvolvimento o caso do Algodão," *Revista Economia Rural*, 18, no. 3 (jul./set. 1980): 383–413

Freitas, Luiz Antonio Rossi de and Oscar Bertoglio, "A evolução da avicultura de corte brasileira após 1980," *Economia e Desenvolvimento,* 13 (2001).

Freitas, Vladimir Passos de, "A constituição federal e a efetividade das normas ambientais," (Phd thesis, Faculdade de Direito da Universidade Federal do Paraná, 1999).

Frota, Antonio Boris and Gilson Jesus de Azevedo Campelo, "Evolução e perspectivas da produção de soja na região Meio Norte do Brasil," in M. A. de Queiroz, et al., ed., *Recursos Genéticos e Melhoramento de Plantas para o Nordeste Brasileiro* (Petrolina: Embrapa Semi-Arido; Brasília, DF: Embrapa Recursos Genéticos e Biotecnologia, 1999), 143–151.

Fuglie, Kleith O. "Productivity Growth and Technology Capital in the Global Agricultural Economy," in Keith O. Fuglie, Sun Ling Wang e V. Eldon Ball, eds., *Productivity Growth in Agriculture: An International Perspective* (Oxfordshire: CAB International, 2012), Accessed http://agecon.unl.edu/9280a86c-342e-4c5a-afab-d350503401b8.pdf.

Fuletti, Darío and Cecilia Petraglia, "Evolución reciente y perspectivas del comercio exterior de productos forestales," MGAP, *Anuario 2018 OPYPA*: 241–252

Furtado, Celso, *Formação Econômica do Brasil,* São Paulo, Editora Nacional, 196.

Gago, Ayelén and Juan. P. Gianatiempo and Martín Lópes, "La cadena de maíz en la Argentina: Evolución del cultivo durante las últimas campañas." Buenos Aires: Bolsa Cereales, 9, 2018. https://www.bolsadecereales.com/imagenes/retaa/2018-12/161-lacadenademaizenargentinaretaapaseeee09.11.2018.pdf.

Galdos, Marcelo, Otávio Cavalett, Joaquim E. A. Seabra, Luiz Augusto Horta Nogueira, and Antonio Bonomi, "Trends in Global Warming and Human Health Impacts Related to Brazilian Sugarcane Ethanol Production Considering Black Carbon Emissions," *Applied Energy,* 104 (2013): 576–582.

Garnica, Maria Fernanda, "Análise retrospectiva e tendências do serviço de inspeção do Estado de São Paulo," (MA thesis, Jaboticabal, SP: Unesp, 2014).

Gasques, José G. et al. "Produtividade Total dos Fatores e Transformações da Agricultura Brasileira: Análise dos Dados dos Censos Agropecuários," in José G. Gasques, José E. R. Vieira Filho e Zander Navarro, eds., *Agricultura Brasileira: desempenho, desafios e perspectivas* (Brasília: IPEA, 2010).

Gasques, José G., Eliana T. Bastos, Constanza V. e Mirian R. P. Bacchi, "Produtividade da agricultura Brasileira e os efeitos de algumas políticas," *Revista de Política Agrícola,* XXI, no. 3 (jul./ago./set. 2012): 83–92.

Gasques, José Garcia, Miriam R. P. Bacchi, Eliana Teles Bastos and Constanza Valdes. "Crescimento e produtividade da agricultura brasileira: uma análise do censo agropecuário," in José Eustáquio Ribeiro Vieira Filho e José Garcia Gasques (Orgs.), *Uma jornada pelos contrastes do Brasil. Cem anos de Censo Agropecuário* (Brasília IPEA, IBGE, 2020): 107–119.

Girão, Raimundo. *Evolução histórica cearense* (Fortaleza: Etene/BNB, 1986).

Girão, Valdelice Carneiro. "As Charqueadas," *Revista do Instituto do Ceará* (1996): 72–92.

Godley, Andrew Godley, "The Emergence of Agribusiness in Europe and the Development of the Western European Broiler Chicken Industry, 1945 to 1973," *Agricultural History Review,* 62, no. 2 (2014): 315–336.

Goga, Sumayya Goga and Teboho Bosiu. "Governance of Poultry Value Chains—A Comparative Perspective on Developing Capabilities in South Africa and Brazil," (Johannesburg: CREED, IDTT and SARChI Chair, 2019).

Gomes, Rodrigo da Costa, Gelson Luiz Dias Feijó and Lucimara Chiari. *Evolução e Qualidade da Pecuária Brasileira* (Nota Técnica; Campo Grande: Embrapa Gado de Corte, 2017)

Gonçalves, José Sidnei and Simone Pereira Gonçalves, "Transformações da produção do algodão brasileiro e os impactos nas paridades de preços no mercado interno," *Revista Economia Ensaios,* 23, no. 1 (2008): 1–34.

Gonçalves, José Sidnei and Soraia de Fatima Ramos, "Da origem à hegemonia e crise do algodão meridional brasileiro no século XX," *Informações Econômicas,* SP, 38, no. 2 (fev. 2008).

Gonçalves, José Sidnei, "Crise do Algodão brasileiro pós-abertura dos anos 90 e as condicionantes da retomada da expansão em bases competitivas," *Informações Econômicas,* SP, 27, no. 3 (mar. 1997).

Goodman, David, Bernardo Sorj and Jonh Wilkinson. *Da lavoura às biotecnologias* (Rio de Janeiro: Centro Edelstein de Pesquisas Sociais, 1990).

Graham, Jim, Tim Gottwald, and Mamoudou Setamou, "Status of Huanglongbing (HLB) outbreaks in Florida, California and Texas," *Tropical Plant Pathology*, 45 (2020): 265–278.

Grossi, Marine Cirino, Flavio Justino, Camilo de Lelis Teixeira Andrade, Eduardo Alvarez Santos, Rafael Avila Rodrigues, and Luiz C. Costa, "Modeling the Impact of Global Warming on the Sorghum Sowing Window in Distinct Climates in Brazil," *European Journal of Agronomy,* 51 (2013): 53–64.

Guedes, Ana Cecília Guedes and Ademir Antonio Cazella. "Arrendamento de terras e agricultura familiar na região do meio oeste de Santa Catarina" *INTERAÇÕES* (Campo Grande, MS), 20: 4 (out./dez. 2019): 1249–1261.

Guedes, Ana Cecília, Ademir Antonio Cazella and Adinor José Capellesso, "O Arrendamento de terras no Brasil: subsídios para políticas públicas," *Revista Grifos,* no. 44 (2018): 105–125.

Guimarães, Carlos Gabriel. "O Instituto do Açúcar e do Álcool e a indústria do álcool-motor no primeiro governo Vargas (1930–1945)." *História Econômica & História de Empresas,* XV, no. 1 (2012): 135–168.

Guimarães, Diego et al. *Suinocultura: estrutura da cadeia produtiva, panorama do setor no Brasil e no mundo e o apoio do BNDES* (Rio de Janeiro: Agroindústria, BNDES Setorial 45, 2017).

Gurlit, Wieland, Eduardo Mencarini, and Ricardo Montealto, "Weighing the risks in South American Basic Materials," *McKinsey Quarterly,* 2, no. 1 (2007).

Gutman, Graciela E. and Pablo Lavarello. "Biotecnología y desarrollo. Avances de la agrobiotecnología en Argentina y Brasil; *Nueva Época*, número 27 (julio-diciembre 2007)

Haber, Stephen and Herbert S. Klein, "The Economic Consequences of Brazilian Independence," in Stephen Haber, ed., *How Latin America Fell Behind* (Stanford: Stanford University Press, 1997).

Hamilton, Alissa, *Squeezed: What You Don't Know About Orange Juice* (New Haven: Yale University Press, 2009).

Helfand, Steven M. and Gervázio Castro de Rezende, "Brazilian agriculture in the 1990s: Impact of the Policy Reforms" (Discussion Paper 98; Brasília e Rio de Janeiro: IPEA, 2001).

Helfand, Steven M., Vanessa da Fonseca Pereira and Wagner Lopes Soares, "Pequenos e médios produtores na agricultura brasileira: situação atual e perspectivas," in Buainain et al., *O mundo rural no Brasil do século 21,* pp. 533–558

Henry, Richard and Graeme Rothwell, *The world poultry industry* (World Bank Publications, 1995).

Herbert-Copley, Brent. "Innovation, Regulation and Environmental Management in the Chilean and Canadian Pulp and Paper Industries," (PhD diss., Carleton University, 1999).

Hategekiman, Bernard and Michael Trant: "Adoption and Diffusion of New Technology in Agriculture: Genetically Modified Corn and Soyabens," *Canadian Journal of Agricultural Economics,* 50 (2002): 357–371.

Herreros Vergara, Javier. "La importancia de la industria del papel y la celulosa y su protección en Chile." *Anales del Instituto de Ingenieros de Chile,* 1 (1940): 31–41.

Hetemäki, Lauri, Riitta Hänninen, and Alexander Moiseyev, "Markets and Market Forces for Pulp and Paper Products," in Eric Hansen, Rajat Panwar, and Richard Vlosky, eds. *The Global Forest Sector: Changes, Practices, and Prospects* (CRC Press, 2013).

Hilgemberg, Emerson Martins and Carlos José Caetano Bacha, "A evolução da indústria brasileira de celulose e sua atuação no mercado mundial," *Análise Econômica,* 19, no. 36 (2001): 145–164.

Holloway, Thomas H., *Immigrants on the Land: Coffee and Society in Sao Paulo, 1886–1934* (Chapel Hill: University of North Carolina Press, 1980).

Hosono, Akio, Carlos Magno Campos da Rocha, and Yutaka Hongo, eds., *Development for Sustainable Agriculture: The Brazilian Cerrado* (London: Palgrave MacMillan, 2016).

Horta, Andre Barros da, *Panoramas setoriais 2030: Papel e Celulose* (BNDES, 2017) https://web.bndes.gov.br/bib/jspui/bitstream/1408/14241/2/Panoramas%20Setoriais%202030%20-%20Papel%20e%20celulose_P.pdf

Ito, Nobuiuki Costa, and Decio Zylbersztajn, "Power and Selection of Contract Terms: The Case from the Brazilian Orange Juice Sector," *Revista de Administração* (São Paulo), 51, no. 1 (2016): 5–19.

Jardim, Cinthya Martins. "Modos de vida em Assentamentos Rurais no Amazonas: Projeto de Assentamento Sustentável Paquequer—Nova Olinda do Norte (AM)." *Somanlu,* ano 13, no. 2 (jul./dez. 2013), 21p.

Järvinen, Joonas, Jari Ojala, Anders Melander, and Juha-Antti Lamberg, "The Evolution of Pulp and Paper Industries in Finland, Sweden, and Norway, 1800–2005."

Jesus Junior, Celso de, Sergio Roberto Lima de Paula, José Geraldo Pacheco Ormond, and Natália Mesquita Braga, *A cadeia da carne de frango: tensões, desafios e oportunidades* (Brasilia: BNDES, 2007).

Jones, Peter G. and Philip K. Thornton, "The Potential Impacts of Climate Change on Maize Production in Africa and Latin America in 2055," *Global Environmental Change,* 13, no. 1 (2003): 51–59.

Juliani, Antônio José, "Aplicação da modernização ecológica no setor de papel e celulose do Brasil," (Ph.d thesis Universidade Federal de Brasília, 2015).

Junqueira, Arthur Botelho, *O algodão* (São Paulo: Est. De Artes Gráficas C. Mendes Junior, 1936).

Juvenal, Thais Linhares and René Luiz Grion Mattos, "O setor de celulose e papel," in Jorge Kalache Filho, ed., *Banco Nacional de Desenvolvimento Econômico e Social 50 anos: histórias setoriais* (Rio de Janeiro , 2002), pp. 49–75, found at https://web.bndes.gov.br/bib/jspui/handle/1408/12975?mode=full.

Kassam, A., T. Friedrich, R. Derpsch and J. Kienzle. "Overview of the Worldwide Spread of Conservation Agriculture". *Field Actions Sicence Reports*, vol. 8 (2015), p. 3. Found at: https://journals.openedition.org/factsreports/3966.

Katz, Jorge, Giovanni Stumpo, and Felipe Varela, "El complejo forestal chileno," in Jorge Katz and Néstor Bercovich, eds., *El desarrollo de complejos forestales en América Latina* (Bogotá: CEPAL/Alfaomega, 2003).

Keck, Margaret E. "Social Equity and Environmental Politics in Brazil: Lessons from the Rubber Tappers of Acre," *Comparative Politics*, 27, no. 4 (Jul. 1995): 409–424.

Klein, Herbert S. and Francisco Vidal Luna, *Brazil, 1964–1985, The Military Regimes of Latin America in the Cold War* (New Haven: Yale University Press, 2017).

Klein, Herbert S. and Francisco Vidal Luna, "The Growth of the Soybean Frontier in South America: The Case of Brazil and Argentina," *Revista de Historia Económica*, 38, no. 3 (Fall 2020): 1–42.

Klein, Herbert S. and Francisco Vidal Luna. *Feeding the World: Brazil's Transformation into a Modern Agricultural Economy* (Cambridge: Cambridge University Press, 2019).

Klein, Herbert S. Klein and Francisco Vidal Luna, "The Development of a Modern Cellulose Industry in South America," *Latin American Research Review*, 57, no. 4 (2022): 753–774.

Klein, Herbert S. "The Supply of Mules to Central Brazil: The Sorocaba Market, 1825–1880," *Agricultural History*, 64, no. 4 (Fall, 1990): 1–25.

Koster, Henry, *Viagens ao Nordeste do Brasil* [1816] (São Paulo: Cia Editora Nacional, 1941).

Krichal, Alexey. "Liverpool and the Raw Cotton Trade: A Study of the Port and its Merchant Community, 1770–1815," (MA thesis Victoria University of Wellington, 2013).

Laerne, Van Delden, *Brazil and Java: Report on Coffee-Culture in America, Asia, and Africa (1885)* (London & The Hague: Martinus Nijhoff, 1885).

Lamberg, Juha-Antti, Jari Ojala, Mirva Peltoniemi, and Timo Särkkä, eds., *The Evolution of Global Paper Industry 1800–2050: A Comparative Analysis* (Springer Science & Business Media, 2012).

Lee, Gyoung-Ah, et al. "Archaelogical Soyabean (Glyne max) in East Asia: Does Size Matter?" *PLoS One*, 6, no. 11: e26720.

Lefevre, Eugênio, *A administração do Estado de São Paulo na República Velha* (São Paulo: Typografia Cupolo, 1937).

Leite, Sérgio et al., eds. *Impactos dos Assentamentos. Um estudo sobre o meio rural brasileiro* (Brasília: Instituto Interamericano de Cooperação para Agricultura, IICA, São Paulo, Unesp, 2004).

Lema, Daniel, *Crecimiento y productividad total de factores en la agricultura Argentina y países del cono sur, 1961–2013* (Washington DC: Banco Mundial, 2015).

Lima Filho, Rafael R. de, Alex S. L. da Silva and Gustavo A. M. Aguiar. "Cenário Favorável para o arrendamento," *Agroanalisys*, 37, no. 4 (2017): 25–26.

Lima, Mendelson, et al., "Demystifying Sustainable Soy in Brazil." *Land Use Policy*, 82 (2019): 349–352.

Lima, Rodrigo C. A., Leila Harfuch and Gustavo R. Palouro, *Plano ABC: Evidência do período 2020–2020 e propostas para uma nova fase 2021–2030* (Agroicone/Input, 2020).

Lima, Valdomiro Antonio de Oliveira, "A reestruturação industrial dos frigoríficos de carne bovina do Estado de Mato Grosso do Sul," *GE Frontier* (vol. 2, no. 4, UFMGS): 143–171.

Lima, Valdeson Amaro, Isabel Cristina dos Santos and João Amato Neto. "Indústria de máquinas agrícolas no Brasil. Uma Análise evolucionária no período 1985–2015," Cidade do México. *ALTEE,* (2017), 16pp.

Lima-Toivanen, Maria Barbosa, "The South American Pulp and Paper Industry: The Cases Brazil, Chile, and Uruguay." in Juha-Antti Lamberg, Jari Ojala, Mirva Peltoniemi, and Timo Särkkä, eds., *The Evolution of Global Paper Industry 1800–2050* (Dordrecht: Springer, 2012).

Lima-Campos, Aluísio G. de. "A crise internacional do algodão". *Revista de Política Agrícola,* XI, no. 3 (jul./ago./set. 2002): 27–32.

Linhares, Maria Yedda Leite, "Pecuária, alimentos e Sistemas agrários no Brasil (Séculos XVII e XVIII)". *Arquivos do Centro Cultural Calouste Gulbenkian, Le Portugal et l'Europe Atlantique, le Brésil et l'Amérique Latine. Mélanges offerts à Fréderic Mauro* (Lisbon and Paris, Dez., 1995).

Lirbório, Lúcia Ferreira, "O circuito espacial de produção do algodão naturalmente colorido na Paraíba-Brasil," (Phd thesis, São Paulo: FFLCH-USP, 2017).

Liu, Yan, Richard L. Kilmer, and Jonq-Ying Lee, "Canadian Orange Juice Imports and Production Level Import Demand," *Journal of Agribusiness* 25, no. 1 (2007).

Llovet, Ignacio, "Tenencia de la tierra y estructura social en la provincia de Buenos Aires," in Barsky, et al., eds., *La Agricultura pampeana: transformaciones productivas y sociales* (Buenos Aires: Fondo de Cultura Económica, 1988), pp. 249–294.

Lohbauer, Christian, "O Contencioso do Suco de Laranja entre Brasil e Estados Unidos na OMC," *Revista Política Externa*, 20, no. 2 (2011).

Lopes, Gustavo Acili, *A Fênix e o Atlântico. A Capitania de Pernambuco e a economia-mundo europeia (1654–1750)* (São Paulo: Alameda, 2017).

Lopes, Maria-Aparecida. *Rio de Janeiro in the Global Meat Market, C. 1850 to C. 1930: How Fresh and Salted Meat Arrived at the Carioca Table* (Routledge, 2021).

Lorenzi, Bruno Rossi. "Etanol de Segunda Geração no brasil: política e translações," (Tese de Doutorado, São Carlos: Universidade Federal de São Carlos, 2018).

Luckstead, Jeff, Stephen Devadoss and Ron C. Mittelhammer, "Imperfect Competition Between Florida and São Paulo (Brazil) Orange Juice Producers in the U.S. and European Markets," *Journal of Agricultural and Resource Economics*, 40, no. 1 (Jan. 2015): 164–178.

Luckstead, Jeff and Stephen Devadoss, "Trends and Issues Facing the U.S. Citrus Industry," *Choices*, 36, no. 2 (2021): 1–10.

Luna, Francisco Vidal and Herbert S. Klein. *An Economic and Demographic History of São Paulo, 1850–1950* (Stanford: Stanford University Press, 2018).

Luna, Francisco Vidal and Herbert S. Klein, *Brazil Since 1980* (Cambridge & New York: Cambridge University Press, 2006).

Luna, Francisco Vidal and Herbert S. Klein, "Nota a respeito de medidas para grãos utilizados no período colonial e as dificuldades para sua conversão ao sistema métrico," *Boletim de História Demográfica*, VIII, no. 21 (março 2001), found at http://historia_demografica.tripod.com/bhds/bhd24/fvl.pdf.

Luna, Francisco Vidal and Herbert S. Klein, *Slavery and the Economy of São Paulo, 1750–1850* (Stanford, Stanford University Press, 2003).

Luna, Francisco Vidal, Herbert S. Klein and William R. Summerhill, "The Characterístics of Coffee Production and Agriculture in the State of São Paulo in 1905." *Agricultural History*, 90, no. 1, (winter 2016): 22–50.

Luraschi, Marco, "Análisis de la cadena productiva de la celulosa y el papel a la luz de los objetivos de desarrollo sostenible: estudio del caso de Chile," (Documents of CEPAL, Santiago, 2007).

Luraschi, Marco, *Análisis de la cadena productiva de la celulosa y el papel a la luz de los objetivos de desarrollo sostenible: Estudio de Caso Chile* (CEPAL, Naciones Unidas. M. 2005).

Lusas, Edmund W., *Soybean Processing and Utilization* in H. Roger Boerma and James E. Specht, eds., *Soybeans: Improvement, Production, and Uses* (3rd ed, Madison, Wisconsin: American Society of Agronomy, Inc. Crop Science Society of America, Inc. Soil Science Society of America, 2004), 949.

Lyra, André de Arruda, "Estudo de Vulnerabilidade do Bioma Amazônia aos cenários de mudanças climáticas." (Phd thesis, Instituto Nacional de Pesquisas Espaciais, São José dos Campos, 2015).

Macau, Flavio Romero, Julio Araujo Carneiro da Cunha, Nawfal Assa Mossa Alssabak, and Januario Souza Leandro, "Food Value Chains: Social Networks and Knowledge Transfer in a Brazilian Halal Poultry Network," *International Food and Agribusiness Management Review*, 19, no. 3 (2016): 211–223.

Macdonald, Andrew, "A crise do algodão tem solução," *Revista de Política Agrícola*, VI, no. 2 (Abr./ Mai./Jun. 1997): 3–4.

Macedo, Luis Otávio Bau "Modernização da pecuária de corte bovina no Brasil e a importância do crédito rural," *Informações Econômicas*, (São Paulo), 36, no. 7 (jul. 2006): 83–95.

Machado, Carlos José Saldanha, "Mudanças conceituais na administração pública do meio ambiente," *Ciência e Cultura*, 55, no. 4 (2003).

Mahar, Dennis J. Mahar, *Government Policies and Deforestation in the Brazilian Amazon* (Washington, D.C.: World Bank, 1989).

Malhi, Yadvinder, J. Timmons Roberts, Richard A. Betts, Timothy J. Killeen, Wenhong Li, and Carlos A. Nobre. "Climate Change, Deforestation and the Fate of the Amazon." *Science*, no. 319 (2008): 169–172, https://doi.org/10.1126/science.1146961.

Mamigonian, Armen, "Notas sobre os frigoríficos do Brasil Central Pecuário". *Boletim Paulista de Geografia*, 51 (jun. 1976).

Margulis, Sérgio, "O Desempenho ambiental do Governo Brasileiro e do Banco Mundial em Projetos Co-financiados pelo Banco" (Textos Para Discussão No. 194, Brasilia: IPEA, 1999).

Martha Jr, Geraldo B., Eliseu Alves and Eliseu Contoni, "Land-saving Approaches and Beef Production Growth in Brazil," *Agricultural Systems*, 110 (Jul. 2012).

Martha Jr., Geraldo B., Elisio Contini e Eliseu Alves, "Embrapa: Its Origins and Changes," in Werner Baer, ed., *The Regional Impact of National Policies: The Case of Brazil* (Edward Elgar Publishing, 2012): 204–226.

Martinelli Jr, Orlando, "O complexo agroindustrial no Brasil: um estudo sobre a agroindústria citrícola no Estado de São Paulo," (MA thesis, FEA/USP, 1987).

Martinelli Júnior, Orlando Martinelli Júnior, "A Agroindustria Citrícola no Estado de Sao Paulo," *Estudos Economicos*, 19, no. 2 (1989): 277–317.

Martínez, R. D., E. N. Fernández, E. R. Género, and F. J. L. Rumiano. "El ganado bovino criollo en Argentina." *Archivos de zootecnia*, 49, no. 187 (2000): 353–361.

Martins, Diego de Cambraia and Felipe Souza Melo, "O algodão do Brasil e a economia atlântica: comparações entre o Maranhão e Pernambuco (c.1750–1810)," 7ª Conferência Internacional de História Econômica e IX Encontro de Pós Graduação em História Econômica.

Martins, Juliane Carneiro and Ana Maria A. A. Attai. "Análise da pecuária Maranhense entre os anos de 1974 e 2017," *IV Congresso Internacional das Ciências Agrárias* (Virtual), 2019.

Martins, Marcelino e E. Johnston. *150 anos de café* (Marcelino Martins & Johnston Exportadores Ltda., 1992).

Masuda, Tadayoshi e Peter D. Goldsmith, "World Soyabean Production: Area Harvested, Yield, and Long-Term Projections," *International Food and Agrobusiness Management Review,* 12, no. 4 (2009): 143–162.

Mattei, Lauro Francisco. "A reforma agrária brasileira: evolução do número de famílias assentadas no período pós-redemocratização no país" (Estud. Soc. e Agric., Rio de Janeiro, vol. 20, no. 1, 2012): 301–325.

Mccook, Stuart, "Cronica de uma praga anunciada. Epidemias agrícolas e história ambiental do café nas Américas," (VARIA HISTORIA, Belo Horizonte, vol. 24, no. 39: pp. 87–111, jan/jun 2008).

McKenna, Maryn. "Coffee Rust is Going to Ruin Your Morning" *Atlantic,* September 16, 2020

McNabb, Kenneth L. and Lineu H. Wadouski, "Multiple Rotation Yields for Intensively Managed Plantations in the Amazon Basin," *New Forests* 18, no. 1 (1999).

McPhee, John, *Oranges* (New York: Macmillan, 1967)

Medeiros, Josemar Xavier de, "Sistemas de produção integrado, contratado, cooperado e independente," in *Produção de suínos: teoria e prática.*

Meira, Roberta Barros, "Banguês, Engenhos Centrais e Usinas," (Dissertação de Mestrado, FFLCH-USP, 2007).

Mello, Fabiana Ortiz T. and Luiz Fernando Paulillo, "Formas plurais de governança no Complexo Agroindustrial Citrícola: estudo de caso na microrregião de Bebedouro," *XLVI Congresso da [SOBER] Sociedade Brasileira de Economia, Administração e Sociología Rural, 2008* found at https://agecon search.umn.edu/record/108523/files/319.pdf.

Mello, Pedro Carvalho de, "The Economics of Labor in Brazilian Coffee Plantations, 1850–1888," (Phd thesis, Department of Economics, University of Chicago, 1977).

Mendonça, Jorge Maurício, "Emergência e consolidação do padrão eucalipto na indústria brasileira de celulose de mercado," (MA thesis, Campinas: UNICAMP, 1992).

Mendonça, Mauricio, "El complejo forestal en Brasil," in Jorge Katz and Néstor Bercovich, eds., *El desarrollo de complejos forestales en América Latina* (Bogotá: CEPAL/Alfaomega, 2003): 83–121.

Mengel, Alexandre "Modernização da Agricultura e Pesquisa no Brasil: A Empresa Brasileira de Pesquisa Agropecuária, Embrapa," (Tese de Doutorado, UFRRJ, 2015).

Merrick, Thomas W. and Douglas H. Graham, *Population and Economic Development in Brazil, 1800 to the Present* (Baltimore: The Johns Hopkins University Press, 1979).

Mieli, Joao Carlos de Almeida, "Sistemas de avaliação ambiental na indústria de celulose e papel," (Phd thesis, Universidade Federal de Viçosa, 2007)

Mielitz Netto, Carlos G. A.. "Modernização e diferenciação na Bovinocultura de corte Brasileira," (Phd thesis, Unicamp, Campinas, 1994).

Milanez, Artur Yabe, et al. De promessa a realidade: como o etanol celulósico pode revolucionar a indústria da cana-de-açúcar—uma avaliação do potencial competitivo e sugestões de política pública, *BNDES Setorial,* 4 (2015): 237–294.

Miller, Kathleen A. Miller and Michael H. Glantz, "Climate and Economic Competitiveness: Florida Freezes and the Global Citrus Processing Industry," *Climatic Change*, 12 (1988): 135–164.

Miller, Shawn William, *Fruitless Trees: Portuguese Conservation and Brazil's Colonial Timber* (Stanford: Stanford University Press, 2000).

Milioli, Anderson Simionato, Daniela Meira, Maiara Cecília Panho, Laura Alexandra Madella, Leomar Guilherme Woyann, Matheus Henrique Todeschini, Andrei Daniel Zdziarski, et al. "Genetic improvement of soybeans in Brazil: South and Midwest regions." *Crop Science,* 62, no. 6 (2022): 2277.

Miranda, João Eustáquio Cabral de and Ary Ferreira de Freitas, *Raças e tipo de cruzamentos para produção de leite* (Juiz de Fora: Embrapa, Circular Técnica 98, 2009).

Miranda, José Ednilson and Sandra Maria Morais Rodrigues. "História do bicudo no Brasil," in Jean Louis Belot, ed., *O bicudo-do-algodoeiro (Antohonomus grandis BOH., 1843) nos cerrados brasileiros: biologia e medidas de controle* (Cuiabá: Instituto Mato-grossense do Algodão, 2015): 9–46.

Mishra, M.K. and A. Slater, "Recent Advances in the Genetic Transformation of Coffee". Biotechnology Research International Volume 2012, Article ID 580857, 17 pages https://doi.org/10.1155/2012/580857

Monbeig, Pierre, *Pioneiros e fazendeiros de São Paulo* (São Paulo: Hucitec/Polis, 1984).

Montebello, Adriana Estela Sanjuan and Carlos José Caetano Bacha. "O setor de celulose e papel na economia brasileira," *O Papel,* 72, no. 4 (2011).

Montenegro, Felipe Santiago, "Spread de crédito no setor de papel e celulose: um estudo da precificação de empresas brasileiras no mercado offshore," (MA thesis, FGV, 2018).

Montesdeoca, Krystal Maria. "Total Factor Productivity of Tropical Soybean-Maize Systems: The Case of the Safrinha Crop System in Mato Grosso, Brazil," (MA thesis, University of Illinois, 2015).

Morator, Nilma de Oliveira, *A história do IPEF na Silvicultura Brasileira* (Piracicaba SP: IPEF, 2008).

Moreno Fraginals, Manuel, *El ingenio: complejo económico social cubano del azúcar* (3 vols, Havana: Editorial de Ciencias Sociales, 1978).

Moreira, Ajax Reynaldo Bello, Steven M. Helfand and Adriano Marcos Rodrigues Figueiredo, "Explicando as diferenças de pobreza entre produtores agrícolas no brasil", *48º. Congresso Sober*, Julho 2010, acessado em 1/04/2007, found at: http://www.sober.org.br/palestra/15/156.pdf.

Moreira, Nicolau Joaquim, *Indicações agrícolas para os imigrantes que se dirigem ao Brazil* (Rio de Janeiro: Imperial Instituto Artístico, 1875).

Moreira, Priscila C., Gustavo C. Moreira, Nicole R. Castro e Rodrigo P. da Silva. "Produtividade e economia de fatores de produção na cafeicultura brasileira". *Revista de Política Agrícola*, Ano XXVIII, no. 2 (abr./maio/jun. 2019): 6–21.

Mott, Luiz R. B., "Os índios e a pecuária nas fazendas de gado do Piauí colonial". *Revista de Antropologia* (1979): 61–78.

Motter, Paulino and Herlon Goelzer de Almeida (coord. editorial). *Plantio Direto. A tecnologia que revolucionou a agricultura brasileira* (Foz de Iguaçu, Parque Itaipu, 2015)

Mundlak, Yair, Domingo Cavallo and Roberto Domenech, *Agriculture and Economic Growth in Argentina, 1913–84* (International Food Policy Research Institute, 1989).

Murakami, Thays G. L. "Trajetórias tecnológicas na etapa de hidrólise enzimática para a produção de bioetnol de 2ª. geração" (Tese de Doutorado, Campinas, Unicamp, 2015).

Narrod, Clare A. Narrod and Keith O. Fuglie, "Private Investment in Livestock Breeding with Implications for Public Research Policy," *Agribusiness: An International Journal*, 16, no. 4 (2000): 457–470.

Narrod, Clare A. Narrod, Carl E. Pray, and Marites Tiongco, "Technology Transfer, Policies, and the Role of the Private Sector in the Global Poultry Revolution," (International Food Policy Research Institute, Discussion Paper 00841, December 2008).

Negri, Barjas, *Estudo de caso da indústria nacional de equipamentos. Análise do grupo Dedini (1920–1975).*

Neves, Marcos Fava and Vinicius Gustavo Trombin, *Anuário da Citricultura 2017* (São Paulo: CITRUSBR, 2017), found at http://www.citrusbr.com/download/biblioteca/CitrusBR_Anuario_2017_alta.pdf.

Neves, Marcos Fava and Vinícuis Gustavo Trombin, eds., *The Orange Juice Business, A Brazilian Perspective* (Netherlands: Wagenigen Academic Publishers, 2011).

Neves, Marcos Fava e Mairun Junqueira Alves Pinto, eds. *A cadeia do Algodão Brasileiro. Desafios e estratégias, safra 2010/2011.* (Brasília: ABRAP, 2011).

Neves, Marcos Fava, *Food and Agribusiness in 2030: a roadmap* (Netherlands: Wageningen Academic Publishers, 2020).

Neves, Marcos Fava, Vinícius Gustavo Trombin, and Rafael Bordonal Kalaki, "Peeling Back the Citrus in Brazil: Mapping and Quantification of the Brazilian Citrus Chain," *Citrus Research & Technology,* 35, no. 2 (2017).

Neves, Marcos Fava, Vinícius Gustavo Trombin, and Rafael Bordonal Kalaki, "Mercado brasileiro de suco de laranja: uma alternativa para mitigar os efeitos do declínio do consumo no mundo," *Citrus Research & Technology,* 35, no. 2 (2017).

Neves, Marcos Fava, Vinicius Gustavo Trombin, Lourival Carmo Monaco Neto and Rafael Bordonal Kalaki, *Orange Juice Chain Past, Present and Future* (Western Cape, SA: KAAP-AGRI, 2019), found at https://www.fruit-processing.com/wp-content/uploads/2019/04/OJC_Neves_et_al_2019.pdf.

Nobre, Carlos A., Gilvan Sampaio and Luis Salazar. "Mudanças climáticas e Amazônia". *Ciência e Cultura,* 59, no. 3, (Julho/Set. 2007): 22–27.

Nogueira, Francisco R. B. e Sara V.D. Simões. "Uma abordagem sistêmica para a agropecuária e a dinâmica evolutiva dos sistemas de produção do nordeste semi-árido". *Revista Caatinga,* Mossoró, 22, no. 2, (abril/junho 2009).

Novelli, Priscilla Zygmantas Novelli, Daniela Cabral Paiva, Nadir Lopes Garcia, and Thiago Brava Izidoro. "Panorama sobre a regulamentação do sistema APPCC em estabelecimentos de carne de aves sob inspeção federal," *Hig. Aliment.* (2016): 139–145.

Nunes, Debora Cristina Leite, "Conservação de água em máquina de fabricação de papel, O caso da Bahia Sul Papel e Celulose S.A.," (MA thesis, Universidade Federal de Itajubá, 2007).

Nyko, Diego et al. *A evolução das tecnologias agrícolas do setor sucroenergético: estagnação passageira ou crise estrutural?* (Rio de Janeiro, BNDES, Setorial 37), 399–442.

Oliveira, Silas Maciel de, Rodrigo Estevam Munhoz de Almeida, Rafaela Alenbrant Migliavacca e José Laércio Favarin. "Importância do Sistema de plantio direto (SPD) para a cultura do milho," *Visão Agrícola,* no. 13 (jul./dez 2015), 40–44.

Oliveira, Almir Leal de "A força periférica da empresa comercial do charque." Found at: http://www.humanas.ufpr.br/portal/cedope/files/2011/12/A-for%C3%A7a-perif%C3%A9rica-da-empresa-comercial-do-charque-Almir-Leal-de-Oliveira.pdf.

Oliveira, Almir Leal de. "As carnes secas do Ceará e o mercado Atlântico no século XVIII". Found at: http://www.humanas.ufpr.br/portal/cedope/files/2011/12/As-carnes-secas-do-Cear%C3%A1-e-o-mercado-Almir-Leal-de-Oliveira.pdf.

Oliveira, José H. F. de, Cláudio de U. Magnabosco and Arnaldo M. de S. M. Borges. *Nelore: Base Genética e Evolução Seletiva no Brasil* (Documentos 49, Planaltina: Embrapa Cerrados, 2002).

Oliveira, Silas Maciel de, Rodrigo Estevam Munhoz de Almeida, Rafaela Alenbrant Migliavacca and José Laércio Favarin. "Importância do Sistema de plantio direto (SPD) para a cultura do milho." *Visão Agrícola*, no. 13 (2015): 40–44.

Oliveira, Wilson José Ferreira de, "Gênese e redefinições do militantismo ambientalista no Brasil," *DADOS Revista de Ciências Sociais*, 51, no. (2008): 751–777.

Olmstead, Alan L. and Paul W. Rhode, "Biological Innovation and Productivity Growth in the Antebellum Cotton Economy," *The Journal of Economic History*, 68, no. 4 (Dec. 2008): 1123–1171.

Ormond, José G. P., Sérgio R. L. de Paula e Paulo Faveret Filho, *Café: (re)conquista dos mercados* (Rio de Janeiro, BNDES Setorial, n.10, set./ 1999).

Ortega, Lucía Emilia, (2017). "Estrategia y estructura empresarial en la expansión de la soja hacia el norte argentino," (PhD diss., Universidad de Buenos Aires. Facultad de Ciencias Económicas).

Osório, Helen, "Para além das charqueadas: estudo do padrão de posse de escravos no Rio Grande do Sul, segunda metade do século XVIII," *3º Encontro Escravidão e Liberdade no Brasil Meridional*. Found at: http://www.escravidaoeliberdade.com.br/site/images/Textos3/helen%20osorio.pdf.

Osório, Helen. "Fronteira, escravidão e pecuária: Rio Grande do Sul no período colonial," *II Jornada de História Regional Comparada* (Porto Alegre: PUCRS, 2005), 1–16. Found at: http://cdn.fee.tche.br/jornadas/2/H4-09.pdf.

Osório, Helen, "Estancieiros d Rio de São Pedro: constituição de uma elite terratenente no século XVIII". *Actas do Congresso Internacional Espaço Atlântico de Antigo Regime: poderes e sociedades*; found at http://cvc.instituto-camoes.pt/eaar/coloquio/comunicacoes/helen_osorio.pdf.

Paanta, Airan Miguel Dos Santos Panta and Valter Rubens Alcantara Santos Sobrinho, "Agronegócio da citricultura sergipana entre 2010 a 2017," *Citrus Research & Technology*, 40 (2019): 1–9.

Pac, S. Nocelli, *Evolución de Siembra Directa en Argentina Campaña 2016–2017* (2018). At https://www.aapresid.org.ar/wp-content/uploads/2018/03/Estimacio%CC%81n-de-superficien-en-SD.pdf.

Padgett, James, "Rebuilt and Remade: The Florida Citrus Industry, 1909–1939," (MA thesis, University of Central Florida, 2018), at: https://stars.library.ucf.edu/etd/6736/.

Paiva, Alexandre Magno Ramos, "A contenda sobre o algodão entre o Brasil e os Estados Unidos na Organização Mundial do Comércio: considerações acerca do efeito para a inserção do Brasil no Mundo," (MA thesis, João Pessoa: Universidade Estadual da Paraíba, 2013).

Paiva, Ruy Miller, "Fatores que afetam a produção de algodão no sul do Brasil," *Agricultura em São Paulo*, SP, 43, no. 3 (1996).

Paiva, Ruy Miller, Salomão Schattan and Claus F. Trench de Freitas. *Setor Agrícola do Brasil. Comportamento econômico, problemas e possibilidades* (São Paulo: Secretaria da Agricultura, 1973).

Paliwal, Ripusudan L. (2001). "Origen, evolución y difusión del maíz," in Ripusudan L. Paliwal, ed., *El maíz en los trópicos. Mejoramientos y producción* (Roma: FAO, 2001), pp. 5–11.

Palmieri, Fernanda Geraldini and Margarete Boteon, "A percepção do citricultor sobre a indústria paulista de suco de laranja: parceria ou conflito?" *Citrus Research & Technology*, 39 (2018): 1–12.

Panagides, Stahis, "Erradicação do café e diversificação da agricultura brasileira." (Rio de Janeiro, IPEA, outubro de 1968).

Panta, Airan Miguel dos Santos and Valter Rubens Alcantara Santos Sobrinho, "Agronegócio da citricultura sergipana entre 2010 a 2017," *Citrus Research & Technology*, 40 (2019): 1–19.

Pastore, Afonso Celso, *A resposta da produção agrícola aos preços no Brasil* (São Paulo: APEC, 1973).

Patricio, Inaldo Sales, Ariel Antonio Mendes, Alcides de Amorim Ramos, and Danilo Florentino Pereira, "Overview on the performance of Brazilian broilers (1990 to 2009)," *Brazilian Journal of Poultry Science*, 14, no. 4 (2012).

Paula, Edson Júnior Heitor de and Merik Rocha Silva. "Melhoramento genético em bovinos de corte," in Amado de Oliveira Filho, ed., *Produção e Manejo de Bovinos de Corte* (Cuiabá-MT: KCM Editora, 2015), pp. 42–58.

Paulillo, Luiz Fernando and Marcelo Costa Neves, "Análise das estruturas de governança de compra de laranja dos maiores packing houses no estado de São Paulo," *Organizações Rurais & Agroindustriais*, 17, no. 4 (2015): 461–478.

Pedro, Rocha, and V. Villalobos Arámbula, *Estudio comparativo entre el cultivo de soja genéticamente modificada y el convencional en Argentina, Brasil, Paraguay y Uruguay* (No. IICA F30 53. San José Costa Rica and Buenos Aires, 2012).

Peixoto, Marcus, *Extensão Rural no Brasil—uma abordagem histórica da legislação* (Textos Para Discussão no. 48; Brasília: Senado Federal, Coordenação de Estudos, 2008).

Penna, Julio A., and Daniel Lema, "Adoption of Herbicide Tolerant Soybeans in Argentina: An Economic Analysis," in *The Economic and Environmental Impacts of Agbiotech* (Boston: Springer, 2003).

Pereira Filho, Israel Alexandre Pereira Filho and Emerson Borghi, *Mercado de Sementes de Milho no Brasil Safra 2016/2017* (Sete Lagoas, MG: Embrapa Milho e Sorgo, 2016).

Pereira, José Matias, "O processo de ocupação e de desenvolvimento da Amazônia". *Revista de Informação Legislativa*, 34 no. 134 (abr./jun. 1997).

Pereira, Luciano Gomes de Carvalho. *Controle fitossanitário: Agrotóxicos e outros métodos* (Brasília: Câmara dos Deputados, Consultoria Legislativa, Estudo fevereiro de 2013).

Pereira, Mirlei Fachini Vicente, "A modernização recente da pecuária bovina em Rondônia: normas territoriais e a nova produtividade especial," *Revistado Departamento de Geográfico UERJ*, 26 (2015): 95–112.

Pereira, Thales Augusto Zamberlan, "The Cotton Trade and Brazilian Foreign Commerce During the Industrial Revolution," (Phd thesis, São Paulo: FEA-USP, 2017).

Peres, Frederico, Josino Costa Moreira e Gaetan Serge Dubois, "Agrotóxicos, saúde e ambiente. Uma introdução ao tema," in Frederico Peres, Josino Costa Moreira and Gaetan Serge Dubois, eds., *É veneno ou remédio? Agrotóxicos, saúde e ambiente* (Rio de Janeiro: Fiocruz, 2003): 21–41.

Pérez, Fernando Resquin, "Producción de biomasa en plantaciones intensivas de Eucaliptus spp. en Uruguay" (Phd thesis, Universidad de Córdoba, 2019).

Pestana, Paulo, "A indústria de tecidos de algodão". *Boletim da Directoria de Industria e Commercio,* São Paulo, Secretaria a Agricultura, Commercio e Obras Públicas do Estado de São Paulo, 17ª Série, abril, n. 4, 1926.

Pestana, Paulo, "Produção agrícola em 1910–11". Boletim Directoria de Industria e commercio, Secretaria da Agricultura Commercio e Obras Publicas do Estado de São Paulo, 3ª. série, fevereiro, no. 2, 1912.

Petrone, Tereza Schorer. "As áreas de criação de gado", in Sérgio Buarque de Holanda, ed., *História Geral da Civilização Brasileira* (Rio de Janeiro: Bertrand Brasil, Tomo I, A Época Colonial, vol. 2, 2008).

Pichelli, Katia Regina, ed., *Embrapa Foreastas: 30 anos* (Embrapa Florestas, Colombo RS, 2008), found at https://ainfo.cnptia.embrapa.br/digital/bitstream/item/51443/1/Livro-30anos.pdf.

Pimentel et al., *Bicudo uma grave ameaça à cotonicultura nordestina* (Documentos 24; Campina Grande, Embrapa, 1983).

Piñero, Valeria, Samuel Morley e Pablo Elverdin. *Los efectos de la Roya em las economias Centroamericanas* (International Food Policy Research Institute, Documento de Discusión 01457SP, 2015).

Pinheiro, Paulo Cesár Ribeiro. *Os carros flex fuel no Brasil* (Brasília, Câmara dos Deputados, Consultoria Legislativa, Nota Técnica, 2009).

Pissón, Horacio Martín Melo, "Estudo geoeconômico da cadeia produtiva de papel e celulose no Uruguai," (MA thesis, Universidade Federal de Santa Catarina, 2018).

Polaquini, Luciano Eduardo Morello, José Gilberto de Souza and José Jorge Gebara. "Transformações técnico-produtivas e comerciais na pecuária de corte brasileira a partir da década de 90", *Revista Brasileira de Zootecnia,* 35, no. 1 (2006): 321–327.

Pollack, Susan L., Biing-Hwan Lin, and Jane E. Allshouse, *Characteristics of US orange consumption* (US Department of Agriculture, Economic Research Service, 2003).

Porte, Juliana Varchaki, Viviane V. de Lacerda, Jose Braccini Neto and Ângela R. L. de Souza. "Análise dos custos da cadeia produtiva de suínos no Sul do Brasil" *Custos e Agronegócio on line,* v. 15, edição especial, abril, 2019. Found at: http://www.custoseagronegocioonline.com.br/especialv15/OK%202%20cadeia.pdf

Poveda, Manuel Moreno Ruiz. "Análise econômica e ambiental do processamento da vinhaça com aproveitamento energético" (Dissertação de mestrado, São Paulo: Universidade de São Paulo, 2014).

Prado Jr., Caio. *História Econômica do Brasil* (São Paulo: Brasiliense, 1972).

Prado Jr., Caio. *A Revolução Brasileira* (São Paulo, Brasiliense, 1966).

Prates, Rodolfo Coelho and Carlos José Caetano Bacha, "Os processo de desenvolvimento e desmatamento da Amazônia" *Economia e Sociedade* (Campinas), 20, no. 3 (43), (dez. 2011): 601–636.

Queiroz, Maria Isaura Pereira de, "Pecuária e vida pastoril: sua evolução em duas regiões brasileiras." *Revista do Instituto de Estudos Brasileiros* 19 (1977): 55–78.

Radicchi, Caio César, "Competitividade das exportações brasileiras de celulose: uma análise do Custo Brasil," (MA thesis, Universidade Federal de Viçosa, 2004).

Ramos, Milton Geraldo, Pedro Nicolau Serpa, Constâncio Bernardo dos Santos and José Antônio Cardoso Farias, *Manual de Silvicultura, I- Cultivo e manejo de florestas plantadas* (Boletim Didático No. 61; Florianoplis: Epagri, Santa Catarina, 2006).

Ramos, Pedro, "Um estudo da evolução e da infraestrutura da agroindústria canavieira do Estado de São Paulo (1930–1982)" (Dissertação de Mestrado, São Paulo, FGV).

Ramos, Pedro e Walter Belik, "Intervenção estatal e a agroindústria canavieira no Brasil". *R. Econ. Sociol. Rural,* Brasília, 27, no. 2 (abri./jun. 1989): 197–214.

Ramos, Pedro, "Os mercados mundiais de açúcar e a evolução da agroindústria canavieira do Brasil entre 1930 e 1980: do açúcar ao álcool para o mercado interno." *Econ. Aplic.,* São Paulo, 11, no. 4 (out./dez. 2007): 559–585.

Raven, Peter H., "Tropical Floristic Tomorrow," *Taxon*, 37, no. 3 (ago. 1988): 549–560.

Redwood II, John, "World Bank Approaches to the Brazilian Amazon: The Bumpy Road toward Sustainable Development," (LCR Sustainable Development Working Paper No. 13, Washington DC: World Bank, November 2002).

Riello, Giorgio, *Cotton: The Fabric that made the Modern World* (New York: Cambridge UP, 2013).

Ripusudan L. Paliwal. "Origem, evolución y difusión del maíz," in Ripusudan L. Paliwal. *El maíz en los tropicos. Mejoramientos y producción* (Roma: FAO, 2001).

Rizzi, Aldair Tarcísio, "Mudanças Tecnológicas e Reestruturação da Indústria Agroalimentar: o caso da indústria de frangos no Brasil," (Phd thesis, Campinas: Unicamp, 1993).

Rocha, Denis Teixeira da, Altair Dias de Moura and Ademir Francisco Girotto. "Análise de risco de sistemas de produção de suínos, integrado e independente, em períodos de alta e baixa rentabilidade," *Revista de economia e agronegócio,* 5, no. 3 (2007).

Rocha, Pedro, and V. Villalobos Arámbula, *Estudio comparativo entre el cultivo de soja genéticamente modificada y el convencional en Argentina, Brasil, Paraguay y Uruguay* (No. IICA F30 53. San José Costa Rica and Buenos Aires MAGYP, 2012).

Rodrigues, Gelze S. de S. C. e Jurandyr L. S. Ross. *A trajetória da cana-de-açúcar no Brasil, perspectiva geográfica, histórica e ambiental* (Uberlândia: EDUFU, 2020).

Rodriques, J. Barbosa, *Hortus fluminensis; ou, Breve noticia sobre as plantas cultivadas no Jardim Botanico do Rio de Janeiro para servir de guia aos visitantes* (Rio de Janeiro: Typ. Leuzinger, 1894).

Rolim, Leonardo Cândico. "O negócio das carnes secas do Siará Grande" *XXVII Simpósio Nacional de História, ANPUH*, Natal, 2013.

Rosetto, Raffaella e Antonio Dias Santiago. "Adubação, resíduos alternativos", Agência Embrapa de Informação Tecnológica.

Rossato, Fabrícia Gladys F. S., Andres Susaeta, Damian C. Adams, Ieda Geriberto Hidalgo, Thais Duekc de Araujo, and Adriana de Queiroz, "Comparison of Revealed Comparative Advantage Indexes with Application to Trade Tendencies of Cellulose Production from Planted Forests in Brazil, Canada, China, Sweden, Finland and the United States," *Forest Policy and Economics*, 97 (2018).

Rudorff, Bernardo F. T., et al., "Remote Sensing Images to Detect Soy Plantations in the Amazon Biome—The Soy Moratorium Initiative," *Sustainability,* 4, no. 5 (2012).

Rudorff, Bernardo F. T., et al., "The Soy Moratorium in the Amazon Biome Monitored by Remote Sensing Images," *Remote Sensing,* 3, no. 1 (2011): 185–202.

Ruiz, Lucas Gonçalves, *Uma Visão Geral sobre a Cédula de Produto Rural (CPR).* Accessed http://www.migalhas.com.br/dePeso/16,MI227850,11049-Uma+Visao+Geral+Sobre+a+Cedula+de+Produto+Rural+CPR.

Sabourin, Eric and Patrick Caron, "Origem e evolução da agricultura familiar no Nordeste semi-árido," in Eric Sabourin and Patrick Caron, eds., *Camponeses do sertão: mutação das agriculturas familiares no Nordeste do Brasil* (Brasília, DF: Embrapa Informação Tecnológica, 2003), 29–45.

Saes, Flávio Azevedo Marques de. *As ferrovias de São Paulo, 1870–1940* (São Paulo: Hucitec-INL-MEC, 1981).

Salibe, Ary Apparecido, Teófilo Sobrinho, and G. W. Müller. "Sinopse de conhecimentos e pesquisas sobre a laranja 'Pêra'." *Laranja* 23, no. 1 (2002): 231–245.

Salinas, Patrícia José de Almeida, "Arrendamento e parceria na agricultura brasileira: condicionantes, contratos e funcionamento," (Phd thesis, Campinas: Unicamp, 2009).

Sandi, Ari Jabos Sandi and Marcelo Miele, "Análise comparativa dos custos de produção de frangos de corte em SC e GO," *Guia Gessulli da Avicultura e Suinocultura Industrial,* 104, no. 9 (2012): 20–29, found at https://www.embrapa.br/en/suinos-e-aves/cias/estudos.

Santiago, Maura M. D. and Valquíria da Silva, "A política de crédito rural brasileira e o endividamento do setor agrícola: antecedentes e desdobramentos recentes." *Agricultura em São Paulo,* 46, no. 2 (1999): 47–70.

Santos, Edna, *Aumento da produção de algodão no Brasil traz novos desafios para a pesquisa"* (Campina Grande: Embrapa Algodão, 2019).

Santos, Brunna da Silva, Natália Patto and Thais Duarte Tavares, "Exportação de suco de laranja pelo porto de Santos," found at https://fateclog.com.br/anais/2019/EXPORTA%c3%87%c3%83O%20DE%20SUCO%20DE%20LARANJA%20PELO%20PORTO%20DE%20SANTOS.pdf.

Santos, Robério Ferreira dos, "Aspectos Econômicos e Sociais da Cotonicultura no Nordeste do Brasil," (Circular Técnica 31; Campina Grande, Embrapa, 2000).

Sartori, Ivar Antonio, Otto Carlos Koller, Sergio Francisco Schwarz, Renar João Bender, and Gilmar Schäfer, "Maturação de frutos de seis cultivares de laranjas-doces na depressão central do Rio Grande do sul *Revista Brasileira de Fruticultura,* 24, no. 2 (2002).

Sayad, João and Francisco Vidal Luna, "Política Anti-inflacionaria y el Plan Cruzado," in *Neoliberalismo y Políticas Economicas Alternativas* (Quito: Corporacion de Estudios para el Desarrolo (CORDES), 1987), 189–204.

Schieber, Eugenio, *Impacto economico de la Roya del cafeto e America Latina* (Guatemala, 1973).

Schubert, Tim S., Shabbir A. Rizvi, Xiaoan Sun, Tim R. Gottwald, James H. Graham, and Wayne N. Dixon, "Meeting the Challenge of Eradicating Citrus Canker in Florida—Again," *Plant Disease,* 85, no. 4 (2001): 340–356.

Schwartz, Stuart B.. *Sugar Plantations in the Formation of Brazilian Society: Bahia, 1550–1835* (Cambridge: Cambridge University Press, 1985).

Sediyama, Aline Fumie, et al. "Análise da Estrutura, Conduta e Desempenho da Indústria Processadora de Soja no Brasil no Período de 2003 a 2010, *Revista de Economia e Sociologia Rural,* 51, no. 1 (2013): 162–182.

Sesto, Carmen, "*História del capitalismo agrário pampeano,* tomo 2: La vanguardia genadera bonaerense, 1856–1900" (Buenos Aíres: Siglo XXI, 2005).

Shimada, Pery Francisco Assis, "A evolução da agroindústria canavieira em Minas Gerais de 1705 a 1955," (Dissertação de Mestrado, Piracicaba, Escola Superior de Agricultura Luiz de Queiroz, 1992).

Shimada, Pery Francisco Assis, "A evolução diferenciada da agroindústria canavieira no Brasil de 1975 a 1995," (Tese de Doutorado, Piracicaba, Escola Superior de Agricultura Luiz de Queiróz/USP, 1997).

Shutheff, William and Akiko Aoyagi, *History of Soyabens and soyfoos in Southest Asia (13th Century to 2010)* (Lafayette Ind., Soyinfo Center, 2010).

Sigerman, Ariel and Pilar Useche, "Impact of Citrus Greening on Citrus Operations in Florida," *EDIS* [University of Florida, Institute of Food and Agricultural Sciences (IFAS)], no. 2 (2016): 1–4.

Silva Neto, Waldemiro A., Carlos J. C. Bacha and Mirian R. P. Bacchi. "Evolução do financiamento rural para a pecuária e sua relação com a dinâmica regional dessa atividade no Brasil," (TD 24; Goiâna, *NEPEC/FACE/UFG,* maio 2011).

Silva, Adriana Ferreira, Geraldo Sant'Ana de Camargo Barros, and Margarete Boteon, "Price Analyses of the Brazilian Citrus Supply Chain," *Journal of Food Science and Engineering,* 7 (2017): 49–58.

Silva, Felipe P., "O Crédito Rural no Brasil," *Animal Business Brasil,* 2, no. 6 (2012): 61–66.

Silva, Francisco Carlos Teixeira da, "Pecuária e formação do mercado interno no Brasil-colônia." *Estudos Sociedade e Agricultura,* 8, abril 1997.

Silva, José Graziano da, *A nova dinâmica da agricultura brasileira* (Campinas: Instituto de Economia da Unicamp, 1996).

Silva, Melissa A. S. da, Nori P. Griebeler e Lino C. Borges. "Uso de vinhaça e impactos nas propriedades do solo e lençol freático." *Revista Brasileira de Engenharia Agrícola e Ambiental,* 11, no. 1 (2007): 108–114.

Silva, Michelle Oliveira, "Inovações institucionais e tecnológicas no setor sucroalcooleiro: arranjo de rede nas interações público/privado, de Planalsucar à Ridesa," (Dissertação de Mestrado, Universidade Federal de Goiás, 2013).

Silva, Rodrigo Peixoto da, "Efeitos poupa-terra e poupa-trabalho na agricultura brasileira". *Revista de Política Agrícola,* Ano XXVII, no. 3 (jul./ago./set. 2018): 69–81.

Silva, Vicente de P., João HBC Campos, Madson T. Silva, and Pedro V. Azevedo, "Impact of global warming on cowpea bean cultivation in northeastern Brazil," *Agricultural Water Management,* 97, no. 11 (2010): 1760–1768.

Silvestre, Alline A. Freitas et al. "Ulitzação da vinhaça na agricultura," *Journal of Agronomic Sciences*, Umuarama, 3, no. especial (2014): 47–62.

Simão, Eduardo de Paula, "Características agronômicas e nutrição do milho safrinha em função da época de semeadura e adubação." (MA thesis, Sete Lagoas: Universidade Federal de São João del Rei, 2016).

Simonsen, Roberto, *História Econômica do Brasil (1500–1820)*. (Brasília: Edições do Senado Federal, 2005).

Soares, Alcides Ribeiro, "A experiência dos engenhos centrais," in Odalia e Caldeira, eds., *História do Estado de São Paulo* (vol. 1, pp. 161–187).

Soares, Sebastião Ferreira, *Notas Estatísticas sobre a Produção Agrícola e Carestia dos Generos Alimenticios no Imperio do Brazil* (Rio de Janeiro: J. Villeneuve e Comp., 1860).

Sobrinho, Barbosa Lima. *A ação do Instituto do Açúcar e do Álcool* (Rio de Janeiro: Relatório do Sr. Barbosa Lima Sobrinho, como Presidente da Comissão Executiva, no Período de maio de 1938 a abril de 1946).

Sobrinho, Raimundo Braga and Maurice James Lukefahr, *Bicudo (Anthonomus grandis BOHEMAN): nova ameaça à cotonicultura brasileira. Biologia e Controle.* (Documentos 22; Campina Grande, Embrapa, 1983).

Sonka, Steven T. Sonka, Karen L. Bender, and Donna K. Fisher, "Economics and Marketing," in Boerma and Specht, *Soybeans: Improvement, Production, and Uses*, 919.

Sorares, Monique H. C., Norme E. S. Beltrão, Cleber A. Santos e Yvens E. M. Cordeiro. "Impacto dos Assentamentos Rurais no Desmatamento da Amazônia," (Mercator, Fortaleza, vol. 17, e17009, 2018).

Sorj, Bernardo, Malori J. Pompermayer, and Odacir Luis Coradini, *Camponeses e agroindústria: transformação social e representação política na avicultura brasileira* (Rio de Janeiro: Centro Edelstein de Pesquisas Sociais, 2008).

Soterroni, Aline C., et al. "Expanding the soy moratorium to Brazil's Cerrado," *Science Advances*, 5, no. 7 (2019): eaav7336:1–9.

Sotta, Eleneide Doff, Fernanda Garcia Sampaio and Juan Vicente Guadalupe Gallardo, eds., *Coletânea dos fatores de emissão e remoção de gases de efeito estufa da agricultura brasileira*. (Brasília: Mapa/Senar, 2020).

Souza, Gabriel Soares de, *Tratado Descritivo do Brasil* (Rio de Janeiro: Typographia Universal de Laemmert, 1851).

Souza, Jonas Soares de, "O Engenho Central de Porto Feliz: subsídios para o estudo dos engenhos centrais do Brasil no século XIX," *Anais do Museu Paulista*, (1971–1974) tomo XXV, pp. 25–43.

Souza, V. C., "História econômica da suinocultura no Paraná: tradição e modernização: depoimento" [10 março, 2016] (Nova Laranjeiras: Entrevista concedida a Odair José F. de Oliveira. 2016).

Stephens, S. G. and M. Edward Moseley, "Early domesticated cottons from archaeological sites in central coastal Peru." *American Antiquity*, 39, no. 1 (1974).

Stolf, Rubismar e Ana Paula Rodrigues de Oliveira, "The Success of Brazilian Alcohol Program (Proálcool)—A Decade-by-Decade Brief History of Ethanol in Brazil," *Engenharia Agrícola*, Jaboticabal, 40, no. 2 (mar./apr. 2020): 243–248.

Storey, Alice A., et al. "Investigating the Global Dispersal of Chickens in Prehistory Using Ancient Mitochondrial DNA Signatures," *PloS one*, 7, no. 7 (2012): e39171.

Strand, Edwin G., *Soybeans in American Farming* (Technical Report no 966; Washington DC, USDA, 1948), 1-8

Summerhill, William R. *Order Against Progress: Government, Foreign Investment, and Railroads in Brazil, 1854–1913* (Stanford: Stanford University Press, 2003).

Suprinyak, Carlos E. and Cristiano C. Restitutti, "Os muares e as Minas: relações entre a demanda mineira e o mercado de animais de carga nos séculos XVIII e XIX," *Anais do XII Seminário sobre a Economia Mineira*. At: http://www.cedeplar.ufmg.br/seminarios/seminario_diamantina/2006/D06A034.pdf.

Suzigan, Wilson, *Indústria brasileira. Origem e desenvolvimento* (São Paulo: Brasiliense, 1986): 331–344.

Szmrecsányi, Tamás e Eduardo Pestana Moreira, "O desenvolvimento da Agroindústria Canavieira do Brasil desde a Segunda Guerra Mundial." São Paulo, *Estudos Avançados,* 11, no. 5 (1991): 57–79.

Szmrecsányi, Tamás. "1914–1939 crescimento e crise da agroindústria açucareira do Brasil. São Paulo." *Revista Brasileira de Ciência Social,* 3, no. 7 (1988).

Szmrecsányi, Tamás, *O planejamento da agroindústria canavieira do Brasil (1930–1975)* (São Paulo: Hucitec/Unicamp, 1979).

Toivanen, Hannes, " Waves of Technological Innovation: The Evolution of the US Pulp and Paper Industry, 1860–2000," in Juha-Antti Lamberg, Jari Ojala, Mirva Peltoniemi, and Timo Särkkä, eds., *The Evolution of Global Paper Industry 1800–2050: A Comparative Analysis* (Springer Science & Business Media, 2012).

Toivanen, Hannes, and Maria Barbosa Lima Toivanen, "Innovation and the Emergence of Brazilian Pulp and Paper Sector," *O Papel*, 72, no. 4 (Apr. 2011): 65–71, found at http://www.revistaopapel.org.br/edicoes_impressas/41.pdf#page=65.

Tommasino, Humberto and Waldemar Annunziatto "¿Cómo mejorar la cadena forestal uruguaya? *Anuario 2014 OPYPA* (MGAP)Tourneau, François-Michel le and Marcel Bursztyn. "Assentamentos rurais na Amazônia: Contradições entre a política agrária e a política ambiental." *Ambiente & Sociedade*, Campinas v. XIII, no. 1 (jan.–jun. 2010): 111–130.

Traxler, Greg, *The Economic Impacts of Biotechnology-Based Technological Innovations* (FAO-Agriculture and Development Economics Division, ESA Working Paper no. 04–08, 2004), https://ageconsearch.umn.edu/record/23806/files/wp040008.pdf.

Turner, A. *Manual do Plantador d'algodão.* (Maranhão: Officina Typographica do Frias, 1859).

Udaeta, Rosa Guadalupe Soares Udaeta. "As hospedarias de imigrantes em São Paulo: o caso da Maçan D'Oro. *Anais do XX Encontro Regional de História ANPUH/SP*—UNESP-Franca (06 a 10 de setembro de 2010).

Vainer, Celso, et al. "As tecnologias do Plano ABC na mitigação de gases do efeito estufa," *Agroanalysis,* FGV, 39, no. 11 (nov. 2019).

Valle, Cacilda Borges do, Liana Jank and Rosangela Maria Simeão Resende, "O melhoramento de forrageiras tropicais no Brasil," *Revista Ceres,* 56, no. 4 (2009): 460–472.

Valdes, Constanza, Kim Hjort, and Ralph Seeley, "Brazil's Agricultural Competitiveness: Recent Growth and Future Impacts Under Currency Depreciation and Changing Macroeconomic Conditions," (USDA, Economic Research Report Number 276, September 2020) found at https://www.ers.usda.gov/webdocs/publications/99427/err-276.pdf?v=347.3.

Valdes, Constanza, "Brazil's Momentum as a Global Agricultural Supplier Faces Headwinds," *Amber Waves* USDA, ERS (September 27, 2022), found at https://www.ers.usda.gov/amber-waves/2022/september/brazil-s-momentum-as-a-global-agricultural-supplier-faces-headwinds/.

Vargas, Jonas Moreira, "Abastecendo *plantations*: a inserção do charque fabricado em Pelotas (RS) no comércio atlântico das carnes e a sua concorrência com os produtores platinos (século XIX)," *História* (São Paulo), 33, no. 2 (jul./dez. 2014): 540–566.

Vargas, Jonas Moreira, "'As mãos e os pés do charqueador': o processo de fabricação do charque e um perfil dos trabalhadores escravos nas charqueadas de Pelotas", Rio Grande do Sul (1830–1885)," *Sæculum Revista de História,* 36 (jan./jun. 2017).

Vargas, Jonas, "'A aristocracia do sebo' Riqueza, prestígio social e estilo de vida entre os charqueadores de Pelotas (Rio Grande do Sul, 1850–1890," *Revista Digital Estudios Historicos* [Uruguay], VIII, no. 17 (Diciembre 2016).

Veloso, Fernando, Silvia Matos, Fernando de Holanda Barbosa Filho and Paulo Peruchetti, "Produtividade do trabalho no Brasil: uma análise dos resultados setoriais desde 1995,"FGC-IBRE, 2003, found at https://ibre.fgv.br/observatorio-produtividade/artigos/produtividade-do-trabalho-no-brasil-uma-analise-dos-resultados-0.

Veneziano, Wilson, *Cafeicultura em Rondônia, Situação Atual e Perspectivas* (Porto Velho: Embrapa Rondônia, 1996).

Vessuri, Hebe, "El hombre del maiz de la Argentina: Salómon Horovitz y la tecnología de la investigación e la fitotecnia sudamericana." *Estudios interdisciplinarios de América Latina y el Caribe,* 14, no. 1 (2003): 89–118.

Vidal Neto, Francisco das Chagas and Eleusio Curvelo Freire, "Melhoramento genético do algodoeiro, " in Francisco das Chagas Vidal Neto and J. J. V. Cavalcanti, eds., *Melhoramento genético de plantas no Nordeste* (Brasília: Embrapa, 2013).

Videira, Raphael Almeida, "Uma análise da concorrência no setor brasileiro de celulose," (MA thesis, São Paulo: Fundação Getúlio Vargas, 2004).

Vieira Filho, J. E. R., "A fronteira agropecuária brasileira: redistribuição produtiva, efeito poupa-terra e desafios estruturais logísticos," in J. E. R. Vieira Filho, and J. G. Gasques (Org.). *Agricultura, transformação produtiva e sustentabilidade* (Brasília: Ipea, 2016), pp. 89–108.

Vieira Filho, José Eustáquio Ribeiro. *Efeito poupa-terra e ganhos de produção no setor agropecuário brasileiro.* (TD 2386; Brasília: IPEA, 2018).

Viola, Eduardo J. "The Ecologist Movement in Brazil (1974–1986): From Environmentalism to Ecopolitics," *International Journal of Urban and Regional Research* 12, no. 2 (Jun. 1988): 211–228.

Visentin, Maria Alice Dias Rolim, "A floresta Amazônica e as mudanças climáticas: proteção da biodiversidade," *Revista CEJ* (Brasília), XVII, no. 60 (maio/ago. 2013): 96–102.

Viveiros, Jerônimo de, *História do Comércio do Maranhão, 1612–1895* (São Luis: Associação Comercial do Maranhão, 1954, Vol. 2, p. 460).

Wadsworth, Alfred P., and Julia de Lacy Mann, *The Cotton Trade and Industrial Lancashire 1600–1780* (Manchester University Press,1931).

Wandel, Jonathan F. Wendel, Curt Brubaker, Ines Alvarez, Richard Cronn, and James McD. Stewart, "Evolution and Natural History of the Cotton Genus," in A. H. Paterson, ed., *Genomics of Cotton, Plant Genetics and Genomics* (New York: Springer, 2009), pp. 3–22.

Watts, Isaac, *The Cotton Supply Association: Its Origin and Progress* (Manchester: Tubbs & Brook, 1871).

Webber, Herbert John, and Leon Dexter Batchelor, *The citrus industry: History, World Distribution, Botany and Varieties.* (2 vols, Berkeley: University of California Press, 1967)

Wesz Junior, Valdemar João, (2014). "O mercado da soja e as relações de troca entre produtores rurais e empresas no Sudeste do Mato Grosso (Brasil)" (Phd Thesis, Rio de Janeiro: Universidade Federal Rural do Rio de Janeiro, 2014).

Wesz Junior, Valdemar João, "O mercado da soja no Brasil e na Argentina semelhanças, diferenças e interconexões," *Século XXI, Revista de Ciências Sociais,* 4, no. 1 (2014).

Wilcox, Robert W. *Cattle in the Backlands: Mato Grosso and the Evolution of Ranching in the Brazilian Tropics* (University of Texas Press, 2017).

Wilson, Richard F. "Seed Composition." *Soybeans: Improvement, Production, and Uses* 16 (2004): 621–677.

Wright, Brian D., and Tiffany M. Shih, "Agricultural Innovation," (Working Paper 15793, Boston: National Bureau of Economic Research, 2010).

Wright, Gavin, *The Political Economy of the Cotton South, Households, Markets and Wealth in the Nineteenth Century* (New York: W.W. Norton, 1978).

Xavier, Thaise Dantas de Almeida, "Avaliação do modelo de negócio para o desenvolvimento das cultivares de algodão transgênico na Embrapa," (MA thesis. Recife: Universidade Federal de Pernambuco, 2018).

Yardley-Podolsky, W. J. Huitt. "Um perfil da indústria de carne e seu futuro". *Revista de Administração de Empresas* (Rio de Janeiro), 21, no. 2 (abr./jun. 1981).

Yavapolkul, Navin, "Three Essays on the International Orange Juice Market," (Phd thesis, University of California, Davis, 2011).

Zanela, Angelo Brião Zanela, "ENsaios sobre business groups: Perdigão e Sadia e a consolidação de grupos econômicos no Brasil (1934–2009)," (Phd thesis, Universidade Federal do Paraná, 2019).

Zimmer, Ademir H., et al., *Degradação, recuperação e renovação de pastagens* (Campo Grande: MS: Embrapa Gado de Corte, 2012), accessed at: www.embrapa.br/busca-de-publicacoes/-/publicacao/951322/degradacao-recuperacao-e-renovacao-de-pastagens.

Zulian, Aline, Andréa Cristina Dörr and Sabrina Cantarelli Almeida, "Citricultura e Agronegócio Cooperativo n Brasil," *Revista Elet. em Gestão, Educação e Tecnologia Ambiental* 11, no. 11 (Jun. 2013).

Zullo Junior, J., Hilton Silveira Pinto, Eduardo Delgado Assad, and S. R. M. Evangelista, "Potential Economic Impacts of Global Warming on Two Brazilian Commodities, According to IPCC Prognostics," *TERRÆ* 3, no. 1 (2008): 28–39.

Index

H. S. Klein and F. V. Luna, *Brazilian Crops in the Global Market*, Palgrave Studies in Economic History,
https://doi.org/10.1007/978-3-031-38589-6

E

G

J

S

The manufacturer's authorised representative in the EU is Springer Nature Customer Service Centre GmbH, Europaplatz 3, 69115 Heidelberg, Germany. If you have any concerns regarding our products, please contact ProductSafety@springernature.com

Printed and bound by CPI Group (UK) Ltd, Croydon, CR0 4YY
28/09/2026
02224062-0002